SchNEWS At Ten

SchNEWS At Ten

Published by SchNEWS, October 2004

ISBN: 09529748 8 6

Printed by Calverts Press, London

SchNEWS is a free weekly news sheet published by volunteers in Brighton. It is obtainable by sending first class stamps (ten for nine issues) or donations (in UK pounds, payable to "Justice?") to SchNEWS, c/o On The Fiddle, P.O. Box 2600, Brighton, East Sussex, BN2 0EF, UK Phone +44 (0)1273 685 913

SchNEWS is also online **www.schnews.org.uk** The website is updated each week with the latest issue of SchNEWS as well as new **Party & Protest** listings: our guide to parties, festivals, demos and actions happening in Britain and elsewhere. (If you would like to put an event in this then contact us...)

You can also receive SchNEWS each week for free in either PDF or text file version by email - see 'Subscribe' on the website.

Also available on the banana yellow website:

* Every issue from no. 1 (Nov 94) onwards, plus other archives.
* **SchMOVIES** - we do movies now - which are free to download.
* **Yellow Pages** - regularly updated contacts list featuring around 800 direct action, community, alternative media, etc etc groups, campaigns & centres in Britain and abroad (a version updated to October 2004 is in the back of this book).
* **DIY guide** - direct action how-to guides
* **Prisoner Support** page
* **Search facility**

c/o Justice?
Prior House,
6 Tilbury Place,
Brighton.
BN2 2GY

Tuesday, 13th September, 1994.

Dear Michael Howard,

We are writing to thank you for the positive effect the Criminal Justice Bill has had on our community.

Your attempt to criminalise our culture has unified it like never before. Thanks to you we are now witnessing the largest grass roots movement of direct action in years.

Your inspiration has made us work closer together: Networking is happening across the nation - Road Protesters and Ravers, Gay Rights Activists and Hunt Saboteurs, Travellers and Squatters and Many More, as we realise the strength of our numbers.

As the man personally responsible for such collective positivity we cordially invite you to open our Ideal Squat Exhibition on Monday 19th September at 12 am, at a location to be confirmed, and furthermore we would be honoured if you would accept the position of honorary mascot for the 'Justice?' group.

We look forward to your reply!

R.S.V.P

Yours Sincerely,

for Justice?

Contents

Part 5 - Behind The Scenes

Part 6 - Grassroots Resistance

Part 7 And Finally...

Just Do It

SchNEWS' strapline has always been 'Information For Action' – which means it is all about arming people with the knowledge and contacts to go out and actually make a difference, in the here and now. It's not supposed to just be an extra bit of roughage for a healthy, balanced news diet.

Since it started in 1994 SchNEWS has always been written and produced by people who have been involved in the various political movements it writes about – so the chain of events you see in these pages is very much the journey we've taken over the last ten years. Others may see these events differently, and that's just fine by us – we've never claimed to be a definitive voice.

While a lot of the stories covered in this book are the latest chapters of struggles which have been going on for centuries – like constant running battles to protect communities and environments from exploitation – others are strange new threats like genetically modified food, or have unprecedented features like the global communication power of the internet. We pick up the thread from a point in 1993 when Michael Howard's Criminal Justice Act was outlawing communities like travellers and free party goers for living in ways that didn't conform to middle England's prejudices, as well as criminalising those whose took direct action where the 'usual' political channels had failed them. But what they didn't bargain for was that the CJA had an unexpected effect, uniting many of the groups it attacked in opposition to the new law. At the same time anti-road protests and Reclaim the Streets parties were springing up all over the country in a campaign of direct action that stopped the government's road building programme in its tracks. A movement was in the making. SchNEWS, amongst others, came out of this movement. The succession of inspiring actions and events in these pages show what was achieved thanks to that not-so gentle nudge from Michael Howard, and how things progressed and moved into new areas since.

But don't expect us to roll all the thousands of things we've covered over the years into a nice neat story - as if you could. It'd be tempting to paint the picture of a political generation which started out with opposition to the Criminal Justice Act and a range of ecological direct action, primarily road protests... And later when the internet came along, the poetic communiqués of Zapatista Sub-commandante Marcos began to circulate and people became swept up in international issues - which were similar to their own, but usually much more severe... Then on June 18th 1999 and with the Battle of Seattle a global movement was born, which 'we' merged into... And post 9-11 all this turned into the anti-war movement. But all that's too 'big picture' – it doesn't represent the full spectrum of smaller struggles which have come from, and contribute to, the international current.

After ten years of being part of the direct action movement, and later the anti-capitalist movement – as well as writing about countless issues in Britain and abroad – you might ask us what's worked and what hasn't? In the nineties the anti-roads movement slashed the Tories' road building plans through sustained direct action. On the other hand you only have to look at the war last year to realise that marching from A to B and listening to politicians' speeches and keeping within police cordons doesn't actually work – because *they* aren't listening. In other words don't bother waiting for an MP or a union to do your bidding – you'd be more likely to get results if you got organised and took action yourself – whether that means trashing a GM trial crop, or setting up a community project in your neighbourhood.

The range of global and local issues needing urgent attention these days is huge, and the diversity of people involved now is just as staggering. The days of the big road protest camps might have quietened for the time being, but ecological direct action still very much exists with a lot of that energy moving into areas like genetics or climate change. Braver souls have taken the international aspect far further than just summit hopping by going to hotspots like Palestine or Iraq. Some have developed the technical skills to get the global Indymedia network up and running (or sort out SchNEWS' email spam problem). Many who had been involved in direct action have turned to working on a community level, practising the same ideas of positive social change, but what they're doing might not register on the political radar.

Rather than trying to be a complete history – which would go on forever - in this book the emphasis has been placed on bringing out some of the most inspiring stories which have happened; amazing stuff which has been achieved by 'ordinary' people just like yourself with minimal resources. The sorts of stories which will inspire people to get off their arses… **and actually do something about it!**

Forward

by Mark Thomas

Flicking through a newspaper recently I saw an article that said the authorities had worries about a potential terrorist attack on the Pope when he visited Lourdes. Well thank God terrorists are stupid enough to target the site of miraculous healing. If the attack happens surely the headlines will read "Bomb goes off at Lourdes! Everyone cured!" In fact the Pope should go one further and challenge the terrorists to have a go. Unfortunately none of the so called newspapers saw it like that. The story was just another log to be thrown onto Blunkett's bonfire of hysteria about terrorism by ever more compliant media.

The tabloids flock around the story of Blunkett's mistress, believing that it important to reveal every grubby detail, but none of them quite having the courage to deliver the headline "David Bonkett !" or the Viz version of "David Spunkett!". Ironically the Home Secretary who has done more than any other to invade our privacy demands that it is a private matter.

And while our right to protest, privacy, to hold the state to account are eroded the popular imagination is not fired by outrage at these preposterous acts, but hi-jacked by the thought of David's pimply arse rising and falling in passion as his dog whimpers in the corner forcing itself to concentrate on a bonio. It's a wonderful world.

Under Blunkett's laws anyone involved in direct action can be classed as a terrorist, both practically and legally. Under the anti terror "stop and search" laws hundreds of protestors were regarded as terrorists when they were detained and searched at the DSEi arms fair protests in London in 2003. Very little of this story appeared in the press, maybe the Guardian wrung its hands on page 9 for 3 column inches before urging its readers to vote Labour in the editorial.

Under the anti-terror laws a terrorist is defined as anyone who uses force or threatens to use force, to cause violence to people or damage to property, for ideological, religious or political purposes or beliefs. That is just about anyone of us. From GM crop protestors, to animal rights, to anti corporate campaigners, terrorists every one of us. Under the legislation Nelson Mandela, Mahatma Ghandi and Jesus would be terrorists. And all the mainstream media can do is endlessly debate "public disengagement in Party Politics".

We don't expect the media to be on our side and that is why SchNEWS, Indymedia, Undercurrents etc are so important. We have to inform ourselves and each other because no one else is going to do it for us. Of course it is a minor miracle that SchNEWS is still going after ten years and the various contributors and authors have not been banged up on a more permanent basis. It is a miracle that a weekly sheet run by volunteers and paid for by readers donations has lasted this long. So Happy birthday SchNEWS!

There has been the most amazing activity over the past ten years and the most imaginative forms of dissent that have flowed across the world. Here in Blighty SchNEWS has been at the forefront of reporting, encouraging, informing and organising the direct action movement. The phoney war on terror has curtailed our rights, the official anti-war movement seems to have dissolved into Respect, the neo cons seem to be gaining momentum and we could be looking at even bleaker times to come.

One thing is that the stakes we are playing for could not be higher. The consumerism and prosperity enjoyed by the west's middle classes is paid for by ecological suicide, worsening poverty and war in the majority world, and growing inequality within the rich countries themselves. It can't go on.

So where will we be in ten years? Fuck knows. What happens next is up to us. I hope we are all up for it.

Mark Thomas

...ind, could be yours for a barga...

FOR AUCTION

PLANET EARTH Slightly soil-stained, sitting tenants, no previous careful owner, gas and water provided, needs some repair, room for redevelopment, suit megalomaniac. Price: the sky's the limit. Applications to your local World Bank.

4 BILLION WORK SLAVES Obedient, well programmed, choice of colours, slight problem with the minor

ANARCHOSAURUS

A handy set of new terms - plus a few old faves thrown in - which we thought were all asking for it.

Anarcho-primitivists
People who dream of living as hunter-gatherers but who have to make do with the occasional camping trip – with their hi-tech outdoor kit and pot noodles.

Anorakist
A politico who spends all his/her time on a computer, and believes that social change begins by posting messages onto online forums.

Argy-Bargy-Ment
Use of physical force when remonstrating with police on demo's. Often involves pushing a police shield violently while encouraging them to go catch some real criminals.

Bimble
To move slowly and aimlessly.

Breatharian
Someone on an extreme diet, which excludes everything they shouldn't eat for health or political reasons. Not to be confused with a hunger striker.

Brewids
Twee merry Englanders who romanticise Celts, Arthurian legends and real ale. Still managing to cling to some rustic fantasy about a green and pleasant land, as the place gets turned into a sprawl of airports, motorways and hyper-store developments.

Counter Culture
Hanging about in your favourite right-on café all day.

Crasstafarian
Person, usually in their mid-thirties, whose primary source of inspiration is the anarcho-punk outfit Crass.

Doof
Aussie word to describe a rave-type event where people dance to sounds wholly or predominantly characterized by the emission of a succession of repetitive… er doofs. Doof doof doof doof.

Fanny Gazer
An anarcha-feminist who has reclaimed the word 'cunt'.

Five-Fingered Discount
Shopping without money. Goods appropriated without consent of the owner. To *half-inch* something.

Fun Mummy
Emerges from their crypt to have a laugh on actions but does nothing useful.

Home Visit
Demonstration held at a person's house to persuade them to stop working for a nasty company. Tactic used mostly by animal rights activists.

Iron Butterflies
The initial release of adrenalin at a big demo when it's just about to kick off.

Kettle
Item used to boil water. Tactic used by police to contain a demonstration by surrounding everyone with riot cops. Nothing to do with a *kettle watcher.*

Kevin Keegan
Rhyming slang for vegan. E.g. is the veggie slop *Kevin*? No but it's *Ronnie*

Lifestylista
Person who has the right clothes, hairdo and mates to be a proper anarchist (see also *Upper Crusty*).

Lunch Out
Failing to get something done. As in, "I was gonna write something for the SchNEWS book, but lunched it out."

Meeting Junkie
One who thrives on tedious meetings, and normally doesn't do anything else.

No Bore But The Class Bore
Someone who goes on and on and on… about class struggle all the time. Usually middle class.

Nostalgic Ravers
How many ravers does it take to change a lightbulb? Ten. One to change it and the other nine to say how much better lightbulbs used to be.

Orgeezers
British travellers and itinerants who live in the south of Spain, typically around the town of Orgiva.

Pacifascist
Someone who professes to being a pacifist and will happily sit there getting the shit kicked out of them by a copper. But strangely physically attacks others for wearing a black hoody or trying to defend themselves against the cops.

Pilton Pilgrims
Someone who goes to one festival for the year - Glastonbury - and seems to think it's the only festival which exists.

Projectile Reasoning
The use of half bricks and other masonry to underline a point being made to the police.

Ronnie'n'Reggie
Rhyming slang for vegetarian.

Slack Bloc
People who stay at home and watch a political demonstration on the news. They're "with us in spirit" though. see *slacktivist.*

Slacktivist
Person who tells you all the actions they've done in the pub and then fail to turn up the for next morning's action. See *slack bloc.*

Summit Hoppers
People who use mobile phones, email and cheap air travel to fight...er globalisation.

Upper Crusties
Like *crusties*, but wear expensive clothes, snorts cocaine and use their 'alternativeness' to make sure they're always on the guest list. Used to speak with a home counties accent, now it's all 'fuck'n'wikid innit'!

Vegan Police
There to make sure everyone around them keeps to their high standards of right-on-ness.

Vertical Non-hierarchies
Hierarchies and divisions of labour which unavoidably occur in non-hierarchical groups due to peoples' different skills and abilities, but which can never be acknowledged.

Yoghurt Weaving
Making a dreamcatcher from an old ball of grey wool? Want some healing crystals (dug up from some poor indigenous peoples land)? A hug for world peace? (sometimes a good chat up line). Sorry, but eating brown rice and organic veg won't get rid of capitalism.

Zapatista Fetishistas
Those obsessed with far-away indigenous struggles (often the Zapatistas in Mexico), at the expense of engagement in local issues.

Part 1 Prehistory

SchNEWS was born in 1994 on a wave of activity that was based around resistance to the Criminal Justice and Public Order Act (CJA) - and therefore the main body of this book looks at events which happened from 1994 to 2004. But obviously neither the CJA nor the resistance to it came out of a vacuum, but was one episode in a continuing battle in the fight for a better world.

The eighties were the era of Thatcher-Reagan economics. The Conservative government took on the trade unions with the full force of the state, smashing the miners and print unions amongst others. For the counter culture, it was the peace campaigners at Greenham Common and the New Age travellers that were the 'enemy within.'

The first article traces the rise of this dynamic culture based around travellers, free festivals and raves, and the state's sustained attack on it. Following this are photo collages which look at another line of activity that would eventually be targeted by the CJA – direct action including road protest camps and hunt sabbing.

ASSEMBLIES OF **CELEBRATION** ASSEMBLIES OF **DISSENT**

Jim Carey reviews the recent political history of Travellers, city kids, raves and festivals and reveals the multi-tactic approach used in attempts to annihilate an emerging culture of celebration and dissent.

Pic: Matt Smith

When the Criminal Justice and Public Order Act (CJPOA) began its passage through parliament in 1993, there were many who were genuinely flabbergasted at the extent of its legislative garrotte. Why were travellers, squatters, ravers, political protesters and public assemblies considered so much of a threat to the nation that new criminal law was required to eradicate them?

In a legislation-paving speech delivered in 1992, the then Home Secretary, Kenneth Baker, broadcast the government's intentions thus: "We will get tough on rapists, tough on armed robbers and tough on squatters". Such wild comparisons became a regular feature of the passage of the new law and, although such selective demonisation was nothing new in British politics, few thought that it would manifest itself in such overtly draconian fashion. By making a "series of repetitive beats" into a legally defined target of criminal sanctions, the CJPOA was the first European national criminal law to target a specific kind of music since Nazi Germany.

Far from an isolated incident however, the CJPOA (commonly shortened to the CJA) was merely one of the more draconian measures in a long and relentlessly executed strategy to destroy a burgeoning and energetic youth culture…

The networking hub of the UK's 'underground' culture were the unlicensed public festivals, which had been proliferating across the British Isles since the early seventies. Primarily designed to provide financially accessible community celebrations, these gatherings also harboured active expressions of rising public dissension; populated largely by disaffected youth determined to create a life for themselves outside the market-myopic. The largest gathering was at Stonehenge each year during the summer solstice - the longest day. Having begun as a small gathering in 1974, the Stonehenge Solstice Free Festival attracted 30,000 people to its last uninterrupted incarnation in 1984.

The Stonehenge Free Festival was an affront to the government, not only were 30,000 people gathering without the presence of the police, they were doing so on one of the largest military training grounds in the UK, and in the highly Conservative county of Wiltshire – and it was getting bigger every

Pic: Tash

Stonehenge Free Festival 1983

year. Also many on the free festival circuit were environmentalists and began involving themselves in direct action, the main focus of which concentrated at the time on nuclear energy and weaponry.

Between 1980 and 1984, convoys of travellers took part in public operations known as Cruisewatch. This involved the overt tailing of mobile Cruise missiles, transported from silos in Wiltshire to secret locations in neighbouring counties. This was a particularly sensitive area for the government. Secretly located nuclear missiles formed a major part of the UK's nuclear deterrent tactics, with mobility designed to confuse the Soviets in the event of an attack. Anti-nuclear campaigners argued such manoeuvres brought the possibility of nuclear war even closer and effectively blew the government's cover by following the missiles everywhere they went with a convoy of traveller trucks.

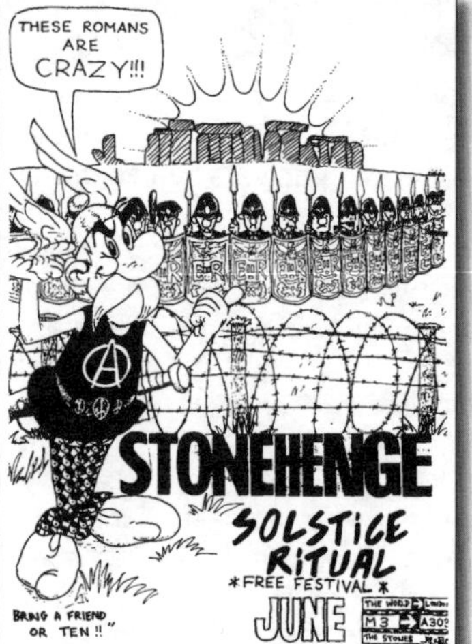

The term 'Peace Convoy' was a generic term coined by the media and, with the continual involvement of travellers in anti-nuclear demonstrations, it was a term that stuck.

In June 1982, a 'peace convoy' left Stonehenge to support the nuclear weapons protest outside Greenham Common in Berkshire; holding an impromptu festival on the perimeter and cutting the fence. In September the same year, another convoy incorporated the Sizewell B nuclear reactor in Suffolk into its itinerary of East Anglian festivals. Once again they established themselves in the car-park and stayed for a week. In 1984, the significance of these stand-offs was brought to a head when another peace convoy took part in a large demonstration outside the US Cruise Missile base at Molesworth in Cambridgeshire. Along with other contingents of anti-nuclear protesters, travellers occupied a perimeter site for five months; planting and reaping crops whilst a group of Quakers built a Stone Chapel of Peace.

Following a High Court possession order granted in February 1985, the entire protest camp was finally evicted using soldiers from the Royal Engineers regiment. Significant to the political escalation subsequent to these protests, the eviction was attended by the then Minister of Defence, Michael Heseltine, famously arriving on site in a camouflage flak jacket. Meanwhile the festival circuit harboured an increasing multitude of campaign groups - particularly those connected with the environment - assembling en masse, distributing information and discussing action. Up until 1985, these burgeoning assemblies of alternative living and dissent stood successfully defiant in the face of Margaret Thatcher's designs on an ultra-efficient market mono-culture. In 1985, however, the 'Peace Convoy' and its associated culture became the target of a multi-strategic campaign of annihilation, inaugurated in bloody fashion at Stonehenge.

Blood In The Beanfield

It is difficult to convey the extent and effect of the berserk circumstances, which occurred on June 1st 1985, but their socio-political ramifications were immense. A convoy of travellers' vehicles left an impromptu park-up site in Savernake Forest to head towards Stonehenge. Seven miles from the Stones, and still some way out of the newly imposed four and half-mile High Court exclusion order,

Pic: Tash

Ethnic cleansing in a Wiltshire beanfield, June 1st 1985 Pic: Tash

police blocked the convoy with three lorry loads of gravel. After a short stand-off, the acting Deputy Chief Constable of Wiltshire, Lionel Grundy, gave orders for his men to begin attacking the vehicles and arresting drivers. When word swept through the convoy that police were smashing windscreens at the front and the back of the line of vehicles, travellers pulled their vehicles off the A303 and into an adjacent grass field. At this stage, many travellers were keen to return to the Savernake Forest site, but were told by Wiltshire Police that those wishing to leave the scene could only do so without their vehicles (homes).

After a tense wait, the pressure cooker finally exploded when over 1000 police, drawn from five constabularies, charged into the field wielding truncheons. In an effort to escape, the convoy drove from the grass field into the adjacent beanfield looking for a way out. A huge number of riot police charged in behind them to commit a now legendary carnage, referred to as the Battle of the Beanfield.

Public knowledge of the events of that day is still limited by the fact that only a small number of journalists were present in the beanfield at the time. Most, including the BBC Television crew, had obeyed the police directive to stay behind police lines at the bottom of the hill "for their own safety".

One of the few journalists to ignore police advice and attend the scene was Nick Davies, home affairs correspondent for The Observer. He wrote: "All of us were shocked by what we saw: police tactics which seemed to break new bounds in the scale and intensity of its violence. We saw police throw hammers, stones and other missiles through the windscreens of advancing vehicles; a woman dragged away by her hair; young men beaten over the head with truncheons as they tried to surrender... the police operation became a chaotic whirl of violence...basic rules of police behaviour were abandoned. The identification numbers of most officers were concealed by flame-proof overalls....I saw a young man's glasses swiped from his face and front teeth break under the raining blows."

The only national television camera crew in the beanfield was from ITN. Reporter Kim Sabido spoke to camera: "What we the ITN camera crew and myself as a reporter have seen in the last 30 minutes here in this field has been some of the most brutal police treatment of people that I've witnessed in my entire career as a journalist. The number of people who have been hit by policemen, who have been clubbed whilst holding babies in their arms in coaches around this field, is yet to be counted...There must surely be an enquiry."

However, when the item was nationally broadcast on ITN news later that day, Sabido's voice-over had been removed and replaced with a dispassionate narrator. The most violent of the film footage was also edited out. When approached for the footage not shown on the news, ITN claimed it was missing. Some but not all of the missing footage has since re-surfaced on bootleg tapes and was incorporated into the 'Operation Solstice' documentary shown on Channel Four in 1991.

Photos taken by press photographers also disappeared. Ben Gibson, a freelance photographer working for The Observer that day, was arrested in the beanfield after photographing riot police smashing their way into a traveller's coach - he was later acquitted of charges of obstruction. Fellow photographer Tim Malyon narrowly avoided the same fate: "Whilst attempting to take pictures of one group of officers beating people with their truncheons, a policeman shouted out to 'get him' and I was chased. I ran and was not arrested." Malyon stored his films with Birnbergs solicitors, but they disappeared. Fortunately, some of Ben Gibson's and Tim Malyon's prints have recently resurfaced.

One unusual eyewitness to the beanfield nightmare was the Earl of Cardigan, secretary of the Marlborough Conservative Association and manager of Savernake Forest. When travellers left

Free Party, Frome, Somerset Pic: Matt Smith

Savernake Forest, he had decided to travel alongside the convoy on his motorbike, "to follow the events personally". Cardigan described some of the scenes at prosecutions brought against Wiltshire Police, including descriptions of a heavily pregnant woman with "a silhouette like a zeppelin" being "clubbed with a truncheon" and riot police showering a woman and child with glass.

After the Battle of the Beanfield, Wiltshire Police approached Lord Cardigan to gain his consent for an immediate eviction of the travellers remaining on his Savernake Forest site. "They said they wanted to go into the campsite 'suitably equipped' and 'finish unfinished business'. Make of that phrase what you will." says Cardigan. "I said to them that if it was my permission they were after, they did not have it. I did not want a repeat of the grotesque events that I'd seen the day before." Instead, the site was evicted using court possession proceedings, allowing the travellers a few days recuperative grace.

In an effort to counter the impact of his testimony, several national newspapers began painting him as a 'loony lord', questioning his suitability as an eyewitness. He consequently successfully sued the Times, the Telegraph, the Daily Mail, the Daily Express and the Daily Mirror for claiming that his allegations against the police were false and for suggesting that he was making a home for hippies. His treatment by the press was ample indication of the united front held by a politically complicit national media. Cardigan says of the papers "I hadn't realised that anybody that appeared to be supporting elements that stood against the establishment would be savaged by establishment newspapers. Now one thinks about it nothing could be more natural."

Largely as a result of his testimony, police charges against members of the convoy were dismissed in the local magistrates courts. However, there was no public enquiry. Of the 440 travellers taken into custody that day, 24 went through the gruelling five year process of taking Wiltshire Police to court for wrongful arrest, assault and criminal damage. They finally won a four-month court case at Winchester Crown Court in 1991, but received compensation almost identical to the legal costs incurred in the process.

To some of those at the brunt end of the truncheon charge, the violence left a devastating legacy. Alan Lodge, a veteran of many free festivals, was one of the twenty four travellers who 'successfully' took Wiltshire Police to court following the Beanfield incident: "There was one guy who I trusted my children with in the early 80's - he was a potter. After the Beanfield I wouldn't let him anywhere near them. I saw him, a man of substance at the end of all that nonsense wobbled to the point of illness and evil. It turned all of us and I'm sure that applies to the whole travelling community. There was plenty of people who had got something very positive together who came out of the Beanfield with a world view of fuck everyone."

The violent nature of the police action drew obvious comparisons with the coercive police tactics employed on the miners' strike the year before. An edition of the Police Review, published seven days after the Beanfield, revealed: "The Police operation had been planned for several months and lessons in rapid deployment learned from the miners' strike were implemented." If the paramilitary policing used on the miners strike was a violent introduction to Thatcher's mal-intention towards union dissent, the Battle of the Beanfield was a similarly severe introduction to a new era of intolerance of travellers, festivals and public protest.

Manufacturing The Case For Crackdown

At the 1995 Big Green Gathering Festival, Inspector Hunt, a member of Wiltshire Police force for 20 years, told a reporter from SQUALL Magazine: "Stonehenge Festival grew too large and out of control, the Beanfield was just the beginning of the process of dealing with it. The laws that came after were even more effective." Indeed the year after the Battle of Beanfield came the Public Order Act 1986, affording police the power to break up any gathering of twelve vehicles or over. This new legislation not only provided the authorities with powers to stop convoys, it also had seriously detrimental implications for both festivals and traveller sites all over the country and was widely used.

On June 5th 1986, Margaret Thatcher told the nation that the British government was "only too delighted to do anything we can to make life difficult for such things as hippy convoys". On the same day, a cabinet committee was formed to discuss new legislation to deal with travellers and festivals. Chaired by Home Secretary, Douglas Hurd, the committee was comprised of the Secretaries of State for Transport, Environment, Health and Social Security, and Agriculture.

Meanwhile, convoys assembling to celebrate that year's Solstice were chased around several counties by police, before finally finding some temporary respite on a site at Stoney Cross in the New Forest. Four days later, Hampshire Police mounted 'Operation Daybreak', steaming in en masse at 4am to clear the Stoney Cross site. Sixty four convoy members were arrested and 129 vehicles impounded after police arrived on site armed with DoT files on every vehicle. Even more maliciously, police had also obtained care orders for the travellers' children, although a tip off reaching the camp before the raid meant the children had been removed.

The Battle of the Beanfield and the increasingly hostile political climate which followed, had a dramatic affect on the travelling community, frightening away many of the families integral to the community balance of the festival circuit. In 1987, people stood on the tarmac beside Stonehenge having walked the eight mile distance from an impromptu site at Cholderton. As clouds smothered the Solstice sunrise, those who had walked the distance were kept on the road, separated from the Stones by rows of riot police and bales of razor wire. As the anger mounted, scuffles broke out.

A year later the anger had tangibly increased and once again at Solstice dawn there were some who found the situation too unacceptable. This time the scuffles were more prevalent with concerted attempts being made to break through the police cordon. Secreted around the area, however, were thousands of waiting riot police and as the frustration of the penned in crowd grew, numberless uniforms came flooding down the hill to disperse the crowd with a liberal usage of truncheons and riot shields. Andy Smith - now editor of the magazine Festival Eye - finally received a £10,000 out of court settlement from Wiltshire Police in 1996 for a wound to his head received after he tripped, fell and was then hit on the head with a truncheon whilst on the ground at Stonehenge in 1988.

The numbers of people prepared to travel to Stonehenge and face this treatment naturally dwindled, resulting in a concentration of those who were prepared for confrontation in defence of what was considered as a right to celebrate solstice at Stonehenge. Successive large-scale police operations backed by the Public Order Act 1986, became stricter in attempts to stop anyone from reaching the stone circle at Solstice. Despite this, the ensuing years would always see a handful of those who would hug hedgerows and dart between the beams of police helicopters in order to be in view of the Solstice sunrise at Stonehenge.

Destroying The Alternative Economy

Up until 1985, the free festival circuit had provided the economic backbone of a year long itinerancy. By selling crafts, services, performance busking, tat and assorted gear, travellers provided themselves with an alternative economy lending financial viability to an itinerant culture. Evidence suggests that the political campaign to eradicate festivals included specific attempts to break this economy.

"As soon as they scared away the punters it destroyed the means of exchange," recalls traveller Alan Lodge. "Norman Tebbit went on about getting on your bike and finding employment whilst at the same time being part of the political force that kicked the bike from under us."

In the years that followed, the right wing press made much of dole scrounging travellers, with no acknowledgement that the engineered break up of the festival economy was a major contributory factor to the increase in itinerant claimants.

Another ramification of this tactic was even more insidious. At the entrance gate to the 1984 Stonehenge Free Festival, a burnt out car bore testament to the levels of self-policing emerging

Pic: Tash

from the social-experiment. The sign protruding from the wreckage proclaimed: "This was a smack dealer's car". However, dispossessed of their once thriving economy and facing incessant and increasing harassment and eviction, the break down of community left travellers prone to a destructive force potentially more devastating than anything directly forced by the authorities: Heroin, the great escape to oblivion, found the younger elements of a fractured community prone to its clutches and its use spread like myxamatosis in a rabbit warren. Once again traveller families were forced to vacate sites that became 'dirty', further imbalancing the battered communities and creating a split between 'clean' and 'dirty' sites.

"At one time smack wasn't tolerated on the road at all," recalls mother of six, Decker Lynn. "Certainly on festival sites, if anybody was selling or even using it they were just put off site full stop."

Lynn, who still lives in her double decker bus says "Heroin is something that breaks up a community because people become so self-centred they don't give a damn about their neighbours." Many travellers report incidents of blatant heroin dealing going untouched by police, whilst other travellers on the same site were prosecuted for small amounts of hashish. "So many times people got away with it and there were very few busts for smack," recalls Lynn. "They must know smack is the quickest way to divide a community; united we stand and divided we don't."

The other manifestation of community disruption was the emergence of the so-called 'brew crew'. These were mainly angry young travellers feeding themselves on a diet of special brew and developing a penchant for nihilism, blagging and neighbourly disrespect. When the travelling community was strong the outflux of youth from the inner cities was well met, absorbed and often healed. The so called 'brew crew' caused constant disruption for the festivals still surviving on the decimated circuit and provided an obvious target for slander hungry politicians and right wing media.

Raves And The New Blood

Towards the end of the eighties a new cultural phenomenon emerged in the UK resulting in an injection of new blood and economy to the festival scene. Free rave parties were similar to free festivals in that they were unlicensed events in locations kept secret until the last possible moment. They offered similar opportunities for adventure and began attracting huge numbers of young people from the cities and the free festival scene began to merge with the rave party scene producing an accessible hybrid with new dynamism.

Once again political attention was now targeted against these new impromptu rave events, resulting in the Entertainment (Increased Penalties) Act 1990. This brought in massive penalties of up to £20,000 and/or six months imprisonment for the organisers of unlicensed events. This pushed event organisation into the hands of large commercial promoters with the necessary sums required to pay for licences and policing. A report produced by market analysts the Henley Centre in 1993 estimated that British ravers were worth a potential £1.8 billion a year to the entertainment industry and said that rave culture was posing a "significant threat" to the market share of drinks retailers, breweries and pubs. The chairman of Allied Leisure - the entertainments section of the alcohol conglomerate Allied-Tetley-Lyons described rave culture in 1992 as "a major threat to alcohol-led business."

As a consequence of legislation directed against raves, the nature of festival and rave promotion swung away from its community based orientation, as big business attempted to commercially harness the public's desire for adventurous festival/parties in the countryside. According to Tony Hollingsworth, ex-events promoter for the GLC and now part of a £multi-million commercial festival outfit Tribute: "The motivation behind these festivals is no longer passion, it is commerce." Relative to the people-led festivals, critics argue that the commercial festival scene now offers little more than another shopping

Castlemorton, May 1992. Pic: Tash

Free party at Hay Bluff, Wales, 1996. Pic: Matt Smith

experience, where an attendant wallet is valued and encouraged far more than participation.

Kick Off At Castlemorton

By 1992, leaked documents from Avon and Somerset Constabulary demonstrated the existence of a clandestine Operation Nomad. A Force Operational Order, marked 'In Confidence', revealed: "With effect from Monday 27th April 1992, dedicated resources will be used to gather intelligence in respect of the movement of itinerants and travellers and deal with minor acts of trespass." An intelligence unit set up by Avon and Somerset Police produced regular Operation Nomad bulletins, listing personal details on travellers and regular festivalgoers unrelated to any criminal conviction. The Order also stated: "Resources will be greatly enhanced for the period Thursday 21st May to Sunday 24th May inclusive in relation to the anticipated gathering of travellers in the Chipping Sodbury area."

This item referred to the annual Avon Free Festival which had been occurring in the area around the May bank holiday for several years, albeit in different locations. However, 1992 was the year Avon and Somerset Police intended to put a stop to it and thousands of people travelling to the area for the expected festival were shunted into neighbouring counties by Avon and Somerset's Operation Nomad police manoeuvres.

The end result was the impromptu Castlemorton Common Festival, another pivotal event in the recent history of festival culture.

West Mercia Police claim they had no idea that an event might happen in their district and were therefore powerless to stop it. However, observers questioned whether it was possible that Avon and Somerset Police had not informed their neighbouring constabulary of Operation Nomad.

In the event, a staggering 30,000 travellers, ravers, festival-goers and inner city youth gathered almost overnight on Castlemorton Common to hold a free festival that flew in the face of the Public Order Act 1986 and the Entertainment (Increased Penalties) Act 1990. It was a massive celebration and the biggest of its kind since the bountiful days of the Stonehenge Free Festival.

The right wing press published acres of crazed and damning coverage of the event, including the classic front page Daily Telegraph headline: "Hippies fire flares at Police". The following morning's Daily Telegraph editorial was headlined: "New Age, New Laws". Within two months, Sir George Young, then Minister for Housing, confirmed that new laws against travellers were imminent "in reaction to the increasing level of public dismay and alarm about the behaviour of some of these groups." One revealing feature appeared in the Daily Telegraph following the festival at Castlemorton. Headlined "From ravers to travellers: a guide to the invaders", it profiled four individuals under the headings 'The Squatter', 'The Raver', 'The Traveller' and 'The career Traveller' - a significant early indication of what was to come. Indeed, the outcry following Castlemorton provided the basis for the most draconian law yet levelled against alternative British culture. Just as the Public Order Act 1986 followed the events at Stonehenge in 1985, so the Criminal Justice and Public Order Act 1994 began its journey in 1992, pumped with the manufactured outrage following Castlemorton.

By the time it reached statute two years later, the CJPOA included criminal sanctions against assembly, outdoor unlicensed music events, unauthorised camping, squatting and 'aggravated trespass' (public demonstrations). The law also reduced the number of vehicles which could gather together from 12 (as stipulated in the Public Order Act 1986) to six.

The news-manufacture used to prepare the public palate for the coming law was incessant, with media descriptions of travellers including "a swarming of human locusts" in the Daily Telegraph and "These foul pests must be controlled" in the Daily Mail .

Police Surveillance and Benefit Clampdowns

The year after Castlemorton Common, the police set up Operation Snapshot, an intelligence gathering exercise on raves and travellers designed to establish a database of personal details, registration numbers, park up sites and movements. This information was used as a backbone for an ongoing intelligence operation begun by the Southern Central Intelligence Unit (SCIU), operated from Devizes in Wiltshire and initially co-ordinated by PC Malcolm Keene. The SCIU held regular meetings with representatives of all the constabularies of Britain.

Leaked documents revealed that Operation Snapshot had estimated there to be around 2000 traveller's vehicles and 8000 Travellers in the UK. In the minutes of a meeting held at Devizes on March 30th 1993 with representatives from many county constabularies, the objectives of the operation included the development of "a system whereby intelligence could be taken into the control room, and the most up-to-date intelligence was to hand"..... "capable of high speed input and retrieval and dissemination of information". At the same meeting the police's National Criminal Intelligence Service (NCIS) requested that it should be allowed "to move in with the Southern Central Intelligence Unit for one or two weeks during the Solstice".

Further intelligence information was gathered via social security offices. The working party report on Itinerant Claimants, prepared for the DHSS in 1986, advised that "in the interests of advance warning and the safety of staff, we recommend better liaison with the police." A National Task Force was set up to "monitor the movements of such groups of Travellers" and to "inform relevant District managers of their approach and numbers".

DIY mutation

The protracted lengths taken by the authorities to eradicate travellers, squatters, raves and free festivals are a sober reminder of how those willfully existing outside the mainstream are curbed: through the use of legislation, intelligence targeted harassment, benefit clampdowns and news-manufacture often strategically coordinated in a multi-tactic approach stretching over many years. Such strategies are mostly achieved without public knowledge; diffusing recognition of their mechanisms and ultimate intention. What is clear is that rather than seek to accommodate an expanding community culture, Margaret Thatcher's government and those who have followed have sought to annihilate it.

However, far from disappearing as a result of these strategic clampdowns, political dissent and unlicensed communal celebrations have in fact mutated and thrived. During the nineties, road protest camps like those at Twyford Down, Newbury and Claremont Road were in many ways evolved versions of festival gatherings and travellers sites. Whilst thousands of people might attend an environmental protest rally at weekends, the very existence of an established protest depends on people living on site all year round; in benders, tree-houses, living around fires, sometimes through the worst winter conditions on the frontline.

Sunrise at an Exodus Free Party Pic: Matt Smith

Imagination fuelled the techniques of dissent in defiance to laws against assembly; spawning ingenious methods of resistance including tunnels, scaffolding towers and aerial walkways. In the mid-to-late nineties and early 2000's, Reclaim the Streets (more about them later) organised a series of street parties in audacious reclamations of the urban environment using tripods, children's play areas and sound systems to block major roads with celebration and dissent. Other groups such as Luton's rave and social justice collective, Exodus, continued their free communal raves and housing action projects whilst facing off incredible levels of insidious opposition from a conspiring cabal of politicians and police. They remained prolific as a free party force until big internal fall outs forced them to disband in 2001.

As a million and half demonstrators poured into Hyde Park to voice their dissent against UK involvement in the war in Iraq on February 15th 2004, there was an added poignancy for those in the know. The music and speeches were all being presented from a large purple-tented main stage of special significance. For above the heads of Jesse Jackson, Ken Livingstone, Tony Benn and Ms Dynamite, dangled the familiar hand painted logo of one Wango Riley.

Back in the day yer see Wango Riley's Travelling Stage was an old flatbed truck parked up at a multitude of free festivals, presenting entertainment to those who would celebrate their dissent with vigorous revelry. These days that flatbed has evolved into a supertent and a main stage.

As many a traveller and festival goer used to say back in the days of the Stonehenge Free Festival .....You Can't Kill the Spirit.

NO MORE ROADS

Anti-road protests 1992-94

In the first half of the 1990's another powerful form of resistance which brought together environmental as well as social aspects mushroomed - the anti-roads, and the broader ecological direct action movement.

While the Castlemorton free festival may have been one of the excuses the Tories were looking for to bring in the Criminal Justice Act, the following pages show just the sort of Do-It-Yourself politics which the government couldn't allow.

TWYFORD DOWN

When a few people set up camp in 1992 to stop the M3 being ploughed through the ancient landscape of Twyford Down, near Winchester, they probably didn't they realise that they would be the catalyst for the anti road and wider direct action movement.

As the protests escalated and work was continually delayed by tactics like digger diving, lock-ons and site invasions, it wasn't long before the full force of the law was deployed. Early one December morning in 1992 while half the camp were in court fighting an eviction order, the combined forces of over 200 police and private security guards moved in. Protestors were physically and even sexually assaulted by the Group 4 guards - the first time private security had ever been used against peaceful road protestors. This became known as Yellow Wednesday after the yellow jackets that Group 4 guards wore. Even some of the security guards were so appalled by what happened that 22 resigned soon afterwards.

Despite this the campaign grew and the government issued High Court injunctions against 76 protestors to prevent them from disrupting work, with seven of those eventually sent to prison for two weeks for defying the injunction. Protests

Pics: Alec Smart

Pics: Alec Smart

continued, with the last big one being a mass trespass on July 2nd 1994, when over 1000 people invaded the building site to protest about the upcoming Criminal Justice Act. Unfortunately the road was completed in late 1994, and is now open, so the Down is lost forever, but Twyford became a milestone not only for the anti-roads movement, but also for protests in general.

See also - www.schnews.org.uk/sotw/twyford-down-plus10.htm

Solsbury Hill

Pics: Adrian Arbib

Pics: Matt Smith

While people were on the roof-tops in Claremont Road in east London, the West Country were 'avin it in the first tree top protest in Britain, Salisbury Hill near bath.

"The Solsbury Hill campaign was a great learning experience for all of us, and was a new way of getting involved in the protest movement. I learnt about new ways of resisting an eviction, about squatting, researching archaeology, SSSI's, wildlife, etc. The CJA came in halfway through the campaign too, so what was civil disobedience at first, became criminal." - Indra

No M11 Link Rd Campaign

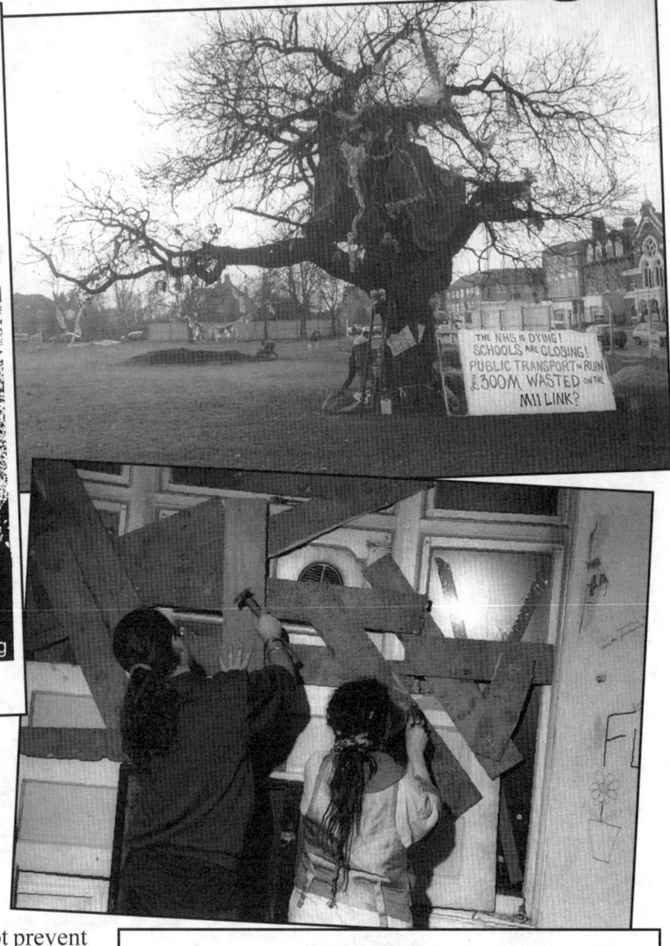

The M11 link road campaign (1993-95), like Jesmond Dene in Newcastle before it, brought the road protests into the city. The motorway extension punched through communities and now stands high on stilts above them. Although the campaign ultimately did not prevent the building of the road it was the first significant step the emerging grass roots environmental movement made in engaging with urban spaces and communities.

Now familiar techniques were used to delay the construction of the road. Site invasions and occupations were combined with sabotage to stop construction work. This led to large numbers of police and constant security patrols being employed to protect the construction sites, at great expense—the delays and security escalated the total cost of construction by tens of millions of pounds.

Groups of the empty compulsorily purchased houses were squatted and fortified. The autonomous republics of Wanstonia and Euphoria were declared and duly evicted by over seven hundred police.

"Claremont road took things to another plane, a crescent off the main drag. The road was blocked to traffic and the site transformed. A sculpture of resistance, made of what the everyday folk left behind. Art in the face of power, a street, a squat and a home. Crowned with a scaffold tower and

skirted with web-like nets it stood; a carnivalesque symbol of defiance. A free -form barricade with no front or back, its sacred geometry defied the profane lines the Metropolitan police drew around it. Eventually it fell but the seven day eviction left shards of its destruction in a thousand hearts, shards that would rejoin, be split again, and rejoin again." - Twos-up Dave

"Claremont Road was so amazingly tranquil and happy. A long street of some 30 Victorian houses, tree lined on one side, houses on the other, these now all squatted and wildly decorated in psychedelic art, except for one house, still the domain of the sweet 93 years young Dolly, looking on in bemusement at her new friends and would-be saviours."

Sofas and chairs in the street, a no-car zone apart from the street's very own green 'Rust in Peace' car, full of art and flowers. A cafe, an office, and a thriving little community, all asking me for "Any spare change". Busking in the sunshine, dogs yapping, the breeze in the trees, and artistic happenings aplenty. It was a very dynamic and yet meditative atmos. I may not be a tattooed punk, but I loved it there."

For further reading see www.schnews.org.uk/sotw/claremont-rd.htm

Nick Cobbing

Hunt Sabbing

"Thugs, Wreckers and Bullies" – Michael Howard talking about hunt sabs in 1993 CJB speech

Disrupting the blood sports of the idle rich was never going to make anyone popular with the establishment. In the early nineties, still clad in the foetid rags of anarcho-punk, sabbing was a force to be reckoned with, with up to a 150 self funded, autonomous groups up and down the country taking direct action to save wildlife every week. Mass hits could see up to two hundred Sabs descend on a single hunt, outfoxing local police.

1992/3 saw an escalation of violence against hunt saboteurs reach its peak when Foxhunts recruited paramilitary stewards to confront the Sabs. The resulting rise in violent incidents was used by the British Field Sports Society (precursor to the Countryside Alliance) to help Michael Howard impose the aggravated trespass sections of the CJA. It became an offence punishable with prison to *trespass on land with the intent to disrupt lawful activity*. Trespass had always been a civil matter, now big landowners were granted another set of rights at the expense of the rest of us.

Used to being at the wrong end of the truncheon in any case, Sabs fought back, joining the anti-CJA movement and dealing with police harassment with the time honoured tactic – running "If they can't touch you they can't arrest you".

National hits were called, using numbers to defy the law, culminating in the infamous Battle of Stagden Cross in Essex where the hunt cowered behind police lines as Sabs demonstrated their defiance.

Despite their best attempts, Mikey Howard and his toff friends never did break the movement and the fight continues to this day.

Testa

Testa

TALLY HO FOR THE CRIMINAL JUSTICE ACT

Anti-CJB March Trafalgar Square, Mayday 1994 Pic: Matt Smith

characterised by the emission of REPETITIVE BEATS

Resistance to the Criminal Justice Bill 93-95

Here are several peoples' accounts of the resistance to the Criminal Justice Bill emerging in Britain, the key events along the way, and some thoughts about the ongoing effects of both the CJA, and the political movements which came together to resist it.

It was in 1992 that the first intimations emerged in ministerial speeches that a new law was imminent, and as 1993 drew to a close it became apparent that the new law would see a major crackdown on travellers, squatters, free festivals & parties, public protest and other activities which had become a regular way of life for thousands.

If you're not outraged, you're not paying attention!

The work of canny media-watchers, like 'SQUALL' (the magazine "for squatters, travellers & assorted itinerants"), meant that we began learning about the Tory Government's latest plans before the Queen's Speech announced them for certain in November 1993.

What had been devised was a gargantuan piece of criminal law entitled the Criminal Justice & Public Order Bill. Its contents covered a wide and seemingly unrelated series of clauses covering everything from increased stop & search powers, the ending of the right to silence, sanctions against public assembly, DNA sampling of suspects, right through to the age of consent for gay men.

Pic: Matt Smith

No Mad Laws

The bits that had the effect of catalysing a generation to stir itself into political dissent were in Section 5 of the Bill: the introduction of all sorts of new criminal offences, blatantly aimed at all kinds of subversive/sub-cultural activities. Hunt sabbing, squatting, assemblies of vehicles, trespassing in order to protest or party, attending large gatherings, playing repetitive beats in public…

'Wholly or predominantly characterised by the emission of a succession of repetitive beats.'

"When I first heard about the Bill, I was living in a squatted house on the route of the M11 Link Road in East London. We used to joke about how they were just trying to make us paranoid. We were jumping onto machinery on the work-sites, living in squats, having big parties, going off to festivals, and it seemed like every single thing we did was being targeted".

Back in those early days, if you sat down and thought about the Criminal Justice Bill, you realised that you had two basic choices: Either stick your head in the sand and ignore it as long as you could, or do something about it…

Aware that it had the potential to affect, but also unite, all kinds of groups and scenes, we organised a networking meeting in south London and invited everyone we could think of that we thought might be interested in somehow opposing it. Our priority after that meeting was to spread the word far and wide, through all our existing networks, and a few more besides.

"We figured that lots of people (including ourselves) had been hearing vague rumours about the new laws, and knew that they were going to affect us, but it wasn't clear exactly what would be involved. Our first task was to go through the actual Bill with a fine tooth-comb, trying to identify which clauses were particularly objectionable and then explain in easier English what they said.

"The comedy value of the legal definitions used in the Bill was fully exploited. Who can forget 'music characterised by a succession of repetitive beats'?!"

Assuming that your wild optimism didn't extend as far as believing that a few well-written letters to MP's would be enough to stop the legislation going through, the next step was figuring out what to actually do.

From the earliest days, these meetings always reflected an almost-impossibly broad spectrum of political background, consciousness, understandings and preferred methods. We were simply a network of groups and individuals fighting a common enemy, and that common enemy was pretty easy to hate regardless of personal political persuasions.

It's nigh on impossible to generalise about the kinds of people who ended up playing a part in the anti-CJB struggle. One writer at the time describes a march of "hunt sabs, ravers, the homeless, Travellers, '88 Chartists, libertarians, children, Outragers, dogs, SWP, Green Anarchists, entertainers and Black Flaggers, as well as plenty of plain ordinary folk belonging to no recognisable group or organization."

There was already lots of natural overlap &

friendship links between the different 'scenes' and networks – instinctive leanings towards do-it-yourself, creative thinking, anarchist methods of doing things. Lots of people wouldn't have described themselves as 'activists' but they were already active in all sorts of ways, experienced in working in collectives, making events happen on a shoe-string budget, doing what they did for the love, or sheer necessity, of it…

A multitude of different groups existed, each focusing on its own field of interest: Advance Party, Road Alert, Forgive us our Trespasses/Earth First!, Hunt Saboteurs Association, Liberty, Friends & Families of Travellers, Squatters Action for Secure Homes (SQUASH) & the Advisory Service for Squatters, a myriad of local FINs (Free Information Networks), the Exodus Collective and other sound systems, festival crews and co-ops. Some of these were much bigger or better established/organised than others; some were made up of people brand-new to political action.

Unlicensed fun will become illegal: Act Up

When we started spreading the info, we knew that there were plenty more people out there who shared our concerns (or some of them) and could be prevailed upon to take some political stance, often for the first time in their lives. A map in the London Freedom Network office showed all the autonomous groups operating locally around the country: it mushroomed from about 15 to about 80 in a few short months in 1994 as knowledge of, and opposition to the CJB swept the UK. By the summer's end, a LOT of people had heard about the CJB, and got involved in some way in the hundreds of protests against it.

People now might reminisce – with either love or frustration - about the sheer diversity of the opposition to the CJB. "The campaign was all about uniting people in their opposition to one last fling of complete Tory madness, and we were all trying hard to get on with each other". The names chosen for each local network may have varied ("Reaction to the CJB", "Defiance Alliance", "Freedom Network") but the vibe was the same – trying hard to work together in a rather delicate alliance, to leave our sometimes deep differences at the door and focus on fighting the planned laws rather than each other. To a certain extent we succeeded in doing this, and the year proved a highly educational roller-coaster for everyone who applied themselves to the campaign.

Freedom Network - and a fair few of the groups that sprung up at that time - enthusiastically embraced the whole "DIY ethos" and the identity of a "disorganisation" (we were strictly no-members; there were no "leaders" or paid staff; our meetings were open to all) but this led to its own challenges.

Many people were new to the murky business of politics, and not experienced enough to recognise or counter the problems often thrown up by structurelessness. We had a touchingly naïve belief in welcoming everybody's contribution, which left us influenced by all sorts of nutters, one-man campaigns (and they always were men), radical peaceniks, the SWP and some very woolly, liberal thinking. However this was the first time that a lot of us had turned into political campaigners and been forced to start thinking about the wider picture, about how the murky world of politics works.

A few people chose to direct their attention to other parts of the Bill – eg the stop and search provisions. Football Fans against the Criminal Justice Bill was a well-organised initiative pretty early on in the campaign.

On Monday 24th January 1994, the Criminal Justice and Public Order Bill entered its commitee stage in parliament. If it goes through you may be arrested for • Tress-passing on land • Failing to leave land • Waiting for a gathering/rave • Attending a gathering/rave • Making preparation to hold a rave • Squatting • Hunt saboteuring.
These laws will contravene the United Nations Commission for Human Rights in respect of your; • Right to silence • Right to peaceful protest • Right to travel freely • Right to free assembly.

March & Rally
against the criminal justice bill
Sunday 1st May 1994 2pm
Speakers Corner, Hyde Park, London

If you don't get involved physically & financially then everything that happens to you over the next couple of years will be your own fault.
Don't talk about it: Do it!

Keep it sweet.
Keep it right.
Remember this is a peaceful fight.
For more information contact The Advance Party 081 959 7525

The circus comes to town, Picadilly Circus, Mayday 1994 Pic: Simon Wheatley

One action is worth a thousand angry words

The "DIY" (do it yourself) ethos meant that we encouraged everyone to take whatever they judged to be appropriate autonomous action (relying on the old anarchist theory that if there's enough natural support/enthusiasm & energy for something to happen then it will happen!) This led to the creation of several now-infamous items: the round "Non-Violence' stickers, and a small leaflet entitled "Keep It Fluffy", each project initiated by a single person.

The North says No

The campaign flourished. Looking back at old 'events listings' I'm still amazed at how much we did. There were several actions every week, info-stalls at festivals & other events, and a full calendar of focused protest activity all over the country.

Most actions involved doing something that might potentially be criminalised, which meant pretty much anything went: mass trespasses, occupations, direct action, squatting, free festivals, carnivals, funeral processions, sit-downs, 'vigils for 'democracy', gatherings, hunt sabotages, visits to MPs' homes, picnics, silent raves, rambles, and much, much more. The campaign engendered oodles of creative energy: billboard-modification (subvertising), comedy nights ("laugh in the face of the CJB"), inventive photography projects, re-enactments of historical events, graffiti, big benefit parties, art shows, squat cafes, clowning & circus, fax-jams…

A lot of it was symbolic, and proved an easy entry for people new to protest. We tried to avoid narrow definitions of 'direct action', excessive macho posturing and exclusivity.

"It was great. People got involved at whatever level they wanted to: there was so much to choose from that they could do what suited them. We were all spinning our own parts of this amazing web of resistance to the State's plans…"

"We did small actions, usually organised by less than ten people, often their first time doing something like this. It was exciting, highly educative, and felt very safe".

"My favourite actions were things like the suffragettes, and this local event we had: 'Brixton Bubbling against the Bill' (basically a procession with a flat-bed truck, that went in and around all the estates). And there were the M11 protestors who got up on the roof of Parliament, that was brilliant". "There was even a song written about that, by the Tofu Love Frogs!"

Other memorable – and cheeky - actions included the surprise visits to Michael Howard's house in Kent,

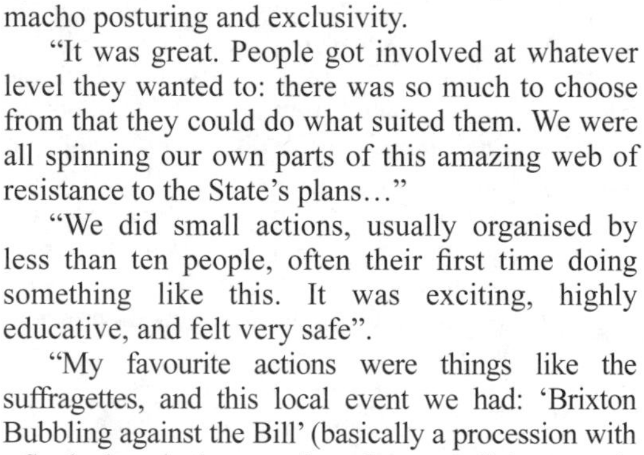

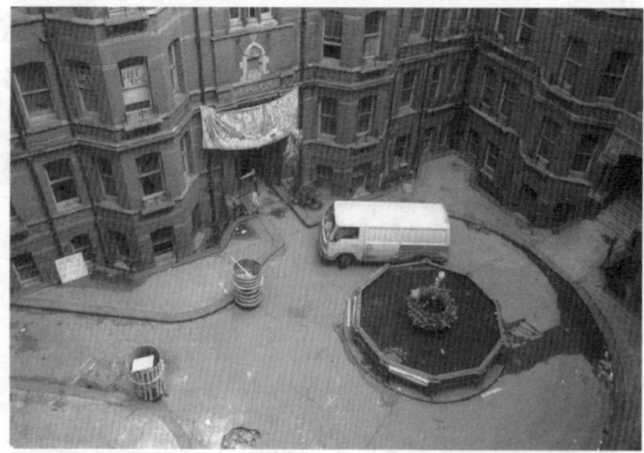

New Squatland Yard - Armoury Square, London, Feb 94 Pic: Alec Smart

and to William Waldegrave's farm, and lots of squatting. One of the earliest anti-CJB actions started in February 1994: the occupation of Artillery Mansions, a huge and criminally-empty building of flats a few hundred yards from the houses of parliament and right across the road from New Scotland Yard police HQ. The building became known as New Squatland Yard and attracted heaps of media coverage as well as offering rough sleepers a flat of their own.

So much for demonstrating about the right to celebrate and dance for free, why not just do it? After the London Mayday demo in 1994, sound systems Sunnyside, Vox Populi and Desert Storm found a forest site at Wanstead Common, East London to carry on the celebration of dissent. Pic: Matt Smith

A lot of what we did was highly symbolic rather than effective (in any sense other than a media-stunt). "We were trying to get the word out to as many people as possible, as cheaply as possible, so we did high-profile, well-thought-through, fancy actions, highly visible, and tried to up the media". "Gettting the word out and influencing public opinion – that's where you need to get the mass media in. That's something we could learn from that time: in terms of using our energy wisely, we focused our efforts on small, direct, actions which aimed to either cause financial damage or get a nice photo on the front pages of the nationals".

There seemed to be less disagreement about the tactic of engaging with the mainstream media, partly because there weren't many good alternatives. SQUALL had set up as a small A5 magazine in 1992 originally to highlight issues of squatting before burgeoning rapidly into a well respected and hefty tabloid-sized tome distributed across the UK four times a year (see www.squall.co.uk). SchNEWS and other local news-sheets were formed as part of the campaign against the CJB with SchNEWS going on to become a relentlessly regular weekly info sheet covering a multitude of significant political issues, and again distributed throughout the British Isles and beyond. These media outlets allowed campaign groups to get an inspiring handle on the size of the movement, helped tool activists up with accurate information, and allowed different groups to understand each other's methods better. The anti-CJB/anti-roads campaigns also inspired activist video-projects, primarily with Undercurrents but later encompassing even more grassroots, low-budget examples. Continuing attempts to broaden our own media and the eventual creation of an Indymedia network followed. Activist journo's from these alternative media outlets would also appear regularly on mainstream radio and television channels to give the political issues a louder voice.

We were hot news for a while, but the mainstream media would often represent us in the ways that suited their pre-agenda more than suited the reality of what was occurring, and this was often a problem.

Did we use them or did they use us? "We used them. Definitely. We picked our journalists, mostly used the freelance ones who'd joined the campaign." "it was a key way of getting the information out, as were our own media as they developed: we used both".

Wake up Democracy's Dying

A similar dynamic existed in our dealings with NGOs and groups like Charter 88, or Liberty. We needed to distribute information about the Bill, and these organisations had the resources to produce buckets of

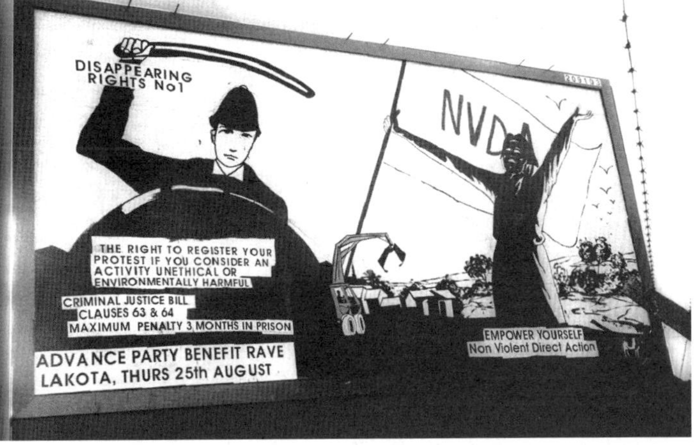

Billboard in Bristol, paid for by the band The Levellers, hand decorated Pic: Matt Smith

Anti-CJB March, London, 23rd July 1994 Pic:Matt Smith

leaflets, but naturally these would reflect more liberal views (and problematic concepts like 'democracy' & 'rights') than many of us actually had.

JCB the CJB

The anti-M11 campaigners in East London launched 'Operation Roadblock', a full-on month of daily direct action against the road-building.

'Forgive Us Our Trespasses' ("Earth First!'s answer to the CJB") began a national scheme to encourage groups to break the new trespass laws in whatever way they saw fit.

Fight for your Right to Party

Advance Party suggested a big march on May 1st 1994, to be a refreshingly different event than most humdrum slogs through the streets of central London. The presence of sound systems and some live festie bands on a truck on the march made a huge difference. It was infected with a new dance-culture energy ("think thousands of cheesy quavers with their hands in the air and smiles on their faces!") that evolved into Reclaim the Streets parties in years to come.

Why march when you can dance?

May 1st "was great, it was vibrant, bright, it felt like we were onto something. Unfortunately that was what attracted the attention of the SWP. July 24th was huge, out of our control, and out of their control too."

The SWP decided it worth their predatory interest to do the usual: set up a front organization called "The Coalition Against the Criminal Justice Bill" (as though we hadn't been coalescing quite well without them, thanks very much!) and make heaps of placards with the name of their newspaper on the top…"

They steamrolled everyone into signing up for another big march on July 24th and turned most anti-CJB campaigners right off. Older hands were already suspicious of them and their insidious tactics, and everyone left disempowered by their methods/unexcited by their tactics. We carried on doing our own things (eg displays & agitation at the Hackney Homeless People's festival, a mass trespass at Twyford Down, and lots of smaller actions) in the run-up to the July march.

What got the media headlines at that march was some scuffling with the police, smoke-bombs, and the fairly thorough testing given the metal gates across the entrance of Downing Street. The incident prompted the construction of the new, improved, and much sturdier gates now in place, and it was later rumoured that the police had planned to use rubber bullets (for the first time on the mainland) if the gates had been breached by protestors.

"The SWP were successful in taking over/influencing the campaign far too much. Basically, they had the financial clout to make hundreds of posters, organise coaches for the national demos etc in a way that we couldn't match. All they really did was those two big demos, and some speaker meetings, it was terribly top-down, not very creative, and ultimately disempowering for us. Decisions were being made by an unelected cabal within the Party, with secret minutes – they'd set their final position before any meetings so there was no real discussion".

However, because the SWP were trying to usurp and take over anarchist inclined campaign groups with no formal hierarchy, they were never that successful. People just got bored of them quite quickly and the SwaPo's, as they were nicknamed, could never quite get hold of the rudder in order to stear the ship their way. They did manage, however, to steal some of the media publicity off the backs of more creative campaigns.

"We undoubtedly suffered the attentions of agents provocateurs, and the organised Left, but to be honest we were quite capable of causing our own chaos and problems."

Criminal Justice Act
FREE ZONE

We assert our rights to:

- Freedom of peaceful assembly,
- Freedom of expression,
- Remain silent under arrest,
- Gather and party.

For more information contact
Freedom Network - 071 738 6721

Fluffy/Spikey Debate

Keep it fluffy keep it right remember this is a peaceful fight Vs Keep it Spiky

One of the big lessons to be learnt from the anti-CJB campaign might be the danger of polarising our movement (whether that's between 'violence' & 'non-violence' or anything else) and inflicting shallow, stereotypical, judgements on each other.

There was a great deal of over-simplified 'debate' over the levels of violence and non-violence that varying groups and individuals were comfortable with. We wasted a lot of time feeling forced to pick between two equally-badly-defined boxes, and failing to find a way for everyone to respect each others' tactical choices.

"Either you were a 'fluffy' and all that implied: you'd gladly lie down and let the police ride their horses over you cos you got off on that kind of thing. Or you were 'spiky': hard as nails and twice as loud, and the kind of person who drank too much Special Brew/Stella at the park, threw things from the back of the crowd, and managed to injure or just offend most of your fellow-demonstrators".

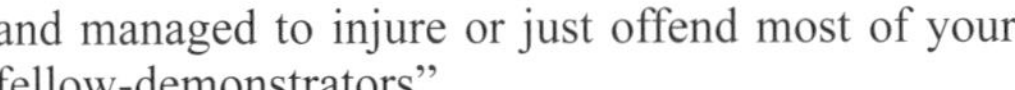
Going overboard at Downing St, 23rd July 94 pic: Alec Smart

Velvet Revolution

"Launched late summer 1994, the Velvet Revolution Tour was an interactive, audio-visual and multi-media explosion of popular resistance to the Criminal Justice and Public Order Bill, which rocked the socks off venues across the country.

Kicking off at The Hacienda, Manchester's famous rave HQ, the tour took in more or less every major city south of the border. It included an unadvertised fake riot Police bust who would try to shut down each gig. On the first night one fancy dress riot copper decided to test the integrity of her disguise; stopping a real riot van full of plod right outside the Hacienda. Fortunately they saw the funny side.

After the first of the tours' London gigs at Middlesex University, tired and exhausted after yet another all-nighter, almost everyone involved headed off to take part in the third and final demo against the Bill, only to find themselves in the middle of a riot in Hyde Park. Later, when the tour moved to Sheffield the police paid a fruitless little visit to try and cancel the performance. In Nottingham, the local force surrounded the tour in a car park and threatened a violent eviction, but backed down after negotiations.

The final date of the tour was November 4 1994 at Heaven, one of London's most famous and long running nightclubs. It was a fitting date for the tour to end, as on that very day, a few miles away the Queen finally put her signature of consent to the legislation making it law. At the time the talk was not so much about the fact that no matter what the public thinks, politicians will always make laws to suit themselves and their hidden agendas, but was more about speculating what would happen the very next day, which just happened to be Bonfire Night."

Part of the Velvet Revolution show included a fake police bust Pic: Matt Smith

Squatting is STILL legal!

The squatters' groups had a reputation for being quite well-organised; they benefited from a background of local squatters' aid groups (in cities like Bristol as well as London) and similar struggles in the past. They were already looking ahead, and trying to plan for the future, eg. monitoring the introduction of the new anti-squatting measures, "because no-one else will do it".

The morning after the... Mother Festival, Smeathorpe, Devon, July 95. This was supposed to be a big free festival in defiance of the CJA, but because of police suveillance ended up in chaos in two locations. Pic: Matt Smith

Squatters were among the first to warn against the dangers of scare-mongering. The worry was that many only heard the bare bones of the Bill, and once they heard it had become law, would probably assume that all squatting was now completely illegal/impossible. We'd been hyping up the dangers of the CJB, trying to inspire outrage & involvement by providing extreme examples of its potential usage, but by the end of the summer 1994, some were trying hard to ensure that more detailed information went out.

By the time the Bill became an Act (3rd November 1994), most groups had changed their approach and we'd formed a massive network of actions in direct defiance of the law and for/against a wide array of other issues at the same time. We tried to keep track of how the Criminal Justice Bill/Act was being introduced, and to ensure that people were equipped with the facts (and often more up-to-date with the new rules than the police themselves). And of course, dealt with a silly number of letters from students doing projects on the subject!

Diversity, Dissent

As predicted, Liberty quietly dropped its much-vaunted "Public Order Monitoring Project" once it had served their aims of finding suitable cases to use in mounting legal challenges at the European Court of Human Rights. Lacking Liberty's paid staff and resources, we had been happy at the thought of them coordinating the monitoring: but now we're left with very little real information about the uses of the Act. SchNEWS proved a more useful (and much more accessible) record of what actually happened, even since the 'Arrestometer' feature disappeared!

The day after the CJB becomes an Act, five climb onto the roofs of the Houses of Parliament unfurling the banner 'DEFY THE CJA'. A still taken from a TV report, 4th Nov 1994

Together we'll crack it!

Different parts of the CJA became law at different times, some on November 3rd itself (prompting good-natured competitiveness between different groups trying their hardest to be among the first few arrests!) and some others not until mid-1995.

Many police forces were reluctant to use the new powers before being issued with guidelines; the exceptions were the 120-odd hunt sab arrests during the first few months, and the incredible enthusiasm shown by Kent Constabulary in nicking both anti-road protestors from the 'Flat Oak Tribe' fighting the "Blue Route" at Thanet Way (who chalked up an impressive 64 CJA arrests between them, and some crap bail conditions, and a spot of remand custody for not following these!), and the new wave of anti-live-exports protests at Dover, Shoreham and other docks.

Disobey the CJA

There was still a lot of activity in 1995. By June, there had been 1000+ arrests at the anti-live export demos. There was direct action against road-building at Solsbury Hill, the Wells Relief Road and the M11 Link (although most of the squatted houses along the route had already been lost), and against quarrying and open-cast extraction. There was a surprise occupation of Stonehenge on VE Day, RTS successfully pulled off their first Street Party in Camden, and another newly-formed group, 'This Land is Ours', began a series of land-squats with a week-long occupation of an old airfield near St George's Hill in Surrey.

Knees up Mother Earth

There is definitely less squatting now that there was a decade ago but the CJA laws aren't the only reason: The increasing pressure on land in the South-East of England, accompanied by rising prices and relentless gentrification in many of the inner-city areas once favoured by squatters, has affected entire working-/under-class communities. On top of that, Thatcher's 'Right to Buy' scheme and the forced privatisation of so many Council services has put many formerly Council-owned properties out on the open market for more 'efficient'/profitable use. There will always be empties, but not as many entire estates/blocks/streets as there once were, making squatting a less 'easy' option.

Free festivals were another of the supposed targets of the Bill. What really affected them was the massive wave of emigration that the proposals generated among New Travellers.

There are thousands of refugees from the once-flourishing free-festival scene who now live abroad, eg in France, Spain & Portugal. They realised the shape of things to come here, were tired of being trashed (physically and in the popular press), and the CJB provided the final impetus they needed to make the decision to get out. Ten years on, they still ain't coming back.

The CJA included the repeal of the 1968 Caravan Sites Act (which obliged local authorities to provide limited – and often expensive and crap - sites for Travellers). There were never enough sites to match demand, and now the situation is worse, with even fewer authorised permanent or transit sites.

No justice, just us

Free parties – both urban and rural – continued, but "People from the rigs had been hearing too much about it – they weren't up for taking the shit – I mean, the party people were still up for it, and parties still happened. But they got pushed underground… meaning, the organisers got much more sensitive… sensitive to people noticing, or bringing it on top, places away from anyone seeing or hearing it or getting annoyed. They happened less often, and were always word-of-mouth". "Squat parties have changed. The law made it theoretically quicker for owners to chuck squatters out, so party crews stopped opening places well in advance of the parties, didn't spend as much time decorating the space…" "….and of course, ketamine reared its ugly head. It fitted perfectly with the nihilism which followed the eviction of all the anti-road camps".

Looking back now, the new police powers and measures can be seen as part of a continuing process of repressive legislation designed to make it harder for any of us to resist the system.

Similar measures were introduced at the same time in other European countries (including France, Germany, Spain & Sweden): cracking down on public disorder, raves, Travellers & trespassing; legitimising police search powers; increasing information-gathering about 'extremists'; introducing prison sentences for some squatting offences; making deportations easier etc.

Did it win?

"Legally the Bill won. It achieved its aims, and has definitely affected what we do, and what sorts of direct action tactics we use. It used to be that you just got done for Breach of the Peace, or something minor like that. I was nicked at Newbury, and after that had to start making careful decisions, because I'd decided I wasn't prepared to go to jail for any length of time at that point". Most people agree that the tactics they use now, and the types of actions that they do, have altered as a result of the new laws."

When we were fighting the Bill, a lot of groups didn't really pick up the implications of the police being allowed to set bail conditions (In the past, you'd either be given unconditional bail, or taken to a court where the magistrate would set the conditions). Once the law was in, there was a bit of a silly season – of both crap arrests and would-be-laughable-except-it's-not bail conditions levied at many anti-road and animal rights protestors.

And, in case you forgot, the CJA also gave the police the right to take not just photos but also DNA samples from suspects. (They didn't do any of that cheek-scraping nonsense till then!) Obviously that was just the thin end of a wedge that's now moving towards full ID cards with biometric recognition technology…

Despite everything, all the hard work and sleeplessness, 1994 was exhilarating, positive, empowering, and mostly fun. "The landscape suffered a political shift in the wrong direction, but culturally it was a draw. We're still here, still active, and still in touch with each other. The anti-roads years were a sort of victory, the anti-GM mass trespasses and crop smashing were very successful, and each locally-initiated campaign benefited from the connections made in fighting the Bill".

We were able to continue networking our actions across this national network, automatically billing them all as 'in defiance of the CJA' and so bringing out the natural instinct of anyone who opposed the Act to come along and do it too! They often did, even if it was something they hadn't dreamt of doing before: dancing in a field or squatted building all night, protesting outside Campsfield detention centre or against live exports, resisting the eviction of a tree-house on the route of a new road or setting up a new 'social centre'.

"That was what got the punks and ravers together for the first time. It brought all the Neds in, got everyone united, got lots of people down to Pollok Free State (the camp set up on the route of the M77 link road through southern Glasgow) who otherwise wouldn't have got involved in something like that"

This was one positive outcome of the CJB. It prompted the creation of squatted social centres in lots of towns and cities without a tradition of this type of community initiative, where squatting for housing is relatively rare. And now the concept of publicly squatting a place (even just for a short time to make a point about a particular issue) doesn't seem as strange or unachievable.

When freedom is outlawed only outlaws will be free

"It'd be hard for anyone to have come away from the anti-CJB times with their opinions and lives unchanged, unless of course they were already a cynical old black-clad anarchist when it started!" The anti-CJB campaign undoubtedly did politicize a lot of people who hadn't been around for (or old enough to remember) the mass struggles of the '80s. As well as altering their views of the Government and its 'Opposition', "parliamentary democracy", political parties, and the entire electoral process, it encouraged a healthy disregard for the concepts of "lawful" & "unlawful", and disrespect for the forces of law and order. It opened their eyes to the possibilities of a different world. The links made while opposing the CJB lasted, and this momentum fed into all subsequent movements which followed…

DISCLAIMER: This is the work and collected thoughts of just a few of the many people who participated in some way in the anti-CJB campaign. Don't take our words and shaky memories for granted as the full story: all sorts of actions happened up and down the country that year, so you should be able to find people near you who were as involved as us. Ask them for their experiences & stories: collect your own oral history!

BATTLE

"At times the atmosphere was almost surreal: Lord Soper, the Labour peer, continued with his regular Sunday spot at Speakers Corner answering such questions as "How can we believe the scriptures?" and "Should Tony Adams be captaining England?" while in the background flaming litterbins were hauled across the road. A jogger, dressed in white top and shorts, entered from the top of the park. To his left, 20,000 people were dancing; to his right 20,000 people were in running battles with mounted police. Like a symbol of ignorant England, he just carried on running as if nothing had happened."

On October 9th 1994 an estimated 100,000 people marched in London in opposition to the Criminal Justice and Public Order Bill, which was slowly but surely edging its way to the statute books. The previous two marches were more like carnivals than traditional demos, but this one, although bigger and more defiant, seemed to be heading towards boring speeches in Hyde Park when… The sound systems turned on to Park Lane and the crowd went wild. This is a recollection of events, as told by the people who were there.

"Hundreds of protestors had crowded around the mobile sound systems, which were inching their way up Park Lane, against the wishes of the cops. A line of police was put across the road to try to stop them, but this soon disintegrated by the sheer force of numbers of the demonstrators. Police vans were swamped, and a few people climbed onto the roof and started dancing - one with a banner 'Stop trying to kill our culture'. This was more like it!"

"One of the great things about rave music is that it winds up the old Bill something chronic"

"Senior officers were aware that agitators planned to start a rave in the park using the sound systems which accompanied the march... The business of allowing large mobile sound systems at political demonstrations is a serious new problem that we will have to deal with" - The Job, the Met's paper.

"The sound-systems are now in the Park, surrounded by dancers. Someone's on the mike, chanting 'Here to dance, not to fight!' Have some people done so much E they're entirely removed from reality? As if a charge of riot cops will stop short when they see how nice they're being!"

"A few minutes later, scores of riot police climbed over the fence and charged. For those who've seen the riot police in action before, their desire to beat the shit out of people at random wasn't a surprise. But for those who hadn't, it was immediately unbelievable, provocative and enraging. At the first baton charge, everyone ran instantly. But the crowd soon realised that we were

OF HYDE PARK

vastly superior in numbers. Each attack became matched with a counter-attack. Every available object was flying at the cops - and they turned tail and ran. The mounted police were sent in but proved themselves next to useless… all police were chased out of the park within an hour."

"I have been at riots before - but this was the first time I have ever felt that violence by protestors was justified, as it was in self defence… I would never advocate the ethics of Class War and I think that their 'keep it spiky' leaflet was pathetic, and bound to be picked up on by the media, but if you are charged by a line of baton-wielding police, for merely dancing in the street, you fight back."

"By about nine o'clock a lot of people had gone home and the Park in the dark did not seem such a safe place. A police helicopter swooped down with a spotlight trained on the crowd and its own sound system broadcasting the message "Disperse now or force will be used". But dispersing wasn't easy even for those who wanted to go home. Lines of riot cops blocked most of the roads out of the area and tube stations were closed. When a gap appeared in the police lines some people took the opportunity to pour up Oxford Street with police charging behind. Shop windows were smashed as a last two fingers up to the cops, before dispersing."

After the riot the Met Police ruled out an investigation into tactics used during the march and rejected criticism of their handling of the situation: "I am proud of the way my officers reacted in the face of extreme violence" - Asst. commissioner Tony Speed.

"I was hit across the forehead with a truncheon. Two other policeman came from behind and swiped me across the legs and then the stomach with batons." - Danny Penman journalist with the *Independent*. "

"I was pushed down on the floor, punched, hit across the back with a truncheon, and then three police were just kicking me and hitting me with truncheons. It took four people to get them off me. I was in agony. They were acting like hooligans." - Vincent Seabrook, Coalition Steward

"I went to Hyde Park and left a different person"

"It was about 10pm I was standing just inside the park fence looking out at the giant fighting scrum that filled Park Lane trying to work out what to do when my boyfriend shouted 'run' and jumped over the fence. I glanced behind just in time to see a group of riot police jump on me. I don't recall how many. They threw me on the ground and started kicking me… they were shouting 'get out of the fucking park you slag' and similar verbal abuse. Then one pulled me onto my feet by my hair and two of them started marching me to the park gates. Another behind me kicked me so hard I couldn't walk, and so was dragged instead by the back of the neck."

Pics: Matt Smith

The lasting effect of the Criminal Justice and Public Order Act and the Battle of Hyde Park was to bring together a range of disparate groups and politicise many people, as the *Independent* editorial stated afterwards: "Yesterday's march marks the discontent of an increasingly vocal and well organised groupings of minorities that challenges the social conservatism now endemic across British politics."

Part 2

JUST US?

To celebrate the tenth anniversary of SchNEWS, Jo Makepeace interviewed some of the original *'Justice?'* crew who helped to spawn SchNEWS as we know it today. Gail, Dave FT and Carly try to shed some light on its origins and weird name among other things...

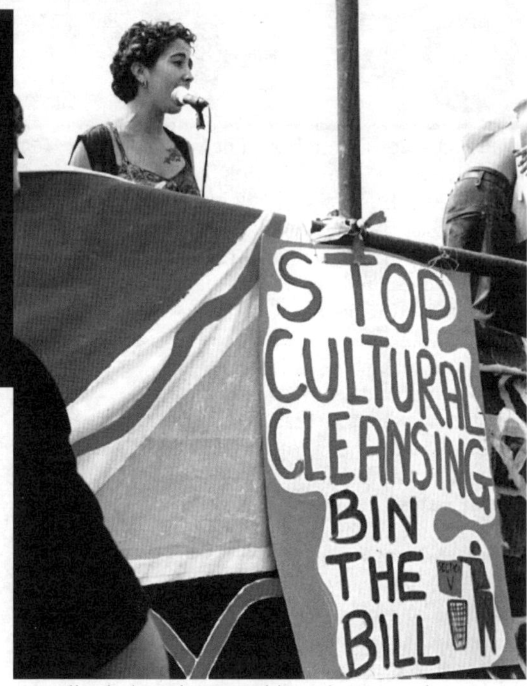

Justice? was a loose collection of like-minded individuals from the Brighton scene who canvassed pubs, clubs and other gatherings to warn people that their rights were in danger from the Criminal Justice Bill. The Prince Albert Pub gave them space for free and the meetings grew. When one woman, Gail, heard about the Bill, she went to Brighton library and read the bill cover to cover. As the need for an office to co-ordinate the many innovative ideas became apparent, Gail decided to give up her job, set up an office in her home and throw herself into campaigning. After a few months of the weekly Justice? meetings, numbers dropped off a little and Gail ended up on her own one Wednesday evening in the Albert pub with 12 people from the Socialist Workers Party who had suddenly become interested.

Gail: "I just didn't give them any jobs to do and got on the phone to get everyone else to come back the next week. The following week when a more diverse group had reconvened, the selling of party material was banned by consensus. They could come and participate, but not recruit. It was essential that Justice? remained unaffiliated to any political group in order to maintain its open, grass roots motivation."

What sort of stuff did Justice? organize?

"We did a couple of marches through Brighton, organized a picnic, coaches for the demos in London, printed up leaflets with information, lobbied the council - that sort of thing. We used to do stalls at a lot of club nights. Most of the clubs in Brighton were quite convivial towards the movement - they wanted to be seen to be doing something good. The Brighton club scene wasn't as corporate as it is now.

After about six to eight months we decided to do a community squat. This was inspired by what we had seen at Cooltan Arts in Brixton and the Rainbow Church in Kentish Town. When it was decided that Justice? would take on this task, the group was divvied up into working groups such as squat cracking, program planning, cafe, etc.

Old Courthouse

Gail: After actually cracking the place it was amazing, with loads of people coming out of the woodwork through word of mouth and helping out - it took on a life of its own! It was only supposed to be open for a week or two. Between the time of moving into the Courthouse and then moving out of the Courthouse, the people involved in Justice? changed quite dramatically. A lot of people were living there the whole time - so therefore they were putting pressure on. But it wasn't supposed to be about housing people - it was supposed to be about raising awareness, having a focus, a constructive community centre where you had a system of events, workshops, and things.

The Courthouse was also very theatrical. Lots of creative things were going on. Gibby was like 'Let's do the news. We'll call it the SchNEWS.' It was 'Wake up Wake up this is the SchNEWS in the Courthouse.' A live run-through of short, snappy stories along a theme with Gibby, myself and others dressed up silly, doing a spoof reading of the news."

Were there conflicts about the same old things - violence/non-violence?

Gail: "Well there are differences of opinion in any group of people you get and even if people are working together against a common enemy or force you'll still have differences of opinion on how you should deal with it. So it wasn't arguments - it was just..."

...healthy debate.

Gail: "Sometimes the meetings were quite lively!"

What happened after the Courthouse?

Gail: "It was up into CJ's on Western Road. Then there was the housing association place down on Grand Parade. It started spiralling a bit, and the energy became a bit unfocused. It wasn't really an energy I wanted to be associated with 'cos it was more about trashing buildings and having a fight with the police instead of doing something constructive and positive. Then there's the problem of self-policing. When you're doing it all voluntarily, and you're getting loads of crap for it, it drains your motivation, so I decided to get a bit of my life back 'cos it had been quite all consuming. The whole idea about Justice? was that it was supposed to be a 'non-hierarchical fluid organization' so that different people at different times could take on different responsibilities, and I thought I'd done my time."

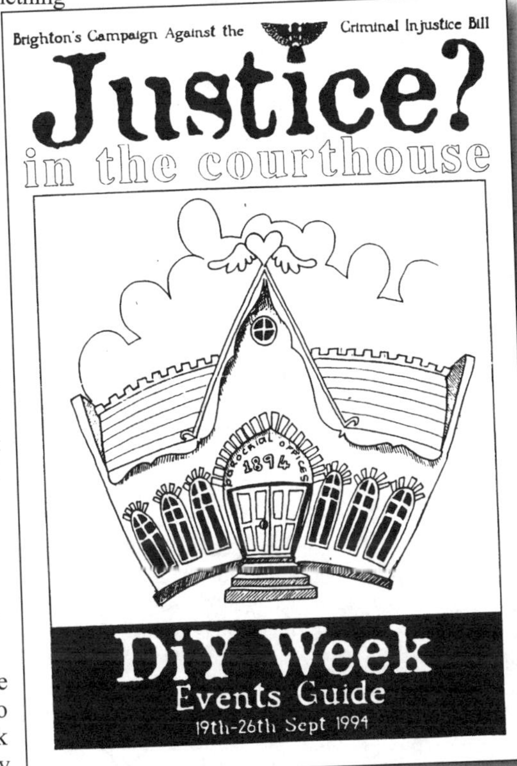

About the same time as the Courthouse, Justice? managed to blag themselves an office. How did that come about?

Gail: "I knew some people who knew the Levellers, so they took me down to talk to them and I told them they should show some support for a local group - give us some money! They weren't prepared to do that, but they gave us an office free of charge. The office has been really useful and stabilising for SchNEWS - it wouldn't have been able to go on if it wasn't for the office. I don't think it would have had the motivation, 'cos it's one thing keeping things together, it takes a whole different energy when you're having to move on all the time."

Did SchNEWS get a bit removed from Justice?

Gail: "Maybe because it was in a separate office and not everyone felt they could contribute, I suppose, so naturally SchNEWS became a separate identity. Another really important, generous help that came Justice?'s way was from Mikey who used to run the New Kensington Pub. He made his way to a meeting and offered up his pub where the SchNEWS could be read at regular Friday night readings - very much in keeping with the theatrical, satirical look at current affairs."

A SchTAR IS BORN

Dave FT decided to get involved with the anti-M11 protest in London. But that was before he was rung up by Gail and invited to a meeting in Brighton.

Dave FT: "This was held in a local pub where I was introduced to a group of around ten people. As I had edited the student union magazine and created artwork for gigs, I was recruited to help print Justice? fliers and posters. In the usual Justice? way - turn up and you've volunteered - I was introduced to Gibby and we left the meeting to work on the 'Deeds not Words' flyer design which we finished at 4am that night. Not bad for our first meeting.

As Justice? developed, I itched to start a newspaper. One of the deciding factors in starting SchNEWS came while attending one of the many meetings that occurred throughout 1994. The DIY movement, and Justice? in particular, seemed to suffer from a lack of collective memory - a continual problem in any kind of anarchist/radical project that has open membership and allows people to drift in and out.

The name SchNEWS itself came from a play on the idea of alternative news, hence 'News? SchNEWS!' Gibby and others originally performed SchNEWS in local pubs around Brighton. Half theatre, half information-broadcast, it was good at satirising the news and telling us what was happening, but not so good at helping us remember what we had done previously.

Gibby and I worked on producing the pilot issue of SchNEWS on 16th November 1994. It grew from a press release/flyer that we were planning to do to explain the closure of the squatted Court House. At that point it was touch and go whether anyone would support it. I think we were both surprised that people were so keen on the idea. In any case, the Justice? structure and decentralised decision making meant that if we were keen to keep it going, it was likely to continue.

A single gesture of defiance is worth more than a thousand angry words!!

FIGHT TRUTH DECAY

I wanted SchNEWS to scream 'Read Me!' and to be engaging. I hoped SchNEWS could be an alternative to the restricted and often biased news that the traditional media published. I designed the SchNEWS logo using the old-looking 'Attic' typeface. The logo just fitted immediately. It still amazes me that this design has been kept throughout SchNEWS' history.

SchNEWS issue 1 was the first time we actually attempted to collect news and information to publish and share. One of our main intentions was to avoid the style of jargon-filled newspapers that took themselves far too seriously. I favoured well laid-out readability, trying hard to balance content and look. Gibby on the other hand always wanted to get as much news into the paper as humanly possible. Indeed this would be the source of never-ending negotiations through the night, often till 6 or 7am. When we were ready to finish, Gibby would still be finding just 'one more typo', just 'one more small change'. I often wondered if readers realised how much effort was spent on creating the text of SchNEWS.

SchNEWS' distribution was a random and amazing thing. Somehow the magazine would be photocopied (people with office jobs would cane their work photocopier). It would turn-up all over the place and I was always astounded by the decentralised manner of its distribution and printing.

The entire nature of the Justice? blagging machine was epitomised when SchNEWS attended Glastonbury. We were given a small vehicle pass for two people. But we took traveller's lorry with as many people as could hide inside. Being questioned by security as to what was in the back and why we needed a 7.5 tonne truck in the first place was somewhat difficult (the windows and doors were suspiciously filled with computer boxes). But when I told them that if they damaged the equipment trying to take it out I would hold them directly responsible, we were let in. As we hadn't thought about the lack of electricity, in the end SchNEWS at Glastonbury had to wait till we got back to be written!

I now look back with amazement at the collective work of SchNEWS and how it continues to push forward without compromising its principles or the quality of its reporting. It still has a commitment

Just the Kick-start SchNEWS needed

"During the squatting of the Courthouse, some women from Women against Pit Closures came down to give a talk. I think they'd just dug up Heseltine's garden and were going round doing direct action against pit closures so we thought we'd ask them down to pick their brains. A couple of hundred people were there.

During the discussion about the inevitable eviction from the Courthouse, a few people were saying, "When the cops come to chuck us out, I think it's really important we keep the moral high ground and leave peacefully" - and the women just laid in. They said emphatically, "No, you don't do that - you stand up for yourselves!" I have this vivid memory of these people looking like they'd just been told off by their mum!

Then one of the women said "And how do you tell everyone what's going on? Have you got a newsletter?" And people were shaking their heads and looking at the floor, and they said 'Well you'd better bloody get one together then!' Quite soon after that SchNEWS started. That was certainly part of the reason it came about." - Colin

to news that is ignored by the mainstream media - written for free, published for free and given away freely, it is a remarkable contrast to our commodified culture of consumption."

In the mish-mash of opposition to the Criminal Justice Bill, Carly was one of those who at the time she got involved described herself as a 'Trot.' Her account shows some of the problems of large groups of people coming from different angles working together! As for SchNEWS, being a mum and having to get up earlier than most meant that Carly got lumbered with printing it up every Friday morning for years.

Carly: "I was on the national committee of a group called Youth Against Racism In Europe which was an offshoot of Militant. At one of these meetings they started talking about the Criminal Justice Bill and what you could do in your area. A lot of it was about lobbying your MPs and having demonstrations outside the town hall. I got really fired up. The meeting was in Coventry and I'd just got off the train in Brighton when I bumped into a friend of mine who said 'Quick - come down to the Courthouse, it's being threatened with eviction'.

I went down there and went up to one bloke all eager, 'I wanna talk about the Criminal Justice Bill and let's do something about it' and stuff like that - still not quite getting the point that they WERE doing something about it and they didn't need some jumped up trot telling them what they should be doing! And he went, 'Hey man, this is a community centre - Criminal Justice Bill – we're not into that now, this is a squatted social centre.' He was just a tosser quite frankly! There were lots of people like that involved in it and I felt quite let down at the time. Others didn't want to fight the eviction and just wanted to leave the Courthouse in a dignified manner! Then I met this other bunch of people - the Autonomous Group who seemed a lot more in agreement with my politics and where I was coming from and wanted to make a stand against the bailiffs."

WHEN FREEDOM IS OUTLAWED
THE CRIMINAL INJUSTICE ACT
TOGETHER WE'LL CRACK IT
ONLY OUTLAWS WILL BE FREE

So - what were the Justice? meetings like?

"It was quite a strange experience for me because I was used to going to meetings where someone would speak on a particular issue and then you'd all discuss it. And then there was a thing called 'any other business' at the end, which, to me, is what the Justice? meetings were! They were just the 'any other business' bit.

The Criminal Justice Act was still the major target, but then people from different groups would come and you'd be told about when there was a hunt sab and things like that. And it got people involved.

For instance I went on a hunt sab which I never thought I would do. But I went on it more because it was defying the Criminal Justice Act. It was the same with the live animal exports down in Shoreham - a lot of people went down there not because of the little fluffy animals: it was because of the politics behind it and because people were getting shat on. Trade unionists would come and talk about their struggles that were going on at the time and things like that - and people would get involved more as a show of solidarity and defiance against the Act that now made what they were gonna do illegal."

Then of course there was the endless fluffy v spikey debate …

"During that time there was a leaflet produced about the imminent eviction of the Courthouse. One line said 'to the barricades.' A couple of the fluffies argued that it would attract people from the estates who just wanted a fight with the police so they threw them all in a skip outside! Someone rescued them, then someone else said they were gonna sit up all night and just draw a line through that one line in it, which just showed you the type of the people there - very middle class hippies.

Still, I very quickly realised that it was extremely patronising for the Trots who'd come in like, 'We're politically pure. We'll show you what's going on. You're all silly little people, we'll show you what to do.' That wasn't what the spirit of the thing was about. It was everyone working together, and all coming to collective conclusions on stuff, rather than someone telling you what to think.

When Justice? was in its heyday, people were getting stopped at the Job Centre by police and pulled aside and told 'We know you're really skint - if you wanna make some more money we'll give you fifty quid and a pager if you infiltrate Justice? and tell us what they're up to', which gave us more of a sense of self importance. Another time there was a free party organised somewhere in the country. On the day, our phones went completely dead - when people were supposed to be phoning us to find out where it was. Another time you'd pick up the phone and you'd be put through to the police control room."

So what happened after Justice?'s Heyday?

"I think the Simon Jones Campaign was what Justice turned into, to a certain extent, because it was one of our own that had got killed. We took it extremely personally."

CJ's on Western Road Brighton - the second Justice? squat

Did you get involved in SchNEWS?

"The main thing I did was the printing every week - which was boring - at the Resource Centre. They used to have a really bad printer that broke down every 50 copies. But I thought this'll die like everything else. We thought we'd all go off and get a life!!! It's quite sad when you see some of the same people still involved now!"

The eviction of the Courthouse November 1994 Pic: Alec Smart

Justice? Brighton's Campaign in Defiance of the Criminal Injustice Act

Weekly SchNEWS

Pilot Issue | 16 November 1994 | Published in Brighton

Big Brother CCTV installed in Brighton

What are we doing to our town? The One State is upon us. We have given in. We accept that when we are out of our own homes, we are - at all times - to be watched, to be monitored. Fourteen CCTV (close curcuit television) cameras are panning across town, like searchlights, looking for any indiscretion, picking out any abnormal activity which may be sen as subversive. They will zoom in on our faces, track our movemnets, the police like legitamised voyeurs watching our activities, silently and detached. We have welcomed them in and we will come to forget them. Part of the street furniture, part of society. The argument for CCTV is strong - stop one rape, stop one murder and it will be hailed as a success.

Nobody *wants* to be watched all the time - it feels wrong. Surely if we are the ones to witness Orwell's prophesy fulfilled than we should look hard for any alternatives.

Firstly, CCTV doesn't solve crime - it relocates crime. And it smacks of a crippling lack of vision that the answer to this problem is to cover Sussex with blanket surveillance at enormous cost. Private business interests, it seems, are a higher priority than the liberties and freedoms of individuals to walk down the high streets without being videoed.

Secondly, Sussex police can say until they are blue in the face that the cameras will not be used for information gathering but by dividing police and public with machines can only create a climate of deep suspicion and mistrust.

However, there is an alternative. It's quite simple. It's called natural surveillance - people watching people. The same cut in crime that we are told to expect from the spies in the sky can be achieved by the relaxing of licensing laws and the opening of the town at night. Last year Manchester City Council experimented with extended liquor licensing and the results were amazing - all reported crime in the city centre down by 43%. All through the night there were people on the streets. People feeling safe in the knowledge that they are being watched by other people. The cost? Zero. The benefits of the 'night-time economy'? Enormous.

Surveillance cameras are an eerie and sinister development not inkeeping with the spirit of Brighton and Justice? opposes them with vigour.

FACTS

Cameras cost £310,000 - Agreement has been reached with Brighton Council that the scheme will not use video evidence in court for petty offences (graffiti/flyposting) but it will use the cameras to pick up such 'criminals' - Scheme to be widened to include Horsham, Worthing, Eastbourne & Hastings within 2 years - Scheme financed in partnership with private business/police/Brighton Council - Cameras can identify an individual at distance of 100m - Monitoring room at John St station next to control room. - Det Supt John Smith on record as saying "there is no intention of using the scheme for information gathering"

If by any chance you would like Brighton Police to know that you are watching them watching you, here's where you are being filmed:

If you are catching a train, messing about on the Palace Pier, wandering past the Clock Tower, strolling along the seafront, shopping on Bond Street, admiring the Pavilion or walking along West St or Russell Rd or Cannon Place or Preston St or Western Rd or Clarence Square or Middle St or Duke St or Martin St or East St or Gardener St or Church St or St James' St or the Old Steine or Black Lion St ... please say hello. Act-up!

SchNEWS live is broadcast at 5.45pm @ Prince George, trafalgar st. every Friday

Justice? evicted from the Courthouse

Q1. What happened to the Courthouse?
We were evicted last Thursday after a rooftop protest. Apologies to anyone who was on the phone tree and didn't receive a call - it was a bit hectic.

Q2. What happened to the Church?
Holy Trinity Church on Ship St was squatted and all the Justice? stuff moved in as a temporary measure. The Church was opened at the weekend for an exhibition on the Courthouse and the Criminal Injustice Act. There are already agreed plans for the church by another group who use derelict buildings and turn them into art centres. Because we didn't want to jeopardise their position (it took them 2yrs to get permission) we agreed with the owners to move out. There was also a problem of fire hazards, dry rot and structural damage which meant the Church wouldn't have been practical as Courthouse Mk II.

Q3. Where's the next squat?
First a bit of history. Justice? was formed to raise awareness of the Criminal Justice Bill in April. Organising a squatted info and action centre was only one element of the work that is done. Although a mad success, the Courthouse did have the effect of neglecting other areas of protest and tied people to one place instead of enabling them to take part in other direct action. It seems a consensus is growing that another centre would be a positive move but at a smaller scale and open 3/4 days a week. The office should be in a sustainable rented building. As the squatting law comes into effect in February and the law is not retrospective it would seem a good idea to mobilise a 'squat-the-lot' campaign. Lastly everyone needs a break to recover before this next action. **A temporary office has been set up. Tel: 691659**

Criminal Injustice Act attacked

from The Guardian 14/11/94

Prison governors warn today that the Criminal Justice and Public Order Act will lead to a huge increase in the jailing of people with unconventional lifestyles for minor criminal offences and amounts to a misuse of the criminal justice system.

The joint statement published today by the Penal Affairs Consortium, a group of 23 organisations involved in the prison system, says the legislation could have the effect of criminalising many of these people.

The consortium appeals to the police, prosecutors and the courts to apply the legislation with discretion "to avoid inappropriately harsh treatment of people who should not be processed through police stations, courts and prison cells."

David Roddan, general secretary of the Prison Governors' Association, said: "Until now the purpose of imprisonment has been to help people to lead law-abiding and useful lives on release. This act is a poorly drafted bundle of prejudices that could lead to a massive increase in people committed by the courts and nowhere to put them.

"Imprisoning individuals whose lifestyle simply does not conform to the norm of society and is rarely of a serious criminal nature is expensive, futile and an abuse of human rights."

"On release squatters will not magically be provided with housing, travellers will not suddenly change their lifestyle and young people will certainly not stop partying."

The Penal affairs Consortium says civil noise abatement powers already exist to deal with large unlicensed rave parties if persistent loud music is causing distress to nearby residents, but a sensible use of these powers is a long way from the wholesale criminalisation of young people by banning their raves, parties and gatherings."

Evening Anus

FIGHT BANAL

THE MONOPOLY OF SUSSEX EVERY DAY 2000 DON'T BUY!

WHO KILLED KENNY?

"Sunday will be the last night that we will open the pub. We are extremely sad about this, as we have loved working in the Kenny for the past five and a half

"The sole purpose of these large corporate pubs is to make money; although the Kenny and the Gladstone are still businesses, they provided a valuable community service.

Christmases back. Bar-workers who tried to get a petition asking for more wages were told by their bosses that if they didn't like it, they could get lost. Throughout the

If the office is where the 'official' SchNEWS work went on, the New Kensington Pub in Brighton's North Laine was certainly where the more popular 'unofficial networking' took place.

Situated smack bang in Brighton's alternative quarter, this is where for six years Brighton's doers, dreamers and dropouts liked to hang out. SchNEWS spoke to the ex-landlord Miki.

"My whole philosophy behind the pub was 'If I can't dance I don't want to come to your revolution.' We don't just want bread, we want bread and roses, and that was my idea of a pub. Sort of – beer and roses! And the roses were not just about making it as exciting a place as possible but also about providing this place where people could speak and have ideas and also where there was no discrimination. In all the time I was in the pub I didn't have to call the police once. Any bother we had, it was totally self-policing. People used to just stop the violence because people had a loyalty to the place.

I got involved with Justice? 'cos I was just so fucking angry about the Criminal Justice Bill. Since I was 11, when I went on my first CND demonstration, I've been protesting, and basically this act was about criminalizing legitimate protest. The Shoreham live animal export protests focused that for me. I'd never seen that level of violence before, apart from the poll tax riot. You'd see elderly ladies with hand-knitted banners being beaten up by police. Just before I came to Brighton I went with my then fifteen year old to protest against the BNP somewhere in South London where they'd set up a headquarters. I saw the police herd people into an alley, and push them against a cemetery wall, and the wall broke, and people were hurt. Things changed after the miners strike: suddenly there was a legitimisation of this violence, and they were actually saying that the people on the protest were the criminals.

I didn't know anything about the planning of the Courthouse but the minute I saw the banners up I was in there. I offered to do food for the kitchens from the pub. I cooked a lentil dhal and a great big bean stew in a big fuck off pot as my donation.

It was about January when we started doing things properly in the pub. There was SchLIVE every Friday and I used to try and liven it up a bit. People came down to it because it was very exciting. And the people who did it were so talented – so funny. It wasn't just the written word – it was spoken, felt with emotion.

It was a very exciting and productive time. I used to have a poster in the pub at election times saying, 'Whoever you vote for, the Government gets in'. This is even more so today when the Blair and Bush can totally ignore the wishes of people and wage war, killing thousands of innocent people. This is why SchNEWS is even more important than ever today. With all the spin and media manipulation that exists, at least we have access to some truth and decency, and that is what SchNEWS provides for us. Long may this continue."

Miki and his daughter Kath were evicted from the New Kensington in March 2000.

Pub Strike

However, the New Kensington wasn't just an alternative community centre - but one of 600 pubs that went on rent strike against their owners Inntrepreneur. Inntrepreneur were forcing publicans to buy barrels of beer from their own suppliers, which would cost up to £100 more than the pubs could get them on the open market. One publican likened it to the old feudal system, when workers would be given vouchers, instead of wages, that they had to spend in their bosses shops! This 'beer tie' was illegal under European Union competition laws and so Britain's first pub strike was born.

Inntrepreneur began a war of attrition with court case after court case, against any landlord or landlady that had dared to stand up to them. The Kenny was in and out of court until Inntrepreneur finally got the eviction notice they desired.

However, in May this year, a pub landlord from Staines became the first to be awarded damages under the anti-competition rules. He was given £250,000, and this ruling against the company may eventually cost Inntrepreneur more than £100m.

Talking of anti-competition rules, Inntrepreneur is owned by Japanese venture capitalists Nomura who also own First Quench – the country's largest off- license chain that includes Thresher, Victoria Wine, Wine Rack and Bottoms Up. Nothing like good old competition in the High Street is there?

SchLIVE

Pic: Alec Smart

Early Doors - 1994 / 1995

If you were to drop into the New Kensington pub in Brighton early on a Friday evening in those years, you would have caught the SchNEWS in another format - SchLIVE! These days everyone assumes that the SchNEWS newsletter came first but it didn't. SchLIVE came before the A4 newsletter and the website.

When Justice occupied the Courthouse in protest of the Criminal Justice Bill, bits of the bill were read out in a mock news reading show. It was an entertaining way of making announcements and getting the information across. After the Courthouse was evicted the SchNEWS was conceived, printed and read in the George but swiftly transferred to "the Kenny" as it became known –and that's where it really took off.

The format for the SchNEWS live was simple. Two or three people sat behind a table and read the SchNEWS, adding and correcting any mistakes, giving updates and so forth. Here, bits that hadn't made the latest edition could be added. It was in keeping with the age old tradition of oral history being spread via word of mouth. And although we didn't know it at the time, ten years on it's become a part of our own history.

SchLIVE back then could be a chaotic affair as nationwide actions against the CJA escalated, the arrests were steadily rising and we found ourselves being a focal point for those wanting to get involved in this DIY direct action movement. A lot of people in Brighton cut their teeth on direct action after going to those early SchLIVE's to get a take on what was really going on. It was precisely what Michael Howard didn't want.

Necessity breeds creativity. The only way we could get the truth out was to read it out in the pub. So we did - loudly!

The SchLIVE became a regular slot for the week and whilst some readings weren't as good as others there was always a feeling of purpose. We were reclaiming the media. The mainstream media had failed us so we simply created our own. There was no conscious decision to do this. It happened because it needed to happen. We couldn't just sit back and take the media blackouts and bullshit.

The SchLIVE could be a drunken mess sometimes. It could be serious thought provoking comment. It could be a debate that nearly got out of control. It was a punk version of Newsnight. It was political cabaret. Well –sort of.

The popular slots that made the SchNEWS a good read went down just as well live. Crap Arrest of the Week, the Arrestometer (chalked up on a slate) was booed and cheered at. Sometimes we dressed up in drag or as newsreaders. We got local musicians or actors to read. Anyone who was up for it or had something to put over was encouraged to have their say or publicise their event. We moved the show around from clubs to community squats slotted in between DJ's or bands. We became the information service for the clued up.

After a few months Conscious Cinema asked us to do the links for their first video magazine, which was a compilation of direct action footage from around the country. We filmed the links and screened it in the Kenny after a SchLIVE, and the use of video and commentary was a powerful combination – it was here that the idea for the tour came about. In one incredible night we screened Operation Solstice for the Battle of the Beanfield anniversary editon. The result was electric. The place was buzzing with energy, enthusiasm and anger.

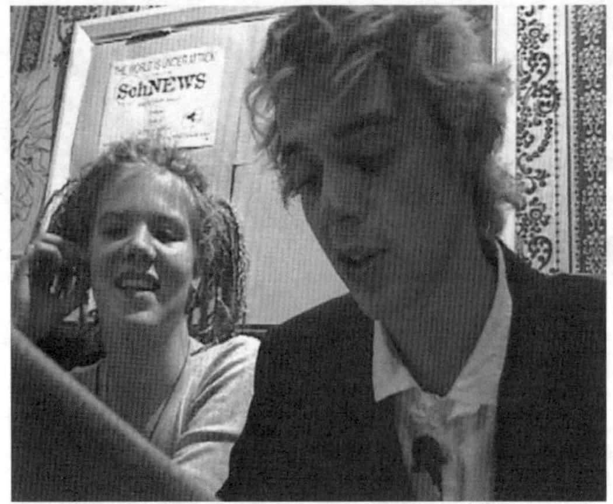

Gibby and Kate reading out the pilot issue of SchNEWS at one of the very first SchLIVE readings. The George pub, Brighton November 1994

So it was in this climate, with the Third Battle of Newbury making the arrestometer defunct and the words 'aggravated tresspass' passé, that we planned the first SchLIVE tour.

The Tour - 1996

We test runned the new SchLIVE at the University of Sussex during the Squatter Estate Agency media madness. It went down fantastically well. A mixture of info and chat with appropriate links to films and a good up-for-it audience. It's strange but I think this was probably the best one we ever did. I don't know, some how the chemistry was right. We struck the right chord or some such thing. It felt fucking excellent. The tour was announced in the SchNEWS. Anyone who wanted us to come to their town or city just had to ring us up and we'd see what we could do. In about two weeks we had venues up and down the country.

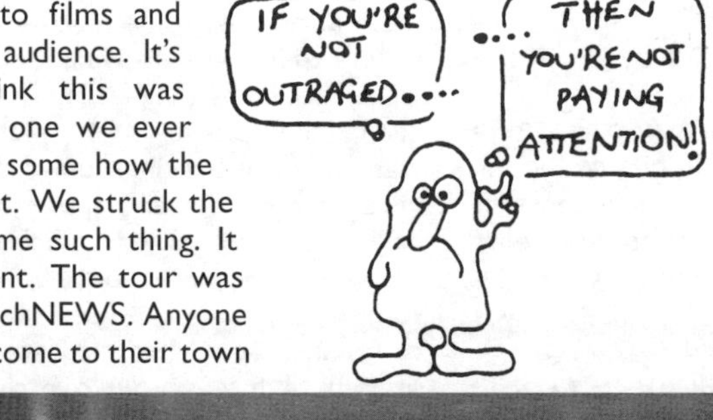

So, in May 1996 we set off. Kev from Conscious Cinema had a big bus that got us around. Inside we had the projector, two VCRs, a crappy screen and god knows how many videos! A special SchLIVE in the UK banner was designed. The Brighton based band Flannel linked up with us for a few gigs.

It was weird at first. Even though we had done a lot of shows outside Brighton it felt odd to be in a completely different environment. Every gig was different from audience to venue. We played pubs, town halls, squats, cafes. We even had a slot at the Green party conference. We had a very lukewarm reception there causing one bloke to shout out –"but if we all did what you're doing we'd all be arrested"

It was quite amazing. Everywhere we went we were so well looked after. That's sounds silly, right? But we were bowled over by the generosity and depth of commitment everyone had. It was brilliant to see others doing the same as us. We were forging links with these other groups. Creating networks. Making friends.

The tour was similar to the SchLIVEs in the Kenny in many ways. At times it was reckless and we soon all became accustomed to being hassled by the cops. The bus was boarded a few times, general intimidation. We soon got accustomed to setting up in new locations without really knowing what to expect from the venue or how we would be received. We got on with it as best we could given the circumstance. Of

Pic: Alec Smart

course we broke down. (the bus, I mean, not us. Well.....) but that was when we were at Fairmile at the height of the Summer. So we all had time off and played in the sun. One night we set the cinema up and played films for the road protesters there. Great stuff.

The last venue was at Strawberry fair and by that time we were all tired, and almost doing the show by remote. It was a real pain in the arse because that was the only time we couldn't get the films to work. The last gig on the list after about twenty-five gigs and the bloody films ballsed up. So it goes.

It's difficult to put it all across by writing it down. Someone tried to keep a diary but after a while there simply wasn't time. We were writing, adapting and living on the road with a show that was constantly changing as the SchNEWS was written or new info came in.

Anyone who has toured will probably know the feeling. It's impossible to get it all over. All that experience condensed into a short space of time. There was the incident when the bus nearly rolled into the sea, getting marooned in Shepton Mallet and having to borrow a hunt sab van to get to the next venue. The crap arrest quiz, the big issue reporter who didn't have a clue, the fucking excellent Cambridge gig with the Off Shore crew and the eight year old DJ, and the personal dynamics of several people living in a confined area, come to mind.

Three tits for the price of two - the final gig of the SchLIVE tour at Strawberry Fair, June 1996.

But the best thing was the fact that we had done it. It was DIY direct action on the move and in-ya-face, and the for the most part it worked. I know we inspired people. I know we got people to get involved in various campaigns. We made people laugh at the bullshit we are fed everyday by the mainstream media. It was a massively inspiring and positive experience.

For our tenth birthday we did it all again.

Conscious Cinema

Also starting during the Courthouse period in November 1994, and for a while being in the office next door to SchNEWS, **Conscious Cinema** produced four video magazines over several years on subjects ranging from forest gardening, to the media ecstasy scare, to direct action protests to graffiti writers. They put on public screenings at public halls and protest sites to front rooms, as well as taking it on the road, and being part of the 1996 SchLIVE tour. From 1999 til 2003 Conscious Cinema had a second phase, aiming to be more financially sustainable, but has now stopped for the moment.

Kev, who was part of the early phase of Conscious Cinema speaks about how he got involved:

Kev: After being involved in road protests for a while I got sick of the way it was being portrayed in the media and decided to do something about it.

Undercurrents was already going but I wanted to be part of something that would be watched in group settings, and be... free. So I got together with Dylan - who already had Conscious Cinema going in Brighton - and we decided to put together videos. The aim was that they would be produced as cheaply as possible using recycled video tapes (our mate used to skip them from the back of production houses in London!) and sent out free to groups.

The idea was that the videos would be shown in community settings - getting away from people watching things by themselves at home – because often you feel unable to do anything as an individual. We wanted people to watch 'em in group setting so they could discuss what they had seen and work together to take action! After the screening a collection would be taken with some money paying local costs, some coming to us towards for the next video and any left over staying with the local group.

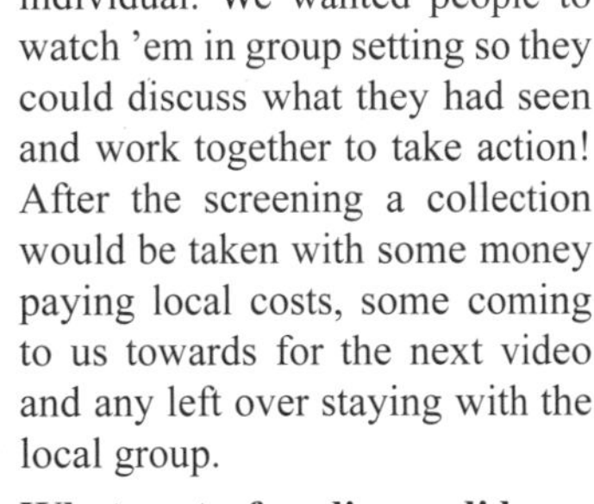

What sort of audience did you reach?

The videos mainly went to direct action groups across the country who used it as a tool to draw people in (everyone likes to see an action movie!), raise awareness and funds.

Have I Got SchNEWS For You

As well as SchLIVE, people got involved in a range of satirical shows, political cabarets and other bits of high-brow performance art. Here Pete and Cosmo recall a few of their adventures...

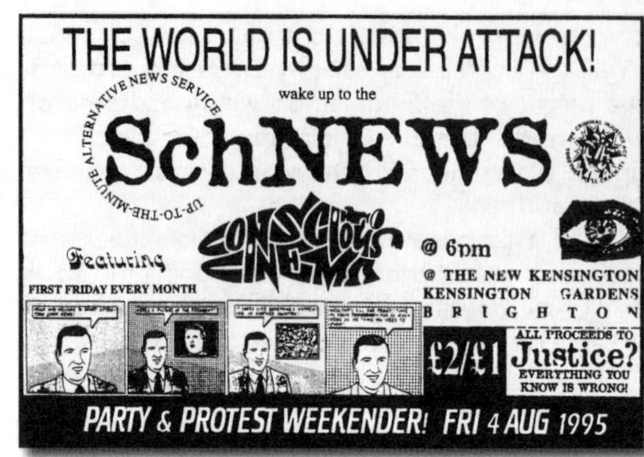

Tell us about the political cabaret nights?

Pete: Right through from '95 there was always stuff going on, some regular events, others as-and-when. SchNEWS Nights were once a month for about a year – it was comedy sketches, music, bits and pieces of everything.

Cosmo: The cabaret nights were mental... films, theatre, music, from people who were involved in the protest side of things and people from outside as well. There was so much talent and ingenuity going into the scene from so many different types of people, and it fed into a lot of the political action at the time. One demo against the imposition of the Job Seekers Allowance in Brighton was pure anarcho street theatre - I don't think Joe Public had ever seen anything like it judging by the looks on some faces!

Tell us about Have I Got SchNEWS For You?

Pete: We were asked during the Brighton Festival in 96-97 to do a quiz show for the Brighton Fringe so I took it up on myself to write the questions …using back issue to get the questions together. It was all part of the tradition of taking all this outside these four walls, outside the office and into the real world.

Cosmo: I didn't really mind getting up in front of people and making a tit of myself so I happily got involved. 'Have I Got SchNEWS For You' ran for two shows in Brighton. The scripts were great, really well written and very easy to perform, with all the gags and cheeky comments written in.

The first show was hilarious - the venue was rammed but all of us were quite chilled so people did some amazing performances. Mark Little, formerly of Neighbours fame (!) was on top form and Chris Turner played the inimitable Sergeant Shitter of the Crap Arrest Squad. This was a mad "arsey cop" character he created and he would just have people in stitches when he did it. I ran into Chris in the bogs just moments before we were due on stage that night and he was in a full copper's uniform - minus the trousers! He was looking worried and said "Cosmo, you wouldn't happen to have a spare pair of black strides on you, by any chance?" I laughed and was like – 'Chris, this is minutes before the gig, what are you playing at?' I went on, introduced him and, fair play to the bloke, he entered just as I'd seen him, baring his legs and boxer shorts to the world. It brought the house down and set the tone for the whole night.

The second 'Have I Got SchNEWS' was memorable too. I had the only working microphone in the whole place so no-one could hear what the contestants were saying. Everyone, audience and contestants alike, were wrecked and I was in full drag with a stoopid wig on.

But Pete found at one Earth First gathering that his humour wasn't always appreciated ….

Pete: We were doing a 'Have I Got SchNEWS For You' type show and one of the contestants - who had done so much, and was one of the main Road Alert people and brilliant geezer - had a Barbie doll on his desk as a University Challenge type mascot. The show got increasingly lairy and whether or not it was to your comedic taste, well this person threatens to shove a Barbie doll up my arse. And I go round my question master's desk and say 'go on then' - fully clothed and he gestures to do it - he didn't actually do it… And then the quiz ended, we all had a good laugh, I remember being covered in Guinness, it was a bit boisterous…

Then the next morning it was the big meeting at the gathering I'd had a few sherbets too many and was nursing a little bit of a hangover. This woman stands up and says… "I am so angry I can hardly speak, and I'm so disgusted I've hardly slept." She said that in her youth someone had obviously abused her and our prank had brought it all back… completely accidentally – but ultimately it wasn't our fault! We said sorry but it turned into this whole feeding frenzy in this field of about 150 people - it turned into a sort of hippy version of Jerry Springer. About 10 Germans left the site in disgust even though they hadn't even gone to the show.

It was all just political correctness gone mad. I for one was in this to effect change on government policy such as the roads programme. But we were expected to deal with some situations that were way above our heads, and this distracted us sometimes from the job at hand. What happened in Scotland that time was a self indulgent free-for-all of new age bollocks masquerading as people trying to solve a problem. I was very angry about the whole thing at the time, and make no apology for my actions in retrospect.

But all in all, without splitting too many hairs, considering the movement as a whole, it was such a varied bunch of people right through from some of the most rational, to-the-point, a sort of … tunnel vision - right through to touchy-feely. You got some of the most random spaced-out people right through to some of the most organised, fantastically efficient people you could hope to meet. How they all fitted into one movement is a testament to everyone.

Anarchist Teapot

The Anarchist Teapot started in 1996 and was the name given to a series of squatted cafes that popped up around Brighton. After squatting eight venues, the collective got more involved in catering for outside events like actions and gatherings. Some of the tea pot crew are behind the Cowley Club, Brighton's collectively owned social centre.

(pic right) One of the Anarchist Teapots on the London Road in Brighton - giving passers-by the choice of free tea... or a McFat burger at McDonald's two doors up.

www.eco-action.org/teapot

the 8th anarchist teapot
taking over disused buildings, creating an autonomous space and offering free tea and radical readings, since 1996 ....
SQUATTING A NEW BUILDING IS ALWAYS VERY EXCITING!
SUCH A BEAUTIFUL BUILDING!
I'M PUTTING THE STEREO.. ..HERE!
DON KING
THE OWNERS WILL START LEGAL PROCEEDINGS TO EVICT US...
NUT KING
EFFECTIVE MASKING UP WITH PANTOMIME COW
HM. IT'S THEM AGAIN.
SMEARY ESTATE AGENT
NON-TOO PLEASED COP
IT'S FUN DOING THE PLACE UP...
REACH.
UH.. WHERE'D THAT NAIL GO ??
ANARCIST
ANARCHISTS CLEANED WINDOWS.
MR. MUSCLE WINDOW CLEANER
WE NEED TO PLAN SOME EVENTS...
AND FILL IN THE SHIFT ROTA!
SHALL WE OPEN TOMORROW?
ANYONE FOR THE PUB?
WE DON'T CHARGE FOR TEA OR FOOD BUT EXIST OFF DONATIONS
THAT'S A DONATION FOR YOU FOLKS!
OH.. LOGS (?) WELL THANKS!
HM MAYBE THEY DON'T SELL DONUTS IN HERE.
CHIAPAS
a fresh day everyday at
THERE YOU GO!
THEY'VE BEEN SAT THERE FOR HOURS..
HOWMUCH DO I OWE YOU FOR THE TEA?
OH IT'S FREE
YEAH THERE'S AN ACTION ON MONDAY 'BOUT THAT
HELL'S VERY LOUD OFFSPRING
HEY LET'S NICK THEIR DONATIONS-TIN!
NAH. THEY'RE NICE.. LET'S NOT!
THIEVING TRUANT KIDS
SWEET GRANNIE (SHE PUTS HEADPHONES ON WHEN THE MUSIC'S TOO LOUD)
ANOTHER SPONTANEOUS VISITOR ASSUMING THIS IS A 'PROPER' CAFÉ

CRAP ARRESTS OF THE DECADE

From issue two there was an **Arrestometer** tallying arrests for those nicked under the new **Criminal Justice Act (CJA)**. This became a running league table of arrestee numbers with Hunt Saboteurs invariably leading the field followed by a pack that included Travellers, Road Protesters, Footie Fans, Peace Campaigners, Animal Rights Campaigners, Tree Defenders, Squatters, Ravers and more.

With Shoreham just down the road and SchNEWS people traveling to demos up and down the country, we started to see and hear lots of ridiculous arrests - and so 'Crap arrest of the week' was born. Pretty soon the flood gates were open, and people began sending more and more in. **'Crap Arrest Of The Week'** became a staple part of SchNEWS and is still this most popular part of the paper. And no, we don't make them up!

Ten years and nearly five hundred crap arrests later, for the many people who have had their time wasted by a jobsworth and/or malicious cop, the only consolation is to send their story into SchNEWS, and let our readers get some gritted-teeth enjoyment out of it.

In recent years, that bastion of equality and liberty the USA has been providing some of the best 'crap arrests' – and many more which warrant a slightly stronger word than er crap.

As for the **Arrestometer** – we tallied the CJA arrests for a year until Newbury, when there were so many people getting their collar felt it became impossible to keep score.

Crap Arrest Of The Week

Issue 224, 20th August 1999

For mooing!

A pantomime cow was arrested and charged with harassment and threatening behaviour after going into a McDeath's in Gloucester and saying MOO!!! The front and back of the cow were held for some 6 hours, and are in Gloucester Magistrates Court, 9.45am 13th September. In the meantime the cops are keeping the skin as evidence.

Crap Arrest Of The Week

Issue 43, 6th October 1995

Possession of a vegan chocolate cake!

Two hunt sabs had baked a cake in anticipation of their friend being acquitted in court but she lost the case. Feeling it was inappropriate to give her the gift they drove home. Police stopped their car for no reason and took the cake to be a bomb (it was in a cake-tin). They were held for 18 hours on "suspicion of carrying dangerous explosives" while the tin was sent to forensics.

Crap Arrest Of The Week

Issue 120, 23rd May 1997

For possession of myrrh!

Head Mix Collective, on tour in Wales a few days ago , were pulled over by Aberwystwyth's finest. Finding out they were a band and obviously up to no good they searched the van from top to bottom and found some..... medicinal myrrh. Unused to alternative remedies, they proceeded to arrest the owner and seize the van, refusing to release either until 3 hours after the gig was meant to begin. Good job Jesus wasn't born in Wales!

Crap Arrest Of The Week

Issue 259, 19th May, 2000

For being pregnant!

A woman from Faslane Peace Camp in Scotland spent two and a half hours in a cell after refusing to stand up during court proceedings. The women had asked the judge if she could be excused from standing as she was five months pregnant and suffering from severe backpain. The Judge told her to stand up or get out, before having her removed for contempt of court.

Crap Arrest Of The Week

Issue 209, 23rd April 1999

With intent to have a cup of tea.

A worker at Faslane Naval Base got talking to peace-camp demonstrators and decided to go back for a cup of tea with them. The MOD police threatened him with the sack if he went to the camp and when he persisted in his tea mission he was taken away by the (Tea)-Service Police!

Crap Arrest Of The Week

Issue 458, 11th June 2004

You've Bin Nicked!

At the Baishakhi Mela festival in East London's Brick Lane on the 9th of May, police arrested a remote controlled wheelie bin for being a public nuisance. When told that the bin had been booked to perform at the festival the police asked 'what's the point?' Hmm entertainment maybe! The bin was later released without charge.

Crap Arrest Of The Week

Issue 385, 13th December 2002

For being the 51st Protester!

Robin Webb, press officer for the UK ALF, was arrested last week in America at the national demonstration against Huntingdon Life Sciences. His crime? Laughably absurd he was supposedly the 51st person to enter the "50 person" protest zone at the lab! American authorities are intent on not letting this hardened criminal escape, his bail was a whopping $10,000 and the judge in the case is holding Robin's passport so he can't escape!

Crap Arrest Of The Week

Issue 261, 2nd June 2000

For being run over…

A cyclist in a critical mass protest in Bristol was arrested for obstructing traffic after an irate driver had knocked him to the ground. A prosecution is set to go ahead. Is cycling a crime, or only if you are knocked off your bike?

Crap Arrest Of The Week

Issue 428, 24th October 2003

For throwing a teabag

Yep you read it right, not a rock, a bottle or even a bomb but a harmless old teabag. A seventeen year old girl was recently nicked, charged and then sentenced to nine months community service (!) for throwing said tea bag at an animal abusers car during a demonstration outside the National Institute of Medical Research, a government sponsored vivisection lab in north London. Another protestor was charged with endangering a driver because he took a picture using a flash! 12 officers came to the house of the teenager to arrest her

Crap Arrest Of The Week

Issue 401, 25 April 2003

For jumping in puddles!

A twelve year old boy was arrested in Florida for "purposely stomping in the water." For his crime, comitted on school grounds, he was handcuffed on his way back to class, taken to jail, and charged with disruption of an educational institution! The boy spent two hours sitting by himself in a police holding cell before being released!

Crap Arrest Of The Week

Issue 293, 16 February 2001

For obscene inflatables!

A pensioner, a schoolboy, a care worker and a middle aged housewife were arrested and charged with harassment of B & K Universal Ltd, a company based in Hull, who breed animals for vivisection. The charges included - and we're not making this up - "holding a placard, making obscene gestures with an inflatable champagne bottle, sending a birthday card", and the best one "staring at a building!"

Crap Arrest Of The Week

Issue 321, 7th September 2001

For wearing a purple hairband!!

Pamela Smith was in Edinburgh Sheriffs Court supporting a fellow Trident Ploughshares banner dropper, when she was told 'the sheriff wants your hairband off.' Pamela claimed her right to wear it, but the Sheriff disagreed and had her locked up for two hours before charging her with Breach of the Peace!

Crap Arrest Of The Week

Issue 417, 8th August 2003

For firing a water pistol

A man in county Durham was CS sprayed and arrested after a policeman driving a vehicle was caught in the crossfire of a vicious water pistol fight. When the copper was squirted 'at close range from a pressurised water gun' into his he car he thought he'd join in the fun - with a can of CS. A police spokesperson claimed the officer was 'temporarily blinded' by the water, justifying the charges of a Public Order offence, resisting arrest and causing danger to a road user!

Crap Arrest Of The Week

Issue 102, 10th January 1997

For impersonating a cat

Lawrence O'Dowd was fined £100 by York magistrates for saying "Miaow" to a police dog. The unemployed 18-year old was arrested by Sergeant Fred Taylor and charged with using threatening and abusive words and behaviour. Poor Lawrence was also bound over for two years to keep the peace. He was unavailable for comment. Obviously the cat got his tongue!

Crap Arrest Of The Week

Issue 142, 7th November 1997

For eating a yoghurt...

Swat teams of vegan police staged a daring daylight raid and arrested 47 people on suspicion of burglary, after a pot of yoghurt disappeared from a fridge in the occupied offices of reviled opencast mining firm H.J. Banks. Thus in the wake of what must be one of the largest amounts of blatant criminal damage ever committed under police officers' noses, Derbyshire coppers had by the end of the day taken people in only for the eating of a dairy product, holding them for 24 hours. Scraping the legal barrel? It is not known whether the yoghurt in question was strawberry or black cherry.

Crap Arrest Of The Week

Issue 11, 24th February 1995

For possessing a sense of humour

Footie fan arrested at Swansea v Middlesborough. Asked a cop 'are you escorting us to the station mate?'. He replied 'Shut your mouth and keep moving'. Footie fan: 'If you or any of your mates are going to police the Shoreham protest could you give me a lift?' Copper 'Shut your gob or you're knicked sonny'. FF: "I didn't realise that being in possession of a sense of humour was a criminal offence In Wales'. He was then nicked and ch arged under s5 of the Public Order Act for threatening and abusive behaviour. In the police van he was told to sit on the floor 'where he belonged'. When he said he was a teacher the cop said 'Yeah, and I'm Mickey Fucking Mouse.'

Crap Arrest Of The Week

Issue 58, 26th January 1996

Pantomime Cow arrested for aggravated trespass!

The said cow was alleged to have broken "through security cordon towards contractors" with the intention of disrupting work at Newbury. Now if a pantomime cow can get through security....

INSIDE SchNEWS

'Inside SchNEWS' is a regular feature, offering news and updates about people we know about who are in prison and could do with support or at least a friendly letter. Like other regular aspects of the newsletter, 'Inside SchNEWS' began by focusing mostly on those arrested for Criminal Justice Act or direct action type offences, sitting alongside 'Crap Arrest Of The Week' and the Arrestometer as a gauge of how the state was busy criminalising dissent.

PRISONER SUPPORT

Why?

Prisons are the bottom line in the state's control over us. Resisting the prison system is part of challenging the status quo, but supporting those who get caught and imprisoned for their beliefs should be a vital part of any movement too.

Writing to Prisoners

Prison is designed to grind you down, and it isolates people from the outside world. Writing to prisoners helps break this down. It might be intimidating to sit down and write a letter to a stranger, but you can keep it short the first time. Just sending a card with a few well wishes and some words about who you are can brighten up someone's day and make them feel remembered. It can also possibly lead on to a correspondence.

Some people, when they write to prisoners are afraid of talking about their lives, what they're up to, thinking this might depress someone locked up or just not be of interest. But prison life is dead boring, and any news that livens it up is generally welcome. Use your sense, don't write about things that are likely to get the prisoner into trouble.

Don't necessarily expect an answer - some prisons restrict the number of letters a prisoner can write or receive, or the person may be out of stationery/stamps, or just not be very good at writing letters.

Passing cards round meetings, the pub or among your friends for people to sign with messages of support is an easy thing to do to brighten up a prisoner's mailtime. Or maybe you have the time to start up regular letter writing sessions with your friends, with the purpose of motivating each other to write.

SchNEWS 6, 20th January 1995
The first Inside SchNEWS

Inside SchNEWS

"they can chain the body but they'll never kill the spirit"

Justice? have received another letter from the growing band of political prisoners in this country. Hunt sabber David De Souza was arrested at Hyde Pk and the anti-BNP Welling demo. He writes: "Hello! Thanks for your card, really good to hear from you all, brothers and sisters! Things are ok here in Costa Del Elmley - a few silly rules but I'm settling into my temporary home. Just to fill you in with the boring bits - waiting for sentence over Welling on Section 1 (Public Order Act) probably in April and awaiting trial for Hyde Pk do last year. Originally charged with Section 2 but had it dropped to Section 3 (affray) - received a few bumps and bruises c/o The Met but remember Keep it Fluffy ??? Seems things are quite busy close to home and 95 is going to be a good year! No Live Exports,Sabbing, McLibel - exciting times. United we stand. Well take care of yourselves and stay free (if not I've put the kettle on just in case!). Anarchy, peace and freedom, Dave." David De Sousa EJ3464, House Block 2, HMP Elmley.

Sending Stuff

If you are up for it - don't offer your help if you aren't - ask what items the prisoner can receive in the post, or give the prison a ring, as this varies from prison to prison. It also often depends on which screw handles your post and what mood they're in!

Books: There are different regulations on this too, so ask. More than often a prisoner can only receive books directly from the publisher - this goes for alternative magazines as well - or via a recognised distributor or bookshop. A friendly bookshop will usually oblige if you buy the book and pay for the postage.

Pamphlets/Zines: These seem to get through to most prisons in the UK okay if they're not too big and folded up inside a normal sized envelope, for some reason. They are often counted as photocopies which are, up to a certain amount, usually allowed.

Visiting

If you are up for travelling to visit a prisoner, mention this to them. But bear in mind that convicted prisoners are only entitled to a limited number of visits (remand prisoners to much more), usually about 2-3 a month lasting up to 2 hours with 2-3 people. You will need to identify yourself at the gate, so take along sufficient I.D., and 'clean up' before you go - getting caught with even the tiniest bit of drug residue or anything else dodgy can have serious consequences for the prisoner.

Other Support

Ask whether the prisoner you are in touch with wants publicity for their case, or protest letters written. If you can raise money, ask where it's needed.

Groups/contacts

There are a number of prisoner support groups around. Get in touch to find out more and to read about some of the prisoners that shouldn't be forgotten.

Brighton Anarchist Black Cross, c/o 6 Tilbury Place, Brighton BN2 2GY mail@brightonabc.org.uk www.brightonabc.org.uk

Earth Liberation Prisoners, BM Box 2407, London WC1N 3XX www.spiritoffreedom.org.uk

Animal Liberation Front Supporters Group, BCM 1160, London WC1N 3XX

Miscarriages of Justice Organisation, www.mojuk.org.uk

Haven Distribution (books to prisoners), BM Haven, London WC1N 3XX

WHITE BOOK

The White Book was the forerunner of the Yellow Pages you get in every SchNEWS book and on our website. It was knocked together by a few people in SchNEWS's brand new office. Two editions were printed and distributed in 1995, funded by the Levellers.

Gibby explains:

"It was originally Mark from the Leveller's idea. There's a music industry handbook called the 'white book'. He said 'why don't you do it for the direct action movement?' So we did. It was the equivalent of a bunch of journalists publishing their private contacts book. It was a bit of a joke apart from the core fifteen contacts on the first page. Just shows you how few people it takes to make a movement.

But that access enabled those voices to be heard in the media. A journo suddenly has a contact number – they call. This was not the era of email and mobiles. I believe it pushed a lot of issues SchNEWS had highlighted into the mainstream, a kind of activist journalism.

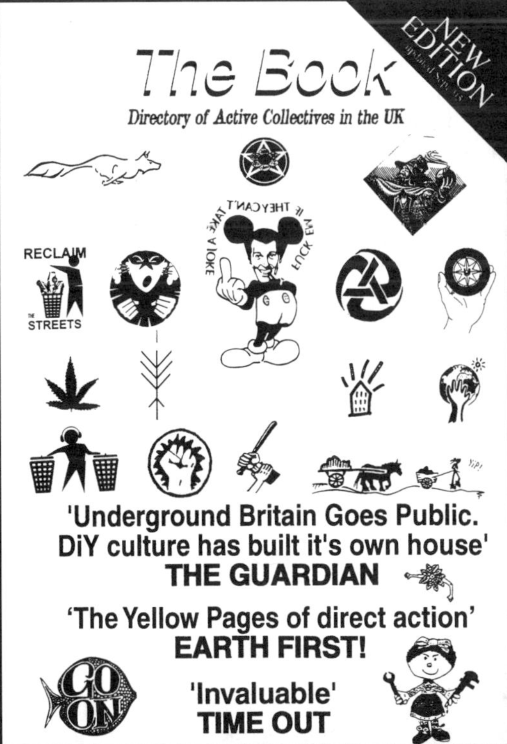

After around 1993 there was a definte sea-change: suddenly all these groups had exploded, completely outside the old guard of socialist and Marxist groups, or NGO's like Friends of the Earth or Greenpeace. But they had nothing to bind them together, no network. So we set about trying to make one.

We just sat on the phone for days calling anyone we could find, doing blind mail outs to addresses scrawled on bits of paper brought back from protests around the country. People heard about it and started sending in forms. Most groups were just a couple of people - like "Useful Climbing Tuition" which was just Mark and Karen and an address in Clwyd who offered "safe techniques on trees, cliff faces, possibly buildings (but not experienced in that area)". I wonder if anyone popped down?

Then there was the 'Bakuninist Firebombing League' with the useful contact "wouldn't you like to know."

Others were more established, like Veggies from Nottingham. Others, like Comrade Vladimir Smith of the Workers Against Nasty Killings Especially Revolutionaries (WANKER'S), we just made up. But only a couple.

We didn't get a lot of response in the first edition from black groups - doh! So we changed the name to 'The Book'. After that it just made sense to put these contacts at the back of the annual SchNEWS book and they became the Yellow Pages of direct action. The big, big plus point was that these numbers were always being checked so it was actually a directory which worked.

I think it made people feel more and more that there was a recognisable movement mushrooming. Sir Ivan Lawrence, the then Chairman of the Commons Select Committee on Home Affairs said "If they incite anyone to commit a criminal act or are conspiring to do so, I am sure that the police would be very pleased to receive copies." We just said: "Fuck 'em if they can't take a joke".

Shoreham

Live Animal Export Protests

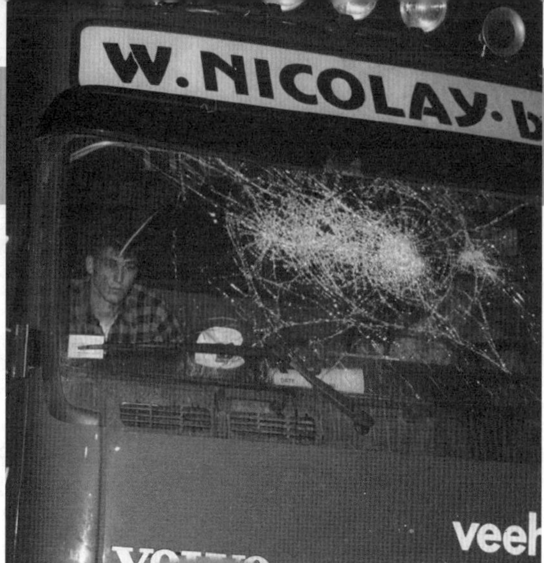

1995 saw the sudden resurgence of the animal liberation movement and its expansion to include people of types and ages previously undreamt of. Local residents and experienced animal rights activists joined forces against the live export trade. The cruelty of live transport, inhumane even by factory farming standards was compounded by the fact that the calves were being transported by ship and aircraft to the continent to be confined in veal crates, which had been banned in the UK. Veal is a profitable part of the dairy industry and is produced by confining calves in boxes just two feet wide so they cannot move and become anaemic, producing the white meat favoured by "gourmets".

A long standing Compassion in World Farming (CIWF) campaign coupled with threats of direct action had combined to force all the major passenger ports to pull out of the trade. Various dodgy entrepreneurs leapt in to fill the gap by using smaller ports for animal transport. Unlike with the major ports the live transport lorries now had to drive directly through local communities bringing many face to face with the horrors of factory farming. Around the country in Brightlingsea, Coventry and Shoreham, people began to physically obstruct the trade.

There were massive demonstrations at Shoreham Harbour (just down the road from SchNEWS' base in Brighton) and SchNEWS interviewed Sue, one of those involved with the protests:

"On the night it started - January 2nd 1995 - there were loads of people down there, some who had been involved with animal rights before, but also all sorts of people, a lot of elderly people sitting down in the road. A large number of people were CIWF members, so I think they mobilised a load of people with the intention of just protesting. However some of the more experienced activists were able to get these people to start blockading the lorries. The police were seriously undermanned and they didn't know how to deal with all these old people sat down in the road in front of them, so what they did was to wade in and start nicking all those with dreadlocks and facial piercings."

On the first day, the police couldn't get the lorries through and they decided to turn them all back.

"Because it went so well, on the next night a lot of people who found out about it on TV, radio or word of mouth, must've thought 'I live down there - let's go'. At that point the police hadn't realised just how it was going to pick up - they hadn't got a full force out. There were four hundred protesters. People climbed on to one of the lorries - one guy got all the way along and starting smashing the windscreen. Everyone was cheering, I was at the front looking up at him and there was nobody saying how disgusting it was. The pictures went around the world."

The next day CIWF told their members to withdraw because of the violence, but not many of them obeyed. Eventually the protests swelled to over fifteen hundred people and Sussex Police took the decision to bring in the Met.

"The Met were disgusting, so violent , attacking old people - pushing over one man who'd just had a hip replacement. A lot of people, Tory voters lost their faith in the police during the protests, it destroyed a lot of illusions."

After a while protests centred around a hard core of two hundred with a continuous presence of at least twenty protestors at the harbour. There was a more "direct" side to the campaign with locks being glued, rocks hurled at trucks and arson. The conflict continued into June when Sussex police, alarmed at spiralling costs, began to restrict the amount of protection they would offer the convoys. When they restricted the exports to two days a week the trade ceased to be financially viable. A local community with a sprinkling of activists had succeeded in outfacing Sussex police and the live export industry..

However the Shoreham Protestors were not about to go away.

"It opened a lot of people's eyes to all sorts of animal abuse, it produced a lot of vegetarians and vegans. We sent coaches to Consort and Hillgrove (see 'New Life For Animal Rights' elsewhere in this book) and to Dover to continue the campaign against live exports. I would say that the live exports campaigns rejuvenated animal rights."

These campaigns provided the model for the fight against the vivisection industry to come. The strength of the animal liberation movement is its broad cross section, and acceptance of different approaches: Letter writers do not condemn arsonists, nor vice versa. Pragmatic strategy, not tactics are all important.

Shoreham Protester - Sue, 7 Stoneham Road, Hove , East Sussex , BN3 5HJ Ph: 01273 885750

PART 3: DIRECT ACTION STATIONS! So - you've got the gist of how SchNEWS happened. We had the office, we had an up-for-it crew of people, it was time to go out and make a difference. Over the next 220 pages are some of the most significant stories we've written about in the past decade.

Justice? Brighton's Campaign in Defiance of the Criminal Injustice Act

Published in Brighton

Issue Fifteen | 24 March 1995 | Free/Donation

YOU'RE NICKED!

POLLOK ATTACK

The shit has hit the fan in Glasgow. Wimpey baliffs along with 32 vanloads of police invaded the Pollok Free State protest camp on Wed. They managed to cut down trees on the periphery of the main camp after an ariel battle in the treetops. Floodlights were set up last night and the eviction went on into the night. 15 arrests were made and one person was injured. The £53 million M77 will cut through the heart of Europe's largest urban green space.

As one protester said "Its a boxing match and this is just round one". The Glasgow community including local schoolchildren are trying to save more than 5000 trees in a seven mile stretch. The remaining protesters are calling for people to get up there now! Call 0141 810 1600/ 0860 728244

POLICE AMBUSH

Ten sabs were ambushed by Sussex Police in a carefully sprung trap last week. They were driving down a public right of way when a police officer directed that they leave immediately and kindly showed them the track to take. As if by magic, approximately 25 police officers appeared out of nowhere, brandishing crowbars and jemmies, and forced an entry into the van. All ten occupants were arrested and handcuffed, during which process several sustained minor injuries. The van itself was completely stripped down. Was it coincidence that they were directed to leave via a private track, and that down that track lay 25 coppers?

THUGS FOXED

Two pro-hunt thugs from the Cheshire foxhunt were given 12 month prison sentences after being found guilty of violent disorder. Geoffrey Park and Anthony Kirkham were part of a ten-strong gang armed with pick axe handles and coshes who trashed a hunt sab van and beat up its occupants. A woman who ran for help was cornered by the gang, punched to the ground and then severely beaten. One sab sustained two black eyes, damaged kidneys, extensive cuts and bruising to the body and head.

SchNEWS LIVE!
@ The New Kensington,
Kensington Gardens, Brighton.
Every Friday 5.45pm
SchNEWS LIVE!

NO ALTERNATIVE

A group of Scottish travellers have been forced by the CJA to dig in their heels to hold a piece of land and keep their children and homes safe for the winter months

The Dengin travellers face **two** court cases, first under the 1865 Highland clearance law known as the Criminal Trespass Act then under sec61 (1 & 4) of the CJA. They are asking for support on 28th April Fort William Sheriff Court 10 am :"These laws effectively make our way of life illegal because there's nowhere in the country we can legally camp...even if we are given permission to camp, the landowners can be prosecuted for breach of planning permission. This applies even if we buy our own land. We have no alternative but to camp wherever we can find disused land. The only time we are not breaking the law is when we are moving from one site to another."

SchNEWS IN BRIEF

The No M65 Campaign is now focused on Stanworth Valley's "Village in the sky" which looks set to be evicted in the first week of April. They need more people URGENTLY 0161 861 7895/0585 165311 (camp mobile) *** Reclaim the Streets who campaign on various issues including pedestrian and cyclists rights, car culture etc. have opened a new office 0171 254 2290 *** the crucial European Parliament vote on the Trans-European Road Network(TERN) is due in early April. Write to your MEP asking him/her to support all amendments calling for more rigorous environmental assessments, and to re-evaluate the whole TERN network *** HELP is needed with a book that is being written on the history of the Stonehenge festivals, their banning, how this led up to the CJA, the party scene and the philosophy of the Conservative Party. Contact Jim Loughran, 146 Cowesby Street, Manchester, M14 4UW. COVENTRY AIRPORT: The campaign against live exports from the airport despite limited press coverage. 20-30 protesters are camping there every night, and numbers are swelled to 50+ during the day. The police attitude is "disgraceful generally." A 14 year old boy was arrested but is now back on site. Please show support by writing letters, giving donations etc. A campaign is also underway in Amsterdam, where the cargo ends up after Coventry.

CJA ARRESTOMETER

Hunt Sabs	148
Road Protestors	16
Travellers	11
No live exports*	3
Tree Defenders	2

*at least 450 arrested under 1986 Public Order Act so far this year! (250 @ Brightlingsea/150 @ Shoreham/100 @ various sabs)

CRAP ARRESTS

• Time-warp! A bloke has been charged for something he did at 10.30 at Shoreham, despite the fact that he did not get there until 12!

• At Coventry airport two women dressed up for red nose day wearing joke plastic police helmets were nicked for "impersonating a police officer!"

RING SchNEWS WITH CRAP ARRESTS!!

INSIDE SchNEWS

How NOT to Write To Jailed Activists

At the Missile Silo Peace School in Missouri last July a number of people were talking about letters they got whilst in prison. They get great bags-full of letters all saying the same thing : "What a wonderful thing you have done. You are so brave! I would never have the courage to do such a thing. Thank God for people like you!"

They all hate this sort of letter. (I must admit I have written letters like that myself). I think the problem is that it makes the activist seem different from other people. They would much rather have letters telling them what you are doing, instead of what you feel you cannot do. One women said, "There was some guy in a Catholic Worker House somewhere who sent me these wonderful chatty letters about what was going on at the house." During one of my (very short) says in jail I got an illuminated letter. Nearly everything in the text was illustrated in colour. It boosted my spirits for the rest of the day. Send me a picture of yourself at the fence of a missile silo."

So, don't tell imprisoned activists how much you admire their courage. Tell them instead about resistance in your area. Tell them about yourself. Be chatty. Illustrate the letter if you are artistic. Be a pen-pal, not a worshipper.

From Nuclear Resister newsletter

Pic: Andrew Testa

MAYDAY! MAYDAY!

VILLAGE IN THE SKY ALL SET FOR EVICTION

That's right folks! From Monday 1st May tree-dwellers in Stanworth Valley near Preston in the way of the proposed M65 are all set to defend this beautiful ancient woodland from the bulldozers.

The woods are home to a wide range of species of flora and fauna including Tawny Owls and Goldcrest, and are also recognised by local nature conservation groups as being part of one of the ten most valuable woodlands in Lancashire.

There are presently over 30 tree-houses with 4 km of aerial walkways which even the Under-Sheriff of Lancashire has acknowledged will be "very difficult" to evict. Hundreds of anti-road protestors are expected to arrive over the weekend.

Why not join them in what could be the UKs biggest eviction ever!

The No M65 Campaign are advising everyone to go to the woods by way of the public footpath from the Sun Paper Mill, nr. Feniscowles, Blackburn by very early Monday at the latest. To be in the trees, safety equipment is essential, for specific details ring 0161 861 7895. Please arrive on Sunday for safety training and to find a space. Self-sufficiency in outdoor clothing, food and water strongly recommended.

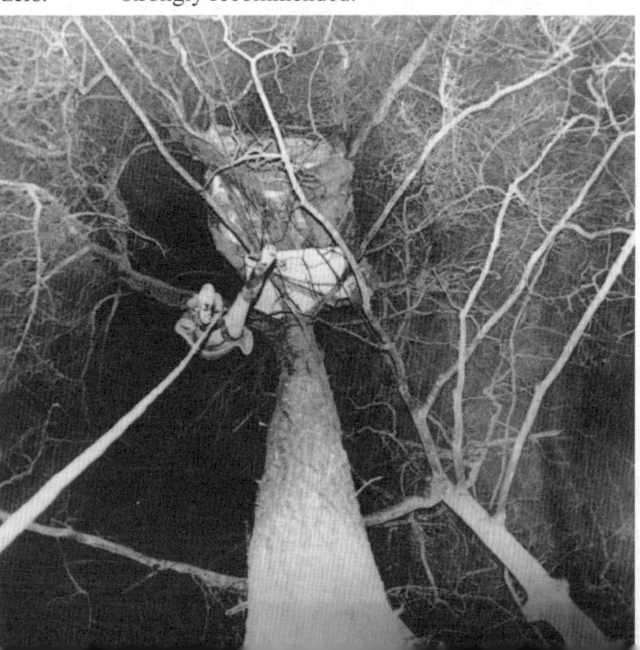

SHAME!

AS BAILIFFS ATTACK VILLAGE IN THE SKY

EYE WITNESS ACCOUNTS FROM OUR PEOPLE 60 FEET UP A TREE

"I have seen many beautiful places get trashed in the name of progress, and I have tried to force myself not to be gutted, but you never get used to the sickening crunching sound that you hear when the trees crash to the ground."

Mayday, Mayday and hundreds of police, bailiffs and security guards moved in to evict 'the village in the sky', as Stanworth Valley in Lancashire became the latest battleground for the anti-roads movement.

The heavily wooded valley carpeted in bluebells with the smell of wild garlic strong in the air is home to birds such as Tawny Owls and Goldcrests. But it lies in the path of the M65 which is being built to link East Lancashire to the motorway network.

As SchNEWS went to press, it was apparent that the (Under) sheriff and his men were becoming increasingly frustrated about the slowness in evicting the tree-people. As time goes by they are taking more and more risks endangering themselves and protesters.

"It's mental, absolutely mental. The sheriff is a liar and he is putting peoples lives at risk. The bailiffs don't know what they're doing. One tree was felled three foot from a tree-house, another branch hit an occupied treehouse. One aerial walk-way was cut with someone still on who managed to scramble off."

It looks set to the longest eviction in post-war Europe, piling up the cost and showing the authorities that they cannot expect to destroy our countryside without determined opposition.

Stanworth Valley Eviction, M65, April 95

Pic: Andrew Testa

RECLAIM

The direct action group Reclaim the Streets (RTS) in the nineties gained widespread recognition. From road blockades to street parties, from strikes on oil corporations to organising alongside striking workers, its actions and ideas attracted more and more people and international attention. This article charts the early years and its impact on popular alternative culture and its underlying philosophy.

The Evolution of RTS

RTS was originally formed in London in autumn 1991, around the dawn of the anti-roads movement. With the battle for Twyford Down rumbling along, a small group of individuals got together to take direct action against the motor car. In their own words they were campaigning:

"FOR walking cycling and cheap, or free, public transport, and AGAINST cars, roads and the system that pushes them."

Their work was small-scale but effective and even back then, had elements of the cheeky, surprise tactics which moulded RTS's later activities. There was the trashed car on Park Lane symbolising the arrival of Car-mageddon, DIY cycle lanes painted overnight on London streets, disruption of the 1993 Earls Court Motor Show and subvertising actions on car adverts around the city. However, the onset of the No M11 Link Road Campaign presented the group with a specific local focus, and RTS was absorbed temporarily into the campaign in East London.

This period of the No M11 Campaign was significant for a number of reasons. Whilst Twyford Down was predominantly an ecological campaign - defending a 'natural' area - the urban setting of the resistance to the M11 construction embodied wider social and political issues. Beyond the anti-road and ecological arguments, a whole urban community faced the destruction of its social environment with loss of homes, degradation to its quality of life and community fragmentation.

Beyond these political and social considerations, the M11 Campaign developed the direct action skills of those involved. Phone trees were established; lots of people were involved in site invasions, crowds of activists had to be manoeuvred to outwit police. The protesters also gained experience of dealing with associated tasks such as publicity, the media and fund-raising.

Then in 1994, a political hand-grenade was thrown into the protest scene: the Criminal Justice and Public Order Act. Overnight, civil protesting became a criminal act, but what the government hadn't counted on was how this piece of legislation would unite and motivate the very groups it was aimed at repressing. The fight of the anti-road activists became synonymous with that of travellers, squatters and hunt saboteurs. In particular, the suddenly politicised rave scene became a communal social focus for many people.

SchNEWS 23 19th May 1995

more info on 0122

STREETS RECLAIMED!

Last Sunday saw a rather amusing little street party in the middle of Camden High St. Protesters and party-goers out-smarted the local constabulary staging a fake crash with two donated cars to block the road to launch a summer season of anti-car actions. Perplexed tourists watched open-mouthed as a cafe was promptly set up and the street, hastily bedecked in bunting and became a circus of jugglers, musicians, cyclists and a vision of a car-free society. Police could only stand and stare as the party swelled in numbers, dancing to the pedal-powered Rinky Dink mobile sound system.

The party pointed to the increasing diversification of road activists, and the growing awareness that it's not just new roads that are a threat to the environment by destroying our green spaces, but that the whole car-owning ethos of the country needs changing. Watch out for more street reclaiming soon! **0171 254 2290**

The M11 Link Road campaign culminated in the symbolic and dramatic battle of Claremont Road. Eventually, police and security overpowered the barricades, lock-ons and the scaffold tower, but the war was only just beginning. The period of the M11 Campaign had forged new political and social alliances and in the midst of the campaign's frenzied activities strong friendships had been formed. When Claremont Road was lost, this collective looked for new sources of expression and Reclaim the Streets was reformed in February 1995.

The years that followed saw the momentum of RTS flourish. Two street parties were held in rapid succession in the summer of 1995 and there were various actions against Shell, the Nigerian

"We are not going to demand anything. We are not going to ask for anything. We are going to take. We are going to occupy."

THE STREETS

The first RTS street party, Camden High St, London, 14th May 1995 **Pic: Nick Cobbing**

Embassy and the 1995 Motor Show. In July 1996 there was the M41 Street Party, where for nine hours 8,000 people took control of the M41 motorway in West London and partied, whilst some dug up the tarmac with jack-hammers and in its place planted trees that had been rescued from the construction path of the M11.

Streets Ahead

At a base level, the focus of RTS has remained anti-car but this has been increasingly symbolic, not specific. RTS aimed initially to move debate beyond the anti-roads struggle, to highlight the social, as well as the ecological, costs of the car system.

"The cars that fill the streets have narrowed the pavements... [If] pedestrians ... want to look at each other, they see cars in the background, if they want to look at the building across the street they see cars in the foreground: there isn't a single angle of view from which cars will not be visible, from the back, in front, on both sides. Their omnipresent noise corrodes every moment of contemplation like acid."

Cars dominate our cities, polluting, congesting and dividing communities. They have isolated people from one another, and our streets have become mere conduits for motor vehicles to hurtle through, oblivious of the neighbourhoods they are disrupting. Cars have created social voids; allowing people to move further and further away from their homes, dispersing and fragmenting daily activities and lives and increasing social anonymity. RTS believe that ridding society of the car would allow us to re-create a safer, more attractive living environment, to return streets to the people that live on them and perhaps to rediscover a sense of 'social solidarity'.

But cars are just one piece of the jigsaw and RTS also raises wider questions behind the transport issue - about the political and economic forces which drive 'car culture'. Governments claim that "roads are good for the economy".

More goods travelling on longer journeys, more petrol being burnt, more customers at out-of-town supermarkets - it is all about increasing "consumption", because that is an indicator of "economic growth". The greedy, short-term exploitation of dwindling resources regardless of the immediate or long-term costs. Therefore RTS's attack on cars cannot be detached from a wider attack on capitalism itself.

RTS is also about encouraging more people to take part in direct action. Everyone knows the destruction which roads and cars are causing, yet the politicians still take no notice. Hardly surprising - they only care about staying in power and maintaining their 'authority' over the majority of people. Direct action is about destroying that power and authority, and people taking responsibility for themselves. Direct action is not just a tactic; it is an end in itself. It is about enabling people to unite as individuals with a common aim, to change things directly by their own actions.

The street parties were an ingenious manifestation of RTS's views. They embodied the above messages in an inspired formula: cunning direct action, crowd empowerment, fun, humour and raving. They have evolved into festivals open to all who feel exasperated by conventional society.

To some extent it is possible to trace the tactics behind the Street Parties in RTS's history. The mobilisation, assembly and movement of large crowds draws on skills from road protests. The use of sound systems draws on dominant popular culture whereas the initial inspiration for Street Parties certainly reflects the parties of the Claremont Road days. However, RTS have retrospectively also realised that their roots lie deeper in history. The great revolutionary moments have all been enormous popular festivals - the storming of the Bastille, the Paris commune and the uprisings in 1968 to name a few.

The power which such activities embody inevitably challenges the state's authority, and

RTS Street Party II, Upper Street, London, 23rd July 1995 Pic: Alec Smart

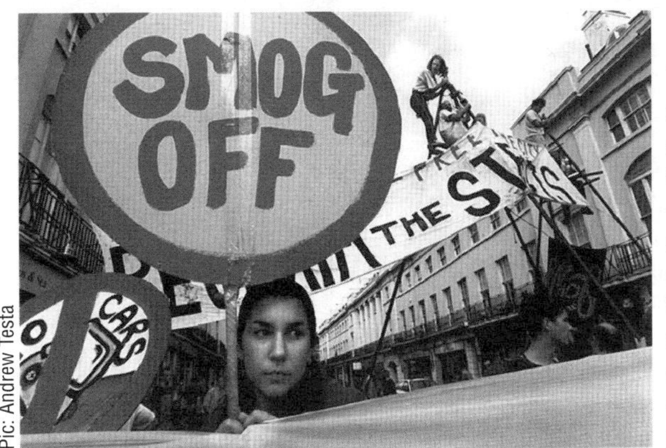

Pic: Andrew Testa

hence the police and security services' attention has increasingly been drawn to RTS. The organisation of any form of direct action by the group is closely scrutinised. RTS has been made very aware of this problem. Vehicles carrying equipment have been broken into, followed and impounded en route to street parties, RTS's office has been raided, telephones have been bugged and activists from RTS have been followed, harassed and threatened with heavy conspiracy charges. On top of this a secret RTS action in December 1996 (an attempt to seize a BP tanker on the M25) was foiled by the unexpected presence of two hundred police at the activists' meeting point. How such information is obtained by the police is uncertain and can easily lead to paranoia in the group; fear of infiltration, anxiety and suspicion which can themselves be debilitating.

Yet RTS was not deterred, they held open meetings every week, they continued to expand and involve new people, and were also frequently approached by other direct action groups. Alliances sprouted with other groups - the striking Liverpool Dockers and Tube Workers to name two - as recognition grew of common ground between these struggles. Throughout the UK and Europe new local RTS groups formed and RTS street parties have taken place all over the world. These new groups have not been created by London RTS, they are fully autonomous. London RTS has merely acted as a catalyst; stimulating individuals to replicate ideas if they are suitable for others to use as well.

Street parties are all very well as a temporary zone freed from the shackles of consumer alienation. But, what could Street parties potentially be? What about beyond the street party? These questions should be answered if the street party, conceived as a means to a free and ecological 'end', is not to become a victim of its own success.

Road Trip

To rescue what is left of the public arena, to enlarge and transform that arena from a selling and increasingly sold space to a common, free space - from controlled locality to local control - is fundamental to the vision of RTS. The logic of this vision implies, not only ending the rule of the car and recreating community, but also the liberation of the streets from the wider rule of hierarchy and domination. From economic, ethnic and gender oppressions. From the consumerism, surveillance, advertising and profit-making that reduces both people and planet to saleable objects.

While four out of five westerners live in the city, while two-thirds of the world's population share the common space of its thoroughfares, it is:

"On the streets that power must be dissolved: for the streets, where daily life is endured, suffered and eroded, and where power is confronted and fought, must be turned into the domain where daily life is enjoyed, created and nourished.

RTS Sheffield, May 1997 Pic: Tash

RECLAIM THE STREETS

Report backs from North and South London

BRIXTON: An orange flare signalled to the gathered 1000's the start of another sucessful 'avin-it' historic street party. Having turned up in relatively small force 'The Old Bill' seemed content to stand back and let it happen. Perhaps this had something to do with the sensitive nature of the locale!

Although the main police CCTV had been skillfully covered-up, by an activist shimmying up a 60-80 foot pole and placing a plastic bag over it, the CCTV unit on McMuck's frenetically swivelled around filming anything it could. McMoney were also forced to shut their toilets as the celebrants took the piss big stylee. For hours a largish swathe of Brixton's streets were given over to fun, jollity and car free space as the RTS red, black and green 'flag'on top of McMurder fluttered in the cooling breeze, making their (McMuck's) Union Jack look grey tattered and from a bygone age. Of course the usual PC Plod 'snatch-squad' lurking about in Brixton tube station made a determined effort to ruin someone's day by arresting people getting on the trains to go home.

Meanwhile a concurrent **NORTH LONDON** street party was in full swing in Tottenham, closing down every single road junction at some point during the day, between Euston and Seven Sisters as 2,000 made their way to the party. Euston tube was closed, so 1,500 people left for Kings Cross and a pig was overheard saying "We're doomed!" ha ha ha. Greater London Radio advised people not to enter north-east London as the Reclaim the Streets movement had taken control of it!!! 5,000 people well and truly reclaimed Tottenham High Road to the tunes of 3 soundsystems which entered and left the party without being pulled. Critical Mass cyclists initially took the site whilst party-goers following multi-coloured flags came forth in their thousands to celebrate the reclaimation of what is rightfully theirs, "Freedom is there for the taking...so let's take it!"

Road Rage at Seven Sisters Pic: Ian Hunter

Local people joyfully joined in the festivities as the high road was taken over with music, laughter, performance, football and kids playing. Local residents said, *"I saw this van pull up with lots of people running after it....the next thing we knew they had blocked the road, started playing music and thousands of people started arriving!"* Another said *"It's great! When we came out of the tube and saw all these people we were completely entranced...I think it's fantastic!"*

At the end of the day two cars used for barricades were set alight and the police baton charged the remaining people making 11 arrests for public order offences. The police were totally out-witted all day.

P.S. Thanks to the intelligent bods who erected toilets over the drains and the litterpickers. Nicely done!!

Bottom pics: Andrew Testa

All pics: Tash

You Take The High Road...

There were Reclaim The Streets events in virtually every large town or city in Britain from 1995 until around 2000, organised by local groups. This sequence of photos from a RTS Street Party in Cambridge on Saturday 14th September 1996 gives a flavour of how they often went...

1. It's a sunny day and around five hundred people - followed by a stupid amount of police - lead a parade from the meeting point to the street to be reclaimed. A tripod goes up, people flood onto the street, then rugs, cushions, costumes, and kids stuff are rolled out. The music starts and it's a street party.

2. At one end of the party is the massive police build-up. They claim they're there after being warned of a right-wing counter demonstration - which didn't happen!!! Busloads of cops from Bedfordshire have been brought in, and a police helicopter chews up £1000 an hour in the air.

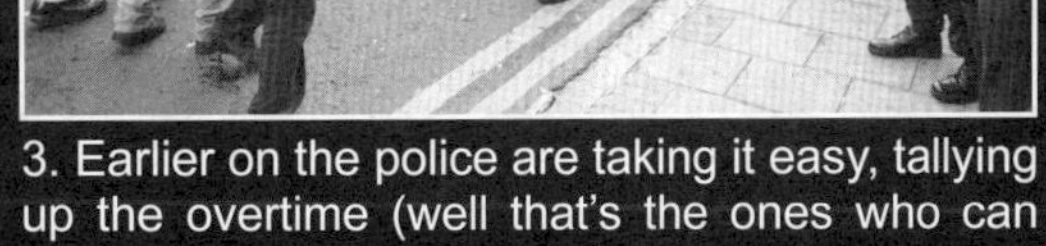

3. Earlier on the police are taking it easy, tallying up the overtime (well that's the ones who can count).

4. Inevitably they get their orders and move in on the party. Forty are arrested.

CODI ETO YN Y CWM!

THE VALLEYS RISE AGAINST OPENCAST MONSTER

Anti-open-cast mine activists were last night holding out, five days into a tree-top battle in Brynhenllys, South Wales, to stop a monster development that will gauge a hole visible front space out of the heart of the Welsh valleys.

Scores of bailiffs, climbers and security hired by Celtic Energy - who stand to make millions from the 'wanton destruction' - have so far failed in their high-risk attempt to evict all the protestors dangling from walkways and makeshift platforms high up in the trees. Watching the chainsaws flying from below are local residents who have been fighting the proposals for 14 years. They've been joined by children on half-term holiday, while police - backed up with a helicopter - and sheriff's men stand guard. Bailiffs stand accused of endangering lives - cutting walkways 40ft in the air with people still on them, and chainsawing the branches of a Corsican Pine from above the heads of protestors clinging on.

One local resident, Nigel Faulkner, told SchNEWS: "Their behaviour has been appalling, putting life and limb at risk, while the decency of the protestors has been a hallmark of the week - they are brilliant people battling every inch of the way."

Brynhenllys Open-Cast, a mind-boggling 770 acres and 200m deep - twice the size of Glastonbury Festival - will be the second largest open-cast site in Europe. The largest by a fraction will be at Selar Nature Reserve near Cwmgwrach, just fifteen miles away, where another troop of tree-dwelling protestors are bracing themselves for possible eviction on Monday.

These two vast holes will wipe out 880 acres of lush watermeadow, ancient oak woodland and a designated Site of Special Scientific Interest, the home of the protected Marsh Fritillary butterfly and nesting places of Peregrine Falcons, and remote wilderness of oaks, beech, ash and , me. A fifth of the development is in Brecon Beacons National Park. Property prices have plummeted as the landscape is ravaged and asthma rates expected to soar. Dr Mark Temple, writing in *The Lancet* reported 30% more sufferers amongst residents at another nearby open-cast site. "Once the ecology has been destroyed it's gone forever." "There are already signs of desertification from previous mining, according to a visiting professor from Algeria" said a spokesman for Wales Against Opencast.

Even police and security are in revolt. Over forty people have been arrested for Public Order offences this week but released with out charge - and without bail conditions, freeing them to continue the protest.

Pic: Alec Smart

Pic: Alec Smart

Dyfed Police have shown their feelings by virtually working to rule, and have been, in the words of one activist, “brilliant”. The private company Reliant Security, well known from the No M11 Link Road campaign - have been bussed in from London to deal with the protests. But many have left in disgust at conditions forcing them to work 34hr shifts with no food or accommodation. On Tuesday night both protestors and security were forced to share the only shelter in the area - the Long Barn - creating the bizarre situation of sitting round the same fire and sharing chips! “Most of the security are being used as slaves. They are predominately black immigrants who don’t know why they are here,” said one protestor.

Local valley communities such as Brynhenllys and Cwmgwrach have been devastated by the closure of all the deepcast mines in Wales. Closed, they were told, because there was no demand for coal. But a week after Tower Colliery, the last pit in Wales, was shut the application was put in for Selar! Tower has since re-opened as a workers co-op employing 300 men and making a healthy profit. The Selar site is only 3 miles away from Tower and could be deep-cast mined creating a further 300 jobs instead of the unskilled handful the open-cast mine will create. Even a Public Inquiry over Brynhenllys found against the proposal but this was overturned and the project rubber-stamped by the Welsh Office. “We exhausted the legal process utterly and direct action was the only option left. It’s been fantastic in fostering a new community spirit,” one Brynhenllys resident told SchNEWS.

IF ORDINARY PEOPLE BEHAVED LIKE- Esso

HAPPY BIRTHDAY CJA!

ONE YEAR ON FROM 'THE POLL TAX ON ACID'

The spark of the largest grassroots direct action movement in a decade, the Criminal Justice Act, is one year old. Happy anniversary. Other struggles come and go, but the fight against Michael Howard's little crowd-pleaser has become a fight for our very own cultural identity. Now that our skin and bones have effectively become the front line in the war on political and social dissent, the choice of whether or not to stand and fight is arbitrary.

But was it ever just about the CJA? Wasn't it about bringing people together at places like the Courthouse, Justice?'s most successful squatted community centre? This not only acted as a springboard for SchNEWS, Conscious Cinema and a million other dreams and ventures, but got people off their arses, thinking about things for the first time, doing things they would normally never do, talking to people they'd never usually talk to. Showing just what we can achieve without the politicians and bureaucrats - creating a so-called DiY culture, but a culture which always seems to flourish when people are under threat or in struggle.

And is *Justice?* really about getting the CJA repealed - end of story? Please write to your MP and sign our petition ... we don't think so.

As political parties lurch further to the right the vacuum becomes ever more clearer for us to fill. Direct action gets results but it isn't just about being against things.

It shouldn't just be about single issues but challenging the whole way it runs:

*** anti-roadbuilding action is now about reclaiming our streets and highlighting the need to end the 'tyranny of the motorcar.'**
*** saying no to out of town shopping centres and endless consumer crap is about growing your own veg.**
*** living in a vehicle or bender is about low-impact lifestyles.**
*** squatting is about recycling the empties.**
*** producing our own newsletters and videos is two fingers up to censorship and about putting out what we think - not what people think about us.**
*** free parties is about saying no to crap clubs with rip-off prices and numbskull bouncers.**

And all of this is about having fun, being yourself and breaking out of the work-consume-die mentality that is killing the planet. It's an organic, evolving energy engaged in celebration as a struggle. A coming together of the people. So what of the future? One year on, there is a vision, a mushrooming of positive solutions. We need to work towards sustainable lifestyles as well as fighting back.

WHAT DO YOU THINK? AND MORE IMPORTANTLY, WHAT ARE YOU DOING ABOUT IT?

The 1st Year - Where Were You?

1994 – NOVEMBER

3.11.94 **Preparing for defiance** as the CJB gained Royal Assent to become the new-born Criminal Justice Act. WHAAAAAAA!

4.11.94 **Up a crane in Manchester** - within 24 hours of the Act becoming law, four people - Ollie, Pete, Chris and Paul - were the first people in the country to be arrested for 'aggravated trespass' for the No M65 campaign. **On the roofs of Parliament**... later that day, five activists climbed on to the roofs of Westminster Hall at the Houses of Parliament and sat silhouetted against Big Ben with a 'DEFY THE CJA' banner for all the world to see. Could've kissed 'em!

11.11.94 **On the roof of the squatted Courthouse,** a community centre in Brighton resisting the eviction. Birthplace of a million dreams...

20.11.94 **In Michael Howard's backgarden**, Folkestone, when 400 people put the Home Secretary and the Government on trial and found them Very Guilty Indeed. While In **Essex**, police made a mass arrest of 31 hunt sabs in an operation costing £40,000 and marred by allegations of serious assault, including one woman who was beaten semi-conscious with a truncheon while she had her hands cuffed behind her back.

27.11.94 **On the top of 'Dolly', a 100ft tower on a doomed squat In Claremont Rd**, East London, at the start of Britain's longest post war eviction. Lasting five days it cost the Department of Transport £2M and involved over 700 police, 200 bailiffs and 400 security guards to evict protestors from houses due to be demolished for the M11 Link Rd.

DECEMBER

17.12.94 **At Crookesmoor Middle School** in Sheffield where 300 activists held a manic DiY conference to plan the New Year of protest after squatting the empty building - and then tatted a Port-a-loo to stink out the visiting namesake and then Employment Secretary, Michael.

1995 – JANUARY

2.1.95 **On top of a lorry in Shoreham, Sussex**, stopping live animal exports in the first action of a

Pic: Alec Smart

Issue 34 –4th August 1995

PIER PRESSURE!

SQUATTERS TAKE OVER BRIGHTON'S DERELICT WEST PIER and have begun repairing floorboards on the 129-year-old Grade One listed building which has been left in shabby neglect since it was closed 20 years ago.

For the last two years a community of, for the most part, happy free peaceful people have been living in the beach chalets next to the Pier - Council-owned chalets which have not been used since 1982. It had become a haven for anyone who needed shelter, food and friendship in the town. However, all this came to an end last Tuesday when sixty police, bailiffs, and heavies gave the squatters two minutes to get out. Any who were not there at the time had their possessions binned. So the community of 30 squatters launched 'Operation Crusty'. Swimming at low tide, they climbed the rusty Pier ladder, forced up the trapdoor and opened a tidal wave of protest. Squatters held the pier for a few weeks but the pigeon shit was overwhelming.

---

six month campaign. Local residents and activists blocked the road forcing the lorries to turn back. The widely-reported window-smashing incident led to 1,500 police turning up the following night, outnumbering protestors six to one.

27.1.95 **On top of a lorry in Brightlingsea, Essex**, as the live animal trade moved into the tiny community of 8,000 and the police waded into protestors....

28.1.95 **On a CJA Defiance Demo in Maidstone**, Kent, where police arrested 33 'ringleaders' (most of the demonstrators) they said had organised the march. All charges were later dropped.

FEBRUARY

2.2.95 **JILL PHIPPS, 31,** ***is crushed to death by a lorry carrying calves for veal transport at Coventry Airport. Anger beyond belief. RIP. The third animal rights protestor killed under the wheels of animal abusers' vehicles. No-one has been prosecuted for any of their deaths.***

13.2.95 **In a Kamikazie car convoy to Pollok, Glasgow**, from Brighton and Oxford via a host of road campaigns, to be burnt out and buried for

> ***"Where the CJA has really bitten hard is the free festival movement and the travellers. There's been a mass exodus to Spain and Ireland, where there is less harassment. Without a strong travelling community, it's impossible to have a viable free festival network"***
> **- Michelle Poole, Advance Party**

'CarHenge' in the path of the proposed M77. At dawn the following day - St Valentine's - treecutters, bailiffs and police moved in to evict tree dwelling activists protecting the largest urban green space in Europe.

MARCH

14.3.95 **Invading the site at Solsbury Hill** with 250 rampant road protestors on the anniversary of the first action.

25.3.95 **On a Cardiff City supporters coach**, halted by a roadblock outside Plymouth, where police stopped and searched all 36 fans and put them the cells for seven hours before releasing them without charge.

And that was sixteen days *before* the new 'sus' sections of the CJA became law.

> ***"Fancy a bite to eat? We won't have a burger, there's a McLibel demo outside the shop. We certainly won't buy veal - RIP Jill Phipps. Can't really go for a spin, since we are boycotting petrol stations and motorway extensions. People are living in trees at the end of the road. Head for a train, past the patchwork of travellers' buses and trucks parked up on wasteground by the station. Give them a wave. Have a laugh at the slogans on the defaced billboards. Catch sight of a TV shop showing the news of the Home Secretary's house being invaded by the homeless. Britain's changing. Great isn't it?"***
> **- George McKay, Senseless Acts of Beauty**

APRIL

28.4.95 **Performing naked at a golf-course on St George's Hill** in a 'St George and the Dragon' play done Donga-stylee, marking the launch of 'The Land Is Ours' campaign, at the site where the Diggers began their land actions in 1649. For a week people camped half a mile away on land by disused Wisley Airfield and transformed it into a little eco-paradise.

MAY

1.5.95 **Up a tree in the 'cosmic village In the sky'** at beautiful Stanworth Valley, near Preston, for the Mayday start of a dangerous five day eviction of over forty tree-houses - linked by aerial walkways - in the path of the M65 extension. Two teams of mountain rescue climbers, hundreds of police, bailiffs and private security, two cherrypickers, two caterpillars, miles of fencing, a press blackout, 63 Public Order arrests and several hundreds of thousand pounds of tax-payers money to plough through ancient woodland and continue the govt's insane £16 billion roads programme. Will they ever get the plot?

8.5.95 **Holding hands in a ring round Stonehenge with 300 people at dawn.** A VE Day celebration with a message. Happy, happy day.

14.5.95 **Dancing on the cars in Camden High Street** kicking off a summer season of anti-car protests with **Reclaim The Streets**. A thousand people enjoyed a car-free day with bands, jugglers, a pedal-powered SoundSystem and free food.

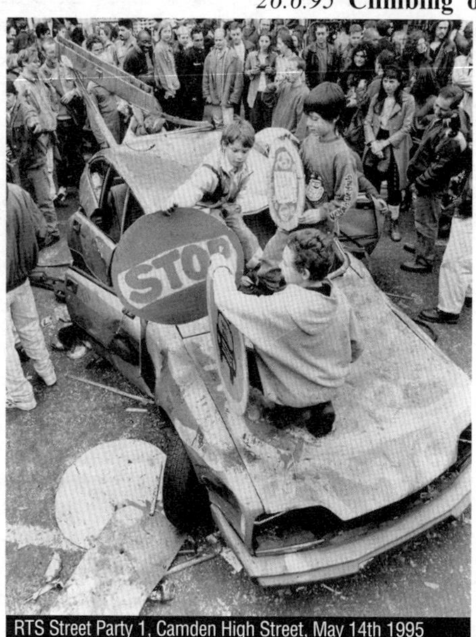

RTS Street Party 1, Camden High Street, May 14th 1995

JUNE

1.6.95 **At an open-cast mine in Garforth**, Leeds, where police arrested 19 people for 'aggravated trespass'- including the press!

20.6.95 **On a tower on the roof of an East London squat** dubbed Munstonia, the last house on the route of the M11, which was taken over when security popped out for a cup of tea....

22.6.95 **Putting two fingers up at the Northern Cruiser**, as the live animals are exported for the last time (?) through Shoreham Harbour. In six months over 300 people had been arrested under the catch-all Public Order Act and police costs put at (a conservative) £4M. Ever seen 400 grannies giving the Nazi salute to coppers?

24.6.95 **Standing victorious on the top of the Brent Spar in the North Sea**, as the world's biggest multi-national, Shell, is forced to back down over dumping the dustbin. "I watched as the tugs started turning slowly round and the biggest rainbow I'd ever seen arced across the sky. I stood on deck in a state of shock, holding a flare, my face agog, going 'Wow!'" - Al Baker.

26.6.95 **Climbing over a fence at Glastonbury Festival** which was declared Europe's biggest free fezzy after 300 yrds of 10ft fencing was ripped down by those who couldn't afford the £68 racket ...I mean ticket....

28.6.95 **At the Old Bailey in court with McDonalds** as the McLibel trial - Britain's longest running libel case - entered its second year. McDs have been regretting suing Dave & Helen ever since as more and more unsavoury McDetails emerge.

JULY

7.7.95 **Driving around in car for 72 hours looking for The Mother** ... the big free anti-CJA festy that never was. A massive police operation of phonetaps, roadblocks and surveillance splintered the party into lots of little babies. Black Moon soundsystem had their rig seized. Eight people were later charged with 'conspiracy to cause a public nuisance' for allegedly organising the non-event - a common law charge which carries a maximum life sentence! Cases are pending.

23.7.95 **Raving Against The Machine,** as Islington's Upper St - London's main Northern artery - is turned into a thumping great Sunday street party with 2,000 revellers and a soundsystem in a tank! On the evening remaining

> ***"The historical fact is that bad laws have been repeatedly overturned by illegal action. In a hundred years time, those involved in protest today may well be regarded as heroes"***
> **- PAJ Waddington, Liberty and Order**

stragglers found themselves on the wrong side of a line of police riot shields.

AUGUST

1.8.95 **Squatting a derelict Pier in Brighton**, as homeless people launch 'Operation Crusty' to highlight their eviction as a community from beach chalets. The collective have since moved into a disused nunnery but are being taken to court by 'The Poor Servants of the Mother of God'!

9.8.95 **Dripping with blood and playing dead at Faslane** at the main gates of the Clyde nuclear submarine base to mark Nagasaki Day - fifty years since the bomb was dropped killing 74,000 in the Japanese city. Police arrested 32 people for Public Order offences.

SEPTEMBER

5.9.95 **In an 8ftx8ft cell on Muroroa in the middle of a Nuclear Test** - that's where one activist was when the French caused a worldwide storm of protest with their first South Pacific explosion. Al, and cohort Matt, managed to stay at large on the island for 31 hours undetected by thousands of crack French troops.

9.9.95 **Digging up the Michael Heseltine's backgarden** searching for coal in protest at the environmental nightmare of open-cast sites.

OCTOBER

2.10.95 **Being arrested for theft of a biro** and other nonsense charges as 31 people are nicked on the first National Day of Action against the Job Seeker's Allowance ...and later infiltrating Newsnight and ruffling Jeremy Paxman to reveal this joke to millions on TV.

8.10.95 **Claiming a right Royal victory** as 400yr-old trees in Windsor Great Park are saved from the chop by people sitting in the trees and refusing to move for two months.

17.10.95 **Driving in a freedom convoy behind a Scottish Pipe Band** as the residents of the Isle of Skye say 'NO TOLL TAX' at the opening of the extortionate bridge to the mainland. More than 30 are nicked for Public Order offences.

24.10.95 **Sharing a barn with security at Brynhenllys**.. as poorly-paid 'slaves' and anti-opencast activists battle for five-days over a monster development that will gouge a hole visible from space out of the heart of the Welsh valleys. More than 40 nicked for Public Order offences.

29.10.95 **Wanting to blow-up Chirac** at Chequers as 600 people run wild at the Prime Minister's country residence as the de-test-able French President flies in to meet his only friend in the world.

The end of the road for a convoy of old cars which have been driven up from Brighton, Oxford and elsewhere to converge on Pollok, Glasgow, to create a Carhenge in the path of the M77

NOVEMBER

1.11.95 **Celebrating in Brightlingsea** as Roger Mills' live export company goes down the pan (we hope). During nine months over 600 people - or one in 15 of the population - were nicked for Public Order offences. Judge Forbes ruling against Mills in a test-case over the validity of direct action drew a parallel with Gandhi.

3.11.95 **Waiting outside a court** where Iggy from the Whitstable Flat Oak Tribe could find himself the first person in the country jailed under the CJA - ironically a year to the day it became law. Keen Kent coppers have been wielding the CJA stick nicking over sixty people for "aggravated trespass" since protests against the Thanet Way road extension in Kent began.

> ***"The Act is, quite simply, a mess. Most police forces have been vary wary of using it, as it is so badly put together it's impossible to put it into practice. The blame for this shambles must be laid firmly at the door of the Home Secretary who introduced the act for the sake of a few cheap cheers at party conference. We anticipate there will be more acquittals, more charges dropped, and that those police forces who seek to use the act in an aggressive way such as Kent and Northamptonshire will be facing a hefty bill for damages with precious little to show in the way of convictions."*** **- Hunt Sabs Association**

AQUITOMETER 90%

At the end of the first year, where we'd been tallying up the arrests every week on the CJA Arrestometer, the final Arrestometer appeared in issue 49. But it turned out afterwards that the vast majority of these cases were either dropped or acquitted.

In the year since the Criminal Justice Act became law over 500 people have been arrested but not a single one jailed (at the time of writing). In fact, around 90% of cases have been dropped or, when they have gone to trial, defendants are acquitted. Many police forces have been wary of testing a poorly-drafted piece of legislation and have opted for a more widespread use of the 1986 Public Order Act - making over 1,200 arrests at live animal export demonstrations alone in the last 12 months. However, the CJA has been used countless times as intimidation. Peaceful protest has, however, been effectively banned by the use of outrageous bail conditions. It seems not to matter whether charges will stand up if the police can bar someone from protest sites until trial. The immobilised protestor then faces up to six months wait when the ludicrous charges are then dropped and no trial takes place and people are acquitted. Many people are now suing the police for wrongful arrest, false imprisonment and malicious prosecution. These figures are as accurate as we can get them. The indication they give is that the police are acting as political servants of the government and their vested interests. It also shows clearly that the Criminal Justice Act is simply not working.

CJA ARRESTOMETER

Hunt Sabs 170
Footie Fans 116
Road Protestors 88
Peace Campaigners 48
Environmentalists 46
No Live Exports* 38
Tree Defenders 14
Travellers# 11
Ravers 10
Illegal Gatherers 3
Druids 1

**1200+ animal rights actives nicked this year*
 # and 125 CJA evictions monitored by FFT

*** Since the riot at Hyde Park last year, when the media first woke up to the CJA, protestors have gone from fighting in the streets to fighting in the courts - and winning time after time:**

31.8.95 **Travellers in Crowborough,** East Sussex successfully challenged an eviction order under Section 77 of the CJA when Judge Sedley announced the law was 'Draconian' and 'unlawful' on the grounds that Councils have a legal duty to safeguard and promote the welfare of children in need under the Children's Act.

13.9.95 **A Druid, King Arthur Pendragon,** beat down Babylon in the first test-case of Section 71 of the CJA 'trespassory assemblies' (where gatherings of more than 20 people are declared illegal by decree from Chief Constables). Back then his annual celebration at Stonehenge was stopped by the boys in blue - but now Excalibur has cut another swathe from the Government's field of Law Und Ordnung.

28.9.95 **Already condemned by the United Nations, Part 1 of the CJA** - the building of children's prisons for 12-14 year olds - was taken to the High Court by the Howard League for Penal Reform who extracted major concessions from the Home Office. Local Authorities in 3 of 5 cases have refused planning permission. Not a brick has yet been built.

2.11.95 **Black Moon Soundsystem** had their £9,000 rig confiscated in July but have had their rave test-case adjourned again - for the seventh time. Are the powers-that-be scared or do the police just wanna have a party? We should be told.

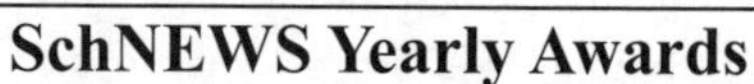

SchNEWS Yearly Awards

'We've got our CJA knickers in a twist' award to **KENT CONSTABULARY**

'Come and have a go if you think yer hard enuff' award to **RECLAIM THE STREETS**

'Builder from Lewes' award to **AL BAKER**

'Best activist age group' award to **UNDER-13s**

'Have I got a sign pointing to my head' award to **LINDIS PERCY** (7 CJA ARRESTS)

"Carry on breaking the law - it's only the only way to beat it" **- Phil Pritchard, Road Alert!**

WHATLEY QUARRY?!

EARTH FIRST! 60 NICKED IN SUPERQUARRY SHUTDOWN!

Each morning one lorry a minute leaves Whatley Quarry fully laden with rocks for road-building... Twyford Down, Solsbury Hill, Newbury... but it's been strangely quiet since Monday.

"I couldn't believe the size of the place,it stretched on forever, the air was full of evil dust and the machinery we headed for was so massive when lit up it looked like a deserted city!"

Five days ago - it's 3.30 am. Bagpipes wake 500 activists. 5.30 am: site invaded from all directions...

Earth First!'s national day of direct action was to shut Whatley Quarry in Somerset for the day - one of the biggest quarries in Europe, supplying stone for much of this government's destructive road-building programme. Amey Roadstone Corporation (owned by Hansons) now want to double it in size - making a hole visible from the moon and swallowing two thirds of the Mendip Hills. It also threatens the local water supply including the source of Bath Spa.

"The action was a total success before the day began, there was nobody manning the office or machinery! All CCTV surveillance cameras were quickly taken out of action. There were people up every crane, on top of offices, up lights, up chimneys!

"The pumps at the bottom of the Quarry were stopped. A section of railway line mysteriously disappeared - the line, as far as Westbury, had to be checked due to pixies on the track. One of the main conveyor belts, which had been mysteriously trashed due to a stray fire extinguisher, made an excellent trampoline!"

With 500 on the action and only 80 security the protestors numbers were too great to control. Yesterday SchNEWS phoned Whatley to find out whether they had reopened the quarry - and to get a figure on the cost of the action. A spokeswoman said she "was not in a position to comment". Estimates have been given at a cost of over quarter of a million.

Pics: Alec Smart

SchNEWSreader

Released 1st December 1995

Rushed out for the Christmas market – the orange book covering the first amazing year – from the single-sided pilot issue in November 1994 up to issue 50 in November 1995. In these pages we can see the format of SchNEWS quickly form, which has remained basically the same ever since, as well as the regular favourite sections coming in such as Crap Arrest Of The Week, Inside SchNEWS, SchNEWS In Brief, Party & Protest, and finally, er '...And Finally'. This book also contains a great collection of cartoons by Kate Evans.

This book is sold out and rare as hen's teeth, but most of it is readable online at

www.schnews.org.uk/archive/index-001-50.htm

BINGO!

Labelled as "one of the most bizarre conferences held in Brighton" last weekend saw the doors of the old Top Rank Bingo Hall flung open for a Justice? organised National Direct Action Conference. Nearly 600 people (CCTV provided police estimates!) schemed, swapped ideas and watched Conscious Cinema as bemused Christmas shoppers trundled by outside.

Opening the conference, Colin from Justice? explained that throughout the world millions of people, mainly poor, were involved in direct action against environmental destruction and attacks on people's rights. Those involved in direct action in Britain are part of a worldwide movement for the planet's future - from Whatley Quarry to Ogoniland, from France to Newbury. Given that a third of people in Britain live in poverty and are offered nothing by a corrupt parliamentary system the direct action movement could grow enormously if it builds more links with those most under attack - unemployed youth, people living in run-down estates, refugees - in their struggles against injustice. Then we could really shake things up for the politicians who are quite happy to see poverty grow, our rights diminish and the world destroyed as long as big business keeps making big profits.

The conference organised workshops on dealing with the media, Non Violent Direct Action, prisoner support, road protests and loads more. Most important of all, people got to talk to others from around the country, plot actions for the coming year and learn how to organise more effectively. Following on from the day and continuing in the great tradition of party and protest the former theatre saw 2,000 people partying until 10 o'clock on Sunday morning.

"Everyone involved in Saturday's Conference and party did it for free. There was security, fire extinguishers, clear fire exits and free water. For a small donation everyone had a storming party that went on all night".

After people spent all day Sunday cleaning, leaving the Bingo Hall better than we found it, it was infuriating to find the Argus printing a picture proclaiming "The message and the mess: the aftermath of the Justice? Conference". We replied "The photograph was like going to the Goldstone ground after a big match, taking a snap of empty terraces and saying "Look - people have dropped litter" before anyone could clear up! And graffiti? Well, I'm sure the children who did some rather nice artwork in the crèche, wouldn't be too happy with that description."

The fact that a squat as well-run and enjoyable for thousands as the Justice? conference was can be attacked by the press doesn't surprise us - the mainstream media usually lines up with the politicians (CJA) and the police (evictions) in attacking people who take over empty buildings and put them to good use. If you want proof of the hypocrisy of it all just keep an eye out over the next week or so for those very same papers crying crocodile tears over the plight of the homeless at Christmas - while quite happily putting the boot into anyone who actually does anything to sort out homelessness by squatting properties left to rot by tax-dodging businesses.

Back of the flyer...

ROUGH GUIDE TO THE DAY

Ring up Friday P.M. or any time after this time to find out exact venue

Workshops > Road Actions: The No M11 Campaign do a practical w.shop on road protesting

Media Tarting: Justice? on writing press releases, media stunts...

Getting Arrested: Shoreham solicitor Des Murphy, gives advice on what to do if you get arrested.

Discussion Sessions > Prisoners Who Use Violence: A debate on why certain groups refuse to actively support prisoners who have advocated violence. Anarchist Black Cross, Liberty and Amnesty debate.

What (Animal) Rights: How important are animal rights? Do groups such as the Animal Liberation Front go too far to protect animals when human rights are neglected all over the world? Come and discuss.

Do We Really Want Agenda 21:
Activ 88 vs Brighton Autonomists

Speakers > > > Duncan Blunkhorn on the history of Direct Action ** Road Alert! on the Newbury Bypass ** Youth C.N.D. on French Nukes ** Nikki Jameson talks about prisoner support ** Also Workshops by the Primitivist Network, Activ88...

Other Shit being Sorted so come....

LATER: Rather Large Party... Sound Systems... Bands

Free Entry.... Café... Creche

Direct Action Conferences

Pic: Tash

Justice? organised three Direct Action conferences in Brighton from 1995-1997, run on a Do-It-Yourself basis with zero budget.

Each conference saw the direct action movement at a different juncture – the first one, held on 9th December 1995 at the old Bingo Hall, North St Brighton, was at the point where all the sections of the Criminal Justice Act were now law, and people were wanting to broaden the scope of direct action. The second took place in a freezing, dilapidated building opposite Preston Park on November 23rd 1996. The venue wasn't ideal but it was a miracle it took place at all after some over-the-top policing. Co-inciding with the 100th issue of SchNEWS, it came at the end of a year which saw a diversity of large campaigns ranging from Newbury to the Liverpool Dockers. The third and final one was held rather ironically at the old Brighton Argus newspaper building on North St, Brighton. Along with the cops, the local paper had been running a witch-hunt campaign against Justice? and the direct action that was happening in town, so when Brighton Fringe offered us the newspaper's old building to host a conference about direct action we jumped at the chance! It took place on 10th and 11th May 1997, just days after Neo Labour had taken power

The following is an interview with Carly, a key organizer of the conferences...

So how did the idea of a Direct Action Conference come up?

At the beginning over one hundred people would turn up for Justice? meetings – it was mad. But as numbers started to dwindle, it was decided that rather than discussing what we were up to, that we'd have political debates to make them a bit more interesting – and to try and get different people involved. So me and a friend, Sara, decided that we'd organise these meetings We went to the office one day and made a massive list of all the discussions we wanted to have and the list was so long we thought we might as well have a conference! The direct action scene was coming from so many different perspectives we wanted to pull it in so there was some sort of focus, some sort of agreement over major issues.

Was Justice? going in different directions at this point (late 95)?

Yeah it was because the people who'd set it up – some of them were DJs and ravers, there were trade unionists, trots and anarchists and the rest which mean't a lot of disagreements over how to run things, and what direction we should be going. We felt we've got to agree what direction we should be going – we can't be so random and all over the place.

What sorts of things did you want discussed at the first conference? Was it discussing theories or tactics, or priority targets for direct action?

It was really diverse. We had prisoner support, environmental issues, trade union issues...

But I think the biggest question at the conference was – where are we going? We squatted the old Bingo Hall in town in North Street, and people came from all over the country. It was just an amazing building – it used to be a dance hall and still had a lot of the original structure in it. We also organised a party for the evening which was wicked - actually one of the best parties there's ever been in Brighton!

Tell us about that radio interview

I'd hardly had any sleep when a local radio rang up

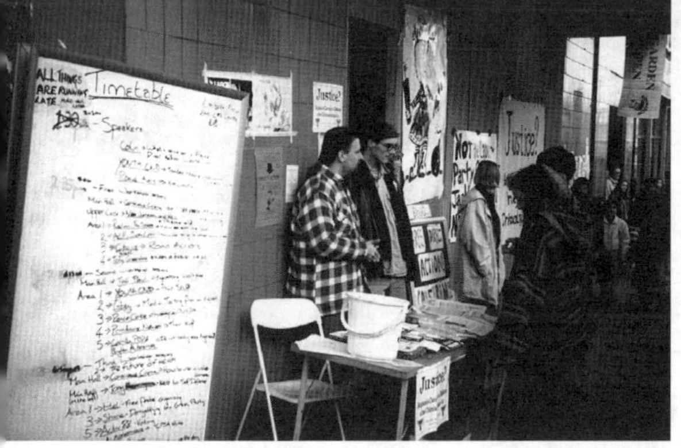

and asked why we were putting on the conference. I told them we wanted to get people like animal rights supporters, trade unionists etc together to …'fight against stuff', which perhaps wasn't too coherent.

What sort of numbers attended?

There would have been a few hundred (and a few thousand for the party!) Some had come to Brighton specifically for the conference, others just popped in for a look. In one of the rooms there was Conscious Cinema putting up video footage – which was good cos it brought people in, but we were trying to have one big meeting in the main hall and some people were more interested in going to watch a video! We were running round trying to get people to go into the meetings.

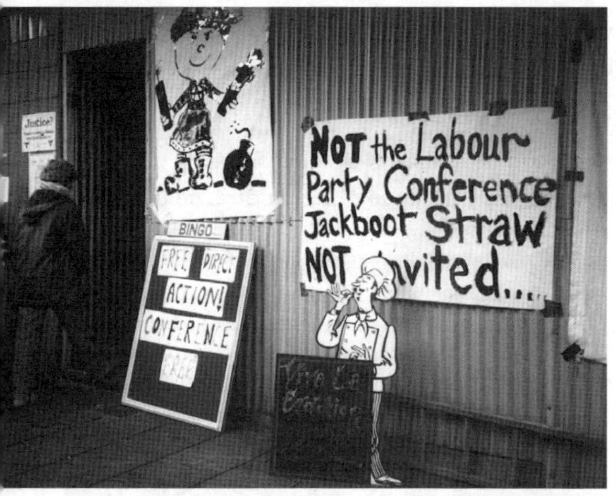

Was there a big focus about discussing the Criminal Justice Act – cos all the sections of the CJA would have come in over that twelve months?

Once the Criminal Justice Bill became an Act people starting moving on and saying 'it's not just about this'… It'd shown people the relevance of the different things that people were involved in and how they were all linked, and how we were all in the same boat together and you couldn't just be an animal rights activist and ignore… human rights or the environment.

Around the time of that conference there must have been a transition point for a lot of people, after the CJA had come in, where they realised 'hang on a minute – it's not just about free parties' or roads or whatever.

Yeah – but for the first one, there were only two of us doing it, and neither of us had done anything like it before, and Sara was so shy she wouldn't ring anyone up or answer the phone!

Colin got involved in the second one, so it was a lot more regimented, and we'd decided much more what we wanted to focus on, what we wanted to get out of it, and what direction we were heading. For the first one, when people phoned up and said they wanted to speak, we just said 'yeah ok', so some of the people who spoke were random nutters really. But we were just so excited that people wanted to speak at our conference. We didn't want to be too exclusive – at first anyway.

So with the second one – twelve months had gone past – things must have moved quite a long way… there would have been Newbury, the Liverpool Dockers and so on in '96…

We were getting a lot more 'left wing' in our influences.

Was that to do with the focus on workers struggles like the Liverpool Dockers?

Yeah. There were all these trade union issues coming up and it was like… Hillingdon (hospital workers – see SchNEWS 136), the Magnet Strikers, the Liverpool Dockers – so we had to be a lot more focused this time and also making it (direct action) more welcoming to people who have had nothing to do with it before – cos we were still seen as dirty hippies and tree huggers. Trying to get more 'normal' people involved was a lot of the focus, and getting the hippy tree-huggers to realise that there was more to life than… hugging trees!

And probably some of them were quite middle class and hadn't had much to do with workers struggles…

A lot of them didn't care. I remember at one of the Earth First! Gatherings – there was a French environmental activist there and, I think we were talking about working class issues and human rights, and he was just saying that… "We're called 'Earth First!' we're not 'People First' – you put the earth before people, people don't matter". But then it's people who are fucking up the earth…

So who was talking at that second one… apart from the Dockers?

The dole workers were on strike as well so we had someone from them to speak. We had a solicitor talking to us about our rights, stuff on squatting, racism and later in the afternoon debates such as 'whose gonna save the planet - corporations or people.'

How long did it take to organise a direct action conference?

After that second one, we sat in the pub that evening

IF ORDINARY PEOPLE BEHAVED LIKE- Burson-Marsteller PUBLIC RELATIONS

and started planning where we'd gone wrong and what we were gonna do for the next one!

With the second one we decided we were going to re-squat the old Courthouse, where Justice? had squatted before the Criminal Justice Bill became law. We managed to get back in there and stayed overnight, but the place had been completely trashed by the bailiffs when they had evicted us first time round.

The police were having none of it - at one point we were on a mobile phone talking to the solicitor, holding up the barricades while the police are trying to smash it down, and the solicitor saying 'they're not allowed to just break in' with me screaming down the phone 'I don't think they care actually'. So the old Courthouse wasn't an option. Time was running out and we needed a venue. But the police knew how successful the last conference was and there was no way they wanted it to happen. And it was getting harder and harder to find buildings and we ended up frantically trying to find empty buildings that'd be suitable for it.

Then we decided – well maybe it doesn't have to be too suitable – just anywhere would be good! So on the morning of the conference, we took this massive empty building – and it'd been used as a shooting gallery by smackheads – it was really disgusting. There was no wheelchair access or stuff like that. It wasn't the most ideal venue. I'd had three and a half hours sleep in the last five days from trying to sort out the squats which ended up meaning that I was the best chair of a meeting ever because I was so sleep deprived! Everyone was trying to talk at the same time and I wasn't having it, everyone shut up when I told them to!

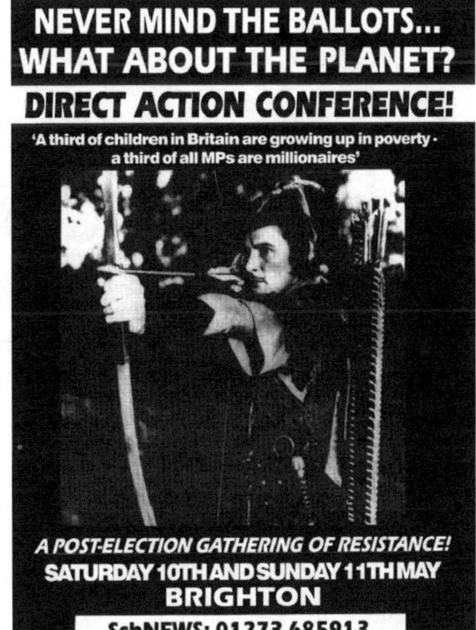

So what was the flavour of the third one?

We had stuff on free parties and surveillance - which ended up half the conference getting up and doing actions on the new CCTV cameras that had been put up around town including someone tieing a blow-up doll to one! We also had this amazing woman speaking from the Magnet workers who were on strike at the time, as well as Liverpool dockers.

After the third one did, you think 'we're not gonna do another one?' Why didn't you do another one?

I think the whole mood had changed... Like when we first started doing the conferences, you'd go to the Earth First! gatherings – and you'd feel like one of the Trots cos you'd be sitting in your corner saying 'look this is going on in the world, you can't just talk about hippy-dippy nice things.' But over the years, you'd find that the people who were saying the more hippy stuff would be the ones in the corner because the mood had changed and people started realising that it was so wide reaching, that you couldn't just be focused on a single issue campaign.

Groups up and down the country were getting quite established by now?

If you get it into context... before, Brighton was seen as one of the main places where anti-CJB stuff was going on, and... people were looking at us sort of saying 'they know what's going on' But by the end of the conferences, they didn't need us ... it would have been really patronising for us to keep going on saying 'hey – we're from Brighton we'll show you what to do.' People were doing it for themselves.

EXODUS COLLECTIVE

We all like a good free party, and the Exodus Collective certainly put on some of the biggest and best parties in the Luton area for 10 years. They even managed to get away with four free festivals despite a raft of legislation to stop them happening.

But although the parties defined the collective and attracted thousands of people, they were more than just about having a dance. They were a unique urban phenomenon offering working, viable solutions to many of society's ills; poverty, crime, drugs, unemployment and the break down of communities. Renovating derelict properties and farmland, showing what people can achieve when they work together, even in some of our most deprived areas.

Of course such utopian actions met with the full force of the law, including a mass arrest which famously led to 4,000 surrounding Luton police station demanding their release. In fact the continuous clampdown got so bad, that eventually even Bedfordshire County Council voted to support a public inquiry into "the activities of Bedfordshire Police and others against the Exodus Collective".

Serious differences of opinions, meant the collective are no more, although some of the crew continue to carry on with other projects, but their legacy is an inspiration to everyone.

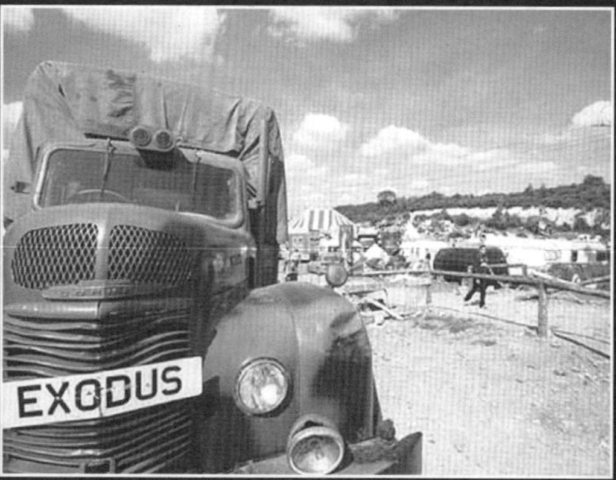

Issue 92, 27th September 1996

COLLECTIVE STRENGTH

At the beginning of September, members of the Luton based party and housing action group Exodus prepared to party European style. Following a successful conference by INURA (International Network of Urban Regeneration and Action) in Luton, the Exodus Collective were invited over to Zurich by a similar Swiss group - Rote Fabrik. Two international gatherings in the space of a month. Both positive, complementary and uplifting. The crew pack up and make the journey home. To what? *"While we were away, 60 police officers raided the Farm... another trick to try and discredit. Yet what did they take away? A bag of sugar and a bag of baby milk. Please."*

But this is just one minor hassle compared to events over the last four years. The collective have fought police harassment, press smears, council skulduggery and an alleged covert freemason campaign. They now face eviction from Long Meadow Community Farm, where school trips are arranged so that local kids on the estates can have first hand experience of rural life and livestock. The Exodus Community dances have faced high court injunctions, equipment seizure, road blocks, even legislation to increase the penalties for people organising unlicensed 'raves'... brought about by local Tory MP Graham Bright.

And yet they continue to grow and thrive.

Haz Manor was first squatted in March 93. A formerly derelict old people's hospice on the edge of Luton, it has been totally rebuilt to house 40 people. Repeated plans have also been put forward to the local council asking for space in which a community centre can be developed. When the first plans were put forward in early 93 Exodus began a promising dialogue with Dunstable Police. Chief Inspector Mick Brown told local press at the time, *"What we need to do is find premises that the organisers need, to come up with the proof that their ideas work."* Shortly after, Luton police swooped on Long Meadow Community Farm, arrested 12 people and seized sound equipment. This led to a 4,000 strong protest by disappointed party people... outside Luton Police Station! Members of the collective believe that the man putting political pressure on police chiefs was none other than...Graham Bright MP.

There certainly seems to be a concerted effort, by persons unknown, to create situations to put the boot in. Hassling their local freemasons probably doesn't help. (Roy Davies, Labour Councillor and Leader of Luton Borough Council was recently 'outed' as a mason, and last week Judge Maurice Drake stepped down from the trial of one of the Collective members after it was disclosed that he was a member of the Royal Arch, an elite order of the freemasons.) Even local brewers Whitbread feel threatened - they lose thousands in pub sales when parties are held.

Exodus is a grass roots community group, providing housing and popular entertainment... that works. It may not be conventional, but real change isn't made by following convention. It's about being able to answer the needs of the community and about taking responsibility and regaining control over our lives. Nuff' respect.

The Collective are currently undertaking negotiations with the Dept of Transport regarding the proposed sale of Long Meadow Community Farm. Despite the promise of first refusal on the property, it has been verbally sold to another party without prior consultation.

Third Battle Of Newbury

"The Newbury bypass. One nine mile road. Which manages to pass three times through the North Wessex Downs Area of Outstanding Natural Beauty, and obliterates three Sites of Special Scientific Interest, an ancient Stone Age settlement, eleven other archaeological sites and two perfectly preserved Civil War battlefields. As well as destroying the habitats of kingfishers, nightjars, hobbies, bats, and dormice, all protected species, and one of the last remaining colonies of Desmoulin Whorl snail. And polluting the river Lambourne, one of the cleanest in the country because the whole thing runs through woodland. To build it means chopping down an estimated ten thousand tress." - Kate Evans in Copse.

The following is coverage of the protests against the Newbury bypass, using the unedited reports by SchNEWS people as they ferried between the dampness of the protest camps and the er, dampness of the office. People can discuss the significance of Newbury for the anti-roads movement, but it was obviously an enormous protest which drew probably thousands of people into direct action. For SchNEWS the sustained involvement and coverage of Newbury was pivotal in the way it was a final break from writing about the resistance to the CJA, and put it more clearly in the role of being what the Guardian called at the time 'The protest movement's national newsletter'.

Issue 56 – 12th January 1996

Security stiffed by rampaging road protesters...

If anything has become apparent over the past few days then it is that the best tool the anti-roads/direct action movement possess is imagination. For three days running, people power has effectively outwitted the Highways Agency in their bid to start trashing work along the proposed route of the Newbury bypass.

Day one. People in tripods block the exits of the security compound so no vehicles can get out. Security are trapped for the day. One-nil.

Day two. Attention is switched to the coach station of the company supplying buses for the security. People chain themselves to the entrance until Horseman Coaches call back the coaches sent to pick up security!

Later on it's stalemate as hundreds of security link arms round a solitary bulldozer which after felling a couple of oaks falls silent as protestors play a new surreal version of British Bulldog.

Day three. More trees are cut but by 10 am work is again abandoned. Three -nil!

Whether this softly-softly approach from the police and security will last long is debatable. When the glare of the media circus moves on to its next fix and the contractors get impatient as the March deadline approaches (under an EC directive construction work should not effect nesting birds) will this 'people have a right to protest' last?

So why the fuss?

"Newbury has a traffic problem why not build a road? Sounds logical enough but unfortunately the easier it is to travel by car the more people

"Sorry darlin', I'll be home late today. Something's come up". Pic: Alec Smart

travel by car, as a result new roads generate their own traffic"

Current forecasts point to the bypass providing relief for just 5-7 years! Even chief supporters Newbury District Council are now saying the bypass won't solve the town's traffic problem only that it will give them a chance to sort it.

"Nightmare scenarios are looming, planning applications have been lodged for more than 5000 houses on the land between the new bypass and the western edge of town. They will need their own roads, out of town shopping centres etc. These new roads are generating their own traffic."

Freedom to drive?

The 13km long bypass will trash 3 sites of Special Scientific Interest, damage a number of local nature reserves, two civil war battlesites, 12 archaeological sites as well as managing to 'pass' three times through the North Wessex Downs Area of Outstanding Natural Beauty. Not bad eh? Along with the road will come 'infill' ....already some 700 planning applications have been submitted.

70% of Newbury's traffic is local so wouldn't the £101 million be better spent on a package of local traffic reduction measures? What about improving public transport, cycle routes, school buses, car-share schemes etc. All of which an Independent transport consultants have shown could solve the towns traffic problems far better and more cost-effectively than a bypass.

For example, upgrading the Southampton to Midlands railway to take so-called piggyback freight services, where heavy lorries travel on specially designed trains would ensure huge savings on pollution and road maintenance. The equivalent Channel Tunnel to Glasgow piggyback line will take 400,000 lorry journeys off the roads every year after it opens in 1997.

Laws? You make 'em we break 'em...

"Over two thirds of the population believe that there are times when breaking the law is justifiable"

The decision to proceed with the by-pass in July 1995 was a direct result of concerted lobbying by local politicians, the roads lobby and those with vested interests. There was no formal consultation or opportunity for debate during the review period.

No proper Environmental Impact Assessment was ever carried out despite the findings of the Government's landscaper Advisory Committee back in 1986 that the road was "quite unacceptable".

Supporters of the bypass claim that it enjoys overwhelming local support, but the quoted 6:1 in favour was estimated through a self-selecting phone in which only a few per cent of local people responded!

Who said this?

"Our priorities are to reduce the need for transport; to put public transport before private, rail before road, less polluting before more polluting forms of transport and to encourage walking and cycling." It's the Liberal Democrats transport policy. But isn't Lib Dem MP David Rendell one of the main supporters of the bypass?

Deeds Not World

Ironically while all this was going on a Conference was being held in Newbury to discuss the Government's White Paper on 'Rural England'.

The Paper talks about the importance of the rural environment and its commitment to protecting the wider countryside, meanwhile a few miles down the road, the same beautiful countryside is under threat. As with all this waffle it is not worth the paper it's written on. Forget the empty words/the writing-to-your-MP - join the protests at Newbury.

DIRECT ACTION STATIONS!

More people needed to beat the bulldozers at Newbury...

"The Newbury bypass was conceived in the 1960's, planned in the 1970's and out of date by the 1980's. Shouldn't the Department of Transport start living in the 1990's?"

"We've got away from the 'let's just cost them loads of money'. The idea is to stop this road and with the preparation and organisation we've got, we can. One of the biggest direct actions ever to take place was against the proposed damming of the Franklin River in Tasmania when David Bellamy got nicked. That succeeded because of the massive amount of planning, preparation and imagination that went into it. If people can do it there, we can certainly do it here."

Week Two of the Third Battle of Newbury

As the March deadline approaches (EC directive means that trees cannot be felled during the nesting season) the cat and mouse game between security, police and people trying to stop the bypass hots up. So far it's been estimated that just half a mile of the eight and a half mile site has been cleared of trees! However more and more security guards are being drafted in and people are needed desperately.

Police have now begun to flex their Criminal Justice Act (CJA) muscles with the catch-all aggravated trespass.

The police are also using their new powers to bail people off site. People being nicked are being told not to return to within one km from where they've been arrested. With trial dates often set months from the time of arrest this results in an increasing number of protestors unable to participate in demonstrating.

"The first week was totally amazing and exhilarating but people didn't get any sleep. People are now getting tired and we desperately need fresh energy and imagination. The best thing people can do is come up for a couple of days a week. There's so many ideas and skills we have that we need people to come up and help make them work."

The campaign is taking many twists and turns and is involving a cross section of people involved for the first time in direct action.

On Wednesday a group of Newbury businessman launched Business Against Bypass. Adrian Foster-Fletcher, an executive headhunter who has attended protests in his Jaguar, said the community had only woken up to this issues when anti-road protesters arrived "We were told the M25 would solve all our problems, but it didn't." And in the post SchNEWS received a letter from Alan Page, a resigning Liberal Democrat sickened by their support for the bypass.

"As a 30 + year supporter of the Liberal cause and more recently as an executive local officer I have no desire to be associated with a movement which has torn up its environmental credibility in such an ignorant manner. My personal observations of British provincial towns, including Newbury is that we have become choked with heavy lorries and single occupant private motor cars. Eradicate this and we have manageable road space for all and we keep our countryside free of destruction. I have informed my bank not to honour the direct debit agreement with the Liberal Democrat Party. I will send the subscription to the Newbury protestors."

And SchNEWS, when questioning the Liberal Democrats Press Office on the contradiction between their so-called 'green' transport policy and their support for the road, were told "The time for protest is over"!

Which just goes to show you that all the main parties show the same contempt for people power and would have us wrapped up in endless debate and passing round bits of paper whilst the Earth's life support systems collapse round our ears.

Forget writing to your MP - get on the direct action tip, get down to Newbury and stop this insane road scheme in its tracks......

A single gesture of defiance is worth more than a thousand angry words!!

Only illegal, in-your-face direct action will stop this road - and everybody knows it. With spiraling costs some of the construction firms are getting cold feet and the police are saying publicly they cannot afford to continue to police the protest. In other words this battle can be won - if people get down to Newbury and stop this road! As one activist told SchNEWS, "We need people who are prepared to get up very early and take the battle to the contractors before they get near the site. We need people who are organised and are willing to get arrested to stop this madness. We need hundreds of them and we need them now. - SchNEWS 58, January 26th 1996

BYPASS THE LAW!

BATTLE OF NEWBURY HOTS UP - COME AND JOIN THE FUN

"With hundreds of security and police this as the Largest mobilisation of state forces yet against the anti-roads movement. If you can only get to Newbury once - do it. It's not only your chance to stop this insane road being built but also to show your defiance of the Criminal Justice Act."

Week three of the Third Battle of Newbury and the imaginative tactics used by the protesters are really worrying the road builders, the government and the police - because they are effectively getting more and more people off their arses and into direct action.

Protesters are continually rethinking their tactics in the face of more and more desperate attempts to ensure the site is cleared before the nesting season in March. Around one sixth of the route has now been cleared and the security cordons protecting the chainsaw gangs are now larger than football pitches. The police are not even giving warnings before nicking people for Aggravated Trespass (you can be nicked for this if a copper just thinks that you are going to disrupt a 'lawful activity' on private land). They then dish out bail conditions which amount to a sentence without trial and virtual house arrest. Protesters guilty of no offence are being told not to go anywhere near the protests and some are having to sign on at police stations in their home towns everyday to stop them demonstrating.

One solicitor told SchNEWS, "Bail conditions are not meant to be punishments in themselves. In this case they are clearly being used as a political means to suppress campaigns" Bindmans solicitors are currently preparing cases to take to the High Court to get these conditions overturned. As one protester told SchNEWS "The police are using these bail conditions to try and break the protest. We've got to make them unworkable by breaking them".

There are now 20 camps along the eight and half mile route and more people are needed now to help build defences. One way protesters are making sure the road won't be built is by fortifying and defending these camps. Four of them are in the High Court today (Friday) faced with eviction notices.

Every morning a convoy of roadbuilders and security flanked by masses of police around three quarters of a mile long converges to the south of Newbury - protesters have successfully slowed up proceedings by driving 10 miles an hour in front of them! The media's big story this week was about the guy who was meant to have cut one of the security vans' brake cables - failing to mention after successfully blockading their coach he was dragged off by security and held onto some wires which snapped. The police later arrested the wrong man for this 'offence'.

Protestors have occupied land, blockaded contractors and security transport. D-locked themselves to anything going and generally put every obstacle in the way of the clearance work. Against this, the police are doing what they've always done - using the law, including their new powers under the CJA, to stop any effective protest. So it's pretty worrying when Friends of the Earth - on behalf of the Newbury protesters - put out press releases condemning "deliberate damage" by protesters and calling for protesters to have a "positive relationship" with the police who are arresting them!

They might read The Sun on building sites, but on protest sites like Newbury the preferred reading is something a bit more high-brow.

When SchNEWS phoned Friends of the Earth to clarify their views they told us that "We don't condemn the police - it's unfortunate that they have to take these draconian actions but they do have a job to do" Friends of the Earth are doing loads of useful work to support the campaign but we should recognise that the police's job is to do what the government tells them, in this case ensure the Newbury bypass is built - and that it's kind of difficult to have a "positive relationship" with people who are arresting you for just about anything.

Issue 59 – 2nd February 1996

AROOOOGA!!

BATTLE CRY AS CAMP GET SET FOR ACTION

"It's hard to comprehend the scale of the Newbury operation (19 busloads of security on Wednesday). It's hard to comprehend that the tranquillity of this beautiful countryside could be shattered forever if this bypass is ever built."

Week Four. The anti-roads movement is piling on the pressure in the face of a continuing escalation of police and security numbers - the latter now nearly doubled to 1,200-strong - while police continue to criminalise peaceful protest via the backdoor with stringent bail conditions.

Under the Criminal Justice Act police can set bail - rather than a magistrate - and people arrested for the catch-all offence of 'aggravated trespass' are being bailed one kilometre away from the proposed route. They must also sign on EVERY DAY at their local police station, or face jail. This is to be challenged in the High Court.

This blanket use of aggravated trespass and outrageous police bail conditions represents an attack on all our rights.

Almost £1 MILLION has been spent on policing the Third Battle so far, admitted Chief Supt Blair of Thames Valley police. PLUS £1 MILLION security costs - rising as more troops are bussed in. Ex- army officers are being recruited to instill discipline to the rag-rag Reliance rent-a-mob.

ILLEGAL! On Tuesday the police were coining new legal terms as protestors were dragged out of their benders near Snelsmore Common despite the contractors having no possession order on the camp. "We are not sure if it was legal or illegal - we are describing it as 'inappropriate' and asking them not to do it again" said Supt Blair. Protestors are planning to take out a private prosecution against Reliance Security.

ILLEGAL! Trees are still being felled dangerously close to protestors and security despite the government's own Health and Safety Executive declaring that felling must be at least two tree lengths away from any individual.

ILLEGAL! Workers set fire to plastics to smoke out tree-sitters - the fire brigade, alerted by protestors, were turned away by the police.

Death threats have been received in the Newbury office - including one claiming to be from a security guard. Media reports of guards injured in violence were, in reality, one guard who twisted his ankle and another who ran straight into a tree.

The police and security are using any means they can - legal or illegal - to get this road built. We can beat them by force of numbers, contempt for their 'authority' and in-yer-face direct action'

Issue 63 – 1st March 1996

NEWBURY UPDATE

It's a Thursday, seven weeks into the Third Battle of Newbury and the evictions have just begun. In the same week that Selar is completely trashed, the climbers move to Snelsmore - the oldest camp on the route of the Newbury Bypass. The bailiffs and climbers turned up at this beautiful camp at 4am and within hours had sealed up the tunnels and cleared ground benders and nearby trees.

Weirdly, climbers cut walkways and pulled people out of the trees but didn't trash the tree houses. This could be because they didn't want to be too heavy on the first day as there was a high press presence. Or it could be so they can just move around trashing bits of different camps so protesters are spread out everywhere not knowing where work will be going on the following morning. Then again maybe, they're just stupid and they don't realise that if they leave the tree houses up, we will climb up them again.

Whatever's going on in their heads, the only thing we can do is GET UP THERE NOW! 01635 45544

Pic: Andrew Testa

600 NICKED AT NEWBURY!

An astonishing 600 people have been arrested since the Third Battle of Newbury road protest began ten weeks ago. More than one hundred have been nicked in the last six days, including 35 yesterday.

Many people, already arrested two or three times, remain defiant and face months in jail if they cop it again. Most are charged for the new 'crime' of 'aggravated trespass' under the Criminal Justice Act. Others are done under obscure ancient laws. Police have been so keen that on some days protestors have filled all police holding cells at Newbury, Andover, Basingstoke and even 60 miles away in Milton Keynes.

But Under-Sheriff Nick Blandy, in charge of the evictions, said this week: *"These protestors don't know how lucky they are. We could be using CS Gas. In less tolerant countries they would machine-gun them from trees."*

This week most of the camps at Great Pen Wood were evicted using the mercenary climbers ostracised by the British Mountaineer's Association. But the tallest tree on the 9-mile route at Reddings Copse stood firm. On Wednesday bailiffs, using the largest platform machine in Europe, went for the 120ft Scot's Pine but an Oak tree felled nearby smashed into its control panel with one bough then landing on a climber. He has a suspected broken neck. Blandy, eating a sarnie, ignored it.

Most of the clearance work has happened. As the warmer Spring weather arrives, the final battles are about to be fought. Rickety Bridge camp faces eviction after court on Tuesday. There's Camelot, home to druid Arthur Pendragon and his cohorts, and, of course, the Scot's Pine. Other one-tree camps are dotted around. Solidarity actions continue across the country.

Pic: Andrew Testa

Kennet Eviction

13/3/96 I'd first walked down the beautiful Kennet River bank in the Summer when the Bypass was given the go-ahead and the first tree-houses went up. I remember the elation in the Autumn when the Mothership landed. Straddling six tree-trunks with enough floorspace to do two forward rolls, Europe's biggest tree-house was a magnificent feat of building work. (It was named after a song by pop icon Julian Cope. Cope had arrived at the camp in January, unaware. "Wow! *That* was named after a song by *me?*") The place thrived through a bitterly cold winter. Today. up in the tree-house, was definitely Spring.

4.30am.WAKE UP! WAKE UP! AROOOGA!

The tree-top village gets up very, very fast. Wild rumours fly. It's still dark. no-one can see anything. They've never attempted a pre-dawn raid. Someone hits the air-raid siren which rings the alarm from Castle Wood to The Chase. The walkway link with the other side has gone. It's not even first light.

5.15am. Climbers on the riverside. The police have thrown a cordon several hundred-strong round the camp, doing the job of the security who haven't yet arrived. Protestors take positions, 'clink, clink', across the treetops.

6.30am Jeers drown out Under-Sheriff Nick Blandy's important eviction announcement. He looks at his important clipboard. He looks so damn small from up here. The chainsaw gangs fire up. The Sheriff's climbers are in the trees.

9.20am After nearly 3 hours of heart-stopping drama the first man is brought down. One woman is clinging to branches 80ft high as the climbers snatch at her heels. A line is thrown across from another tree and she ties it on and escapes in spectacular commando-style across the sky.

11.29am. The Cat & Mouse game is proving fruitless. No-one gets picked. In one tree the small huddled figure of a young girl wrapped head to toe in a pink blanket sits motionless, freezing but dignified. Hooded, faceless, she reminds me of an Ewok. (She stays all day. solid as the trunk, a tower of strength.) Enter the forces of darkness. Sheriff's Officers, dressed as Storm troopers in full black riot gear. head for The Mothership. The Skywalkers shout encouragement to those locked-on inside. Only George Lucas, or indeed anyone with a camera, is nowhere to be seen. I can see through the foliage, in the distance, lots of people shouting and waving. I listen to the megaphone pleas from the locals: *"I've lived here all my life. I was born here,"* shouted one, her Home Counties accent breaking up with emotion. *"What you are doing is sick. You are criminals."* The crowd start chanting: *"Scum. Scum. Scum. Scum."*

2:30pm Crash! The Mothership is still being dismantled. Possessions cascade into the mud. Some security guards pick through the debris for pathetic bonuses to top up their £3-an-hour job. It makes you sick for humanity. The climbers are still being out-manoeuvred at every step. The protestors rally. but the tension is relentless. Someone shouts, not for the first time, *"Gaia is behind us 200%!"*. Moments later Gaia appears, as if by magic, as a young deer running through the devastated Matchstick Land below, past the idle fluorescent patches of police and security. There are cheers. There's maybe a dozen people left in an island of fifty trees.

4:30pm After 12 hours of buzzing chainsaws, the assorted forces give up and leave us to the massacre. People cry uncontrollably. tears streaming down painted faces. I'm dumbstruck. It's difficult to comprehend the loss. Not just the loss, forever, of an idyllic piece of English Countryside. Not just a Site of Special Scientific Interest. For the last year these trees were homes. The protestors, a community. People lived here. Goodbye sweet Kennet and a curse on all those who made you fall.

Pic: Andrew Testa

Issue 66 – 22nd March 1996

AND FINALLY...

Castle Wood, the final camp on the site at Newbury was evicted on Tuesday. 85 days, 29 camps and 770 arrests after clearance work began, and at a cost of £1.5million (three times the estimated cost) the roadbuilders have completed one phase of their precious bypass. Cocky Under Sheriff Blandy organised a press conference to announce his "victory" over the protesters - and was promptly run outta town by protesters who did not look very "beaten" at all! Blandy and his mates obviously aren't as confident and victorious as they like to make out - they are now looking at spending £6 million on putting 20 miles of fencing around the route! Apparently there's an end of spring term school feeling at Newbury as protesters have a break before the next stage of the actions. Lotta continua!

So far, £12 billion pounds has been axed off the roads programme. The roads programme, once the pride of the DoT's mad-cap scheme to Tarmac this sceptred isle, is now seriously hobbled, perhaps, in the long term, fatally wounded. The trees at Newbury may be gone, but construction work will not commence until the summer, due to budgetary difficulties. As yet, no-one has (dared volunteer) been selected to carry out this dirty deed.. Many contracts around the country, including the next stage of the M11, and several of the 'DBFO' privately financed schemes have not been tendered yet.

It's looking as if all the time, energy and arrests have been worth it! Despite massive provocation, (to be a bailiff, climber or security guard is basically to be granted a licence to beat people up) the anti-roads movement has (virtually) always responded in a non-violent manner. This has, at times, taken quite phenomenal powers of self control given what has been meted out to us. At a time such as the end of the first phase at Newbury (seconds away, round two!), it is good to pause and evaluate what we have achieved, and give ourselves a bit of mutual congratulation....

Pic: Andrew Testa

As the evil, planet trashing forces of Babylon smash their way through our native countryside, it is time to bid a fond farewell to Newbury.
Three months, thats thirteen weeks, or ninety-four days, or in fact a whole bloody 1996 of stressfulcoldhungry chainsaw massacre.
A nine mile route, and we fought for every inch.

Newbury was my flowering, it was where I shone:
Battles with busses, stopping security guards going to work;
Street stalls and shouting;
Collecting money from noisy bars at chucking out time;
Meetings where everyone listened - no one yawned and 20
decisions were made by consensus in 1 1/2 hours;
Arguments over 'tree spiking' and the sanctity of workers
verses the sanctity of the trees;
Visiting prisoners, supporting prison visitors with tea and talk;
Putting on gigs, performing on stage,
Hiring PA's, halls, lighting rigs and god knows what else,
Working with Prima Donna's, committed hippies, stars, lovers of
the land and friends;
Cooking for weekend protesters, collecting wood for tree houses;
Going with Marie to buy her first ever climbing harness;
Building 'lock-on's' at Snelsmore;
Building a water store for a garden there, too;
Flirting outrageously and finally getting, or should that be sharing, a shag?
Training in Non violent Direct Action (history lessons on the Suffragettes,
Ghandi, Mothers of The Disappeared, Greenham, CND);
Training in Stress Management and Community Building;
Then later on, training on court procedure and learning from our mistakes;
Making press releases, then being on the radio, on TV, in the press;
Making phone trees, making 3am phone calls;
Standing around, watching friends be evicted from trees,
Feeling cold, useless and angry,
Swearing, "I'll never do that again,"
Going home, learning from it, resting, resting and resting,
Coming back better prepared, hopefully;
Arguments with work colleagues, discussions with friends;
Talking in pubs after meetings, having socials, parties, video evenings, food;
Deciding on what to spend our funds on (rope and tilley lamps for Snelsmore's
Gotan camp);
All of us using our lifetimes experience on this,
And from it we got a lifetimes worth of experience.
Newbury was our flowering, it was where we shone.

The first poem SchNEWS has ever published. Pic: Snelsmore eviction

MONSTER MUNCH
as Selar set to be swallowed whole!

Are you laughing at my moustache? Pic: Andrew Testa

The tree village at Selar nature reserve in South Wales was evicted this week after a three day battle involving around 200 police, security, bailiffs and professional climbers. The site was set up in May 1995 when protesters built a tree village on this Special Site of Scientific Interest near the village of Cwmgwrach, in the valleys of South Wales to prevent Celtic Energy trashing the site to make way for an open cast mining site.

Open cast mining is more profitable than the deep pit mining traditionally used but far more environmentally damaging as the whole landscape is gouged away until the coal is reached. This is particularly galling for the local community, as it is still suffering from the year long miners strike of 1984-5. Thousands of miners and their families in South Wales - the vast majority of whom have been supporting the current protest - were brutally oppressed by the police and state, simply for trying to protect their livelihoods and striking against pit closures.

The National Coal Board and Conservative government said at the time that there was no demand for coal, and that deep mine pits were uneconomical. So why this need to open cast if there is no demand? And if deep mining pits are so uneconomical why did Tower Colliery now a workers co-op and the only deep mine pit left in South Wales make a £3m profit last year? The minimal landscaping that is done afterwards fails to cover up the enormous damage done and whole areas are changed forever. The site at Selar - 88 acres - will be the biggest in Europe and will be visible from space.

There was a fierce battle to evict a similar site at Brynhenllys 15 miles away last October - this week they moved in on Selar. It was a completely full-on eviction. At dawn each morning they arrived and set to work for ten whole hours, with up to 18 climbers and bailiffs, cherrypickers and chainsaw crews. Safety guidelines were often totally ignored as tree houses were trashed. Yet again, it is a miracle that no one was killed or seriously injured. One woman was grabbed by a climber, and taken to the ground upside down.

Various ingenious schemes delayed the eviction. A quarter ton of metal was welded into a geodesic dome, which would have fallen apart if any part of it was tampered with. It eventually had to be lowered to the ground and the occupant removed. A net draped between the trees caused bailiffs some difficulty and one climber was briefly captured by protesters in the net! However by Wednesday the whole site had been evicted and another beautiful place had been trashed in the pursuit of profit...

There are numerous lessons to be learnt from the eviction of Selar. One is that the bailiffs and cops are getting good at evictions and we need to constantly be thinking up more imaginative tactics - an eviction team composed of climbers used at the evictions of Stanworth, Brynhellys and Selar, and under the command of Andrew Wilson, Undersheriff of Lancashire, has been established and is getting quite experienced at evictions. Perhaps the most important lesson is the need to build local support, involving more and more people in actively defying the vandals destroying our countryside. If we learn lessons from evictions like the one at Selar then the courage and determination of the brave individuals involved will continue to be an inspiration to us all.

Evening Argus

NIGHT FINAL

THE CHOICE OF SUSSEX THURSDAY, FEBRUARY 15, 1996 28p

BATTLEGROUND!

Face to face: Confrontation at the dem *Pictures: Simon Dack*

But we're taking no chances next time, warn police

IAN CARTER PHIL MILLS

POLICE today warned they may use tougher tactics next time street demonstrators try to blockade Brighton.

During yesterday's protest in North Road, they resisted issuing riot shields and NATO-style helmets to avoid being accused of being provocative.

But four people, including one police officer, were injured and senior police said they won't take chances again.

Chief Insp Martin Bailey, second in command of the police operation, said: "We had no indication it was going to be violent but a hard core of about 75 people turned it that way. That means we may have to use different tactics next time."

A total of 36 demonstrators were arrested and 12 were later charged with public order offences. Some demonstrators were from London and the Newbury bypass protest group.

PC Mark Emery from Rye suffered a cut head after being hit by a coin and a baby was cut when it was hit by a beer can.

TURN TO PAGE 3

Save Our Surgery

The Argus backs the Hurstwood Park campaign

Editorial (01273) 544544 Advertising (01273) 544300

DO YOU KNOW WHO WE ARE?

WHAT REALLY HAPPENED AT THE SQUATTERS ESTATE AGENCY

It's February 26th (1996) and Shelter have just announced "National Homelessness Week" - where you can wear a badge or send a postcard - all to aid the homeless. Realising that throw-away campaigns like this don't help, and fed up with the fact that despite a huge homelessness problem squatters in Brighton are being seriously harassed, Justice? reveal plans to open a *Squatters' Estate Agency.* A place to drop in, have a cup of tea and find a home. A place where you can go for squatting advice and subversive literature. With pictures of empty properties in the window complete with handy hints: "Three bedrooms, nice garden, window open at rear."

Justice? weren't new to Squatting. Most people in Brighton could remember "The Courthouse", our most famous and long-lived home (still boarded up and derelict). But we'd also had short spells in an old jeans shop, the Council's old housing advice centre, and a bingo hall. In all these places lists of empty properties were available (the SchLETS), along with practical advice for would be D.I.Y. Homeowners.

And so it came to pass... The Estate Agency was planned, plotted and schemed - a few faxes sent off to local TV, newspapers and radio. BOOM! All hell breaks loose, and suddenly the whole idea becomes a media monster. Radio 1, 2, 3, 4. The Mail, Independent, Telegraph, Newsnight, Meridian, Central - all jockey for a position on the story. It goes international as media from Canada, Australia, Russia, Germany, Belgium and the USA cover the story.

Local politicians weren't so keen, as Tories and New Labour queued up to slag off the idea that people were actually getting off their knees and doing something practical about homelessness. Tory MP Sir Derek Spencer said "We need this in Brighton like a hole in the head." This was swiftly dealt with by a Justice? spokesperson countering with "Brighton needs Sir Derek Spencer like a hole in the head."

New Labour's Brighton Council leader Steve Bassam (himself an ex-squatter) showed his true colours by stating that there was no need for such action, and that there was "adequate legislation" to deal with homelessness!

***"WE NEED THIS SORT OF THING IN BRIGHTON LIKE A HOLE IN THE HEAD!"* - Derek Spencer MP (Brighton Pavilion)**

OPERATION ARGUS

Originally there were plans to have the agency at an established squat that was facing eviction the same week. A couple of phone calls were made to the County Council and it looked like the building was secured for a time by trying to apply through the housing co-op mechanism. This got trashed however when the BBC found out the location and filmed through the windows, broadcasting the same day. After an interview with the Big Breakfast, bailiffs turned up and the verbal agreement with the Council was suddenly null and void. Eight people were made homeless. Cheers. Enter Operation Argus: a meeting was held and a hand-picked team of crack Direct Action commandos swung into action. A building cracked and secured under the very noses of a CCTV camera.

The press were still relentless, as what most thought of as a prank had become real. The opening day was incredible. There was more media than punters. The interviews didn't seem to stop all day, and all but the most hardened media gateaux got a bit sick of mikes and cameras. A mock ceremony in front of the Agency was staged, a couple of custard pies were stuck into a certain face and the ribbon was cut. We were open.

"NO POLICE, BAILIFFS OR ARGUS REPORTERS!"

It came as no surprise when we got our court date to be evicted. An Eviction Notice was served on the Estate Agents within hours of opening. Christine Simpson, the chair of the Housing Committee said that we were causing harm by offering people temporary, unstable accommodation (so they would have been better off sleeping rough waiting to be housed by the Council then?). She had promised in a public meeting a few months earlier not to evict anyone unless they were causing a nuisance or the building was needed for something. Strange how quickly things can change.

Brighton Council had managed to fly the eviction through the courts in less than 24 hours. Amazing what they can do when they try. But really it didn't matter, we were cramming a hell of a lot into that short time. The Advisory Service for Squatters came down and did a talk on the new squatting laws, a SchLIVE was performed, and the regular Justice? meeting was held there.

A BBC film crew doing a documentary on the DiY culture in Brighton decided to do a little experiment and invite some people with differing opinions than us for a civilised debate on the issues. They didn't tell us that the people they invited were some of the most bigoted individuals we had ever met, who refused to even sit down and chat with us, but instead wandered around aggressively demanding where we were from and why didn't we go back there. Apparently we had no right to complain about homelessness if we weren't born and bred in Brighton, and we were encouraging homeless people to move down here!

Cheap food and tea were constantly on the go and the writing of the SchNEWS transferred to the Agency with a wicked attack on the local rag. The Evening Argus ran a whole series of articles attempting to blame the Agency for any break-ins in the whole country. Or so it seemed. It was therefore decided that it was time for our love-hate relationship with the Argus to end. All Argus journalists were banned from the Estate Agents, and Justice? refused to talk to them. Oh what joy to escort one of the journalists off the premises as they pleaded to be let in, saying that we needed them to cover our story, or we would get no publicity Yeah, right. With 3 journalists from national papers, and 2 film crews inside that argument didn't hold much water.

And so a new sign above the front door was erected - "No police, bailiffs or Argus reporters".

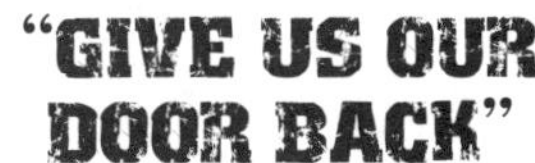

"GIVE US OUR DOOR BACK"

The syndrome known as activist burn-out had hit everyone by then. Fuelled by the media, the Agency had much longer opening hours than we had planned for, and the threat of the bailiffs meant that many of us were up each day at 6am waiting in case they arrived (lazy dole scroungers, eh?) Early Friday they came. About 6 or 7 bored looking bailiffs, a policeman acting

EVERY HOME IS FREE IN THE ALTERNATIVE PROPERTY MARKET

Paul, the estate agent to the squatting classes

Daily Mail Reporter

Situations vacant: Squatter rights campaigner Paul

SQUATTERS are setting up their own estate agency to advertise empty properties for the homeless to descend upon.

Photographs of vacant shops, offices and houses will be displayed in the window of the agency, which is itself a squat.

Inside, volunteers equipped with the latest technology will supply 'clients' with information about the size and condition of hundreds of vacant buildings.

The Squatting Estate Agents, due to open in Brighton later this week, is thought to be the first of its kind.

Sir Derek Spencer, Tory MP for Brighton Pavilion, described it as 'outrageous'.

'We want this like a hole in the head,' he said. 'It just adds to the reputation of Brighton as home for a collection of drop-outs and will drive away all the holiday and conference trade that we need.'

> 'This will attract drop-outs and drive away the trade we need'

The agency will be based in a town centre office owned by Brighton council which is occupied by squatters.

Members of Justice — a pro-squatting campaign group behind the scheme — were yesterday searching for empty properties to advertise.

Although their dress and hairstyles are in stark contrast to their High Street counterparts, they will go about their business in much the same way.

They can be contacted by their office telephone, fax, mobile phone and on the Internet.

They even have their own PO Box — named On-The-Fiddle.

'Paul', one of the scheme's organisers, said the idea sprang from a regular directory of empty buildings suitable for squatting produced by a group of friends.

'I would say there is a hard core of about 100 people squatting in Brighton and Hove, but there is a lot of other people who just drop in and others who come down from London,' he said. 'The town has the highest population in the country for homelessness yet there are more than 1,000 empty commercial and residential properties.'

Sporting a mohican haircut and brandishing one of the agency's leaflets, Paul said he hoped the scheme would attract attention to the homeless problem.

He said: 'We are not going to hand people a load of tools and say, "Get out there and break in." And we certainly do not advocate breaking into private property and moving in while the owners are on holiday. We are talking about taking buildings which have been empty for a considerable period. 'Often owners are just waiting for places to rot and fall down so they can grab some land money.

'Sometimes people can live in a building for a year or more before the landlord even notices.

'If squatters do not cause any criminal damage inside a property or change the locks then they are legal and there is nothing the landlord can do apart from apply for an eviction order through the courts.'

But Brighton Council leader Steve Bassam warned that the group could face eviction themselves.

He admitted that he had been a squatter during the 1970s, but said that was before the introduction of 'adequate legislation' to deal with homelessness. Brighton and Hove chamber of commerce chairman Frances Hix branded the idea deplorable.

She said: 'Owners of properties who have to evict these people often end up with legal bills running into hundreds or even thousands of pounds.'

Brighton police said they would monitor the effect of the agency.

Inspector Grenville Wilson said: 'Squatting is not itself a crime, but when it involves breaking into a property, that is an offence.

'If instances of breaking and entering are reported to us, we will take action.'

R
te
pa

A WHIT
tion case
yesterday
Ursula C
award but
that was i
The 4
mother o
Lambeth
industrial
failing t
shortlist
tutor's jo
had been
terms on
basis.
The tri
that Mrs
Liddingto
was raci
nated aga
member o
panel was
She said
of the t
excellent.
found tha
not been
which is
opportu
about.
'I have
ed. I'm de
During
the Sou
council cl
of word

as an observer and a very worried looking council official turned up at ridiculous o' clock. Inside both doors had been sealed and barricaded. About 20 of us were there when the bailiffs piled in. They concentrated mostly on the main entrance door, wedging in chocks to prise it open. But fast as the chocks were put in they were knocked out again. A couple of buckets of water from the upstairs window gave them much pause for thought (local Tories later said that it was full of urine and excrement - well okay we may drink a lot of cider, but even we couldn't fill that much.)

The cameras rolled. The journalists scribbled. They tried a new approach. The plan was to actually remove the door itself, and this nearly worked. For a time it was a battle for the door as it swung inside and out. Everyone started shouting "give us our door back!" and for some reason, they did! Perhaps they were knackered, or more likely the build-up of shoppers had increased - and the Council don't usually like to be seen doing such things in public. Whatever, they disappeared. Once again it proved that defiance works. We knew they'd be coming back but the fact that we'd antagonised Brighton bailiffs to the extent that they'd had to earn their money for a change, and they went off with their tails between their legs was a top feeling.

SQUATTING IS STILL LEGAL

The Squatters Estate Agency remained active until Tuesday morning, ten days after it had opened. The previous night it was decided to leave whilst we were ahead. We tidied up, recycled the empties and left via the upstairs window. Downstairs a formidable barricade was left at the front door. The bailiffs turned up at 8 in the evening, and smashed their way in to be confronted with an empty shop devoid of people.

"NEVER MIND THE MEDIA, DID YOU ACTUALLY HOUSE PEOPLE?"

One of the more touching moments happened when a man walked in saying his friend had just died and did we want to let his house, as it was empty. At the same time a young couple walked in with a child saying they were homeless. We introduced them to each other, and off they went to sort it out. A lot of people found homes or at the very least somewhere to crash.

To be truthful, we did make a couple of honest mistakes, as two properties were advertised that were inhabited. This gives some indication of the state of some of the properties in the town - one was awful; an old couple living in squalor upstairs in a boarded-up shop. As soon as we found out our mistakes the properties were immediately removed from the list, and we took the owners a bunch of flowers.

What had started out as a small Brighton protest had stretched around the country and across the seas.

Rather than being manipulated by the media, we had set our agenda, and got the message across that homelessness was a major problem, and that despite the Criminal Justice Act, squatting was still legal in England and Wales, and a practical solution to sleeping rough. The fact that so many supported and helped us dispelled the tidal wave of misinformation and myths about squatters ten-fold.

Most importantly we showed that homeless people no longer have to see themselves as passive victims waiting for patronising handouts from the state, but can get out there, and find themselves somewhere to live, instead of rotting on some Council waiting list.

MOTORWAY SANITY!

RTS Street Party III
Issue 82 July 19th 1996

"Carnival is not a spectacle seen by the people; they live in it, and everyone participates because its very idea embraces all the people... But the most important thing is that we won't be asking the politicians to create a future for us, we will create it ourselves"

A 30 foot pantomime dame was playing the bagpipes; a green-winged fairy was busy granting wishes; there were fire jugglers, bongo players, sandpits and sound systems. So what? Just another festival? Well, yeah but this was a party with a purpose. And it was being held on a section of the M41 near Shepherds Bush roundabout. Reclaim the Street's Street Party III was in full effect as approximately 8,000 filled the streets. A space usually prohibited to pedestrians became an autonomous none of party and protest for the day: road cage became road rave.

"Streets once the open forum of daily life are now the open sewers of car culture"

Under the dame's skirt, drowned out by the nearby techno music, four men and a pneumatic drill were busy digging up the motorway and two trees were later planted in the hole. It was Tuesday before things were back to normal. As

Pic above/below: Tash

the Reclaim The Streets flyer said "There are many ideas of what a green future could be like - a street party offers glimpses of possibilities..." The vibrancy of the party contrasted sharply with the bleakness of the nearby Shepherd's Bush high rise flats. Local kids from the estates came and joined in, at first unsure of their new environment, but soon fully in the swing, and showing party goers where the nearest standpipe was so they could fill their water bottles.

"The Street Party, itself reclaimed from the inanities of royal jubilees and state 'celebrations' is just one recent initiative in a vibrant history of struggle, both to defend and to take back collective space. From the Peasant's Revolt, to the resistance to the enclosures - from the land occupations of the diggers to the post war squatters movement on the recent free festivals, peace camps, land occupations, and the struggle against roads. In this country alone, extraordinary people have continually asserted not only the need to liberate 'the commons', but the ability to think and organise for themselves."

Pic below: Alec Smart

ANYONE FOR TRIDENT?

OPEN SEASON ON THE ARMS TRADE AS PLOUGHSHARES WOMEN WALK FREE

"If British Aerospace sold stakes to Vlad the Impaler, and Vlad went out of business today they'd start selling sabres to Genghis Khan tomorrow" - Terry Egan trade unionist.

The decision by a Liverpool jury to clear four women of writing off a £23m Hawk jet is making a lot of people in the 'arms industry' very nervous indeed. The women had gone to Warton airbase in January armed with just hammers and smashed up the Hawk control panels. In court they successfully defended themselves against charges of criminal damage by arguing that they were disabling the plane to stop a more important crime, genocide, from being committed. They have set a remarkable precedent – it's now legal to destroy jets, missiles, weapons and anything else made in Britain for export to dodgy regimes for use against their people! The Hawk jet was due to be sent to Indonesia where the dictatorship has killed a third of the East Timorese population and continues to oppress its people. As one activist, Mick, told SchNEWS, "It's all go for real direct action now. They'd better be increasing their security around all those bases and factories because there's a lot of people very keen on destroying the products of this sordid little industry bit by bit."

"Outside, people were saying that we couldn't go around smashing up other people's property. But people in prison don't have hang ups about that. They accepted that if planes are going to kill people, then you stop them."

With rioting by pro-democracy demonstrators in the Indonesian capital of Jakarta at the weekend followed quickly by a new 'shoot to kill' policy from the military regime, focus has once again been turned towards the world's fourth largest country. Britain is quite happy to sell weapons to a country which according to Amnesty International has killed "hundreds of thousands of civilians" and illegally occupied East Timor since 1975. And it is East Timor where the jets are being used to kill and terrorise the people. As John Pilger, a journalist who, posing as a travel consultant entered the country in 1993 and made the documentary Death of a Nation, told the jury *"I have reported from places like Cambodia and Vietnam, but I have never seen anything like East Timor. The country was like a vast cemetery, its landscapes covered in crosses with the names of entire families on them".*

In 1991, just after 270 peaceful demonstrators were massacred in East Timor, the British government approved "aid" of £81m to the Indonesian government. In 1993 Foreign Secretary Douglas Hurd flew out to Indonesia to congratulate the regime on "recognising human rights as an

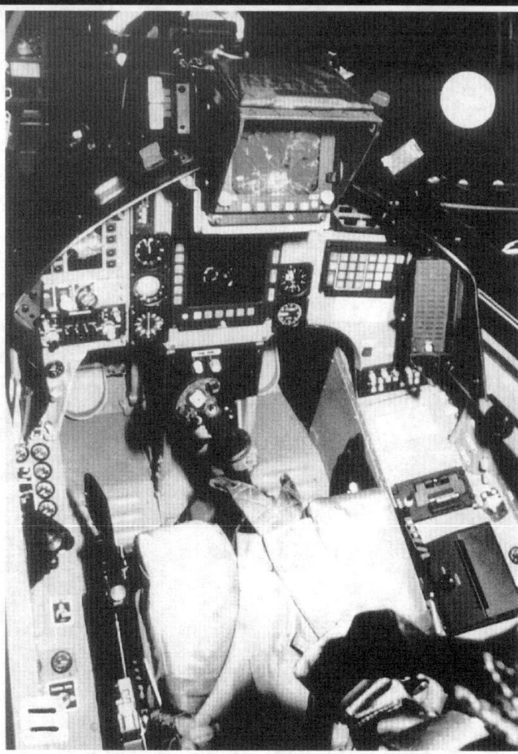

important element in man's freedom" and gave them another 63 million quid. Six weeks later 24 British Aerospace Hawk jets were sold to Indonesia.

Labour sold the first Hawks to Indonesia in 1978, and Shadow Defence spokesman, David Clark recently said that a Labour government "would definitely be willing to supply military equipment to Indonesia". With an official 'opposition' like this thank God there's people willing to take direct action against this dealing in death - and juries willing to support their right to do so.

"To the media, terrorists are crazed, masked loners or political extremists. In reality, the real terrorists are governments and corporations waging war on people and the planet for the God of Money."

It's nothing new: secret files just declassified in the US show that Britain aided the slaughter of more than half a million people by the Indonesian army in just a few months in 1965. The covert aid of arms were dubbed 'medicines'. The documents reveal that the then British ambassador, Sir Andrew Gilchrist, wrote to London: *"I have never concealed from you my belief that a little shooting in Indonesia would be an essential preliminary to effective change."*

If 500,000 deaths is a 'little', what else don't we know?

LIVERPOOL DOCKERS

The Liverpool Dockers were, for many of the newer people who had been part of the direct action movement, the first workers struggle they had been involved in (which isn't surprising as most of us have never had a proper job). Like most struggles it brought together several issues at once from working class communities to globalisation and labour casualisation. Here we cover the 'Reclaim The Futures' event in Liverpool in September 1996 and reproduce an interview with a Docker when they were down in Brighton in 1997.

On September 25th 1995 eighty men who worked for Torside Shipping Company on the Liverpool Docks were ordered to work for a disputed overtime rate. They refused and were all sacked. They mounted a picket and dockers from another company refused to cross it. The 329 men of Mersey Docks and Harbour Company were also sacked. Within 24 hours their jobs were being advertised in the local press.

> ***"My message is simple. If they beat us, they'll be coming for you soon" - A Liverpool Docker SchNEWS 47-48***

The roots of the strike go back to 1989 when the National Dock Labour Scheme was abolished, and casual labour crept into ports across the country - except Liverpool.

The dockers were members of the Transport and General Workers Union, which refused to make the dispute official because they broke the anti trade union laws introduced by Thatcher. When SchNEWS contacted the (still in opposition) Labour Party about the docker's plight, they replied "We don't normally comment on industrial disputes". So what do they comment on?'

The struggle became an important resistance to privatisation and the new flexible way of working. They were living proof that the usual crap from politicians about how great globalization is looks a bit different on the ground to workers facing worse working conditions or redundancy. Ignored by the corporate media, and let down by the British trade unions, the Dockers had to be more imaginative... which included working with troublemakers like Reclaim The Streets and SchNEWS and using direct action tactics.

For example on 20th January 1997 an international day of action took place around the world in solidarity with the dockers. In Liverpool eight dockers and seven helpers occupied three cranes at the grain terminal, preventing the unloading of the "Lake Erie" which was delayed for a total of 35 hours. The activists were arrested and charged with aggravated trespass.

Invaluable support during the strike came from abroad with actions occurring in Australia, New Zealand, Japan, the United States, Mexico, Brazil, Canada, Quebec, Sweden, Norway, Russia, Denmark, Holland, Belgium, Germany, France, Switzerland and Greece – which ranged from stoppages and occupations, to even a general strike of transport workers. The rank and file membership of the West Coast Dockers Union in America alone donated half a million dollars

The dock dispute against casualisation became even more real for the people of Brighton, as one of SchNEWS' own writers Simon Jones was killed on his first day of work at Shoreham port, doing one of the most dangerous jobs in the country with no health and safety training (see page 124).

Unfortunately, the port bosses did beat the Liverpool dockers with the strike ending in January 1998 after 850 days.

As for the men themselves, some of them got together to set up their own nightclub and the Initiative Factory in central Liverpool, which in their own words "Acts to mobilise talent, to combat uncertainties, to reduce material and spiritual poverty and help to build a caring, compassionate society. Resistance, human spirit, creativity, energy, resources and organisation are the watchwords which guide our activities."

Contact dockers@gn.apc.org 0151 207 9111

DOCKS AND DREADLOCKS COME TOGETHER

"It was an excellent day for us, the best day of the strike so far. You lot coming up here has meant so much to all the dockers and their families. We've grown in strength through this and our morale is really high again." **- Striking Liverpool docker**

Last weekend hundreds of direct action activists headed for Liverpool for three days of protests, parties, pickets and solidarity to mark the anniversary of the start of the Liverpool dockers' strike. And what a weekend! Flags flew from the roof of the dock offices taken before dawn; climbers cheered from the lop of the giant gantries as they lay idle; Turkish communists and Kurds arrived with their circle dancers to show support; and on the picket line dockers and road protesters, trade unionists and direct action veterans showed the scab lorry drivers what they thought of them.

WITH A LITTLE HELP FROM MY FRIENDS

The weekend kicked off with a march through Liverpool's city centre. Striking dockers and their families mingled with Kurdish dragons, trade unionists, flags, drums and sound systems. Neil Fox, the young son of one of the striking dockers, told the rally, "Friendship is a precious gift that cannot be bought or sold. It is worth more than a mountain of gold". Speaker after speaker, all involved in different struggle, came to say they were involved in the same struggle - and were there to support the dockers.

"The others talk about doing something – this lot actually do it." - a Liverpool Docker.

That night hundreds of activists squatted a disused customs building by the dockside. Police nastiness was in evidence, with riot police at the rally blocking off roads, and vehicles carrying sound systems finding their tyres mysteriously slashed. Sunday was for organising, discussing where we were going and meeting dockers.

Monday 6am and everyone in the squat gets an early morning call. By 6.30am the docks are invaded, the gantries and the office roof are taken and hundreds arrive at the picket line. The tugs strike for the day in solidarity and no ships come in.

HERE COMES THE SCUM

Dozens of vans with dogs, horses and the leather clad S&M freaks of the Operational Support Division arrive to intimidate the picket and assault and arrest people at random. There were 47 arrests, almost as many as throughout the whole year of the strike. Minibuses of trade unionists were stopped under the CJA (they got through in the end!), one picket got a broken collarbone, someone else was held for 48 hours and another was remanded to Lancaster Prison. All day dockers and their families provided food and drink for their supporters and people discussed this new found unity. 15 people stayed up cranes for nine hours. Ten flew a red black and green flag from the top of the docks offices all day and, icing on the cake, the docks offices in town were occupied by protesters.

As protesters walked from the picket to the squat 10 riot vans drove up, cops sprung out and nicked people for that dreadful crime of 'walking along a street'. A UNISON rep was nicked and beaten up in a van (having his hand burnt with a cigarette lighter and getting hospitalised). The filth smiled. One family who came out their house to cheer the crowd got a police car screeching to a halt in front of them. We arrived at the squat and walked though lines of police trying to intimidate us and just waiting to have a go. The dockers and their families and friends were there in force to make sure we were alright, cheering and clapping. Solidarity is a two way street.

That night there was a kicking party (does everyone in Liverpool know all the words to every Beatles song or what?) with speeches, drinks and food laid on by the strikers. The forces of law and order, thoroughly pissed off by now, resorted to slashing the tyre of a van parked outside where we were staying and asking the driver if he "needed any help". Not good losers.

"Single issue politics is well and truly dead now. The scumbags who these dockers have been on strike against for a year are the same people who make millions out of polluting the planet and want to force us all into shitty jobs so they can make even more money. Us and the dockers have got a lot more in common than a lot of people think. This unity is going to grow and grow, I'm telling you " - Rent-a-mob outside agitator on her way to Liverpool

The dispute was provoked when a docker, who had already worked a 12 hour shift was told to do overtime. He refused, and was sacked on the spot. The strike then ensued, with 500 men staying solid behind the principle of resisting the erosion of their working rights. Some of the men had been working for 35 years or more and have refused to take the £25,000 redundancy offer from the Mersey Docks and Harbour Company. Not one has yet gone back to work.

Liverpool dockers have had enormous international support throughout the dispute. Mersey Docks profits have fallen 17% in the last year and on the action day their share price dropped 14 points. On Monday Swedish and Danish dockers organised a 24 hour blockade of main ports in support of their Liverpool comrades. Loads of other dockers throughout the world continue to give support - more than they've got from the 'Labour movement', and their own union.

Nothing could illustrate the difference between those who want to defend basic rights and our children's future and the cynical, power-seeking manipulation of the 'official opposition' better than this week's events in Liverpool and Blackpool. In Liverpool people stood shoulder to shoulder against scabs and the police. In Blackpool the most right-wing Labour Conference ever supported Tony Bleurgh on every vote, even refusing to support index-linking for pensions.

Funnily enough, Bill Morris, head of the dockers' union (the Transport and General Workers) was in Blackpool with his middle class friends rather than on the picket line with his members. This didn't stop him denouncing the weekend's events and calling on the dockers to 'disassociate' themselves from the groups that actually got to Liverpool to show their support. He might as well have whistled in the wind - the dockers immediately put out a statement praising "the principled courageous and peaceful support given over many weeks by the Advance Party, Reclaim the Streets and other grassroots environmental groups. This unique unity between Trade Unionists and environmental groups will continue to be developed in the future."

Seaforth docks, Liverpool invaded on September 30th 1996

Why Reclaim the Streets and the Liverpool Dockers?

What is the link between 'anti-car activists' and 'sacked dockers'?
Both argue for social change, although for different reasons and perhaps with different goals. We must recognise the common enemies we are fighting against in order to combine forces and achieve real social change.

The power that attacks workers through union legislation and casualisation, is the same power that attacks the planet with over-production and consumption of resources; the power that produces 4 million cars a year is the same power that attacks workers through the disempowerment of the unions. This power is capital. As long as society is run for profit, social and ecological exploitation will occur. The question is: can we combine these movements to effectively challenge this power, before we are led into a social and ecological catastrophe?

That we even ask 'Why Reclaim The Streets and the Dockers?' shows the common perception that ecology does not include social issues. This separation and presentation of the ecological crisis as unconnected to other forms of exploitation serves the interests of capital, and needs to be overcome if society is to survive. Industrialisation itself is what separated us from ourselves, each other and the earth.

So how did we get from the car to the dockers?
Street parties are gaining in popularity as a form of direct action, while picketing has not been very successful in the last few years. After a year of daily pickets at the gates of the Port of Liverpool, the dockers were entering their second winter with little hope of success. They had been abandoned by their union, the TGWU, and sought support outside the union movement.

When RTS supported striking tubeworkers in August 1996, the dockers had little left to lose in asking for their support. The result was an empowering action that involved activists from all over the country and a fascinating shift in the direct action movement. The occupation of the gantries and office roof meant that the picket refused to disperse until all activists came down without arrest. 150 pickets stormed the port and a docker got on the roof, throughout the day we all stood up for each other and the right to determine how we live. The dockers showed they were prepared to take the opportunity to innovate and take action, and (although only briefly), take over the means of production. As one docker said, "it was like a blood transfusion."

The dockers revitalised their struggle and made links with other movements; we enhanced our movement by extending boundaries for direct action. Suddenly, direct action was not just a fringe sport for extremists.

In uniting with the Liverpool Dockers we laid some foundations for the future growth of a movement for radical and lasting social and ecological change.

As Dockers join the KLF, SchNEWS asks...

WHAT TIME IS VICTORY?

On a recent trip to Brighton for the Trades Unions Congress (TUC) SchNEWS cornered Dockers' Shop Steward Bobby Morton and asked him a few questions over a couple of beers.

SchNEWS: With Tony Blair telling the TUC "we will not go back to the days of industrial warfare, strikes without ballots, mass and flying pickets, secondary action and all the rest of it" and banging on about "the flexibility of the present labour market" isn't your dispute a throwback to the past. Aren't your tactics old fashioned and irrelevant?

Bobby: No, I think they are extremely effective. Yesterday's editorial from Lloyds List (influential shipping journal) says that the ship owners representatives are crying foul over our international day of action saying this is a terrible thing to do, is old fashioned and out of sync with the Labour Party. But what they are basically saying is that these bastards are hurting us, and it shouldn't be allowed to happen, so I think the tactics Blair condemns are very effective weapons and ones that should be used on a more regular basis.

Sch: The Labour government is the major shareholder in Mersey Docks and Harbour Company, but in the first six months in power, they have shown complete disinterest in intervening to settle the dispute. Before the election, Labour said they would introduce legislation to reinstate sacked workers, and now they have reneged on that - where do you go from here?

B: When the Labour Party were talking of reinstating people who were unfairly dismissed they were talking about disputes which would have been deemed to be official. One that would have had a legally organised strike ballot, and of course we never got the chance to do that because we were faced with a picket line and had to make an instant decision. To have a ballot it would have taken us probably a month to organise, and during that month we would have been crossing the picket line on a daily basis, which we wouldn't do.

Sch: What do you think of the support internationally compared to the support in Britain?

B: Apart from financially there is no support in Britain. People say nice things to us, and give us the money, which we appreciate, of course, but physically there is no action whatsoever taking place in the UK. I've got friends in industries all over the UK who would like to help but find themselves incapable of doing so because of fear - particularly in my industry if you lose your job and you're over 40 you'll never work again, and people are afraid of losing life's comforts.

However, the most amazing thing for me - especially when we listen to the claptrap Tony Blair is spewing up all the time - is that all of the countries which have been mentioned as part of the international day of action, they all have strict anti trade union laws and yet they still supported us. For example people in Canada, have been threatened with suspensions and the sack and the West Coast of American Union threatened with being sued for millions. Yet they all went to great lengths to tell the newspapers and the employers that regardless of any legislation they were going to take that secondary solidarity action in support of the Liverpool people.

Sch: So why do think the unions here in Britain are running scared - do you think that if the dockers won, it would be a thumbs up for militancy, which is exactly what the unions don't want?

B: The unions are terrified of that. They've grown comfortable. If you're a general secretary and you've got militancy running through your union, and strikes everyday, then obviously you're going to have a greater work load and there's gonna be more expenditure of your members money. Everyone wants a peaceful life -it's human nature. They just wanna draw their wages and are terrified of any type of militancy that may grow out of the Liverpool docks dispute

Sch: People have now obviously got greater expectations of the Labour government. Do you think people will start to get angry and take action once they realise these expectations aren't being met?

B: Well there will be a little bit of both. I'm talking to people this week who voted Labour who genuinely believe that after the honeymoon period, when things settle down, the government will change their stance and become more mellow towards the trade union movement. But they are living in a dreamworld, cos you're stuck with this for as long as long as the electorate allows them to get away with it and the only time you will see a change is if there's a moodswing.

Sch: Have you got any idea why you get more support from comedians than politicians?

B: Well to me, all politicians are comedians so I don't know where you draw the line. The comedians that support us are working class people with working class values and ideals. For example a son of Liverpool, who is a very very rich so called comedian is Jimmy Tarbuck and he wouldn't fart in our direction and neither would Cilla Black. But when you get down to the likes of someone Lee Hurst and Jo Brand with a working class background these are the people that support us, cos they speak the same language as we do.

Sch: You said that there hasn't been much physical support in England. How important do you think the direct action movements' involvement with the dockers has been, especially the 1st year anniversary actions in Liverpool?

B: It's so important, because when I describe the lack of action in the UK, I was talking specifically about industrial action. Reclaim The Streets and the other groups that converged on Liverpool in September 1996, well that was a marvellous experience for us - and it does no harm to say it here, that a lot of our people who are more traditional, didn't want the involvement of the Reclaimers. However, we carried the day and extended the invitation and after you lot had left Liverpool everyone was delighted; even the ones who had been sceptical about it, suddenly turned round and said 'that was a good idea when are they coming back again?' It gave us a very important lift at a very psychologically important moment because it began to dawn on our people - 'hell we've been out of work now for a year, its a milestone in our lives' and there is a tendency when you reach a milestone you start to go downhill and become depressed. Because of the action of the reclaimers on that weekend it gave our people a real boost.

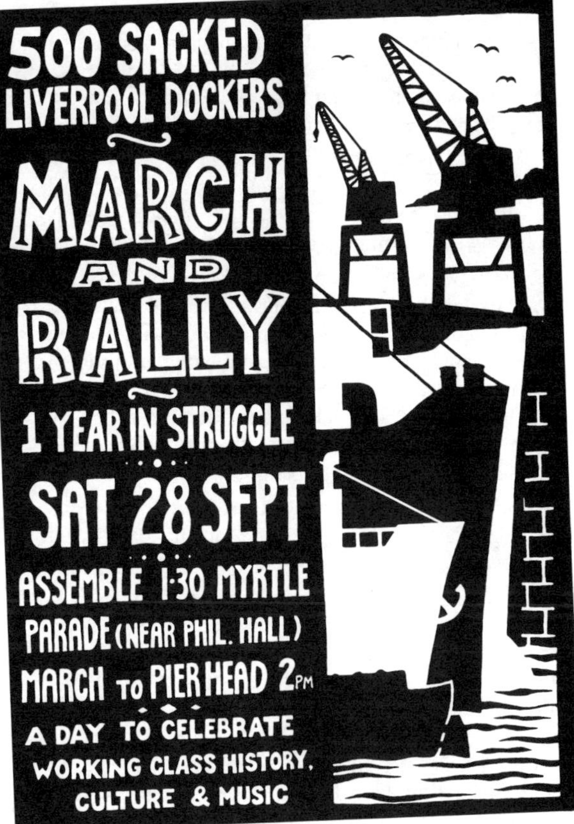

Sch: Why do you think that your dispute has captured the imagination of people involved in the direct action movement? I mean down in Brighton we can hold meetings on prisons or asylum seekers and there's not a lot of interest, but the dockers dispute seems to cut across the divide. Why do you think that is?

B: I think there are two different reasons for that, the first going back to your traditional industrialists. They have this romantic idea of international solidarity which we have always boasted we have. On another scale one of the things we've said right from the very start is that we won't take the easy way out and take the severance pay of £30,000. I mean here we are now, we've got no money and we could take the easy option, take that money and walk away, but we've always said that its not about money. You could make it £100,000 and it wouldn't make a difference. We are looking at getting our jobs back not just for ourselves but to pass it down to the youth of Merseyside, and the types of jobs we are wanting to pass down are full time, well paid jobs with good conditions not the type of jobs that exist in the port of Liverpool now.

So with the international action it's looking to the past, but when we're talking about the youth, were talking about the future, and this is where we found we had a common bond with the Reclaimers, and the environmentalists - because those groups want a better future for themselves, the children, for the planet, and its something that just gelled together.

Sch: That's what we try to do with SchNEWS, to bring all the different struggles together and say to people 'look - these issues are they same, despite our petty differences we all want the same thing.' Recently in Brighton they've introduced Project Work-for-your-dole scheme, and because people are being forced onto it, and we need action now it has meant everyone from trade unionists to claimants to anarchists to socialist workers has to work together.

B: The key word is action. When we were earning say £20,000 a year, in full- time employment and could go to the pub every night, when we met at trade union meetings we used to argue like cat and dog about Marx, Lenin, Trotsky - fuck me these people had been dead for 50 years ! But all of a sudden, once you're thrown into the dispute and taking part in action we don't talk about them anymore, thank God, we have to sort out day to day activities - when your taking action your mind is working and you're not dwelling on the past.

Sch: Coming back to the trade union movement, it does seem to need an injection of imagination at times. In the British Airways dispute workers were threatened with the sack if they took strike action, so did a mass sickie instead. It was a good example of getting round the anti trade union laws. What do you think?

B: There are all kinds of ways to skin a cat. Several years ago the air traffic controllers in Greece were threatened with the sack if they took strike action so they merely informed their employers that they were going on hunger strike! With imagination you can let it run riot with any number of things, but you've got to have the ambition and the will to do it, and again going back to your question traditional trade unions have got no imagination.

Sch: What's your relationship with the local constabulary - they are the scariest bunch of cops SchNEWS has come across apart from Belfast!

B: We have a dual relationship, some of the local constabulary are actually human beings and then you've got the other half - who belong to the Operational Support Division, and with that division one of the qualifications is that you've got to have a lobotomy before you can be considered for the job. With the latter we have no relationship whatsoever apart from being beaten over the head.

Sch: What about the good aspects - you lot get loads of holidays abroad? Come on admit it, that's what you did it for.

B: You might have noticed that I have an all year round suntan! Before the dispute I've mainly travelled round Europe, then early in the dispute there came an occasion where I had to go to the East Coast of America. Three of us went there to picket the entrance of a dock, in the middle of the worst blizzard they'd had in New York for 70 years! Then we get invited to a convention in Florida - the business only took half an hour and we spent the rest of the week relaxing in the sun waiting for our plane! We got away with going to Florida, but then we got an invite to go to Honolulu. How the fucking hell were we gonna tell our lads who have been in dispute for months about that one!

Sch: How do you decide who speaks at meetings - isn't it really important that as many of the dockers as possible have a chance to go round the country so they can see just how much support they have got? At our direct action conference the lads who'd never spoken before at a meeting couldn't believe that all these crusties and punks gave a shit about their dispute.

B: It's very difficult to come back from the West Coast of America where we are treated like gods, and go to a mass meeting of our people, and transport the feelings and emotions from the other side of the world. So now we've encouraged the rank and file to go round and speak and experience the support as it helps lift the spirits.

Sch: Bill Morris (the Transport and General Workers general secretary) has not only told you to disassociate yourselves from those activist troublemakers, but he has also made derogative comments that the dock dispute has become more a political movement. It does almost seem like a new political movement - what do you think?

B: I don't see it as a political movement. I see it as helping people, a level of awareness. For example, two years before we were sacked environmentalists went into the port to stop wood from the rainforest being offloaded. People arrested were put in a cage in the docks. The minute that happened all dockers stopped work. We approached the police and said 'unless you release the people from that cage within the next half an hour all the dockers will be going home.' When we came back from our teabreak 20 minutes later, everyone had been released. What the Merseyside Dock Company really hated about us was that if an injustice was perpetrated on one person then the rest of us would turn round and say - 'we're not having that, unless you stop the injustice then we will all go home. You sack him - you sack me.'

Sch: What would you say to people who've got casual jobs, working in service industries, with short term contracts and no union representation?

B: I've got a son who is 17 and will soon be looking for work in Merseyside where there is nothing except McDonalds. I would advise him wherever he ends up - get organised.

Sch: Where do you think the dispute is going ? We've heard rumours that some dockers want to call it a day and that donations aren't as good as they were some months ago.

B: We've got to be honest about it, none of us thought it would go longer than three weeks - and when the first offer was made some of the men wanted to accept it. But we're not gonna settle for a deal unless it involves everyone. We've got to see it out until every single one of us has an alternative. Last night I was talking to a Bosnian miner and I realised that compared to them we've had nothing like the hardship they have suffered. At one stage they had no wages, and there are no state benefits - and I asked him 'if there was no money coming into the house how did you survive?' He replied 'if there's no money coming into your house how do you survive?' And we both realised that we all rely on the same sort of miracles.

Sch: Cheers, Bobby - here's to the overthrow of capitalism! XXX

Liverpool footballer Robbie Fowler lifts his shirt to reveal a message supporting the Liverpool Dockers after kicking a goal – bringing the issue to a TV audience of millions. He was fined by UEFA for 'displaying a political logo' at a match – advertising a brewery or sweatshop sportswear is ok.

 *Issue 72 –3rd May 1996*

RECLAIM THE GROUND!

As Brighton & Hove Football Club's home ground gets flogged off

Just 15 minutes into the game dozens of fans ran onto the pitch, quickly followed by hundreds, which turned into thousands. People of all ages and backgrounds joined in, including the opposing York fans who swapped shirts with their Brighton counterparts, and united in chants of 'sack the board.' Fans sunbathed in the centre circle, played frisbee, and a mass beach ball game broke out. Surrounded by a bemused line of fully clad riot police, the crowd refused to leave. The ground was reclaimed! The match was abandoned (for only the third time in football history due to crowd involvement). The occupation played on for a symbolic 90 minutes (the duration of a normal match) and ended peacefully as subdued fans left the Goldstone for perhaps the last time.

Ex-manager Liam Brady called the demo 'a plea for help from the Brighton supporters'. Tony Lake, Assistant Chief Constable of Sussex Police said, "The main thing is there was no significant public disorder".

Football may or may not interest you but events in our national game are reflected in our nation at large. The money men have taken over, and they care about nothing but money. Their money. "Football is a business now. We're in a business world" (Richard Costabady, Sports Correspondent). It's the people who lose out. "Fans have been treated with contempt", said Chris Caplin, former Brighton manager.

By direct action Brighton fans may have scored in injury time, but it only takes the game to extra time. Chairman Bellotti's press release on Monday was priceless: "Our club does not want those yobs who've bought shame on our club". This from a man whose sold Brighton's home ground – and along with it peoples' memories and dreams - off for a retail park. It's enuff to make you sick as a parrot.

SchNEWSround

Published December 1996

"Reclaim the streets... Newbury... the Squatter's Estate Agency... as 'Direct Action' became media buzzwords, SchNEWS published the inside story from the activists themselves! Along with copies of Issues 51-100, it includes a quarter of a million words plus excellent full-page photos, the 1996 activist's database and 60 extra pages of stuff!"

ISBN 0 9529748 0 0

Now sold out

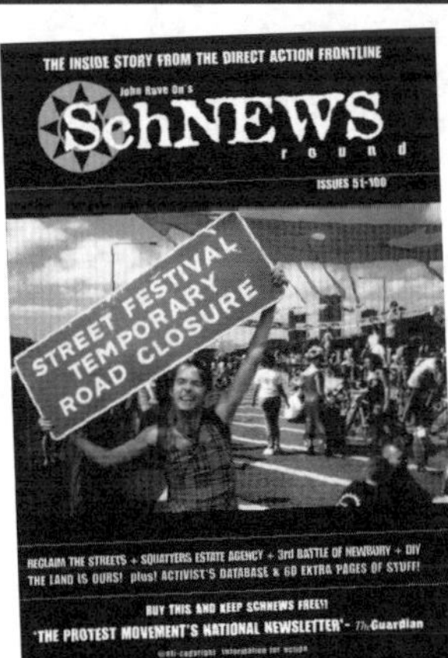

This book nearly never made it to the printer... Pete, one of the producers of SchNEWS Round, tells the story:

"...We were all out celebrating putting it together on the night we finally finished, and it was my job to drop it off at the printers the next day. We were in a pub in Kemptown and ... I'd had too much to drink. I had panniers –so I had half the book in one pannier, half the book in the other pannier, and I cycled home. Cycling when you're drunk not a good idea: I did it and must have fallen off the bike two or three times on the way home. And the next day I woke up with a hangover to find that one of the panniers was missing.

And I'm like – oh no. I rang up a couple of people and I'm going "...er er I've lost half the book..." – and it was the only copy. I'm thinking – do I leave town? Are people going to send Harry and the boys after me? But people were very understanding. I was thinking there was no way I'd get it back.

It just so happened that an old phone bill from my house was in the lost pannier... and I got a phone call from someone saying 'I've got something of yours – it might be quite important...' I was very very thankful to them."

How long did they make you wait?

"About three or four days. And then – soberly –I took the folders up to London the next day."

Diary of a Direct Action Conference Organiser

Wednesday night 2 a.m. The phone rings... they're in. 4 people have managed to get through a broken window and re-enter the old Courthouse building. It had lain empty for years before Justice? squatted it in 1994 to protest against the CJB. During our occupation we fixed the roof plumbing, electricity; toilets and set up a community centre. 51 days later it was all over. Alford Developments got an eviction notice, promising in court to use the place as a homeless hostel over Christmas (they didn't). The bailiffs came in and trashed the place... 2 years on and it's still empty. Brighton Council have threatened the owners that if immediate repairs aren't made to the Grade II listed building, the council will start work and send the owners the bill.

Thursday morning 8.30 a.m. - the police show up, and despite a huge section 6 banner hanging from the roof letting the authorities know it's been legally squatted, they're ready to move in. Chief Inspector Martin Bailey tells the occupiers he doesn't care about the law; the squatters have committed criminal damage by allegedly breaking a window getting into the property. But what about the criminal damage the owners are causing, letting water pour through the roof?

Panic stations as we activate the phone tree - there's fifteen police, with dogs, and a battering ram smashing their way in - the irony that they are doing this in order to arrest people for criminal damage isn't lost on us! A solicitor is telling one of the occupiers on the mobile that the police can't evict, they need a court order – "But they are evicting us now!" she yells back down the phone!

Three brave souls hang from a window ledge in the cold for nearly 7 hours, by which time we can get a crowd of people, a band playing, a mobile café, lots of media cover-age, a solicitor and local green party councillor - Pete West - who tells the press: "It's a pity the police don't take as much action when there's a burglary." Lydia Dagostino from Bindmans Solicitors tries to reason with senior officers but gets nowhere: "The overall response was totally disproportionate to the alleged offence. It seems that senior police officers are willing to go to any lengths to stop this sort thing happening in Brighton even they are acting illegally."

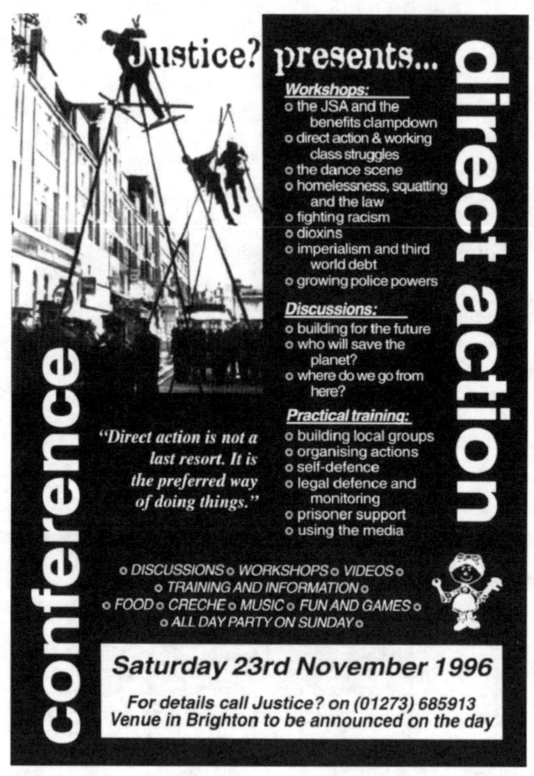

12 noon Friday and about 50 of us assemble in a pub and walk en masse to another squat cracked in the early hours of the morning. Strength in numbers we hope. We're followed by two undercover police, and within minutes a police helicopter is flying overhead. We're in. but the place is too small, so a few of us go searching for another venue. By now the town is crawling with cops - why? We only want to hold a Conference!

Months of planning... but it's 7 a.m. Saturday before another venue is found: a 14 storey office block that's been derelict for a decade. Its grim inside, and only 2 floors are useable and there's no water or electricity But by noon, its been made habitable, and the Conference is underway.

5 hours later, and up to 400 people have been discussing everything from green parenting to prisoner support; genetics to the ever increasing powers of the police - and stuffing their faces with Vegan chocolate cake. The planned party is off - the building is too dangerous, and back at the other smaller squat the council have slapped on a noise abatement order before a note of music has been struck - but some acoustic bands still play and people party.

The theme of the Conference was about uniting different people in different struggles - about the fact that the DiY protest movement was never about single issues but against a system that puts profits and property before people. About getting off your arse and doing it for yourself. Voting with your feet and actions 365 days a year rather than crossing a box every four years. About not just fighting back but putting down positive building blocks - visions of the future.

- Special edition for the Brighton Direct Action Conference 2 -

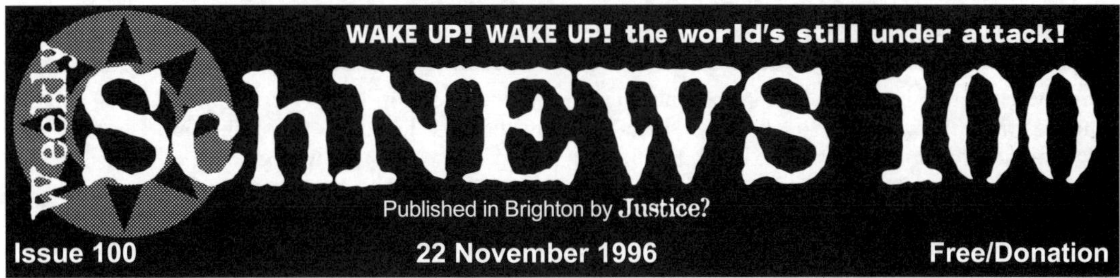

SchNEWS REACHES THE BIG ONE HUNDRED AND ASKS...

WHERE DO WE GO FROM HERE?

"If you go to one demonstration and then go home, that's something, but the people in power can live with that. What they can't live with is sustained pressure that keeps building, organisations that keep doing things, people that keep learning lessons from the last time." **- Noam Chomsky**

Over the last few years, thousands of people have got involved in direct action of one kind or another for the first time. People have protested and partied realising that life isn't something that just happens - each of us can make a difference, and together we can change the world we live in.

Nice one! It has been conservatively estimated that, in the last year alone, there have been at least five hundred separate actions carried out by direct action activists - that's ten a week. At places like the Newbury Bypass, it's been one big long direct action since January, costing the authorities newly £10 million, seriously hampering work and bringing into question the whole idea of the car culture we live in - at a cost of over 1,000 arrests. In South Wales 'eco-warriors' descended on the Welsh valleys and joined with locals to breathe life back into the fight against open cast mining. Across the country roads and motorways have been turned into street parties and streets have been gridlocked by cyclists. Politicians' gardens have been dug up and genocidal jets destroyed. People have fought their way onto TV programmes while producing their own newspapers, newsletters, videos and pamphlets to let everyone know what's going on.

The campaigns and actions that SchNEWS has covered over the last hundred issues have been enormously varied. But what they have in common is that they have all been about people who have got off their bums and refused to be passive in the face of injustice, oppression, and the destruction of our planet. And by being active - by doing instead of talking or waiting for someone else to do things for us - enormous lessons have been learnt.

DIRECT ACTION STATIONS!

Creativity, imagination, humour and energy are the name of the game as activists have realised that what passed for 'left-wing' and even 'revolutionary' politics in the 70s and 80s was stale, boring, and ineffective - marching from point A to point B once a year shouting slogans and then going home was never going to change the world. Not even a wee bit.

The ingenuity, imagination, and organisational skills of anti-road campaigners just keep on making things more difficult for the police and bailiffs. Where do you go after tanks start pumping out techno at the security at Fairmile? Most people now see the importance of physical self-defence and good legal support on actions as ways of defending themselves. People are learning to use the media instead of having the media use them to produce sanitised 'lifestyle' reports that ignore the important questions we are raising.

SINGLE ISSUE NONSENSE

"Ultimately, the idea of SchNEWS is to encourage people to get off their bums, go see things for themselves and make up their own minds.... And sure we're putting in our slant - but at least we're saying it without bosses and advertisers breathing down our necks." **- SchNEWSround introduction**

The British media have constantly tried to emphasise the 'lifestyle' aspect of what we do in order to trivialise the issues we raise.

When Justice? set up a squatters' estate agency to highlight the reality of mass homelessness in Britain (and the fact that it was possible for people to do something about it), we were deluged with reporters wanting to know about the 'alternative lifestyle' scene in Brighton. We even ended up on the fashion page of the Daily Mail. Road protesters trying to explain the insanity of the government's road building programme are smiled at politely by journalists who then asked how they go to the toilet up a tree!

In the face of this attempt to trivialise and isolate us we have learnt probably our most important lesson - that the battles we started off fighting - against profit-producing car culture, against attacks on our right to party and protest - are linked with many other struggles in Britain and abroad. Over the last year SchNEWS has covered struggles well beyond the 'alternative' style issues we are, according to lifestyle journalists, meant to

"The concept of a single issue group is now meaningless. We're making more and more links all the time."

limit ourselves to. The miners' strike, revolutionary struggles from Bougainville to Kurdistan, Britain's occupation of the north of Ireland, football, attacks on the unemployed, uprisings in Brixton and Paris, prisons, attacks on asylum seekers, sacked Liverpool dockers - the list goes on.

Making these links, destroying the myth of 'single-issue' politics, is probably the most important step we have taken over the last year. And it's about time - because if things are gonna change then such movements have got to grow.

"We were moving on, growing, making links. Liverpool dockers and their families may not wear the same clothes as your average road protester, but in Liverpool we found out that we had a lot more in common than many a middle class commentator might think. We came together because we saw our struggles were interlinked and the solidarity displayed on both sides, in the face of vicious police intimidation, was inspiring. But then what could be more natural than groups of people fighting this sick system coming together?" ***SchNEWS 85***

Monday 30th September, 1996. Same country - two very different worlds. Seaforth Dock, Liverpool, on the first anniversary of the sacking of the 500 dockers fighting against casual labour. Largely deserted by the labour movement, the dockers - inspired by the party on the M41 motorway in July - turned to Reclaim the Streets and other direct action groups for support. Activists from across the country descended on Liverpool, squatted a building to lip in and raided the docks. Flags flew from the roof of the dock offices, climbers took over the giant gantries which lay idle all day, and activists swelled the picket line when they weren't running in and out of the gates. Meanwhile up the road in sunny Blackpool, it was lots of blah as the Labour Party - the official opposition - held their most right-wing Conference to date.

POVERTY, WHAT POVERTY?

The living standards of the poorest people in Britain, the real working class that makes up the poorest third of our society and has no political voice, have been slashed in the last few years. The disparity between rich and poor in Britain is now greater than in Nigeria. A third of all children in Britain grow up in poverty - that's 4.1 million kids. One in three households in the East End of London have an annual income of under £4,500. If the poorest 60% of people in Britain had the same share of earnings they had in 1979 each such family would be £3,000 a year better off than they are now.

Half of Britain's workforce works for less than the European Union's decency threshold of £6.03 an hour. Several million work for under £3.50 and one million for less than £2.50 an hour. Benefits have fallen from 40% of average male earnings in 1979 to 17% today. At the same time, some people are doing very nicely, thank you. Deputy Prime Minster Michael Heseltine, for instance, has a personal fortune now growing at two million pounds a week. He is already worth £170m, putting his family amongst the hundred wealthiest in Britain.

The Job Seekers Allowance (JSA) will make things even worse. If you refuse an offer of a job or training scheme you will lose all your benefit instead of the 40% you used to lose. Unemployment Benefit claimants under 25 will have their benefit cut from £48.25 to £37.90 to pay for tax cuts for the middle class. Loads of us will be forced to choose between shitty 'jobs' that give multinationals slave labour or losing all entitlement to benefits. Already nearly half a million people under 25 are earning £2.50 or less an hour. Perhaps unsurprisingly, the suicide rate amongst young men has increased by 75% since 1979.

Those who work will also find themselves worse off under the JSA as employers will be more likely to sack their workforce and look for those given the choice of either working for pittance or having their benefits cut.

THE WORLD WE LIVE IN

"We can't let people just march in and do what these people are doing. We have to look after the interests of our shareholders" Guinness told *SchNEWS*, describing what it thought about the Land is Ours campaigners who took over derelict land in Wandsworth to turn into a low impact eco-village.

"The world's largest 500 companies produce 50% of the world's greenhouse gases. Shell connive with the murder of human rights and environmental activists in Nigeria and BP help fund Colombian death squads to secure access to the £23 bn Colombian oilfields. Between 1972 and 1985 only one per cent of World Bank funding for urban transport in the third world went to pedestrian facilities. Almost 80% directed to road vehicle schemes - nothing to do with the needs of the people in these countries, but much more profitable."

Multinational capitalism is the most destructive, inhumane system ever known to humanity - but funnily enough no political party of any importance in Britain opposes it. It is a system where a few massive, transnational companies control the production and distribution of most of the world's goods. These massive companies need to expand or go under. They need profits like people need air, and will do anything to get it. Politicians, states and governments are not really the main problem - they only do what they're told to by big business, driven by its own macabre logic. It is not through mismanagement or badness that the world is as it is - it is simply the working of a logic, the logic of capital, that cannot produce anything other than huge inequalities, wars and ecocide.

"One per cent of the world's population now controls 60% of its resources while 80% of the world's people scrabble for 15 % of its resources."

It is not really surprising that it has been people concerned with defending the environment that have been amongst the keenest to take action against this system. Whether in Britain where children from estates are far more likely to get asthma than children in the leafy suburbs, or in the third world where the fight for social justice is integrally linked with resistance to the multinational rape of their countries' resources, the link between social injustice and environmental destruction is obvious. You cannot seriously campaign to defend the existence of our planet's ecology without challenging multinational capitalism and its never-ending hunger for profit - a hunger that has brought us to the brink of ecological collapse. As one US delegate to the 1992 Rio Earth Summit commented, *"Environmental protection has replaced communism as the greatest threat to capitalism".*

Millions of people throughout the world are involved in life and death struggles against capitalism and its unending attacks on their ways of life and environment. They usually face repression that makes what we face at present seem like a tea party. As Under-Sheriff Nick Blandy, in charge of evictions at Newbury, has touchingly put it, "These protesters don't know how lucky they are. We could be using CS gas. In less tolerant countries they would machine gun them from trees". The people waging these struggles win or lose by building sustainable organisations of resistance that fit the conditions they live in.

USE YOUR CROSS WISELY – CRUCIFY A POLITICIAN

So what about the 'official opposition', the Labour Party? Will they at least be slightly better than the Tories? You decide. Jack Straw's 'opposition' to Michael Howard's law and order crusade, for instance, is more like a who-can-be-more-like-Judge-Dread competition rather than a defence of civil liberties against a state determined to crush the last remnants of our freedom..

There are some who think that electing a Labour government will make things slightly better. For instance the organisers of a recent 'green left' conference stated that *"The immediate priority is to help defeat the present Conservative Government"* (i.e. elect Blair). Surely the immediate priority is to involve lots more people in actions, in doing things, rather than getting people to vote for a scumbag party like Labour. An exaggeration? Hardly. Blair has been completely straight about the fact that he's offering bugger-all to the worse off and has talked of his admiration for Thatcher. In the 80s under Thatcher things were bad enough - but she had North Sea oil and the profits from numerous privatisations to pay the social security bill for mass unemployment. New Labour will not have that money and have made it clear they will do anything - dole cuts, workfare, health cuts, whatever - to keep their middle class voters happy. Frank Field, Labour's hot-shot benefits expert, even wants every adult to be given a smart card encoded with a DNA fingerprint to make the benefit system more secure.

Don't expect any better from the Liberal Democrats. They like to parade themselves as the most environmentally friendly party but David Rendel MP is staunchly in favour of the Newbury bypass in a pathetic attempt to save his seat at the next election by going on an anti-protester offensive.

The coming election will be an opportunity to show the contempt we feel for the politicians - Labour, Tory and Liberal Democrat - who run this country on behalf of profit-guzzling big business. As one activist put it at the summer Earth First! Gathering *"We can harass them around the country, break up their set-piece TV appearances and generally make life very difficult for them. These politicians treat us like shit and it only seems right to return the compliment."*

NEVER MIND THE BALLOT – LETS GO OUT THERE AND DO THINGS FOR OURSELVES

"Direct action is not a last resort. It is the preferred way of doing things."

- Reclaim The Streets flyer handed out at the M41 street party.

People are voting - with their feet and actions 365 days of the year. Take the Exodus Collective. They were formed out of the need of people on the council estates of Luton to gather and find housing. In the last four years they have gone from putting on small parties in woods to huge gatherings, attracting up to 6,000 people. All donations collected at parties are pumped back into the collective. They have housed over 40 people at the HAZ Manor and run the Community Free Farm where school kids regularly come to sample the rural atmosphere. Despite such community-minded activities (or more likely because their activities are community-based rather than done for profit) they have been seriously harassed by the police.

Credit Unions in Liverpool are now so numerous they are available to half the population. In these not-for-profit banks, people pool their own resources and draw on them for small loans to lots of people not considered 'credit worthy'.

Plants For A Future are growing 1,500 edible and useful plants on a 26 acre farm in Cornwall, and are now planning Britain's first sustainable eco-village somewhere in the south west.

UNDER ATTACK – 'DIVIDE AND DESTROY'

***"The anti roads campaign Reclaim The Streets is in danger of being hijacked by anarchist lawbreakers, transport campaigners warned yesterday."* - Evening Standard August 96**

The politicians, large businesses, multinationals, and the media are terrified of people getting together in opposition to their rule and are busy attempting to demonise and isolate anyone who tries to do so. Road protesters have been described as a *"threat to national security"* by the security services who now openly admit to targeting such groups. There are few people involved in any actions who will not have their face on a photo or video taken by the Met. Police Forward Intelligence Team. *Justice?*, by squatting an empty shop and being associated with one or two bike rides and street parties in Brighton, has been described by one of the town's MPs as creating a *"mini-revolutionary situation"*. The attempt to label those most involved in direct action, particularly environmental activists, as 'terrorists' illustrates the way in which the state intends to divide and destroy us.

Hundreds of thousands have been involved in some sort of protest at some time or other - environmental groups in Britain, for instance, have a combined membership of over five million. The state does not want to alienate these people - it just wants to make their protests ineffective. It tries to do this in two main ways: by isolating the most consistent and active campaigners from the majority of those involved through harassment, imprisonment and whatever else it takes; and by encouraging activists to follow 'moderate' (i.e. ineffective) leaders within the movement by giving these figures money, media-time and so on.

We have already had a taste of this strategy. When 7,000 people took part in Reclaim the Street's street party on the M41 in July the police didn't try to arrest everyone for 'conspiracy to obstruct the highway'. Instead, they raided the offices of RTS soon after, stole a computer and threatened two RTS members with conspiracy charges. The aim of such operations, is to intimidate and isolate those most involved in actions from the majority - and thereby stop the growth of a movement that has the potential of being really effective.

General Frank Kitson, a British Army expert on 'subversion', laid out this strategy in *Low Intensity Operations* way back in 1971. He wrote the book while he was busy waging war in Britain's oldest colony, Ireland. British rule has ruthlessly suppressed struggles of oppressed peoples throughout the world, but more than anywhere else Ireland has been used as a testing ground for the 'counter-insurgency' strategies now beginning to be used against us - repressive legislation, frame-ups, intensive information gathering, and other 'dirty tricks'.

In his book, Kitson emphasises the importance of intelligence gathering, *"psychological operations"* such as propaganda against opposition groups, use of the media to target individuals, and the use of infiltrators. The aim of all this is *"to discover and neutralise the genuine subversive element"* and *"to associate as many prominent members of the population, especially those who may have engaged in non-violent action, with the government"*. Divide and destroy is the name of the game.

***"Some of those taking part were anarchists dedicated to destroying society. They should not complain if next time society takes a dimmer view of their actions."* - Evening Argus editorial after Brighton Reclaim The Streets, 17 February 96**

PRISONER SUPPORT

The state will inevitably use its more extreme sanctions against us, and we need to support those who are subjected to its so-called Justice and retribution. Since its early days, *SchNEWS* has highlighted the importance of defending prisoners, especially jailed activists. We have learnt a lot about the barbarity of the British prison system and the importance of supporting those unlucky enough to be trapped inside it.

By now most of us probably realise that it's a lot more useful writing to a prisoner than to an MP. Many prisoners have written back to say how much they appreciate getting the *SchNEWS* and letters sent to them - and how much hearing about what's going on outside has stopped them feeling demoralised and isolated inside.

A HISTORY OF STRUGGLE

For the last two years *SchNEWS* has covered in detail the tooling up of the police and their nasty activities against us. But we've also drawn the links between what we're up to now and struggles in the past - because we've got a lot to learn from them.

The 1930s saw massive working class struggles involving rent strikes, pitched battles with the police, mass anti-fascist demos, and the organisation on a mass scale of the unemployed against workfare schemes and other government attacks. Thousands of working class people went to fight fascism in Spain while the British government did nothing.

More recently, the uprisings of black and white youth throughout Britain in 1980 and 1981 sent shock waves through the British establishment. It was felt that the traditional British Bobby needed to be toughened up to counter this threat. The thin blue line suddenly started to get thicker. Our counter-insurgency expert General Kitson was hurriedly transferred from Ireland to become Head of the Army's UK Land Forces and Kenneth Newman, the Chief Constable in Northern Ireland, was transferred to become Chief Constable of the Met. Gerry Northam's enlightening book *Shooting in the Dark* shows how the British Police have become a near para-military force along the lines of colonial Police Forces from the good old days of the Empire.

The miners' strike of 1984-85 was a major, and almost successful, challenge to Thatcher's government. A national police operation was mounted against the miners involving 20,000 officers. Every dirty trick in the book was used to beat the miners' strike including illegal roadblocks, massed attacks by riot police, MI5 infiltration of the highest levels of the miners' union, and a personal smear campaign against the miners' leader Arthur Scargill. Over 12,000 miners were arrested. Thatcher described the miners as *"the enemy within"* and Manchester's Chief Constable James Anderton called miners' pickets *"acts of terrorism without the bullet and the bomb"* (familiar, eh?). Tens of thousands of people joined miners' support groups throughout the country. But in the end, largely due to the failure of the labour movement and Labour Party to support the miners, the strike was eventually defeated. The Police were given more opportunities to try out their new strategies and new toys - the Battle of the Beanfield, Wapping and Tottenham riots are but a few. Within a few years, hundreds were to join anti-poll tax groups that successfully defeated the poll tax and brought down Thatcher. This was the biggest ever show of direct action in Britain for years with at one point over 17 million people not paying, or refusing to collect the tax.

However, despite all these struggles, no sustainable organisations have been built to learn the lessons of the past and make the links we need to make between different struggles. In that sense, probably more than any other, the divide and destroy strategy has worked well. Popular movements, some extremely active and involving hundreds of thousands of people, come and go - but the strong, sustainable organisations we need have not been built.

IS THIS A LAUGH OR IS THIS FOR REAL?

We now face important decisions about where we go next. On our own we can at most be an irritation to those in power and an interesting object of study for journalists and cultural studies students. Linked with others, we can build something of real importance. As George Jackson, black working class revolutionary and Black Panther member shot by guards in a U.S. prison, put it, *"It isn't just a matter of trusting the good will of other slaves and other colonies and other peoples. It is simply a matter of common need. We need allies. We have a powerful enemy who cannot be defeated without an allied effort".*

We need to build real unity with others, to learn from others. We will find our natural allies, as we did in Liverpool, amongst the millions of people in Britain suffering poverty, racism, police harassment - and fighting back, like us, in pockets of resistance. When the JSA starts to hit, and thousands simply lose all of their benefits, we have to have organisations there to do support each other. Because no one else will do it for us.

We have always been at our strongest when we've been most active, doing actions and organising imaginative campaigns that involve new people. In doing this, we have learnt that you don't get very far if you are constantly trying to impress the media and convince politicians that what you're doing is 'reasonable'.

As the eviction by Guinness of the Land is Ours occupation in Wandsworth showed, those in power don't give a shit about what's reasonable - they're only interested in money, not people. Next time The Land is Ours or whoever squats some derelict land maybe a few lessons can be learnt from the women on *EastEnders* who got nicked fighting their council for a playground for their kids - that sort of local DiY self-help is going to become more and more important as facilities for people on estates become even more non-existent. We can't allow those who try to narrow the effectiveness of actions by constantly trying to keep things legal and 'acceptable' to those in power to stop us from being effective.

By their nature, most actions we've been involved in have come together very quickly and then moved on, to different places with different people. That's fine in its place - at road protests, for street parties, for one-off squats - but now we need to adapt the way we organise in order to meet new challenges. We need to build locally, getting to know and linking up with unemployed groups, black and refugee groups, strikers, and people living on estates forgotten about by corrupt councils.

We need to start to build sustainable organisations to meet the sustained attacks that are coming our way soon. Open, democratic organisations that are welcoming to new people, that discuss what we're doing and learn from past struggles and the loads of other struggles across the world that are fighting the same enemy we are.

If, over the next few years, we don't start uniting the pockets of resistance that already exist - if we allow ourselves to retreat into secretive sects that slag each other off and are endlessly suspicious of anyone new - we will simply be picked off struggle by struggle. If we do get it together with others, if we do start to involve new people in in-yer-face direct action in their hundreds, in their thousands, then the sky's the limit - and we can start having some serious fun as we party and protest and build a real mass fightback against a system that has long outlived its welcome.

"We need to start to build sustainable organisations to meet the sustained attacks that are coming our way soon".

REUNION RAMPAGE!

"What's worse? The temporary end of a bit of replaceable machinery or the permanent end of one of Britain's most beautiful landscapes? They had it coming." - Newbury resident.

The anniversary of the beginning of work on the Newbury Bypass was marked with a rally of around one thousand people last Saturday. SchNEWS had gone along with bits of ribbon to tie onto the fence in "symbolic protest" but as the day unfolded rather more "decoration" happened than many of us bargained for. Fencing was breached, a trickle of activists entering under cover of heavy fog. The trickle became a flood, as more fence surrounding the old Middle Oak camp was cut and pulled down. As police and security looked helplessly on people got more and more cheeky, culminating in a spectacular fireshow provided by a dumper truck, a portacabin and the cab of an enormous crane. Youthful campaigners and middle England alike registered their disgust at the wasteland that is now Newbury.

When SchNEWS asked Costain to comment on the action they replied, *"We have always supported peaceful protest, but unfortunately after Saturday's events we can no longer support the protesters."*!

Who are the real vandals?

Over the last year some of the most beautiful countryside in the South East has been trashed. Wave goodbye to 3 Special Site of Scientific Interest, an area of Outstanding Natural Beauty, a registered battlefield, 12 sites of archaeological importance, 10,000 trees, a snail's habitat and a colony of

Pic: Andrew Testa

dormice. All this for a £101 million road which even the Dept of Transport and local council admit will not solve Newbury's congestion problems.

So was it just 'outside agitators' that joined in the damage? One Newbury woman said "it's about time something like this happened", and later a middle-England resident actually asked one protester, sitting on a digger, "is there some way I can damage this?"

Rally organisers Friends of the Earth, sang a different tune *"the few malicious hotheads who ruined what had been a wholly peaceful rally..... betraying the values of the green movement."*

Much has been made of how the roads protest movement has shown its true colours and become violent, descending into "chaos and crime".

"Violence" is a very emotive word, and easy to band about. No security guards or police were injured, but one protester was hospitalised and another run down by a police horse. In fact the lead up to the 'Reunion Rampage' saw overkill police tactics continually harassing anyone in the Newbury area stopping and searching vehicles and nicking people for the most minor offences. So far 950 people have been arrested in a year of protests, some spending time inside on nonsense charges, like breaking the ridiculous bail conditions and High Court injunctions stopping their right to protest. People had obviously had enough...

Now *SchNEWS* would never encourage its readers to take part in such activities, but why is damage to property considered violent? The "Swords into Ploughshares" women were never considered violent for causing £23 million worth of damage to a hawk jet on its way to Indonesia...

Pic: Andrew Testa

DIG THAT!

Sheriff Sore After Seven Day Shafting

They came in at 9.40 on Thursday evening. A wierd new time for a wierd new type of eviction where the old cast of baddies
God, there aren't very many of you are there? - Can't you run about a bit to give us something to do?
We are being paid by the hour y'know
(give me strength!)
the Sheffield Climbers
are joined by sinister new figures THE CAVEMEN
(actually, they're rather friendly mine rescue workers who just don't want to be identified)
and The-Man-with-the-sheets-of-8x4-Plywood and-T Square
as well as the evil Sheriff of old.
Mr Coleman how long do you think the eviction will last?
I can confidently predict that the trespassers will be removed from the camp within 24 hours

"It's the only way to get a voice these days. I feel if I had just written to my MP, would I have achieved all this? Would you lot [the assembled media] all be here? I think not." **- Swampy, yesterday**

The last protester along the route of the A30 in Devon emerged from the tunnels at 8:45 p.m. last night after a week underground - setting a post-war eviction record.

Fairmile, the last of the three camps on the A30 route to be evicted, was established over two years ago (pre-dating Newbury) to block Britain's first private road from being built. Not only does it cover more countryside in tarmac but it's also a symbolic starting point for a disastrous new government policy. Swampy, Animal and the now-famous moles didn't put the Earth first for the media to focus on their lifestyles; they did it to expose this scandal. So here are the facts:

In 1992 the Chancellor announced a private finance initiative which would give a new lease of life to the road building industry. The Design, Build, Finance, Operate (DBFO) scheme was announced. This meant that companies who build roads are not paid immediately, but instead after a 30 year period are given an undeclared amount based on pre-set shadow tolls. In other words the road builders get paid for each vehicle that uses their road. Responsibility is then given to the road builders to encourage motorists to use the road - flying in the face of the government's own admission that new roads create more traffic. This would be done by sign-posting and by encouraging development along the route. Devon County Council has already set aside land along the route for a new town with an expected population of 10,000, a technology park, a power station and an extension to an existing quarry, effectively extending the urban fringes of Exeter to the east by eight miles.

This DBFO scheme, dubbed Destroy, Burn, Fell, Obliterate, is the first road of its kind (its nearest cousin is the Channel Tunnel). It's a financial nightmare and one with a dubious safety record. The new roads programme means that safety and environmental protection are of little relevance to the private sector profit-making companies who are responsible for the construction of this and many other roads. And just to show they mean business, the Government chose this week to announce the widening (to dual-carriageways) of *another* section of the A30. European super-trunk route here we come.

The main problem facing bailiffs were the complex tunnels into which protesters have dug - *"Built by gypsies with candles",* as the Deputy Under-Sheriff put it on Thursday. Meanwhile police have been hassling tunnellers' parents for information. But this has

been countered by devious actions from activists determined not to let the forces of darkness get away with the abuse of the planet for profit.

Last week the Under Sheriff and his men were woken at 4 a.m. by a hoax fire alarm and were forced to wait in the cold car park while the building was subject to an intense safety inspection.

Another group of activists targeted *Balfour Beatty*, the company who are building the road, by climbing a crane opposite Parliament owned by the company and unfurling a banner saying *"Privatised Vandalism - stop DBFO roads. We Love You Fairmile!"* The crane was held for most of the day, and all the crane's occupants were arrested for offences including Aggravated Trespass.

The demands made by the protesters include: removal of harsh bail conditions; secrecy behind DBFO schemes be dropped; and what's left of the beautiful site is preserved until an unbiased & open public inquiry looking at all secret information surrounding the scheme.

Pic above & bottom left - Andrew Testa, pic below - Alec Smart

Muppet Dave & Animal/Eleanor in the tunnels.

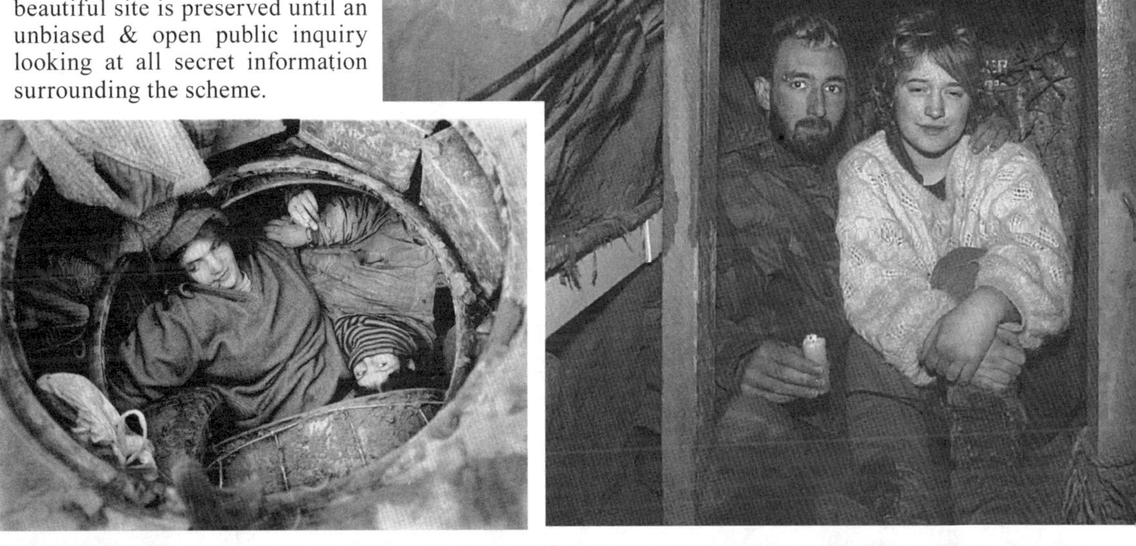

The Spectacularisation of Fairmile

It's worth nothing that, more than any other eviction, Fairmile became a media spectacle, and that was partly our own creation. Which isn't necessarily a bad thing; I'm not a person who believes in not talking to the press at all; I just believe that we've got to try and remain in control, and know when to pull out. We've gained a lot of good publicity, and have, hopefully, changed some consciousness in people. There were national press articles that copied sections of our press releases verbatim.

Part of what we do is try and make an issue which is otherwise boring sexy, make politics real. That's what has happened, exemplified by the M11, where we began to realise and harness the fact that our resistance to the roads was graphic, was real, and that people could relate to its immediacy. The tunnels were the end of that process - the ultimate insane thing to do.

On the day we were going to issue our demands, the Under-Sheriff cut off our intercom communication with the tunnel, which the press had been filming and using directly; "And now we go to the people down in the tunnels". We put out these demands and they just cut off all the communications! In the end it was probably better than if they hadn't!

The demands were 1) All the Design Build Finance Operate (state organised private road building) documentation should be made open to public scrutiny; and 2) All road-building should cease until they'd been reviewed. At a critical time when media interest was slacking off, putting the tunnelers in danger, the demands got us loads of media interest. You looked at the demands and just thought, "Well that's pretty fucking reasonable. They're just asking for a few bits of paper to be made available to the public." But the reality was that the DBFO is a cover-up by the state and making those documents public is something that the state wouldn't be able to do.

We asked for them because we knew that they wouldn't be able to give them to us, or if they did, then it would open up a can of worms for the roadbuilding industry. We knew from day one that they were never going to meet the demands. We'd deliberately balanced them so that they appeared reasonable but in no way were actually meetable by the state. We didn't ask for a plane to Cuba, but then nor did we give them something that they could do, like "Don't arrest us" or something like that.

We were able to say that the demands were us opening the negotiations, and the state's response was to cut our communication lines. We managed to present ourselves as the reasonable ones and the state as being the nutters. We were the ones asking for negotiation, and they were the ones in balaclavas!

It was at this point that the media attempted (quite successfully) to turn our struggle to defend life into a personality story. They wanted to know the backgrounds of all the people down the tunnels, and all we'd tell them was their names and age. There was quite a diverse range of ages there - everything from early 40s (John) down to sixteen (Animal). Which was why we decided to say the ages, because we thought it would shatter that media-generated impression that it was just young activists that were doing these things. In the end they created a situation where millions knew what colour socks Swampy wore down the tunnels, but not the name of the site the tunnels were in.

This was nicked from Do Or Die #6

Fort Trollheim

Pic: Andrew Testa

Allercombe

Pic: Andrew Testa

A Tale from Allercombe, A30

"Allercombe was the third and lesser known protest site of the A30 campaign. Built around the copse, situated in rolling down farmland, where an entire tree village had been constructed, complete with a 40ft tower rising from the canopy. A large expanse of cargo netting strung through the trees and a massive communal tree house. Attempts were made to construct a tunnel system, but constant water logging meant it never became as sophisticated as the Big Mumma network at Fairmile. It became so muddy in the winter months that the activists became like mythical swamp creatures. It was a magical and inspiring time." OJ

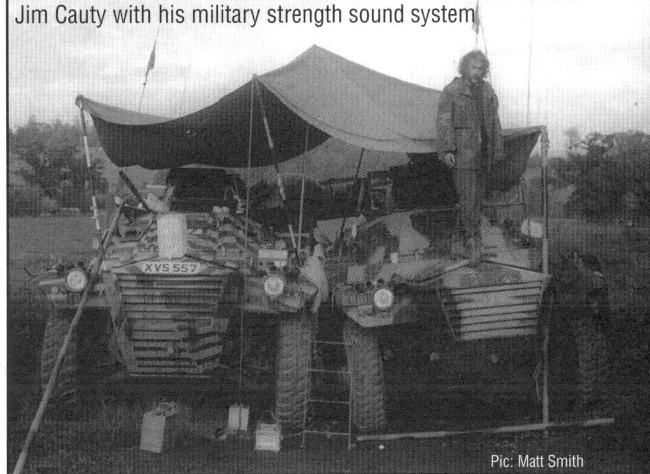

Jim Cauty with his military strength sound system

Pic: Matt Smith

Pic: Alec Smart

A POLITICAL PARTY?

Matt Smith

It's not all sweetness and light in the SchNEWS office, we often have arguments about coverage of issues. But one subject that caused a big fallout was the reporting of the Liverpool Dockers/Reclaim the Streets march in London on April 12th 1997. Upset that their version of events had not been reported in that week's issue, a few people put out a spoof SchNEWS. While some of the points raised were petty and based on personal conflicts, there were valid points that we've reproduced here:

Schnooze

Published in Brighton not by Justice? 22/4/1997

The demonstration on the 12th of April was a joint effort between the sacked Liverpool Dockers, Reclaim the Streets and various other groups. The following account is an attempt to understand some of the issues that were brought up on the day and hopefully serve as a starting point for debate and discussion.

Arriving at Kennington Park at midday felt like walking into a carnival. The atmosphere was electric, and the knowledge that something beyond a traditional demo was in the offing lent the whole day an air of expectancy and anticipation. As we reached the breakaway point the sight of rows of TSG vans and lines of foot soldiers subdued the buzz for a moment, but then as we were walking along Whitehall a smoke bomb went off outside Downing Street, which re-galvanised sections of the crowd and a party began to grow outside the gates. The drums were going, flags flying, people dancing, whistles blowing and lots of other things best left unmentioned! There was a feeling of excitement and as the numbers grew, but just as this was going on a whisper spread through the crowd saying that people were needed at Trafalgar Square. This split the numbers, but the sound system was ensured entry into Trafalgar Square.

The sound system in Trafalgar square.

After a couple of false alarms which had people, and the police, running up and down the Square, a white truck careered into the top end of Trafalgar Square, to shouts of 'surround it, that's the sound system'. The mass of bodies wanting it in the Square totally outnumbered police and they backed off a tactical retreat. People then went crazy, euphoric at having got one over the cops.

In the excitement of getting the sound system in, however, the fact that someone was arrested was largely bypassed. Initially, he could have been easily de-arrested with the number of people that were there. But by this time people were too busy dancing to the sounds pouring out of the truck to consider the fact that someone had lost their liberty in trying to get it in.

This raises questions about the use of a party, especially a street

Andrew Testa

Alec Smart

party, as a form of protest. Is the party, in itself, the protest? Or is it the means to protest? Reclaiming the streets for a party is a great idea and it brings in heaps more people than you could otherwise assemble for a protest. But were the majority of people there to protest, or simply there for a party? At Trafalgar Square some people were clustered around the sound system, dancing, and then there were those, on the outskirts defending the space that we had created. Being at the party probably politicised some people, but is it enough? How much longer can we go on attempting to create temporary autonomous zones, when the majority of people are simply content with that?

After the sound system had gone.

Having been kept out of Trafalgar Square for most of the day, people were finally allowed back in at about 7pm. The reason being that the sound system had gone, and with it, the vast majority of people. In the northeast corner of the Square however, there were skirmishes going on between protesters and riot police.

Reclaiming the bridge

Finally about a hundred people went up onto Waterloo Bridge and occupied it. At first the crowd halted traffic, then people bounced a parked car across both lanes. A Jaguar was trashed and as someone went on to do the next car a voice shouted out 'No, leave that one. Just do the posh cars!' The police had been left on the Embankment able only to watch, and the blockading of traffic served the purpose of stopping any vans coming across the bridge from the north end. They chose not to come down on foot, probably because they would have had to walk single file to get to us. People then took the roundabout at the bottom, which was held for quite a while but as it was so big, it left people in small, isolated groups.

Afterthoughts

Looking back at the day, issues were raised: Firstly, people seem obsessed with the media but in truth what does the media matter? They were already reporting Downing Street as a riot before the majority of people had even entered Trafalgar Square. In any respect, they are going to use the angle which will sell the most copies of their paper. This approach by the mainstream media also seems to be used to try and shift copies of the alternative newssheet - SchNEWS: Write what you think the punters want to read, at the lowest level you think they are capable of understanding and hey presto you've got three thousand copies of pulp.

We cannot simply congratulate ourselves on the excellent party; the hype over the links that were made, also need to be questioned. Beyond being in the same physical space, what links were made? It seemed like the Dockers were in the centre of the Square listening to speeches, and when these were over they left. The arty-heads were around the sound system, dancing, and the politicos were in confrontation with the police. Though it may not have been quite as stark as this, the divisions were very much apparent.

There is a real need for self awareness within the direct action movement and for a deeper understanding of issues which are continuously brought up and use this to inform future actions. By constantly appealing to the lowest common denominator, and simply talking about how great we were, you put yourself in a position of never moving beyond that. We need to take encouragement and satisfaction out of the victories we do have, but as those are never complete victories, we need to look at ways to move beyond them. Not being aware of oneself and one's actions, nor the actions of others, or the motives for those actions, is the greatest obstacle to moving beyond the limitations we are confronted with. And nowhere, is this lack of real political awareness more accurately captured than in the headline of the SchNEWS: **'They wanna fight! We wanna party!'**

Alec Smart

DOWN T'CAKEHOLE

...and up the duff, Denise takes Swampy's record

Pic: Alec Smart

"Three of my grandchildren have got asthma. I used to walk through here for years with the dogs. It's disgusting." - **Joyce, local resident**

At 8am this morning six Manchester Runway 2 tunnellers will have been underground for seven days and one hour - beating Swampy's Fairmile record and costing Manchester Airport £200 a minute. Destined for fame is mother-to-be Denise with Muppet Dave, Matt and Neville who have spent more than a week `downstairs' in Cakehole at the Flywood Camp. Jeni and Blowpipe are holed up in Paul McCartney's Cavern.

Swampification!

But the Swampification of protests is all lifestyles and no issues. So SchNEWS brings you the facts behind the Britain's first anti-airport direct action protest. One thousand acres of greenbelt at beautiful Bollin Valley in Cheshire - double the land destroyed by the Newbury bypass - will be Tarmac'ed. The development is pointless - Runway 2 would provide a third more flights, yet one third of all seats from Manchester are empty. It would be used at first for just five hours a week. Fifty miles away, Liverpool Airport is idle. The Airport claim 50,000 jobs will be created. In fact it will create negligable local employment for £200M of gross environmental destruction. In February, Manchester Chamber of Commerce and Industry estimated it would be more like 5,000.

In January the first people took to the trees after 20 years of letter-writing opposition in nearby Mobberly, Styal and the well-heeled Wilmslow. A 101-day enquiry was "loaded in favour of the developers from the start" according to former Beirut hostage and local Terry Waite. New Labour MP Graham Stringer was simultaneously leader of Manchester City Council and the chairman of Manchester Aiport plc - the Council owns 55% of the Airport. Funny that. Yet Stringer has accused the protesters of *"coming from the same political tradition as Mussolini and Pol Pot."*

Terry Waite headed a team of independent legal observers but Stringer denied access to the eviction site. Police vans patrol the four-mile razor wire exclusion zone in a £6 million security operation. The press corps are penned in 100 metres out of sight of the action, only able to report that they could not see anything. Evidence gatherers film and photograph everyone.

Nameless ex-SAS balaclava'd `Men In Black' are employed to dig the protesters out, but are working at a painfully slow rate of a tunnel door a day, which makes those in the know laugh at how long it will take.

Pic: Andrew Testa

"Are we going to tell lies against our enemies who lie? Don't the facts speak enough?" Chai Ling, Tianammen Sq. '89

Pic: Alec Smart

Under Sheriff Randall `The Vandal' Hibbert, backed by hundreds of security and bailiffs, hit the first of the seven tree camps at 3.45am on Tuesday May 20th. Protestors sat around the campfire at Zion Tree say they were subjected to an unprovoked truncheon attack by Greater Manchester Police. They deny involvement but are `investigating'. It took 15 days before the last man was pulled from the branches at Sir Cliff Richard OBE Vegan Revolution, Jimi Hendrix, River Rats, Wild Garlic, and The-Camp-Of-Many-Names. `Leery' Flywood, the first camp to be set up (known also as Babylon's Council Estate) featured Battlestar Galactica, a multi-levelled tree fortress holding 14 people. It took cherry pickers to get people out - and would have been unevictable had a tunnel been at the base.

One man, Carl, nailed his ear to a tree, and another was tied to a trunk in a wheelchair. Russ and Tangle, who fought it out 80 feet up, announced they were getting married as they were released from Wilmslow police station. There have been 160 arrests during the campaign. One protester, Sharyn, who was jailed for refusing bail conditions, went on hunger strike demanding proof that the prison food was not genetically engineered. Local support is fantastic and half the security are on our side.

Zero Tolerance, a London kamikaze soundsystem, was tied into the trees in the `We are Over Here' camp providing a surreal aural backdrop with the likes of Girl from Ipanima, Vivaldi and banging techno ringing out depending on the mood, while Sea Sabs mounted attacks down the Bollin River (owned by the Rivers Authority not Manchester Airport). Now protesters say they will take their campaign direct to the Airport itself, while others head South to fight Rank's Centre Parcs development in Lyminge Forest, Kent.

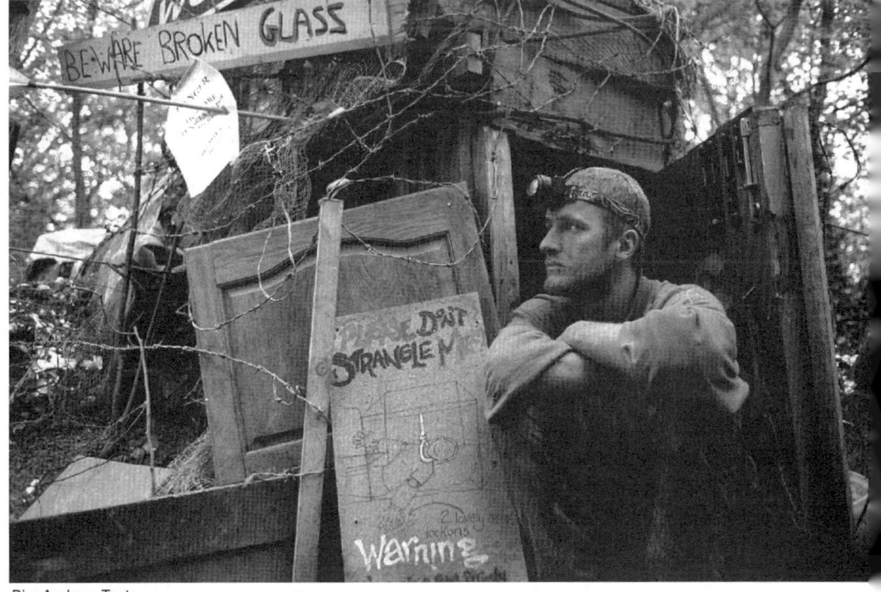

Pic: Andrew Testa

A Proper Grilling:

The McLibel Trial

The McLibel trial was one of the most vociferously fought and successful political trials in modern times. A gargantuan battle between one of the world's largest corporations and two penniless British activists, becoming an inspirational breakthrough at the rise of anti-corporatisation. Jim Carey presents a summary of a stunning saga as it draws to a final close.

"The reason Japanese people are so short and have yellow skins is because they have eaten nothing but fish and rice for two thousand years," said Den Fujita. "If we eat McDonald's hamburgers and potatoes for a thousand years we will become taller, our skin become white and our hair blonde."

Were these not the words of a Japanese native, this statement would surely have been slammed as racist. But, as president of McDonald's Japan, Fujita's sense of national identity runs a subordinate second to his loyalty to the corporation. And Paul Preston, head of McDonald's UK, displayed a similar character when he asserted: "McDonald's isn't a job, it's a life... McDonald's employees have ketchup in their veins."

Far from being just the ludicrous ramblings of a few shortsighted corporate individuals, however, Preston and Fujita's skewed sense of personal priority is in rapid ascendancy and increasingly influential as multinationals control ever-larger portions of the global economy.

However, most of the convoluted multi-million pound strategies driving these manoeuvres rarely escape the confidentiality of the boardroom. And so, majorly influential though they are on our lives, we get to know little of their insidious design until long after the horse has bolted.

But there are exceptions and none more so than one of the most extensive corporate grillings ever - the McLibel trial.

McDonald's must bitterly regret the day they threatened one libel suit too many back in 1990 and so precipitated what Channel Four News subsequently referred to as "the most disastrous PR exercise ever mounted by a multinational company".

In its attempt to cut the tongue from even the smallest of its critics, the burger giant sued Dave Morris and Helen Steel, two penniless political activists, for their alleged involvement in distributing a leaflet called 'What's Wrong with McDonald's?'

The Corporation were confident their notorious legal department would triumph with ease against such small fry. After all, the McDonald's Corporation had forced grovelling public apologies from everyone they'd ever sued largely because no one could afford to fight them in court. But Helen Steel and Dave Morris were made of sterner stuff and decided to fight all the way.

Their determination resulted in acres of media coverage adverse to McDonald's reputation as the longest trial in British legal history resulted in two dramatic years of corporate cross-examination and forced disclosure. The 314-day trial was followed with a 23-day appeal hearing and finally a day in the European Court of Human Rights.

McDonald's hired one of the best libel QC's in the UK at the cost of over £2000 a day, spent over £10 million on the case, and made two unsuccessful attempts to buy the defendants' surrender. With legal aid denied to any defendant under British libel law, Steel and Morris fought the convoluted legal case themselves, wading through 18,000 court transcripts and 40,000 pages of documents and witness statements. They relied on a fund amounting to just £35,000, donated and raised by sympathisers. As a result of their tenacity, the strategies and tactics of one of the world's largest and aggressive corporations were revealed to the public in High Court Room 35.

FOOD FOR THOUGHT

The McDonald's Corporation generates an annual turnover of US$26 billion, operating 18,500 burger bars in 89 countries and opening nine new outlets a day. The strategy behind such global expansion is ambitiously aggressive; its success envied and emulated throughout the corporate world. McDonald's is a new global superpower in a world where the economies of multinational corporations have overtaken that of small countries.

The critical leaflet central to the McLibel trial contains information on a wide variety of issues, ranging from McDonald's involvement in rainforest destruction to poor employment conditions, the insidious strategies of child advertising to the poor treatment of animals. With such a wide variety of urgent social issues subjected to the close scrutiny of a high court, the two defendants used every opportunity the trial presented to force disclosure of revealing internal corporate documents.

"In the witness box they can't turn around and walk away, ignore your questions and avoid telling you what's going on," says Helen Steel. "You can force them to give an answer, so it is a unique opportunity."

David and Helen versus Goliath

One of the key issues investigated by the trial was the advanced techniques used to inflate the corporation's product image. McDonald's spends a massive US$1.4 billion each year on marketing. According to a recent survey of two thousand people in several different countries, the corporation's golden-arches logo is now a more globally recognised symbol than the Christian cross. Delving deep beneath the mechanisms of McDonald's branding, the McLibel trial spent many months investigating the reality behind claims found in the Corporation's adverts, as well as the psychological techniques adopted by their marketing strategists.

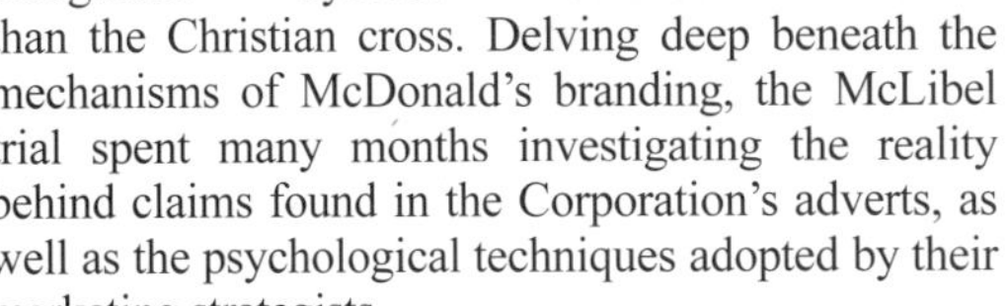

Chief among the claims is McDonald's insistence that their products provide a 'nutritious' and 'healthy' meal. When Dr Sydney Arnott, a top cancer expert, appeared on behalf of McDonald's, he found himself agreeing that: "A diet high in fat, sugar, animal products and salt, and low in fibre, vitamins and minerals is linked with cancers of the breast and bowel, and heart disease." The court then heard that this statement had come from the allegedly libellous leaflet – scoring a massive own goal for McDonald's. Dr Neal Barnard, president of the US Physicians Committee for Responsible Medicine then told the court: "Many of the products sold at McDonald's are high in fat and cholesterol and low in fibre and certain vitamins", and as a result "contribute to heart disease, certain forms of cancer and other diseases".

For the Corporation, these were embarrassing testimonies, exacerbated further by the court disclosure of an internal company document from a high-level meeting in 1986, stating: "McDonald's should attempt to deflect the basic negative thrust of our critics... How do we do this? By talking 'moderation and balance'. We can't really address or defend nutrition. We don't sell nutrition and people don't come to McDonald's for nutrition." However, in the McDonald's Nutrition Guide, which is still given to the public at its outlets, the corporation claims: "Every time you eat McDonald's, you'll eat good, nutritious food."

Such inconsistencies resulted in three US state attorney generals sending a warning to the corporation. Stephen Gardner, former Assistant Attorney General of Texas, appeared in the McLibel witness stand to read from their letter: "The Attorney Generals of Texas, California and New York have concluded our joint review of McDonald's recent advertising campaign which claims that McDonald's food is nutritious. Our mutual conclusion is that this advertising campaign is deceptive. We therefore request that McDonald's immediately desist further use of this advertising campaign. The reason for this is simple: McDonald's food is, as a whole, not nutritious. The intent and result of the current campaign is to deceive customers into believing the opposite... The new campaign appears intended to pull the wool over the public's eyes."

PESTER POWER

The unmasking of McDonald's hidden strategy was then complemented with a thorough examination of its designs on the most vulnerable consumer age group. According to David Green, senior vice-president of McDonald's Marketing, "[Children] are virgin ground as far as marketing is concerned." The McDonald's internal Operations Manual was read out in court: "Children are often the key decision-makers concerning where a family goes to eat... [offering toys] is one of the best things... to make them loyal supporters", using McDonald's birthday parties as "an important way to generate added sales and profits and the clown Ronald McDonald as a strong marketing tool."

Despite UK advertising codes forbidding commercials which "manipulate the emotions" of children, the provocation of what is known in the industry as 'pester power' is widespread. The Operations Manual further states: "Ronald loves McDonald's and McDonald's food. And so do children, because they love Ronald. Remember, children exert a phenomenal influence when it comes to restaurant selection. This means that you should do everything you can to appeal to children's love for Ronald and McDonald's."

In conjunction with its advertising, the corporation also runs a wide variety of strategic schools projects, including education packs, free teacher-resource materials and good behaviour schemes with free burgers as a reward. These, and many other such schemes, fortify the McDonald's experience in the minds of children, an intention clearly admitted to by McDonald's advertising executives under cross-examination. The court then heard how Geoffrey Guiliano, the actor who played Ronald McDonald the Clown in the 1980s, eventually resigned and went public with his regrets: "I brainwashed youngsters into doing wrong. I want to say sorry to children everywhere."

EAT YER GREENS

Each year in South America, an area the size of Wales is stripped of virgin tropical rainforest, primarily to provide land upon which the global beef market can indulge its appetite for low-cost cattle. As the world's largest single user of beef, McDonald's has worked hard to avoid implication in what is widely recognised as an issue of major public concern. All hell broke loose in the McDonald's camp when Prince Philip met a McDonald's executive at a World Wildlife Fund function in Canada in 1983. According to a letter disclosed during the McLibel trial, Philip said to the executive: "So you are the people who are tearing down the Brazilian rainforests and breeding cattle." The executive apparently told Philip he was mistaken, to which the reply was "rubbish". According to the letter, Philip then "stormed away".

To avert a potential PR disaster, Fred Turner, chairman of the McDonald's Corporation, sent out a worldwide edict that no McDonald's plant was to use Brazilian beef. The corporation then sent a letter to the World Wildlife Fund saying: "McDonald's worldwide is not involved in any manner in dealing with rainforests, or their removal, or in buying beef as a result of cattle that have been grazing in areas that formerly were rainforests." The World Wildlife Fund later wrote saying the corporation was "exonerated". However, a letter disclosed in court during the McLibel trial revealed that despite the 'political' ramifications of ignoring the worldwide edict, the managing director of McDonald's UK gave covert permission to McKey meat suppliers to provide its UK burger bars with Brazilian beef. Furthermore, letters from McDonald's Costa Rican meat suppliers reveal the company reared cattle on former tropical rainforest land. The court was then shown film footage in which a representative of the Costa Rican company stated that they had supplied beef for use in McDonald's US outlets.

"Libel cases are brought to censor and silence the 'truth'. The fact that we've gone through three years of the case, and come out the other end, maintaining distribution of the leaflet, launching the McSpotlight web site and seen the growth of the campaign means we have won! The real court is the court of public opinion, and we won't accept the stifling of our voices. The public are the jury in this case." - Dave Morris

An expert witness in animal rearing, appearing on behalf of the corporation, also admitted that chickens reared for chicken McNuggets and McChicken sandwiches are packed into vast windowless sheds, with 44 per cent of them developing leg abnormalities and other health problems. Young chicks, he told the court, were routinely dosed with antibiotics in an attempt to reduce disease. The court also heard how hens providing eggs for McDonald's Egg McMuffins were kept in battery cages with no access to sunlight and less than an 'A4 sheet of paper' as space for each bird. Under cross-examination, McDonald's UK chief purchasing officer unbelievably described these conditions as "pretty comfortable".

SITUATION VACANT

Poor conditions then became the subject of a different investigation, this time concerning the corporation's employees. The term 'McJobs' is now so commonly used it is only one step away from English dictionary citation. Deployed throughout the media in a variety of contexts, the word has become synonymous with poorly paid, dehumanising work devoid of employment rights. However, when the Oxford English Dictionary (OED) revealed it was thinking of putting the word 'McJobs' in its dictionaries, McDonald's threatened to sue once again and the OED went quiet on the matter.

During the McLibel trial Sid Nicholson, McDonald's UK vice-president, admitted in court that for staff aged 21 or over, the corporation "couldn't pay any lower wages without falling foul of the law". Also appearing in the witness box was an ex-McDonald's employee from Canada who recalled how McDonald's management ordered its employees to lie down in the snow to form the word 'no', affirming the corporation's view of unions. Indeed, despite claiming that McDonald's is not anti-union, the corporation's UK vice-president disclosed under cross-examination that the company did not allow its workers to "collect subscriptions... put up notices... pass out any leaflets... organise a meeting for staff to discuss conditions at the store on the premises... or to inform the union about conditions inside the stores". Contravention is considered "gross misconduct" and a "summary sackable offence". An ex-McDonald's employee and representative of the French trade union CFDT also informed the court of how five McDonald's managers were arrested in

Lyon in 1994 and charged with trying to rig union elections. However, when right-winger Jacques Chirac became president in 1995, he pardoned all five without the case going to court.

Interestingly, Sir Bernard Ingham is hired for his PR advice as non-executive director of McDonald's UK. As press secretary to Margaret Thatcher, Ingham was the propaganda architect behind the strategic disempowerment of British trade unions. Indeed, Thatcher formally opened McDonald's UK headquarters in her Finchley constituency, and her constituency manager at the time, Mike Love, is now head of public relations for McDonald's UK.

In a separate but related case, the tenacious McLibel Two sued the Commissioner of Metropolitan Police, claiming damages for misfeasance in public office, breach of confidence and breach of their right to privacy. The actionable case came to light during the full McLibel trial when Sid Nicholson, McDonald's ex-head of security in the UK and a former Met Police officer, admitted in court that McDonald's security team were all ex-policemen who still had easy access to police records and had made use of that access. He inadvertently informed the court that McDonald's security department had obtained specific information about Dave Morris and Helen Steel from currently serving met officers. The case concluded with the Metropolitan Police issuing a public apology and stumping up £10,000 in an out of court settlement.

McNUGGET OF TRUTH

When Mr Justice Bell delivered his verdict on the full trial in June 1997, there were some damning indictments of McDonald's practices in his two-hour disposition. He ruled that the Corporation did indeed "exploit children" with their advertising strategy, are "strongly antipathetic" to unionisation, are "culpably responsible for animal cruelty", have published claims about their fast food which "pretended to a positive nutritional benefit which their food (high in fat & salt etc) did not match"; and "pay low wages, helping to depress wages in the catering trade." However he also ruled that not all of Steel and Morris's accusations had been proven with primary source evidence and that they had therefore libelled McDonald's and should pay damages of £60,000 (half the amount sought by the Corporation).

When the McLibel Two appealed the verdict in 1999, they achieved significant advances in the judge's original ruling when the appeal court ruling strengthened the condemnation of McDonald's practices contained in the original judge's verdict. Lord Justices Pill, May and Keane ruled that it was fair comment to say that McDonald's employees worldwide "do badly in terms of pay and conditions", and that it is true that "if one eats enough McDonald's food, one's diet may well become high in fat etc., with the very real risk of heart disease.'" The £60,000 damages was reduced to £40,0000 but with the McLibel Two refusing to pay, the Corporation cut its heavy losses and announced that it would not pursue the matter any further.

But for the McLibel Two this was not yet the end of the matter.

In September 2001, they took the British government to the European Court of Human Rights (ECHR) claiming heavily imbalanced libel laws in the UK were an affront to free speech. Without any access to legal aid, the defendants had been required to prove every one of their allegations with primary source evidence. This, they argued, meant that large corporations were effectively beyond public criticism even though their strategies and executions have a majorly significant impact on the lives of the British public. This time qualifying for legal aid and therefore professional legal representation, Steel and Morris's case was presented to the ECHR in Strasbourg in September 2004. A verdict on the matter, which could completely overhaul Britain's archaic libel system should it to go against the British government, is expected at the end of 2004/beginning of 2005.

There are very few genuine forums for corporate accountability and scrutiny in which money has not bought allegiance and bypassed the truth. Indeed, with the massive amounts of money available to corporate marketing departments, the only significant trouble on the horizon for any corporation is the public exposure of embarrassing truths; brand image being both the strength and the Achilles' heel of any corporation. For this reason McDonald's made two separate settlement offers to the McLibel Two, flying over US executives and offering sizeable sums of cash if the defendants would finish the case. In refusing their offers, the two defendants proved themselves to be different from the likes of Den Fujita, Paul Preston, Sir Bernard Ingham and other money grabbing corporate cronies. Positioned beyond the reach of even the largest multinational corporation, their loyalties are not for sale. And for the last fourteen years those loyalties have been deployed on the absolute frontline of the struggle between community and corporation.

This article first appeared in SQUALL Magazine (www.squall.co.uk). Further information on the McLibel trial can be found at McSpotlight www.mcspotlight.org

Issue 142 - 7th November 1997

Trick Or Treat

On Friday 31st, Hallowe'en, a nasty big opencast coal mine in Derbyshire was put decidedly out of action by the amassed forces of miners, ex-miners, radical ecologists, ghosts, witches and vampires. The action kicked off at 6am at the Doe Hill House site, and enjoyed the passive co-operation (if not support) of the Derbyshire constabulary, whose scant number of officers looked on as an estimated £350,000 of damage was joyously wreaked upon machinery.

Laughter

One activist told SchNEWS "*machinery was dismantled, engines clogged, windows broken, tyres slashed and wiring ripped from vehicles. Several generators and the security lighting rigs 'fell' over the side of steep cliff edges as bemused workers stood back and laughed.*" Rumours that the larger scale damage only began after the proprietors of the mine refused to proffer up sweeties to trick or treating activists are unconfirmed. What is known, however, is that by the time the protesters made good their escape after two or three hours of industrious activity, the site had been pretty comprehensively trashed; a spokesperson for mine owners HJ Banks confirmed, "*every item on site was damaged.*"

Nasty

Opencast mining is nasty - it continues to devour as many acres of prime UK countryside as it did miners' jobs when the deepcast mining industry was killed off (see SchNEWS 139). After a clean get away from the mine, some of the activists moved on to occupy the firm's regional offices where they were eventually arrested on suspicion of burglary. On the day tasty vegan fare was laid on by Manchester's very own Counter Culture Collective - caterers for the frontline.

IF ORDINARY PEOPLE BEHAVED LIKE- BNFL

WHY DO YOU KEEP BUYING STUFF WITH DODGY CHEMICALS IN IT? THIS CUPBOARD'S STUFFED WITH LEAKY CANS OF TOXIC SHITE!

RELAX, WILL YOU? THE KIDS CAN CLEAN IT OUT WHEN THEY'RE OLDER...

Polyp

POLICE ENTER DEAD WOMAN'S BOTTOM

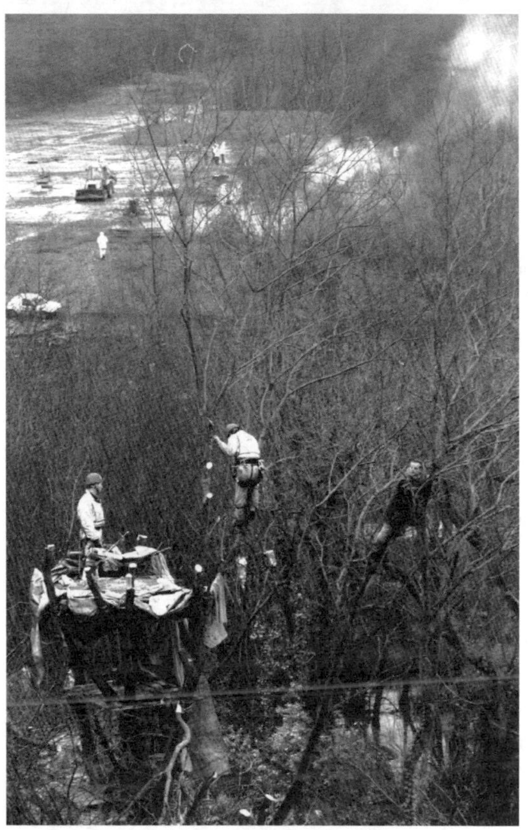

"This area of the East Mendips is the centre of Somerset's major quarrying industry. Virtually one-fifth of the national requirements are met from Somerset." **- Somerset County Council**

As SchNEWS went to press, a game of cat and mouse between protesters, bailiffs and the police is taking place at **Dead Woman's Bottom** near Nunney, Frome. The five protest camps are being illegally evicted by the Under Sheriff of Somerset and his merry men who moved in early Tuesday morning. The protesters are trying to stop the proposed Bull's Green Link Road being built. Although there are only 30 to 40 people on site they are proving impossible to evict effectively.

The authorities are having real problems evicting because some of the camps are on private land, and local landowners who are opposed to the road are refusing to support the powers that be. One told SchNEWS: *"There are vans and vans and vans of riot cops but the Section 69 (a formal warning from a senior cop to leave the land) that they're handing out is basically a get-out-of-jail-free card."*

Despite the fact that there were children on site, no prior warning was given of the eviction. One woman was dragged off and her kids were left alone screaming, while a doctor was assaulted by bailiffs on his *own land.*

INVISIBLE PIXIES

As fast as the bolts for the perimeter fence are set in concrete, they are being mysteriously ripped out by invisible pixies... *"This protest will last for months. We are conducting a guerrilla warfare from the woods."*

Everybody's favourite environmentalists Tarmac are paying for approximately two-thirds of the £3.2M road-scheme - the rest is to be met from the tax-payer. If built, it will give Tarmac easier access to the Halecombe quarry, as well as enable them to trash previously inaccessible areas of the Mendips. The road will cut through Asham Wood, one of the last two ancient woodlands left in the area and home to the endangered Greater Horseshoe bat and Fresh Water Cray fish (no, the fish aren't up a tree, they're in a stream clever-clogs). But don't worry, according to the County Council's Structure Plan this part of the Mendips is a Designated Special Landscape Area! Ironically, while the Council are arguing that the road needs to be built to divert heavy lorries away from five villages, 30% of Halecombe Quarries output is for asphalt for roads and road maintenance.

The Mendips have been the scene of the longest running ecological direct action in the country. The mining causes massive destruction to the environment, lowering and polluting the water table and producing material for large construction projects. As one activist told SchNEWS: *"It is ridiculous that the Mendips are supplying stone to the whole country. Mining should be small-scale and supplied on a regional basis"*

Both pics: Andrew Testa

Brighton Argus February 10th 1998

One paper that does not want to sell out

ACTIVISTS from the controversial Brighton-based national protest newsletter SchNEWS were celebrating this week after launching their 150th issue.

Widely regarded as the bastion of the British underground press, the magazine is run by volunteers who operate a strict no advertising policy, and correspondents have filed copy from as far afield as trees near the Newbury bypass and tunnels under Manchester airport.

A spokesman for the magazine said: "It's amazing that from its humble beginnings, SchNEWS has gone on to do so much.

by RICHARD FORSHAW

"Here's to the next 150 issues, but hopefully some sort of global sanity may occur and make our activities unnecessary."

But direct action organs have often courted controversy in the past, and at a press conference to launch the new 200 page SchNEWS annual, editorial staff were disguised as the Teletubbies in a bid to escape recognition by the authorities they love to hate.

The spokesman pointed out the case of three journalists who wrote about direct action events and were subsequently jailed for three years for conspiracy to incite criminal damage.

"We wore the masks and disguised our voices as a statement to promote a free press in Britain," he said.

Comedians Mark Thomas and poet/musician Attila The Stockbroker recently performed a sell-out benefit gig at the Pavilion Theatre for the birthday celebrations.

The new SchNEWS annual, a compilation of issues 101 to 150, goes on sale tomorrow (Saturday) priced £6 and is available from the Peace Centre in Gardner Street, or by sending an SAE and a cheque payable to Justice?, SchNEWS, c/o On-The-Fiddle, PO Box 2600, Brighton BN2 2DX.

wake up to reality

SchNEWS annual

issues 101 - 150

A MESSAGE TO THE GOVERNMENT...

FROM OUR PANEL OF EXPERTS

WARNING! YOU ARE BEING WATCHED BY CLOSED CIRCUIT TELEVISION

BUY THIS & KEEP SchNEWS FREE!

THE THIRD SCHNEWS COLLECTION FEATURING ISSUES 101 - 150 PLUS: ACTIONS · ARTICLES · REPORTAGE · CONTACTS · CARTOONS & MUCH MORE

SchNEWS Annual

Launched on 10th Feb 1998 with a Mark Thomas gig at the Pavillion Theatre, Brighton.

Covering issues 101-150, Dec 1996-Jan 1998

ISBN: 0-9529748-1-9

Still available see back of book

This annual was mostly the labour of a single minded woman... She recalls...

"...It was such a pleasure to do. The help from people I didn't know that well cemented friendships I still have now. It was a slow process at first, trying to collate the info needed for funding, as SchNEWS had no money in the account to fund it: funding was the first and biggest hurdle as no funding = no book.... we had a meeting in the local with the accounts people of SchNEWS and 3 out of 6 said I should pull the plug as I had no money. This pissed me off soooo much as I had put soooo much work into it already and these "no faithers" were telling me not to bother!!

The very next day there was a letter waiting for me from one of the organisations I had blagged for money, with a fat cheque of 3500 Quid!!!! So I remember walking on air and waiting for the "no faithers" to waltz into the office and passing them the cheque....ha ha... and that was it we were all steam ahead!

One of the funniest things I remember when doing the book was getting about 15 people in the pub for a meeting so we could get captions for the photos that were going into the book. Most of the people who were asked actually turned up (that usually happens when the venue is the local!!!) then I showed each picture and they were passed around and the captions came flooding out. Obviously the more pissed we got the better the captions. It was a fantastic evening and such a bloody laugh!

I'm a technophobic so most of the page layouts were done by hand - the printers thought it very 'quaint'."

Pic: Andrew Testa

From Issue 143, 14th November 1997... South London Tree Camp

Local people have set up a camp at Canbury Gardens in Kingston to protect 76 poplar trees. The trees, that were originally planted to obscure the view of a power station, will be cut as part of a plush housing development, to allow residents a better view of the park. Permission has been given by the Liberal Democrat MP Alan MacMillan. He has been forced into admitting his "conflict of interests", by sitting on the Environment Committee that has given the development permission, and living on the affected street which will "benefit" from the enhanced view of the Thames.

The Gandalf Trial

After a four year police operation, five people who wrote for the radical magazine Green Anarchist and the press officer for the ALF were arrested and charged with ***"conspiring to incite persons unknown on unspecified dates over a five year period to commit unspecified criminal damage".*** Such wide catch all conspiracy laws were aimed at making reporting direct action illegal.

In November 97 three Green Anarchist editors were jailed for three years and the trial for two others was set for spring 98. But, in March 98 in a shock move the three originally convicted were released on bail from prison. One of those released, Steve Booth, told SchNEWS: *"When I was told I could go the lads in the cells were cheering. People inside have a defeatist attitude - but this time it was like "Yes! You've fought the system!". I'm completely shocked and stunned by the whole thing. The guard said he'd never heard of this happening before. We've heard a rumour that the reason we've been let out was that Amnesty in the US was about to list us as political prisoners."*

He was also praised the prisoner support he got commenting: *"I went into prison with bar of soap, biro and toothpaste. I came out with four huge binbags of letters and books!"*

A couple of months later the High Court quashed their convictions. The High Court judges strongly criticised the original judge for misdirecting the jury and giving excessive sentences. One of the three Noel Molland told SchNEWS *"Thanks to all your readers and staff for all the support while we were inside, its been really appreciated, but let's not forget their are still activists in prison who still need our support."*

This didn't stop Hampshire Police and the Crown Prosecution Service carrying on with the prosecution of Animal Liberation Front Press Officer Robin Webb & Green Anarchist General Editor Paul Rogers - with the original trial judge, who had been criticised by the High Court!. It seems that in the weeks following the successful appeal, the CPS came under intense pressure to continue prosecution from the Hampshire police force, desperate to save face.

But in November 1998 the conspiracy trials finally collapsed leaving Hampshire constabulary with serious egg on their face with an estimated bill of around £10 million spent during the four and a half years of Operation Washington. Robin Webb told SchNEWS *"I'm delighted at what the National Union of Journalists referred to as 'an extreme vendetta against me by Hampshire Police' has finally come to an end."*

Read more about the trials on the SchNEWS website: www.schnews.org.uk/hotstuff/gandalf

SIMON JONES

Simon Jones was a writer for SchNEWS, and a close mate of those around Brighton. In 1998 the dole were hassling him so he took a shit job - and on the first day of that job was killed in a work-related accident. He was a victim of casualisation: bring in untrained people because you can pay them less. The company responsible have tried to get away with it. They soon found out they'd picked the wrong people to mess with. The Simon Jones Memorial Campaign was set up by his family and friends to bring this company to justice. This is the story, told using excerpts from SchNEWS

 ***Issue 182 –4th September 1998***

'Casual Killers'

***"Some employers seem to treat their workers like machinery. They're not. They have families and friends who are torn apart when things like this happen to them."* - Anne Jones, Simon's mother**

***Tuesday 1st.* Some people have climbed the 80 foot floodlights and unfurled banners which say 'Simon Jones RIP' and 'Casualisation Kills'.**

On the ground thirty people who have gathered at the docks to commemorate the death of their friend place a wreath. A banner reading "murderers" hangs from the dock gates, which have also been d-locked to stop trucks going in and out. Leaflets explaining what is happening are handed to mainly sympathetic workers. Simon would have been celebrating his 25th birthday today. Eventually the company are forced to close the docks down for the day. Workers are sent home on full pay, probably the first time Euromin have coughed up holiday pay.

Euromin Docks 1st September 1998: Some of Simon's mates climb the crane, and drop a banner from it.

Thursday 3rd. People occupy the offices of Personnel Selection, the temp agency that sent Simon to the docks when he was clearly unsuitable to do such a skilled job. The "murderers" banner is hung from the window, while outside his friends leaflet passers-by. The leaflet asks *"Why should agencies such as Personnel Selection take half your wages when you're doing the work?"*

Eventually Personnel Selection are also forced to shut down for the day, again sending the workers home on full pay with a notice in the window saying this is out of respect for Simon.

Euromin Docks 1st September 1998: Friends and family of Simon Jones blockade and close down the docks on what would have been his 25th birthday

3rd September 1998: The offices of Personnel Selection in Brighton are blockaded and closed down for the day

So what happened to Simon Jones?

Four months ago Simon was sent by Personnel Selection to work at Euromin as a stevedore. But as Emma Aynsley, his girlfriend at the time pointed out *"Simon had no experience of working inside a ship and should never have been allowed to work there. He was doing one of the most dangerous jobs in the country for about £5 per hour, with no training whatsoever. It was like asking someone without a driving licence to drive an articulated lorry."*

Simon had only been working on the ship for about an hour unloading stone when his head was crushed by the grab of a crane. He died instantly. The death of Simon is tragic, but was no accident. In fact it was a direct result of the low paid 'flexible' market workplace which is now endemic throughout the country.

Along the waterfront casualisation has returned to all British docks since the abolition of the National dock scheme in 1989. No holiday or sick pay, no job security, more injuries and deaths. Within four years the accident rate at British docks had leapt by a third. However, the advantages to the companies involved were enormous - a 41% saving in wages caused by 5,000 redundancies and cheaper labour with fewer rights.

Joining Simon's friends on Tuesday was Bob Ritchie, one of the 500 sacked Liverpool Dockers, who told SchNEWS *"We went on strike for over two years to prevent deaths like this, which are inevitable with an untrained, casual workforce. Before casualisation, this sort of thing would never have happened. If these companies are allowed to get away with employing casual staff to do skilled jobs the death toll will just keep rising."*

Which it has. There were 302 deaths from accidents at work last year, 17% more than the year before. Meanwhile the record of Health and Safety Executive is appalling. Out of 50,000 major injuries at work last year 48,000 weren't even investigated by the Executive. Despite New Labour talking about being 'tough on crime, tough on the causes of crime' when it comes to companies like Euromin it goes decidedly soft.

Simon had gone to the agency after hassle from the dole. Under the Job Seekers Allowance unemployed people are forced to take any jobs, however unsuitable or unsafe, under threat of losing benefits. Employment agencies boom in this environment - there are six pages of them in the Brighton Yellow Pages alone. Bharti Patel of the Low Pay Unit believes Simon's situation was not unusual. *"The sanction of benefit withdrawal can mean that people will take any job at any price".* The situation is set to get even worse with the introduction of the New Deal".

The Liverpool Dockers' strike, which continued for longer than the miners' strike of 1985-86, received little media coverage, being viewed by many as a last ditch defence of dinosaur ways that were now a thing of the past. The New Britain of the late 1990's has little time for such 'labour market inflexibility'. During the dockers dispute Tony Blair was already voicing his support for the Tories' creation of *"a more restricted trade union legislative framework than any other country in the western world."*

Simon wrote for SchNEWS, and was a supporter of the direct action movement's decision to join the Dockers in a mass picket on their first year anniversary. Whereas some people couldn't see what we had in common, Simon thought the connection was obvious - the Dockers were fighting the crap-jobs-for-crap-pay system that affects just about everyone. In the end it was a connection that became all too real for him.

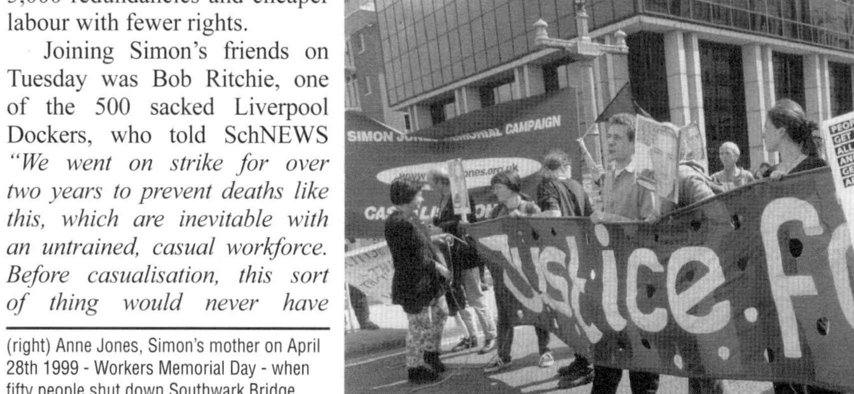

(right) Anne Jones, Simon's mother on April 28th 1999 - Workers Memorial Day - when fifty people shut down Southwark Bridge for an hour to protest against the continued failure of the Health and Safety Executive to bring her son's killers to justice.

As Emma told SchNEWS *"Simon was killed by the bosses he hated. I suppose there was a time when you had unions that went on strike over things like this, but not anymore. You've got to rely on yourselves, on each other, because there's no big organisations out there anymore that are going to make things right. If we want to make things better, it's up to us."*

By closing down Euromin and Personnel Selection for the day we showed that if we work together then we can make a difference. Simon would have been proud.

Issue 203, Friday 5th March 1999

'Casual Killers Part 2'

The Simon Jones Memorial Campaign swung into action again on Wednesday invading the Department of Trade and Industry and occupying the lobby for an hour (*see pic below*) to demand the prosecution of employment agency, Personnel Selection. Nearly a year on and despite every legal channel being exhausted as well as a series of high-profile actions no-one has been prosecuted over his death.

Meanwhile on the same day in Parliament George Galloway MP thundered "James Martell's (Euromin manager) contempt for the laws of health and safety in this country, his greed and hunger for profit, his negligence and carelessness, slaughtered this young man just as clearly as if he had pushed him off the dock with his own hands."

Simon's death highlights the spread of low-pay and casualisation across Britain; as a spokesperson from the Memorial Campaign told SchNEWS "If you want to kill someone, the easist way to get away with it is to do it at work."

Issue 210, Friday 30th April 1999

'A Bridge Too Far'

On Wednesday (Workers Memorial Day), fifty people including Simon's family, gathered outside the Health and Safety Executive HQ in London to pay their respects with a minute's silence. Health and Safety have done nothing to bring Simon's killers to justice, so people decided to occupy Southwark Bridge for an hour, stopping the traffic by unfurling banners across the street and blowing whistles and shouting. Despite this direct action, when Simon's parents and a few of the group gained access to the director of the Executive, Jenny Bacon, she fobbed them off, telling Simon's aunt to "shush"! This high ranking government official denied receiving 5 letters sent by Simon's mum, and claimed that investigating 1 in 20 serious injuries in workplaces was acceptable due to budget restrictions. Jenny Bacon chose not to respond when asked what chance people would have of having their grievances heard, if they didn't occupy bridges in central London.

Issue 252, 24th March, 2000

High Court Victory

Supporters of the Simon Jones Memorial Campaign are celebrating a landmark victory in the High Court. Simon was killed on his first day of work at Shoreham docks, yet the Crown Prosecution Service refused to prosecute the company responsible saying they didn't have enough evidence. One jubilant supporter told SchNEWS that the CPS "were torn to bits" in the courtroom at their decision not to prosecute Euromin for corporate manslaughter. "Every decision the CPS have made about corporate manslaughter is now open to re-examination."

Issue 333, 30th November 2001

'Licence to Kill'

"The judge has decided Simon's life is only worth fifty thousand pounds." **- Tim Jones, Simon's brother.**

"The law's refusal to punish these serious crimes is just one more indication of how little importance our law makers give to casual workers' health, safety and right to life." **- Simon Jones Memorial Campaign.**

Bosses up and down the country were yesterday celebrating the fact that killing your workers won't get you locked up behind bars after a jury trial at the Old Bailey. Richard James Martell, general manager of Dutch-owned Euromin, based at Shoreham, was found not guilty of manslaughter and his company found not guilty of corporate manslaughter over the death of Simon Jones in 1998. Instead they were given a £50,000 fine with £20,000 costs for breaking health and safety regulations.

Simon was just another statistic, one of the hundreds of people who die at work every year, while the companies that employ them get off scot-free or have to pay pathetic fines. As the Simon Jones Campaign said, "We are painfully aware that in 21st century Britain the fight for the most basic of workers' rights - the right not to be killed or injured at work - is still being fought. The Crown Prosecution Service has put obstacles and obstructions in the path of this prosecution at every turn. The Health and Safety Executive have consistently shown themselves to be either unwilling or unable to take the necessary action against employers to ensure the safety of workers."

It took over three and a half years from the day Simon was killed for the trial to get to court. The Crown Prosecution Service (CPS) had to be dragged kicking and screaming every step of the way until in an historic U-turn they were told by two High Court judges that they were adopting an approach that was "baffling" and "beggared belief" over their refusal to prosecute. That it even got this far was because of a relentless campaign by family and friends.

So what does this now mean? That scumbags like James Martell can carry on cutting safety corners to squeeze an extra pound of flesh, and temp agencies like Personnel Selection will carry on sending anyone anywhere as long as they can keep half their wages?

SchNEWS knows that under the present law it is almost impossible to find anyone guilty of corporate manslaughter charges and no doubt there will be calls for the laws of the land to be changed. But we also know that it isn't just laws that need to be changed, but a whole new world built, one where people are more important than profit, where people like Simon Jones aren't killed just to make some boss or shareholder a little richer.

Issue 351, Friday 26th April 2002 update

12 towns and cities took part in Wednesday's day of action against casualisation organised by the Simon Jones Memorial Campaign. In Brighton 80 people including a band, lots of balloons and an old dragon demonstrated outside Personnel Selection, the temp agency that sent Simon to his death. The company decided to shut down for the afternoon 'as a mark of respect'.

After word: Direct Action's role...

It is significant, as one of Simon's friends said, that perhaps the most high-profile campaign about a workplace death in this country has had no union involvement. "Direct action basically grew out of the inaction of the left and the unions. As one of the Liverpool Dockers said when we occupied Euromin, 'A few years ago, it would have been workers coming out that shut that dock, not protesters going in.' Direct action is seen as something slightly eccentric - admirable, but 'single issue', cut off from 'real' politics - whereas, in fact, it's just doing what working-class and progressive organisations have always done, but have now been effectively stopped from doing with a mixture of carrot and stick. It's pretty scary that protesting when some capitalist bastard kills your mate is considered unusual."

For more visit www.simonjones.org.uk

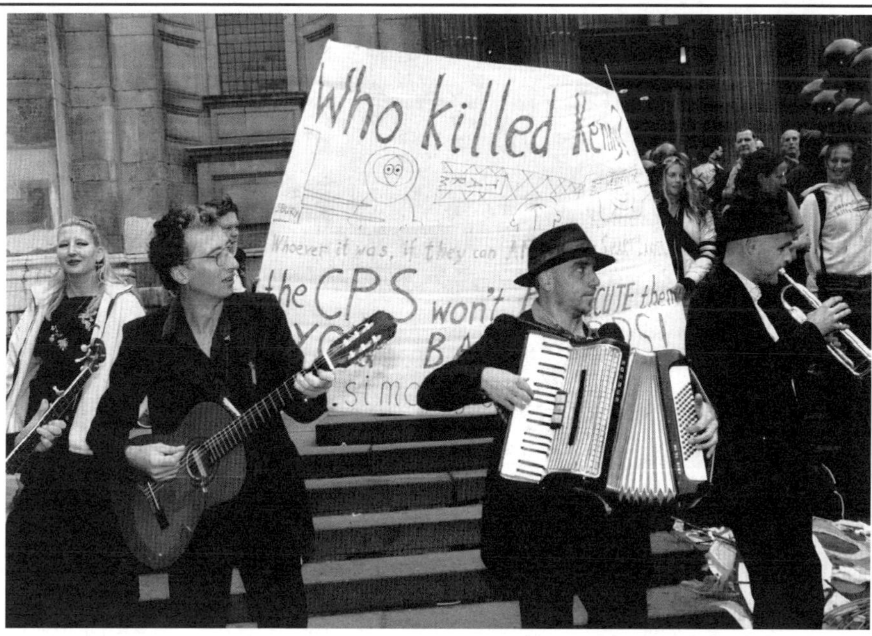

(right) On what would have been Simon's birthday, 1st September 2000, perennial rent-a-lairy-mob Tragic Roundabout belt out a tune outside St Paul's Cathedral, where a crowd have gathered to march on the London offices of the Crown Prosecution Service, who were yet to bring charges against Euromin. This didn't stop the police arresting one protester for affray on the day!

Pic: Richie Andrews

Knowing Who Your Friends Are

Our son, Simon Jones, showed us a few articles he had written for SchNEWS, I guess it was late 1997 or early 1998. He had been to Lyminge Forest in Kent, where some big firm was trying to buy up hundreds of acres of ancient woodland, which people had wandered freely in for centuries, fence it off and build a holiday village. After Simon was killed at Euromin in Shoreham in April 1998, the obituary in SchNEWS described him as "a sane, sharp geezer", well I wouldn't mind that for an epitaph. A lot of the SchNEWS people made the long return trip from Brighton to Banbury for Simon's funeral; this was the first time we met them. They struck us as stark, uncompromising and totally honest, both in appearance and ways. We soon found out how much they cared about Simon and the callous way he was killed. They were at the occupation of Euromin, of the department of Trade and Industry, and many other demos and court cases.

If you rely entirely on donations to run a newspaper, you can print the truth as you see it. Obviously the mainstream media have serious constraints; even basically decent organisations like the Guardian, Independent and Channel 4 have to keep their advertisers happy, and those are all driven to some extent by greed. Private Eye is particularly disappointing: it claims to be satirical and anti-establishment, but it's a very depressing read because it says in effect that various organisations have got the country sewn up, and there's nothing you or I can do about it. SchNEWS can make you feel angry, but not despondent, because it reports on those people who are trying to stop corporate greed and government corruption, and who sometimes, as at Lyminge Forest, succeed.

As for trade unions, they have bitterly disappointed us. When the Simon Jones Memorial Campaign needed money for either a judicial review or a private prosecution, we got £1000 from one enormous, powerful union, £250 from a very much smaller one, and lots of inventive excuses from the rest, including "Simon wasn't a member of a union" and "We have to be careful not to encourage direct action; we could have our funds sequestered". You can imagine how well this one went down with people who were putting their health and liberty on the line confronting the police at demos.

We wrote a leaflet for jobseekers, which a person fairly high up in PCS union had said they would help to distribute. We sent it, together with a photo of Simon, to their head office. Three months later they replied to our e-mail, denying all knowledge of our letter. We e-mailed the leaflet, they said OK we'll use it, another six months passed, we got in touch again, they said sorry, we can't do it, it won't be effective, here's your photo back. Cheers, guys.

Remember a left-wing union activist in the1960's, name of John Prescott? Look at him now, Blair's hired thug. Thirty pieces of silver and he's anybody's. Do you suppose today's so-called militants are any different?

With Schnews, what you see is what you get. No hidden agendas, plenty of effective protest. If the police stop harassing you, you'll know you're not doing your job. As Alan Dalton, the asbestos and work safety campaigner, who died last year, summed up his life: "Be annoying".

Anne and Chris Jones
16 August 2004

NEW LIFE FOR ANIMAL RIGHTS
lethal injections for vivisection labs

"Experience of the past should remind us that governments - no matter what their persuasion - are great at making pre-election promises in order to get themselves into power, but once in the coveted position, will only deliver on them if they see potential political gain or if they are pushed so hard they cannot resist."

- Arkangel Website.

When Neo-Labour published its document, *"New Labour, New Life for Animals"* before the 1997 general election, it hoped to gain a few more votes from animal lovers up and down the country. This document promised, amongst other things, to set up a Royal Commission of Inquiry into Vivisection, which was a complete lie - it has never happened.

While many were persuaded by Neo Labour's empty promises, others were more sceptical. The fights against **Consort Beagles, Hillgrove Cat Farm, Shamrock Monkey Farm, Regal Rabbits, Huntingdon Life Sciences, the Cambridge primate vivisection lab, Harlan Firgrove** and more are all inspiring examples of people not believing government lies and taking it upon themselves to stop animal cruelty.

Shamrock Monkey Farm Pic: Alec Smart

Consorted Effort

In 1997, animal rights activists were in the middle of a campaign against Consort Beagles, a supplier of dogs to the vivisection industry. The campaign saw the adoption of new tactics - to hit Consort wherever they could and cost them as much money as possible. The campaign against Consort included regular large, angry demonstrations – these demonstrations brought together campaigners from across the country - these were inspired by the massive demonstrations against live exports that had given those involved in animal rights a moral boost.

At the World Day for Laboratory Animals demo held at Consort in April 1997, 500 people turned up. One eyewitness told SchNEWS, "People were pretty upset at seeing the beagles and started ripping the fences apart. Riot police turned up as people got through the perimeter fence and into the building". Police responded with the usual baton charges, but also used their new weapon - CS spray. A sixteen-year-old asthmatic described the effects of CS spray: "I could hardly breathe, my eyes and nose were streaming. It was like I was having a fit. Someone called an ambulance, but the ambulance personnel hadn't a clue what to do - they were asking the police how to treat it. They had obviously had no training with CS spray."

At the next national demonstration against Consort, 200 people turned up and were attacked by riot police. Police tactics included hitting a 71year-old woman over the head and then arresting her for Affray. A police dog, after biting two protesters, turned on its handler, obviously realising the police weren't there for the benefit of his canine comrades inside. Some protesters then moved on to the home of Gordon Gilder, who is involved in animal transportation. Here police deployed CS gas with deliberate cold, calculated vindictiveness. The police went up to groups of protesters and sprayed them point blank in the face for such hideous crimes as leaning on a gate. 30 people later received upwards of £1,000 fines for Kidnapping, Assault, Wrongful Arrest and Malicious Prosecution. One woman received £10,000 after she was repeatedly sprayed in the face, hair, and mouth while handcuffed. The good side to all of this is that after much struggle on the part of animal rights activists, Consort was finally closed down.

Coming From All Angles

The closure of Consort Beagles in July 1997 gave the animal rights movement a massive boost. Next to go were Hillgrove Cat Farm and Shamrock

Monkey Farm. Hillgrove was especially notorious for supplying kittens as young as thirteen days old to vivisection laboratories. When the campaign against Hillgrove started up, Chief Inspector Charles Pollard of Thames Valley police said, "The numbers of protesters will dwindle and fade away." Ooops, I think you were wrong there mate. Numbers certainly didn't fade away. In addition to the big regular regional and national demos, there were daily demos and night vigils at the entrance to the farm, and firms supplying all sorts of materials to the 'Farm' were persuaded to stop their dealings.

Concerned members of the public flooded Hillgrove with phone calls and faxes during office hours so that genuine customers couldn't get through. Mr Brown, Hillgrove's owner, and his wife found themselves receiving all sorts of things they had never ordered, from books to porcelain statues of Elvis (sent to them after people had 'mistakenly' put Brown's address on the 'send no money now' forms found in magazines). When Brown received a letter bomb courtesy of the Justice Department it was clear he had become a major target.

"Thank god there are people willing to sacrifice their liberty for the sake of defenceless animals, and prove that common humanity does still exist in this so-called civilised society."
– Marilyn Tyrrell, 94-year old Hillgrove supporter – Oxford Mail 27/1/98

At many demonstrations, the protesters often had the upper hand. At one demo, thousands of people tried to storm the farm, ripping down fences and pelting Brown's house with rocks that smashed probably every window as well as extensively damaging the roof. The policing costs were massive amounting to £1.5 million by the end of the campaign.

Shamrock Farm had been the target of low-level campaigns for years, but the Consort and Hillgrove campaigns inspired the people involved to take it further. Shamrock was a hell hole for primates that had been exposed by an undercover investigator from the BUAV who worked at Shamrock, keeping detailed diaries of goings on and filming conditions. He exposed the day to day brutality, where monkeys were punched, pulled out of the cages by their tails and repeatedly stabbed with a needle to try and take a blood sample.

When police imposed exclusion orders around Hillgrove and Shamrock, campaigners instead went to the city centres of Brighton and Oxford. There was no way they were going to simply go home. They had a message to take to the public and they certainly made it heard. If the police think that by simply stopping campaigners from going to the hell-holes that the campaigners will simply give in, then they have been proved wrong. At one Oxford demo, police took to arresting journalists. Thames Valley Police press officer Janet Malcomson claimed, "Press cards are forged by animal rights activists and they pose as reporters." Er, right, all press cards are registered at Scotland Yard with PIN digits known to the reporter in the event of a police query.

Once the campaigns really got going there was no stopping them. The companies were hit from every angle. If someone supplied a product to Hillgrove or

Hillgrove Cat Farm 18th April 1998 Pic: Andrew Testa

Shamrock, they were persuaded to stop. A constant presence at the premises made day to day business uncomfortable. Those staff that weren't wise enough to leave immediately found themselves receiving mass demos outside their homes. One Hillgrove worker finally gave in after her house was taken over for the day by a bunch of cops awaiting a home demo - apparently the mess they made with their muddy size elevens was just too much! Lynda King, vet and Managing Director of Shamrock, had many windows smashed at the stroke of the new millennium. A couple of months later there was an arson attack on her garage which destroyed two cars.

Both campaigns succeeded: After many rumours Hillgrove closed on 13th August 1999. 800 cats were saved from vivisection and re-homed. The closure of Shamrock was more sudden, on 10th March 2000, Shamrock announced that it was to close as soon as all the monkeys were re-homed. Although this turned out to be a lie as all the monkeys were sent to labs, no more animals will suffer there anymore.

Campaigners from Shamrock then turned their attention to Regal Rabbits. After a site invasion and a raid by the Animal Liberation Front, it took a mere 12 days of campaigning to close down Regal Rabbits, who had supplied rabbits to the vivisection industry for 22 years. The owner asked what he could do to stop the protests. 'Close down' came the simple reply - and he did.

Love Shac

But other nuts have been harder to crack. After Consort and Hillgrove closed, the campaigners involved turned their attentions away from the suppliers of animals to the users of animals – they targeted **Huntingdon Life Sciences** (HLS), Europe's biggest contract animal-testing facility. The (soon to be) notorious **SHAC (Stop Huntingdon Animal Cruelty)** was born.

HLS kill around 500 animals each day in order to test agrochemicals, cosmetics, potential drugs and other products for humans. And while they defend their activities saying that they are conducting essential medical research, the majority of their work is for the chemical industry – testing things like oven cleaner and pesticides. HLS has been exposed five times by undercover investigations showing animal cruelty, have a criminal record from a British court of law for breaking the Companies' Act and are the only UK laboratory to ever have their animal testing license revoked by the government – although they got it back later.

This was a much bigger target than the previous animal suppliers and the campaign has been going for nearly five years. But SHAC are not daunted and say, "We never give in and we always win!" They have had a massive impact: Huntingdon are the only commercial company in existence that has been forced off the New York stock exchange and the London Stock Exchange. No commercial insurance company or bank in the world will touch them and they have had to be rescued by the government from immediate closure – the Bank of England now provides their financial services. Animal rights activists have been able to do what anti-capitalists have failed to do – bring a huge corporation to its knees. In 1992, Huntingdon was valued at $500 million dollars. Today they are valued at about $30 million and are $89 million in debt. In 2006 they

ANIMAL RIGHTS PRISONERS

The success of the animal rights movement has been paid for by many who end up serving lengthy prison sentences, for anything from minor public order offences through to arson. But the animal rights movement has an extremely good prisoner support network, which includes the Animal Liberation Front Supporters Group and the Vegan Prisoners Support Group. There is an anecdote that a fascist in prison for a racist attack became disillusioned with his movement when he saw the amount of letters an animal rights prisoner was getting. Which just goes to show you should write to a prisoner, not your MP!

One prisoner worth mentioning is Barry Horne. Barry Horne had carried out an arson campaign against Boots and Boots subsidiaries to force them out of animal testing. He was given a massive eighteen year sentence for the attacks, in which no one was hurt. He tried to carry on the struggle in prison and went on hunger strikes.

His first hunger strike was when the Tories were still in power; he ended that after Labour promised action when they came to power, outlined in the 'New Labour New Life for Animals' leaflet. His third hunger strike was the longest - he went on hunger strike to make Labour live up to their pre-election promise of a Royal Commission on vivisection. After 60 days, the Home Office met with Barry's representatives. On day 66, a fax from Labour MP Kerry Pollard promised a parliamentary consultative body. Barry's hunger strike finished after 68 days, but he was extremely ill and his body never recovered from the effects. Soon afterwards, George Howarth, the then Home Office minister responsible for animal experiments, told the media that there had never been any negotiations. On a hunger strike three years later which only lasted two weeks, Barry died of liver failure - a legacy of that third hunger strike and Labour's broken promise.
For more on Barry Horne see:
www.arkangelweb.org/barry

will have to pay back $50 million in bonds. The future looks bleak for HLS.

Once again, it is the commitment of activists and the tactics involved that have proved to be the conclusive factor in the campaign being so successful. Many of the actions taken don't need you to belong to any group or need you to be an up-for-it activist. SHAC say that emails and phone calls to HLS and their customers and suppliers are very effective: "Never underestimate how important these calls are. Many companies that have dealt with Huntingdon have ditched them due to the calls they have received from members of the public voicing their concerns and talking to their staff." Demonstrations are of course a major factor in the campaign; they "can be anything from 2,000 people marching round Cambridge city centre to one person putting stickers up - the point is they all count."

The belief that every action that is performed is another blow to HLS is central to much of SHAC's campaigning. But to increase the effectiveness of individual actions, there are co-ordinated days for people to phone or email a particular company.

SHAC knows that static demos alone are not effective - large demonstrations are routinely followed up with home demonstrations at the homes of workers. Moving around like this makes it harder for the police to keep up, and also stretches their resources. It also means HLS and their customers and suppliers never know where they are going to be hit next.

The targeting of suppliers has been effective with hundreds of companies pulling out, many after only being informed that they are a target of SHAC. The targeting of "secondary" targets, rather than HLS itself, is a tactic that has proved remarkably effective. HLS aren't gonna give in because they've had a few demos, but suppliers and investors realize that HLS is only a small part of their business.

The SHAC campaign has also been met with police and legal repression. One of the most common pieces of legislation used is the Protection from Harassment Act. This act, despite being touted as being designed to protect women from stalkers, was first used against animal rights protesters. Many injunctions have been granted to HLS and their customers which inhibit a large number of previously legal activities - like making phone calls and having demonstrations. Also used heavily by the police is Section 42 of the Criminal Justice and Police Act 2001, which was specifically brought in to deal with demonstrations outside someone's home. The police can move you on and if you don't, then you face arrest. Another tactic of the police has been the use of Anti-Social Behaviour Orders (ASBOs require a lower burden of proof than a criminal conviction, although the penalty for breaking an ASBO can be up to five years in jail). ASBOs have been targeted at particularly vocal activists in order to try to restrict their activities. Animal rights activists have been at the forefront of having the law tested out on them. The inventiveness of the campaign and its meticulous research into targets, however, has meant the campaign tries to stay one step ahead of the authorities at all times.

Monkey Wrench

After a period of attrition for the Animal Rights movement, another victory has recently been achieved that gave it a new boost. In January 2004, Cambridge University announced that it would not be building a primate vivisection lab. The SPEAC campaign, who had campaigned tirelessly, said, "It was the threat, often put into action, of constant protest at the entire University, and the negative impact we were having on their donors worldwide. We hit them where they were most vulnerable - their finances - and left them with no choice."

The case of the primate vivisection lab is a study into government corruption. Planning permission for the lab had been refused twice. The Planning Inspector who declined permission said, "I could not conclude that need in the national interest is demonstrated insofar as this pertains to the scientific/medical research and procedures undertaken by the University." In other words, an independent person who looked at all the evidence said there wasn't any need for the centre. But this didn't stop John Prescott overruling the Inspector's decision and giving the go ahead. Prescott's decision was based entirely on the word of Lord Sainsbury who is the Science Minister, Neo Labour's biggest financial backer, and who has a vested and personal interest in the biotechnology industry.

The SPEAC campaign is now concentrating on opposing a vivisection lab being built by Oxford University and halted construction when building firm Montpelier pulled out, forcing Oxford Uni to find another builder.

Following on this success, another breeder closed soon afterwards - Harlan Firgrove in East Sussex, which bred rabbits and guinea pigs for vivisection. Harlan Firgrove closed after a four year campaign by a handful of dedicated people. After the demonstrations started, the company erected a huge galvanised steel fence around the whole perimeter and bought 12 security cameras. They also took out an injunction to try and stop some of the protesters - it cost them £70,000 and they failed.

The recent upsurge in animal rights success has brought a flurry of media lies from the vivisection industry and tough talking from the Home Secretary about cracking down on animal rights extremists. But still no news on that Royal Commission of Inquiry into Vivisection. New Labour, New Life for Animals? Don't hold your breath.

Hunt Sabbing: Upping The Anti

The Hunt Saboteurs Association - the first direct action animal rights group in Britain - reached its fortieth birthday this year. Forty years of groups of concerned individuals with no central funding or command intervening in and disrupting the sport of the aristocracy and the establishment.

Pic: Nick Cobbing

Of course sabbing is all about saving animals from a cruel death at the hands of hunters, shooters and anglers. When the fox bursts from its hiding place in the cover, scant feet ahead of the lead hounds whose baying and yelping presage the kill to come, the adrenalin kicks in and you run forward with your whip raised preparing to drive back them back. In that moment you're not concerned about land ownership, police bias or the class composition of the hunt. All that comes later. Saving a hunted animal in this way is one of the most direct and satisfying political actions it is possible to take. It's not a media stunt or a form of indirect lobbying; it's simple direct intervention.

The HSA, under the wonderfully named Johnny Prestige, split from the lobby-based League Against Cruel Sports in 1964. As soon as they got into the fields and began saving lives instead of waiting for Parliament to ban cruelty, they encountered the heavy hand of the state. The first hunt sab to end up before the courts was Norman Redman, who was bound over to keep the peace following an incident on the Chiddingfold Hunt in Sussex. It was felt that he should leave the movement in order to avoid negative publicity, something which seems hilarious in the light of how arbitrary arrest is now considered an occupational hazard by sabs. Ever since then despite the fact that almost everything sabs did was legal until the Criminal Justice Act 1994 the police and local squirearchies everywhere combined to combat the activities of the hunt saboteurs.

Street (Somerset) Hunt Sab Association pose for the press during the Culmstock court case, 1964. In the first year of the HSA, there were 120 strikes, mostly in the West Country, and the Street HSA - run by Joyce Cebo - had 40 members

http://hsa.enviroweb.org

Cut To The Chase

No sab expects a fair deal from the police and the movement has produced many more anarchists than have ever joined it. The sight of a red-coated toff protected by the boys in blue as he embarks on a killing spree on his vast estate is enough to produce a lurch towards the black and green in anyone.

Early sabbing missions sound like chaotic affairs with road blocks and abuse and smoke bombs being hurled at the hunt and a lot of experimentation with methods of disruption. It took sabs a few years to understand the arcane mysteries of hunting - that it is the hounds under the control of the huntsman that do the killing - that the terrier-men are in control of the grim business of digging out - that a terrier will be placed into a burrow where a fox has taken refuge and they will fight until the terrier man digs them both out and throws the fox to the waiting hounds or shoots it. The majority of the hunt are simply spectators. Once this was understood sabs began to learn the skills of horn blowing and how to misdirect hounds by covering the fox's musky scent with citronella spray. As a last resort home made whips can be used to make the loud crack which drives back the hounds and keeps their quarry alive. This remains the day in day out business of sabbing fox or hare hunts.

In the late eighties and early nineties there were up to 150 autonomous groups of sabs operating across Britain, often going out three or four times a week. The same period saw a take off of Animal Liberation Front actions .The message of veganism and revolution was being spread by the likes of Conflict (Personally I used to hate punk at four o'clock on a hungover morning but it certainly seemed to get a few folk going).

This network meant that a system of regional and national hits emerged, where different groups would back each other up in the face of hunt violence and heavy policing. Hunts know that an assault on a sab can lead to them being targeted by a much bigger group the next week or in the case of a national hit being descended on by hundreds. This became necessary because of hunt immunity from the law (O.K some hunt supporters have been arrested for assault but a conditional discharge is usually their fate). Over the years two hunt sabs Mike Hill and Thomas Worby have been killed - both by being run over - yet neither of the drivers was proseceuted for anything other than careless driving. Assaults from huntsmen which would land any ordinary criminal and certainly any sab in jail are routinely dealt with very leniently by the courts.

Pic: Alec Smart

As the prospect of a hunting ban looms closer (Although I'm not holding my breath, we've been here before), people continue to intervene on behalf of hunted wild life, simply because once you've seen them kill (and there is no quick nip to the back of the neck) and witnessed the brutal arrogance of a countryside elite who consider it their god-given right to do as they please with the land and its inhabitants it's difficult to stop. There is great pleasure in disrupting the hunt and watching the red fox run free in the face of the police and hunt thugs. Join us and help wipe the smile off a huntsman's face.**www.huntsabs.org.uk**

 ***Hunt Sabbing*** ***Issue 274 –8th September 2000***

RIDING ROUGH SHOD

Croydon hunt saboteur Steve Christmas lies fighting for his life in intensive care this week after being run down last Friday by a thugs' Land Rover in what appears to be a premeditated attack at one of the first hunt meets of the season. Steve was one of four sabs disrupting the Old Surrey, Burstow and West Kent foxhunt near Horsted Keynes, where the hunt were 'cubbing'- the cuddly term for letting your dogs tear foxcubs to bits to get a taste for blood. Tired of killing small woodland creatures, the hunt apparently thought they'd turn their hand to something bigger.

Steve was airlifted to Haywards Heath hospital with four broken ribs, a crushed pelvis, a damaged lung and severe internal bleeding. He's had to have two operations- one to remove a metre of his intestine and one to fit a metal plate to his pelvis- and is breathing through a ventilator. Tubes are inserted in his heart and doctors fear his lung may have collapsed. His condition remains critical.

This was the second assault sabs had suffered that day: twenty minutes earlier, three inbred thugs (from the same 4x4 which later ran o ver Steve), aided by huntsman Mark Bycroft, started attacking the protestors. One sab was knocked over by the vehicle as they tried to flee the field; luckily they got away uninjured and briefly carried on sabbing, until the scum in the 4x4 returned - with tragic results. After nearly killing Steve the driver came back to taunt Steve's mates as they tried to help him.

Dawn Preston, spokesperson for the Hunt Saboteurs Association, stated: "This incident shows both the hunters and hunt supporters blatant disregard for life - whether it be human or animal. It must be a sick and twisted individual indeed who is so fearful of his favourite 'sport' being banned that he tries to kill those who seek to prevent him from torturing our wildlife. Do not forget that two hunt saboteurs have already been killed in the last ten years - and at one stage today I was terrified that another name could be added to that list. How many lives have to be lost before we see an end to this abhorrent sport and those that partake of it?"

Sabs congregated the following day outside the hunts' kennels in Felbridge, Surrey to 'discuss' the matter with hunt staff - and were met by country chaps wielding pick-axe handles. The cops were there, predictably - and equally predictably made no arrests. The kennels are home to huntsman Mark 'One Ball' Bycroft, convicted in 1991 for assaulting a sab and notorious for his violent overreactions to the presence of 'antis': a man so unpopular his own mother wrote to sabs to inform them of her beloved son's genital inadequacy. A further demo happened on Wednesday evening, at the home of the hunt master, and passed without incident.

What a load of horseshit

Pic: Andrew Testa

Sussex police have apparently arrested, interviewed and released a man on police bail in connection with the 4x4 incident. The hunt has claimed he is 'nothing to do with them'. Obviously random passers-by have developed the habit of driving into fields, exchanging matey greetings with complete strangers on horseback and then beating the crap out of anyone with non-leather footwear.

Thankfully, incidents as serious as this are very few and far between. Sabs are needed out there in the field NOW- the full hunting season doesn't start until October, but the brutal spectacle of cubbing is now in full swing.

HUNTSMANBALLS...

...to replace Mark Bycrofts' missing one perhaps? A few gems of foot-in-mouth from the hunting set:

"Tolerance, understanding and dialogue are what we all seek. Indeed, confrontation is not the country way." - Countryside Alliance, January 1999

"Horsewhipping a saboteur is rather like beating a wife. Both are personal matters." Master of Essex fox hunt in 1970

"The huge majority of hunt saboteurs are urban dwellers and several appear not to have washed for quite a while" - David Greenwood, ex-master, Ampleforth Beagles. Hmm maybe they've got us there.

STEVE CHRISTMAS UPDATE

Steve has survived but is left with permanent injuries including a double groin hernia that is inoperable due to previous hernia operations. He was recently awarded £18,500 compensation for his injuries, but his four year legal fight has cost him £22,000.

The driver of the vehicle that ran him over, Matthew Maynard was found not guilty by Judge Thorpe, who said: "The only thing I will say to the defendant is this was a regrettable accident because he has a slightly unfortunate antecedent history [i.e he has a record of violence] so he is going to have to be fairly careful in support of the hunts and I say that because I have just seen the press have come into court." He got off with a £75 fine for driving without insurance or license.

Steve says "My feelings are that the hunt thugs have shown their true colours to the whole country recently and it is disgusting that I had to wait four years for recognition that I was the victim of this incident. However I feel vindicated in that the Criminal Injuries Compensation Board has been forced to accept that I was the victim of a violent attack in which a vehicle was used as a weapon"

A demonstration at the kennels the day after the attack resulted in an incident where some windows of the huntsman's house were broken. Following this 26 protesters were later arrested in a series of dawn raids for 'violent disorder', subsequently changed to 'conspiracy to commit violent disorder' as there was no proof who committed any acts of violence. The prosecution argued that this 'conspiracy' happened in the minute walking up the lane to the kennels! Proof of this conspiracy was people wearing black hooded tops (which is what most sabs wear all the time, even down the pub) and that the protesters weren't carrying placards (don't you know that's the only way you're allowed to protest) and a leaflet produced AFTER the incident happened!

Despite the wide ranging investigation only five people were convicted. The five escaped jail sentences but had to do community service instead; the judge said they would have gone to jail if he thought they had committed any violence. But if they didn't commit violence why were they found guilty – because someone else was violent?

Justice? It's a question we keep asking ourselves.

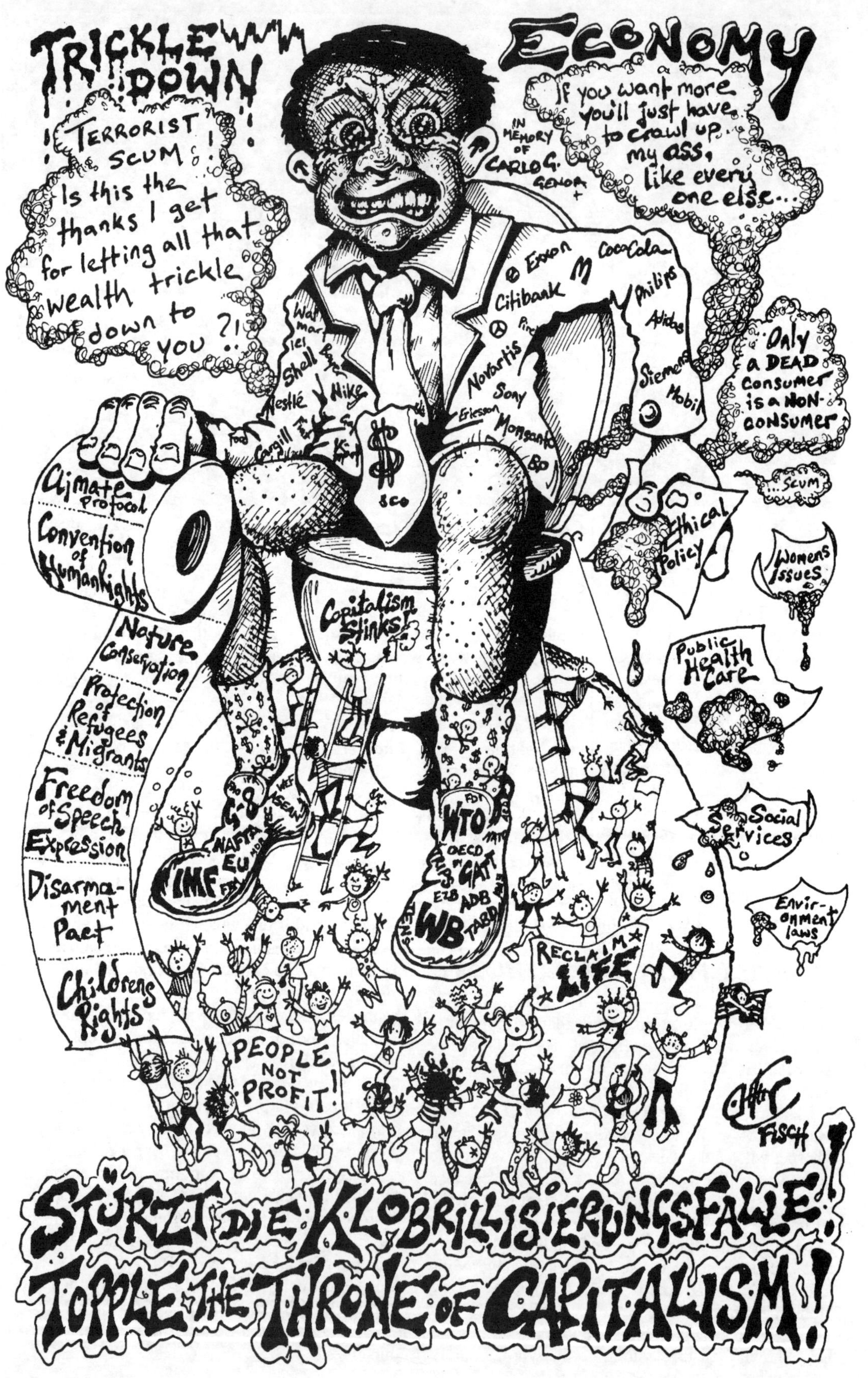
TRICKLE DOWN
ECONOMY
TERRORIST SCUM! Is this the thanks I get for letting all that wealth trickle down to you ?!..
If you want more you'll just have to crawl up my ass, like every one else...
IN MEMORY OF CARLO G. GENOA
Only a DEAD consumer is a NON-CONSUMER
...SCUM
Exxon
CocaCola
Citibank
Philips
Adidas
Novartis
Shell
Nike
Nestlé
Sony
Ericsson
Monsanto
Cargill
Siemens
Mobil
Climate protocol
Convention of HumanRights
Nature Conservation
Protection of Refugees & Migrants
Freedom of Speech Expression
Disarmament Pact
Childrens Rights
Ethical Policy
Womens Issues
Public Health Care
Social Services
Environment laws
Capitalism Stinks!
IMF
NAFTA
EU
WTO
OECD
GATT
ADB
WB
RECLAIM LIFE
PEOPLE NOT PROFIT!
FISCH
STÜRZT DIE KLOBRILLISIERUNGSFALLE!
TOPPLE THE THRONE OF CAPITALISM!

Part 4
SchNEWS Goes Global

March 1998 was the first meeting of the People's Global Action (PGA) in Geneva, which SchNEWS people attended, along with others from around eighty countries. Roughly from this point SchNEWS – along with many others – began to become part of a global struggle fighting the targets of global capitalism and neo-liberalism. Coinciding with the rise of the internet and web access, the PGA began organising international days of action against specific targets.

We then started having to buy the Financial Times so we could get our heads around the alphabet soup of free trade acronyms like the IMF, WTO, GATS, TRIPS, etc. Of course, this doesn't mean we abandoned covering ecological direct action or local stuff...

This meeting was the direct follow on from the first 'Encuentro against Neo-Liberalism' held by the Zapatistas in Mexico in 1996, and brought these currents to Europe for the first time. This meeting was the forerunner to the Peoples Global Action

Close Encuentro

"The voices and words are like many springs of life, water in a world being scorched by greed, cruelty and neo-liberalism. We have begun to dig the channels for the water to flow amongst themselves so it may reach all corners of the planet." - Zernep, Turkey

In the killer heat, amongst the giant mosquitoes of El Indiano, the conference in a squatted farm begins. Meanwhile in a Spanish bullring, two masked Mexicans take to the stage. In an intoxicating atmosphere, these representatives of the Zapatista rebel army are given an ecstatic welcome. This is Plaza de Toros, in a rundown district of Madrid, and the inauguration ceremony of the Second Intergalactic Encuentro for Humanity and Against Neo-Liberalism (catchy!). More than 3,000 people have travelled from over 60 countries for nine days across Spain to create a 'network of resistance'.

The sheer scale and concept of this remarkable conference is difficult to describe. With such a multilingual gathering of tribes, translation itself is a key problem, but, it is said, "we speak many languages, but ours is the language of Utopia". It is a gathering of people "who dared to dream"- an open, embracing encounter for the oppressed people of the world. And the oppressed people of the world are having one helluva Fiesta! "We are here to discuss how the current economic policies are affecting our everyday lives all over the world," says Lucia, eyes twinkling above the red scarf disguising her identity. "We need to find a way of creating a global network of organisations that have the power to resist these economic polices."

The Zapatista Army of National Liberation (EZLN) came out of the jungle on New Year's Day 1994 to occupy six towns in Mexico, taking their name from the unfinished revolution of 1910 led by Emile Zapata, and inspiring those fighting for a better world. Or as Andrew from Ireland told SchNEWS "It came after the fall of Communism, the Gulf War and general feeling of helplessness. This was a new struggle. It became a focus of the left as a successful movement, free from labels such as Marxist."

This Encuentro is unparalleled. Like a global DiY conference, there is no top-down organisational structure and the people are from poor, unfunded groups. "This movement is about hope," says Lucia. "In this world hope has gone down, down, down....but now our heart exists and we are gonna get together and empower ourselves and go to the streets and say to everybody we exist." The Brazilian 'Movimento Sem Terra' (the landless Brazilians) are here. So too are 120 Mexicans, who have raised the equivalent of three months wages each to fly in, and twenty-five indigenous people, who have had their flights paid from Colombia, Chile and Argentina. Squats, schools and sports halls accommodate the masses in a staggering feat of hectic organisation.

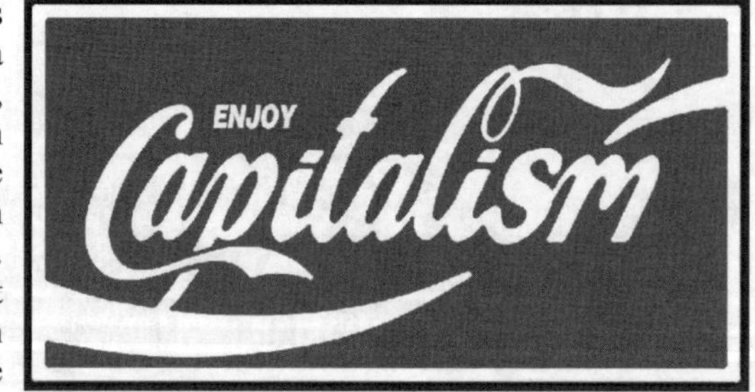

The Encuentro has also been swamped by 800 activists from Italy, adding a dash of style and techno know-how. "The Zapatistas have given a shake to the revitalised left in Italy," explains Maloop from the Centro Sociale Occupato Autogestito Forte Prenestino (got that?). In June, four thousand Italians had descended on Milan train station and demanded transport to join the march against the Euro Summit in Amsterdam. After eight hours of deadlock they got their way. He adds, "After this we are very strong." This is a gathering conducted in a truly epic style. From the first meeting place in Madrid, the participants were spread liberally around the Spanish state. Six tables, or sub-conferences, were arranged by theme and situated as far apart as El Indian on the South coast to Barcelona in the east coast. In something as ambitiously broad and all-encompassing as a gathering "against neo-liberalism", the descriptions of the various themes give concrete focus for discussion. Culture, education, information, land rights, ecology, labour... in all 25 sub-themes. One of the well attended tables is on patriarchy - reflecting an awareness of women's issues in the EZLN itself, an army comprised of more than a third women.

Regular communications arrive via the internet from Chiapas, a medium without which perhaps the Encuentro wouldn't exist. But it's not all talk. The police pulled out of evicting the Vakeria squat ('Cow shed') in Barcelona on Tuesday night when they realised an international force of 1,000 activists would march to the building's defence. "The most impressive thing is that rather than being overwhelmed by the number of people here, and all the cultural and political differences, everyone is really getting down to it", says Richard from Cambridge. "The sense of purpose found here will spread back across the world. It brings a new meaning to the word globalisation."

UNITED COLOURS OF GLOBAL ACTION

> *"We are writing the constitution of a single global economy"*
> **- Renato Ruggerio, World Trade Organisation**

There's a woman from the Peruvian guerrilla group Tupac Amaru chatting to a Russian environmentalist. Nearby, activists from the Brazilian land squatters movement are doing some funky moves on the dance floor with a guy from the Filipino seafarers' union. Then some Brits brashly challenge a bunch of Maori indigenous people activists to a drinking contest. To where on earth have all these people come?

This is Geneva; city of Rousseau, banking, and the U. N. But alongside the city's international stature as the `capital of capital', there exists the lesser-known reality of a place with more squatted social centres than probably any other European city. And now many of these have become venues for the first People's Global Action conference, for which grassroots activists from over half the nations of the world are trickling together; a confluence of radical currents taking place where Geneva nestles between the mountains.

Attending the gathering is like a political shot in the arm. So maybe just because half the world's radical movements are clinking beer glasses here, doesn't mean that tomorrow afternoon will see the downfall of global capitalism. But the breathtaking diversity of folks here are all awakening to each other's struggles, and sizing up their common globalised enemy with a fast sharpening sense of purpose. Beneath the flaming Spanish guitar and ethnic drumming of the evening's entertainment, its possible to hear the tantalising sound of people's perspectives broadening.

"We were all fingers, now we're going to make a fist", enthuses Olivio, one of the organisers of the gathering. The 400 or so participants are taking forward the same process of determined international networking that was going on at the Zapatista-inspired Encuentro (`encounter') in Spain last summer, where the idea for the People's Global Action was born. This time, the focus is clearly defined: action against the World Trade Organisation as it celebrates its 50th anniversary in May. In Geneva we are lathering up our collective forearm; the UN's institutional lackey of global capital is about to receive a global grassroots fisting.

On Wednesday in Geneva 500 people marched in carnivalesque style to the headquarters of the WTO, blocking major roads. The effervescent mixture of some of the world's most marginalised peoples came directly to the heart of the beast - the very building from whose corridors a handful of suits quietly plot the onset of world corporate domination. Activists blockaded the car exit and scaled pillars, dropping anti-free trade banners over WTO's gateway. A handful of cheeky activists sneaked into the building, eventually being chucked out after bringing up their concerns with people inside.

An inspiring few days then. Look out for actions and campaigns coming outta this one over the months to come. In the words of another of the PGA participants

"We must realise our small struggles are part of the global struggle. 1998 must be a new spring, such as that of 1848 and 1968"

Yer SchNEWS scribes felt so inspired by the experience that they're just dying to spread around some of that international energy. So we're putting together a booklet of interviews with many of the amazing people who were in Geneva, packing those diverse struggles told in their own words, into one easy-to-read volume, with plenty of subversion, and loads of pop pix n' fax.

& present

Cost: Priceless!

1998 SPECIAL REPORT
on the United Colours Of

PEOPLE'S GLOBAL ACTION!

www.agp.org

STOP THE KILLER CORPORATIONS!

Snapshots from the voices of global resistance.

EAST TIMOR, CANADA, ARGENTINA, SOUTH KOREA, INDIA, AOTEAROA/NZ, AZTLAN, USA, GENEVA, MEXICO.

Over half of the top 100 economies of the world are not countries, but corporations. The World Trade Organisation, 50 years old on May 18th 1998, is the cosy home of their free trade bliss. General Motors is bigger than South Africa, Shell mightier than Norway, IBM eclipses Pakistan. Mitsubishi, for example, is now the fifth largest "country" in the world. "We are writing the constitution of a single global economy," boasts the WTO's Renato Ruggerio. Welcome to the new world government. Welcome to the united colours of global resistance.

"Multinational Corporations are... the shock troops of the imperial powers." *John Pilger, Hidden Agendas, 1998. (Vintage: ISBN 0-099-74151-2)*

@nticopyright
INFORMATION FOR ACTION!

Disclaimer: This leaflet is not designed to inspire to conspire. Stay at home and watch TV. Then you will feel content. Honest!

@nti-copyright - global information

Nevermind May '68

Here comes May '98 and a new global movement of movements is born

From SchNEWS & Squall 1st PGA Conference Special Report pamphlet.

"In the short term the future's really good. I couldn't have foreseen this in my dreams. There is going to be a shock around the world, I mean it is gonna be like an earthquake. It's the first stirrings of something really massive across the world. The fuse has been lit on a really big piece of dynamite, y'know. Sometimes the fuse goes out or someone cuts it, but if it goes on like this we are gonna have a real explosion of a movement. Since '68 we haven't had this kind of special smell in the air."

Olivier de Marcellus, a grey-haired Swiss lecturer, is positively throbbing with excitement. He's one of the coordinating team of a new ad hoc international group called People's Global Action, where more than 300 delegates from 71 countries came to Geneva to share their anger over corporate rule.

"It is difficult to describe the warmth and the depth of the encounters we had here. The global enemy is relatively well known, but the global resistance that it meets rarely passes through the filter of the media. And here we met the people who had shut down whole cities in Canada with general strikes, risked their lives to seize lands in Latin America, and destroyed Novartis's transgenic maize in France. The discussions, the concrete planning for action, the stories of struggle, the personalities, the enthusiastic hospitality of the Genevan squatters, the impassioned accents of the women and men facing the police outside the WTO building, all sealed an alliance between us. Scattered around the world again, we will not forget. We remain together. This is our common struggle."

Over half of the top 100 economies of the world are not countries, but corporations. And the World Trade Organisation (WTO) is the cosy home of their free trade bliss here in Geneva, the capital of world capital. General Motors is bigger than South Africa, Shell mightier than Norway, IBM eclipses Pakistan. Mitsubishi, for example, is now the fifth largest 'country' in the world. "We are writing the constitution of a single global economy", boasts the WTO's Renato Ruggerio. Welcome to the new world government. Welcome to the united colours of global resistance.

"We have to start aiming at the head," explains Olivier. "We have been militants fighting against nuclear power, against housing, sexism. Different tentacles of the monster. You are never really going to do it that way, you really have to aim at the head."

The process began with the Zapatista-inspired 'Encuentro' in Mexico in 1996. "The Encuentro launched the idea of people working horizontally across the world, this international of Hope.

International trade treaties have become the most important phenomenon in globalisation. The latest scam is known as the Multilateral Agreement on Investment. The respected writer and broadcaster John Pilger describes the MAI as "the most important imperial advance for half a century".

Inside a Parisian bunker, every six weeks since 1995, representatives of the 29 richest countries on Earth - including the UK - have been plotting this new deal in secrecy and in haste. It is an agreement that would, at a stroke, legally bind together these countries for a minimum of 20 years and seek to invalidate all domestic environmental, social and labour protections to the greater 'rights' of money in the international 'free' market.

The real clout in the MAI is the right it gives companies to sue governments for large damages. In what is known as the 'pay the polluter' case, the Ethyl Corporation of America is suing the Canadian government for $367 million dollars for banning the use of MMT, a controversial gasoline additive, which it makes in Ottawa. It wants "immediate compensation for imposing legislation which hinders its operations [profits]" under free trade rules identical to the MAI.

But across the globe resistance is growing. In May this year actions were taking place across the globe to mark the rage against the WTO celebrations of their 50th anniversary. The fury ranged across all continents from Canada to Columbia, Bangladesh to Aotearoa/NZ. Over 30 cities, from Ankara to San Francisco were holding the first global street party on the same day with the slogan: "our resistance will be as global as capital!"

And in Geneva itself several hundred Indian farmers, Italian train-jumpers, French unemployed marchers and German caravan convoyers were spoiling the party. The united colours of global action are serious, but when I asked a smiling Olivier to give his statement to the world he summed up the spirit: "This," he said, "is really fun!"

MIND THE GAT!

WTO, NAFTA, MAI, FTAA, GATS... on and on they go, the alphabet soup of 'free' trade agreements, as they confuse and bore us into submission. SchNEWS hasn't just been covering the protests against these agreements but looking past all the government spin and trying to explain in simple terms that there's nothing free or fair about them, that they are just another corporate carve-up of the planet.

"The GATS is not just something that exists between governments. It is first and foremost an instrument for the benefit of business." - ***European Commission website***

"If GATS gets the green light Europe can kiss goodbye its public health services" - ***Susan George, economist***

It's just over a year since the World Trade Organisation (WTO) got a good kicking in Seattle (see SchNEWS 240). But behind the closed doors of the world's most powerful trade organisation, bureaucrats backed up by their mates in big business have been busy plotting.

What they've come up with is a few new ways of expanding the General Agreement on the Trades in Services (GATS). First signed in 1994 the agreement is all about eliminating 'barriers to trade' (see below)

So they've come up with a cunning plan to privatise the world's public services. Everything from water to housing to education to hospitals, and a whole lot more are now 'barriers to trade' creating unfair competition that must be put on the open market to the lowest bidder.

A European Commission representative singled out the European health service as ripe for 'liberalisation' (that's corporate chat for privatisation), with a US healthcare industry lobbyist complaining that health has "largely been the responsibility of the public sector (making it) difficult for US private sector health care providers."

"Globalisation is not about trade. It is about replacing local or democratic government with corporate rule." - ***Bob Olson, anti-globalisation campaigner***

Now that would make a hell of a lot of difference in the UK where New Labour are pressing ahead with handing over hospitals, schools, prisons, council houses etc. to the private sector. Hey, last week the UK even became the first country in the world to part privatise Air Traffic Control.

Elsewhere European water and energy companies are keen to expand their interests in the Third World. This is of course out of a noble sense of duty in wanting to help developing countries obtain things like clean water and not as the more cynical amongst you might think about further lining shareholders pockets.

Trickle Down

Imagine getting a water bill that cost you one third of your wages. Or needing a permit to collect rainwater in rooftop tanks. This was a reality for some of Bolivia's poorest families when the Government sold the public water system with Bechtel taking a major share. The charges that the company imposed on peasant families were so crippling that they sparked mass protest. Hundreds of thousands took to the streets of Cochabamba City in April. Soldiers sent in to quell the protests killed six and injured hundreds of others. The Governor of the State resigned, saying he did not want to be responsible for the 'bloodbath' that would follow the Bolivian Government's refusal to reverse the privatisation. But in the end, the protestors won – Bechtel were kicked out of Bolivia and the Government accepted the protestors' demands to put control of water in local hands.

But it's not just been protests in Bolivia. Around the world this year there have been mass strikes in Indonesia, calling for the government to end contracts with private water companies, while in Costa Rica huge demonstrations took place against the privatisation of the country's energy and telecommunications sector. In South Africa, protests and strikes are taking place in response to privatisation, with the ANC government taking a heavy stance against protestors.

However, if the new GATS agreement had been in force, all these protests would have been futile, because as the WTO Secretariat points out, one of the benefits of GATS is helping "overcome domestic resistance to change." What that means is that once a country signs up and decides to open up a particular service to WTO rules, it would be practically impossible to go back on any agreement . Any change of heart – tough. Change of government – tough. Popular protest – grin and bear it. Or face the trade sanction consequences.

In effect, the 'new world order' way of running the world is being forced on every country and every person on the planet, whether they like it or not. SchNEWS reckons its time to give the WTO and its friends another good kicking...

INSTITUTIONALISED VIOLENCE

This is stolen from the 'Financial Crimes', the spoof paper produced by Reclaim the Streets in the run up to the Prague World Bank protests in September 2000 which confused lots of city suits with its pink paper and likeness to their favourite rag. And it seriously wound up the real Financial Times!

Call us paranoid, but one of the key weapons used by those at the top against the rest seems to be boredom. They deliberately make their institutions sound so dull no sane person would want to read about them. Just seeing the name Organisation for Economic Co-operation and Development is enough to send anyone to sleep.

Acronyms are part of this plot. Just think, if asylum seekers renamed themselves TMPs (transnational migratory persons) they might get left alone by Britain's institutionally racist press. Nowadays reading an article on international politics is akin to a trip through the human genome: IMF, TABD, WTO, NAFTA, IBRD, IFC, ERT, TRIPs (okay, that one's funny), UNEP, G-7, ILO, OECD, UNHCR...

It wouldn't be so bad if these bodies and treaties were politically irrelevant - sports societies, perhaps, or flu-like diseases (I'm sorry Mrs Jones, I think you're coming down with a nasty case of WTO). But unfortunately for anyone interested in the way the world works, they are important. Each has a specific role to play in keeping the march of the global economy onwards.

G7/G8 (Group of 7/8)

The G8 is the 'Group of 8' industrialised nations: the USA, Britain, Japan, France, Canada, Italy, Germany and, since the fall of communism, Russia. Given Russia's poor economy, the cabal is often still referred to as the G7. This is where serious discussion and economic policy-making takes place, and its influence spreads throughout all the major international bodies.

WTO (World Trade Organisation)

Now this one's really naughty. The World Trade Organisation's main aim is to eliminate 'barriers to trade'. It might be easier to think of barriers to trade as barriers to profits. These can include decent worker's rights, environmental standards, and human rights concerns. National laws can be overturned if they interfere with a corporation's divine right to make money.

OECD (too long to fit!)

The Organisation for Economic Co-operation and Development is 'Diet **WTO**'. It pushes free trade and economic liberalisation, but lacks enforcement powers. Most of its members are in the rich North, but some lucky industrialised outsiders such as Mexico and South Korea have been invited in. It is most notorious for developing the **MAI**, which acronym lovers can read about below.

UN Security Council

The United Nations Security Council is intended to maintain international peace and security. There are five permanent members - the USA, United Kingdom, France, Russia and China. Ten elected members also sit on the Council. They pass resolutions that can be vetoed by any permanent member and ignored by US allies such as Israel. The security council can order military action.

NATO (North Atlantic Treaty Organisation)

The North Atlantic Treaty Organisation is a military alliance linking Western Europe with the US. A cold war institution, it now provides a living for arms dealers (as new members from Eastern Europe have agreed to increase their military spending). This is useful for the US as an alternative route

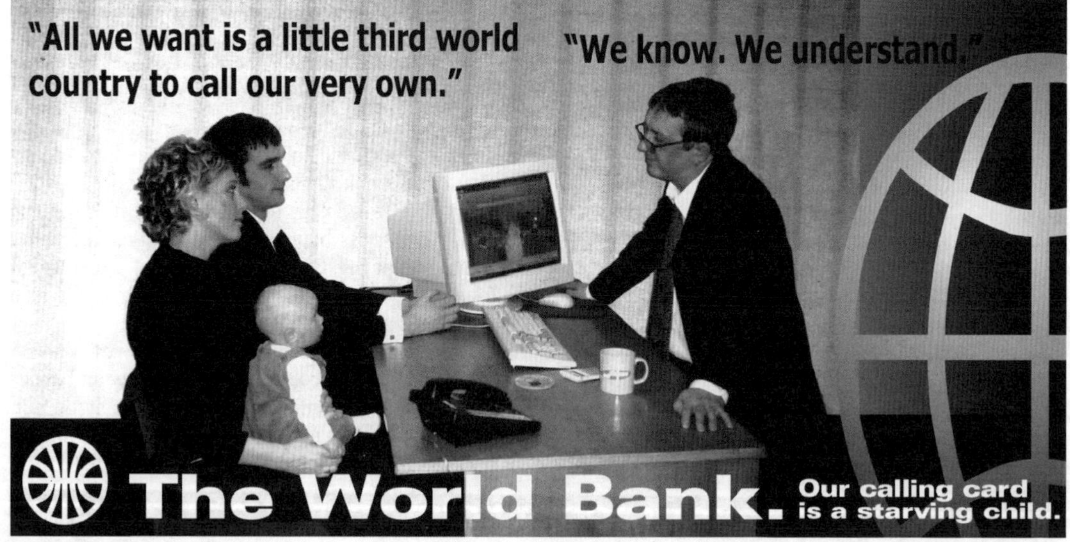

Polyp

for action when a **UN Security Council** member would otherwise block it, as happened over Kosova.

ICC (International Chamber of Commerce)

The International Chamber of Commerce is little known, but extremely influential. In brief terms, it is a collective lobbying body made up of corporations that are powerful in their own right. Their stamp is all over the policies of the institutions already mentioned, and they even wrote large chunks of the draft **MAI**.

ERT (European Round Table)

Business leaders of Europe. The European Round Table of Industrialists write and put forward ideas that become European Union legislation. An example of which was their blueprint for a trans-European road network. This road network is now EU policy.

This next bit is by schnews people

IMF (International Monetary Fund) and WORLD BANK

Celebrating sixty years this month - happy fucking birthday. Recently this pair has been used to force countries to adopt right wing neoliberal economic policies. Loans are offered if governments agree to privatise, offering these for sale to western business interests. Of course these governments have no choice: they wouldn't be asking for the cash unless they were desperate. Meanwhile the corporations create new monopolies, forcing up the cost of basic services. The World Bank also does a good line in lending cash for ecologically disastrous schemes across the world, and seem to especially like big dams and road building projects.

NAFTA (North American Free Trade Agreement), was supposedly a harmless 'free trade' deal struck between Canada, Mexico and the United States. Calling **NAFTA** a "trade" agreement is misleading, **NAFTA** is really an investment agreement. Its grants multinationals loads of new rights and privileges and encourages the relocation of factories and jobs to Mexico and the privatization and deregulation of essential services, such as water, energy and health care. For example, its allowed the US to export 820,000 expensive unionised workers on $17 an hour just across the border in Mexico where they are paid $5 a day. It also guarantees US patent rights, opening up Mexican agriculture to US biotech firms. This is likely to put four million farmers out of work, trash the environment and reduce the types of Mexican maize grown from 150 varieties to one.

Since **NAFTA** was signed, wages in Mexico have declined by 10%, while labour productivity increased by 45%, mainly due to the fact that many workers have increased their hours of work from 8 to 12 hours a day.

According to Canadian political economist John W. Warnock, "Neoliberalism and NAFTA have been good for the rich in Mexico and the large corporations. The banks, privately owned and robbed by the Mexican rich, have been bailed out of bankruptcy twice by taxpayers. The illicit drug industry flourishes and is now more important than the oil industry, and free trade and cross-border trucking have made marketing much easier. Aside from incomes, spending is very low on education, health, agriculture and rural development plus research. It is not surprising to find that most people, including academics, do not believe that so-called "free trade" has been good for their country."

And that's without even mentioning the environment. According to the Sierra Club total pollution has doubled in Mexico since NAFTA was introduced. Under NAFTA corporations can sue governments for getting in the way of business with daft stuff like pollution laws and safety regulations. In August 2000, following a NAFTA ruling, US corporation Metalclad won $16.7m compensation and the right to pollute an area in San Luis Potosi after local protests delayed the building of a waste treatment and disposal site which would poison the local water supply.

As Kevin Danaher from Global Exchange put it "The free market ideology is this bullshit that they put out there to pry open Third World countries and to keep people here stupid and think, "Oh, get the government out of the way. Let capital decide how the world will be run." Well, duh. If you let capital decide how the world is going to run, they'll cut down every tree, they'll kill every fish, they'll push our wages down to zero, they'll pollute the shit out of everything, because all they care about is making money."

FTAA – Free Trade Agreement of the Americas is intended to be the most far-reaching trade agreement in history covering the whole of the Americas (except Cuba) - basically NAFTA on steroids.

GATS - The General Agreement on Trade in Services. Part of the **WTO** grand plan.

TRIPS - Trade Related Intellectually Property rights, which give the big boys the go ahead to patent life. The 'gene rush' includes highlights such as American corporations buying up blood samples of the indigenous peoples of Ecuador!

ECGD - Export Credit Guarantee Department

This scam works a bit like this. If you are an arms company and you want to sell your weapons to a dodgy regime, but are worried that the dictator wont pay you, the ECGD will guarantee you your money. If the dictator doesn't pay, guess who has to fork out? Yep, the taxpayer! The ECGD are currently £10 million in debt, and financing British arms deals, dams, and dodgy investments all over the world.

NEO-LIBERALISM

All the above is part of the corrupt ***neo-liberal*** agenda legitimized by the so called **Washington Consensus**, which is nothing more than an agreement between the White House, IMF and World Bank. Elites from all countries knock together **FREE TRADE** agreements, which enable rich countries to carry on exploiting from poorer regions.

Such trade agreements remove "barriers to trade", inconvenient little things like environmental protection and workers' rights and push the way for the privatisation of everything.

Supporters of neo-liberalism talk of 'free market' policies that encourage private enterprise, consumer choice and personal initiative, and use these arguments to justify everything from lowering taxes on the wealthy, to dismantling and privatizing education and social welfare programmes, attacking workers' rights and scrapping environmental regulations (often referred to as **RED TAPE).** They prattle on about a level playing field where a small Indian peasant farmer can compete with a multinational corporation.

The reality though is that neo-liberalism encourages a massive increase in inequality and severe deprivation for the poorest nations, whilst killing the environment and encouraging instability in the global economy. But, and here's the key to its popularity with its supporters, it creates an unprecedented bonanza for the wealthy.

When these pioneers of righteousness, are presented with some of the rather large downside, they claim that the spoils of the good life will invariably spread to the broad mass of the population This is known as **'THE TRICKLE DOWN EFFECT'** as long as the neo-liberal policies that exacerbated these problems in the first place are not interfered with! Or, as one commentator put it, "at their most eloquent, proponents of neo-liberalism sound as if they are doing poor people, the environment and everybody else a tremendous service as they enact policies on behalf of the wealthy few." According to the neo-liberal zealots this is all human nature, we've hit the jackpot and there is no alternative to the status quo ... but millions of people thankfully beg to differ.

ANTI GLOBALISATION PROTESTORS

This is a bit of a nonsense label, 'cos people against these free trade corporate shin-dig like to communicate and get together with people across their world to globalise their protests. The problem is economic globalization which makes the rich richer (free movement of money and corporations is good, but the free movement of people is bad!?) that maintains the dominance of a few western multinational corporations. So maybe that's where the **ANTI CAPITALISTS** come in. Not that they're a new phenomena, just like globalization, they've been around for hundreds of years. They protest against the increasing international power of big capital concentrated in the hands of very few people and companies.

Then there's those bloody **ANARCHISTS** – A group hell bent on the destruction of society by removing all laws and getting rid of governments ... or is that the Neo-liberals? Anarchists come in many colours (such as black and slightly faded black) and political persuasions. They reject authority, preferring to organize themselves, and empowering others to do likewise. In Brighton can often be found in offices working long hours in poor conditions for no pay...

NON GOVERNMENTAL ORGANISATIONS (NGO's)

Join in the protests against 'free' trade but spend too much time encouraging us to write to our MP's. Now being used to do governments' or international organizations' work for them on the cheap, often using volunteers. They are weakened by their reliance on money from governments or organizations such as the **World Bank**, which means they can only carry out work which the rich and powerful agree with. Drinking fair trade tea and coffee is only polite, but it ain't really a solution to capitalism.

NEO-CONS (Neo-Conservatives)

These are the nutters who cut their teeth in the Reagan administration and are now running Bush's White House. A group of fundamentalist Christians, they want the US to wage a perpetual war in order to ensure unchallenged domination of the world. They've got their own bible, the 'Project for a New American Century', a scary megalomaniac plot for world control, which, amongst similar suggestions, recommends preemptive war with nukes launched from space against oil rich countries.

FAT CAT SLIM

Neo Labour Carries On The Good Work Of The Tories

"The Private Finance Initiative means paying more for less." **- Dr. Jean Shaoul, accountancy expert Manchester University.**

Public services sold off to big business. Private firms in our schools. Worse pay and conditions for workers. Adverts on fire-engines. Who could possibly be behind such dastardly schemes? New Labour, silly.

Welcome to the world of the Private Finance Initiative (PFI), which in plain English means privatisation by the back door.

FIRST THEY CAME FOR THE TUBE...

The London Underground is already the most expensive in Europe, and with plans for it to be sold to private companies, fares will spiral even higher. As with the fragmentation of British Rail, health & safety will be put at risk, services will be cut, and large scale redundancies and casualisation are on the cards.

THEN THEY CAME FOR OUR SCHOOLCHILDREN...

In Haringey four private companies have been short-listed under the PFI to take over schools, including Rentokil Initial (who in the past have been removed from one in three of its school cleaning contracts). School buidlings will effectively be privatised, as private companies will take control for up to 30 years, and they will decide how schools will be used outside of school hours, to make profits.

In Haringey this will mean the privatisation of cleaning, caretaking and repair and maintenance work, threatening jobs, pay and conditions. Despite widespread opposition, the Council is pushing ahead spending £250,000 just to prepare its bid.

If that's not enough New Labour have also come up with Education Action Zones, allowing big business to get involved in running education. In Sheffield the main sponsors are Midland bank and Yorkshire Water. Meanwhile in Surrey, the council have announced plans to privatise the teachers of one of its schools.

THEN THEY ATTACKED OUR BRAVE FIREFIGHTERS...

"It's privatisation through the back door. All companies work for profit and this is just not appropriate within a public service." **- Fire Brigade Union spokesperson**

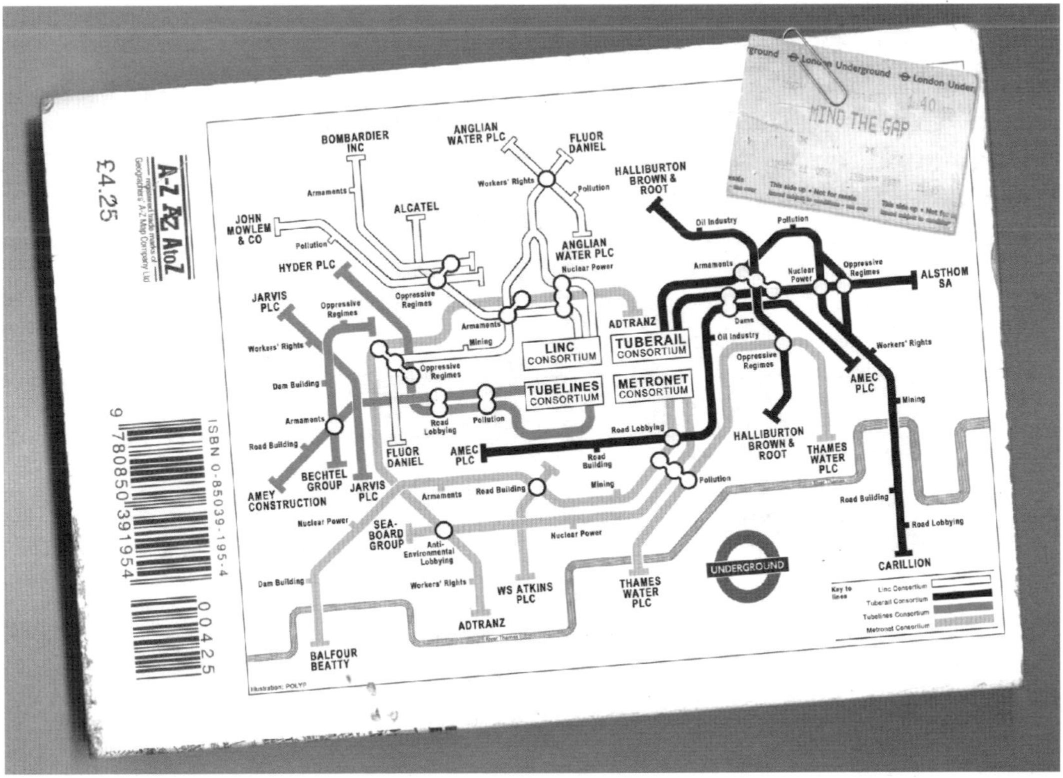

Fire-fighters are on the brink of their first national strike since the seventies over plans to break up the national framework, which sets a minimum standard of working conditions around the country and replaces it with "local bargaining." Fire-fighters rightly see this as a first step towards privatisation. One union spokesperson commented "*We've seen what damage local bargaining has done to our public services,our railways and our ambulance service. First they carve up the workforce then they sell bits off and the public end up paying for a worse service.*"

Just to show how keen they, the London Fire Brigade this month made a multi-million pound Private Finance Inititave deal to fund their fire-fighting fleet and equipment.

And there's more…London are also looking into the raising cash through private sponsorship, which could include advertising on the side of fire engines!

NEXT IT WAS THE HOSPITALS...

"It's (the PFI) like taking out a mortgage from a loan shark to buy a house which you already own - and then discovering, 25 years down the line, that the property has been repossessed by the lender anyway." - Francis Wheen, journalist

Dryburn hospital in Durham due to open in 2001 will be built, financed and owned by a private sector consortium, Consort Healthcare. In return for use of the hospital, the local health service trust will pay the consortium £7 million every year for the next 30 years. Consort will also provide most of the hospital's ancillary staff, at a cost of an extra £5 million a year.

Offically, PFI schemes are given the go-ahead only if they offer better value for money than other options. But a study by the union UNISON shows that the cost of the PFI scheme over 30 years will be over £22 million more than if the public sector had built and owned the hospital.

There will also be a reduction in services with only half the hospital beds originally planned and a 22 per cent cut in clinical staffing budget over the next two years

Workers at the University College Hospital in London recently went on a two week all out strike over privatisation plans.

THEN THEY WENT FOR THE HOUSING BENEFIT DEPARTMENTS

Housing Benefit and Council Tax staff in Brighton and Hove are preparing to take strike action after the Council revealed it's plans to sell off their department to a private company called Capita. The announcement, made only three weeks ago, was followed by an immediate meeting where 180 people voted unanimously for a strike ballot to defend their jobs, and two mass pickets of the Town hall while the issue was debated left Councillors in no doubt as to what the mood was. The proposals, which will remove the entire Housing Benefit operation to Falmer, will mean an inevitable drop in the quality of the service: long delays in processing claims, no local service points, no flexibility when it comes to overpayment demands.

Capita have a past history of incompetence (in one mistake 4,600 pensioners were accidentally sent a letter informing them that their housing benefit was being cut, along with an increased council tax demand!), lying about their efficiency rates -and redundancies. The most interesting thing about the company is that Labour Council leader Lord Bassam lists a consultancy with Capita in the House of Lords Register of Interests! When news of the privatisation broke, Capita's shares rose 39p-more money for Bassam's chums.

The Council, worried that this is becoming a local election own-goal have decided to 'review' the decision-a stalling tactic if ever there was one. But with Unison deciding to introduce a voluntary levy on all its Brighton and Hove members to support a prospective strike, the Council may have bitten off more than it can chew.

LIFE AFTER PRIVATISATION

"Strikes in the future are not just going to be won by the withdrawl of labour - they are going to be won by employing other methods. Having people like Reclaim The Streets(RTS) involved could go a long way to winning other disputes in the future. RTS get publicity and cause the bosses serious financial distress - and they can't be sacked." **- Steve**

Steve Hedley was on strike with other railway maintainance workers and engineers over pay and conditions. Since privatisation the companies that bought British Rail have been making around £1million a day profit and Railtrack a similar amount. Meanwhile, maintenance workers are taking home around £135 a week after tax for a 37-39 hour week.

Everytime the firemen go on strike Neo-Labour has to bring in the army - and the ancient 'Green Goddess' fire engines - to do their job. In November 2003 the postal workers were on strike, as were the firemen - both strikes about 'modernisation' (read privatisation and deregulation). We were wondering if the Green Goddesses were going to start delivering the mail as well...

During the dispute Steve was at Euston Station on a picket line when a scab van drove straight at the picket line. On its way past it was alledged that a wing mirror was cracked on the van and Steve was blamed. However two independent photographers and even Railtracks own CCTV showed that Steve wasn't the vandal to blame. Still, the Railtract sub-contractors sacked him and even though the case was thrown out of court, the company have refused to give him his job back.

• A recent report which studied 41 local authorities involved in Private Finance Initiative schemes, has concluded that 150,000 jobs will be transferred to the the private sector in the next 10 years. Job losses are estimated at 30,000.

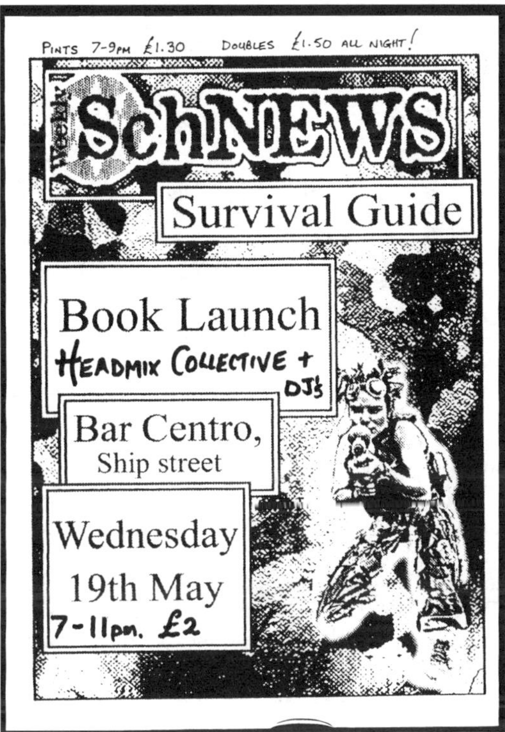

IF ORDINARY PEOPLE BEHAVED LIKE- Microsoft

Crystal Palace Pic: Alec Smart

Tales From A Road Protester 1997-99

Some people think that the protest camps were dying down after Fairmile in '97, but there were still lots of protest sites going on - and enough up-for-it nutters to keep 'em going. Here is one of their accounts...

I was politicised through parties, despite an uneventful stint in St Albans Earth Action Group when I was 16, where the most radical thing I did was to appear on a five minute programme called Thames Help campaigning about the benefits of low energy light-bulbs. My environmental considerations took a back seat as I discovered the joys of the free party through the likes of Spiral Tribe. Inspired by this, when I moved north to go to college, we bought a little sound system and started having parties in the woods around Keel University, much to the dismay of the head of the university.

Politically isolated at college in the back waters of Stoke on Trent, the advent of the CJB dusted us down, brought new energy, and suddenly having parties was a political act! A talk in our students union about Battle of the Beanfield and the importance of fighting the CJB, from an old traveller whom I now know to be Tash from Nottingham, was enough for me to move to Brighton after college and duly volunteer my services to SchNEWS.

Admittedly, after Stoke, moving to a Siberian labour camp may have had its positive sides, so to move to Brighton in 1995 when the Squatters Estate Agency was in full swing was beyond words. On good advice, on my first Friday night I went into the New Kensington Pub and was first introduced to SchNEWS Live. I found a tenna in the toilets, which I since found out has never happened in the history of the pub. It was enough to get me hooked.

A few SchNEWS lines and visits to sites later, I finally decided to leave the office and join the nomad tribes holed up in tunnels and trees that I had spent so long phoning and writing about.

First port of call was Lyminge forest where I met the new eco-pin-up Blue, and where Stig was given a camera by the BBC to create a video diary of 'Life in the woods' (this is the same Stig who found herself at the Thanet Way road protest on her own. The one where security phoned the SchNEWS office to ask for more people to come down to the protest site, cos numbers were so low they were about to lose their jobs!) It actually became an incriminating collection of clips, a comprehensive 'Drink Diary' for those on the site, and was eventually discarded when it became hard evidence of who actually drunk the Vodka one evening when Flannel came to lift our spirits, so to speak!

The site was full of lots of wierd and surreal lock-ons. Included was an underground chamber, in which the infamous ACAB would be stuck in a separate chamber behind bars. As the bailiffs entered from the roof, red lights and sirens would be triggered, and they would enter the chamber to find ACAB clad in a nightie, screaming at them from behind his cage. On another camp, an arm chair was sunk in the ground, part of a wider lock-on, and measured perfectly for an 80 year old local volunteer to sit in when the imminent eviction arrived. The prospect of such scenes almost make me disappointed that we won the campaign and never had the eviction.

More surrealism prevailed as I went to Dead Woman's Bottom, and looked at the OS map and discovered that this really was the name of the place. I was introduced to the various farm animals on site and taken into the woods adjacent and shown the remains of one of Alistair Crowleys alters. During the eviction, while helicopters were flying overhead, we were tucking into fried egg sandwich's, each of which consisted of about 12 donated quales eggs.

Crystal Palace Pic: Alec Smart

But possibly the strangest episode was one morning in the tower in the Crystal Palace eviction. Outside the site was the relatively unknown Ali G, and we were hearing reports from rather serious protesters of some local nutter in a track-suit taking the piss! After three days, with Barnaby as the police liaison in his wedding dress, the banter started with the resident line of riot police at the foot of our tower. We'd previously refused the police requests for us to sing Happy Birthday to their fellow officer, much to their disappointment. But I couldn't believe my eyes as we were greeted that morning with the eight cops, shields and masks at their feet, giving us a Mexican wave! Obviously all changed as they finally dragged us out of that tower.

On another positive note was the successful campaign of Teigngrace in Devon, where the local clay quarry was to be expanded so the world could have more toilets! The delicate nature of the campaign in its fight for a public enquiry meant that defence work was temporarily halted on site. While some spent the summer of '97 in the Teign and Bovey rivers canoeing and swimming, others decided to take to the road and walk to the Ministry of the Environment in London and demand the enquiry. Obviously the intention was to do an action when we arrived, but 242 miles later, while elated from the success of the walk, the enthusiasm for an action waned somewhat. While most boarded the coach back to Devon, some of us sat in the pub opposite to plan a banner drop for the following morning. We needed the seats that overlooked the entrance, which were currently occupied by two yuppies. Undeterred, one bloke took off his socks for the first time in 242 miles, and rolled them down the table, perfectly halting at the wine glasses of the yuppies. To such cries as 'You are disgusting!' the couple dutifully upped and left, and we were able to plan what turned out to be a lovely day on top of the DoE. It made front page news of the Western Morning News that week, despite the fact that the image used was of me holding aloft the glorious golden can of Special Brew in victory. Ah well!

On a less chirpy note, I visited the Birmingham Northern Relief road one week in the heart of winter. The communal bender was built off the back of a trailer, with the burner the heart of life for the dwindling few left at this particular point. The final evening came when Sgt Belcher (no really, this was his name) the community copper who 'befriended' the protesters, arrested someone on site who he knew had a warrant out for him. While others went to do prisoner support, I was left in the bender on my own. Little did I realise that no-one was now in the vicinity, except for the 30 or so police that had amassed outside the bender door, waiting for the easy picking to take both myself and thus the site.

Fast forward to today: I was on a coach last week back to London from Manchester, and felt a dark sinking sensation when I slowly realised where I was, as I saw for the first time the lights of the toll approaching.

Some of us went to India for the peoples Global Action Conference, hosted by the Karnataka State farmers Association. A completely inspiring time, we met activists from all over the world fighting against the free market economy and global capitalism. While we were there, the people of the Narmarda valley in the north requested any available activists to come and give their support. They are fighting to stop a series of dams flooding their homeland, and during the raining season the dams already built are opened and the waters start to rise in their villages. The villagers are prepared to die for their lands, and stand in the waters as they rise.

On my return to England, after a series of talks and actions in solidarity with the people of the valley, I wanted to do more work with people. I now work in central London with homeless people who have drug and alcohol problems…nuff said!?

You can read about the protest camps mentioned in this article at www.schnews.org.uk/archive

Lyminge forest - issue 114
Dead Woman's Bottom - issue 151
Crystal Palace - issue 203
Teigngrace Quarry - issue 241
Thanet Way - issue 36
PGA Conference, Bangalore, India. August 1999 - issue 226

Pic: Simon Chapman

AVON RING ROAD

In December 1998 **STARR** (Stop the Avon Ring Road), the campaign to stop Bristol's answer to the M25 being built, began as fifteen protesters d-locked onto and occupied diggers at Siston Common, halting work for the day (pic above). Not only was this going to be another road, it also meant urban infill of 3000 new houses and a supermarket on unspoilt countryside. A camp was set up and buildings due to be demolished for the road squatted in a direct action campaign which went on for 8 months.

ESSEX TUNNELLERS BREAK RECORD

Essex, January 2000 - motorways, suburbs, a housing development and shopping centre hell-hole ruled by Essex girls and Mondeo men. Hey, that's not really fair…

Gorse Wood and Hockley protest camps near Chelmsford were busy defending woodland and wildlife threatened by the building of a six lane motorway, an expansion of the A130 and 800 new houses, oh… and another much needed golf course.

At Hockley the battle was to stop a shady mob with the nice oat-meal-coloured name of Countryside Residential from trashing a wildlife rich woodland for 66 luxury houses. The site contained endangered species but clearing began before the legal agreements with Rochford District Council were signed.

Fighting this destruction on a legal basis was made difficult by the fact that despite the project violating the Wildlife Protection Act, Country Residential were funding the Essex Wildlife Trust, causing a hopeless conflict of interest.

The developers' hired security used medieval siege tactics and violent intimidation. Protesters were imprisoned on site with only a trickle of supplies being allowed in. Locals stormed the barricades and a few managed to get through the fence to join the protesters.

At Gorse Wood, five protesters set a new record for the amount of time spent underground - remaining in the tunnels for 40 nights. They were evicted on January 17th 2000, and all the camps were evicted in spring 2000 having cost Countryside Residential an arm and a leg.

SUITS YOU, SIR!

"Booze-fuelled hardcore anarchists turn anti-capitalist protest into orgy of violence."
- Daily Star

It all started *nicely* enough - 500 cyclists staged a Critical Mass blockade of the streets, Lloyds and NatWest banks were occupied and animal rights activists shouted at an empty building. No-one - least of all the police - could anticipate the mayhem to come.

"Just heard that the boys at Tullett and Tokyo whose office overlooks London Bridge have been waving their gold cards and shouting 'Wankers' at the eco-warriors going past."
- E-mail circulating City

Liverpool St. Station, 12 noon

Ten thousand ungrateful, work-shy dole-scroungers gathered to bite both the hand that feeds them and the free sandwiches provided to lure them away from consumer Utopia; colour-coded party masks distributed amongst the crowd resulted in four separate columns of protesters winding their way through the city streets to converge on the belly of the beast - The London International Financial Futures and Options Exchange (LIFFE). At this point the Carnival - organised by and for a coalition of nice, peaceful anarchists- was hijacked by the disgraceful, masked-up, beer-swilling, black-clad, cop-hating psychopaths that give anarchy a bad name.

And then the fun *really* began.

"We're being beseiged by open-toed-sandalled hippy vandals. We have armed our doorman, Bernard, with a shotgun." **- Partner at Maclay, Murray and Spens ('The Lawyer')**

To the noise of pneumatic drill gabba from a sound-system, a trained Class War hate mob trampled on the bare toes of decent liberal protesters and embarked on a systematic redesign of the urban environment. *'Imagine London with its rivers unearthed and its valleys revealed'* they screamed as CCTV cameras were bagged up, revellers danced in a four-storey fountain of their own urine and the front door of LIFFE was bricked up with breeze blocks and cement hauled in by crack-fuelled chaos junkies. Punk band P.A.I.N.- *at least one member sporting an outrageous mohican haircut-* baited rioters with angry hate music- with added percussion from boots going through the windows of a Mercedes showroom.

"Five activists are reported to have shaved the head of a besuited City type, while pinning him against Freshfield's wall." **- 'The Lawyer'**

Dreadlocked crusties disguised in Oxfam suits stormed their way into the reception of the Liffe building, showering traders- cowering behind piles of photocopied tenners- with fountains of diseased blood as bare feet demolished the plate-glass reception. The masked middle-class mayhem mongers stormed the escalators in pitched battle with salt-of-the-earth Cockney dealers before being squirted back out on the street with champagne cannons.

"Bankers, traders and stockbrokers are the real working class." **- Daily Telegraph editorial**

Other demonstrators attacked branches of McDonalds; kamikaze vegans hurled themselves through the windows and bombarded police with frozen burgers, urging customers to eat Edward and Sophie instead. Others covered themselves with ketchup and deceitfully claimed police brutality.

"Schroeders were attacked by climbing nuts, who attempted to scale the building with ropes and crampons, but were thwarted when traders urinated on their heads."
- E-mail circulating city traders

Thankfully, citizens, such spontaneity is unlikely to happen again. Assistant Chief Constable James Hart of City Police has stated: *"We may, if conditions call for it, be more assertive next time; we'll come in harder, at significant risk to innocent members of the public peaceful protesters and police officers."* Or maybe they'll just ban dissent altogether. Meanwhile…

"Next Friday will be the International City Day of Action. On this day, we ask you all to don your finest pinstripe, knot the Italian silk tie, booted with British brogue, apply your monocles, glue mobile phone to ear and then head off down to Brighton to disrupt as many dreadlocked soap dodging men and women with dogs on string as possible."
- E-mail circulating City traders (unfortunately everyone in Brighton will be at Glastonbury).

Our Resistance Becomes as Transnational as Capital

Friday June 18th 1999 was the opening day of the G8 Summit in Cologne, Germany. It is no coincidence that it was also the day 10,000 people converged on London's financial centre for a 'Carnival against Capital'; that the streets of Port Harcourt, Nigeria's oil capital, were brought to a standstill; that 'the Eugene anarchists' sprang to international fame after riots erupted in a small, North American university town; and the day before the* Financial Times *declared that anti-capitalism had returned.

What follows is an attempt to try to de-mystify the process which led up to the Peoples' Global Action (PGA) - inspired Global Day of Action on June 18th 1999 and to reflect upon some of its impacts.

The Emergence of the Global Anti-Capitalist Movement

The **Zapatista** uprising on 1st January 1994 - the day, on which the North American Free Trade Agreement (NAFTA) was supposed to pass, unnoticed, into effect - sent a wave of hope around the world. It was a reminder that despite the widely hailed victory of "neo-liberalism" and the proclaimed "end of history" symbolised by the fall of the Berlin Wall, capitalism still had its enemies. It was a reminder that there were people who still dreamed of another world and, moreover, that this dream had already begun to be realised.

Inspired by the bravery and determination of the Zapatistas, and by the new language in which they were speaking - posing revolution as a question, rather than an answer - not only did solidarity groups spring up across the globe, but loads of different people began to open themselves to the ideas and experiences of others, to "walk asking questions".

As proof of the inspirational impact that the uprising and 'Zapatismo' had had, and much to the Zapatistas' surprise (they thought that no one would come), in July 1996, 6,000 people gathered deep in the Lacadon Jungle in Chiapas, Mexico for the first Intercontinental Encuentro (or, encounter) for Humanity and Against Neo-Liberalism. People from every continent gathered for eight days and discussed politics, economics, society, culture and identity. Swapping ideas and experiences inside a giant conference centre built by Zapatista communities deep inside the conflict zone.

One year later, in the summer of 1997, thousands converged once more for the second Intercontinental Encuentro, this time spread over four locations within the Spanish State. Much like the first event, the Encuentro was seen as a huge success in providing a forum for much needed dialogue between the world's social movements. Yet those in attendance had already begun to desire more. They wanted this dialogue and exchange of inspiration to continue and - importantly - for this to translate into action which would mutually reinforce day-to-day struggles worldwide.

A three day meeting following the second Encuentro resulted in an invitation being issued for the world's social movements to attend the founding conference of **Peoples' Global Action** (PGA) - a network intended to fulfil this role - in Geneva, Switzerland in February 1998. It was here, only a few kilometres from the headquarters of the World Trade Organisation (WTO), that PGA was born. After days of discussion between representatives of the Indian Karnataka State Farmers' Association (KRRS), Movimento Sem Terra - the Brazilian landless peasants' movement, Maori from New Zealand, indigenous movements from South and Central America and activists from Europe, North America and Australia, a basis for co-operation was established in the form of a set of 'hallmarks'. It was agreed that the network would be open to all of those who agreed upon the importance of working in a decentralised and non-hierarchical manner, who recognised the importance of the principles of autonomy, who rejected the principles of 'free' trade (this developed into a more general rejection of capitalism at the second global conference one year later) and who were committed to the use of direct action as a means of achieving social change.

PGA came into being at a time when 'globalisation' was a word on everybody's lips. The neo-liberal politics of the Washington Consensus were spreading across the globe. NAFTA and a number of other regional trade agreements had recently come into effect. The Multilateral Agreement on Investment (MAI) was being discussed, and the fifty

year old General Agreement on Tariffs and Trade (GATT) had just been formalised into an institution, the World Trade Organisation (WTO) - a body with the power to force the removal of protectionist barriers upon member states and to sanction those which resisted. As such, it appeared logical that PGA, whilst embracing a wide range of struggles, would focus upon the co-ordination of resistance to the WTO and other such institutions.

In May 1998, only three months after the first PGA Conference, actions against the G8 (Group of Eight, most industrialised nations) Summit in Birmingham and the Second WTO Ministerial in Geneva erupted across the globe. In Hydrabad, India 200,000 farmers called for the death of the WTO, in Brasilia, 50,000 peasants and unemployed workers took to the streets whilst Reclaim the Streets parties took place simultaneously in over thirty cities around the world, all under the banner of PGA. In Prague, the biggest single mobilisation since the 1989 Velvet Revolution, brought thousands into the streets, leading to several McDonalds being 'redesigned' and running battles with the police, whilst thousands took over the streets of Birmingham forcing the G8 to retreat to a more tranquil location. The following day, as the WTO Ministerial began, the streets of Geneva exploded. Thousands from across Europe took to the city's streets, smashing bank windows, overturning the WTO Director General's Mercedes and unleashing three days of the heaviest rioting Geneva had ever seen.

Harry Cleaver, an academic at Austin University in Texas and involved with Zapatista solidarity movements, once wrote, "In a very real sense, the Zapatista movement emerged as a tentative and transitory solution to precisely the problem which confronts us everywhere: how to link up a diverse array of linguistically and culturally distinct peoples and their struggles, despite and beyond those distinctions, how to weave a variety of struggles into one struggle that never loses its multiplicity." By May 1998, this process of weaving a fabric of global struggle had well and truly begun.

Global And Local

Whilst the Zapatista uprising, the Encuentros and the formation of PGA had been developing global networks, a similar process was underway nationally in the UK.

In Britain, a direct action movement had emerged and grown in strength throughout the 1990s. Thousands had become involved with the anti-roads movement, most famously resisting developments such as the road through Twyford Down, the M11 Link Road in East London and the Newbury Bypass. Thousands of others had taken part in Reclaim the Streets (RTS) parties around the country. The practical solidarity which had been offered to the striking Liverpool Dockers and other battling workers, along with the direct confrontation with the state experienced by those involved in resisting the road building programme had served to turn the movement radical. By the mid/late-1990s the beginnings of a whole anti-capitalist movement could be seen.

At around the same time as the social movements gathered in Geneva for the founding conference of PGA, an invitation was issued by people who had been involved in the recently disbanded Class War Federation for un-dogmatic, anti-authoritarian groups and individuals to attend a Reclaim Mayday event in Bradford on May 1st 1998. The event, attended by several hundred, was widely regarded as a success, especially in terms of bringing together the radical ecological direct action and the traditional anarchist movements in the UK. Amongst other things, the conference was as an opportunity to network the hastily-prepared actions against the Birmingham G8 Summit which was to take place a couple of weeks later.

It was from this position of strength, with people meeting up, talking and working together both nationally and globally, that discussion about the Global Day of Action on June 18th (J18) began.

An Idea is Born

In the early summer of 1998, an informal chat between London Reclaim the Streets and London Greenpeace (an anarchist organisation, no relation to the other 'Greenpeace'!) began. Both groups had begun thinking about how to build upon the position of relative strength in which they found themselves. London Greenpeace had been involved, along with many other groups, in organising the large, and at times militant, Stop the City demonstrations in the City of London (London's financial centre) in the 1980s. The idea for a similar, but globally co-ordinated, day of action began to take shape.

An initial idea was thrashed out, suggesting "A Global Day of Action in the World's Financial and Banking Districts on the Opening Day of the 1999 G8 Summit in Cologne, Germany", and was taken to the Earth First! Summer Gathering to be discussed. Some were doubtful about our ability to get into 'The Square Mile', (the nickname given to London's financial centre), notorious for its high security, with armed police check points on all roads going into the area and surveillance everywhere. Nevertheless, most were both enthusiastic and optimistic. A few weeks later, the first national meeting was held in London to discuss the idea, draft an international call to action - which was later taken to a meeting of the PGA Convenors in Finland where it was endorsed and further networked - and to set up working groups.

From this point on the idea began to snowball. Working groups, consisting of people from different cities across the UK took on different tasks. One group began to research how the City functions, which companies had offices where and exactly who was investing in what. They produced an excellent booklet entitled *Squaring up to the Square Mile*, with a full colour, pull-out map showing everything of interest from police stations and company head offices to tube stations and McDonalds'. Another translated the international call to action into eight different languages and took on the laborious task of posting it, via 'snail mail' to thousands of groups around the world. Others organised accommodation for those arriving from outside of London, legal support for those arrested and a website to distribute information and to collect reports of actions as they took place (remember, this was in the days before Indymedia!).

Meanwhile local June 18th groups began to spring up around the country, organising benefit gigs and information events about everything from global resistance to capitalism to the technical functioning of the City. They began planning autonomous actions and advertising the 'Carnival against Capital' being organised by Reclaim the Streets.

The Day Draws Closer

As June approached and articles with headlines such as "City Fears Threat of Eighties Riot Re-Runs" started to appear in the press, a plan for the day began to emerge.

Like almost everything else important to capital, the functioning of the City relies heavily upon its workforce. This was a weakness we hoped to exploit.

In the week preceding June 18th, and coinciding with the visit of hundreds of Indian farmers taking part in the PGA Inter-Continental Caravan, tens of thousands of *Evading Standards* newspapers (a spoof of London's *Evening Standard*) were distributed throughout the City and beyond. Explaining the reasoning for the day of action, the history of the movement and the importance of day-to-day resistance to capitalism, they asked workers to 'phone in sick' and stay at home - or better still, to come to the Reclaim the Streets Carnival.

Whilst encouraging workers to skive off as widely as possible, plans were also forged to prevent the more dedicated City workers from reaching their offices. Key points of access to the City were identified (major roads, bridges, train and tube stations). Local groups took

responsibility for disrupting different access points. Plans were made for pulling emergency stop cords on trains and tubes, blockading bridges with old cars and smoke bombs, chaining off roads and hanging banners across streets. All of these actions were to take place simultaneously, during the peak of the morning rush hour and at the same time as a Critical Mass bike ride designed to further congest the City streets.

Those groups who managed to evade arrest during these early morning actions were then invited to carry out further actions throughout the rest of the day, or to help out with the various aspects of the increasingly elaborate plan being formulated for the Carnival.

Pic: Nick Cobbing

By the middle of June, a dozen or so monthly national co-ordination meetings had been held in London. Most of which had been attended by around 40 people from across the UK, reporting back to various local and working groups. Almost 100,000 flyers and 1,000s of posters had been produced and distributed advertising the 'Carnival against Capital'. Tens of thousands of flyers calling for the simultaneous occupation and transformation of the world's financial centres had been distributed around the world. Hundreds upon hundreds of emails had been sent via the J18 email list, and tens of thousands of stickers advertising the day of action had been distributed across the UK. Meanwhile, local groups had been busy producing and distributing their own leaflets, posters and newsletters, making stickers and 'subvertising' billboards. *The Source*, a Brighton-based commercial listings guide (a kind of cheap, local imitation of *Time Out*), even carried an article about how one would have to be blind not to have noticed all the publicity. The day had been prepared as best as possible (or almost), and it had certainly been well advertised, but there were still a lot of uncertainties. Would the police allow us to meet? How many people really would show up on a working day? Would the weather be OK?

The Big Day Arrives!

As dawn broke on the morning of the long awaited June 18th, dozens of activists, with trepidation about whether the year of preparation would pay off, began to arise from their beds and head off for action.

The decentralised actions during the morning rush hour caused minor disruption. A few tube trains were delayed when people pulled emergency cords, a couple of streets were briefly blockaded, the Critical Mass was a little larger than had been expected and a few arrests were made. The overall impact of these co-ordinated actions was somewhat overshadowed by what was to unfold throughout the rest of the day.

As midday arrived, people began to assemble at Liverpool Street Station on the outskirts of 'The Square Mile'. The meeting point had been chosen partly because it was a big, open space, but more importantly because it gave very little clue as to where the crowd would be heading off to once the Carnival began. Over the preceding months, a relatively small group of people had worked out an intricate plan as to how the multiple tube lines running through Liverpool Street, and the various streets leading from station could best be used to create maximum confusion amongst the police's ranks and keep the final destination of the party a mystery for as long as possible.

J18

The LIFFE Building

The London International Financial Futures and Options Exchange (LIFFE) is one of the largest futures exchanges in the world and was the destination of the Carnival against Capital on J18. The exchange was subject to a cyber-attack from European hackers and a simultaneous 'conventional' attack by a crowd which had gathered before its doors.

For those of you not acquainted with the technical words of the global financial markets, 'Futures' and 'Options' are basically insurance policies for suppliers and purchasers of commodities. Over time, the prices of commodities tend to fluctuate. To overcome this uncertainty, traders began to sell 'futures', i.e. a contract to deliver an agreed commodity (or commodities) at an agreed time in the future, for an agreed price. 'Options' are similar to futures, except for the fact that they are not binding - they provide the option to buy or sell at an agreed price in the future. Got that?

As thousands of people began to gather, and the rhythms of the samba band began to vibrate throughout the station concourse, the tension mounted. The plan which involved four teams of three affinity groups (each having around ten members) taking responsibility for leading a section of the crowd in a different direction. The four sections would then - all going well – meet up in front of the LIFFE (London International Financial Futures and Options Exchange) building, the final location of the party. Each of the four teams had been given a colour code - red, green, black or gold - and had been issued with around 2,000 colour coded carnival masks to distribute and a set of streamers. On the back of the masks was a short text explaining that the City was under heavy surveillance and that wearing the masks was advisable, and that on the signal, you should follow the streamers which corresponded to the colour of your mask.

Six giant puppets, each one representing a different revolutionary movement or figure from a different continent, had been brought into the train station. Hidden under the papier mache were sound systems. The idea was that the masks and streamers would remain hidden until exactly 1pm, one hour after the advertised meeting time, when they would then be distributed amongst the crowd as quickly as possible. Exactly five minutes later, the hidden sound systems would kick in, playing the *Mission Impossible* theme tune, followed by a voice saying "Follow your colour! Into the streets! GO, GO, GO!" The affinity groups leading each group would then hold up their streamers and begin to leave the station and head towards the LIFFE building along their pre-arranged route (two teams were to travel by tube, the other two overland.) Each team had one affinity group at the front, one in the middle, and one at the end, all of which were equipped with streamers and some knowledge as to where they were supposed to be leading the crowd in case the group broke down.

Despite the *Mission Impossible* theme tune being drowned out by the noise of the crowd, one set of masks being distributed far too early and the beautifully anarchic nature of the crowd meaning that people didn't 'do as they were told' and follow the colour they had been assigned, but rather followed the group leaving in the direction closest to where they were standing, the plan worked surprisingly well. The complicated and novel idea of splitting the crowd, combined with the spontaneity, ingenuity and militancy of the crowd in responding to tube stations and streets being closed down succeeded in outwitting the police. Their central control point was receiving messages from cops stationed miles apart from each other all saying "They're here, they're here!" The chaos was increased by the fact that there was no real co-ordination between the City of London Police, the main cops in the City, and the Metropolitan Police, in charge of policing in London in general and who had been called in for back up.

After around an hour, three of the four groups had arrived at the LIFFE building. The fourth group had become involved in a prolonged battle with police after a woman was run down by a riot van. As the crowd arrived, sound systems, stages and PA equipment for bands which had been hidden in vehicles parked nearby were driven into the crowd and giant, beautifully painted banners were hoisted between lamp posts. A fire hydrant was opened, sending a 40 foot fountain of cold water into the air, much to the joy of the crowd dancing beneath it in the hot afternoon sun.

As the day progressed sound systems played, bands performed, nearby banks and car dealerships were 're-designed' and a concerted attack upon the LIFFE building was launched with the glass entrance and lobby being completely destroyed and an attempt to storm the trading floor being made. Meanwhile, news began to arrive of other sections of the City being taken over, and of small street fights breaking out well away from the main Carnival. Announcements were made in the Underground that all the City stations had been closed "due to civil unrest".

The day began to draw to a close as the police managed to regain control of the area in front of the LIFFE building, pushing people out of the City and toward Trafalgar Square, a place in which the police feel much more confident of being able to control crowds than in the narrow City streets. As we

A Truly Global Day of Action

Whilst the corporate media in the UK, predictably enough, focused upon the militancy of the events in London, what they didn't explain was the extraordinary international nature of the day. In response to the call issued by a number of radical groups in the UK which was then endorsed by the Convenors of PGA on every continent, tens of thousands of people in over 40 different countries, from Argentina to Bangladesh, Nepal to Belarus and Zimbabwe to Israel realised their common enemy and took co-ordinated action against it.

For a full round-up of what took place around the world see: *Do or Die #8* p.30-34.

retreated, we watched as the plumes of smoke rose above the City. I think those of us who had invested so much time, energy and hope in the day felt a combination of a smug sense of victory and a dawning realisation that someone was going to be made to pay for this.

Conclusion

In the days and weeks which followed there was a feeling of optimism, excitement and apprehension. We felt victorious. We had outsmarted the police. We had brought thousands of people onto the streets, and we had reached a new level and intensity of struggle. Dozens of local groups around the UK had been formed in the process of organising for the day. Thousands had taken part in their first anti-capitalist action. Real functioning networks of resistance, across the UK and globally, had been developed and consolidated. Perhaps most importantly of all, however, was that capitalism itself had been put well and truly back on the agenda. The very fact that the *Financial Times* headline the following day read, "Anti-Capitalists Lay Siege to the City of London", whilst the *London Times* – as if predicting the events soon to unfold in Seattle, Prague and elsewhere – declared, "capitalism's enemies will return", was seen as a tremendous victory.

Finally something had begun to develop which meant that the press could no longer be so complacent that capitalism was the only way to organise society. They had been forced into a position in which they felt the need to publish articles defending capitalism as a social system and, thereby, admitting that alternatives existed. A debate had begun about the possibilities of another world. This was something very, very new. But the boys at the top realised that the social order was not just being questioned. Attacks upon their centres and symbols of power, such as the City, showed a new level of awareness, determination and challenge. Their response was swiftly and efficiently prepared.

A full-time team of 60 officers at Scotland Yard were assigned the task of examining 5,000 hours of video footage and identifying and apprehending those accused of taking part in the day's activities. They published photographs in newspapers and on the City of London Police's website. Meanwhile on Fleet Street, the thesauruses were dusted off as journalists competed for the most ridiculous adjectives to describe those who'd taken part in the Carnival ("open-toed sandled hippy vandals", "booze-fuelled hardcore anarchists" and "evil savages" were amongst some of the best), providing a political atmosphere where heavy sentences could be dished out without controversy. More generally, post-J18, policing policy at large actions in London underwent an enormous change, with the City of London Police - Britain's oldest police force - almost being disbanded. Strategies were rethought and tactics were imported from elsewhere, perhaps most significantly, that of surrounding entire crowds and refusing to let them move until either the situation has de-escalated or everyone has been searched, filmed, photographed and intimidated out of considering taking part in anything 'risky'.

Resources

Squaring up to the Square Mile

A booklet containing information about how the City works, produced by Corporate Watch during the run up to J18 is available at: www.corporatewatch.org.uk/publications/squaringup/intro.html

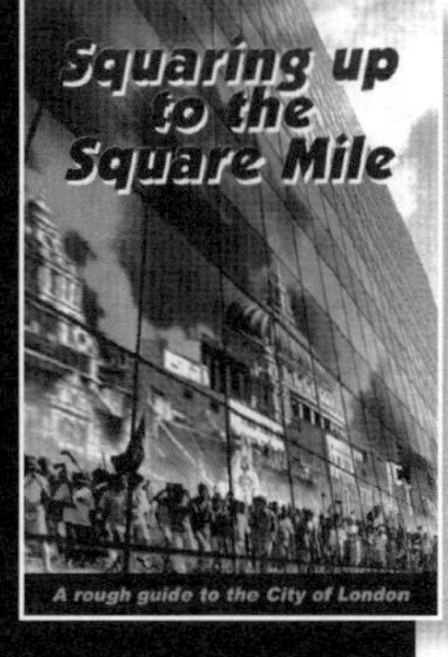

Reflections on June 18th

A pamphlet produced post-J18 with some very interesting reflection on the politics behind the day of action. It can be found online at: www.infoshop.org/octo/j18_reflections.html

Debate within the UK social movements about the day and its significance also began to develop in the weeks and months following J18. Things focussed upon criticisms of such 'mass mobilisations', firstly regarding how much time, energy and resources they consume (which could otherwise be directed into other, perhaps more local or immediate issues) and, secondly, regarding the extent to which these mobilisations were being given priority over smaller actions. Other critics, whilst praising the identification of 'capitalism' as the problem, argued that the J18 event had largely misunderstood what this meant. In other words, capitalism, rather than being identified as a 'social relation' had been presented as being either big banks, big business, finance centres or whatever. This argument, that capital has no centre and so cannot be occupied, or 'an action' taken against it, was something brought up a few times in the run up to the day of action.

Indeed, it was the theme of a conference held in a squat in North London in February 1999 as part of the whole J18 thang. The feeling that a clear and coherent analysis of capitalism wasn't particularly visible in the propaganda and literature produced in relation to the mobilisation (in the *Evading Standards* newspaper, the *Squaring Up to the Square Mile* booklet, the flyers produced by Reclaim the Streets in London or by other groups around the country) is, in the author of this article's opinion, valid. Nevertheless, that capitalism had been identified as the problem, which until this point hadn't been done by many people central to organising the day, whose backgrounds were largely in environmental, peace and animal rights movements, has to be seen as having been a step in the right direction.

A further weakness of the day was that prior to J18, there was very little thought put into what to do next. In Britain, unlike in many other European countries, there is very little infrastructure - in terms of social centres and autonomous spaces - which are able to provide permanent spaces where people who become involved or interested in radical politics can meet other like-minded people and start to take part in ongoing struggles. J18 had been a success in terms of showing that 'anti-capitalists' existed, but failed (despite the efforts of a few) in offering real opportunities for the thousands of people who showed up on the day to develop meaningful, ongoing contact with people involved in day-to-day anti-capitalist activities. This weakness was recognised by many, and a lot of effort has gone into developing stuff in the following years - the London Action Resource Centre (LARC), the Cowley Club in Brighton, the Sumac Centre in Nottingham and numerous other projects. Indeed, one of the focuses of the mobilisation against the 2005 G8 Summit - well underway at the time of this article being written - has been the setting up of permanent and semi-permanent social centres which can, hopefully, fulfil exactly such a function.

For all its strengths and weaknesses, it cannot be denied that the day had a significant impact on the growing global anti-capitalist movement. In particular, it was a major inspiration for those organising against the WTO Ministerial which took place in Seattle a few months later. Some US activists had been in the UK on June 18th, others had heard about the day and the process leading up to it via long term contacts, others still went to talks and workshops held by UK activists who travelled to the US to explain how the day had been organised, what took place and what it was thought could be learned. In particular, the idea of carnival as revolutionary and revolution as carnival was something heavily picked up on in Seattle and elsewhere. And, of course, the events in Seattle themselves proved to be an even greater inspiration to those resisting capitalism worldwide.

It is, perhaps, this worldwide spread of inspiration, made possible by the formation of networks such as PGA and 'advances' like the internet, which makes the new anti-capitalist 'movement of movements' so unique. Some of the most inspiring events which have taken place over the last decade are those which have taken inspiration from other mobilisations, whilst adapting them to suit local conditions, and leaving behind those aspects thought to have been limiting. This was certainly the case with J18 in the UK, which was inspired by, yet managed to move beyond, the successes of the Stop the City demonstrations in the 1980s and the more recent protests against meetings of the international elite such as that against the 1998 EU Summit in Amsterdam.

In order to continue evolving and strengthening our local and global networks of resistance - particularly in relation to mobilisations such as that against the 2005 G8 Summit to be held in the UK, where the temptation to merely produce what is expected of us is so high - this process of looking at ourselves, of „walking asking questions“, as the Zapatistas say, is of primary importance

They're Inside for Us! Are We Really Outside for Them?

Despite a number of press articles claiming (largely wrongly) to reveal 'the organisers' of the day, some police harassment of individual people and one court case against an 'organiser' (he was found not guilty), it was by and large those who simply turned up on the day and took part in the festivities who were subject to the most extreme repression. 16 people were arrested on June 18th itself; another 50 had been nicked by the end of the year following an enormous police operation. Dozens of court cases were held against people accused of committing offences on the day. Numerous people received multiple years in prison; others got lighter sentences and fines. Apart from the excellent work done by the Legal Defence and Monitoring Group (LDMG), a couple of ABC groups and a few individuals, the prisoners received fairly limited support. There was certainly no attempt to build a solidarity movement and demand their release as, for example, happened with the seven people imprisoned in Thessaloniki following the 2003 EU Summit. Offering practical and political solidarity to those subject to repression is something which needs to be taken far more seriously by our movement.

Five years on, at least two people remain in prison for their actions on J18. Rob Thaxton was sentenced to 88 months in a US jail after throwing a single rock at a cop whilst trying to avoid arrest. James Borek pleaded guilty in January 2004 to causing GBH to a policeman and two violent disorder charges, plus an additional charge of skipping bail in 2000. He received a four and a half year sentence. Both deserve and would appreciate our solidarity.

MCCF, **Rob Thaxton,** #12112716, 4005 Aumsville Hwy, Salem, OR97301. USA.
Donations to and information from:
AAA, PO Box 50634, Eugene, OR97405. USA.

James Borek LL6803, HMP Blundeston, D-108, Lowestoft, Suffolk, NR32 5BG. UK
Info: anarprisonersupp@hotmail.com

Updates about these and other prisoners are available from **Brighton Anarchist Black Cross** (ABC): www.brightonabc.org.uk

SchNEWS POSSE HIT SEATTLE

Just when you think flying over to the US for a street battle would be all glamorous - here comes Brits abroad Vs Robocop. This is a personal account from one of the crew...

We all met at Amsterdam airport where we were to wait in transit until we boarded our flight. Our motley crew consisted of a millionaire's brother who suggested he was only going for the people, which roughly translated meant he'd acquired a cheap ticket and just like 96% of the British population at the time he had no idea who the World Trade Organisation were, a Slough Town football fan, my girlfriend, my ex-girlfriend, Yorkshire's answer to Arthur Daley, a bright intelligent woman who had lips that Kylie would die for, and amongst others a girl called Air who arranged us in a circle so we could hold hands and think positively about getting through customs in Seattle - anarchy! We boarded the flight. Arthur Daley saw to it that we were supplied with copious amounts of free alcohol from the friendly Dutch air staff, we all got pissed and sailed through the other end, dived into a petrol guzzling taxi with an engine the size of Botswana, and arrived at our destination.

With a day or so to spare, we met up with more ardent British revolutionary types intent on causing mayhem and destruction - well, actually we all went sight-seeing. After commenting on what a lovely city Seattle was and all agreeing that the locals were really friendly, we decided to put our subversive arses into gear and visit the centre of resistance. There was a beehive of activity going on when we arrived, with huge puppets being made, 'how to be non-violent' workshops and a peculiar group that sold coffee and believed Elvis was God. 'Have you been in touch with your inner Elvis today?' an Elvis look-alike asked. Yeah right! Anarchy American stylee! Still, if this was a squat, it was the strangest one we'd ever seen. There were signs up everywhere: 'No drugs' 'No drinking' 'No smoking'. No poxing smoking!! Give me a break! My last little avenue of prejudice was beginning to show. How on earth this lot were going to stop the gargantuan WTO conference, I had no idea. We made a democratically thought out collective decision at this point to venture into a gay bar across the road and get pissed.

The first time I saw the Robo cops was at the 'people dressed as turtles' march. The 'I'm here for the people' man was standing next to me when out marched a line of robots who had obviously never had the chance to dress up when they were children. They were certainly making up for it now by being in the 'I'm going to put on as much body wear as feasibly possible (without falling over)' department of the American police squad. If it was a contest as to who had the most armour, the obese looking cops beat the turtles hands down. I remember a comment by a protestor stating that, 'We'll never beat these people by dressing up as turtles.'

The day of reckoning came and the American resistance was organised with military precision, blocking every entrance to the conference by sitting in the roads with face masks laced with vinegar. The first car that tried to get through had his tyres punctured by a protestor and while the deafening hiss of the escaping air bellowed out, a super hero in a red cloak began running around the car and jumping up walls in robotic movements that mimicked a police siren which was wailing away for no particular reason. Then

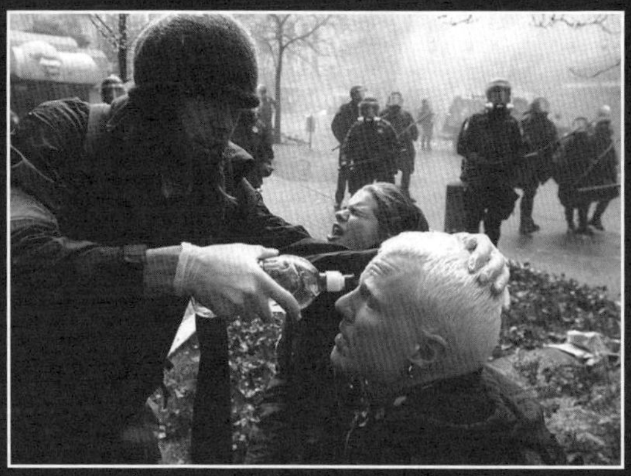

things really began to hot up with the arrival of 'the peacekeeper,' which was a huge armoured car lined with gun wielding mental cases. The peacekeeper began firing tear gas at protestors peacefully sitting in the road. Through the clouds of toxic shite we could see people just sitting there, being shot at, pepper sprayed and gassed, while we looked on in awe.

Post-Seattle, I've heard a lot of people suggest it was people smashing windows that stopped that meeting - bollocks! If that's what you want to believe, fine. I'm not making any judgements on the black bloc or anyone else, everyone has to do their own thing, but if we just take out the bits that we want to believe and ignore the truth, we may as well go and read tabloid papers and talk the same kind of shite! What stopped that conference were the bravest, most peaceful, most organised protestors I'd ever seen. I realised then that my biased comments earlier were based on British protestor ignorance - like a hang over from June 18th.

The Americans weren't the only ones being organised though. In the event of anyone getting lost in the clouds of gas, people in our affinity group were supposed to shout out 'Palace Pier' until we all regrouped. On one occasion when we were doing just that we bumped into masked people going in the opposite direction shouting 'pizza'. In a scene that was reminiscent of the 'Life of Brian', we all unmasked and promptly discovered other mates from Brighton! After getting gassed for about the forty-fifth time in a day, we all decided to go down the pub and get pissed again.

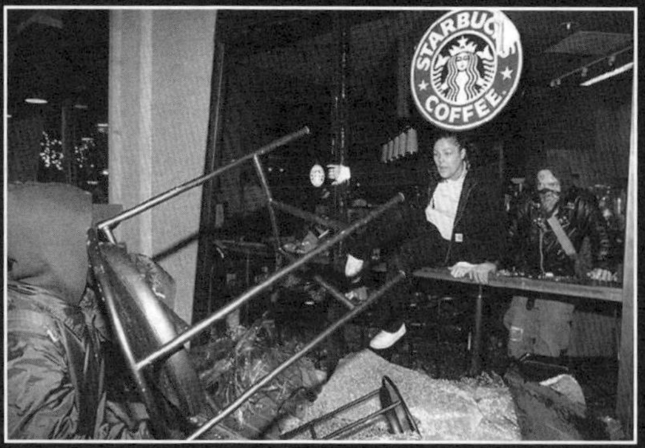

After days of gas, pepper spray, and everything else they could throw at us, I was quite relieved to go to a meeting of the Steelworkers in a local park. After a couple of hours of talking, people began to shout, 'Down the town!' 'Down the town!' I must admit, I really could not believe they were going to walk back into the town after all that had happened. These people were 'avin it big time! More and more people began to shout and before long a huge body of people began to move towards town. Hundreds of people then marched straight into Seattle, blocking the traffic, which was hooting in solidarity, and as we got round the first corner, people began chanting, 'We're waiting for the Union.' Just as the buzz of the crowd began to die down, I looked back to see a collection of colourful union banners coming into view from around the corner about a quarter of a mile behind. That was one moment I'll never forget. We were all there - a solid, indestructible force, the people, a unified collection of protestors, environmentalists, workers and anyone else with a conscience. The chant went up 'The Power of the people won't stop' and then the bastards came round the corner in their shitty peacekeeper mobile and bloody gassed us.

The last day though, the police were beaten. The conference had been stopped. McDonalds was now a drive-in (through the window), Starbucks was more airy and the Mayor had been heavily criticised from all corners for the treatment of peaceful protestors (especially as the eyes of the world were now watching).

We surrounded the prison while an army of excessively armed defenders of hell looked on, drooling at the mouth. After it was promised that the imprisoned protestors would have access to legal representation, which I thought was a bit of a cop out (excuse the pun), the crowds at last began to disperse. Our lot decided the best course of action was to team up with eight Santas we'd met on the march, go down to a bar where we had promised an American guy we would watch his band, and get pissed - for a change! After a week of protesting, being gassed and general adrenalin rushes, some bright spark suggested tequila would reawaken our senses. By the time we left the bar there were Santas lying everywhere, people wearing white beards that shouldn't have, someone stuck in a phone box and peanuts and beer all over the shop. As I was dragging an unconscious person past the stage I looked up to see our American guitarist friend looking down on a scene that must have resembled Keith Richard's fortieth birthday party. It was at that point, on reflection, especially after witnessing the non-alcohol policy of the Seattle protestors and their impressive ability to get up early (we are talking 6.30am) that maybe, just maybe, we may have learned something, even if it was just not to be so cynical.

THE WTO SUMMIT IN SEATTLE IS SHUT DOWN BRINGING WORLDWIDE ATTENTION TO BOTH THE INSTITUTIONS OF GLOBALISED CAPITAL, AND THE GATHERING INTERNATIONAL MOVEMENT OF MOVEMENTS BUILDING TO RESIST THEM...

BARE BREASTS & RUBBER BULLETS

SPECIAL REPORT ON SEVEN DAYS THAT SHOOK THE CORPORATE WORLD

'They never knew what hit them. They had assumed it would be business as usual, the way it had been for decades. Rich men gather, meet, decide the fate of the world, then return home to amass more wealth. It's the way it's always been. Until Seattle.' - Michael Moore, U.S comedian (not director general of the WTO)

'The very fact that the World Trade Organisation is global headline news is a sign of our power, for the high priests of capital fully expected their summit to be convened in the usual frat boy secrecy. We have done our part to help blow away both their cover and their aura of invincibility. Never again will the economists and technocrats be able to decide the fate of the world...in anonymous tranquility.'* - The Aggressive Panhandlers**

'They are worried about a few windows being smashed. They should come and see the violence being done to our communities in the name of liberalisation of trade.' - A Philippino leader

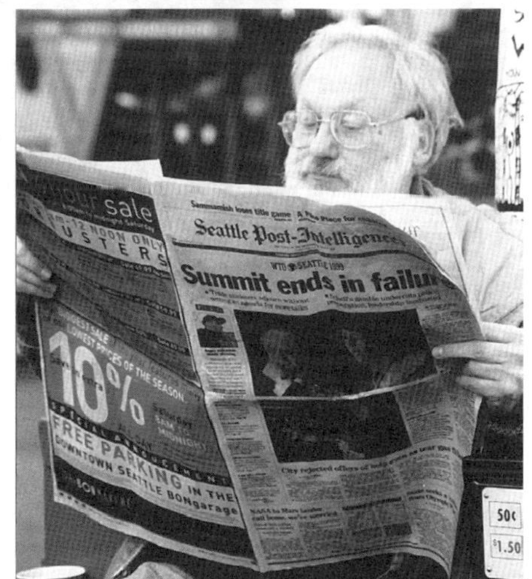

As the gas cleared over Seattle after another uneasy stand-off with the black clad robo-cops, word on the street last Friday was that the talks had collapsed. There would be no millennium round agreement by the World Trade Organisation (WTO). The people on the streets had won a stunning victory.

And what a victory it was. Who would have thought, even a year ago, that sixty thousand people would turn to greet delegates of the World Trade Organisation. Who'd have thought that trade unionists would be marching with environmentalists – people dressed as turtles marching with sacked steelworkers, the topless lesbian avengers mingling with farmers. Churchgoers with the anarchist black-block. The mass protests helped focus worldwide attention on what the WTO really stands for – and it crumbled under the pressure. Forget all their talk about 'free trade,' the WTO is nothing more than a nasty little organisation fighting for the rights of multinational organisations to dismantle every country's labour and environmental laws.

Groups like SchNEWS have been shouting from the rooftops for ages about this, but no one seemed really bothered cos let's face it economics is hardly the sexiest subject in the universe. But last week's event changed all that, with seven days of protest that shook the corporate world.

'It is important to acknowledge the fact that we made history this week. No amount of corporate spin doctoring or liberal hand wringing can diminish this reality.' **- The Aggressive Panhandlers**

WHERE'S THE ORGANISATION ?

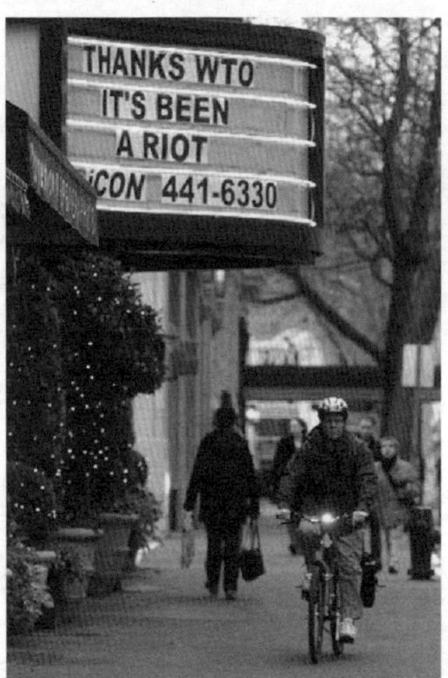

"My mother's a member of the Women's Institute and they organise their fetes better than this." U.K Trade Minister Steven Byers who went to the WTO and got hit with pepper spray for his trouble.

It started quietly enough on the **Sunday** with a few hundred people demonstrating outside The Gap over the sweatshop conditions workers have to endure to produce the company's clothes.

Then on the **Monday** there was a demonstration by the turtle posse pointing out how the WTO had ruled America's Endangered Species Act illegal. Later, French national hero Jose Bove, who recently demolished McDonalds, demonstrated outside his favourite store as a protest against U.S sanctions on French cheese. Things were hotting up. The last thing the U.S President must have expected was to be flying into a city under a state of emergency with the National Guard on the streets?

***'If you were alive, the police gassed you. People coming back from work, kids, women, everyone. People would go out of their houses to see what was happening because these tear gas guns sound like a cannon – and they would get gassed.'*- Eyewitness account from Jim Desyllas**

TUESDAY

Tuesday morning and already thousands are on the streets blocking roads and stopping delegates from getting into the WTO Conference centre. The opening ceremony is abandoned and talks delayed for more than five hours. Around 10 a.m we have a taste of what's to come as riot cops, with 3 foot clubs & dressed like Darth Vader, start spraying CS gas into the faces of people peacefully blocking the roads. One man commented, "When the gas masks came out we knew they were planning to use pepper spray on the people sitting down. The crowd was pleading with them. We locked legs and arms and I pulled a bandana over my face, covering my mouth and eyes. People began screaming in pain. I felt a blow from a club, the cops were beating people as well. A police officer pulled my hand away from my face and pepper-sprayed me in the eyes. The rest of the crowd pulled people to safety and began washing their eyes with a solution of baking soda and water to counter the effects of the blinding pepper spray."

By midday 30,000 trade unionists join the demonstrations, "I'm not a trade barrier" reads the marching turtles' banner; giant puppets weave their way down the streets, superheroes slide round corners, cloaks flying, a group of Father Christmases march along waving at the crowd, doubling over with laughter, "WTO? Ho, ho, ho!" A Reclaim The Streets sound system blasts out funk, rappers rhyming "WTO, it's gotta go." SchNEWS meet Mexican, Indian and French farmers, Tibetan refugees, steelworkers, striking cabbies, anti logging and deforestation protesters, all experts on the WTO, its power and its direct repercussions on their lives.

Mike Moore (then director general of the WTO) calls the whole thing off at Seattle.

These people are no random mob, they have gathered from all over the world to be heard and no matter how many issues are at stake here they speak with one voice, united in their opposition to an institution which has no respect for the ordinary people of the world. They are calling for an end to sweatshops, to child labour and the erosion of environmental laws and the third world debt. These people are well informed, well organised and determined.

"I never got on with environmentalists until I realised we were all fighting for the same thing," - Dan Petrowski, a Michigan steelworker who was made redundant four months ago. Still, what did that matter to the police who lost patience with the crowd spraying them with jets of gas like water cannons again and again?

SCHNEWS US-UK VOCAB WATCH
* Frat – fraternity, secret student society.
**Panhandlers-beggars.

Pic: Nick Cobbing

Meanwhile, groups of anarchists went shopping. McDonalds, Niketown, Gap, Starbucks and the American Bank all had their windows smashed. One man from the U.K. told SchNEWS, *"Even as a pacifist I was pleased. No-one was hurt. It seemed trivial in comparison to the scenes I had witnessed earlier. This wasn't violence against people it was violence against the property of some of the world's most hated multinationals."*

As early evening approached with the crowds remaining on the streets, and the Clinton adminsistration leaning on the mayor to do something quick, the National Guard were called out for the first time in Seattle in modern times. A no-protest zone and a 12 hour curfew were imposed in the downtown area – for the first time since the second world war. This seemed to be a signal for the robo-cops to unleash an arsenal of weapons against anyone who got in their way for the next 24 hours. SchNEWS is used to a bit of argy-bargy with the police but this was something else.

BUTT-PLUGGIN' IN THE USA

"Hey! Check it out – these motherfuckers are firing butt-plugs at us," called out one grinning member of the crowd brandishing a two by four inch rubber bullet.

As night drew in the forces of darkness began pushing people into the the city's bohemian/gay district, the Capitol Hill residential area. This was way out of the no-protest zone, and it infuriated locals who came out of the streets in their hundreds. Seattle Gay News takes up the story. 'Numerous accounts from witnesses all describe excessive force by police who appeared to have no real reason to be on Capitol Hill. The area is outside of the curfew and no-protest zones. One resident told us, 'I haven't been marching, but when the cops turn your neighbourhood into a war zone, it's time to get involved.'

WEDNESDAY

"*The intolerance of democratic dissent, which is a hallmark of dictatorship, was unleashed in full force.*" -Vandana Shiva, director of Research Foundation New Delhi.

Early morning and the mass arrests begin. If yesterday's show of force by the authorities was meant to scare people from demonstrating then they were mistaken. Thousands of people are regrouping at a steelworkers rally. People grow restless at the speeches and start leaving for the no-protest zone. "Whose streets? Our streets!" everyone chants. One man explained to SchNEWS what happened next, "*Eventually we were pushed onto the main road with shoppers, protesters, cars, buses. They're not going to gas us here, are they? I thought. A second later an explosion followed by a barrage of plastic bullets, gas, pepper spray, concussion grenades. Mental. People sitting in their cars were gassed, people leaving work. Everyone.*"

The police say they are using non-lethal weapons but one man reports listening to a local radion station when a man calls in weeping – his wife had been attacked by the police while leaving work and she lost their child – she was 4 months pregnant. A doctor blamed this on the gas.

It's getting scary, the town centre is emptying of people as the curfew approaches. The police are roaming around everywhere, kitted-out in the most bizzare Stormtroopper meets Ninja Turtle outfits and riding everything from bicycles to a huge tank-like thing, inappropriately named the 'Peacekeeper'. If you aren't falling head over heels with laughter, your legs are being shot out from under you by rubber bullets!

Still, if it's scary for the demonstrators at least the WTO delegates aren't having much fun. One New Zealand delegate confides in us that there is confusion inside the conference, and in the evening everyone is holed up in their hotels unable to leave.

THURSDAY

Residents and students march, chanting, from Capitol Hill to join a farmers rally, "Ain't no power like the power of the people 'cos the power of the people don't stop." Thousands then march towards the County Jail where hundreds of protestors are being held, most not giving even their names. The jail is surrounded by

people holding hands. A temporary autonomous zone is established as people keep vigil, sleeping, eating, making music and speeches demanding the release of our brothers and sistas. A party evolves outside the jail as people drum, sing, juggle and dance, chanting "This is what democracy looks like". At the windows we can see the silhouettes of prisoners arms waving as they dance in solidarity.

FRIDAY EVENING

These people just don't give up. A couple of hundred have gathered at the Westin Hotel to support people who have D-locked themselves to the entrance.

It's here that SchNEWS hears the news – the talks have collapsed. There will be no millennium round. It doesn't quite sink in. Inside the Conference centre, the delegates from the poorer countries complained that they were being sidelined, while the world's elite held secret 'green room discussions'. Most of the world's poorest countries have neither the capacity nor the means to implement even the previous round of talks which finished five years ago, let alone take on board a whole new round of negotiations, and couldn't even afford to have a permanent representative in Geneva where the rolling talks are held. (30 countries couldn't even afford to send delegates to Seattle!)

One high-level U.S. journalist said, 'The talks failed because of the protests. They failed because of the chaos. They failed because Clinton pushed the labour working group. And they failed because the Southern hemisphere rebelled.' The U.S. labour movement forced the Clinton Administration to ensure

a working group on labour, which would, in particular, seek to eliminate all global child labour and encourage unionisation. Clinton's speech served to enhance the irony when the Mayor of Seattle declared a 'no protest zone' around the Niketown and Nordstrom department stores but encouraged people to keep shopping there. The citizens of Seattle were free to shop for merchandise made in sweatshops, they just couldn't complain about it.

WE WON, YOU BASTARDS

"We want a new millennium based on economic democracry, not economic totalitarianism. The future is possible for humans and other species only if the principles of competition, organised greed, commodification of all life, monocultures, monopolies and centralised global corporate control of our daily lives enshrined in the WTO are replaced by the principles of protection of people and nature, the obligation of giving and sharing diversity, and the decentralisation and self-organisation enshrined in our diverse cultures and national constitutions." - Vandana Shiva

What SchNEWS did see last week was how the thin veil of democracy so easily falls away when those in power are really threatened. That the Chief of Police has since resigned gives some indication of how out of control the robo-cops were.

But what was far more important was that ordinary people made history last week. The thousands of diverse groups that had come together to challenge the corporate power that is taking over our world. And for a week at least, we won.

ACTS OF SOLIDARITY

- The Longshore and Warehouse Union shut down the Port of Seattle and dozens of ports along the West Coast.
- Seattle taxi-drivers chose November 30th to strike over worsening pay and conditions. When SchNEWS asked one taxi-driver about Starbucks he told us us, 'I don't drink there – they're capatalist bastards.' And what if other taxi-drivers break the strike? 'They'll get shot buddy!' Just like English cabbies eh?
- The Firebrigade Union refused to turn their fire hoses upon the protesters despite repeated requests from the police.
- One delivery boy handed over his pizzas to the demonstrators outside the Westin Hotel, rather than give them to the right-wing talk radio station presenters who had ordered them.

ENTER... INDYMEDIA

The international support and attention the Zapatistas have had since the uprising in 1994 has played a big part in limiting what could have been even harsher repression from the Mexican government, and their use of the internet has played a big role in building that international support.

Since then, the internet has provided a useful forum for people seeking an alternative space away from the advertising-ridden fat-cat corporate agenda setting mass media. As well as that it's a way to reach large audiences instantly and cheaply.

Indymedia is an international network of websites which provide an on-line interactive media base, which gathers reports from the struggles for a world founded on freedom, cooperation, justice and solidarity, and against environmental degradation, neo-liberal exploitation, racism and patriarchy. Created through a system of open publishing, anyone (with computer access) can upload a written, audio or video report, or a picture, directly to their screens.

Through this system of 'Direct Media', Indymedia erodes the dividing line between reporters and reported, between active producers and passive audience: people are enabled to speak for themselves. At bigger actions, Indymedia have established 'Public Access Terminals' on the streets, giving protestors direct access to the technical equipment to upload directly to the website. It has shown itself to be able to take the corporate media head on – for instance during the G8 Summit in Genoa in 2001 Indymedia Italy was getting over a million visits a day.

The seeds of Indymedia were sown by the worldwide J18 protests in June 1999. At the massive demonstrations in London (see page 151) protesters organized a flow of information direct from the streets to a web-uploading facility in the south of the capital. At J18 Sydney, Catalyst created 'active' websites [www.active.org.au] which allowed for the participatory open publishing format. Five months later at the WTO summit in Seattle, the 'active' code was used to create the first Indymedia site, instantly publishing coverage of events by the array of independent writers and camera-people on the street. On its world debut at Seattle, Indymedia got more hits than the CNN website for the duration of the event.

Since then Indymedia centres/websites have continued to pop up around the world. Reflecting the political movements which Indymedia has been born from, many of the initial Indymedia sites were created for specific events – often mass demonstrations – and then continued on as permanent fixtures. UK Indymedia was launched under the shadow of a mohicaned Winston Churchill amidst the chaos of the Guerrilla Gardening action in Parliament Square on Mayday 2000.

The first Indymedia centre at the WTO summit, Seattle, November 1999

The network reports on regional struggles that have been largely forgotten about (or purposefully ignored) by mainstream media. A few examples are:

* Indymedia Argentina reporting live from the Latin American state in 2001, as its economic and political system collapsed after the IMF imposed policies which drove poverty-stricken Argentineans to the point of starvation.
* Indymedia Jerusalem was launched in 2002, days before the brutal invasion of Palestinian territory by the armed forces, and provided crucial information from the besieged state.
* In April 2002 Desert Indymedia set up in the back of a truck at the Woomera protest camp in Australia, and provided incredible footage and photos of the breakout and detained refugees (see page 224).

Check out www.indymedia.co.uk for UK news or www.indymedia.org the international site.

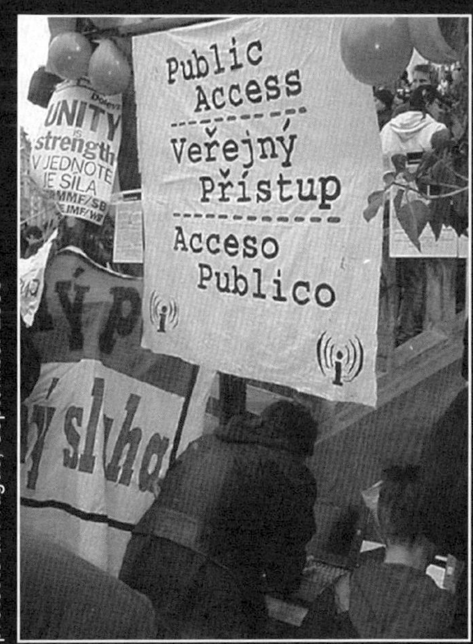

Public access Indymedia at the World Bank/IMF Summit protests at Prague, September 2000

THE MURDERING FUND

The Washinton DC protests against the International Monetary Fund/World Bank spring meetings were billed as Seattle II, and so of course SchNEWS' rovin' riot reporter decided to take another Anarchitours package holiday.

Anarchitours – "5 days of non-stop chanting, marching and police brutality, all in the idyllic setting of the USA's most deprived city: stimulate yourself with in depth discussions of global monetary policy, explore the charming teargas clogged alleys of the 'capital of the world' before relaxing with a luke-warm bowl of lentil stew in the luxury of a crumbling squat; or perhaps simply get stuck round the back of the White House in a turtle costume, cop a face full of pepper spray and spend the next week being beaten up in police custody.......".

In the week before the DC's finest practiced their legendary intimidation tactics – heavy police presence, circling helicopters, arresting 600 people at an anti-Gap demonstration, motorbike charging a critical mass bike ride, closing down the direct action convergence centre for 'fire violations' and confiscating bikes, puppets, pipe-bomb making equipment and home-made pepper spray ingredients. The last two turned out to be, er, a propane cooking stove, gasoline and spices, but you can't be too careful these days, especially in Bill Clinton's back yard.

FOGGY BOTTOM

Despite the heavy policing, and the obvious media headlines ("blood-stained terrorists that trashed Seattle vow to burn DC to the ground and slaughter everyone in it" etc), this was not a re-run of November 30th (SchNEWS 240). Although shed loads of activists, gutted that they missed all the fun in Seattle, turned up for the festivities and sports shops sold out of goggles as everyone geared up for chemical warfare, there were no massive battles or Seattle-style rampages.

Washington DC is designed for riot control, having seen more protests than the South African embassy. Despite this, and the fact that the Seattle shut down has been closely analysed by every police force in the world, some bright spark decided to repeat the exact same plan – affinity groups forming clusters and committing to shut down 'pie-slice' sections of the city. Oddly enough this meant that when everyone dragged themselves out of their soggy sleeping bags at some ungodly hour of the morning and headed down to IMF headquaters in Foggy Bottom, they found shit loads of rozzers waiting for them behind barricades two blocks away from their target.

As the police had kindly shut down the city for them, the protesters concentrated on what they do best: dancing, chanting, singing god-awful hippy songs and arguing about whether kicking in McDonald's counts as violence. There were a few scuffles, and the odd gassing, but few succeeded in their goal of getting nicked. The next day was more serious. As the World Bank's Development Committee met inside a 100 block exclusion zone,

IF ORDINARY PEOPLE BEHAVED LIKE-

a column of protesters managed to penetrate the perimeter. When riot cops blocked them in and ordered them to turn around, they insisted (!) that the police arrest them. Rather reluctantly the police agreed, and so several hundred protestors walked up in pairs and got on the jail busses!

I M FIRED

The poor old bureaucrats and politicians of the IMF and World Bank just can't understand why nobody loves them, despite enforcing poverty, exploitation and environmental vandalism around the world for over fifty years. James Wolfensohn, head of the bank that helps maintain the debt stranglehold that kills 15-20 million people a year, confessed to being "nonplussed" that anyone should want to protest against his admirable efforts to ensure that rich creditors get their money back five times over, with a controlling stake in southern countries economies thrown in for good measure. And Britain's own goodwill ambassador Gordon Brown pointed out that the protestors had nothing to complain about as the IMF's International Monetary and Financial Committee had spent "almost the whole afternoon discussing poverty reduction." So we can relax, because good old Gordon is "determined to ensure that the benefits of globalization reach all countries." So don't think you can hide.

However, not everyone is so keen to be reached by the 'benefits' of globalization. A few days before the power elite met in Washington, the leaders of the Group of 77 – representing the 133 poorest countries in the world, or 80% of Earth's population – got together in Havana to give their verdict on the joys of IMF and World Bank sponsored Structural Adjustment Programmes. Funnily enough they didn't share Gordon's enthusiasm, nor were they impressed by Wolfensohn's commitment to reducing poverty: in fact, they were down right pissed off. "One day, humankind will be called to account: How come you never made no connection between growing poverty for the many and booming wealth for a few?" said Musa, Prime Minister of Belize. And Arthur Mbanefo of Nigeria, said "I, for one, support the demonstrators."

Structural Adjustment is as painful as it sounds: the heady cocktail of privatisation, deregulation, mass redundancies, and currency devaluation that the rich nations impose on poor countries has predictable consequences. As unemployment soars and prices double overnight as a result of devaluing the currency, guess what, people get one fuck of a lot poorer.

And seeing as 'fiscal prudence' also requires slashing social programmes, there's nothing to stop rural people being driven off their land and sliding into urban poverty. Because this means that wages are now more 'competetive' (ie lower), the country is now ready to be a home for export-geared sweatshop industries and cash crop cultivation, which provides the necessary hard currency to keep paying the interest on those loans that the World Bank gives them to tide them over the 'adjustment process'.

This cosy stitch-up, which can turn a food sufficient country like Somalia into a famine wracked, war torn mess in a few years flat, is known as the 'Washington Consensus,' and forms the basis for the expansion of the neo-liberal economic order we all know and love. But all over the world this 'consensus' is being challenged.

Even before September 11th, governments have always used the word 'terrorist' to demonise opposition. Two years before the twin towers were attacked, Neo-Labour introduced their own Terrorist Act, spreading a climate of fear where civil liberties needed to be taken away to protect our... er freedom.

STATE OF TERROR

Are you digging a tunnel to prevent a road from being built through your neighbourhood? Have you pulled up a few Genetically modified crops from your local test site? Maybe you spoke at a meeting where a member of the Animal Liberation Front, for example, also spoke? Well I'm afraid to tell you that you are soon to be deemed a TERRORIST!

The government are starting to realise that protests are not going away, that people are getting more advanced and organised by using such new technology as telephones and the internet! To combat the outrageous behaviour of people meeting up in public spaces and discussing issues, the government have introduced the glorious, updated, newly improved… Terrorism Bill!

Terrorism, in it's hot off the press state, is now "the use of serious violence against persons or property, or the threat to use such violence to intimidate or coerce the Government, the public or any section of the public for political, religious or ideological ends."

This new Bill, which is being fast-tracked through parliament, is targeting environmental groups, animal rights protestors and anyone who shows a social or moral conscience.

If you intended to destroy GM crops coz they are contaminating your local organic farm, you will have less rights than a person who was involved in deliberate assault and robbery. Basically, you will be classed as the same in law as the Soho nail bomber!

FIT THE BILL?

At present, the only organisations listed are those associated with Northern Ireland. But the Bill gives the police or government the power to add to this list. Reclaim The Streets, Earth First!, and Animal Liberation Front have all hit the headlines recently forleading persistent and destructive campaigns against property. By demonising a group, organisation, or sector of a community, you can legitimise a treatment of them that is seen as 'fair punishment' by the general public. This is exactly what happened with Northern Ireland, the coal miners, the anti-poll tax demonstrators, etc.

Under Clause 3 of the new legislation, it will become an offence just to be connected with the new definition of 'terrorists'. If direct action organisations are being targeted as potential terrorists, then it is only a short step to 'proscription'. Once an organisation has been proscribed as 'terrorist', it will become a

The weekend before Mayday 2000 saw several days of meetings in London around the pending Terrorism Act. Activities included this photoshoot featuring a group of people – some of whom were well known – who were about to be classed as 'terrorists' by the new law. Pic: Ian Hunter

criminal offence to belong to that organisation, to openly support it, or to speak out at a meeting where members of that organisation were also speaking. The Bill is scare-mongering people against joining organisations, regardless of whether or not they personally take part in criminal activity.

In fact, you won't even have to be directly involved with the organisation. The Incitement clauses of the Bill (clauses 57-59) would make it an offence to support by words alone an armed struggle in a country outside the UK. Those supporting such struggles as the Zapatistas in Mexico, or the Tamil Tigers of Sri Lanka, will be under investigation.

Under the same clauses, there is a danger that refugees who have fled from repressive regimes to this country will become a legitimate target of the police merely because they support the overthrow of that regime.

CLAUSE 38/39 states that the police will be able to arrest, without a warrant, anyone they reasonably suspect as being a 'terrorist'. You won't actually need to have *done* anything. The powers of 'stop and search' will be extended to include strip searches without a warrant, and failure to co-operate can result in a three month sentence.

As well as this, new rights are being given to the armed forces regarding searching premises if there is reasonable suspicion of the property containing munitions and 'wireless transmitter or scanner'. Does this mean that we could be listening to Pirate Radio Terrorism FM? Or that John Peel and Jimmy Saville were terrorists in their early career? The wording of the Bill is ambiguous and open to misuse through misinterpretation.

Clause 18 states that it will be an offence not to report any knowledge of 'terrorist activity'. This has far-reaching implications for investigative journalists who could face up to five years in jail for not grassing people up.

HISTORY OF THIS BILL

The Bill is going through its Parliamentary stages at an alarming rate, and looks set to become law this autumn. It will replace both the Prevention of Terrorism Act, 1974, and the Northern Ireland Act, 1973. These two Acts have led to some of the worst human rights abuses in this country over the last 25 years, contributed to miscarriages of justice and have led to the unnecessary detention of thousands of innocent people, mainly Irish. This new Bill blatantly ignores the European Convention of Human Rights.

The original Prevention of Terrorism (Temporary Provisions) Act was rushed through Parliament in 1977 in record time – first presented to Parliament on a Wednesday, it was law by Friday morning. Not a single Labour MP voted against it.

Despite what the government said at the time, the PTA wasn't meant to convict people or prevent bombings – it was introduced to prevent the Irish community in Britain from expressing support for a united Ireland. Less that 7% of the more than 5,000, mainly Irish, people arrested under the PTA in Britain in its first seven years were charged with any offence, although many were detained for days.

The PTA has been widely used to expel innocent Irish people from Britain and prevent Irish republicans from speaking in Britain – In 1982 Sinn Fein's Gerry Adams and Martin McGuiness were both banned from entering Britain to speak. The Act has also been used to remove prominent opposition figures during 'difficult' times for the government – the week before the death of hunger striker Bobby Sands, 30 leading republicans were arrested under the PTA, subject to 'extended detentions', then released without charge.

If you think SchNEWS is getting its knickers in a twist for nothing then here's an example of the PTA working in Ireland.

Bernard O'Connor, a teacher from Eniskillen, was arrested under the PTA in 1977. His first interrogation session in Belfast lasted for over three hours. He was forced to stand on his toes, bend his knees and hold his hands out in front of him and was hit in the face when his heels touched the ground or he lost balance. Every time he denied taking part in bombings and shootings he was hit again. That afternoon, three detectives tried to get him to admit lesser charges to avoid 35 years in jail. Then at night the brutality really started. He was stripped naked, beaten up and forced to do press ups continually. His underpants were placed over his head and he was threatened with being choked, then threatened with being handed over to the death squads of the Ulster Volunteer Force. These interrogations continued until he was released without charge on Monday night.

THE GAFTAS

Politics doesn't have to be deadly dull. There's nothing better than a good prank - and here's a few choice ones to show you what's possible with a bit of bottle and sense of humour...

Just deserts - James Wolfensohn, president of World Bank, gets pied in Helsinki Finland, April 2001

The Biotic Baking Brigade

Their web site blurb goes: "As multinational corporations accelerate the plunder of our world, a militant resistance has formed in response. Diverse in philosophy and targets, diffuse in geography and structure, the movement comprises freedom-loving folks with a sense of aplomb and gastronomics. Fighting a guerrilla media and ground war with the titans of industry, these revolutionary bakers and pie-slingers have achieved in short order what can truly be called a Global Pastry Uprising (GPU)".

Belgian anarchist Noel Godin, the Godfather of pie-throwing, who inspired the BBB and others around the world by pie-ing Bill Gates says "Everything is awful around us, so let's try to have fun". Quite. The BBB have thus thrown pies in the faces of some of the most deserving scumbags including Milton Friedman and Anne Widdecomb.

www.bioticbakingbrigade.org

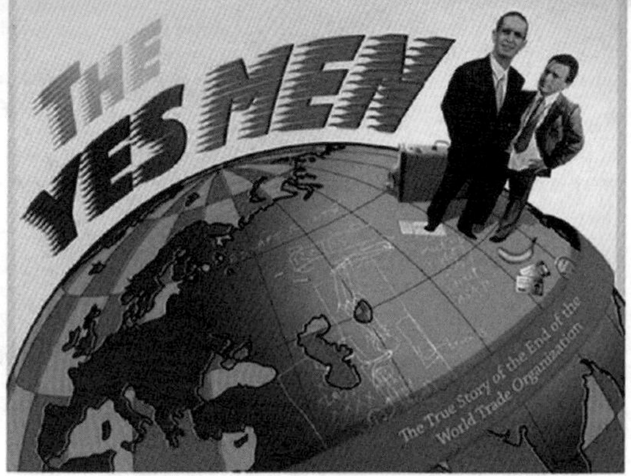

The Yes Men

In 1999, just before the big protests in Seattle, Mike and Andy (a couple of semi-employed, activists with only charity-store suits and no formal economics training) set up a parody of the World Trade Organisation website at the domain gatt.org. Some people mistook it for the real thing and wrote in with questions about all sorts of trade matters. Finally, Mike and Andy found themselves invited to conferences to speak as the organisation they opposed. They scrounged up their savings, bought plane tickets, and went.

At the World Trade Organization, Andy and Mike delivered shocking satires of WTO policy to audiences of so-called "experts." At an international trade law conference in Salzburg, Austria, they proposed a free-market solution to democracy: auctioning votes to the highest bidder. On the TV program CNBC Marketwrap Europe, the WTO announced that 'might equaled right' and that there ought to be a market in human rights abuses. At a textiles conference in Tampere, Finland the WTO unveiled a three-foot phallus for administering electric shocks to sweatshop employees. At a university in Plattsburgh, New York, they proposed that to solve global hunger, the poor should have to eat hamburgers—and then recycle them up to ten times. And at an accounting conference in Sydney, they announced that in light of all its mistakes, it would shut itself down, re-founding as an organization whose goals were not to help corporations, but rather to help the poor and the environment.

For the 2004 presidential election the Yesmen went on a 'Yes Bush Can' national US tour in a painted up coach.

www.theyesmen.org

Dot Con

What a lot of fun you can have with an internet domain name (rights to use a website name). Ian Jones gives us an example...

"We purchased new-labour.com just before they got into power, and a few years later when Jack Straw brought in the Terrorist Act, we launched the website with a not altogether serious take on what it takes to be a terrorist.

Visitors (which were high in numbers) were asked to fill out a questionnaire to in order to check their terrorist rating with questions including:

• *"Did the suppression of human rights protests during the Chinese premier's visit signal the government's determination to champion trade over human rights?"*
• *"Do you believe the starvation of, and refusal of medical aid to Iraqi children is unjust?"*

Those foolish enough to answer "yes" to more than a few of the questions discovered their terror rating was sufficiently high – at least by Straw's standards – to warrant their being asked to report themselves to him, which of course many conscienscious people did as a result. 24 hours after the site went live, a "security consultant" from the Home Office telephoned the owner of the internet server and threatened legal action if the site wasn't pulled immediately. Being more aware of internet law than the Home Office would have liked, and not un-used to such threats they didn't budge!

Unfortunately, little changed as a result of all this, but those involved had a bloody good laugh!"

SHORT SHARP CROP

How GM Crop Farming Was Killed In Britain

"US chemical giant Monsanto are about to pull a fast one. They're growing Genetically Engineered foods which are going into shops without labelling or adequate testing. They are playing Russian Roulette with our lives, and the lives of all species on the planet... Luckily there is time to stop it – if we convince farmers, food-makers and retailers we don't want it." – SchNEWS 96, October 25, 1996.

SchNEWS first mentioned Genetically Modified (or Genetically Engineered) foods eight years ago. In those eight years what looked like the inevitable introduction of GM foods into our food chain has been turned round, with the GM industry fleeing from this country. Two of the three biggest GM companies have pulled out of Britain; the other, Bayer, has been the target of a sustained campaign over the past year and has abandoned plans to grow any crops in Britain till at least 2008. There is only one trial GM crop being grown in this country this year, when in 2000-2001 there were 159. Most food retailers have now removed GM ingredients from their products.

The success of the campaign against GM food in the UK has largely been due to the diverse range of tactics it has encompassed. Supermarkets have been targeted, with aisles jammed with trolleys and shoppers demanding to know which foods are GM free. GM crops have been trashed at night by groups of friends or ripped-up in broad daylight in front of the cops. Farmers have pulled out of planting crops because they would be none too popular with the locals. And pantomime cows have locked onto lorries at supermarket distribution centres.

The best efforts of the biotech industry, the pro-GM zealot Tony Blair and his Science Minister and bankroller Lord Sainsbury (of that well known supermarket chain) have totally failed to convince the public that GM crops are anything other than a money making scam for the companies involved. And while "independent" scientists (who just happen to get funding from the biotech industry and a pro-GM Government) have repeatedly told us that there isn't any risk to health or the environment, a clued up public, wary of bland reassurances following the BSE crisis, just isn't swallowing it.

This article won't investigate why GM food is a threat to health and the environment, that has been covered elsewhere. Anyway the public has already made up its mind: The results of a government consultation into GM foods revealed that 86% of people weren't happy eating GM food and 84% thought it would damage the environment, with 93% of people thinking that the technology was driven by profit rather than public interest.

Instead, this article will focus on the actions that have almost rid this country of GM food – proving that direct action works. As Jim Thomas, a veteran anti-GM campaigner from the ETC group says, "Campaigners rarely get the satisfaction of so clearly winning – a win for the thousands and thousands of people who spent cold nights pulling up crops, long weekends talking to shoppers and farmers and years of emotional and intellectual energy countering the bullying, lobbying power and financial clout of the gene giants".

STOP THE CROP!

GM crops didn't first appear in 1996. Resistance to GM crops first started in the place where they were born – the USA. The first recorded trashing of a GM crop occurred in 1987 when Earth First! activists pulled up 2,000 genetically modified strawberry plants. This inspired other activists to do the same – the first European crop trashings were in Holland back in 1991. In the early '90s in India, a strong anti-GM feeling developed amongst peasant farmers, which resulted in the mass destruction of a Cargill (world's largest seed company) facility and a demonstration of 500,000 people. In Germany in 1996, activists squatted fields to prevent them from being planted with GM crops. This resulted in a third of trials not taking place and many more being destroyed by activists.

The first decontamination of a GM test field in Britain occurred on 8th June 1997, when SHAG (the Super Heroes Against Genetics) played a game of night-time cricket using GM potatoes as the ball. The problem with playing cricket in the dark with potatoes is that the balls keep breaking up or getting lost – what a shame! This year also saw the first action by the Confederation Paysanne in France against genetically modified crops. From then on in Europe the number of actions increased dramatically.

In July 1998 a new campaign was launched – Genetix Snowball. The idea behind Genetix Snowball was to "...safely remove a small, symbolic number of GM plants from the ground and then to encourage others to take similar action." This gained some sympathetic publicity in the mainstream media, which was useful for the whole anti-GM campaign. But the campaign had severe limitations: firstly, the action was largely symbolic and only damaged a small amount of the crop, therefore not really affecting the companies involved (apart from bad publicity); secondly the idea of Genetix Snowball was that one would take "responsibility" for one's actions by informing the farmer and police beforehand – leading to people getting arrested very quickly. The police however were not keen on pressing charges, as this would give Genetix Snowball more publicity. The biotech companies, though, were keen to take out civil injunctions preventing named individuals and Genetix Snowball from damaging GM crops. Unfortunately, the penalty for breaking an injunction can actually be worse than the sanction for criminal damage. A lot of time and effort went into fighting injunctions in the courts and while all the publicity was good, a lot of activists thought that getting on with destroying GM crops and staying out of court was the best option.

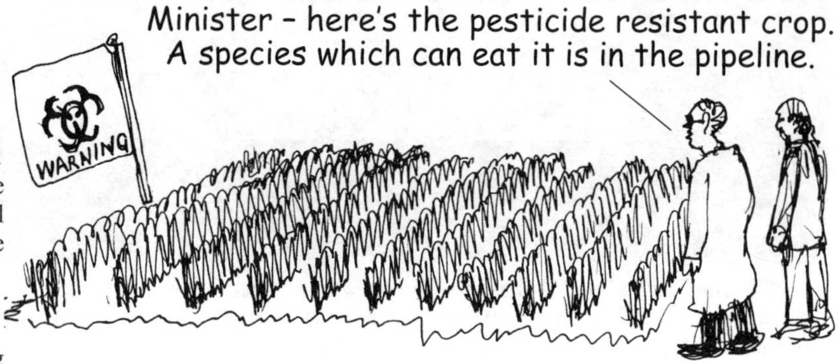

Minister - here's the pesticide resistant crop. A species which can eat it is in the pipeline.

When in 1999 the government started its four year Farm Scale Trials to evaluate the safety of GM crops, campaigners were sceptical that these were anything other then a public relations exercise – the trials were incredibly limited in the scope of what would be studied, and as campaigners pointed out, the trials themselves would cause contamination. These fears led the trustees of Lushill Farm in Swindon to order the farmer to destroy the trial due to local opposition and fears of contaminating nearby organic farms. Greenpeace famously trashed a crop in Norfolk and pictures of people in white biohazard suits ripping up GM crops were beamed around the world. The biggest action happened in Watlington, Oxfordshire, where over 600 people held a rally and after listening to speakers, the crowd realised that more was required than marching from A to B – everyone from direct action novices to hardcore eco-anarchists walked onto the test site and in an hour and a half almost destroyed the whole crop. Placards, bare hands, boots and even space hoppers (!) were used to damage the plants. The police turned up late and made a mere six arrests. While these daytime mass actions provided a good spectacle, the majority of crops that were damaged were done at night by small groups of friends just going out and doing it for themselves.

Throughout 2000 and 2001, both daytime and night-time actions continued. The main target of the anti-GM activists was not the large farm scale trials, but the National Seed List (NSL) trials. Before a crop can be granted commercial approval it has to go through NSL trials to show it is a unique, consistent strain. Disruption of these trials means that is difficult for the seed to be approved. In 2000-2001 all the NSL trials of winter oil seed rape were either destroyed or the crop failed, putting back for a year the development of that crop, which must have cost the company developing it millions. In response to this increased damage to GM crops, the companies started employing more security measures. Syngenta does a lot of its research work at Jealotts Hill, a large complex in the Berkshire countryside. This high security installation is protected with barbed wire fences, infrared cameras and mobile patrols, but that didn't stop a research crop of potatoes being 75% destroyed. One person was arrested after security (finally) realised what was going on, but everyone else vanished into the night. The unlucky person was charged with causing £10,000 worth of damage, but charges were later dropped despite the accused being covered in mud and caught on CCTV.

Nether Compton, Dorset, 16th July 2000 Pic: Simon Chapman

Similar measures were employed at Wivenhoe and Arlesford in Essex where infrared sensors, cameras hidden in bird boxes, and security patrols protected the two maize trials. Again

activists laughed in the face of such a challenge and 95% of the Arlesford and 10% of the Wivenhoe crop were destroyed! The Wivenhoe site was also the focus of a 200 strong demonstration. At this demo some people who tried to enter the field were arrested by very up-for-it aggressive police. Three people were charged with causing a staggering amount of damage – 20p. Not 20p each, but 20p between all three. The keenness of Essex police to press charges probably related to the fact that earlier in the year 11 people had been found not guilty of criminal damage. The '20p three' later had their charges dropped.

Ooops the sun's come up, time for a quick photo and we'll finish it another night

Very few people have ever been arrested for destroying a GM crop, yet alone been successfully prosecuted. For example, in 1999 twenty-seven Greenpeace activists were found not guilty of theft and criminal damage after a re-trial and later in 2001 two people were found not guilty of criminal damage. There was a bizarre scenario in court where the two tried to claim they had caused more damage than the prosecution claimed. The reason for this is that if there is more than £5,000 damage, then the defendants can ask for trial by jury. And with the public so hostile to GM foods, a jury trial almost guarantees a not-guilty verdict.

But what happens when the biotech companies break the law? Are they hauled before the courts? Of course not! On 16th August 2002, the government announced that at least 25 farm scale trials of oilseed rape (planted over a four year period) had been contaminated with unlawful varieties which contained genes for antibiotic resistance. The government said a clear-up would be needed and so two days later the good folk of Dorset decided to help – twenty people tried to decontaminate a GM field containing the offending variety, but were arrested for their public spirited efforts. Four months later they had their charges dropped. Bayer, the company responsible for the contaminated seeds, had known about the problem since June, but didn't bother to tell anyone until August. In the end there was no withdrawal of the crop and no prosecution of Bayer. But Bayer would later suffer seriously at the hands of protesters (see below).

PREVENTION IS BETTER THAN CURE

While it's all very well destroying crops after they've been planted, a better tactic was persuading farmers not to plant the crop in the first place. Many farmers gave in to local pressure when they realised that they weren't popular with their neighbours. This is what happened near Hailsham, Sussex in spring 2001, when after local meetings and a couple of demos against him, the farmer pulled out of the trial before the crop was planted – realising he was none too popular in his village and the rewards just weren't worth the hassle he was getting. Maybe the farmer was worried that he might suffer the same fate that affected some farmers in autumn 1999 who were hosting GM trials – they had agricultural machinery damaged and spray-painted. One of those targeted was the National Farmers Union spokesman on biotechnology and this fact was reported in Farmers Weekly.

Other attempts to stop crops being planted were a bit more last minute, in Munlochy in the Highlands of Scotland, three women were paying a visit to the field before the crop was due to be sown and found the farmer actually out planting the crop. So they jumped in front of the tractor, forcing him to give up for the day. The next day the farmer arrives with back-up from the police to start planting again, but more protesters had turned up to try and stop him and for several days waves of locals, most of whom had never done direct action before, were there to try and stop the crop being sown. An information caravan was set up and the Munlochy Vigil started. The caravan was joined by a toilet and a yurt and amazingly the local council granted the protest camp temporary planning permission. The Scottish courts however took a stronger position against GM protesters (unlike their English counterparts) and jailed a number of people. One of those jailed commented, "I believe that my imprisonment was a political tactic to try and intimidate other protesters against taking direct action against the iniquitous GM crop trial at Munlochy." Such tactics failed to intimidate anybody, as actions against Munlochy continued and much of the trial was destroyed. The Scottish executive later cancelled all GM trials in the Highlands, therefore creating a GM free zone.

Crop squats on the site of a GM field trial have also proved a very useful tactic and were pioneered in Germany with much success. The aim of squatting a field is to occupy the proposed field long enough so that it is too late for the seed to be planted – a group of protesters turn up at a field, erect some barricades and living shelters and put up Section 6 notices forcing the farmer to go through the courts to evict them. One good thing about squatting fields is that it can work as a good focal point for people to learn more about GM crops and for seasoned campaigners to make links with locals opposed to GM crops.

TROLLEY JAMS

Many people opposed to GM haven't got the time or can't risk arrest by going into a field and destroying GM crops. But every little town in Britain has a supermarket and these are soft targets. Actions against them have proved remarkably effective at getting supermarkets to drop GM food.

People descended on supermarkets armed with leaflets to alert the public to the presence of GM foods. Once the British public realised that 60% of their processed food contained genetically modified ingredients (in the form of soya products), they became alarmed.

Supermarkets and major food manufacturers were targeted and many quickly announced their own products would be GM free. Public support was high for direct action against GM food – imaginative activists were cruising around their local supermarket filling their trolley with goods, and then at the checkout demanding to know which products were GM and which weren't – pity the poor confused person on the checkout. At least it makes for a more interesting Saturday afternoon on the tills! Even more effective was coordinating trolleys reaching the tills, totally jamming up a supermarket and costing them money. A less confrontational tactic was to fill a trolley with food and just abandon it in the supermarket with a letter to the manager explaining your opposition to GM food.

Supermarket action at Sainsburys, Exeter, 2004

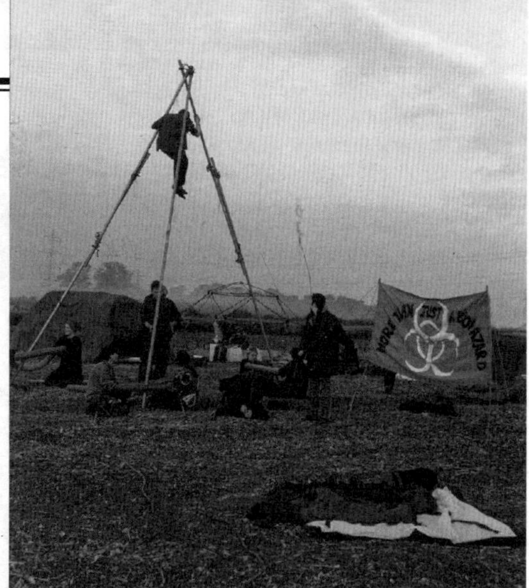

Crop squat on the site of GM trial field

Other tactics included good old-fashioned blockades and chaining supermarket doors shut. Stickers also proved to be a useful way of informing the public and troubling a food retailer who wouldn't listen to public opinion. Stickers placed over barcodes caused maximum disruption. One ex-stickerer recalls the fun that was had: "Three of us spent a couple of hours roaming round our local Safeway. We'd fill up our baskets and pretend to be studying the ingredients when in fact we were placing stickers on the barcodes, and then putting the items back on the shelves. The stickers were simple ones printed with a home computer. We did it for so long, I'm surprised we didn't get caught. A mate of mine got caught a few days later and the police were called, but the supermarket decided not to press charges. They just didn't want the publicity."

Supermarkets, being large monolithic organisations, have centralised distribution depots and operate "just-in-time" restocking systems. Disrupting these distribution centres can cost supermarkets a lot of money and cause them a headache trying to clear the backlog. These distribution centres have been hit on numerous occasions; using classic blockading techniques such as D-locking gates or trucks or using scaffold tripods to block roads.

Under massive consumer pressure, within a couple of years of the introduction of GM soya, most supermarkets and major food suppliers had dropped all GM ingredients from their products. Now all GM foods in Europe have to be labelled by law. Not that you'll find many products labelled as such. Unfortunately the regulations allow 0.9% contamination of GM ingredients. This is better than in the US, the largest producer and consumer of GM food in the world, where there is no labelling of GM foods. The USA isn't too happy that European shoppers are allowed to know what is in their food and want the World Trade Organisation to rule labelling an illegal "Barrier to Trade", 'cos corporations have Human Rights you know.

Mind you it's not just Europeans that don't like GM food – there are massive anti-GM campaigns in places like Brazil, where the Landless Peasant's Movement have occupied Monsanto test sites. In India, farmers have burned down and destroyed Monsanto research crops and labs. Japanese public hostility to GM foods was the reason that Monsanto abandoned producing GM wheat – the Japanese had said they wouldn't buy any wheat products from the US for fear of contamination.

Recently, campaigners have been going back to supermarkets to get the removal of meat and dairy products from animals fed on GM animal feed (of which there is no mandatory labelling). The imported feed is the biggest market for GM products in Europe. If the GM-animal feed business is defeated then it could be the final nail in the coffin for GM in Britain.

BAYER BACK OUT

In October 2001, Aventis washed its hands of GM and sold its Crop Science division to German pharmaceutical giant Bayer. If Bayer thought they had acquired a great asset and that by being the biggest GM company they could make loads of money, they were sadly mistaken. On the day Bayer floated on the New York Stock Exchange (23rd January 2002) their offices in Newbury were blockaded. But this was nothing compared to the campaign that started up against them 18 months later. Bayer became the focus of a national campaign to target Britain's number one GM company. Although Monsanto is the biggest global player, it was Bayer who was leading the way in the UK, owning nine crops out of a total of eleven that could potentially be commercialized (with the other two owned by Monsanto and Syngenta).

In total there were over fifty different actions over an eight-month period. Bayer suffered numerous office invasions, demonstrations and acts of sabotage against their property. The campaign also targeted the top scientists and directors of Bayer directly – demonstrations were held at their homes and wherever they went they were hassled. Paul Rylott, Bayer's top GM scientist had a pie in his face at a conference in London – he was sacked a few weeks later!

Pink Castle, Dorset, April 2002. An Aventis GM maize trial field is squatted for seven weeks and the entire crop destroyed

The first action against Bayer was to jam all the locks at their facility in North Yorkshire with liquid metal. The second was to invade their offices in Newbury, set off fire alarms, cause a bit of mayhem and talk to the employees. A couple of days later Dystar (a textile company who is a subsidiary of Bayer) had its locks glued and anti-GM slogans painted on it. Bayer then had a stand at the British Potato 2003 event trashed by campaigners. All of this within the space of one week!

Commenting on the action at the Potato Event, Bayer Spokesman Julian Little said, "This demonstration shows that these campaigners have lost their argument against GM." But unfortunately for Julian, a month later the results of the government survey of public opinion, GM Nation, were announced with a massive thumbs down for GM crops and the companies behind them. The protesters had won the argument, it's just that Bayer and the Government weren't listening.

Actions continued – night-time visits spraying slogans and causing sabotage, more conferences targeted, visits to directors' homes, virtual blockades (with email, phone and fax jamming), and more demonstrations at Bayer facilities – continually keeping Bayer on their toes and sapping their energy.

A month into the campaign and the first victory came – Bayer announced that they wouldn't be conducting anymore field trials of GM crops in Britain. The reason given was that the government had refused to keep the locations secret. Bayer announced: "In the absence of any moves to ensure the security of trials, Bayer CropScience has no choice, therefore, but to cease its variety trial activities in the UK for this coming season." This was a massive victory for everyone opposed to GM crops – Bayer had admitted that it was the fact that test crops kept on getting destroyed that made it impossible for them to develop any new strains.

In March 2004, Bayer got what it wanted – it was given the go ahead to plant its GM Maize (Chardon LL) commercially in Britain. This was seen as a victory for Bayer, but it was a victory on the back of dodgy farm scale trials – in the trials, GM maize had been compared with a conventional system treated with a pesticide that had just been banned by the EU. In short, the trials didn't compare like with like. The trials of Bayer's oilseed rape and beet showed that these were more damaging for the environment than conventional varieties, and in the face of public scrutiny and pressure, the government couldn't give the go ahead for these crops, much as they'd have liked to. Out of nine, Bayer now had only one crop left (they had withdrawn a couple of others months earlier), but three weeks later Bayer announced they wouldn't bother with the not very good GM maize that farmers really didn't want to plant in the first place. They had only been given a two-year licence and decided that it wasn't worth the effort. They'd soon get ripped up anyway. The government, despite being pro-GM, was probably relieved that Bayer had pulled out – a leaked memo had warned the Prime Minister that there could be "pitched battles in the fields" during the general election campaign the following spring. This is probably why the government placed such tough restrictions on the crop in order to make it unattractive for Bayer. Syngenta and Monsanto were soon to follow Bayer's pull-out, and even went one further, announcing they were closing down their GM research programmes in Britain.

Bayer are bloodied and bruised, but not out – they have stated that they still have a long-term interest in developing GM crops in Britain. No doubt they are behind the scenes, furiously lobbying the government to allow them to plant more GM crops and keep the locations secret. But if they dare, they must surely realise that the wrath of the anti-GM movement, with the full backing of the wider public, will come crashing down on them.

Anti-GM turkeys invade the Dartford distribution depot of Asda 19th December 2000 Pic: Hugh Warwick

Lord Cheque-Out

Since 1994, David Sainsbury has bankrolled the Neo-Labour Party to the tune of over £11m. In 1997, six months after bunging Labour £1m to clear their overdraft, Sainsbury was made a Lord. By 1998, and a few million quid later, he was made a science minister. As science minister, Lord Sainsbury has been busy promoting GM crops, biotechnology and vivisection. Sainsbury not only has a massive share in the supermarket chain, but also wholly owns Diatech, a biotech company, and owns the worldwide patent rights over the "translator enhancer" gene currently used in the genetic modification process.

Sainsbury also partly funds the Sainsbury Laboratory, which, since he became Science Minister, has seen funding increase by 400% from the Biotechnology and Biological Sciences Research Council (BBSRC). Sainsbury appoints everyone to the board of the BBSRC and it has now spent more than £18m on research into GM-related crops.

SchNEWS would like to point out, however, that all of this of course has no influence whatsoever on the Government being in favour of GM technology.

NIPPED IN THE BUD

In the end, the whirlwind of direct action against the biotech companies forced them into a retreat while a pro-GM Tony Blair, in the pocket of Lord Sainsbury, looked on helplessly, complaining that anti-GM protesters were anti-science, when in fact the results of the limited farm scale trials showed that GM crops did in fact damage the environment.

The issue of GM crops however has never been one of just human health or the environment. It's also about who controls the food chain, about the patenting of life and about the pursuit of profit, regardless of the consequences, by a few multinational corporations. It is about the power of the scientific establishment who tried to pull a fast one on the public. The anti-GM movement has empowered many ordinary citizens to fight back against the biotech bullies and the government.

For once we can say that in Britain, for the time being at least, we've won a small battle against the capitalist machine that seeks to control our everyday lives. Proof that direct action works.

* More information about GM food can be got from any of the groups listed under "Genetics" in the Yellow Pages at the back of this book.

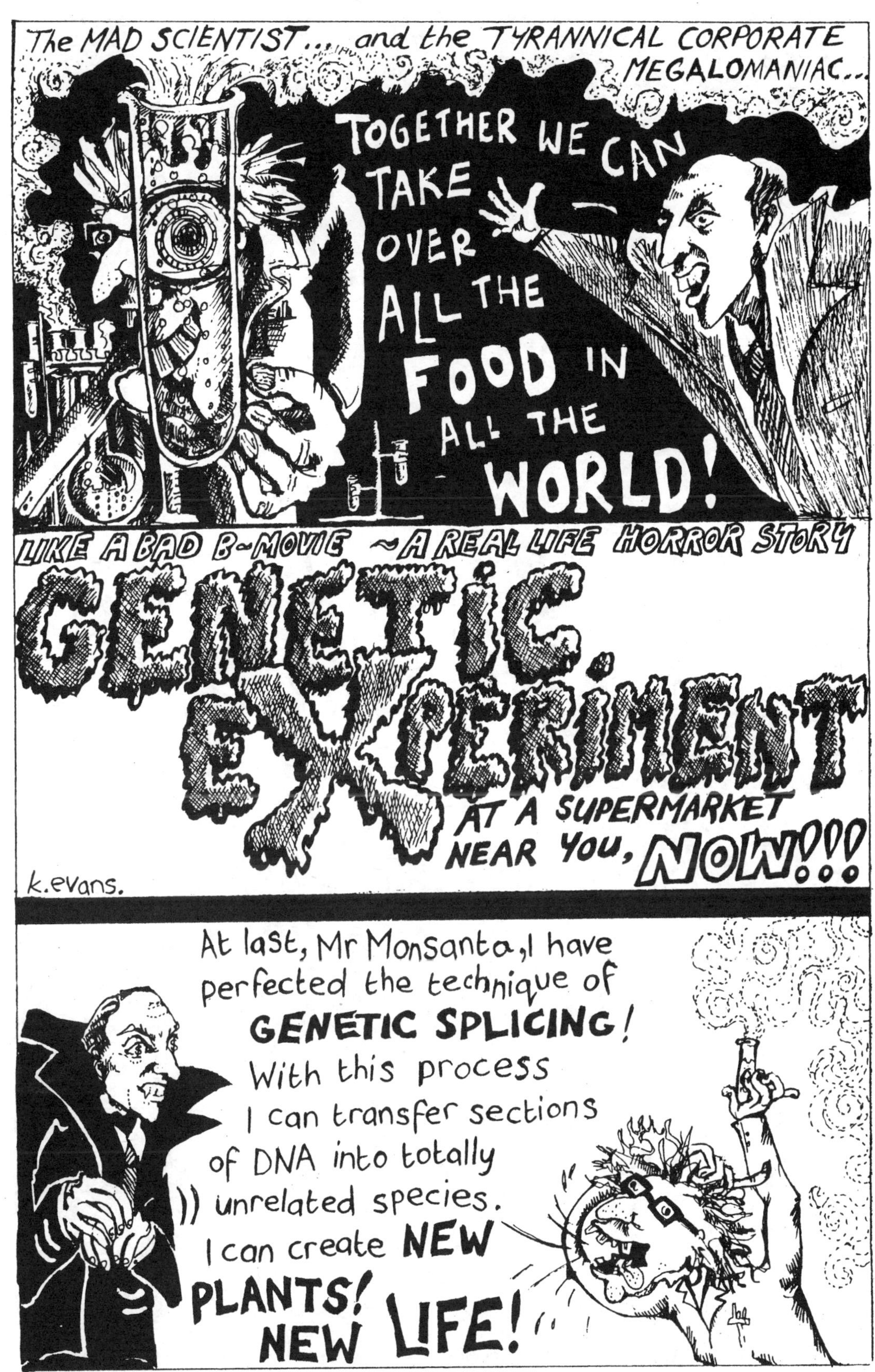
The MAD SCIENTIST... and the TYRANNICAL CORPORATE MEGALOMANIAC...
TOGETHER WE CAN TAKE OVER ALL THE FOOD IN ALL THE WORLD!
LIKE A BAD B-MOVIE ~ A REAL LIFE HORROR STORY
GENETIC EXPERIMENT
AT A SUPERMARKET NEAR YOU, NOW!!!
k.evans.
At last, Mr Monsanto, I have perfected the technique of GENETIC SPLICING! With this process I can transfer sections of DNA into totally unrelated species. I can create NEW PLANTS! NEW LIFE!

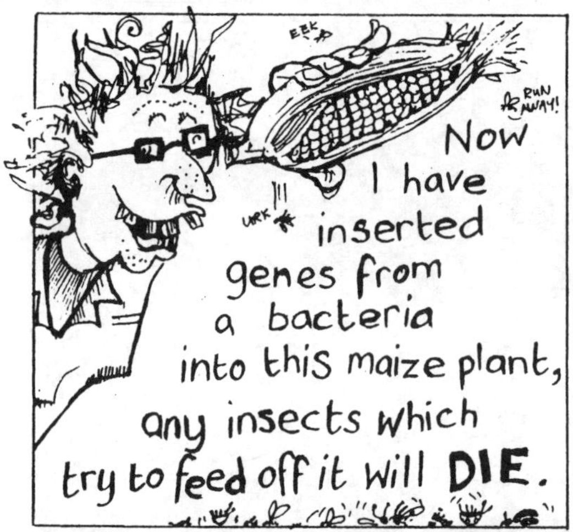
EEK
RUN AWAY!
URK
Now I have inserted genes from a bacteria into this maize plant, any insects which try to feed off it will **DIE**.

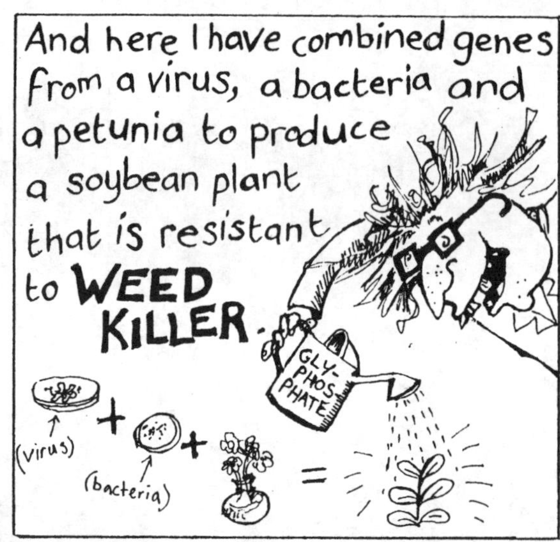
And here I have combined genes from a virus, a bacteria and a petunia to produce a soybean plant that is resistant to **WEED KILLER**.
GLY-PHOS-PHATE
(virus)
(bacteria)

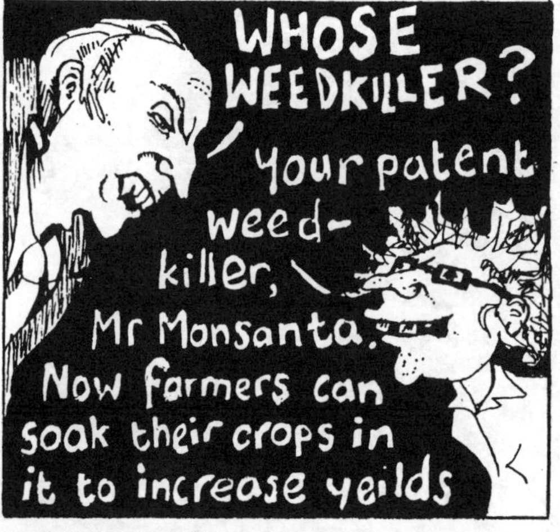
WHOSE WEEDKILLER?
Your patent weed-killer, Mr Monsanta.
Now farmers can soak their crops in it to increase yeilds

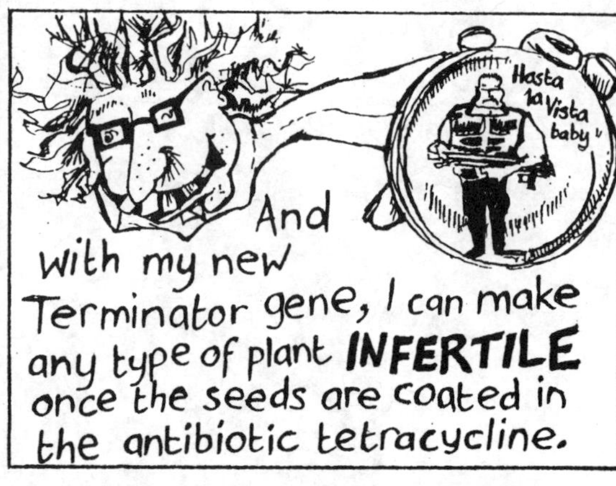
Hasta la Vista baby
And with my new Terminator gene, I can make any type of plant **INFERTILE** once the seeds are coated in the antibiotic tetracycline.

BRILLIANT! No more problems with pesky Third World farmers saving seeds from their crops and planting them again.
My new seedvarieties will be MORE PROFITABLE
ALL farmers will have to buy them or GO BUST!
a ha ha ha
SOON ALL WORLD FOOD WILL BE MINE!!
ha ha ahaha

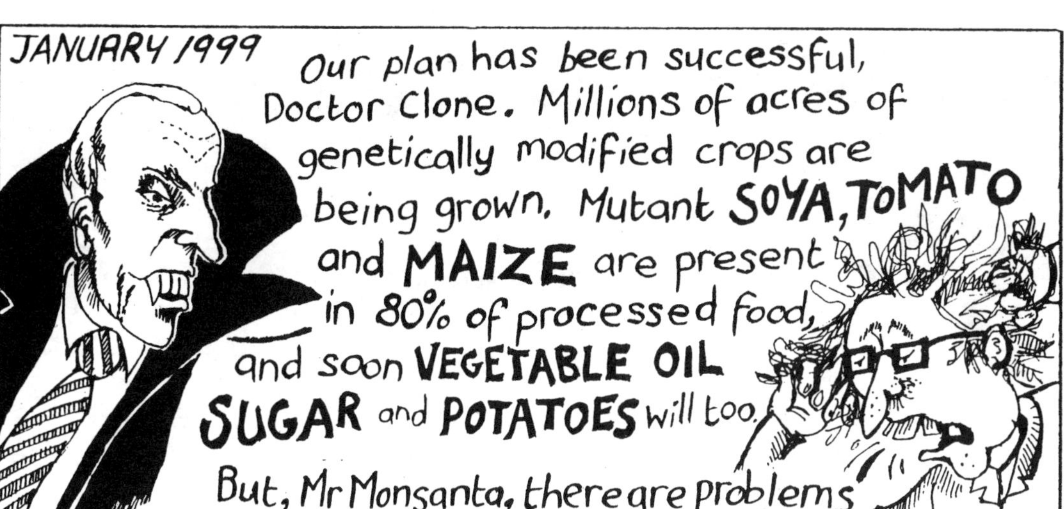

THE NEW TECHNOLOGY IS **UNPREDICTABLE**, AS PLANTS INTER~BREED AND CROSS~POLLINATE, GENETIC MATERIAL IS TRANSFERRED TO OTHER SPECIES...

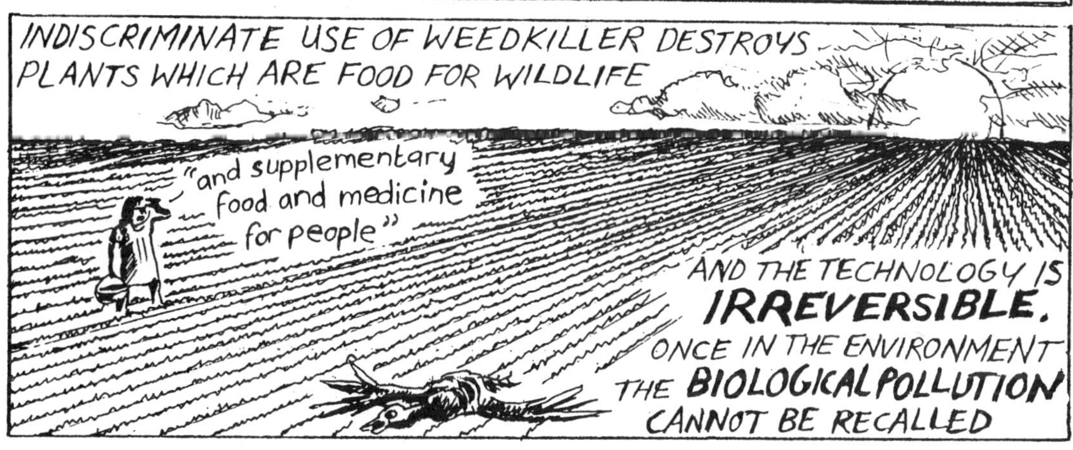

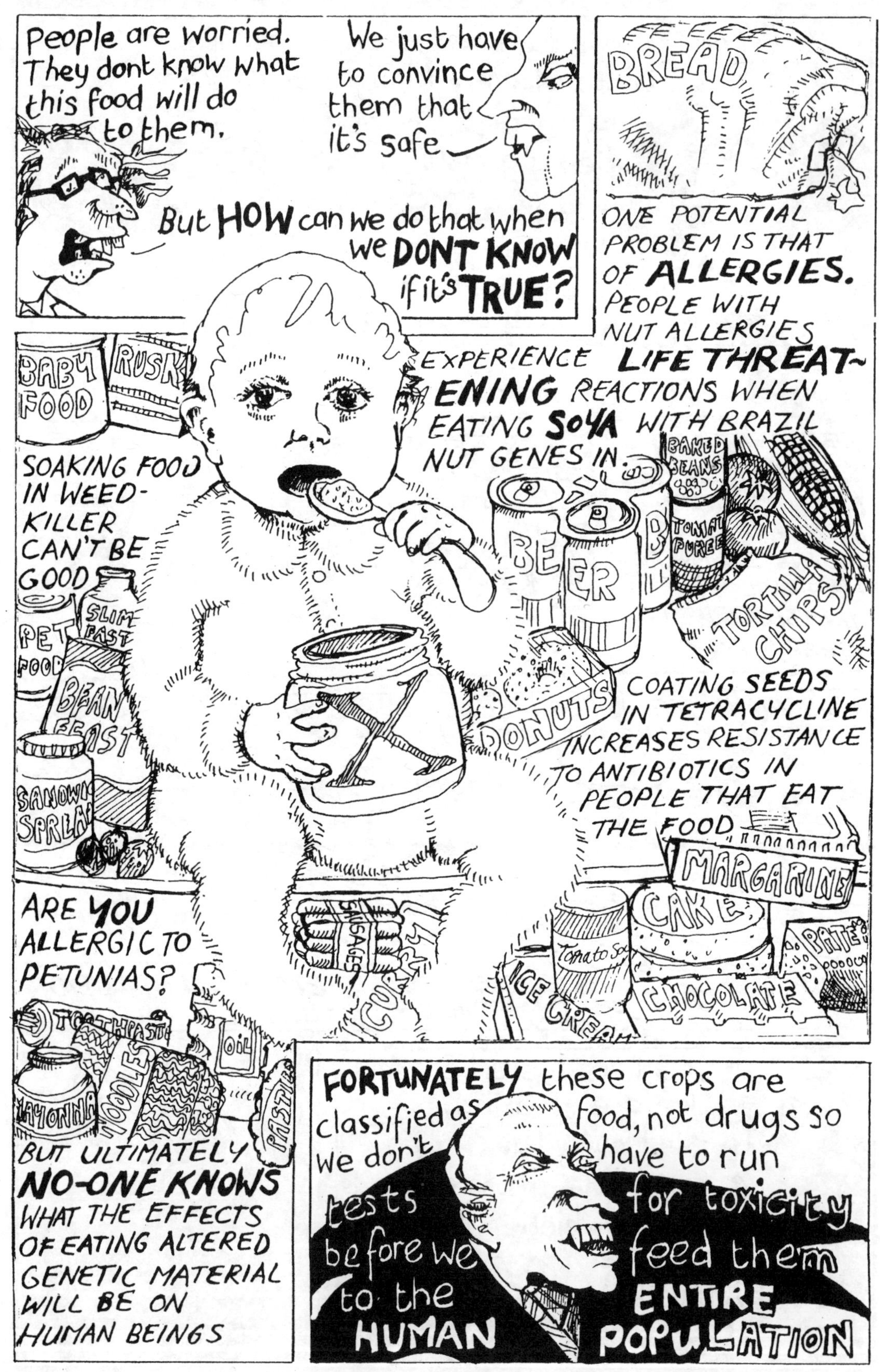
People are worried. They dont know what this food will do to them.
We just have to convince them that it's safe
But HOW can we do that when we DONT KNOW if it's TRUE?
BREAD
ONE POTENTIAL PROBLEM IS THAT OF ALLERGIES. PEOPLE WITH NUT ALLERGIES EXPERIENCE LIFE THREAT-ENING REACTIONS WHEN EATING SOYA WITH BRAZIL NUT GENES IN.
BABY FOOD
RUSK
SOAKING FOOD IN WEED-KILLER CAN'T BE GOOD
SLIM FAST
PET FOOD
BEAN FEAST
BAKED BEANS
TOMATO PUREE
BEER
TORTILLA CHIPS
DONUTS
COATING SEEDS IN TETRACYCLINE INCREASES RESISTANCE TO ANTIBIOTICS IN PEOPLE THAT EAT THE FOOD
MARGARINE
CAKE
PATE
ARE YOU ALLERGIC TO PETUNIAS?
SAUSAGES
CURRY
Tomato Sauce
ICE CREAM
CHOCOLATE
TOOTHPASTE
OIL
NOODLES
MAYONNAISE
PASTIES
BUT ULTIMATELY NO-ONE KNOWS WHAT THE EFFECTS OF EATING ALTERED GENETIC MATERIAL WILL BE ON HUMAN BEINGS
FORTUNATELY these crops are classified as food, not drugs so we don't have to run tests for toxicity before we feed them to the ENTIRE HUMAN POPULATION

Anyway, it doesn't have to be TRUE for us to CONVINCE people.

We'll present the case for G.M. food as ONE SIDE of a DEBATE...
FULL PAGE ADVERT
Here at Monsanta we are extremely NICE and REASONABLE people who only produce wierd food so we can all feed starving Third World babies.

before we FORCE it down people's THROATS:
What happened to consumer choice?
Simply MIX the mutant crops in with normal ones, CLAIM that they cannot be separated, and then RESIST all attempts at labelling them correctly.

Don't worry Doctor Clone, We are WEALTHY; We are INFLUENTIAL.
And if anyone seriously disagrees with us we can SUE THEIR ASS

But some people won't be silenced by the threat of legal action.

They lobby their **M.P.s.**

They target **SUPERMARKETS**

PUBLICISING the dangers of genetically modified food for **CONSUMERS.**

They even take **DIRECT ACTION DESTROYING** our precious **TEST CROPS.**

..Here at the **HUMAN GENOME PROJECT** we are mapping the structure of every part of human **DNA.** All we have to do

DON'T WORRY Mr Monsanto **SCIENCE** will provide a **SOLUTION...**

is to **IDENTIFY** those sections of genetic code which are responsible for **RATIONAL THINKING, ARGUMENT** and the **ABILITY** to **PROTEST** and then we simply **REMOVE THEM** from the **GENERAL POPULATION!**

Heh Heh nothing will stop us now!

THE END of food as we know it?

My First... Genetic Crop Trashing

This is a shortened version of an article that originally appeared in Do Or Die #8.

Actions on genetics test sites were increasing and our group thought it was high time we took part. Walking to the meet up point I still felt a pang of misapprehension. I met up with my friends and after waiting for someone who was (as usual) horrendously late, we set off.

After about quarter of an hour on the road the little voice in my head saying *'this is madness'* became less audible. If you've never been involved in risky direct action then you may have a view of those of us who do it as 'brave and courageous'. The reality is that everyone gets scared – you just learn to ignore the nagging voice in your head. In truth it's only our fear that holds us back.

Halfway to the target site we met up with another full van. We didn't know everyone but we trusted those we did to bring only sensible accomplices. We still had a few hours of driving ahead of us so those of us in the back went to sleep. Awoken from our dreams with the news that we were fifteen minutes away from the target we gobbled some chocolate and psyched ourselves up.

One of us had recced the site out beforehand so despite the rather vague grid refernces on the government register we knew exactly where to go. We parked up a nearby lane and our ragged looking army piled out. After our eyes became accustomed to the dark we started trudging through the fields. Walking along the side of the hedgerow, we ducked down so that any cars passing on the (now deserted) country road would not see us.

When we arrived at our target – a test site of genetically engineered wheat – we got to work trashing the crop. We all had different techniques – some edged forward kneeling on the ground and breaking armfulls of wheat – methodical but slow. Others simply trampled the crop, while some munched a path through the experiment with gardening shears. A house was in sight, but we were all dressed head to toe in black and it being late, we hoped the inhabitants were wrapped up in bed.

Suddenly the halogen security lights on the house came on – shining with surprising force directly onto us. After a moment of panic we realised they'd probably just been set off by a fox or something and we got back to our work. Soon afterwards the lights blinked off. After a while boredom set in – then someone realised that the crop would be destroyed quicker if we all lay down in a line and rolled over it – this produced much silent laughter as we kept bumping into each other. As we came to the end of our 'mission time' every minute seemed to go quicker. By now it was pouring and we were all pretty weary but a third of the crop was still intact. Breaking our own (sensible) rule we stayed ten minutes extra.

We finished off the crop and happy but tired from our manic work we trudged back to our vehicles. Walking bent over, a sudden rash of cars drove past – oblivious to our little tribe five feet away on the other side of the hedge – we hoped. Just as we got to the car someone realised they'd left a pair of shears – with their fingerprints on – in the middle of the field. (Always wear gloves!). After a moment of worry we realised another one of us had picked them up – phew!

Driving off, our different vehicles in different directions, we remained tense until we were around ten miles away. Then the smiles and giggling started. Too buzzing to sleep we chattered about future plans and took the piss out of each other for being too jumpy. In the early hours of the morning I was dropped off at home. A contented sleep followed.

The sabotage was both successful and fun. It was one of the first actions our affinity group had done and therefore unsurprisingly we made a few mistakes. Mistakes we've learnt from. Having done a few more site trashings, we've refined better techniques. The biggest mistake we made was leaving our vehicles in a nearby layby. Their number plates if spotted would have led the cops right to our doorsteps. In subsequent actions we've been dropped off by the drivers, meeting them again at a prearranged pickup point and time. For this reason we have not overstayed our 'mission time' again, even if it has meant not entirely finishing the crop.

Trashing genetic test sites has really helped our group. New activists are now expeirenced and willing to go on, and organise, more actions. Activists who have been around for a while have also been re-empowered.

The Mayday Guerilla Gardening event in London is best remembered for McDonald's getting redecorated and Winston Churchill getting the best haircut he's ever had.

LAWN AND ORDER

Tash

***"As you would expect the MayDay message about why people were there got kind of lost. But what is a few smashed windows and some daubed paint compared to what global capitalism is doing to the planet?"* - An anonymous demonstrator**

Monday's MayDay demonstration in London nearly brought about the collapse of the British way of life. Apparently. SchNEWS was there and has a slightly different story to tell.

In the morning landscape gardeners arrived for a spot of planting at Parliament Square. Bananas and magic mushrooms popped up amongst the pansies and spinach, while large banners declared 'The Worms Will Turn!', 'Let London Sprout', and 'Capitalism is Pants'. The cops had helpfully flooded the square the night before, making it easier to roll up the turf and start laying it over the road. Up went a Maypole and the celebrations began. As Big Ben chimed, SchNEWS wondered how long it was since such traffic-free revelry had happened in front of the Houses of Parliament.

Further up the road a McDonalds was getting the customary trashing, before riot police moved in, splitting the crowd in two and trapping hundreds of people in Trafalgar Square for hours.

The police had taken a bloody nose at last year's Carnival Against Capital on June 18th (see SchNEWS 217/8) and were in no mood for a repeat performance. Even the army were apparently on standby (eh, aren't the army always on stand-by?), while according to the Financial Times, more than 80 per cent of financial institutions were "concerned about the damage to the City's standing" if there was any repeat of last June's Carnival Against Capital. As one person from Reclaim The Streets commented, "The police made sure that everybody knew they were planning the biggest operation for 30 years. Just to keep some gardeners in fancy dress under control."

The police and press hyped the event, and eventually they got what they wanted. A few smashed windows, some graffiti, some people throwing beer cans and hey presto!

'MAYDAY BLOODBATH ORGY – END OF CIVILISATION AS WE KNOW IT – HALF CHEWED BABIES RIPPED APART BY ANARCHISTS FROTHING AT THE MOUTH.'

And what about the cenotaph. Maybe it needs a little bit of perspective. Tony Blair talks about the "mindless thuggery" of Monday, yet didn't he personally invite Russia's President Putin over to Britain, conveniently forgetting that on the orders of the President, Russia has bombed Chechnya back into the Dark Ages? Forget about the 20,000 dead Chechnyans, as Putin gets whisked off to have tea with the Queen. And it's gonna take a lot more than a little detergent to clean up Chechnya. So let's keep this in proportion, no one at the Mayday celebration is to be charged with genocide, child killing or mass murder.

Yet behind the hysteria, comments from the politicians reveal that something else is on the agenda. Blair says "This kind of thing cannot happen again", while Home Secretary Flan Widdecombe asked in the House of Commons the day after MayDay "Would the groups concerned with yesterday's disorder be covered by his new definition of terrorists under his (Jack Straw's) new terrorism legislation?".

SchNEWS reckons the public is ripe to accept that no more anti-capitalist protests will be allowed to happen again. For more thoughts on the day check out www.indymedia.org.uk

Alec Smart

Guerilla Gardening
Mayday 2000
Nick Cobbing
Nick Cobbing
Tash
Ian Hunter
FRIDAY
with ES Magazine
ARMY ON
STANDBY
FOR
LONDON
RIOT
Evening
Standard
www.thisislondon.com
Tash
Tash

RISING TIDE

A MOVEMENT FOR CLIMATE JUSTICE

During the COP6 meeting in Den-Haag, a Critical Mass is held at the Spuiplein, which later converged on the conference centre. 19th November 2000. Pic: Boyd Noorda

The Story So Far

In November 2000, as the UK fuel protests were reaching their height, an aircraft hangar-sized exhibition hall in den Haag, Netherlands, opened its doors to the Kyoto Protocol travelling circus. More accurately if long-windedly known as the United Nations Conference of the Parties to the Framework Convention on Climate Change, or COP6, this was a trade fair poorly disguised as an environmental conference.

While most participants in the Kyoto charade were saying that this was the only hope of making meaningful reductions in carbon dioxide emissions, it became increasingly plain that the process would never achieve such reductions. The real agenda was the creation of a free market in carbon: inventing new profit-making opportunities for the corporations and governments that were responsible for the problem in the first place.

Disappointed at the limp analysis and green groups allowing themselves to be hijacked by the process, a small but determined group of people from all over the world came together to show how that process was dominated by vested interests. This group – known as the Rising Tide coalition – was there to say "It's time for climate justice", this being the right of everyone on the planet to clean air, a long-term future and social justice, all of which are threatened by the onset of climate chaos. It also rejected all attempts to privatise the atmosphere, i.e. the trading of emissions between countries and companies. After all, when you consider that climate change is caused by the over-consumption of fossil fuels by the rich, and that the first people to feel the effects of climate change are the poor; when you consider that the process to prevent climate change is dominated by the rich, who come up with solutions that impose upon the poor... then you stop seeing climate change as a problem of atmospheres and gases and start seeing it as a problem of social and ecological justice.

With the aid of some forged passes, a few of us entered this glorified shopping mall to drop banners, throw pies and disrupt meetings, these were staged alongside street protests and a Climate Justice summit. The Sierra Club and Greenpeace USA went to the trouble of issuing a statement disassociating themselves from the pieing of US delegation corporate top dog Frank E. Loy, presumably in order to protect their right to the baby chair at the table of power.

COP6 ended in deadlock, which pleased no one except the radical interlopers and the oil industry lobby groups (for markedly different reasons!). In grassroots resistance terms, we hoped that actions in and around COP6 would catalyse the creation of a strong movement of resistance to climate change and the economic and social system that is causing it.

Oil Watch

Some of the UK people who went to the Netherlands were inspired enough to kick-start a creative, radical, diverse and long-term movement on this issue. In 2001 the Rising Tide UK network was born and it is still thriving in 2004. Rising Tide's scattered national contacts are supported by a small team of (low-) paid staff in Oxford to organise gatherings, actions, media and outreach. Particular projects in 2004 include helping to inject a creative, radical take on climate change at the ESF and surrounding events in London in October and against the G8 in 2005, the setting up of a coalition calling for 'No New Oil' (or coal or gas) development, producing a regular email newssheet sent out to over 1000 people, and making a short film (called 'Cheeky Apocalypse') looking at

the deranged way TV covered the record-breaking UK temperatures of August 2003.

London Rising Tide has focussed much of its energy against BP's Baku-Tbilisi-Ceyhan oil pipeline. The pipeline, once a jewel in the tarnished crown of US foreign policy, is set to run from Azerbaijan to Turkey via Georgia. It will be a human rights disaster and produce over 150 million tonnes of CO2 each year for 40 years, causing untold damage to the world's climate. Fortunately, and thanks in part to a persistent campaign of lobbying and direct action against it, the pipeline is now mired increasingly in controversy and damaging publicity for BP.

Apart from regular stalls and other outreach, and lending a hand to a successful occupation of the International Petroleum Exchange during the Iraq invasion in March 2003, London Rising Tide has concentrated exclusively on BP. There are several dangers to this form of activism. It can encourage the illusion that the oil industry has the occasional bad apple or bad practice which campaigning and boycotting can remedy. However, while the whole industry has to be dismantled, it is still strategically and psychologically useful to go up against one company or pipeline, particularly if it is vulnerable and there is some chance of victory. The Baku-Ceyhan pipeline's chief vulnerability, apart from the shoddy arrogance of the construction process itself, is the fact that BP sought over 50% of the US$3.3bn construction costs from UK and global taxpayers. This is where much of the campaign has focussed on international banks and obscure semi-privatised government departments like the Export Credits Guarantee Department.

Rising Tide have stuck to BP like a leech, or rather, stuck leechlike to those companies working alongside BP. The reason for this is a pretty good one: BP is Britain's biggest company and its employees are mostly ridiculously loyal. Companies dealing with it though, are often smaller, more vulnerable either economically or in terms of public relations, and its employees are more liable to be receptive to our view (especially if we present it accessibly and

Climate Change is proudly brought to you by these companies.

non-judgementally).

A group as small as London Rising Tide can't expect to have a direct economic impact with the occasional short-term blockade of a refinery or petrol station, but it can damage BP's public image. Ever since BP invested millions of pounds in a complete re-brand, with a new logo and its pathetic 'beyond petroleum' slogan, and started pumping serious money into sponsorship, it has been dancing on highly profitable but dangerously thin ice. With every dubious claim to be a good corporate citizen (i.e. hiding its support for, say, Colombian paramilitaries) and its hypocrisy over renewable energies (i.e. not telling the public that it is solidly committed to expanding its oil and gas output by 3.5% every year), it has laid itself open to brand damage. Which is where we come in.

For two years, Rising Tide has been present at pretty much every event where BP has shown its face. We've disrupted presentations by its boss and chairman, we've brought a Baku-Ceyhan presentation at a corporate carve-up conference to a standstill, we've targeted Tate Britain, National Portrait Gallery, Natural History Museum, Science Museum, British Museum and Royal Opera House (all BP-sponsored, as is the Barbican, which we haven't got round to yet!), and we've shamed charities like Save the Children, Flora & Fauna

International and WWF for their willingness to collaborate with and sometimes take cash from the company on specific projects.

London Rising Tide 'celebrated' BP's Annual General Meeting (AGM) in 2003 by holding a Carnival Against Oil Wars and Climate Chaos and an alternative AGM outside. Several concerned members of the public also entered the meeting in order to make absolutely sure their concerns hadn't been swamped by the mile high tide of greenwash that had engulfed the Oil Festival Hall for the day.

In 2004, Rising Tide and friends again targeted BP, the main event of the year so far for us has been 'Greenwash or Us: the 1st Annual Exhibition of Resistance to Big Oil and the Corporate Hijacking of the Arts'. This was a squatted Camden shop, transformed into an 'art not oil' exhibition of paintings, photographs and sculptures to coincide with the BP-sponsored National Portrait Award, held at the National Portrait Gallery in June. As well as collaborating with local people to run the thriving Camden space well into the autumn with an exhibition, infopoint, cinema, party and workshop events, there were a series of successful actions at the Portrait Gallery during June, including a blockade of the imposing front entrance on the night of the announcement of the winner. Media coverage was conspiratorially sporadic, apart from a very tasty piece in the Financial Times which signed off with this paragraph: "Pride of place goes to a portrait showing Lord Browne's 'benign mask' slipping to reveal 'a satanic look'. Organisers claimed the artwork paints a true portrait of an oil company."

In the pipeline

In many ways, Rising Tide in the UK is in pretty good health, though it has still to make a strong connection with those with links to communities threatened by sea-level rise and those campaigning for better resourced (and un-privatised) public transport. Sadly, the mostly Europe-based Rising Tide International network has withered. There were inspiring actions at COP 6.5 in Berlin in 2002, and a buzzing gathering in Barcelona in 2002 came up with among other things a 'political statement' which is still the basis of the non-hierarchical, anti-imperialist, direct action-based Rising Tide philosophy. But as of August 2004, things are very quiet.

Hope is hovering on the horizon, however, as there is now a climate justice-led initiative to set up a new Europe-wide network of action and communication, inspired to some degree by the southern-based Oilwatch network. The plan is for 'European days of action against the oil industry and for a fossil fuel-free future', to coincide with the European Social Forum and related events in London from October 14-17, 2004. This will allow people attending the ESF etc. to join a feisty action as well as the usual workshops and discussions. It will also with any luck help the launch of said Europe-wide network of resistance to Big (and small) Oil.

Human-triggered climate change is here; our children will be unlikely to see the back of it, even if we drastically cut emissions tomorrow. We need to deal with it, and soon. Solutions need to accept the right of the majority of the world's people not to be washed away for the profits of a very few. The atmosphere – not to mention the earth itself – is a common treasury for everyone not to buy and sell but to share. Our species has forgotten that message at its great peril, but maybe the wake up call that is climate chaos will jog us out of the psychosis (i.e. capitalism) that currently calls the shots.

Read about Rising Tide at the COP 6.5 meeting in Bonn in July 2001 further in this book...

Harmondsworth Detention Centre — Issue 267 – 21st July 2000

"IS IT 'COS I IS BLACK?"

Last saturday, the CAGE anti-prison kick-it-off massive hit the mean streets of Staines. They went to give a big up and say 'nuff respect to the people in the Harmondsworth Detention Centre, only a couple of miles down the road. There, the foreign refugee massive is locked up in prison until someone decides what's to happen to them. We have heard that the UK immigration service says they is not being racialist, even though the refugees are hardly any of them white boys and many are from Kurdistan and countries like that that no-one's even heard of.

These refugees have had the cheek to try and seek a better life in this country – apparently they are not just trying to get banged up without doing anything, so they can get a real hard reputation and bit of cred. The detention centre is conventiently placed right outside Heathrow Airport, and can hold up to 95 detainees. It seems the police don't even need to plant a stash on any of this lot, as the inmates can't leave, don't have none of the normal rights of detained suspects and, surrounded by barbed wire, they are guilty until proven innocent.

Well Fit Inmates

The Harmondsworth hardcore picket crew had been in the Staines area anyway, occupying the site of a proposed women's prison in the heart of the notorious rural Spellthorpe district. They was hangin' there all weekend as part of a real campaign against to the government's prison-building programme, and apparently not because they'd heard the inmates were going to be all well fit. Last Friday was the anniversary of Bastille Day, when all the way back in 1789, people in France stormed into a prison to release the prisoners. All of the people knew they better had not mess with those revolutionaries, who ruled the streets for a whole period called the Terror. Since 1993 the UK prison population has shot up from 45,000 to a record breakin' 65,000, boosting our image as the number one gangsta territory.

Pretty Useless

Indra was one of those present at the Harmondsworth picket. She told us what happened: "Some of the 100 demonstrators climbed onto the top of the fence surrounding the centre and made contact with the refugees. They ignored pleas by the police to come down and stop damaging the fence! It felt pretty useless just standing around the fence, so I climbed it too. I had to see the refugees' faces. But what the hell are you supposed to say to them? 'How's the food, oh and sorry our country treats you like shit!'

"Next day, 12 of us armed with phone cards, propaganda and cherries entered Harmondworth with the names of people we had managed to get to speak to. I wanted to meet those inside, though the idea scared me. The security had a little freak-out, confiscating our literature and cherries. But they had to let us meet the inmates. We encountered people from Algeria, Kosova, Albania, and other war-torn beneficiaries of the British arms industry. They welcomed us warmly.

"One refugee, Salim Rambo, had been caught up in the civil war in Zaire and now fears for his life if he returns home. Salim had been living in London for nine months waiting for his case to be heard. He told us that he had been taken to Hermondsworth by policemen who jumped him, after he responded to an invitation to tell his story to a solicitor. He still has not seen a solicitor or had his case listened to.

"Salim told us that inmates who come to understand too much about what rights they have, are moved elsewhere so as not to stir up the other detainees. We learned that he was due to be deported on Tuesday to Germany. Germany had already refused his asylum application, so from there he would be deported striaght back to Zaire and possible death. I will never forget the look of confusion and terror in his face. We could only get him a solicitor."

A bit o' human beat-box

Early on Tuesday morning 11 people from CAGE leafleted other passengers about to board the same flight as Salim was on. One passenger was arrested after standing up and refusing to let the flight depart. The flight was delayed for two hours, until eventually Salim was removed at the demand of the pilot. Immigration officials threatened him with a beating, but he is now back in detention in London.

Salim's new solicitor believes his deportation order was illegal as he did not have proper legal representation. By deporting him in this way, without access to legal representation, the Home Secretary may have been in breach of international law. This is being taken up in court.

Similar actions in Belgium have led to commercial airlines refusing to deport asylum seekers. A spokesperson from CAGE said: "It is unbelievable that BA and its shareholders are profiting from the forced removal of people from the UK. This is the ultimate in putting profit before life, and it is nice to see that people here are standing up to it... literally!"

Hospitality Industry

Brighton No Borders group visit detainees in Haslar Detention Centre

As the state continues to pander to the media-manufactured anti refugee hysteria, there have been enacted a range of increasingly repressive asylum measures and a rise in deportations and the arbitrary detention of migrants. In Brighton a few of us have got involved in **No Borders** politics after going to the No Border camp in Strasbourg a couple of summers ago. Inspired by the Sans Papier, No One is Illegal and other groups around Europe fighting against immigration controls and deportations we thought that it was time we got off our arses too. The No Borders argument is simply that people should be free to move and live around the world unhindered by national boundaries and governments. Freedom to live where you wish in order to escape persecution or to build a better life for yourself or your family should be a basic human right. But in a globalising world this means that capital and people with wealth are free to move across borders, but most people are not.

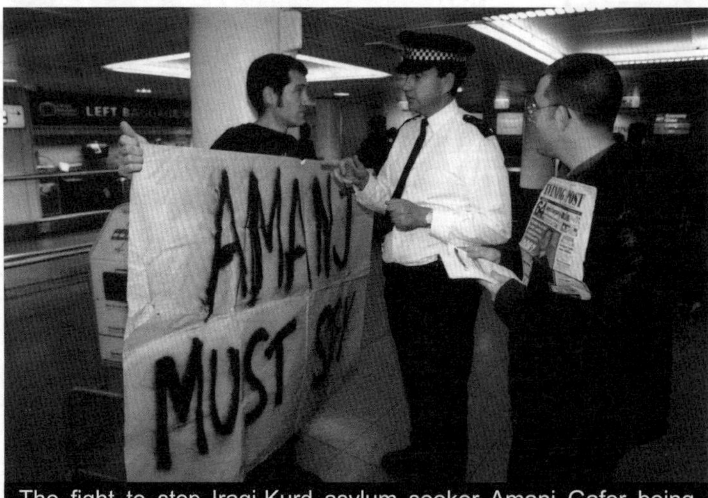

The fight to stop Iraqi-Kurd asylum seeker Amanj Gafor being deported included three successful actions of disrupting the plane he was due be deported on by planting someone on the same flight to stop it taking off – plus leafleting passengers, circulating communiques to airport staff, and demonstrating in the airports. Eventually Amanj was deported by sea in August 2000 to Germany, where he was sectioned as a schizophrenic.

When we got back from Strasbourg we found out about Haslar prison in Portsmouth, where male migrants are detained indefinitely, without any sentence and in grim conditions, and were on hunger strike. I called one of the detainees on hunger strike and around eight of us turned up at Haslar a week later to visit four men from Pakistan, Chad, Eastern Europe and the Congo. The day before we went a Chinese man had thrown himself off the roof, and they had neither seen nor heard what had happened to him.

They told us that they live in dorms and have no privacy at all, are fed inedible food and are subjected to random full body strip searches and a harsh prison routine. Some of them had just arrived in the UK, some had been there for over 10 years. One guy there had been there for over a year and a half living with the stress of having been told since he was first detained that his deportation is imminent. The men we met were picked up by the immigration police for a variety of reasons, but none of them had been convicted of anything, nor told how long they would have to stay in prison for.

I chatted with the guy from Pakistan who had been in the UK for a number of years but had been picked up by the police for working in take away in London without papers. He was gay and had been involved in radical politics in Pakistan and knew that he couldn't go back. His English was impeccable, better than mine, and he spent his time translating legal documents and the instructions that came over the loud tanoy for the other detainees. He was also hilarious and had loads of stories about how he entertained himself in prison. There had been a fire alarm the previous week, following an announcement on the tanoy in English that when the alarm sounds the detainees were to go in silence and single file to the exercise yard and line up. The other guys asked him what had been said and he told them that when the alarm sounds they have been instructed to run round in circles with their arms in the air screaming as loudly as they could, and under no circumstances go into the exercise yard.

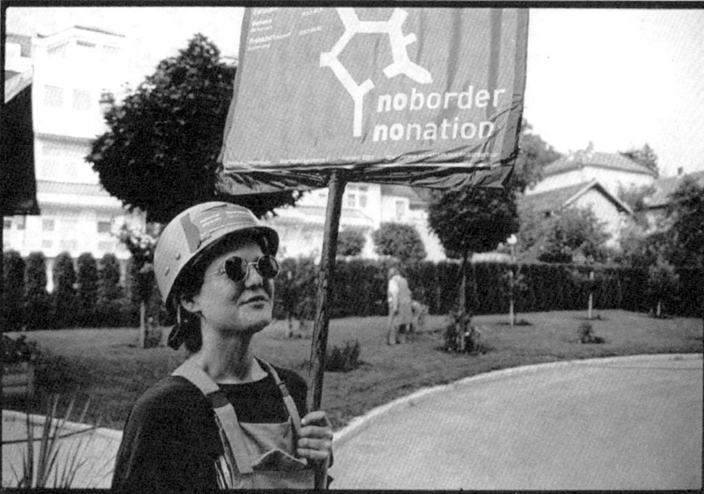

The UN High Comission on Refugees estimates that there are 12.1 million refugees world wide, with around 3 million living in Europe ***sans papiers*** (without visa papers) – the real figures would be much higher. In 1999 the EU began an agreement whereby immigration policy was transferred to the European level – becoming another aspect of 'Fortress Europe'. That year the European Noborder Network came together, and since that time has held Noborder camps along the the edges of Fortress Europe (and worldwide), and at detention centres or airports where refused asylum seekers are deported from. The picture above is from the No Border camp, Petisovci, Slovenia, July 2001. for more see www.noborder.org

There were some awful stories too, of men self harming and suicidal, being beaten up by Wakenhut security in the vans transporting them between prisons and of disgusting acts of racist abuse by the prison service and organisations such as Group 4 who run the detention centres. As we left later that afternoon we saw the prison guard who had shown us in drive off, the bonnet of his white car transformed by red tape into a St Georges cross. We later heard that the men we had met had been strip searched after we left.

I kept in touch with the guy I met that day, he kept me up to date with their hunger strikes and his attempts to teach the African men to line dance, but I was careful not to talk about the demo we were arranging on the phone. We went back to visit and they sneaked out the draft of a leaflet that would advertise the demo, we returned and they sneaked in a copy of the final leaflet. The next time we went to Haslar was for the demo, which was a huge let down. All the guys that we had met and become friends with and had been moved, the Police wouldn't let us anywhere near the perimeter fence, there were loads of socialists trying to sell their papers and the phone lines had been closed down after our initial call to them. We'll go back sometime though.

More recently we have set up a project in the Cowley Club, Brighton's autonomous social centre; the Migrant English Project. The idea was to create a space in the club where migrants would be actively invited to become part of it. This feels important because the more migrants are locked up and deported the less we get to really know what's going on. Lots of the groups that work with refugees have taken on government contracts and we can no longer rely on them to be impartial or able to take a more political stance. The Migrant English Project will never have a government contract or funding that means we can't be political.

The project runs every week for an afternoon, people come and hang out and chat and have English lessons. We also have an immigration solicitor who gives advice. Some of the refugees come each week and have started helping in the Cowley Club café and bar, and we are able to find places to stay and money for refugees who are given nothing by the state. We've yet to have anyone we know deported or detained, but for sure we have the full force of an anarchist social centre behind us when it happens.

There's loads more we'd like to do in the future, more visits to detention centres and keeping the project at the Cowley Club running, but we also hope that others around the UK will also be inspired to get a credible No Borders movement together. Mass direct action and the dismantling of all nation states and borders….that kind of thing anyway.

SUMMIT HOPPING SILLY SEASON

"An anarchists' travelling circus that goes from summit to summit with the sole purpose of causing as much mayhem as possible" - Tony Blair. (the first thing he's ever said that we agreed with)

Between the IMF Summit in Prague in September 2000 and the G8 Summit in Genoa in July 2001, it was summit hopping silly season, with one being disrupted nearly every week.

In every city hosting a summit, invariably there were months of preparation and a build-up of infrastructure, including forums for negotiating tactics, bringing together people and equipment for legal support, and creating alternative media networks like Indymedia.

In places with strong traditions and histories of resistance, like Barcelona or Rome, these resources were readily available. In other places with lesser established anarchist networks and libertarian social centres like Melbourne or Québec, the build up to the demonstrations meant creating networks which have not only long outlasted the original event, but have been the catalyst for the rise of new communities of resistance and even political movements.

During this period groups in Europe such as Italy's 'Ya Basta!' were very mobile and capable of getting large numbers to disrupt summits all over the continent – and from the same faces going to a lot of the events, bonds were formed and a strong Europe-wide network emerged.

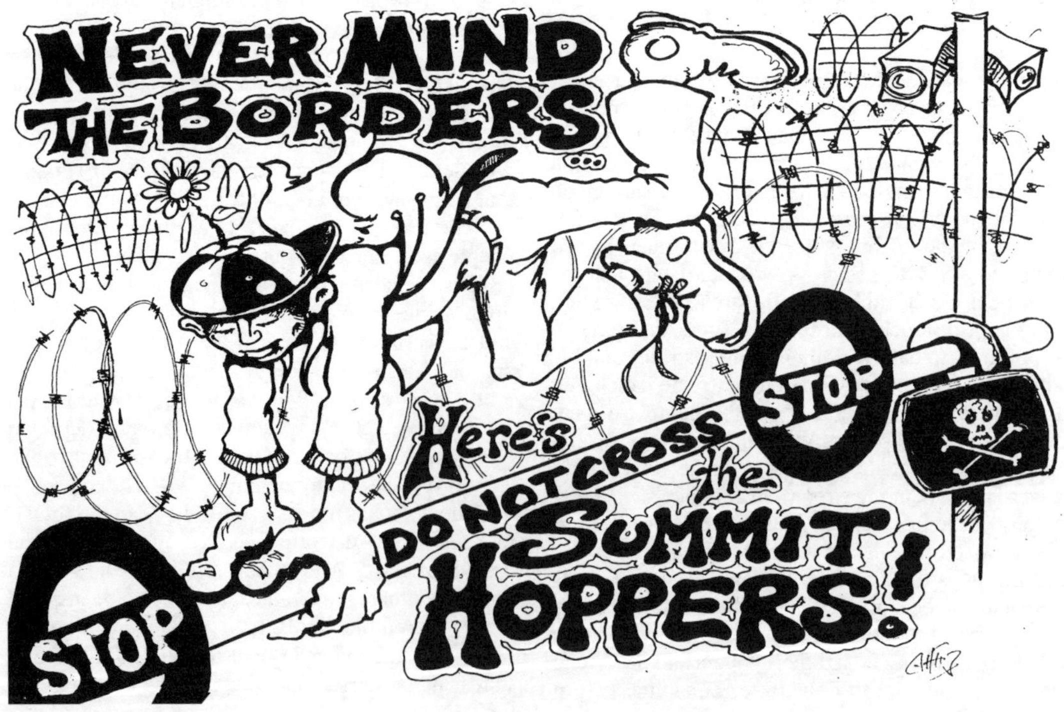

CZECH MATE!

"Don't worry, they won't get anywhere near us here, there's 11,000 police and only 5,000 protesters... I think we can safely ignore them today" - IMF delegate, September 26 – morning!

Another international day of carnival against capitalism, this time in Prague. Cameras rolled, the TV showed the usual tear-gas riot scenes and McDonalds got its customary kicking. But what didn't make the news was that across the globe 45 cities in 20 countries took part in solidarity actions against the World Bank and International Monetary Fund (IMF). What hardly got mentioned were the hundreds of people stopped from entering the Czech Republic or those beaten up and abused in police stations. Also convenientally ignored was why thousands of people took to the streets of Prague last week. But don't worry yer SchNEWS crew were there to give you some nuggets of truth.

FAT CATS & CHUBBY CZECHERS

Maybe it was a bit of an ambitious demand: 'We will lay siege to the World Bank and IMF until they dissolve themselves."

But with the Conference abandoned a day early and the previous day's meetings poorly attended, there's no doubt that last week's mass demonstrations in Prague were a success.

SchNEWS was lucky enough to talk with a 'mole' who spent the day inside the Conference Hall, chatting with delegates over champagne and canapes. One IMF employee told our insider, "I don't care about anything really... apart from how good the food is when I go out on missions to third world countries. You must be very bored if you are interested in the World Bank." Bored? Fifteen thousand people coming together from all over the planet to lay siege to institutions that have been blamed for "harming more people than any other non military organisations in human history", (*David Korten, People Centred Development Forum*). Boredom doesn't really come into it.

The protests were also a success because they drew attention to institutions that have thrived on anonymity. As the chairman of the World Bank inspection panel told our mole, "The only thing the World Bank is afraid of is publicity. These protesters are creating that." A Deutsche Bank employee from New York was even more frank: "The protesters are right of course. We are just interested in the money. The World Bank and IMF are just helping people like us to cream it in. Isn't it great?"

The protests were also a success because they give the poorer countries more courage to stand up and complain about what the IMF/World Bank are doing to them. One told our mole, "It's great to see them here. These protests definitely help us in our fight." Another Southern delegate added, "These protests are the inevitable result of policies being imposed on the world like a religion. Thatcherism has led to this. G7 governments and especially the US are responsible. In G7 countries there are still some safety nets for the poor but in the South, which has almost no voice, there is less and less for the poor. That's why it's great to see the young Europeans doing this. It's the only way."

TEARIN' UP THE CZECHS!

Up to fifteen thousand people mobilised from every corner of the planet; Bologna's Michelin-man stylee Ya Basta! mingled with Czech Solidaritska, Catalonia's CNT and blocs from Poland, Germany, Greece and beyond. Latin Americans, Bangladeshis and Maoris traded resistance tips as the sound system kicked in. Groups divided into yellow, blue and pink-silver blocks and approached the Conference Centre from different directions. As the groups got near to the police lines all hell broke loose, with protestors trading cobblestones with stun grenades, tear gas and water cannons. The bankers couldn't get out, and we couldn't get in, and eventually delegates were taken out by underground – probably the first time a lot of them would have used public transport for a while.

A DROP OF TRUTH IN AN OCEAN OF BULLSHIT

As darkness ebbed in, the remaining pink and blue crew wove their way northwards through the valley to meet the Italians who had blockaded the Opera house -the southern European anarchists obviously craving some higher culture after a hard day's street fight. However, the opera got cancelled and the bankers instead headed to the city limits for a banquet. These people really are down with world's poor! Protesters drifted to Wenceslas Square, scene of the Velvet Revolution, where ten regular cops stood sheepishly in front of a beckoning McDonald's. Within a minute and a half it received its ritual trashing. KFC followed suit, and by the time the IPB Bank got its share of broken paving stones several dozen Prague locals had joined in to reclaim a little power from the bankers who had foreclosed their business or refused them loans to feed their families.

The riot police took their time getting there; just enough damage was done before the cops ran riot and the crowd melted away to pubs with decent prices…

The next day you couldn't move in Prague without being pounced on by police. The WB/IMF cancelled the last day's meetings saying it was nothing to do with the protests. Honest guv, it was just that they had nothing more to talk about…

S Issue 277 – 6th October 2000

PRAGUE PRISONER SUPPORT

"I was arrested and taken into custody. As they led me down the stairs to the cells I noticed blood on the walls and heard cries from other cells… The police searched me and the others, putting all our possessions in one pile on the table in the room. They told us not to move – anyone who did was hit with truncheons across the back. The police were more violent than intelligent; they didn't know where anyone had been arrested, or what for. I was terrified, they did not allow access to a lawyer or a phone to let my friends know where I was. I didn't know what would happen. The people I was in the cells with will be friends for life."

The standover tactics started at the borders: At least 600 "undesirables" were refused entry, including an American, Lee Sustar, who has no criminal record, yet was described as "a threat to public order and health". The Czech authorities have a list of 300 activists not allowed into the country and have the help of the FBI, Interpol and the British Police. A German woman was refused permission to leave Germany under an anti-hooliganism law, the first time this law has been used against anyone except footie fans. The local authorities mounted a massive operation with some 11,000 police supported by armoured personnel carriers, troop trucks, fire engines, helicopters, tear gas, concussion grenades and water cannons.

On the day itself there were few arrests but as night fell and in the following days, police started to pick people up arbitrarily and soon nearly 900 people had been nicked. Many of the arrests were made by masked-up plain clothes cops who were one minute leading attacks on uniformed police and McDonalds and the next dragging activists away. Amongst the random arrests were two German schoolboys who had bunked off a school trip in order to savour the delights of Czech beer!

In custody arrestees were routinely not told why they were nicked, were denied access to food, warmth and medical attention and even denied a phone call or a solicitor. Water often had to be paid for. In some cases up to 20 prisoners at a time were crammed into a cell measuring just nine feet by nine. Some protestors were handcuffed to walls and beaten, others forced to lie spread eagled on the floor and prevented from sleeping.

The treatment of some women was particularly degrading; they were strip-searched and humiliated by male prison guards. The worst case was Chris, an Austrian woman cartoonist, who was nicked and beaten till she lost consciousness. In the nick she was so scared for her life that she jumped from a second floor window. She now has a broken leg and hips, a destabilised spine, and permanent damage to her foot. Her location was only revealed when a nurse in the hospital broke the information embargo imposed on her by police and telephoned her friends. She has now been deported to a Vienna hospital, charged with attacking 3 policemen. Her van, which is also her home and contains her life's creative work, has been impounded by the Czech police to ensure she comes to the trial.

So while most of us are safely away from Prague now, we should remember the people who live there. Over half of all the arrests were of Czech citizens and it's likely that police harassment of Czech activists will continue, so it's important not to leave them to suffer; they really need our help and solidarity. There are at least 20 international activists still in jail and another 70 are missing but presumed in jail. Up to 600 other Czechs are also suspected detained. They will almost certainly have to stay in prison until their trials, which could be three months away.

Pic: Simon Chapman

Direct from frontline Prague

27/9/00: International Blocs rock the Eastern Blockades S26 in the city of 100 fires. Si Mitchell e-mailed this on-the-spot report.

The SQUALL posse are still at large on the streets of Prague, despite the secret polis pinning a tail on their donkey asses, and one cameraman catching a cobblestone around the noggin. Don't worry about what you read in the papers – S26 was a total success – what meetings they managed to hold were backed by a chorus of concussion grenades and the whiff of CS gas. On the streets a well organised, hierarchy-free bloc did what they came to do – and more. Unbreakable links have been formed. We have seen the future of international solidarity. There is no going back.

We hit the square at eight, shin pads and sticks gaffer-taped to every limb as body armour. The SQUALL crew were in good company. A global call to arms had mobilised anarchist blocs from every corner of the planet, Bologna's 'Ya Basta' mingled with Czech Solidaritska, Catalonia's CNT and blocs from Poland, Germany, Greece and beyond. Latin Americans, Bangladeshis and Maoris traded resistance tips as the sound system beat adrenal glands into action.

An elaborate route and splitting plan had been formulated in internationally attended multilingual street meetings. Months of preparation brought 20,000 well-focused justice hunters onto the streets of Czech's capital to blockade the World Bank and IMF's annual carve up. Aware that the real decisions are made well before such glutinous shindigs, the kids on the street set out to blockade the assembled bankers, funders and corporate delegates inside the city's fortress-like Congress Centre – which squats imposingly on top of a city centre hill.

The blockade divided into three groups – yellow, pink and blue. The yellow took the bridge – a four lane viaduct 300ft above the valley, which splits the city – the only northern exit from the Conference Centre. The pink and blue were to head south on the east and west sides, to siege all other exits. Despite plans for tactical amalgamation, by September 24 it was apparent that Pink was red, Blue was black and yellow would be fronted by Ya Basta.

With a 500 strong international hardcore anarchist bloc heading the blue route, we felt obliged to go blue. Mass chants of "Oh Ay, Internationale Solidarite!" mingled with drums and whistles and cacophonous laughter. It was as close to the morning of Culloden as you'll get in a built up area.

The police seemed content to let us plough down to the Centre. However, with our target in sight the cops had made a blockade at the narrowing point of a steep hill. A line of riot cops and a water cannon truck blocked the road. Left was into the valley, and right was blocked by the Vysherad Castle. It was forward or bust. The 'clava posse didn't miss a step as the cobblestones that paved the street began raining on the police line. The cops responded with stun grenades and water cannon (the smarter 'activitsky' wore black waterproofs – the rest of us were instantly soaked to the skin). Within moments the molotovs were coming over the front lines. Blood was spilling on both sides. We fished one geezer – completely spark-out – from the river of water flowing down the hill, as the cop line was replaced with water-firing armoured cars. The police sprayed some kind of skin-

burning paint, perhaps to pick people up later, perhaps just to hurt them now. Concussion grenades exploded repeatedly and the now familiar sting of tear gas filled the street (why do the SQUALL editors keep sending us to these places?) While half the crowd donned gas-masks, the Greeks piled up to the front: "Let us through," they said, "we're used to it!"

After a pitched battle lasting an hour or more (American veterans of Seattle looked on in awe at non-violent direct action – European stylee), the police pushed the blue bloc down the hill. Steel fencing barricades were erected in the streets and fires lit. Small masked groups stoned caged canon trucks. It was Jihad without the religious bollocks. The western exit was sealed. Leaving half the bloc and a burning car to hold the line, the other blues (complete with new riot shields, helmets and sticks... er, dunno where they got them from...) followed the Infernal Noise Brigade Marching band around to help siege the south side.

A renegade pink and silver bloc headed by a UK Earth First! samba band had got within poking distance of the Centre's eastern flank. Meanwhile Ya Basta's military machine was holding the bridge in style (not to mention the attention of the world's media.)

Moles on the inside of the conference relayed information to the mob. Half the delegates hadn't made it and the other half were running round like headless chickens (nowt new there then). The meetings were bungled and we knew it, though the next day's Financial Times would paint another picture. IMF representatives from Bangladesh commended "the young people" for being so effective.

After realising their tacticless strategy of road clearance was doomed, the old bill shut the tube line to the public and took the delegates out by underground – the first time most of them would have used public transport.

As darkness ebbed in, a joyous and united pink 'n' silver and blue crew wove their way northwards through the valley to meet the Italians who had blockaded the Opera house where the IMF delegates were due to spend the evening. However the opera was cancelled and the bankers headed to the city limits for a banquet (these people really are down with world's poor.)

Not wishing to waste the walk, the two thousand strong crowd headed down to Wenceslas Square. Ten regular cops stood sheepishly in front of McDonald's; a semi-circle of activists stood looking at them tapping on the railings. Bang! – one window went and they legged it. Within a minute and a half, the shop was an insurance right off. KFC followed suit, and by the time the IPB Bank got trashed several dozen Prague locals had joined in to reclaim a little power from the bankers who had foreclosed their business or refused them loans to feed their families.

The riot police took their time getting there and SQUALL's agent six won himself a two inch head wound filming what used to be a Mercedes garage – and had to retreat to the nearest "low quality hospital". Karlovo Central had already seen a good few broken limbs and smashed heads – though activist medic teams of doctors and nurses had been on the case all day treating casualties in the field. As daylight dawns in Eastern Europe 460 well battered folk are waking up behind bars as police are stopping and arresting arbitrarily in the streets. As is always the case – a police operation that fails to protect corporate targets is followed by extreme over reaction. The army's coming out to play. We ain't out of the trees yet – but the woods... the woods belong to the activists.

from SQUALL – www.squall.co.uk

AWAY FIXTURE

Brits mobilise to Prague

Apparently, the protests in Prague were "the biggest self-generated mobilisation of British people to a political situation in another country since the Spanish Civil War." Obviously people weren't preparing to go and fight and possibly be killed when they prepared to go to Prague. But the comparison struck me: I had been involved in making history. And while we didn't exactly stop the World Bank and the International Monetary Fund in their tracks, the action was a success both practically (the meeting was halted a day early, delegates were scared to leave their hotels, their social events were cancelled) and symbolically. The Prague protests continued to inspire people beyond the few days around 26th September 2000.

Dredging through my very murky memory of the build up to Prague, I remember it being a time when there was a buzz round the activist scene. The global (!) anti-globalisation movement, as it quickly became known, was rising, and everyone wanted to be part of the next big thing. The Peoples Global Action had begun in 1998, and later the same year, the first global street party happened simultaneously here and in 37 different cities around the globe to coincide with the G8 meeting in Birmingham. June 18th the following year both gave confidence to British activists and inspired our US counterparts. Then came Seattle, which shook the world, upped the ante, and spawned a whole new era of global anti-capitalist protests.

At around the same time, it was becoming increasingly difficult to organise large protests in this country as the state closed the chink in its armour in which J18 had happened. A16 (the World Bank meeting in Washington on April 16th 2000) offered more inspiring images, but few could afford to go stateside for a protest. The next big action in London, the May Day guerilla gardening, was problematic. There seemed to be little motivation for organising an inspiring action in this country. It was in this context that the build-up to Prague began in earnest. There was a tangible sense that if we could get enough people there, we really could win – we could stop this meeting, or at least cause so much disruption as to have a huge impact on it. If they could do it in Seattle, where they didn't even have crazy Greek anarchists, the 'up-for-it' German autonomes, or the Italian Ya Basta, then we had a damn good chance in Europe.

THE NEXT BIG THING

The initiative came directly from the grassroots, from autonomous, non-hierarchical groups, though again, Jubilee 2000 were also organising around the World Bank/IMF meeting. (The hype around the 'next big anti-globalisation riot' however, meant they organized for a peaceful demo on September 25th, the day before the main protests, and then shipped most of their members home again.) A huge number of people organised with their friends or their own groups and got themselves to Prague, without any direction or assistance from any national organisation. The old-style lefty parties did mobilize, but Globalise Resistance was still just an evil twinkle in some SWP members' eyes, and they hadn't yet started to try and take over the British contingent of global protest. I'm sure that part of the appeal of Prague for many was that no one group had ownership of the planned protests. And it is perhaps a reason why more Brits went to Prague than Genoa or other protests and forums since.

It is indicative of how genuinely grassroots this was, that it was one lone person who set up the British S26 website, entirely independently of any group or network. Small groups of friends designed their own leaflets, and the posters advertising Prague were different in every town in the UK. A small group (working under the PGA name) put together a booklet covering the planned protests in Prague, including things like useful Czech phrases. Another individual took it on themselves to research where to buy gasmasks and went to Prague in advance to reccie possible action targets such as corporate offices.

S26 collectives (the truly awful J18 style moniker stuck among the anti-globalisation protesters – presumably only because it was suitably neutral) sprang up around Britain. I'm not in a position to say who or what groups were involved in other places, but if my city was anything to go by, it was a 'random assortment'. Begun by activists loosely from the Earth First! network as a way of reaching out beyond the usual suspects, our S26 collective descended quite rapidly into a fairly useless body. There were only a couple of 'non-aligned' people, a representative from Jubilee 2000, one from Workers Power and one from the SWP. Initially, the group's main aim was organising transport to Prague, which according to one of the few EF! types who persisted with the collective, "felt really weird, as it turned out we were just organising coaches for the SWP". But paranoia about coaches being turned away at the border meant most of us sorted out our own transport arrangements and besides, the SWP only wanted to be there for the one day and then to get back in time for work.

Aside from a public meeting and some solidarity stuff while we were in Prague (and I'm not even sure these were organised through the auspices of the S26 collective), this was the extent of the 'network'. Different politics, the fact that Jubilee 2000's protest was September 25th, and the fact that the SWP only wanted to turn up in Prague, march around and leave asap, meant that there was no joint activity in Prague itself and there wasn't much of a coming together of groups at all. This highlights the question of whether it is worth trying to work with these groups or not. On the one hand to bail out and not bother to go to these coalitions means that you can become ghettoized and allow the SWP to push all other groups out. But, on the other hand, perhaps it is more useful to put your energies elsewhere and build a separate organization. There isn't an easy answer to this.

There must have been a whole host of people who made it to Prague off their own back. And who knows what motivated them to do it. Inspired by June 18th, or Seattle, or a local street party? Looking for the next big protest? Didn't want to miss an opportunity to make history? Read it in SchNEWS or Indymedia, or saw a leaflet? It must be true that a large percentage of Brits (including those linked in to such as the EF! network or left-wing groups) went to Prague because they could. Fifty quid got you there with accommodation. Food and beer were cheap too. It was the first major global protest since Seattle that was accessible to many of us. Within the EF! network there was recognition of the inadequacy of one-off protests, where it seems to the world that people show up in a city, riot, and then melt away. There was a desire to do more outreach, awareness and follow-up stuff, and to some extent that did happen. In my city, people leafleted the centre on September 26th, explaining what was going on in Prague and how it related to life here.

The post-Prague public meeting was rammed, and with many new faces. Even in tiny towns, articles appeared in local papers with headlines along the lines of 'Local lass to fight World Bank in Prague', so to some extent outreach, awareness, and follow-up stuff did happen. Inevitably, aside from the excellent prisoner support done by some Brits, less energy was devoted to follow-up stuff than to the exciting protests themselves. As far as I'm aware, Prague was the first time the radical ecological networks had mobilized together, as a group, for a situation abroad. And we did pretty well. It certainly felt when we arrived in Prague that we were one of the best prepared groups.

Whatever 'avin it' is in Italian, Ya Basta were doing it on the bridge

People were sent to Prague in advance to scout potential targets, find accommodation, and meet with INPEG (an umbrella group of protest organisations). A planning weekend was organised to discuss logistics of how we would work together. Gas masks were bought and distributed. Basic communication was set up. An EF! office was rented in Prague and staffed in advance. Everyone was given the same map of Prague to work from. Spare mobile phones were sourced, and Czech sim cards bought. The law and our rights were researched, and not least, funds were raised (being from a relatively wealthier nation, it was felt we should contribute a considerable sum to INPEG). I could go on, but basically, we were about as logistically organised as we could be.

We were also about as paranoid as we could be. There had been so much hype and scaremongering about this event that it had rubbed off on us. We were imagining secret police around every corner, and I'm sure the 'James Bond' element added to the fun. However, some paranoia was totally justified. Many long time dreadlocked activists cut their hair and wore chinos, worried they might get stopped at the border. On each ordinary commercial coach from Victoria there were many people going to the protest, and everyone travelling on those coaches must have had that 'approaching the border moment'. Nasty as it was for the people concerned, we all heaved a collective sigh of relief when they dragged the one dreadlocked or pierced bloke/woman off the coach to be searched (many of us were carrying gas masks / maps etc). Our ultra-preparedness for this action meant that many of us planned to be in Prague for days or even weeks in advance.

This resulted in quite a few Brits becoming engrossed in the overall organisation of the protest, which was quite a challenge. We had to sit through tortuous meetings, as each point had to be translated into several different languages. Decision-making was incredibly difficult, not least because the people there beforehand were only a tiny fraction of the number of people who would be there on the day and how could we make decisions on their behalf? It also felt bad that the British and US activists dominated the main organising meetings. English was the common language for most Europeans, and so it made sense that all the big meetings were conducted in English, but it felt a bit too colonial for comfort. It didn't help that some of the US 'facilitators' had a style so worthy and earnest (and not particularly democratic in fact) that it made the more cynical Europeans cringe.

Tactical Frivolity

HIT THE GROUND RUNNING

Most British people arrived just before September 26th, and quickly decided to form a splinter group from the main demo plans. Not being party to this decision, I was a bit miffed that it might seem to everyone else that the Brits show up, decide that no-one else's plans are good enough for them, and swan off in a different direction. It did make sense however: we wouldn't want to be with the yellow route for a futile set-piece confrontation between the cops and Ya Basta on the bridge. The red route was full of socialists wanting to chant and march and not much else. Blue had a difficult route, and was very 'black block', leaving little room for our samba and carnival.

The idea then was to form a new route, Pink and Silver. The colour scheme and probably the desire to have a carnivalesque atmosphere was largely influenced by the Samba group and the Tactical Frivolity crew. Already bedecked in flamboyant pink and silver costumes, this latter group, who'd travelled in convoy in vans from Britain were intent on bringing a lighthearted touch to potentially angry situations. A route using back streets to the rear of the conference centre was worked out, and the plan was for the samba band to attract others beyond our own network. This didn't really work, and we only had several hundred mainly British and a few assorted others. This was unfortunate because our choice of route proved good, and with more numbers, we would have had a real chance to get through one thin police line to the conference centre.

This raises one of the most problematic aspects of the way the British EF! network organised in Prague. The decision made during organising weekend, to all work as a group despite quite different politics and styles, and despite some reluctance from more black block types, was in retrospect not the best. Because we'd never really discussed whether we were actually going to try and get through police lines into the conference centre, which would have either required an act of god or some level of violent confrontation with the police, we were not at all prepared for it. And had we got in, what were we planning to do? Dance samba at the delegates till they ran away with their tails between their legs? A flimsy 'black block', prepared to attack police lines, behind a group of exhibitionist dancers, with a slow-moving samba band in between just led to confusion and recrimination.

It is funny that although we were ultra prepared in some senses for a riot, (the costume be-decked dancers even had gas masks painted silver) we lacked experience in dealing with the way the Czech police operated. The Czech police tactics were shock grenades, tear gas and water cannons – which virtually no-one from Britain had experienced. We were thoroughly shaken by the shock grenades, with many mistaking it for CS gas and running. Many people were similarly intimidated by the water cannon and backed off. By the time we saw that the water cannon had actually just run out of water and realised that shock grenades weren't gas, the police back-up had arrived, and we'd missed our opportunity. (A fuller account of the pink & silver experience is in Do or Die Issue 9.) The excellent cycle scouts were one really positive aspect. This was a group who'd cycled to Prague from Britain, and whose role on the action was to cycle ahead to determine where police lines were, to find different routes to the conference centre and see what was happening elsewhere. This tactic, borrowed from Seattle, proved invaluable.

END GAME

The following days were intensely frustrating, as a police clampdown prevented us from organising any more actions. We were hoping to try to target one of the corporate nasties or do some prisoner support action. But with the convergence centre closed by the cops, and any group larger than 4 or 5 people being stopped and dispersed outdoors, planning anything became impossible. We tried squeezing a meeting into the poky flats we'd rented, or cramming into dormitories, but circumstances made it hard for us to organise anything as a group. Some people did get into the delegates hotels, to set off fire alarms etc, but nothing much more. (It is one of the failures of the Prague protests that no good contingency plans were made for actions on the successive days.) However, in the weeks and months afterwards some of the most dedicated prisoner support work was done in Prague by British activists and it is very much to their credit.

It wasn't with a sense of frustration that I left that city. I can never forget, as dusk descended, meeting up with the US Infernal Noise Brigade, and marching heads held high, fists in the air, through Prague's cobbled streets. We felt successful then, even before learning the following day's meeting was cancelled. Even before realising that we had the delegates running scared. Even before we realised that our actions would inspire others to continue to force institutions like the World Bank and G8 into ever more inaccessible venues.

You're The Voice: S11

September 11-13th was the WEF Asian-Pacific Forum in Melbourne.

The networks which built up around the country to shut down this business meeting were successful on the day, but more than that, the connections and infrastructure built up for S11 have long outlasted the event itself, and caused a sea change in libertarian politics in Australia. The organizers of this WEF Forum might have assumed that Melbourne would be a nice, easy going place to have such an event, not counting on 10,000 people blockading the venue and preventing ⅔ of the delegates from getting in.

Amongst the myriad autonomous groups, unions, campaigns and others who had a reason to be there, two groups featured strongly at S11 – S11Alliance, and AWOL (Autonomous Web Of Liberation). S11Alliance was dominated by two socialist groups (the International Socialist Organisation and Democratic Socialist Party) and their big plans for the day were along the lines of getting unions involved, staging speeches, selling papers and getting new members. Eventually people who preferred autonomy and consensus stopped going to these meetings and formed AWOL whose mission became 'blockade and stop the forum' – but the first job was to hook up with the nebulus of groups all around the country ready to come together…

A huge number of people organised themselves into affinity groups and communicated through spoke councils. A S11 road show toured the east coast for two months, and along with other weekend forums, training days, the formation of Melbourne Indymedia, the www.s11.org website and other alt media, thousands converged on Melbourne for S11. For a laugh the nike.com webpage was hacked redirecting 900,000 websurfers automatically to S11.org!

On the 7th of September AWOL organised convergence centres and direct action, legal and medical training. On Sunday the 10th two alternative conferences were featuring speakers including Indian eco-feminist Vandana Shiva.

Monday S11

Because of the blockade many delegates just couldn't get through – protestors saw buses of delegates circling the casino for much of the morning, and helicopters were buzzing. Premier of Western Australia Richard Court (conservative) had attempted – against advice – to enter the conference by car: he found himself bailed up in his car for an hour in the throng with an aboriginal fella dancing on the roof! (see pic below)

By afternoon the crowd swelled out to over 10,000 who enjoyed a street festival with a roving sound system and free food from Food Not Bombs.

Tuesday S12

By the second morning police were under instructions to 'get the delegates in', and attacked sit-down protesters blocking the entrance with batons, injuring 50 and hospitalizing 11. At 11am there was a 10,000 strong union march, but the cops stupidly chose to attack just as this rally was ending, provoking the dispersing crowd to join in the ruck. 3,000 or 4,000 people were back blockading the entrances – but the tension was much higher after the violence during the morning, and again later 30 people holding one of the entrances were injured when police baton charged them.

Wednesday S13

The conference is in tatters and apparently 600 delegates have given up. The blockade is low key because of the police violence the day before and a more carnival style march circles the conference centre, but later in the day a police car runs over a protester and doesn't stop (she had serious injuries but survived).

Aftermath

It's predictable what the mainstream media said about the event, seeing as most of the media companies had delegates inside the forum. The S11 Alliance courted the media, who reported them as the 'leaders', and AWOL was rarely mentioned. S11 saw the rise of a new anti-capitalist network across Australia, very much tied into international struggles.

Links

www.melbourne.indymedia.org

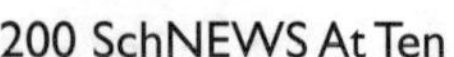

NICE BUT NAUGHTY

"(Enlargement) will bring great economic benefits. These countries will bring... material resources including land and energy, and they will bring markets for our products."
- European Round-Table of Industrialists

Up to 70,000 demonstrators rallied last week on the streets of Nice before the European Union summit. At the same time as a charter of fundamental rights was being discussed counter-summit meetings were being cancelled or raided while others fought battles with police who wouldn't let them into France!

On the day of the summit a few thousand people tried to storm the centre and were met with the usual greetings of tear gas and stun grenades. A bank was burnt, a few shops were trashed and the French President Chirac said the anti-capitalist demonstrators were "contrary to democratic principles." Yet behind the clouds of smoke, the un-elected and unaccountable faces of big business were once again pushing their agenda onto the centre stage, using the EU as a Trojan horse for more corporate global carve-ups.

Carve Up

European Union Plc

Countries, we are told, are desperate to join the EU club. However, before any can play, their economies must be 'harmonised', y'know, public services slashed and privatised, etc. In fact, you could call it the European version of the Structural Adjustment Programmes (SchNews 256) forced onto the 'Third World'. As Green MEP Caroline Lucas points out "In short, governments are expected to give up control over their own economies – spelling destruction for local businesses."

Take Slovakia. With approximately 50,000 staff, the Slovak Railway Company is the biggest employer in the country. In 1998 the Slovak government announced plans to sack nearly half the workforce, and a year later they signed a loan agreement with the European Investment Bank. With strings attached.

The strings will result in a rise in fares of 30%, a cut of two thirds in both state subsidies and in staff pay, a reduction in rail freight and a cut in railway lines. There was no public discussion about these conditions. Instead the media reported that the government and the rail company were given two weeks to accept: if they agreed to meet them, the Bank was ready to provide the loan immediately.

When a Slovakian environmental NGO sent a protest letter to the President of the Bank, he replied: "The proposed restructuring measures in this case mirror those agreed over recent years between the Bank and virtually all railway companies in the ten Central and Eastern Europe Countries which have applied for EU membership." So that's all right then.

Fast Track To Profits

They call it 'qualified majority voting', which basically means countries can't individually veto decisions. Instead the European Commission gets to make decisions without having to answer to anyone. It's called 'fast-tracking' and is popular with big business who are fed up with their great ideas being watered down or blocked altogether by interfering governments or nit-picking protestors. They want swift, centralised decision-making, making it easier to push their demands through an already industry-friendly European bureaucracy. Up to a point, they got their way with more trade decisions passing out of national control. National and the European Parliaments now have little control of Trade-Related Intellectual Property Rights or some services.

If you think this is all confusing, EU bureaucrats estimate that it will take two months to produce a consolidated text of the Nice Treaty, i.e. to come to agreement about what has been agreed!

Cinders In Snow

Switzerland hadn't witnessed such police and army forces deployed since last century's workers movement.

Many activist groups got stopped, body searched, photographed and not allowed to enter the Swiss territory. Others got the same treatment all around Davos including residents and independent media (later allowed in).

24th Jan: Demonstrations take place, including the locking up of a police station in Jura to protest five police being sent to Davos to bolster numbers.

25th Jan: The local government of Tessin is occupied to protest against repressive policing. USB (the 3rd biggest Swiss bank) is occupied in Lugano and Lausanne, banners are deployed calling for demos the next day.

26th Jan: In Zurich, a stink bomb action targets a Globus supermarket. Activists still arrive at borders and 100 Tutte Bianchi (white overall-wearing Ya Basta) block the frontier post of Chiasso for a day and night after their entry is refused. Swiss activists block another frontier post in the afternoon in solidarity.

27th Jan: 200 activists occupy WTO offices in Geneva. Between Lugano and Davos, more than 20 busses close the road in both directions, with 600 people reclaiming the motorway and creating a 10 mile traffic jam, while 200 reclaim the A-road. After being charged, they are allowed to get back to Zurich. 500 are blocked in Landquart train station and block all platforms for trains to Davos. They then try to join the motorway group but get attacked by police forces with plastic bullets and gas. 15 minutes later, the activists obtain a train to go to Zurich which stops by the motorway in solidarity with the road blockage.

Swisscom telephone network is sabotaged to disrupt the forum.

400 demonstrators get through the police line and march towards the Forum. They're stopped 500 yards from it by police barricades and watercanons. In Bern, 150 to 200 activists block traffic on a bridge to protest against the cancellation of trains to Davos.

Everyone gets back to Zurich. As the train is stopped before the centre, a demo starts towards it. Banks, multinational offices and posh cars get trashed on their way while police try to attack the protesters. In the evening there are riots for 2 hours against police attacks and refusal to let the protesters come to the city centre. 130 are arrested through the night.

29th Jan: McDonalds in Lausanne is blockaded, and 200 people demonstrate in Geneva against police repression and occupy the Police and Justice department until they know the whereabouts of unreleased prisoners and assurances that they will be let out that day.

30th Jan: 50 people are deported from Switzerland, while solidarity actions take place in France, Brasil, Spain, Italy & Finland.

Sources: "Davos – account of the events", Rézo Maloka: www.chez.com/maloka (site in French.)

The Swiss Police have expanded on the Storm Trooper tactics of the Corporate Police State with a great new invention: the Shit Cannon, also known as a Shit Sprayer (SS)! Although resistance from local manure suppliers made it impossible to put together for the World Economic Forum protesters in Davos this time around, in the future they'll be ready to send the SS (Shit Sprayers) wherever the people rise up.

Getting sprayed with shit won't be nice but there'll be a certain irony to it. It will be hard for anyone to ignore how much this Corporate Capitalist Police State shit stinks. The People will match shit with shit. There's no shit power like the people's shit power.

15–17th March 2001 

Naples Global Forum

Delegates from 188 countries arrived in the city of Naples for the Global Forum, a group that has the potential to create an e-governmental institution which could control and regulate internet and telephone communications globally. The particular focus was increasing and spreading internet technology to the third world – and topics on the agenda included Italy's first electronic ID card.

15,000–20,000 people arrived in the city to protest against the three day conference. The crowd was a diverse mix of political elements: Kurdish refugees, a myriad of anarchist groups, COBAS (a federation of trade union syndicalists), pacifist and student collectives, communists, and everyone else in between – many arriving on squatted trains, and a university faculty building was squatted for accommodation.

A major clash with police arose in the Plaza Borsa during the conference, where hundreds of demonstrators came prepared to fight with helmets, masks, giant plexiglass shields, sticks, rocks, and a few Molotov cocktails, and the police responded with gas, and charging the crowd. After much gas and fighting – with injuries on both sides – large groups of protesters surrendered and were led out of the plaza by the police.

From Indymedia Naples

Pics right: 17th March – crowd tries to break past the security line around the conference centre

SchNEWS SQUALL Yearbook 2001

First available at Strawberry Fair, Cambridge, June 2001.

"The Zapatistas march into Mexico City, thousands disrupt the World Bank meeting in Prague, Churchill gets an anarchist make-over: from Bognor to Bogota, Dudley to Delhi, and Kilburn to Melbourne, resistance has become as global as the institutions of capitalism."

A written and visual record of the events of the period March 2000 – April 2001 bringing together SchNEWS issues 251–300, articles and photographs from SQUALL magazine, plus extra articles, cartoons, satire etc.

ISBN 09529748 4 3

Still available for a bargain price of £3.00 inc. p&p direct from us

We nearly had all the copies of this book confiscated by police under the Terrorist Act within five minutes of leaving the printers...

"The printers were near Liverpool St station, and little did we know we were driving into the 'ring of steel' as we headed south towards Brixton for cannabis day with the vanload of new books. Just past Liverpool St Station we were pulled over – a dodgy looking old white van, two geezers in it. Two coppers became about five or six very quickly, as the side door of the van was torn open. 'Ello ello, what have we here then? We are searching you under the Terrorist Act' which was barely a month old at the time. What did they find? Boxes of books with the word 'terrorist' and Winston–with–a–mohawk on the cover. They said 'do you know we could confiscate these books under the Terrorist Act? I said yes, knowingly (see page 106 officer). They thought they'd stumbled on a cache of terrorist literature, and started passing copies to one another. All I wanted to do was get to Brockwell Park and get completely stoned, but we had this palava on our hands. Eventually their attention was diverted when they found some magic mushrooms in the van, which they arrested the driver for."

MAGICAL MEXICAN TOUR

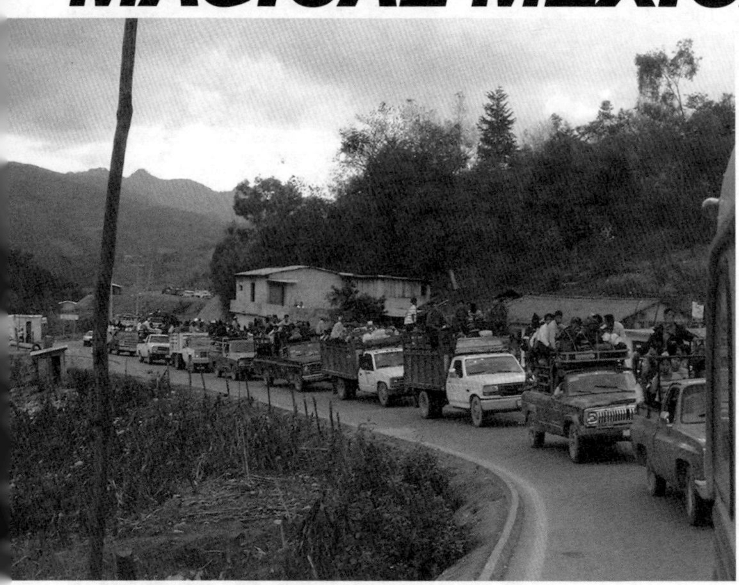

"Our general, Emiliano Zapata taught us not to struggle for power, because power poisons the blood and clouds the mind."

- Subcommandante Marcos

The Zapatista Army of National Liberation (EZLN) marched triumphantly into the main square in Mexico City last Sunday to crowds of over 200,000. The 24 commanders, in full uniform & masks but no weapons, are now refusing to leave the city until all Zapatista prisoners are released, Mexican troops are withdrawn from the state of Chiapas and a bill guaranteeing the political and cultural rights of the 10 million indigenous Mexicans is passed.

The march into the capital was the last stage of a tour which has seen the Zapatistas stopping and speaking to thousands of supporters in towns and cities across the country. As a result, 50 of the 56 indigenous ethnic groups have now united with them to form a National Indigenous Congress.

This has been overshadowed by some in the media who would have us believe it's merely some sort of rock tour with politics; a personality duel between Sub-Commandante Marcos and the new President of Mexico, Vincent Fox. But it isn't about personalities or only about indigenous peoples rights. The Zapatistas struggle has shown graphically that not everyone is happy with the 'neo-liberal privatise everything' version of the world that is being forced down our throats and that we all have the right to say NO!

ZAPATISMO!

"It is the self-activity of the Indians, above all else, that defines this struggle." - Aufheben magazine

On January 1st 1994, the same day the North American Free Trade Agreement (NAFTA) came into force, the Zapatistas emerged from the Lacandon jungle and occupied four towns in the state of Chiapas (see SchNEWS 250). The government response was swift and brutal, but the Zapatistas responded by dodging the army in the jungle, cutting off their supply routes, and when the army retreated, seizing the land from the landowners that had kept them as virtual slaves for years. Eventually a stand-off was established with the Mexican government signing, but never ratifying the San Andres Peace Accords, while surrounding the state of Chiapas with 90,000 troops. Over the next 7 years the Mexican Army conducted a low intensity war against Zapatista communities including the butchering of 45 indigenous men and women in 1997.

The difference that distinguishes the EZLN and every other guerrilla uprising is that the EZLN don't bark commands from a central committee. Instead they take their orders directly from the civilian communities from which they get their support. Before the Zapatista uprising began every Zapatista community was consulted beforehand to see if they supported it and over 98% were in favour. These one and a half thousand communities which cover nearly a third of the area of Chiapas, still exist today, despite suffering continual harassment from over 90,000 troops from the Mexican army who are based there. They are divided into 35 autonomous municipalities that organise and operate collectively. The role of women in particular has changed dramatically, with women taking part in the decision-making process on an equal level with men, and a third of the EZLN made up of women. As Infantry Major Anna Maria says, "It is just not the Zapatista men who have their rights, but now the women as well"

Making Waves

The Zapatistas have helped broaden their struggle by recognising the need for international solidarity. In particular foreign peace observers have helped to lessen the worst offences of the Mexican army, giving birth to a living, evolving internationalism. They also organised the first Intercontinental Gathering for Humanity and Against NeoLiberalism (Encuentro) where 4,000 delegates from many different countries attended.

More importantly, as we all struggle to articulate the way we want the world to be, the Zapatista are living and breathing examples of what is possible.

SUMMIT WRONG?

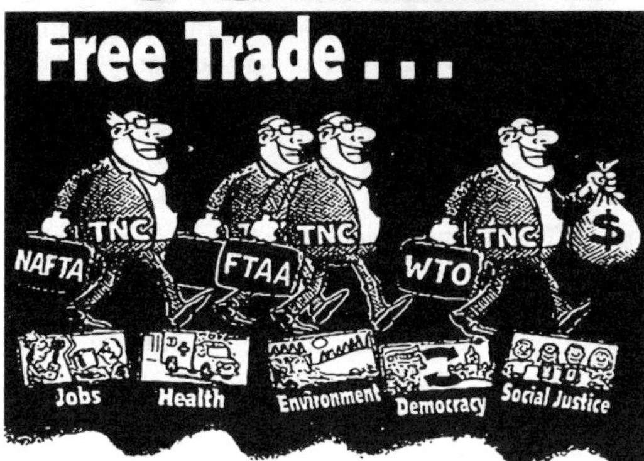

. . . Trampling on our rights

"When laws are unjust, it's criminal not to resist them." **- José Bové, the anti-globalisation French farmer who helped demolish a McDonalds.**

"The truly violent are those who prepare for the summit by accumulating tear gas, plastic bullets and pepper spray. Those who enact laws and measures that will put hundreds of thousands of poor in the street, those who let pharmaceutical corporations make billions on sickness causing the death of millions of people, those who are copyrighting life and creating dependence and hunger. In a word, those who put their profits before our lives. These are the ones we should fear, not the anarchists." **- Black Bloc communiqué**

It was the largest and most expensive police operation in Canadian history. People were turned back at the borders. Ninety people even received the honour of being named on a "preventative detention list" to be rounded up shortly before the Summit began. Six thousand police dressed in thick body armour and heavy shields, with water cannons and guns that fired plastic bullets, tear gas and smoke rounds were protecting a no-go zone. This zone, surrounded by a four kilometre long, ten-foot-high chain-link fence, was unapproachable unless you had special residents ID; otherwise you could expect a tear-gas canister in the face for your trouble. Inside this fence was the Citadel, an actual fortress that was built in 1820 to defend against an American assault. Except this time the Americans with their free trade neo-liberal agenda were the guests of honour.

"Don't worry about the Black Bloc; worry about the Blue Bloc [the police]...These leaders are not committed to non-violence." Jaggi Singh, CLAC

Last weekend leaders of 34 nation states were in Québec City for the **Summit of the Americas.** Amongst other things they hoped to achieve was to put the finishing touches on the **Free Trade Area of the Americas (FTAA)** which aims to establish a "free trade" zone extending NAFTA (the North American Free Trade Agreement – see SchNEWS 200) to the tip of South America. It's been described as 'NAFTA on steroids'.

Unfortunately, every time the world's elite have a corporate knees-up, their meetings are met with resistance. Tens of thousands of people from all walks of life faced the usual barrage of rubber bullets, mass arrests and a thick white blanket of gas. No matter if they were masked-up black bloc trying to pull down the fences or peaceful protesters sitting in the road, the treatment was the same. As one protester pointed out, "The scene looked and felt like war, yet only one side had any real weapons. After the extreme police violence I'd witnessed the past few days, a few broken windows didn't merit a second thought."

But, as Professor and author John McMurtry put it, "The corporate media will continue to block out the life-and-death issues at stake, focus on the saleable spectacle of a large public confrontation, blame and trivialise the thousands of opponents who are assaulted for putting themselves on the line, and return to selling other images and distractions once the violence entertainment is over."

* **Lots of behind-the-scenes activity** happened in the build up to the Summit that you wouldn't have seen reported. CLAC (anti-capitalist convergence), CASA, and affiliated groups travelled across Ontario, Québec and northeastern US to do countless teach-ins on the demonstrations and what the FTAA will mean. Commité Populaire de St.-Jean-Baptiste distributed 10,000 copies of a 4 page tabloid in the neighborhood where most of the action would occur and set up an "adopt-an-activist" program which encouraged local families to put up visiting demonstrators (hundreds of demonstrators were housed this way).

For a report from the barricades: www.schnews.org.uk/sotw/quebec-coming-off-the-fence.htm

SEND IN THE CLOWNS

"An anarchists' travelling circus that goes from summit to summit with the sole purpose of causing as much mayhem as possible" **- Tony Blair.**

It's the Euro Big Top and the main attraction is 'mayhem-causing anarchists'. Step right up and try your luck at the 'decipher the EU political bullshit' stall. See three protesters get shot with live ammo. Applaud European leaders with their 'time to get tough' announcements. Boo and hiss the anti-capitalist critics and ignore the mostly peaceful rally on the Saturday. Still, that's the name of the game.

Before the European Union Summit had even begun in Gothenburg, police had surrounded one of the Convergence Centres rented from the local council for people to sleep in and take part in the 'For Another Europe' Conference. One person who was trapped inside told us, "They barricaded about 400 activists in by putting freight containers all around the school. They didn't let anyone in or out and said they would arrest everyone inside, which in the end, they did." Inge Johansson of the International Noise Conspiracy added "Everybody involved in the protest saw this as very provocative and it was clear that the police had set the tone for how they wanted the rest of the weekend to be."

After that, anytime people gathered to demonstrate they were either arrested en masse or attacked with police batons, dogs and horses. Some cops threw rocks and some of the angry protestors replied in kind and kicked in stores like McDonalds for good measure. But it was during a Reclaim The City street party that the police fired shots into the crowd, injuring three people – one of them critically. At the last update, the protestor was in 'critical, but stable condition', but there has been a blackout on official information about him. Finally on the Saturday 25,000 people gathered in a peaceful demonstration. But that isn't really newsworthy now, is it?

WOT A BIG 'UN

From Stockholm came words that European leaders hoped would be music to environmentalists ears, with them boasting that Europe will become the most sustainable society in the world. There's just one slight problem with this: the EU's over-riding priority remains ever-increasing international trade and competitiveness. At the Lisbon 'Jobs Summit' in March last year, European leaders talked about "greater regulatory freedom" for corporations, asking the European Commission to find ways of simplifying all those bloody rules and environmental regulations that are burdening business.

Meanwhile, 13 countries, mainly from Central Europe, want a piece of EU action. Membership will come at a price, with the Polish Prime Minister talking about selling "difficult measures to the people." That's because they must get their economies 'harmonised'; y'know public services to be slashed and privatised, social services dismantled, restrictions on land purchase by foreign companies relaxed, etc. You could call it the European version of the Structural Adjustment Programmes that are forced onto the 'Third World.' (See SchNEWS 287).

Pushing for these reforms are business lobby groups, the most powerful of which is the European Roundtable of Industrialists (ERT), made up of 45 'captains of industry'. Its former secretary-general boasted about phoning European leaders whenever he wanted policy changes and its web-site claims "every six months the ERT makes contact with the government that holds the EU presidency to discuss priorities." They usually get their way. Take a paper published in the 80s demanding a tunnel under the English Channel, a road bridge connecting Denmark & Sweden, a European high speed train system, and a new Europe-wide roadbuilding programme. Hey presto, they got the lot.

Now they've got all guns blazing for "a minimal regulatory system with the maximum of flexibility," which roughly translates as "sod the environment, sod workers rights, where's the cash?"!

So when Blair talks about this 'undemocratic travelling circus' let's point the finger at big business pulling the strings behind the scenes, going from country to country causing mayhem in the quest for more profits.

Paul Robinsons 'inside account' of being arrested and given a 1 year sentence for 'violent riot': www.schnews.org.uk/sotw/gothenburg.htm

GENOA: YOU MAKE PLANS, WE MAKE HISTORY

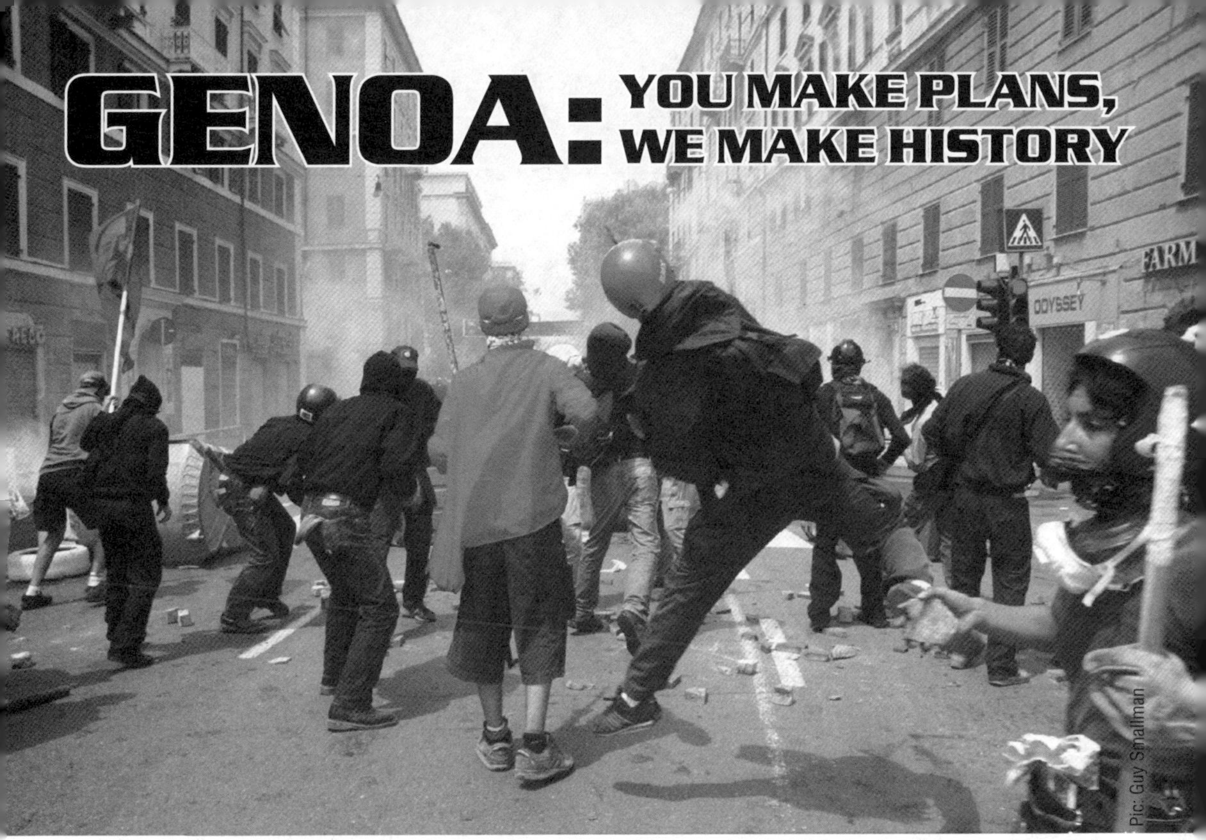

Pic: Guy Smallman

EYEWITNESS ACCOUNTS

When the G8 met in Genoa, 19th-21st July 2001 it was the most violent anti-capitalist protest in Europe. It resulted in the death of Carlo Guiliani, shot by a police conscript. The media made much of this saying it was the first death of the anti-capitalist movement, but this forgets that people are killed regularly in the "third world" fighting against capitalism.

The Build Up

By Wednesday, 18th July – the day before the first mass demonstration – the Convergence centre was teeming with activity. The sports grounds, parks and schools made available by the city council, needed to accommodate the tens of thousands flooding into the city, were filling up. The Genoa Social Forum (GSF: the umbrella group who were overall organisers of the Anti-G8 event) was in full swing: welcoming newcomers by handing out food, bottled water and maps from under marquees; the schools on Via Cesare Battista were buzzing with GSF volunteers, many holding legal or medical passes, as well as Indymedia people who had one floor of the building.

Arriving at Genoa were a spectrum of the usual suspects – lefty, anarchist, green, liberals and the rest from around Europe plus Kurdish activists, Indians, Africans and many others. Also jetting in were some high profile 'anti-capitalists' such as José Bové, the McDonalds-smashing French farmer, who was speaking in the public forum talks around the topic of 'Another World Is Possible' which had been running since Monday.

Convergence Centre with police compound directly behind it. For most of the week it had the atmosphere of a mainstream-ish festival with overpriced food and a concert by Manu Chau. On Saturday it was all sizzling tear-gas canisters and armies of boot-boys.

DAY ONE: THURSDAY JULY 19TH

MIGRANTS MARCH

Today kicked off proceedings with a 70,000 strong march through the town in solidarity with the millions of asylum seekers getting universally-stiffed across fortress Europe. An international soup of banner-waving, wall-tagging, trumpet-blaring, cop-taunting anti-imperialistas meandered through the streets, giving Genoa's multi-faceted police response the chance to air their newly painted firepower.

Meanwhile, as the Japanese PM touched down at Genoa airport, all was quiet inside the forbidden 'Zona Rossa', the high-security area where the delegates were to meet. Dark-windowed motorcades monopolised the roadways save only for cop cars and camera crews. Every entrance point is manned by a mob of gun toting cops. A four metre high steel fence – set in concrete and nailed to the tarmac – blocks all access points to the sacred square mile where the world's most powerful justice-dodgers plan to trough on marinari and the misery of millions. Armoured cars, bulldozers and scores of horses line the Via 20th Septembre, the main artery heading straight for the Ducalo Palace (the conference centre). This is the spot where every fucker in town knows the cardboard-covered army of the Tute Bianche intend to make their entrance.

Pic: Guy Smallman

Meet The Players...

The Italian resistance is more than ready for the G8. The Genoa Social Forum, is a loose coalition of surprisingly varied forces. At one end of the scale is the Jubilee, Drop the Debt reformist lobby and at the other end is the militant Tute Bianche and COBAS (themselves a coalition of street-fighting anarcho-syndicalists and marxist trade unions.) Despite all parties signing up (crossed fingers behind backs stylee) to the GSF "No sticks, no stones, no fire" manifesto – it's well accepted that once the old bill start cracking heads, anything goes.

The organised anarchist groups massing in Genoa have more self respect than to get involved with dubious liberal coalitions and have stayed well clear of the GSF. But, unlike previous incarnations of similar coalitions, the GSF are not dissing anyone else's tactical or ideological approach.

The White Overalls – or Tute Bianche – who include well-padded crews from all over Italy have decided er... not to wear the white overalls after all – because they've linked up with Social Centre activists from Naples and the COBAS militants to form a single attacking block. However, other COBAS contingents are linking with the anarchist black blocks tomorrow. Other anarchists are joining the not provocatively-violent-but-willing-to-defend-themselves-pink-block for another fence breach elsewhere. Confused?

The liberators gathered in Genoa are in positive spirits. Despite the cynics questioning their support, the 70,000 who marched tonight are being continually joined by trainload after trainload of equally dedicated comrades. There is a storm coming and this time it ain't heading for bankers or bureaucrats, this time it's the shot-callers on the slab. No more fucking around. Leaders, it is time to meet your world.

DAY TWO – FRIDAY JULY 20TH

Friday was to be the day of direct action. A whole range of groups were to approach the Red Zone from different directions, but when the tear gas and police charges started the separate groupings soon disintegrated and merged into new blocks – it was hard to distinguish which group you were with. Besides many on the streets didn't join any block but did their own thing.

The Point Of No Return

"Protesters awoke on Friday morning to find that the red zone leapt four blocks east overnight. An anarchist block assembling in Piazza Paolo di Novi had barely started filling their bins with cobblestones when the state police volleyed in the first CS rounds. A street battle ensued pushing us eastwards – away from the target zone."

Pic: Alec Smart

"We then crossed the railway and headed to the northern limits of the red zone, stopping on the way to rearrange some banks and feed the masses thanks to a helpful supermarket (on the return journey the shutters were still off and local residents were taking shopping trolleys full of free groceries home)."

"Another surge, everyone rushed forward on 2 or 3 different streets. Some riot cops got stranded in their retreat and hand-to-hand fighting ensued. Those fighting are not necessarily in black, though they are masked. Some have helmets. This is a militant energy driven by people who have said – Ya Basta!, Fuck the police! rage! energy! resolve!"

"Hundreds strong, they poured into the expansive Piazza Alimondo. Two armoured police Land Rovers drive recklessly into the crowd, one drives away, the other stalls; obviously it didn't want to scratch its paintwork by ramming the wheelie-bin out of the way. It was attacked, the cop at the back began waving his gun around, deliberately pointing it at different people. Some saw it and retreated. Some didn't. Carlo Guilliani walked across the back of the van and picked up a red fire extinguisher lying on the ground. He turned and advanced on the police Land Rover and was shot in the head."

Tute Bianche: What A Gas

"Resembling an army preparing for war, the 10,000 of them spent all morning taping up their bodies with foam and padding. We finally set off on the four km march to the city centre – an endless sea of bopping helmets interspersed with a vast array of flags of every hue and color behind a wall of plastic shields.

Two kilometres from the Red Zone, the police attacked us. First a barrage of tear-gas canisters were lobbed over the front lines, deep into the heart of the demonstration. Nobody had gas masks (doh!) The people, packed in tightly, panicked and surged backwards. We retreated up the road. A water cannon blasted away, throwing bodies around like paper bags. What now? People looked to the Ya Basta leadership in all this disarray but there was no Plan B – the microphone that issued commands during the march was now silent.

The non-violent, active defence tactic crushed in the face of decisively brutal police tactics. As the majority of the march sat down further up the road, thousands of others streamed off into the side streets. The north side was blocked by the railway track, to the south lay small enclosed streets. "Open new fronts! Break through police lines at 2, 3, 4 different points!" Spontaneous and enraged, thousands ran into the sidestreets. Meanwhile, the Ya Basta loudspeaker requested people to stay put on the road, far from the Red Zone."

Pink Block

"On the day the pink block wove through the Genoa streets, singing and dancing and exchanging waves and smiles with people in their houses. The pink march breached police lines and attacked the fence – the first tear gas of the day scattered us, we tried again – more tear gas. Behind the fence were armoured tanks with machine guns on top. We have no doubt that if we had succeeded in getting over we would have been shot. More tear gas, so much we couldn't breathe, but this time savage beatings for the people who couldn't run fast enough. We were all in shock and traumatised by this point.

The police blocked everywhere – someone told us that there had been a death nearby. Eventually we managed to get round and back to where we had started from – passing random groups of traumatised, injured and angry people as we went.

We ended the day in shock and pain, watching slow motion shots of the death of Carlo Guiliani repeated over and over again, interspersed with Bush, Blair, etc looking grey and distant and somehow irrelevant, and wondered where we would go from here."

DAY THREE - SATURDAY JULY 21ST

Sight For Sore Eyes

On the third day was the 'International March'. This march was to be the big, non-confrontational event. Big it was – 200,000 – but with the police having assassinated a protester the day before, it was bound to be a bit edgy...

"Although this march was supposed to be completely non-confrontational, and in spite of the relaxed mood of the morning, there was a lot of tension

on the march. As well as the sizable numbers of people with white-painted hands, there were a lot of people carrying sticks (and thousands more carrying red flags). Every time a police helicopter flew overhead (at least every five minutes), the chant of 'Assassini' would go up from hundreds of voices, and a wave of arms would go up to give the police the finger.

The first mile or so was fairly uneventful. Then, but still a good distance from the GSF convergence centre, the march stopped, and then surged backward for a second. Nobody was sure what was happening, but all around us the goggles and face-mask bandannas started coming out. It was another few minutes before we found out what was going on. Down at the GSF convergence centre the 'Carabinieri' were out in force, making sure that the march turned where it should, instead of carrying on towards the zone. But as the march turned into the city, a pitch battle between hundreds of people and police erupted, with teargas filling the street as more and more people joined the attack (though the largest section of the march continued away from the GSF, away from the fighting).

The crowd attempted to build barricades and hold back the advancing cops. The sky filled with stones. They held the police and those behind them had a few moments more to retreat. Those who needed to get away from the zone could. All afternoon the streets were mad with tear-gas, with stones, with burning banks, burning cars, barricades. The air was shrill with screams, of beatings, violence and fear.

Eventually the barricades were overrun. The police advanced ferociously, beating people indiscriminately. A helicopter overhead fired gas into the fleeing hordes. Further up, people jumped off the rocks into the sea. The huge march ended in absolute mayhem."

"We were being pushed east by armoured vehicles and constant gas, into the flow of the march, which was still coming. You almost got used to the gas, kicking the canisters as they fizzed around your feet. By this stage any thoughts of stopping to photograph were gone, and we were really running. The police had us penned in on the beach – and were letting us through in single file with our arms up. One guy let his arms drop, and was heavily truncheoned right in front of me – instantly he was lying in a pool of his own blood and paramedics came out of nowhere to attend. Eventually some locals led a group of us up the side alleys of the old town and into an enclave which they said we would be safe. After an hour or so we had the all clear, and I walked back to the Indymedia rooms – by this stage the big raid was only hours away".

MIDNIGHT SATURDAY JULY 21ST

Dark Night: GSF Building Raid

On the Saturday night police raided the two schools – one operating as a base for the GSF, legal & medical support as well as Indymedia, and the other across the road, Diaz School was used mostly as an accommodation space. The GSF/ Indymedia centre had computers and films seized or destroyed and in a violent assault on the Diaz School 93 people were arrested with 63 hospitalised. The

Genoa beachfront, Saturday: All the ice cream shops and bars along the beach are closed for the day so these little fascists can have their bit of fun. Think: a tank and an army of bootboys charging past Brighton Palace Pier. Pic: Alec Smart

Pic: Hamish

Pic: Alec Smart

(left) Para-military Carabinieri police enter the School Diaz armed with batons and shields ready to deal with perillous swarms of... knackered people in sleeping bags. (right) Pretty soon most of the sirens wailing are ambulances.

GENOA

raid was supposedly to look for violent protesters – two molotov cocktails were 'found' but it would later emerge that these were planted by police, with the officer who planted them saying: "I brought the molotov cocktail to the Diaz school. I obeyed the order of one of my superiors." The following day TV news broadcasts repeated footage of the police displaying tables of implements allegedly recovered from Diaz like sledgehammers (remember Italian leader Berlusconi owns half the TV channels, and controls the rest).

In the legal cases which ensued after the violent raid, none of the ninety-three protesters arrested that night ended up being charged for any offence. On the other hand twenty-nine police have been charged with inflicting grievous bodily harm, falsifying evidence, slander and abusing police powers. Whether or not the police will be successfully prosecuted remains to be seen.

Eyewitness Accounts Of The Raid:

Marcus Cavell, an IMC UK journalist, described the police attack on him: "It was just endless, I really thought I was dying. It's a horrible thing when you feel your bones breaking inside you. And after a while I just tried to keep one eye open, trying to stay alive. I finally blacked out and couldn't remember anything else till I woke up in hospital."

From the vantage point of the 4th floor of the GSF building looking across the street to the School A. Diaz: "I could see at least 100 cops kick the door in of the school, and we could see through the windows police truncheoning people sleeping. I saw one man held down while two bashed him. Tear gas was used. Nobody was getting out. We stood in total fear, then after watching this, at 12:10am news came up that they were now breaking through into our building."

"At 12:20 I climbed up to the roof of the building and lay face down for 1½ hours, with a helicopter spotlight scanning around, and sound of screaming coming from the school. At some point we found out the Carabinieri had left our building, and we went back to look at the scene across the street. At least 15 people were stretchered out."

A photographer outside: "I was taking pictures of the injured. I thought some of them were dead. Then I got a truncheon in the stomach. The cop took the camera, another held my arms behind my back, pinning me to a wall. I had him thinking that my Indymedia pass was actually an official media pass and he let me go." "I heard a policeman say 'there's too much media'."

"At 4am, after the police had gone, I walked around the school witnessing the aftermath: large pools of blood along the corridor, smears on the walls, and personal objects, clothing and bloodied bandages. Peoples' possessions just thrown around the room on the ground floor where they were sleeping. Some people were still weeping and trembling."

Later we got stories back from arrestees: "We know that they have arrested everyone they hospitalised, taken people to jail and tortured them. One young French man had his head badly beaten on Friday in the street. In jail, they took him into a room, twisted his arms behind his back and banged his head on the table. Another man was taken into a room covered with pictures of Mussolini and pornography, and alternately slapped around and then stroked with affection in a weird psychological torture. Others were forced to shout, "Viva El Duce!" Just in case it wasn't clear that this is fascism, Italian style."

Pic: Gday John

Pic: Alec Smart

AT THE END OF THE DAY...

"Genoa was gutted. No city will host the G8 for a while. 34 banks burnt. 83 vehicles both police and civilian destroyed, 41 businesses torched or looted, 6 supermarkets, 12 government offices – illustrating the belief which some protesters have that targeting the economic organs of the enemy is the most effective tactic. (No buses were burnt, apparently because the bus drivers' union was in solidarity with the protesters, ferrying everyone around for free during the whole week). With Genoa in ruins, the G8 left quietly with a few empty promises to give some money to Africa.

During the whole event some 200 people were arrested, and 600 injured. In the jails, the protesters were tortured while police mocked them with pictures of Mussolini and Nazis. They tortured them, as they have done in Seattle, Prague and Québec; as they did in Pinochet's Chile. They attempt to destroy the movement by spreading panic and fear. To break the back of the militants of this totally unarmed global protest movement."

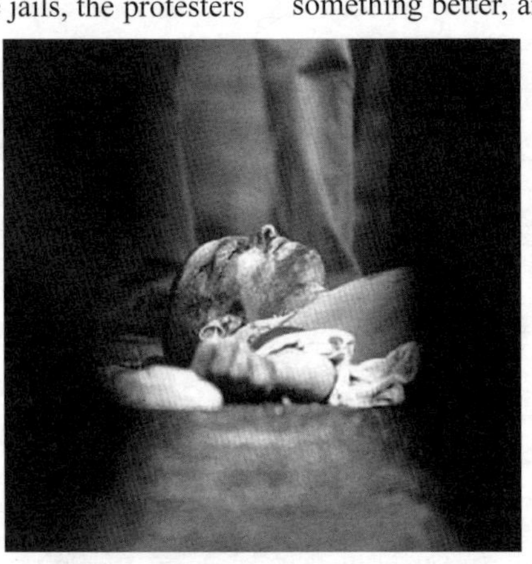

Officer Plannica – the police officer who shot Carlo Giuliani was investigated for manslaughter but charges were never brought. As a final sickening note to Carlo's murder, he sold his story for 30,000 euros (£20,000) to one of Italian Prime Minister Berlusconi's TV channels.

"Seattle had been touted as some sort of watershed, but Carlo's killing in Genoa is a turning point for the anti-capitalist movement (if such a thing really exists). How we play it from here will have repercussions far beyond the blood-stained streets of Northern Italy. It was no freak cub-cop overreaction that left one mother mourning and several others preparing to, as the sun hit the sea on July 20th, but a deliberate act of terror – in the most basic sense of the word.

The snowball that's been gaining weight and speed as it rolled through Geneva, Prague and Gothenburg has become far too jagged a spike in the side of those steering the planetary carve up. Young people are shot dead for daring to think there can be another way. The message from the world's authorities is clear: "go back to your homes, do not meddle in what doesn't concern you, return to your televisions, to smoking dope and stealing traffic cones and leave the intricacies of global economics alone – because if you don't we will kill you. The same way we killed Carlo Giuliani".

If we believe in making changes and creating something better, and if we are prepared to take the risks and put in the time, then let's do it. Let's not let Carlo's death be in vain. Because when one of us catches a bullet, a club or jail sentence, a little bit of all of us dies. But together we are alive and together we can, and we will, win.

This summary of Genoa is an edited version of the coverage we gave it in SchNEWS Of The World. To read the complete thing visit www.schnews.org.uk/sotw/genoa-eyewitness.htm

---

IF ORDINARY PEOPLE BEHAVED LIKE- *NIKE*

SPOOF PAPERS

Spoof publications have been around for a long while, but in recent years they've been a drop of fun in an ocean of worthy propaganda. In 1997, the '*Evading standards*', was published in support of the striking Liverpool dockers, and distributed at the Never Mind The Ballots street party in April 97. The issues were originally seized by police, and the publishers arrested for affray. After successfully suing the Metropolitan Police for wrongful arrest, they were awarded a five-figure sum with which to finance future editions. Hooray! Following the successes of Evading Standards, other hilarious, spot-on copies of newspapers have sprung up, including *The Spun,* and the spectacular broadsheet *Financial Crimes.*

20,000 copies of the *Financial Crimes* – printed in the same pink paper as the real Financial Times – were distributed to rush hour commuters in London and elsewhere on September 22nd for events around the World Bank IMF meeting in Prague in September 2000. Its companion website financialcrimes.com was closed down after legal threats from the FT.

The subversives responsible for the regional South Coast effort, the Brighton & Hove *No Leaders*, received this glowing tribute from the proprietor of the real thing, 'The Leader' (after issues were delivered through residents doors): "We have evidence that substantial confusion has already taken place. We are not against parody and satire as such. However, we believe your publication goes a long way too far."

Another one of Newsquests' publications, the local Brighton rag the Evening Argus, gets mimicked as the 'Evening Anus' occasionally by SchNEWS whenever there's a particular local story to cover. In Bristol, the Evening Post is now variously the Evening Pissed or Pest. Not very subtle, but the monikers have stuck locally.

Giving the paper out on the streets was the only distribution method available to UK pranksters, but when the concept crossed the Atlantic, the game moved on. Protesters against the World Trade Organisation produced a quality copy of the awkwardly named Seattle Post-Intelligencer. Squads of early morning paperboys and girls simply opened up the street boxes with a quarter, replaced the outer four pages and put them back. They were attacked in an angry editorial the next day.

Evading Standards: **www.mcspotlight.org/beyond/evading/** – *The Spun:* **www.the-spun.org**

IT'S GETTING DARK OUT THERE

One SchNEWS writer who's put himself in the middle of some argy-bargy during the last few years at numerous summit riots around Europe discusses tactics...

Pic: Guy Smallman

The human race has only one or perhaps two generations to rescue itself (as it drags every other species down with it), according to the 2003 State of the World report by the Washington-based Worldwatch Institute.

The longer that no remedial action is taken, the greater the degree of misery and biological impoverishment that humankind must be prepared to accept, the institute says in its report.

As the destructive forces of the corporate rulers accelerate the rush toward ecological holocaust, our initiatives to neutralize these forces need to be freed from the shackles of the false dichotomies of right/wrong, left/right, violence/non-violence. Instead we should look foremost at what works, what is effective. We should embrace a range of tactics in the developing "movement of movements", which is rising up in order to fight against a common enemy – corporate capitalism.

One of the most high profile expressions of this has been the flurry of protests and riots that began to accompany almost every major business and government summit since the G8 Summit in 1998. Chaotic, innovative and often intensely violent, these events saw a number of different tactics being tried, tested and developed on both sides. What the mainstream media refer to as the Anti-Globalization Movement has launched a range of approaches like the white-overalls padded block, the Black Bloc, and the Pink and Silver Bloc onto the world stage. In response to this, the Dark Side have hardened their laws and launched a war on "terror", with us among their targets.

After the J18 Carnival Against Capital where the police were overrun, came a clampdown on large anti-capitalist protests in Britain. The N30 demo (the same day as Seattle) at Euston Station was easily contained by the police, which was probably down to three factors: the location of the venue enabled police to easily coral protesters, police preparedness having learnt lessons at J18 and a lack of numbers of protesters. Mayday 2000 despite being touted by the media as "The biggest riot since the Poll Tax" was fairly tame in comparison to J18, but many people got sent down for long stretches, the location was in Parliament and Trafalgar Square – home territory for the police and a location again easy to contain.

WOMBLING FREE

It was in this context that the Wombles were formed, inspired by their involvement with Ya Basta / Tutte Bianche in Prague 2000, a group of London-based anarchists came together to try and devise a new tactic to get round, or go through, the police's tactics of "kettling" everybody in a police cordon. This police tactic of containment, rather than dispersal had effectively made Reclaim the Streets-style street parties impossible in the UK, and was nipping anything new in the bud. Using the padded-up/shield carrying tactics of Tutte Bianche, a dozen or so Michelin-man Wombles managed to force their way safely through police lines, many were freed from street detention and the Wombles as a tactic was showcased in the UK. However the police, state and media have had it in for the Wombles from the start and a massive clamp down on anyone using their tactics followed – with pre-emptive arrests at DSEi arms fair protests and the Labour Party Conference, this tactic in the UK – for the time being – seems to have failed.

Seven weeks later and many British activists joined the hundreds of thousands on the streets of

Pic left: EU Summit, Brussels, December 2001. Pic above: An early trip up from Wimbledon for the Wombles at a London demo on the tenth anniversary of the first Gulf War, January 18th 2001.

Genoa to protest and strike at the G8 Summit taking place there. Genoa was the most violent protest against global capitalism in the west, resulting in the destruction of large parts of the city and the death of Carlo Giuliani shot in the head by a police conscript and then run over by a police landrover. Carlo's assassination was a shot across the bows to the "movement" as a whole and, to its more militant expression in particular. "Keep coming like this and we'll shoot… here's an example."

Months later, back in the UK on September 11th, 2001, DSEi was marketing death at the Excel Centre in east London. Outside, 60 or so padded-up Wombles attended the protest, pushing the police lines at the centre's entrance. Having had the shield wall busted en route and heavily outnumbered, the padded bloc failed to break through police lines. As news of events in New York and the Pentagon filtered through to friend and foe the crowd dispersed. Our lives since 9/11 have been characterised by increasingly intimate state surveillance. You can't send lyrics from a Clash song over your mobile without getting a visit from Special Branch these days. (See SchNEWS 458). Mayday events have died a death in London and large militant anti-capitalist street protests in Britain seem to be at an all time low – with many people concentrating on the war in Iraq. Overt, brazen direct action at demonstrations may be an adrenaline rush and can be inspiring but it's getting increasingly risky.

UNDERGROUND OR OVERGROUND

So what of Direct Action from here? The short history of this "movement of movements", this flurry of events that have brought us to where we are now, has much to teach us, and we would do well to listen.

One need only look at the grassroots Animal Rights movement in Britain to see how effective covert direct action can be when coupled with a vocal above ground ally. The night-time sabotage of the ALF adds weight and force to the arguments and initiatives put forward by the legally operating campaign groups, and vice versa.

Psychologically, and this is an often understated factor, covert direct action helps to bridge the gap between the enormity of the problems facing us and the need to feel that one's actions are having an effect. The destructive urge is also a creative urge. It's possible something similar to the grassroots Animal Rights movement could be applied to other areas of the struggle. Anarchist Liberation Front, anyone?

Covert eco-action works best as an effective challenge to illegitimate forms of power, however, when it is used in combination with overt and public action. If only covert direct action exists and no other kind of action is occurring, there will be some retribution for the injustices being carried out by companies or governments, but for little or no political effect. The economic damage with covert direct action is usually small. But its effect is greater when combined with public campaigns that explain the reasons for the action taken and provide a base for mobilizing a wider opposition. The lessons learnt from the anti-GM food campaign was that a combination of tactical destruction of GM crops set back and cost the biotech companies millions, while the overt campaigns educated the public and exerted political pressure.

The nature of covert action means it is often unseen, unexpected and often unclaimed. This type of action can have tremendous impact on the visible institutions of capitalism (whether these institutions choose to admit it or not). The aim of these covert actions is not to create publicity but to hurt the company financially and psychologically.

Euston, London, November 30 1999

The targeted company may well keep the action to themselves, not wanting the publicity – if someone is attacking a company then people may ask why? This is a question the company may prefer not to answer. Of course, covert direct action is as old as the moon and has long been a tactic of social movements. The Luddites, Captain Swing and other groups throughout history have used sabotage as a means of defence against new forms of capitalist politics, and this heritage is celebrated by contemporary eco (and other) activists.

Mass daylight forms of direct action also have their place. The Genetix Snowball campaign adapted a tactic of open, daylight attacks on GM crops and used any arrests to challenge the legitimacy of these crops in the courts. This publicity was useful for the GM campaign, but most of the damage to crops were by anonymous night time raids which severely hampered the development of GM crops in Britain. Trident Ploughshares use similar tactics against the military establishment, and these have often been very successful. It would be foolish, however, to take this approach in other spheres of sabotage .The jury that would find you not guilty over a GM crop trashing would not be so sympathetic if you were up for smashing up a McDonalds on an anti-capitalist protest.

There is a big build-up to the Gleneagles G8 Summit in Scotland in 2005. The huge expansion in Social Centres over the last few years is providing a vital continuum of action and presence, offering real chances to develop our ideas on a consistent basis in a community setting. The G8 provides us with a focus within Social Centres nationwide and may help us to refine and spread our ideas and tactics, as well as providing us with yet another wonderful target for covert and open direct action. Let's choose the terms of engagement as much as we can.

V IS FOR VIOLENCE

One question that has to be asked is: Are acts of sabotage violent?

Well if physical force is used to cause damage then this is clearly a violent act. Yet people in the movement often go to great lengths when explaining to others how a particular act of sabotage was not violent… how it was done for the greater good, or in defence of the planet, or that it was confined to property damage.

Perhaps it would be more honest to admit that causing property damage is a violent act. This needn't be a problem. The world is filled with all forms of largely accepted violence: The torturous and brutal violence of the factory farm and slaughterhouse; the carnage of the "patriotic" war; the destruction of huge sections of the planet for dams and cities, these everyday acts of our societies are quite okay in most people's minds. Violence is seen as a sometimes-necessary means to an end by the great bulk of humanity. People will have more time for our ideas if we are honest and upfront about what it is we do, what it is we believe needs to be done, and why we perform these actions.

However whether or not an act is violent is ultimately based on an individuals' perception, which is usually distorted through the eyes of the corporate media. What is the difference between Trident Ploughshares disabling a hawk jet and an animal rights activist slashing the tyres of a vivisectionist's car? More economic damage is done to the hawk jet than the car, yet the animal rights activist gets labelled as violent and the Ploughshares activist as non-violent – there is no logic to this reasoning. By admitting that both acts are justified acts of violence it will help break down the media and police's tactic of dividing up protesters into good, i.e. non-violent and bad, i.e. violent. Ultimately, it is other's perceptions of what activists do that we must challenge, rather than what we do as saboteurs.

www.dissent.org.uk

COMING SOON TO A TOWN NEAR YOU

FROM THE MAKERS OF 'GOOD MORNING KOSOVO'

BASED ON A TRUE STORY

GROUND ZERO

THIS TIME IT'S PERSONAL

BEN KINGSLEY as OSAMA BIN LADEN CHEVY CHASE as GEORGE W BUSH MORGAN FREEMAN as COLIN POWELL

BILL MURRAY as RUDY GIULIANI HUGH GRANT as TONY BLAIR CHARLTON HESTON as DONALD RUMSFELD Directed by DICK CHENEY Executive Producer GEORGE BUSH snr Screenplay by the CIA

WARNING: This film may contain scenes of genocide

'I came to Hollywood to be in moofies like Ground Zero. I'll be back in the sequel.' - Arnold Schwarzenegger

'I stand by the claim that this film is forty-five minutes long' - Tony Blair

'Mr Blair had no way of knowing that the film was more than forty-five minutes long' - Lord Hutton

'I love the smell of depleted uranium in the morning ... smells like ... a darn good war film. ' - Infotainment Weekly

VICIOUS CIRCLE

***"What is the alternative? More bombs? More security? More cameras in the streets? More phone taps? More subsidy to the arms industry? ... Is that where we're going? On a race to the bottom trapped between GW Bush and the CIA-created Osama Bin Laden? Because it seems that's what is wanted."* - Adam Porter, Year Zero magazine**

While the SchNEWS crew with hundreds of other protestors were being hemmed in by police for the bare-faced cheek of wanting to shut down an arms fair, news came filtering through of the attacks on the World Trade Centre towers and the Pentagon.

As always, the deaths of innocent people are terrible and harrowing but carnage happens around the world every day of the year. The difference this time is that for once it is happening in the US, on the doorstep of corporate and military power. The Archbishop of Wales, only a few blocks away when the World Trade Centre were hit said, "It's given me a vivid sense of what people around the world live with daily."

Adam Porter, the editor of Year Zero magazine puts it this way:

"The loss of innocent lives is more disgusting than words can express. The office workers, the cleaners, the lift repair men, the people who jumped to their deaths perhaps hoping against hope that they would somehow survive ... those incinerated in the building by thousands of gallons of aircraft fuel ... ordinary US citizens ... just like ordinary people in Paris, Amsterdam, Bangkok, Tripoli and Baghdad. But look, and look hard, this is what men of violence do to cities, what British and American planes did to Basra in Iraq, what British and American planes did to parts of Belgrade.

When I spout on about missiles slamming into the side of escaping Kosovan women, children and pensioners packed into a train I mean it. They died terrible, flesh-ripping deaths.

When you fire cruise missiles into packed shelters full of women and kids in Baghdad they too died terrible deaths.

When you kill 5.8 million Vietnamese, carpet bombing their rudimentary homes whilst leaving the centre of Hanoi and Saigon clear so you had somewhere nice to stay when you invaded they too died terrible deaths. When you rounded up every socialist and liberal in Indonesia and had them killed and tortured they too died terrible deaths. We can add Panama, Honduras, Guatemala, Colombia, Ecuador, Nicaragua, Laos, Cambodia, Israel..."

And if the superpowers' expensive bullets and bombs don't get you, then their economic policies will. Just think – the income of the richest 20% of the world's population is at least 75 times greater than the income of the poorest 20% (it was 'only' 30 times greater forty years ago). Third world debt, enforced by the military might of the United States, Britain and other rich countries, is simply a racket to keep this inequality entrenched. Every day £28 million flows from the poorest countries in the world to the banks of the rich countries. These are the economies of the winner-takes-all capitalist mentality where millions die in a world of plenty through hunger and disease.

Linking Arms

We were protesting about an arms fair where a brand new Trimaran warship is docked for show, and where the latest hi-tech weaponry is being flogged to any country with a big enough national bank account or International Monetary Fund loan – and bugger the human rights record. But straight away, the police violently pushed us into a cordon and completely surrounded us, confiscating water pistols and searching people for ammo to 'prevent a breach of the peace', even trying to snatch musical instruments as potential weapons! Er, excuse us officer, but maybe you should take a look inside the Excel building – we're sure a section 60 weapons search in there would result in a satisfying 'nick'. But of course the delegates and salesmen of flesh-ripping devices are not only creating breaches of the peace for profit, they are doing it with the endorsement of governments the world over.

Change of Tactics

The police weren't going to let us get away with trying to shut down the arms fair. They'd even raided two squats in south London the Friday before where they smashed up props for the demo and nicked four people for 'conspiracy to commit violent disorder'. The 'evidence'? A stick with a nail in it!

Individuals and affinity groups that broke away from the main demo had slightly more success. Some valiantly tried time and again to get through security whilst wandering delegates were told just how much their work was really appreciated. Local support was excellent – people lapped up SchNEWS and slagged off the rozzers: some, once aware of the arms fair, also decided to join in with hounding delegates. Later, kids picked up all the discarded white overalls and pink accessories and had a pop at the old bill themselves!

But we need to seriously reassess our tactics. Firstly, why didn't thousands of people want to come and protest about the arms trade? – do people think, after Mayday, that big London demos aren't worth it, or was the publicity poor? Secondly, if we can't get the numbers and if we continue with the same tactics we'll become increasingly demoralised as we find ourselves in 'the kettle', surrounded by the police. The cops are now used to this style of protest: they can see how events will unfold so they act swiftly and crush them. Thirdly, don't expect a single group or organisation to take the lead. The more successful actions on September 11th seemed to be by smaller affinity groups who used their initiative, and seized opportunities. It's a lot harder for the cops to keep track of lots of small groups, and they're a lot more mobile, so even if one group gets surrounded there are still plenty more on the loose. Get together, use your imagination and creativity, and – most importantly – take responsibility for yourselves.

* Just what sort of a disgusting world these arms companies live in showed itself pointedly the next day, after the bombing when BAE systems shares went up at the prospect of America tooling up even more. While in true capitalist style computer company Cisco Systems said "This is a good opportunity to sell kit to accommodate these financial institutions needs."

Give An Afghani Child A New Life

Help children like Abdul become refugees.

"With your help, we can continue to make poverty and starvation in Afghanistan an issue."

POST THIS COUPON TO YOUR LOCAL MP

YES, I am happy for public funds to be diverted into supporting the effort to keep children like Abdul in refugee camps. I therefore donate £.......-........................

Name..

Address...

Town.. Postcode..................

Smallprint: the money doesn't go to the refugee camps as such, but rather into arming the regime we've put in to replace the Taliban as well as our continuing efforts to track down Al-Qa'ida – which have been unsuccessful apart from causing the deaths of 5000 Afghanis civilians, and displacing hundreds of thousands from their homes – like Abdul and his family.

Cheers Mr Bush: half of my family is dead, our house in Kabul has been destroyed and looted, and we have spent the winter in this camp on the Pakistani border. Nice one. Good luck with the oil pipe you're putting through our back yard.

Monopolise Resistance

How the Socialist Workers Party (SWP) want to hijack Revolt...

"The protesters are winning. They are winning on the streets. Before too long they will be winning the argument. Globalisation is fast becoming a cause without credible champions."
- Financial Times, 17th August 2001.

This article is based on a pamphlet written a few years ago by people involved in direct action from a number of organisations and groups. It grew out of discussions led by SchNEWS and people involved in direct action in Manchester at the Earth First! gathering held in Derbyshire in the summer of 2001. After this, it was discussed amongst people from SchNEWS, Reclaim the Streets, Earth First! and others. Everyone didn't agree on everything - but did agree that we needed to say something along the lines of what follows.

You can find the full length original pamphlet and references for all the quotes at: www.schnews.org.uk/monopresist/monopoliseresistance/index.htm

Anti-capitalise me!

The Anti-capitalist movement has become powerful despite constant attacks from government, the police and the press. The anti-war movement has sprung up in response to the oil wars of the USA, and has helped bring in more people to resistance and protest against the capitalist world order. These movements are alliances, loose networks of groups with differing ideas and aims; and their strength is in diversity, creativity, and subversiveness. But they are at risk of being hijacked. This is why we're expressing our fears that all this good work could be undone by people who have nothing to do with this resistance but instead want to take it over for their own ends.

What's wrong with the SWP?

This is an attempt to show how and why the Socialist Workers Party (SWP) is trying to take these movements over for its own ends. While working with respectable anti-capitalist and anti-war groups, the SWP increasingly attack those involved in direct action, describing us - as the gutter press does - as disorganised, mindless hoodlums obsessed with violence. They are willing to make these attacks so they can portray themselves as more organised and, therefore, the best bet if you think capitalism stinks and want to do something about it.

As they put it in Genoa, "*Remember, we're the only people here with an overall strategy for the anti-capitalist movement. So I want five people to go out with membership cards, five to sell papers and five to sell bandanas.*"

The SWP has attempted to dominate these protest movements in Britain and got involved in the anti-capitalist movement for their own cynical reasons. Their aim is to turn them into ineffective, pro-Labour pressure groups to increase the influence and membership of the SWP.

They see the anti-capitalist and anti-war movements as made up of well-meaning but muddled people who will not be able to achieve anything significant until they are led by the SWP. They want to lead us for our own good: *"Mass movements don't get the political representation that they deserve unless a minority of activists within the movement seek to create a political leadership, which means a political party that shares their vision of political power from below"*.

Full frontal lobotomy

The group Globalise Resistance was set up mainly to increase the influence of the SWP within the anti-capitalist movement. Stop the War Coalition was set up to harness the widely held anti-war feelings across the nation and political spectrum for the SWP's use. These organisations use these issues to increase their brand recognition. Stop the War Coalition would no more take part in an action without prominently displaying its banners and placards than an oil company would give money to an environmental project without telling everyone.

These 'coalitions' are front organisations run by, and in the interests of, the SWP. This does not mean that all their supporters are SWP members, far from it. The whole point of a successful front organisation is that it involves people who wouldn't otherwise join the party while at the same time fulfilling the aims of the party. A successful front organisation will have lots of non-party people involved in running it while remaining politically dominated by the party controlling it. As a speaker put it at the SWP's Marxism 2001 conference, *"The united front is a way for a tiny minority to win over lots of people; Globalise Resistance is a united front."*

Unity or dilution?

The SWP do not share the views of the movements they now claim to be a part of and want to lead:

* They vote for the government.
* They oppose confrontational direct action.
* They consistently argue for activists to moderate their activities to suit the prejudices of the Labour Party.

There is a big difference between winning people over to a cause and watering down that cause so as not to upset the government. The problem is that the SWP are actively conning people attracted to anti-capitalism and opposed to neo-imperialist wars away from direct action and into compromising with the Labour Party. All their activities are geared towards making our movement less confrontational and less effective.

The instinct for unity in mass protest movements is strong, even amongst people with very different political outlooks. Some people see no problem with the SWP's involvement, viewing criticism of their politics as splitting the unity we need to be successful. But this is to misunderstand what the SWP are up to - if the SWP's aggressive selling of their sect's politics is successful, our protest movements will be significantly weakened.

"Vote labour where you must"

The SWP use the language of direct action but take part in it as little as possible. They prefer legal, ineffective demos - preferably with Labour councillors or MPs - because they are more acceptable to the Labour Party supporters they are trying to win to their party.

The SWP have always supported the Labour Party. Their approach in elections is to: *"vote Socialist where you can, vote Labour where you must"*. When they tell us that *"many who were on the anti-capitalist demonstrations or sympathised with them will also be members of the Labour Party"* and *"anti-capitalists have to build bridges towards these outraged Labour members"* you know that they're not calling on Labour Party activists to adopt direct action - they are trying to convince anti-capitalists to tone down their activities so as not to upset these people. This also ignores the fact that Labour is a capitalist party!

Of course, there are loads of people who've got involved in SWP front organisations because they really believed in the cause. But it's not effective, it's a cynical power grab obsessed with market share and ultimately ineffective. The real world's messier, less straightforward and sometimes downright confusing - but it is the real world.

We need to re-think our tactics and organise better. Globalise Resistance organised transport to Genoa and meetings within days of coming back from Genoa, while (we?) did not. We need more debate about how to grow; how do we meaningfully involve new people in activities? How do we learn from our mistakes and pass on our experiences? How do we get our message across faced with a hostile and manipulative media? How can we continue to effectively resist and protest against capitalism and its military enforcement?

Getting our act(ion) together

Direct action has inspired and mobilised millions of people to protest against the injustices of the world. People have continually and creatively adapted their tactics to meet new challenges and changing circumstances. Alongside big actions, people are organising locally in their own communities. Small local groups are building links with other people fed up with what capitalism has to offer. The internet has been important for this, and helps us connect the local with the global - building things solidly, connecting with the spirit of resistance you find in communities up and down the country, while never forgetting how our struggles - and the struggles of millions of people across the world - are linked.

Here are some of our ideas and principles that will help protest movements evolve in the spirit of the dynamic, diverse and effective direct action movements of the last few years:

* *Resist practically*

Our movements are firmly based on the principle that direct action is central to resistance. Capitalism and wars are practical things; you can't stop them by proving that they're not very nice; you take actions to prevent their destruction of lives, communities and ecologies.

* *Build practical alliances with others*

Our movements have been inspired by the struggles of peoples in the south, the majority of humanity, against capitalism and oppression. Massive social movements in many countries fight life and death battles against global capitalism and its enforcers. We see our struggle and theirs as one and the same.

Anti-capitalist and anti-war movements encompass a wide range of groups and campaigns with overlapping activities and ideas. While there are constant discussions and disagreements amongst people, our organic, decentralised way of organising minimises the extent to which abstract ideological debates prevent us from working together.

People are always developing new, practical links with others fighting capitalism and its military enforcement. The way we organise allows us to minimise the state's targeting of individuals as leaders and encourages new ideas and tactics to develop in a way that would otherwise not be possible.

* *Get yourself connected*

One way of encouraging cooperation between people is to have meetings bringing together different groups in an area. In Brighton the Rebel Alliance is an irregular get together of the various direct action/ non-hierarchical groups in the town. Many different and varied groups are given a couple of minutes to say what they are up to. This allows new people to see what's happening locally and decide if want to get involved. Similar stuff happens in London with CItY and in Manchester with the Riotous Assembly.

Our aversion to hierarchy is healthy, but too often it just means that there's some inner circle making the real decisions. This is not non

-hierarchical - it is often the very opposite. Ask yourself - how easy is it for someone new to your town to get in touch with your group? Do you have meetings where newcomers - and not just people from your own social circles - are made to feel welcome and involved in things? The easier we make it for new people to get involved, the more we connect with the day-to-day struggles of people around us, the more successful we will be.

* *Show a healthy disregard for legality*

The law has always been used as a weapon to prevent effective opposition to capitalism and war. Anti-union laws prevent picketing, the Criminal Justice Act stops people dancing, squatting and protesting and the Public Order Act attacks basic rights of assembly - to name just a few. Laws are constantly brought in by those in power to stay in power. We shouldn't treat these laws as anything but an occupational hazard to be got around.

This doesn't mean its okay to go around attacking and robbing people everywhere - that's what governments do to enforce their capitalist world order. It means recognising that the state and its laws are there to defend the capitalist system and we shouldn't be surprised when it does exactly that. It means showing that we will not play by their rules of 'legitimate' protest because they are their rules, not ours, and if we play by them we will lose.

* *Break with organisations and parties that hold our struggles back*

Many people support capitalist governments and their wars. The cheap commodities produced by slave labour in the south, the massive debt repayments to the north, the manipulation of world markets by the rich countries contribute to a high standard of living for many people in the rich countries. It's not just merchant bankers and multinational directors that gain from Britain's financial power - many middle-managers, professionals and others benefit significantly.

It is from the majority of us in Britain, who benefit from global injustice, that the Labour Party and the trade unions draw their membership. Working class people in the Labour Party and trade unions do not determine their political standpoints.

The Labour Party has always played an important role in sabotaging and undermining effective opposition to capitalism, allowing people to feel they 'have a choice', without anything changing. This is not a party that offers an alternative to the injustice, violence and destruction in our world, it is a thoroughly pro-capitalist organisation that is backed and funded by major corporations.

Unions today are little better. They are major financial institutions in their own right, holding assets of billions of pounds. Unions are more interested in providing financial services for their members, they fear facing the prospect of having their assets taken from them. Less than a third of British workers are in unions and those that are tend to have more secure jobs.

This isn't to say that we don't support strikes and other actions by direct action groups who occupied and blockaded docks during the Liverpool dock dispute and took action in support of striking tube workers. In contrast many strikes in the last few years - the Liverpool dockers, the Hillingdon hospital workers, the Tameside care workers, the Dudley hospital workers - have been denied the support they needed to win by their own unions.

* *Watching them watching us*

We all know that the mainstream corporate media is controlled by people who don't exactly take kindly to anti-capitalist ideas. We have our own media, from small, local newsletters to international Indymedia sites - Italian Indymedia was getting over a million hits a day during the G8 summit in Genoa in 2001 - we certainly have ways of getting our message across.

But we can't avoid the mainstream media altogether. In the past we could often let our actions speak for themselves, nowadays our silence is being used by groups like Stop the War Coalition to speak on our behalf. It's true that journalists can stitch you up and misrepresent what you say, but it's important to consider talking to them, on your own terms - so that someone else doesn't come along and claim to speak for you.

So how can you get your message across?

Well, when Justice? set up a Squatters Estate Agency in Brighton in 1996 to advertise local empty property to potential squatters and draw attention to homelessness, there was incredible international media interest. Justice? had a media training day a month before, learning how to deal with dodgy interviewers, so were well prepared for the onslaught. "We got half a dozen of us together, went through the basic points we wanted to make - so many empty homes, so many homeless people, why? - and did the interviews sticking to those points. Because there was a group of us, no one got seized on as leader - and it was great being able to beat MPs and government ministers in discussions by keeping to the basics."

Movements never stay the same for long - they either grow or fade away. If we fail to continually improve the way we organise and get new people involved, there is a real danger that people will turn their backs on direct action and self organisation; and let themselves be swallowed and used as minions by electoral politics. We can't allow that to happen.

BALFOUR BEATTEN

"We are delighted. We were not expecting this, because Balfour Beatty was fighting hard for the dam. This Ilisu campaign is a great example of environment and human rights groups fighting together to be effective."
- Kerim Yildiz, spokesman for the Kurdish Human Rights Project.

Hasankeyf – 10,000 year old town threatened by the Ilisu dam

Balfour Beatty have announced they are pulling out of the Ilisu Dam project in Turkey this week. As the chief executive of Balfour Beatty, Mike Welton, explained "Balfour Beatty believes the project could only proceed with substantial extra work and expense and with considerable further delay. Accordingly, in concert with Impregilo of Italy, it has decided to withdraw from the project."

The Dam planned for the Kurdish region of Turkey and would have made more than 30,000 homeless and affected up to 78,000 people. It would have drowned dozens of towns and villages including the world historic site of Hasankeyf, submerging a total area the size of Greater Manchester. This massive dam would also have made it possible for the Turkish government to control the flow of the Tigris river into Syria and Iraq – no prizes for guessing that this would've been seen as fightin' talk. As part of an international Swiss-led consortium including seven multinationals and eight governments, Balfour Beatty were seeking $200 million in export credit guarantees from the British Government to build the dam – that's British taxpayers money that would have been used to pay for the ethnic cleansing of Kurds in Turkey.

The World Commission on Dams (WCD) published a report of large-scale hydroelectric dams in November last year saying, "in many cases dams have led to the irreversible loss of species populations and ecosystems." It went on to explain that "Impacts of dam building on people and livelihoods have been…devastating." In other words, Dams are NOT environmentally friendly and they are NOT a viable answer to increasing energy demands if you care about anything other than profit.

Comedian and activist Mark Thomas, who has been directly involved in the campaign to stop the Ilisu Dam, happened to be on tour in Brighton when this news came out. His current show already features the story of the Ilisu Dam, and uses his wit to turn the very dry issue of Export Credit Guarantees (the UK government department using taxpayers money to underwrite this and other dodgy projects) into something accessible. His hilarious first hand accounts of shutting down Balfour's Annual General Meeting was delivered that night with extra glee and relish: "The Kurdish Human Rights activists were raging about the atrocities being committed by Turkish government in the Ilisu area, and Friends of the Earth, they were really angry too. I mean they were tutting – loudly – and looking very cross…and the Quakers normally pacifists to the end shoulder-barged their way onto the platform. At this point a couple of big, mean looking Group 4 security thugs started pacing towards us with intent and in the blink of a eye two very skinny, attractive environmental activist women had rugby tackled them to the ground…"

The Ilisu Dam is now not likely to go ahead. But, there are 22 other dams planned in the Tigris and Euphrates basins in Turkey that must be stopped. Amec, another British construction company, want to build a dam in Uyseffely in the Jordanian minority region of Turkey. If their plans go ahead they will displace 12-15,000 people and its predicted environmental impact goes off the scale. They are trying to secure a £68 million export credit guarantee from the taxpayer – that means if Turkey defaulted on the payment, taxpayers will foot the bill.

See www.ilisu.org.uk for updates

Ilisu Dam Campaign members disrupt Balfour Beatty's AGM, 9th May 2000.

Escape From Woomera

Woomera 2002 - Autonomadic Caravan and Festival of Freedoms

By Alex Kelly (June 2002)

Woomera – Autonomadic Caravan and Festival of Freedoms was held from 29th March to the 2nd April 2002 in Woomera, South Australia. Woomera is 500km north of Adelaide and is a poignant site due to the variety of issues which intersect here. It's a strange military town, established as a service town for a rocket testing range and a (now closed) US spy base. Also nearby is the Roxby Downs Uranium mine and proposed site for a nuclear waste dump. The Woomera Asylum Seekers Detention Centre (since shut down) is one of six in Australia – not including new off-shore 'initiatives'. They are managed by Australasian Correctional Management (ACM), a subsidiary of US corporate prison giant Wakenhut Corrections.

Preparations began for an Easter 'festival of freedoms' at Woomera. People talked about 500 people coming, but it was hard to imagine – right up until buses started to arrive at the camp site – that over a thousand people would come...

Despite determination that the festival would be about several issues, the detention centre became the major focus of the five day camp. Attempts were made to forge links with local indigenous groups – a task to which great importance was attached, but not achieved that smoothly.

The Melbourne>Woomera network made contact with a number of Kokatha people, and to my knowledge, were the only group who did. Although the organisation of the 'festival' was decentralised in nearly every aspect – this contact represented the entire camp. A letter from a Kokatha woman to the protesters asserted, "When you mob come up to Woomera please think about how we have been fighting for a long time against Roxby Downs (uranium mine on their land). We have been busy all these years, trying to get control over our country". Woomera raised many issues with regards to 'indigenous liaison' which remain unresolved, but were an important learning process.

Benefit gigs and workshops were held around the country – buses were booked, tents, trucks, a water tanker, a shit-pit digger hired, a convergence booklet put together and legal and medical information gathered. It was time to make the journey!

MEET AT SPUD'S

Thursday 28th March: Organizers and activists gathered at Spud's Roadhouse at Pimba to discuss establishing a camp site. Initially the Dept. of Defence lackey pointed us to a disused sports ground – equipped with portaloos and fresh water – but he neglected to mention that it was two km from the detention centre, and behind a 2.5 metre fence with only one access gate! We chose another location – much closer to the detention centre, formed a circle with vehicles and bedded down. An evening police raid failed to move the camp, and the site was held by a small number of protesters until the buses arrived the following morning.

WHOOPS THE FENCE FELL DOWN

Friday 29th March: After hundreds arrived at the site, we had won the first battle – deciding where to camp. More infrastructure was set up; various workshop tents were put up, the desert Indymedia centre established, soundsystems wired up and a vast array of banners, kites, flags and costumes emerged. Locals set up the 'Kokatha Peoples Embassy' near the site. At midday, we received word that the detainees were going to do a 'sound action' and they wanted to see if we could hear them. We headed straight down to the federal check point where 200 metres of temporary fencing blocked the road - around a kilometre from the detention centre itself. We could see them on the roofs of the buildings in the centre, and when the megaphones were shut down (!) we could hear them.

Later in the day 'No-one Is Illegal' had a meeting to discuss the civil disobedience action called for the following day, as props and banners were made, including a giant pair of bolt cutters!! Detainees alerted us via mobile phone - which I assume was smuggled inside and subsequently confiscated - to an action planned at 6pm inside the centre.

We headed across the desert to the detention centre – and the following hour is almost impossible to describe…

Forming a long parade with music from a sound system on a truck, we reached within 500 metres of the centre - with no sign of police. Then at a five metre fence topped with razor wire we could see detainees well enough to wave and shout to each other. Still we couldn't believe how close we'd come. Next, unbelievably the fence came down!!

I was uneasy, I wanted to know where the police were, whether we were going to be hemmed in. But we continued towards the detainees and next thing we knew we were at the last two fences which separated us from the detainees. For a moment we stood on either side of the fence - straining our arms through the fence to touch, talk, cry and… then - the unbelievable happened:

A bar was used to open a gap in the fence and people began to escape! One after another they stage-dived into the arms of stunned protesters. The police finally arrived but detainees were still able to leap over them into the crowd - as soon as they hit the ground they were surrounded and given clothes as a disguise and rushed back towards the campsite. After fifty had escaped, police horses regained control of the fence. Police tried to pick detainees out of the throng, and arrested a protester of Bangladeshi descent who they banged up for two hours.

That night at the campsite, protesters kept detainees huddled in their tents as escape plans were discussed. Some cursed that they hadn't developed escape plans, because they hadn't dreamed that they were actually going to break detainees out. The police set up road blocks around the camp and 200kms south at Port Augusta, and sent undercover and uniformed police through to sweep the camp for detainees. Without speculating about their whereabouts or even how they got away - for fear of jeopardising their freedom - to date the official figures are that eleven are still free.

HOW DO YOU FOLLOW THAT?

Saturday 30th March was surreal, but much calmer than Friday night. Lots of people had not slept, people were dazed, trying to get their heads around the magnitude of the previous night's events. This time we went straight up the road and knocked over the fence at the check point, some people heading all the way to the centre, other opting to block the road and dance on the "No Entry" signs that were now lying in the dust.

A number of people were arrested for "trespass" and taken away to Woomera lock-up where protesters and detainees who had been captured the previous night were being held. Several were charged with harbouring a detainee. Detainees were charged with escaping and most of the 39 recaptured have been moved to Port Headland detention centre.

Sunday 31st March: A Critical Mass bike ride went to the Roxby Downs uranium mine, and despite a much greater police presence, we were still able to get near the perimeter fence.

A note was thrown over the fence in a rubber glove saying "Australian people, we are hostage in our rooms we can't move anywhere and also the ACM give us sleeping tablets in the food, nobody can do anything, please help us."

At least two former detainees made the journey to Woomera. One of them spoke to fellow Afghani Hazara people on the Sunday, and later translated what he had said to them: "We can not pull down all the fences today, it would be too dangerous for you and for us. There are people here from Germany, America, England, Spain, every state in Australia and we are going to go back and tell everyone, everywhere about this, and we are going to do everything we can to help you. We will never forget you." This man had only been freed from this centre two weeks before, and now had a temporary protection visa (which does not guarantee sanction into Australia).

A publication Desert Storm was produced to record this dramatic action. See the online version at www.antimedia.net/desertstorm

We are all illegal until no-one is illegal.

Argy Bargy

The economic rout of Argentina, and the grassroots fightback.

At the turn of the twentieth century Argentina was the world's seventh largest economy. Throughout most of the twentieth century workers wages and conditions improved and welfare provision was universal (at least if you were a member of one of the corrupted trade unions.) By the turn of the twenty-first century the economy was the basket case of Latin America. During the economic crisis of 2001-03, poverty in Argentina affected 58% of the population and over a quarter earned too little to feed themselves.

How come such a turnabout in fortunes? This was, after all, the Neo-liberal's model economy. The instructions given by the White House, IMF and World Bank were followed to the letter. Perhaps the reality is that Neo-liberal economic policies are really designed to enrich local and international business elites whilst economic growth actually becomes a secondary consideration. Although one of the main players, Citibank, initially lost some $2bn during the crisis, it was but a small blip, with profits rising 36% during 2003. Meanwhile during each day in 2001, 20,000 Argentineans slid below the poverty line.

With Carlos Menem taking the presidency in 1989 the sale of Argentina began. More briberisation than privatisation, companies like Enron picked up some real bargains, for example paying just 1/5 of the real value for the country's natural gas industry. Menem and his successors followed the fundamentalism of the 'Washington Consensus' (a 'consensus' between the IMF, World Bank and White House) beginning by 'pegging' the Argentinean currency to the dollar. This meant that for every Peso spent the government had to have a dollar to back it up in its coffers. Of course Argentina didn't have any dollars and needed to borrow, but the banks lending the cash thought that doing so was a risky business, so they charged 16% interest on such loans.

And the rip off didn't stop there. When the economy looked like it was about to collapse, the IMF offered the government $20bn in return for further reducing wages and cutting pensions. But these policies stripped the country of its assets and left them with few alternatives and huge debts. When the loans looked perilous more were given. The bigger the debt the bigger the interest repayments: the more for the bankers, the less for the people. Despite following instructions the Argentineans never got their hands on the $20bn. It lingered in New York bank vaults and was used to pay the interest on loans made by firms like Citibank. $130bn left Argentina for Western banks during the crisis.

Pissed off that the 'solution' to be followed was the very same set of policies that led to the crisis in the first place, people took to the streets. Food riots began in the provinces but spread into Buenos Aires, banks were destroyed and the Israeli embassy attacked. In Cordoba, Argentina's second biggest city, civil servants set fire to the city hall in protest of the government's economic plans. One protester said, 'I have never seen anything this intense in Argentina in all my life'.

20,000 people marched on to the presidential palace. Police issued warnings of arrests for an illegal gathering, after 15 minutes they opened up with plastic bullets. "The incredible thing is that not a soul is on the side of the police, so everyone who drives by honks, people walking by try to help, clap, boo the cops, throw things." A state of emergency led to hundreds of arrests and numerous deaths including a 15-year-old boy shot by a shopkeeper.

Workers, convinced they could do a better job than their bosses, began to occupy factories. People, pissed off at government corruption, started to create popular assemblies to resolve local problems – from faulty sewers to insufficient hospital budgets. Four-star hotels were being run by cleaning staff, a supermarket was taken over by its clerks and pilots and cabin crew aimed to turn a regional airline into a co-operative. During the crisis there were 'assemblies of the assemblies', with over 4,000 people from rich and poor districts meeting to resolve daily problems. Signifying the move from party politics to grassroots activism, the greeting 'compañero' or comrade has been replaced by 'vecino' or neighbour.

But surprise surprise the new president Nestor Kirchner isn't living up to his promises. Although he's made some real attempts to uncover the crimes of the dictatorship, it's business as usual, as the Argentinean economy begins to boom once more. Ignorant of this natural 'boom follows bust' cycle in capitalist economies, Kirchner, who had once promised not to pay more than 3% of GDP in loan repayments to the IMF, is, once again, playing ball with Washington.

Elected on just 22% of the vote, Kirchner models himself as a populist Peronist and like all good Peronists, accusations of corruption have dogged his previous position of former governor of the largely uninhabited province of Santa Cruz. The challenge now is whether the factory occupations and popular assemblies can continue to grow before Kirchner, like the authoritarian Peronists before him, decides to clamp down on this challenge to his authority and business-friendly policies.

Check out:

* **'Taking back Control: A Journey Through Argentina's Popular Uprising'** by Natasha Gordon and Paul Chatterton (email paul_chatterton@yahoo.co.uk for copies).
* **Que se Vayan Todos** - Argentina's Popular Rebellion. An eyewitness account of the financial meltdown and ongoing grassroots rebellion. www.nadir.org/nadir/initiativ/agp/free/imf/argentina/txt/2002/0918que_se_vayan.htm
* Read SchNEWS' account of the dramatic events of December 2001 in Buenos Aires www.schnews.org.uk/sotw/Arge-taking-peso.htm

For Peat's Sake

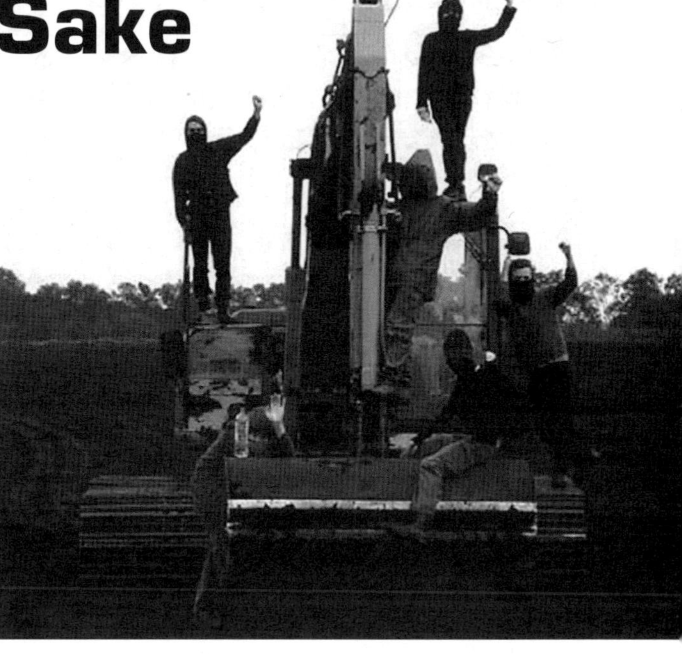

A direct action campaign has been causing enormous problems and expense for companies destroying peat bogs in the north of England so they can flog bags of peat to gardening shops.

Thorne Moors and Hatfield Moor, which are the two largest surviving mires in Britain and make up a total of 3,000 hectares of peat land, are currently being destroyed by a company called Scotts. After a rash of direct action which has cost the company millions of pounds, the two moors could soon become conservation areas, as opposed to something people use to keep potplants in.

Although there'd been campaigning to save the moors for decades, the latest round of trouble started in April 1992 when Earth First! caused £100,000 of damage to digging machinery on Thorne moors. Fast forward to the summer of 2001 and the peat extracting was still going on so northern EF! groups began carrying out monthly actions including stopping work in the factories, trespassing on the moor, filling in draining ditches, slashing bags of peat, sabotaging machines, and shutting down the processing computer to name just a few of the shenanigans.

Then Peat Alert! – a network of eco-activists – called for a national day of action on 18th February 2002. A range of Scotts sites across the country were to be targeted simultaneously: activists D-locked themselves to head office doors in Surrey; there were office and factory occupations in North Wales and a lorry blockade at their fertiliser plant in Suffolk; drainage ditches were filled on Hatfield Moor; interfering dams were built on a bog in Cumbria and an office was occupied in East Yorkshire.

On 27th February Scotts surprised the rest of the peat industry by announcing a deal with DEFRA and English Nature which essentially bought Scotts out of their rights to extract peat, but also gave them until September 2004 to help themselves to nearly a million cubic metres of peat. Though the campaign of direct action clearly seemed to influence the deal, more direct action was needed to curb this last burst of destruction.

So in Easter 2002, a peak time for gardening shops as they shift loads of peat to weekend gardeners, a four day blockade and camp was set up near Hatfield Moor. In August £100,000 worth of damage was done to Scotts in another series of actions, and the campaign's continuing efforts have seriously disrupted Scotts operations, costing them lots of money.

Since then other peat bogs have been receiving the same treatment – with some quite serious "ecotage" at Solway Moss and Bolton Fell bogs. Those pesky pixies!

See www.peatalert.org.uk

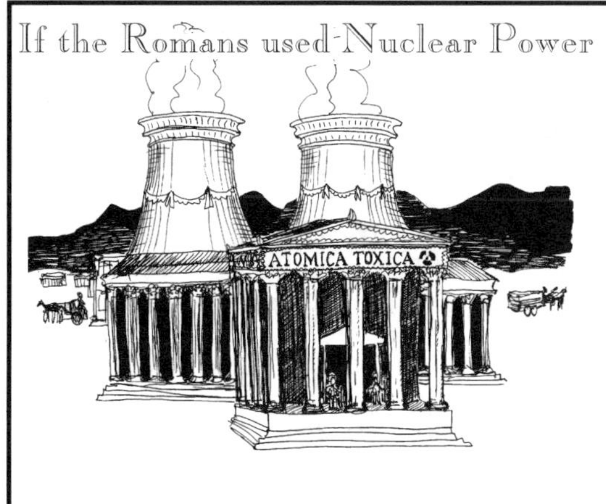

BUSMANS HOLIDAYS

British Activists Working Abroad In International Solidarity

"If you have come here to help me, you are wasting your time... But if you have come because your liberation is bound up with mine, then let us work together." - Lilla Watson, Aboriginal activist

"My ideal would be for there to be a massive global movement for social justice, built on international solidarity, so that when people anywhere were being abused, people everywhere would know about it, refuse to tolerate it and prevent it." - Jo Wilding, peace activist

"Our resistance is as trans-national as our holidays" - Rebel Irrelevance leaflet

The economic globalisation of the world brought in its wake a communications revolution, transforming the awareness of social movements around the globe. Disparate groups were able to raise their voices in unison (and discord) in a way never before seen. The shape of common enemies could be discerned.

As the British D.I.Y movement, especially after June 18th 1999, began to embrace a more international and specifically anti-capitalist outlook, increasing numbers of people started to look at how we could broaden our scope and build genuine solidarity with movements in the Majority ("third") World. So far this has been expressed in forms of practical help, fundraisers for emergency aid, prisoner support, and actions taken against multi-national corporations and embassies of countries involved in oppression and environmental destruction. This article looks at a selection of British people involved in a range of international solidarity work in recent years, but is in no way the full picture.

To venture into other countries as part of autonomous groups or as individuals to assist in struggles is of course not only a recent phenomena; in the thirties anarchists and socialists left Britain to fight Franco's fascism in Spain. In the sixties and seventies people travelled to and took part in armed Majority World national liberation struggles. The tradition continued with the likes of the Peace Brigades who worked in Nicaragua to aid the Sandinistas, and the many other efforts which are the precursors to those in action today.

But why travel around the globe looking for trouble? Is there not enough oppression, dispossession and environmental destruction in the British Isles to keep any self respecting activist busy? What happened to "think globally–act locally"? As the Zapatistas have continually attempted to hammer home, our best form of solidarity is create revolution at home. One rather ironic reason why people travel is that the privileged children of the West can have a more direct role to play in Majority World struggles, thanks to the racist double standards of the New World Order which perceives their lives as more valuable. Certainly the western media considers their suffering more important. The murder of International Solidarity Movement (ISM) activist Rachel Corrie in Rafah, Palestine in March 2003 became internationally famous, but on the same day she died, so did nine Palestinians – which of course got zero coverage.

"...as disgraceful as it is, having a white face can protect you where just being human ought to be enough." – Jo Wilding.

This exaggerated importance of the presence of Western foreigners can be used to deter aggression. A British peace observer on a farm squatted by landless peasants in Guatemala commented on how "for whatever reason, the [Guatemalan] authorities tend to tread very carefully around gringos." The reason is probably because the amount of aggravation, negotiation and media attention that can be generated by the death or injury of a westerner can act as a deterrent to some governments or paramilitary groups.

Another valuable asset is our relative wealth: a benefit gig or jumble sale here can make a huge difference to an impoverished community. Our proximity to the centres of power gives us unique opportunities for action, for the acts of true solidarity, where we use our unjust privilege to ultimately erode it.

Working with individuals and movements from other countries, springing from other roots with different struggles and ways of engaging in those struggles is not just an adjunct to our fight here, it is a necessary and vital part of it. By building connections with majority world movements we can come closer to the realisation that we are not alone, that we are many and that we have the strength to change the world. The more grass roots unmediated experience of life as it is lived by most of world's population we possess, the better our understanding of the true situation we face. By returning their stories and experience to our movement we learn and enhance our own struggle.

In this article are accounts from British activists who have gone to a range of different situations to do international solidarity work: several of which are high profile like the Zapatistas in Mexico; the support for Palestinians resisting the Israeli occupation; and the people of Iraq in the face of the Saddam regime, the UN Sanctions, and now the US occupation. We also hear from people working in countries which get very little media coverage – like the tribespeople in West Papua's fight for autonomy from Indonesia; and hands-on aid convoys to Kosova and Ukraine.

But it is important to avoid the trap of focussing on western activists: the main experts on Zapatismo remain the Zapatistas not the peace observers, and the true victims of the Israeli occupation are the Palestinian people, not the orange-jacketed ISM.

CHIAPAS, MEXICO

On New Years Eve 1994, the previously unheard-of Zapatistas seized towns across the South-Eastern Mexican state of Chiapas. From the balcony of an occupied municipal palace in San Cristobal de las Casas a call went out for international peace observers. Many Mexican and international organizations answered this call, forming civil brigades – which visited different regions of the state – and documenting human rights violations. Huge military retaliation against the indigenous rebels was forestalled by the combination of actions of "civil society" within Mexico, such as strikes, and international pressure.

Realistically, despite their declaration of war, the Zapatista Army of National Liberation (EZLN) forces were never going to be able to fight the Mexican army and the survival of the revolt depended heavily on solidarity from within and outside Mexico.

The EZLN's pronunciations were almost tailor-made for the ideas bubbling up inside British D.I.Y. culture. The Zapatistas explicitly distanced themselves from any attempt to seize state power. "We do not struggle to take power, we struggle for democracy, liberty, and justice. It is perhaps for this reason – the lack of interest in power – that the word of the Zapatistas has been well received in other countries across the globe, above all in Europe" stated Subcomandante Marcos in 1995. The land seized from rich landowners in the uprising was being settled and cultivated by indigenous peasants, who had organised themselves into autonomous municipalities based on collective decision making. To many this seemed to be a model of anarchy in action.

In February 1995 the Mexican Army launched a massive assault on the indigenous communities, forcing a significant proportion of the population to flee their homes and take refuge in the mountains. Several communities asked the Fray Bartolome de Las Casas Human Rights Center in San Cristóbal to help create a security corridor that would protect the civilian population and document human rights abuses. In response to this request and fearing that without an international presence in the conflict zone a greater number of human rights violations would occur, Bishop Samuel Ruiz, the founder of the Centre, issued a call to international civil society to help establish a permanent international peace presence in threatened indigenous communities. This would not only allow the return of the displaced to their homes, but also help protect the communities from further abuses. The peace camps remain to this day and there has been a steady stream of volunteers making their way to Chiapas, eager to help protect but also to learn from the Zapatista movement.

Peace Camp volunteers have two key functions. First, by their mere presence they discourage military aggression against the lives and property of the indigenous communities (the communities are surrounded by up to 70,000 troops.) They are literally the physical personification of international preoccupation about the rights of the indigenous peoples – unarmed civilians using their status as foreigners to support and protect the position of the indigenous people. By showing this international support and solidarity, and linking the communities to the outside world, the observers help counteract the low-intensity counter-insurgency warfare perpetrated by the Mexican government against the EZLN, its bases of support or Zapatista sympathizers. Second, they act as witnesses to human rights violations, documenting and then reporting them to concerned local and international groups. By publicizing these abuses abroad, the observers bring the threat of international diplomatic and economic pressure to bear against the Mexican government.

The fact the peace observers are a serious problem for the Mexican state's counter-insurgency effort is shown by the continual harassment of internationals in the conflict zone including mass expulsions in 1998. The state has continued its 'Low Intensity War' against the Zapatistas, funding paramilitary groups such as that which carried out the massacre of 45 Zapatista sympathisers at Acteal in December1997. Violence of this nature is a constant threat and international presence can act as a deterrent.

The first international *Encuentro*, (encounter or meeting) took place at La Realidad in 1996. Over 3000 activists from around the globe attended to show solidarity with the Zapatista cause and to open up a new space for discussion of opposition to neo-liberalism. This lead to a collective declaration: *"That we will make a collective network of all our particular struggles and resistances. An intercontinental network of resistance against neoliberalism, an intercontinental network of resistance for humanity."* There is a clear line to be drawn from this *Encuentro* to the creation of People's Global Action, so although the Zapatistas remain in the jungles and mountains of south eastern Mexico their ideas have influenced many activists around the world, especially the round of global days of action against capitalism. The call for these protests arose at the *Encuentro* and is part of the reason for the 'anti-capitalist' demonstrations around the world on June 18th 1999 , kickstarting the whole "anarchist travelling circus/summit-hopping" phenomena (see other articles in this book).

Not all direct solidarity with the EZLN has been based around peace observation. Although the Zapatistas are continually under threat from military and paramilitary incursions they are also struggling against extreme poverty. This has been used as a weapon by the Mexican state in the "softer" side of the war. Communities are bribed with access to water, electricity and access to basic medical care to leave the Zapatista fold. The Mexican state hopes to break the movement through blackmail. Various international organisations help provide the autonomous communities with the wherewithal to sort these facilities out for themselves.

Chiapas has over 30% of Mexico's entire drinking water reserves. Annual rainfall amounts to 14,000 cubic meters per person, the highest figure in the country. However, thousands of communities throughout the state have no clean drinking water. U.K based solidarity group Kiptik has been working in Chiapas since May 2000 primarily concentrating on providing clean drinking water to Zapatista communities. In the wake of the revolt a lot of communities moved from the less fertile hillsides to the valley bottoms, previously used for beef farming. However this meant in many cases leaving the original source of spring water behind. Kiptik

---

Issue 250, 3rd March 2000

YA BASTA!

Reproduced here is an interview from 2000 with a SchNEWS bod who'd just returned from spending time in Zapatista communities in Chiapas. Although some of the situations have moved on since then, it still paints an accurate picture of life for the Zapatistas.

Q: HOW DO THE ZAPATISTAS ORGANISE?

A: The Zapatistas control 35 autonomous municipalities, and each municipality covers a huge area with thousands of people in it. The scale of the area is something people don't appreciate. What is important is that the Zapatistas have broken away from the old guerrilla style of organising where the central committee tells you what to do. Instead each village in the municipalities has its own assembly to run its own affairs. For example, some communities have decided on completely communal ownership of the land, while others have a mixed system with common and individual land. Each village sends a delegate to the Clandestine Indigenous Revolutionary Committee, where important military decisions can only be made after all the communities have been consulted. For example during the San Andres Peace Accords, when the Zapatistas talked to the government, every single community was consulted, and these debates can go on for days – they talk it out, till everyone who wants to say something has said it, and then some kind of consensus is made. We were in one community where they had called a congress to decide the education structure

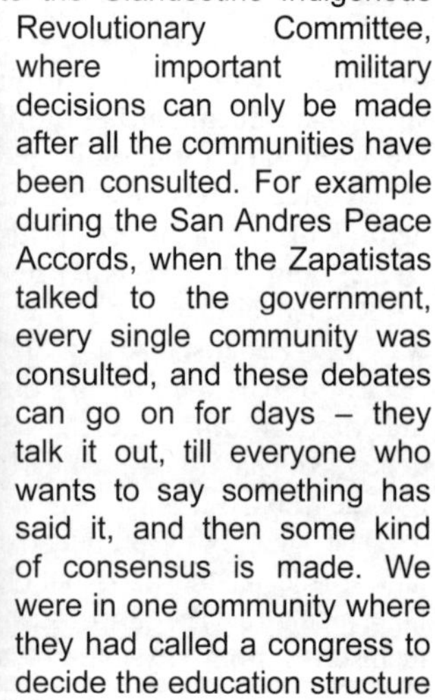

helps to finance and build pipelines bringing this water down to the new settlements. Communities are left with the tools and knowledge to maintain their own water supply, directly increasing their level of autonomy.

Kiptik say "Ensuring a supply of clean water is the most important preventative health measure for a community: incidents of giardia, amoebic dysentery, diarrhea, cholera, and hepatitis can all be drastically lowered." To this end, the organisation also builds dry compost latrines. "We want to keep our projects small and human-scale, and to promote self-sufficiency by leaving skills and materials in the hands of the people in the communities. Wherever possible, we try to use appropriate technology solutions – i.e simple and low cost."

Bristol-based Easton Cowboys on an away fixture.

Foreign volunteers have been left astounded by the strength and endurance of these people, especially when digging holes, mixing cement or trying to carry objects with the meka-paal (a sort of head-yoke/torture device). One international volunteer warned, "Don't try to out work the Zapatistas – it'll only end in tears!"

In addition, Kiptik provides assistance in obtaining medical equipment for remote rural clinics and health posts, as well as helping install solar panels for clinics which need electrical power. Recent projects also include touring the autonomous municipalities with a cinema, showing such revolutionary classics as *Robin Hood*, *Braveheart* and *Tai Chi Master.*

No article about British involvement in Chiapas would be complete without mention of the *Easton Cowboys,* a Bristol-based amateur football club who pioneered the concept of solidarity through sport. They've travelled as a team to play the Zapatistas on two occasions to advance the idea of "freedom through football". Their appearance caused a certain amount of amusement in the communities, where they were described as "the whitest white people ever seen." Alfredo Jimenez, a team captain from Morelia said: "We are very emotional and excited. This is the first time anyone from far away has come to play us and we hope this isn't the last time football teams from other countries come here." One of the Cowboy's commented "never has the old saying that football breaks down barriers been so true."

Links

www.kiptik.buz.org

Chiapas Indymedia:

http://chiapas.mediosindependientes.org/

---

for the whole of the municipality and the meeting lasted two days!

Q: TELL US ABOUT THE LAND OCCUPATIONS

A: I think the mainland takeovers started around 1995. Just three landlords used to control the municipality we were in. The landowners had passed land to each other for generations, until they were kicked out, and the area put under Zapatista control. Before, in many places instead of being paid wages, the Indians were given credit for the landowner's shop where everything was priced really high, so reinforcing their poverty.

Many communities have debated what to do with the old landowners' houses because no Zapatistas will live in them. Some have been used as warehouses, some have been demolished. In one community they took down a house brick by brick when they heard the landlord and his heavies were coming back. They sent him a Christmas card with a picture of where the house once stood and said don't bother – there's nothing to come back to!

Q: WHAT IS THE STANDARD OF LIVING?

A: They are dirt poor, they haven't got any money, but they haven't got anyone to tell them what to do now. They always come out with "we have dignity". Their standard of living probably hasn't changed that much since the uprising, but at least now they are farming the land for themselves.

Q: WHAT'S THE ATMOSPHERE THERE LIKE?

A: Schizophrenic! You get the feeling from some that they can take on the whole world, but at the same time army planes are flying really low every day, there's troop carriers and police helicopters, military bases next to some municipalities – it all causes a certain desperation. What the army and police do is come into some communities on the pretext of looking for someone. It's always the women who are there, with these big sticks and little babies on their backs, fighting them off. A Mexican general recently complained that he didn't join the army to fight women and children!

Q: TELL US ABOUT THE ROLE OF WOMEN

A: My experience was that the women are tough as hell. They take part in the command structures of EZLN, for example the occupation of San Cristobal was directed by women. One third of the army are

women. When I was in San Cristobal there was this huge women's march against militarisation in Chiapas. Women insisted on alcohol being banned in the whole of the Zapatista controlled region. Landowners used to make sure the Indians got addicted to alcohol, which got them into tremendous debt until they were basically slaves. If they tried to leave they would be shot or punished, so this alcohol thing was a really useful form of control and it had an effect on the women as there was a lot more domestic violence then.

Now, each community has got a little jail just big enough for one or two people and if any of the men turn up pissed they stick them in the jail for the night. And it works, people don't drink. Another example of the influence of women is the story of one guy who organises clean water projects for the communities. He put a proposal to the men in one village and said for the water project to work, it would take a lot of hard work: three weeks of solid digging a four mile trench from the mountain to the village. The men decided not to bother, and let the women continue to go down to the river and bring water back in buckets. However, when he went back to the village a week later, he was approached and told by one of the elders that the women had had a meeting and told the men in no uncertain terms that they were gonna dig the pipeline!

However, in the assemblies there is still a hierarchy and it is still often the men who do the talking; the women's revolution has happened, but it's not all the way there yet by any means.

Q: DO YOU THINK THE UNITED STATES SEES THE ZAPATISTAS AS A THREAT?

A: Yeah, definitely. The US use the excuse of the war on drugs to arm the Mexican army and most of that weaponry is being used against the Zapatistas. And of course the US is worried because the Zapatistas are setting an example in not accepting poverty and injustice. The Americans spent millions destroying guerrilla movements in El Salvador, Guatemala and of course Nicaragua. And now a whole new rebellion has happened in Mexico, a country the US has always had a high level of control over.

The region is also rich in oil. The Mexican government wants to get its hands on it, but this revolutionary movement is in its way, so at some point there is gonna be a conflict. There is also huge bio-diversity in the forests, and the American bio-tech companies want to get into the jungle and start copyrighting the genetic codes.

Q: HOW IMPORTANT DO YOU THINK THE INTERNET HAS BEEN TO THE STRUGGLE?

A: I had this vision of them all tapping away on their computers in the jungle and that was rubbish – most communities don't even have electricity. It is Zapatista supporters in Mexico City and America who have been invaluable in terms of getting the message out and creating a public mood where the Mexican government feels it can't intervene because it would be too controversial.

Q: HOW IMPORTANT DO YOU THINK IT IS THAT PEOPLE LIKE YOURSELVES GO ABROAD TO VISIT AND SHOW SOLIDARITY WITH THE ZAPATISTAS?

A: To be honest, in terms of material support, the most useful thing that could happen is some solidarity movement in America to try and stop the weaponry getting to the Mexican army. In the absence of that, it's a morale booster. We went over as a football team, and in every community we visited we had to get up on stage and introduce ourselves, say where we are from – they're all like 'where's Europe?' However, if their grasp of geography isn't very good, they are politicised and they understand why we are there.

Q: HOW IMPORTANT DO YOU THINK THE ZAPITISTA STRUGGLE IS FOR INSPIRING PEOPLE?

A: With the collapse of 'communism' there was gloating about the triumph of capitalism. If you want to get rid of the way the world is now being run, you've got to have some kind of idea about what the new world will be like, and the Zapatistas are vital because they are not only saying it, they've actually done it. They're running the municipalities communally, they're organising their own education projects, their own water projects, have their own army, they're reaching out to the other indigenous people of Mexico – it's inspirational.

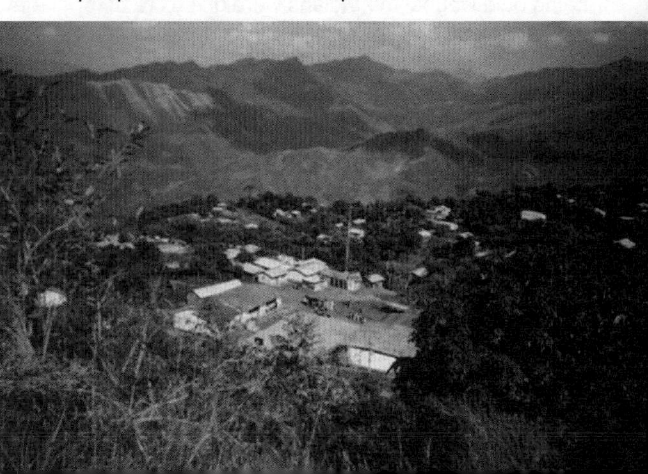

Busmans Holidays II
KOSOVA

While media attention has long since left the wars in the Balkans, the process of rebuilding communities and shattered lives there goes on. As well as the major NGOs being involved in this work, there are also independently run aid projects. Kieran Turner, who was involved for years with SchNEWS, has since been running aid convoys to Kosova and Ukraine. Below is an interview with him about this, but before is SchNEWS' take on the Kosova war, from issue 207, 9th April 1999.

WAR IS PEACE

"We are taking this action for one simple reason: to damage Serbian forces sufficiently to prevent Milosevic from continuing to perpetrate his vile oppression against innocent Albanian civilians" **- Tony Blair**

"The first casualty of war is always the truth" **- Traditional**

On 24th March, two weeks after Poland, Hungary and the Czech Republic joined NATO, NATO launched massive air strikes against Serbia. As ever, superpower aggression was dressed up as a humanitarian exercise, this time to defend Kosovan Albanians from Serb terror. As ever, this was a lie. Since 1992 the desire of Germany, Britain and the United States to expand their influence into eastern Europe at the expense of an enfeebled Russia has brought war, genocide and 100,000 dead to the peoples of the former Yugoslavia. Those dying now in Kosova and Serbia are the latest victims of these western powers' bid for control of the region.

There is no doubt that Milosevic is engaged in mass murder of the majority ethnic Albanian population in Kosova. Ethnic Albanians account for over 80% of Kosova's two million population – well over one million of these Albanian Kosovans are now refugees, either inside Kosova or in neighbouring countries. It is still unclear how many have been killed by the Serbian army, police and fascist paramilitaries.

Until 1989 Kosova had been an autonomous province within Yugoslavia, but with the rise of nationalist hatred fuelled by the super powers, Milosevic was able to use his assertion of Serbian nationalism in Kosova to grab power for himself in Serbia – and lay the basis for war, ethnic cleansing and genocide in Bosnia and, now, Kosova. There is no doubt that Milosevic's warmongering, encouraged and payrolled by western powers when it suited them, needs to be opposed.

But NATO's attacks on Serbia are nothing to do with protecting Kosovan civilians – their plight is now worse than ever. For less than a tenth of the cost of one bomber, NATO could have supplied significant amount of arms to the Kosovan Liberation Army or supported what is left of the democratic opposition in Serbia. Of course, they did neither – because they are concerned with global power struggles, not the plight of those they cynically exploit to justify their warmongering.

If the United States, Britain and the other massive military powers currently bombing the former Yugoslavia were concerned with defending "innocent civilians" they have had numerous opportunities to do so recently – and not done it. In Turkey, the Kurds have had their villages burnt, their culture outlawed, their people killed and turned into refugees by the thousand without any action from NATO – maybe because Turkey is a key strategic member of NATO. When one million Rwandans were systematically slaughtered in a hundred days Clinton did nothing to prevent it because it did not suit US global interests to do so.

The air strikes NATO are carrying out are aimed at ensuring that Serbia, with its strong economic and political links to Russia, does not get in the way of growing western influence in the region. A staggering amount of air power is being used. 80 fighter bombers and 100 cruise missiles – costing £800,000 each – were launched on the first night alone. You can only wonder at the technology contained in the B2 stealth bombers, which cost $2.1bn each.

NATO tells us that these weapons are so expensive because of their ability to minimise civilian casualties – in fact, they are designed to increase their destructive power while minimising any risk to those using them. Each cluster bomb being dropped from an RAF Harrier jets, for instance, spreads 147 small bombs over an area of up to 100 acres – many do not explode, creating unregulated minefields wherever they are dropped. The RAF is currently dropping cluster bombs on Kosova.

For four decades following the second world war, socialist Yugoslavia was able to maintain peace amongst the various nationalities making up the country. The Balkans had always been a region where major world powers fought out their battles at the expense of the local population. The anti-fascist militias that became the Yugoslav state after the second world war were determined to prevent the rise of national tensions and fascism in the area again.

The death of Yugoslavia's President Tito and the collapse of the Soviet Union in the late 80s allowed western powers to expand their influence in the region by encouraging the national tensions that would lead to the present horrors. They consistently backed local politicians stirring up national hatred – like Serbia's Milosevic and Croatia's Tudjeman – against those trying to keep Yugoslavia united.

The powerful multinationals that NATO represents are interested in global power, profit and control of natural resources – not Kosovan refugees. The peoples of the former Yugoslavia, like so many other millions of people from South America to East

Timor, can expect no help from these warmongers except for PR purposes. Organising practical support for the victims of the war in Kosova and building serious opposition to the multinationals' war machine in Britain is the only way we can show solidarity with the millions so cynically used to justify this latest European war.

Further reading:

- *The death of Yugoslavia* by Laura Silber & Alan Little
- *Kosovo – a short history* by Noel Malcolm

AID CONVOYS

Kieran was one of those who in response to the plight of the Kosova Albanians in 1999 began organizing autonomous voluntary aid convoys to the affected region. Five years later he's still actively involved in humanitarian work.

What made you decide to undertake aid work specifically for the Kosova Albanians at that time?

The appalling stories and images that were in the media constantly. The Guardian was running "War in Europe" as the heading for the first five pages every day. We realised that this terrible stuff was happening really close to us, and we were close enough to really make a difference without spending a fortune, or going somewhere so alien we couldn't hope to understand it in a hurry. And we just felt it would be awful NOT to try.

We did, initially, try things like visiting Tinsley House detention centre, at Gatwick, to talk to refugees and establish if we were right to think we could help. We wanted to know, also, if we'd be better off spending our effort on helping the people who'd made it here. However, we decided with their encouragement that we could indeed do some good "out there".

What happened?

We made lots of contacts with existing aid organisations very quickly, as we tried to avoid re-inventing the wheel, but were determined to be driven and directed by real, local people and to avoid all the waste and red tape which scares people about charities. We had a fantastic response. Experienced aid workers were quick to give advice, and we've been able to see the realities of how different sized organisations are *all* essential, complementary parts of the picture. We make real friendships between UK and foreign communities, and we are certain our aid goes where it is intended for.

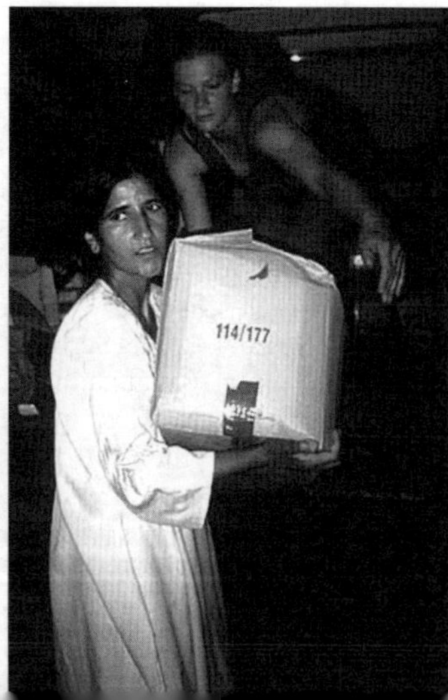

Our first convoy delivered its aid to Kosovan refugees in Albania in April 1999. Since then we've delivered to refugee camps and villages in there and in Macedonia, and volunteers have spent several weeks in Kosova itself, meeting with (and delivering aid with) families,

During an aid run to Kosova, volunteers from the convoy are taken on a tour of Skanderaj, the village where our host grew up. These are the ruins of the local school.

Trades Unions, the students of Prishtine University, doctors and nurses at Gjlane hospital, and politicians from the provisional Kosovan government. Given the ethnic divisions, it is important to note that we do not only deliver aid to Albanian communities. With no hesitation, where there are still Serbian people there – who have suffered from the war as much as anyone else – we work with them too, of course.

What's happening with the organisation now?

The project is still happening, and there is so much still to be done. We intend to keep on working to help the people of the region, paying particular attention to Macedonia and Albania, where they have received less concentrated international support than Kosova itself. We must work with them after the fighting to help them rebuild their lives. Make no mistake – over ten years of apartheid and systematic rape and murder have been perpetrated against these people. Our volunteers have heard chilling stories, and seen the evidence in grim detail. In many villages every home was burnt. Every sizable town has *hundreds* of orphans. Children of rape victims require special attention and care. Schools and Universities are re-stocking libraries for the first time in ten years.

What form does the aid take?

It varies enormously. There are four main categories and we get involved in all of them:

1. "Humanitarian relief" – this is emergency stuff like food and clothes for refugee camps. It also gives us access to people so we can hear their stories first hand and report them back home (or wherever they're not being heard.)

2. Equipment for longer-term projects, like sewing machines, computers (for schools and hospitals), gym stuff for orphanages, medical equipment, tools (for self-reliance!), water-purification stuff and so on.

3. Community development... not necessarily physical stuff at all. We support a Ukrainian youth group

right now with a little equipment, a few ideas (in consultation with them, and their ideas), a bit of moral support, and some "protection" against being harmed by local bureaucratic corruption.

4. Empowerment here in the UK. I don't collect second-hand clothes any more, except from a few special friends who come up with all that we need. But those few friends include a network of retired people who feverishly knit wonderful babies' clothes for us. I honestly believe that it helps people in the target country feel more connected to us and less patronised, but I also think it's very important that we're saying to people here – who don't have money to give and won't ever want to travel with us – that they can, nevertheless, make a huge difference in other people's lives.

Have you ever had any hassle out there?

Hah! Well, if you count being shot at, being in a town being shelled, standing on a landmine, being arrested, and having meetings in darkened rooms with arch-capitalists who're trying to persuade me that the Serbs are all really Ku Klux Klan by means of proving it to me by showing me the axe, with blood still on it, then yes we've had hassle!

Mostly it comes from jobsworth or worse, corrupt, customs officers, although there were some hairy moments in the Albanian mountains too. On the whole it's not politically motivated, just theft-related.

Approximately how many people have been involved with traveling to Kosova, Ukraine etc?

Enormous numbers. We've had a convoy with 38 vehicles! But that's not the bulk of people – I also have to count the youth group and other volunteers at the far end and also all those who come along to benefit gigs and stuff here. But it's a hard core of maybe 20 in Ukraine and maybe 10 here in the UK, and sadly pretty much just me, with a music producer called Ting who's working on music equipment for the kids in Ukraine, and the pensioners who knit, still working in Brighton.

How do you react to suggestions that effectively you were aiding the U.S. propaganda effort, which allowed them to present the war against Milosevic as a "humanitarian" one?

Even if aid is that "sticking plaster", I believe in helping to alleviate the suffering of real people, and can't be callous enough to give time to the thought that they'd be better off in the long term without aid – after all, lots of them would be dead or at least miserable by then.

As for the propaganda element – what happened was hugely influenced by spin and jingoism. You could have got rid of Milosevic (the clear objective) with NATO ground troops in a few days with very little loss of life, instead of the gratuitous bombing which devastated the lives of lots of totally innocent Serbian people – and their economy. That just looked better in the right-wing press, seemed more palatable to Western soldier's parents, and so on. It also left industrial plants wide open for U.S. "investment". That's a nightmare for the local people now because they're grateful for the jobs, but under no illusions about where the profits are flying back to.

Maybe we, the aid teams, helped in that, but it was much bigger than us, and didn't need us to justify it! I think we did more good than harm so the accusation doesn't worry me, it just makes me want to take the people suggesting it, and show them the realities on the ground.

Why small scale autonomous aid? Why not support the more mainstream organisations operating in the region?

Fundamentally because of scale – we carried on in that style because we got to work directly with real people and heard the truth, not the organisational propaganda. We also built up much, much more trust with the people we were helping because when they finally understood we were volunteers, they realised they could be much more honest with us. We did in fact contact lots of the big agencies like the Red Cross. In the early days they misunderstood us and just asked us to send them money we'd raised. We eventually demonstrated that we had more to offer. At one point Oxfam were giving out our number to people volunteering in Brighton. And several times we delivered our aid to the International Medical Corps who were delighted, especially at how quickly we were able to bypass political considerations because we didn't have huge vested interests in government funding to protect.

What do you think is important about International Solidarity?

The world will be a better place if we all know each other!

Links: *www.aidconvoy.net*

Kosovan kids proudly show off an assault rifle they recently found. They were also finding bodies – they're spared no details of ethnic cleansing.

Busmans Holidays III

WEST PAPUA

from Issue 377, 18th October 2002

S-Pacific Target

The people of Bougainville are attempting to sue British mining giant Rio Tinto over the genocide and environmental devastation that were a regular part of Rio's 25 years of operations on the small South Pacific island. The lawsuit seeks compensation for every person who suffered during the nearly three decades of mining that went on at the giant, now-defunct Panguna copper mine located smack in the middle of Bougainville.

Bougainville is only a small island, but it's one that has been under siege since Papua New Guinea (PNG) took control of it from Australia in 1975. Even before this, CRA, an Australian subsidiary of Rio Tinto, had forced its way onto the island to build the Panguna mine. 220 hectares of rainforest were destroyed to build Panguna, and after 20 years, the mine had grown to a huge crater half a kilometre deep and nearly 7 km in circumference, creating over a billion tonnes of waste. This waste was dumped in the Jaba River Valley, creating a wall hundreds of metres high and turning one of the island's biggest river systems fluorescent blue.

By 1988, the islanders had started to fight back, successfully closing the mine. The PNG government, which relied on the mining for 45% of its export earnings, responded swiftly and violently with Australia's help. But despite ten years of violent oppression, the Bougainville Revolutionary Army managed to keep the mine closed and eventually PNG got out. Bougainville is now in the midst of seeking its independence.

In solidarity with all indigenous peoples of the South Pacific, there was a week of actions from October 5-12 targeting companies and groups involved in ecological and cultural destruction in the region. Rio Tinto was the first to be targeted. Entrances to Anglesay Aluminium, a North Wales subsidiary of Rio Tinto, were blockaded for most of Thursday 10th. A Toyota office in Redhill was paint-bombed, highlighting Toyota's involvement in logging in the South Pacific. On Wednesday, the Indonesian embassy in London was forcibly entered in protest over the country's continued occupation of West Papua and the murder of an estimated 100,000 indigenous people. And last but definitely not least, the New Tribes Mission offices were paid a visit at their UK headquarters in Grimsby. The missionary group has stated that it is their intent to reach and preach to every "dark corner" of the planet. But the people of West Papua have declared missionaries to be one of the 4 biggest threats to free peoples – one of the biggest reasons being that they build airstrips in remote jungles which are eventually used by businessmen, corporations and military personnel. First comes Christianity, then comes Coca Cola.

Sitting On A Gold Mine

West Papua is the western half of the island of New Guinea, located north of Australia. It is home to some 2.5 million people, around 1.3 million of whom are indigenous West Papuans. The country is rich in minerals and resources and has enormous tracts of untouched wilderness. It is also has some of the most diverse bird and marine life in the world. But now West Papua has become another East Timor. The land was integrated in to the Republic of Indonesia against the wishes of the Papuan peoples. Terrible human rights abuses and massive environmental destruction has been taking place since the early 1960s.

In 1969, the Indonesian government, with assistance from the United Nations held a referendum to allow West Papuans to decide whether they wanted to become part of Indonesia, or remain independent. This was referred to as the "Act of Free Choice".

The referendum did not represent the true aspirations of the West Papuan people because less than 1% of a total population of 700,000 were permitted to vote in the referendum. Those who were allowed to vote were threatened with having their tongues cut out if they did not vote in favour of becoming part of Indonesia. Unsurprisingly, they voted unanimously in favour of becoming part of Indonesia. West Papuans refer to the referendum as the "Act of No Choice". Since 1969, the Indonesian military has waged a campaign of terror and violence against the West Papuans, killing, raping and torturing people struggling for basic human rights. West Papuans are killed even for the simple act of raising their national flag, the morning star. The killings are on such a scale as to threaten the very survival of the West Papuan people.

To defend themselves and fight for their basic freedoms, West Papuans have engaged in a campaign of guerilla warfare against the Indonesian military. Its West Papuan name is Organisasi Papua Merdeka (OPM). Every leader of the Free West Papua Movement has been murdered by the Indonesian military.

Indonesia derives vast amounts of money from West Papua through the gold and copper mines that are located there. The largest of these is jointly owned by the US mining giant Freeport and the UK/Australian company Rio Tinto. Every year, the Indonesian military receives around $11 million from the Freeport mine. Other companies operating in West Papua include BHP-Biliton and BP.

Interview with Billy Banjo of Brighton based South Pacific Solidarity.

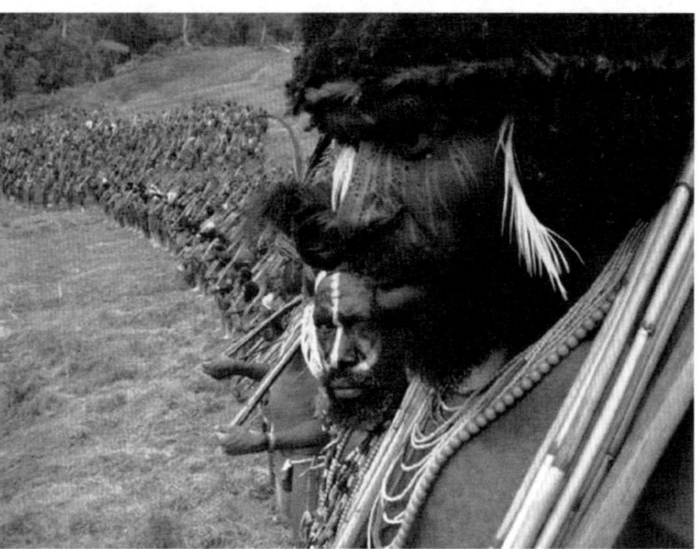

Why Solidarity with the South Pacific?

Throughout the Pacific Rim wild nature and wild culture are under attack. Capitalism is an ongoing genocidal invasion which must be fought. Solidarity South Pacific is concentrating on giving direct aid and taking direct action on behalf of various tribal, anarchist and ecological groups in the South Pacific. Our main areas are in West Papua, which is one of the most culturally and ecologically diverse regions on earth and one which is facing a massive onslaught of industrial destruction. We're also active in the Phillipines with groups there and also in Bougainville as well as Papua New Guinea [the eastern half of the island].

What sort of actions and solidarity has this involved?

Some people from our group have gone to the Phillipines, to PNG and West Papua and obviously the situations on the ground have been quite different so the reasons have been quite different. I went to New Guinea for instance to deliver directly a number of medical supplies which had been requested by resistance organisations in West Papua, and trained them in their use. Other people have gone there with much more detailed mission statements such as linking up different tribes or researching companies which are active over there. Also we're involved in trying to buy land for tribal people in ways that the tribes themselves find difficult.

Specifically what I was doing was going out there, not with equipment for everyday health care but with medicines for trauma. In West Papua we're dealing with a situation where 200-250,000 people have been killed in the last thirty years in the ongoing war of conquest by the Indonesians. Of course their traditional tribal cultures have evolved forms of medicine based on herbalism and mysticism and this has served them well. But of course it wasn't designed to deal with phosphate grenades or machine gun injuries. While I'm critical of western medicine and western technology in general, given they're in a war I felt it was very important to give them specific tools to help them survive the onslaught.

Do you feel that you could use your western perspective to help the people of West Papua ?

To some extent, maybe, but I think – and perhaps this is peculiar to some of the groups that we're working with – these groups are very much on the outside of the capitalist system. They're living in the forest, quite often they're peasants living on the land. It's quite clear what's happening with the onslaught; it's airstrips being built and it's roads being built. Trees being cut down. Police in areas where no police have ever been before. So really in a way their position gives them a clearer insight into our system than many of us here on the inside. Saying that, some of the understandings we have as activists within the capitalist core can be useful in this moment. For example I know that there was a request to send out quite detailed reports of the internal workings of an organisation on the internet. Now the people who requested this really had very little clue what the internet was, i.e. that the information would definitely get through to the people who were trying to hunt and kill them. We refused to do those kind of things, so while I don't think we should be in the position of telling tribal people or the groups we struggle alongside what to do, we also shouldn't be shy of using our knowledge to say "that's a blind alley" or "that's going to be dangerous". To a certain extent that's an important part of our role.

We made sure when we went there to be critical of western technology and that we were saying that this was particularly for war and crisis situations. That's when western medicine really works, it wasn't for general health care and we discouraged its use. So yes, our knowledge of the West is very useful to them in that struggle and you find that many of the groups we're working with and insurgencies around the world in general are from the least technologically developed cultures on Earth, quite often fighting with bows and arrows against helicopter gunships. While personally I've got no knowledge of fighting or weaponry or anything, because I've got some medical experience I can give that.

One of the things that helped these tribes from West Papua to understand what was attacking them was the fact that they sent out one of their number from New Guinea for the first time in a generation to find out, 'What is this "WEST" thing that's attacking us?', 'What are "corporations"?' 'And "God" – is it a good or a bad idea?'

This guy he lived in the West, he lived in Britain for a while and his understanding was crucial to the success or otherwise of their struggle. He clearly articulated to them in their own language when he returned that it was governments, corporations, religious and development organisations that were their enemies and trying to either destroy them or incorporate them into the system. His position as somebody who lived half way between those societies was very useful in illustrating to them what was going on.

Would you say that you were following an agenda provided by these groups?

Myself and our group all come out of the *Earth First!* scene in Britain, which fundamentally is about defending wild cultures and wild peoples from the onslaught of industrialism. To a certain extent in America where Earth First! started, many of the campaigns were inspired by native American resistance. While those struggles continue there are no Red Clouds today. The Wild West has moved to New Guinea. If you go to New Guinea now there are mining corporations, there are crazy missionaries, there's alcohol being used to disrupt tribal cultures, there are massacres and all the things that were seen in the Wild West in the 1850s, happening now in 2004. So to a certain extent our agenda is quite clear and set by the trajectory of our society. Of course it's up to us and we chose which groups to support and once we'd chosen them we made sure we carried out solidarity work which they requested..

What about the direct action taken against the missionary organisation?

In general you won't find many people who like missionaries – most people think that they belongs to the past. These evangelical Christian sects are literally wiping out cultures and massacring people and are at the forefront of "civilisation". When we started working with some of these tribal organisations they said that the first people they meet are people who get their tribes to build the airstrips and once the airstrips are built the soldiers come in and then the government and then the corporations. The church organisations are always telling people to be passive, to not resist. The missionaries are really the beginning of this process of destruction. There are huge networks of missionaries and they're very well organised.

Because of that people in the UK decided to take action against New Tribes Mission, a Christian sect running "Project 2020", which is an attempt to put a church in every currently uncontacted tribal village on earth. They are literally flying aircraft over primal rainforest all over the planet to try and find these last people and bring them the word of Jesus Christ, on the basis that once they've done this to everyone on earth then Judgement Day will come. These people are fucking lunatics, but they're lunatics who work carefully with corporations and have been publicly linked to the CIA. One action involved about fifty or sixty people going into the headquarters of the New Tribes Mission and removing lots of important information and money, and damaging equipment. A device was left which flooded out the place and trashed it later in the day. As far as I know this was the first action which took place in the capitalist core against missionaries and it was done as a result of a request from tribal peoples in New Guinea.

Interestingly after that, people from our group were in the Highlands of the Philippines dealing with another tribe, and when they heard about this action against New Tribes Mission, they were really happy about it as they'd been dealing with these fuckers for years; so that was definitely an action taken as a result of leadership from those communities in the struggle.

If the most important thing is to create revolution in your own homeland then why maintain contact with these groups?

Sandline International, a mercenary company based in London, were planning to entirely incinerate the Bougainville Revolutionary Army in Papua New Guinea, one of the most inspiring ecological revolutions that's happened. They were planning it from plush offices in Kings Rd and Bougainvilleans were literally waiting in the forest to die. But you've really got to look at it through the eyes of that person in the jungle in Bougainville: If they could jump ten thousand miles from the forest to Kings Road where these mercenaries are based, what would they do? And if we're inspired by these people, if we feel linked to them in some way in struggle, then in these moments of crisis we have an obligation to carry out action against these people here. What that action is; well it depends on the situation. I think this is an obligation. Not to do it, not to participate in solidarity and resistance in those situations is really just a reflection of our own very limited privilege and the remarkable lack of civil war here in Britain.

What about prisoner solidarity?

We're very involved in prisoner solidarity with these groups, one of the few ways we can have a significant impact on these movements. Two prisoners illustrate this. Raoul Zapata who was a forest official was in jail for shooting dead – in self defence – a mayor, who was involved in illegal logging. This guy was an ecological prisoner. He had very little support, and his wife was hundreds of miles away from the prison he was in and could hardly visit him. A fairly small amount of money raised here meant that at the very least his wife could go to see him. Things got better than that, there were a load of letters from Britain to the government and that apparently was the "swing" factor which meant that he was released from jail without charge. So our position in the West means that while we might be seen as scum by the elite here in Britain, in the third world there's an inverted racism in the bureaucratic systems, and there's a perception that these people must have some level of power, at least more so than the guy who's living two doors down the street from the prison.

We think that activity in Britain and in Europe is one of the main reasons why one particular guy is still alive. Benny Wenda, who was a leader of an organisation called DeMakk, had been jailed for organising pro-independence, anti-logging activities. He was kept in a cell which was literally a toilet, manacled and blindfolded for days. He was expecting to be executed in prison in an unofficial and brutal way. He wasn't really eating very much because previous prisoners from the organisation had died after being poisoned by the warders. So we sent money so that people could bring food into the prison. We organised lots of people to write and ring and harass the prison. As a result of that he was moved from that small cell in solitary confinement to the general prison population. Once he was moved there the prison population conspired to have a riot purposely so that he could escape. He made it over the fence into the forest and across to PNG, where we had contacts for him and arranged his flight and some documentation to get him to Britain to claim refugee status. So I think that's a very good example of how a relatively small amount of work by a dozen or so people can result in the saving of a life.

When Benny was in jail we did a picket outside the Indonesian embassy about him. We later did another picket but by that time we had Benny with us instead of a photo of him behind bars. So Solidarity can have a real effect."

Solidarity with the South Pacific: www.eco-action.org/ssp/

For more Bougainville history, check out the excellent film **"The Coconut War".**

Busmans Holidays IV

PALESTINE

International Solidarity Movement (ISM)

Issue 349, 5th April 2002
HOLY SHIT! IT'S YER FAITHFUL

STATE OF TERROR

***"History is repeating itself...This is fascism, how they [the Israeli soldiers] are dealing with people, detaining them in big schools and interrogating each one, writing numbers on them...people are terrified. The Israeli soldiers are shooting everything. Life here has totally stopped; it's dead. This is terrorism against civilians. It is organised terrorism by the state...this is an organised war against a whole people who have no weapons to resist tanks, and helicopters and F16s."* - Ashraf, a Palestinian imprisoned in his home in Ramallah.**

It's Monday in Beit Jala, a small town near Bethlehem and 150 people from the International Solidarity Movement and dozens of Palestinians are marching peacefully in the deserted streets. They are attempting to visit families besieged in their homes, before Israeli tanks block their path. Two of the marchers start to move towards the tanks with their hands up in order to negotiate, but soldiers open fire at both the crowd and the reporters that are there. Eight people are injured, one seriously.

Other activists are holed up with Yasser Arafat in his headquarters. Mario Lill from Brazil's Landless Workers' Movement (MST) is one of those who are acting as a human shield and has become a sort of war correspondent broadcasting live to Brazil. Others such as anti-globalisation French farmer Jose Bove were arrested in the compound by Israeli troops.

Wednesday and two thousand people including internationals, Israeli and Arab civilians gather at a checkpoint near Ramallah trying to get humanitarian aid delivered to the besieged town. Soldiers fire tear gas and baton charge people. One of the protestors was Yehudith Harel. "Two Israeli faces surfaced today. One is the decent and humane face of the Israeli Anti-war movement – an alliance of Israeli citizens – Jews and Arabs, adamant to struggle together for Justice for the two peoples. The second is the ugly and brutal face of the Occupation mentality and practices threatening to crush us."

CASUALTIES

People from around the world have been volunteering in the occupied territories of the West Bank for over a year. Invited by Palestinian activists, these international supporters live and work in solidarity with them – a similar call out to the one made by the Zapatistas in Chiapas, Mexico.

People from abroad can often get away with a lot more when protesting, partly because they have the eyes of the international press on them – until Monday that was, when live ammunition was fired at the international observers for the first time.

As for the Palestinians, even the doctors, nurses and paramedics are being used by the Israeli army as human shields or forced to strip and sit on their knees at gunpoint in the streets. Israeli forces have stopped ambulances delivering aid or picking up the wounded and are detaining the Palestinian Red Crescent society and aid workers. 120 Palestinian paramedics have been killed in the last 18 months.

As Israeli tanks roll in to Palestinian settlements, they destroy telephone lines and cut electricity and water supplies. All men between the ages of 16 and 50 are rounded up. Some homes are destroyed, others have their windows blown out and walls dynamited as soldiers move from home to home. Soldiers occupy other homes forcing the residents to live together in a single room, with little or no access to telephone lines, news coverage or even food and water.

An entire civilian population is being openly terrorised after over 50 years of occupation by the Israeli State.

Michael Ben-Yair, former Israel attorney general said, *"The Intifada is the Palestinian people's war of national liberation. We enthusiastically chose to become a colonist society, ignoring international treaties, expropriating lands, transferring settlers from Israel to the occupied territories, engaging in theft and finding justification for all these activities...we established an apartheid regime."*

Lev Grinberg (Director of the Humphrey Institute for Social Research at Ben Gurion University) sums up the situation: *"Suicide bombs killing innocent citizens must be unequivocally condemned; they are immoral acts, and their perpetrators should be sent to jail. But they cannot be compared to State terrorism carried out by the Israeli Government. The former are individual acts of despair of a people that sees no future, vastly ignored by an unfair and distorted international public opinion. The latter are cold and "rational" decisions of a State and a military apparatus of occupation, well equipped, financed and backed by the only superpower in the world."*

"The Palestinian non-violent movement today faces an unprecedented situation, a level of violence that is unimaginable. The Israelis don't see it. I want to show you a day of siege in Jenin, basically a "non-news" item, where tanks roll around, shooting in the streets to announce curfew as people run in fear. This happens every single day and it's not news because most journalists don't leave Jerusalem except occasionally to go to Ramallah or Bethelehem. In an environment like this people won't join a non-violent movement. That's why we need Internationals. We need people to join, to bring the attention of the international community to the situation."- Neta Golan - Israeli peace activist

"You are all invited to Palestine. When they see Internationals who have come, Palestinians feel hope, that others have come to feel their hardship. Hope is very important for a people who feel their pain ignored, their voice unheard, their land taken away every day."- George Rishnawi - Palestinian peace activist - 20 November 2002

Rafah, Gaza, Palestine –March 2003

A house pockmarked with bullet holes stands at the end of a street looking out over a rubble-strewn waste land (see pic, right). An Israeli army watchtower stares back. For months the Israeli Occupation Forces have tried to drive this family from their home, terrorizing them with continual gunfire until they have abandoned the front of the house. Bullet holes through the kitchen at head height bear witness to how the inhabitants could be killed with impunity at any time. Then signs are hung from the roof by international volunteers announcing in Hebrew & English, "Don't shoot! Internationals and children live here." The firing continues nightly but is no longer directed at the house. For one family the nightmare of occupation has been eased.

From the point of view of an anti-capitalist, Israel/Palestine can seem problematic. It doesn't immediately seem to fit into neat ideological box. For a start, in its current form the conflict is being waged for a Palestinian state, surely an anathema to those of us who long for a world without borders.

Why support a nationalist struggle which might create an Islamic state?

The fact is that the Palestinian people have long been the grist in the mill of the capitalist world order. Since Israel's establishment in 1948, the Arab population has continued to lose its rights, its land and its access to resources. Israel is the main U.S. strategic partner in the Middle East, supported to the tune of $4 billion a year – despite having a population of only six million – and has one of the world's most sophisticated militaries. The Israeli state is currently building the "apartheid"

16th March 2003: ISM volunteer Rachel Corrie uses NVDA tactics to block armoured Israeli bulldozers from destroying Palestinian homes in Rafah, Gaza. Within an hour of this photo being taken, she was killed by one

wall around the Occupied Territories: a nine metre high barrier which snakes through what remains of Palestinian land, dividing communities, cutting off children from school, workers from employment and farmers from their land. The Occupation has been likened to a cross between ethnic cleansing and the construction of a giant prison camp.

International Solidarity Movement (ISM)

It is the very fact that this conflict is so lop-sided that opens up the space for Non Violent Direct Action in a warzone; in the ISM's own words "a movement of Palestinian and International activists working to raise awareness of the struggle for Palestinian freedom and an end to Israeli occupation, utilizing non-violent, direct-action methods of resistance to confront and challenge illegal Israeli occupation forces and policies". Crucially the ISM is Palestinian led, and actions are undertaken according to what the local population feel is most likely to aid their resistance. Also while the ISM itself is non-violent it supports the right of Palestinians to resist the occupation.

The first ISM campaigns took place in 2001. Foreign civilians, many from Britain, answered the call to action and took part in witnessing and protesting the brutality of occupation and the injustices perpetrated by the Israeli occupation forces against Palestinian civilians. These activists then returned to their home countries to report on their activities and on what they witnessed. These campaigns focused on key towns and villages in Occupied Palestine in which non-violent resistance is active, and included solidarity visits to villages that had recently been hard-hit by Israeli forces using tanks, helicopters and F-16s.

The third ISM campaign was scheduled to start on March 29th, 2002. That week, however, Israeli forces stormed into each Palestinian city in the West Bank (with the exception of Jericho), imposing weeks of curfew and full military occupation. International activists continued to arrive and by the end of April hundreds of foreign civilians had come to the Palestinian Territories to help with the delivery of food, accompaniment of ambulances and medical personnel, and to act as human shields in cities, towns and refugee camps. ISM activists were the first to start documenting the human rights abuses perpetrated against Palestinians though interviews and documentation of destruction.

International activists were present when the Israeli Occupation Forces (IOF) besieged the Church of the Nativity in April 2002. Four Brits were among those who forced their way through IOF cordons. Alistair Hillman, who was arrested and deported after the action said *"Our presence in the church eased the situation. Obviously the delivery of food, medical aid and cigarettes was appreciated. It was clear that the morale of the Palestinians was improved by our presence. We were able to use the media interest generated to draw attention to the plight of those inside and counteract the IOF claims about the siege."*

ISM work continued with a permanent presence in Palestine as volunteers engaged in ambulance accompaniment, dealing with Israeli soldiers at checkpoints, clearing roadblocks and all the time acting as "human shields", putting their bodies in between Palestinians and IOF violence. Help was given with harvesting olives from groves which had been there for hundreds of years but were now under constant threat from violent Israeli settlers. Volunteers stayed in houses threatened with demolition (often the family homes of suicide bombers), which were scheduled for demolition as a form of collective punishment, contrary to the Geneva Convention. Throughout all of this activists dealt with intimidation, tear gas, arrest and shootings from the Israeli military.

During March-April 2003, within a five week period (which were also the first weeks of the invasion of Iraq), one international activist Rachel Corrie was murdered by an Israeli military bulldozer, another Tom Hurndall was shot and later died in an irreversible coma and a third, Brian Avery was shot in the face. A Channel 4 journalist, James Millar, was also gunned down in Rafah. The Israeli state had seized the opportunity of the smokescreen offered by the invasion of Iraq to eliminate a troublesome thorn in their side. This was the moment when the ISM finally gained the full attention of the world's media. This was the headline grabbing stuff that to a certain extent the movement existed for, to attract attention to and explain the plight of the Palestinians, to give an insight into a situation so horrific that suicide bombing seems a valid response. On the day that Rachel was killed so were another nine Palestinians in the Gaza strip, a routine escalation in the death toll. After the shootings of Tom Hurndall and James Millar it became clear that the IOF intended to drive out all international witnesses from Gaza. In the West Bank there was a wave of arrests and deportations against internationals.

The ISM has not bowed to the pressure, there are still Internationals engaged in work in the Occupied territories, witnessing, recording and broadcasting unwelcome truths. New allies have been found as many Israelis have been moved to take action against the building of the apartheid wall and increasing numbers refuse to serve in the Occupied Territories. Israeli activists have been shot by the IOF for taking action against the Wall, raising the question of what purpose it serves.

The war being conducted against the Palestinians is not just one of rocket fire and house demolitions, helicopter gunships and midnight incursions. It is a psychological war where the aim is to wear the population down through unemployment, poverty, destruction of sewage and water infrastructure and the squeezing out of communities from land they have inhabited for generations. Effective solidarity can be as simple as actually just being there:

"As Internationals, we come as spanners in the corpse machine. We come as a small chance to free up new possibilities, for resistance and imaginings of a new reality – whatever that will finally be. It means walking with people, listening to them, absorbing their stories and their pain, then speaking it out to death-numbed Western audiences . It means accompaniment, witnessing atrocity – often with no powers to stop it – staying with the kids in the street when they're fighting back and dying. All that camera grabbing stuff – the placing of your body between soldiers, guns and tank fire – that's minor compared to the living with, daily non-spectacular emotional support solidarity is all about" - British activist Ewa Jasciewicz.

* To find out about more about the **International Solidarity Movement** see www.palsolidarity.org

Bypass the corporate media

www.jerusalem.indymedia.org - www.zmag.org - www.palestinechronicle.com - www.alternet.org - www.electronicintifada.org - www.rafahkid.net

Rafah, Gaza, March 2003 – ISM activists place their bodies in the way of Israeli army destruction

Busmans Holidays V

IRAQ

International solidarity in Iraq was going on in the years before the invasion, including the British group 'Voices In The Wilderness' campaigning around the UN sanctions and going on missions to the country. These sanctions, which had been imposed since the end of the first Gulf War in 1991, were estimated to have killed up to 1.5 million by limiting the country's access to anything deemed to have potential military 'dual use' – which included everything from pencils to medical equipment, water purifying equipment etc. This sent health, education, energy and sanitation services in Iraq back to the dark ages. The sanctions were a way of holding Iraq in check before the 'regime change' plan was instigated in 2003.

In the lead up to the invasion – and during the US-led occupation since – some very brave and together activists have gone to Iraq to help on the ground, to observe, and to broadcast information back to the rest of the world. Jo Wilding has made several trips to Iraq, and in the past year her regular communiqués from the country have reached audiences in the millions over the internet.

Interview with Jo Wilding February 2004

Jo Wilding, a 29 year old Bristol based activist has gone to Iraq and undertaken the multiple role of journalist, peace activist and stilt walker! Her involvement with Iraq began with Voices in the Wilderness, travelling in 2001 to Iraq to campaign against the UN economic sanctions. She returned in February 2003 and stayed for the month before the war and the first eleven days of the Coalition assault. Her weblog provided an up to the minute account of the true situation in Baghdad under the intense bombardment. She was later expelled from the country by the Iraqi foreign ministry. She returned for six months between November 2003 and May 2004 and was involved in several projects including the Circus to Iraq. Her visit culminated with a dramatic intervention in Falluja, where during intense fighting, she and others braved sniper fire to accompany ambulances and negotiate with Occupation forces.

You travelled around Iraq with circus performers. Some (well, Richard Littlejohn, the arsehole right-wing columnist in the Sun) might say that taking balloons and face paint into a warzone is trivialising the issues involved. What's your response?

Some might say that because they are ill-informed and have no imagination. The kids – and the adults – who are caught up in a war zone are traumatised, distressed, depressed. As well as all the physical reconstruction that has to happen here, there is a huge need for psychological reconstruction.

As an example, there are thousands of people who have fled Falluja and the kids living there have been terrorised by bombing, ripped out of their homes and shifted from place to place, ending up in a crowded, dusty place where the toilets are still being built and there's no school, no play things and no activities to take their minds off what they're going through. We turned up and spent a couple of hours playing with them, using bubbles, balloons and parachute games, and it transformed them. They had fun for a couple of hours, they thought about something other than bombs.

At one of the places we worked in Nasariya, the teacher told us that before our show, when they gave the kids drawing materials, they always drew planes dropping bombs, tanks, explosions. After the show they started drawing clowns and jugglers. It helps to displace those violent and frightening images as the most vivid memory. Another place in the south, one of the women who worked there said it was the first time she'd seen the girls smile since the war. She said it made her think there was still hope. In that way it's powerful and healing for the adults as well as the kids, especially in the squatter camps where people are living in really miserable conditions.

The thing that trivialises a war is the ignorant reporting propagated by some of the media, the failure to analyse, to criticise, to question, the focus only on political and military issues and not on what

Circus2Iraq entertaining kids at Haifa Palestinian refugee camp.

Guy Smallman

it means to live in that situation. I'm not so arrogant as to say the circus solved problems or changed the world but for sure it made a difference to the people it came into contact with, kids and adults.

Going to play games with those kids doesn't trivialise what they experienced. People are weighed down by what they've gone through and play is an essential part of the healing process. The cynicism that says it's trivial is part of the problem – and that criticism has never come from any of the Iraqis that we've worked with.

You were in Palestine with the ISM. Did you find that your experiences there were helpful with your activities in Iraq?

My time in Palestine was brief: I was only there a day before being arrested in Bethlehem and jailed and deported, so I didn't experience much about organising or working in an international setting, although being on hunger strike was an intense experience that I think taught me quite a lot.

Having said that, when we talked about going into Falluja and I was deciding whether or not to go, I thought about the action at the Church of the Nativity and the fact that, when that action was talked about, I thought it was impossible. I thought there was no way we were going to get food and people into the church without being shot, never mind arrested. So I suppose the big thing I learnt from Palestine was that an outrageously cheeky non-violent action even in a heavily armed siege, can work and that, as disgraceful as it is, having a white face can protect you where just being human ought to be enough.

I think the big similarity is that we were using the racism of the occupying forces to protect the people being occupied, in that, in both cases, it hasn't been seen as a problem to kill Palestinians/ Iraqis, but to kill a foreigner is a much bigger issue. I think it's appalling that an attitude like that can exist, that one life is worth more than another, but it definitely helped in Falluja to be able to shout to the Marines that we were foreigners.

At the checkpoints we were able to argue for the people to be let through and I think part of that is facilitation of communication between the troops and the locals and another part is that people are less inclined to behave outrageously when they know they're being watched.

Are there any other conflicts where you think it might be possible to intervene this way?

After I wrote about what we did in Falluja I got quite a few emails from people wanting to come and do the same sort of thing, including several US military vets. A small group from the US contacted us for advice and then came over and went into Najaf. I think there is interest in doing this kind of activism and there is a use and a need for it over here.

Wherever there are non-combatants caught up or trapped in a fight between two sides, and where a white face or a foreign passport is some kind of protection, there is potential for this intervention. Groups like Christian Peacemaker Team have been doing it for a long time, negotiating or observing at checkpoints and providing advocacy within the country for example.

I read an article by Amy Goodman, who runs Democracy Now, a TV/radio station in the US, about being in East Timor during the Indonesian occupation. She and a colleague went on a demonstration with the East Timorese people, marching at the front in the hope of giving some protection. They were beaten to the ground and the troops opened fire on the marchers. The troops first asked if they were Australian, then found out they were from the US. They'd killed some Australians a little while before. It really depends on being from a country that "matters" enough.

I think there's already a lot of it happening as well in places like Chiapas where international observers spend time in the Zapatista communities. It could be more widespread though. I think that there also needs to be a focus on situations where the conflict hasn't yet erupted: what could we have done to protect civilians in Saddam-era Iraq? What could we do now for the Kurds in Turkey, for the Iranians? Could we have done this kind of work in Northern Island when our country's troops were brutalising people at checkpoints?

How can you make journalism tie in with activism?

Amy Goodman is a journalist, but I think sometimes we blur the boundaries between activism and journalism, because knowing that their actions will be reported can moderate the behaviour of the troops, so the journalist is proactive in the situation, and because as activists part of what most of us do is to spread the stories about what's happening.

Certainly here, among those of us who live outside the media bureaux, CPA and fortresses, there is a crossover. The first group of us that went to Falluja consisted of some who'd call themselves journalists, some who'd call themselves activists, some who'd say they were both or neither, but the ambulance crew consisted of me, a film maker and a translator.

What sort of reaction have you had from the occupation forces? Does speaking the same language as the occupying forces make your work easier?

The US soldiers just try to flirt. They often assume that you support them because you're a foreigner. At the checkpoints, because they were so pleased to meet English speakers, especially women, some of them were getting a bit careless with what they said and started to boast about how many people they'd killed in Falluja and say they didn't want to let people out of the town because it would be easier to "kill them all in there."

As well, though, I know that the life of a foreign activist doesn't mean that much, that the military commanders would only say we shouldn't have been where we were.

Are there any Iraqi groups who are interested in developing ideas of non-violent resistance to the Occupation?

There has been some industrial action but part of the problem is that there are vastly more unemployed people than jobs. There are a few new independent trade unions but not many and the protection for trade unions, though it unambiguously exists in international law, seems a bit flimsy to people clinging to jobs in a country with no effective court system.

Beyond that, the main form of protest is marching. People talk about a massive campaign of non-cooperation but again the problem comes back to jobs. The majority of people with jobs are essentially government employees so they are all, to some extent, working for the Americans.

It's very hard to talk about solidarity with most Iraqis, even on a demonstration. They have given massive support to the people fleeing Falluja, offering food, money, space in their own houses, and so on, but this is seen as an act of charity. The concept of standing by someone is difficult for a lot of people because for decades, that was likely to get you killed.

What ultimately do you want to achieve with your solidarity work?

Ultimately? World peace and non-violent social revolution.

No, seriously, I came here during the sanctions and before the war to try and make visible what was happening to people in Iraq and to try and find out what people outside Iraq can do to help. I came back here in November partly for the same thing and also to facilitate practical solidarity projects such as links between university students in the UK and Iraq so the students in the UK can help rehabilitate the libraries and labs and the two groups can talk about the issues in all of this.

I don't know whether I'd call what I do 'extreme'. Being in Baghdad, knowing that all

Guy Smallman

Guy Smallman

the killing of civilians, shooting of ambulances, closing of roads and so on was going on in Falluja, a few kilometres up the road, seeing and hearing the injuries and the stories of the refugees and the doctors who'd been working there, I don't know what else I could do besides go there, do what I could to help and then tell as many people as I could what I saw there. The alternative was to hide out in the apartment in Baghdad and fret about the possibility of getting kidnapped.

I suppose it's the same thing that motivates me to train as a lawyer, to use whatever skills and advantages I have to try and give people practical support, to fight for justice in an unjust system, that values the testimony of a couple of white foreigners more than the same story coming from thousands of Iraqis, that says the shooting of an Iraqi doctor is a lesser event than that of a foreigner. What else could I do?

Is there any way that you'd ever consider that your work was done? What would make you stop?

Since I started doing all this, and doing talks around the country, I've met people who were active in the Philippines in the 1950s, people who were part of the civil rights movement, people who have been working for a lifetime on peace and social justice and have never given up. I can't imagine the point in my lifetime when there will be no injustices that need to be fought.

I suppose my ideal would be for there to be a massive global movement for social justice, built on international solidarity, so that when people anywhere were being abused, people everywhere would know about it, would refuse to tolerate it and would prevent it and that's why it's important to try and empower people, to let people know that whatever skills they have, they can take action, they can do something about the things that piss them off.

But probably the thing that would make me stop is tiredness."

Links

www.wildfirejo.org.uk
www.circus2iraq.org

Guy Smallman

Pic: Simon Chapman

March 22nd 2003 – a few days after beginning of the invasion of Iraq – a spectrum of protesters descend on the Fairford airbase in Gloucestershire. It's from here that US Air Force B52s continually launch on bombing sorties to Iraq.

BOMBS AWAY

Direct Action And The Anti-War Movement

As was reported at the time, the movement against the second Gulf War produced some of the biggest mass marches in history. On 15th February 2003 about 20,000,000 people marched in towns and cities around the world. But there were other aspects of the movement that went almost unacknowledged – individual acts of refusal and sabotage, direct actions, illegal protests, and mass disobedience.

Before the dust had settled after the 9/11 attacks, it was already obvious to some that the Neo-Conservatives (the bunch of crazies with the real power behind George W. Bush) were going to take the opportunity to go after what they wanted in Iraq. By autumn 2002 it was obvious to everyone. As the grim reality of what was happening dawned on the world, pockets of resistance began appearing all over the place.

We went on the marches like everyone else, but (like most people) we didn't hold out much hope that marching by itself was going to be effective. Most people involved with SchNEWS thought that the only real hope lay constant and massive acts of disobedience. In the SchNEWS produced for the September 28th anti-war demo in London, Jo Makepeace wrote, "It won't be union leaders or paper sellers or 'organisers' that will stop this war. It will be ordinary, angry, active people – us, you, your neighbours, your mates – taking direct action. Stopping high streets at rush hour. Shutting down government and military buildings. Having sit down protests on marches instead of moving on whenever the police tell us to."

In the months following people took direct action all over the place. There was so much going on that SchNEWS set up a section called War Briefs, where we could report the coolest actions that we heard about, and the callouts for people to get involved with actions and groups. There were also a lot of front pages devoted to the anti-war movement that year, as was the 2003 Annual (Peace de Resistance), which we crammed with all the stuff we hadn't managed to fit in the weekly issues. Looking back over it all, a lot of the most inspiring things that happened seemed to come out of nowhere. Small groups of people taking it upon themselves to throw a spanner in the works where they knew they could make a difference. Kids and teenagers all over the world causing chaos in schools and city centres. When the war started there were spontaneous and angry protests all over the world; cities were closed down, and government and military buildings took a richly-deserved kicking.

We didn't stop the war from happening, but that was always going to be a tall order. This is a fight that will be going on for a long time, and the only real hope that we have of changing things is still direct action. The war is a part of daily life now – resistance needs to be part of daily life as well.

War Briefs

18th October 2002: An anonymous caller to a San Jose, California TV station took credit for a pre-dawn fire at a military recruiting office on Monday. Three military cars were set on fire, and the words "pre-emptive strike" were painted across the front of the office in red lettering.

10th January 2003: Two Scottish train drivers refused to move a freight train carrying ammunition destined for the Glen Douglas base on Scotland's west coast, Europe's largest weapons store. Railway managers had to cancel the Ministry of Defence service after the crewmen, described as "conscientious objectors" by a supporter, said they opposed Tony Blair's threat to attack Iraq.

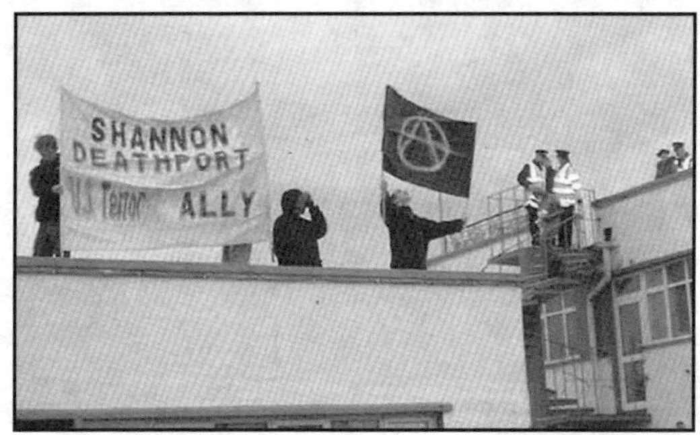

January 18th 2003: A week after a permanent peace camp was established there, around two thousand converged on Shannon Airport in Ireland – where at that stage 7,000 US troops a week were already passing through to the Gulf. This came after 150 protesters had previously torn down the fence and a Hercules plane had been sprayed with anti-war messages. The event began with a march out of the town and, being called by the SWP, was supposed to just involve marching and listening to speeches, but some had other ideas and a group climbed onto the roof of an airport building to make some noise and drop banners, and a portable sound system was wheeled in making the speeches difficult to hear. Later another group broke past police at a gate to enter airport warehouses, getting out without arrest.

Think Global, Act Volkel

Actions at NATO Airbase, Volkel, Netherlands

January 18th: Around 100 break into the airbase for a weapons inspection, entering in small separate efforts. All were arrested, but released later without charge.

9th February: Barbara Smedema breaks into Volkel and smashes three satellite dishes with a sledgehammer, in protest against the war, and the existence of nuclear weapons housed at the airbase. She served two months imprisonment for this, and upon release was surprised by her sister with the gift of a new sledgehammer.

February 6th: Six lock-on to block the entrance of **RAF Lakenheath,** a diversion while others break into the base for a weapons inspection at the largest US Airforce controlled base in Britain.

31st January 2003: On Wednesday a peace activist was arrested at Shannon Airport, Ireland after she was found causing damage to an American military plane parked there. Although she didn't manage to disarm the plane, she did manage to cause 500,000 Euros (£350,000) worth of damage.

14th February 2003: Army reservists who've been receiving their call-up papers during the last few weeks have been **refusing to go in record numbers**. So far one in three have either applied for exemption or have just ignored their call-up papers.

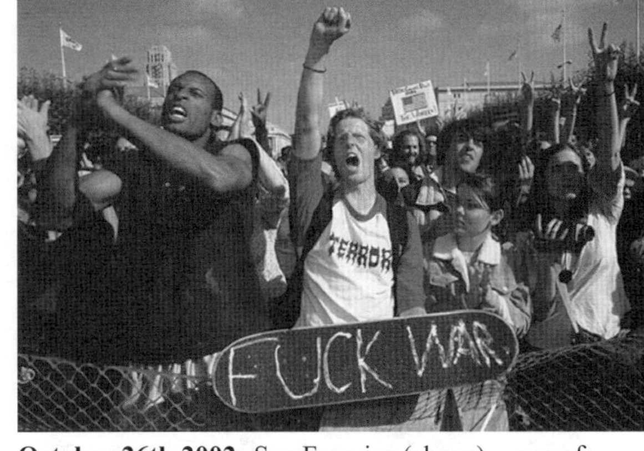

October 26th 2002: San Franciso (above) – one of the countless city-centre marches across the world

Having achieved their objective of drawing attention to the unconstitutional use of **Shannon airport** for US war preparations, the victorious **Shannon Peace Camp** has now been dismantled and in a major victory for them, the US aircraft which used the base have now been moved to Germany.

15th February 2003: As the international anti-war movement gained momentum, a series of international days of mass demonstration organised mostly by lefty groups crescendoed with February 15th which goes down as the biggest ever day of protest in history (pic right – Hyde Park London).

Pic right: Simon Chapman

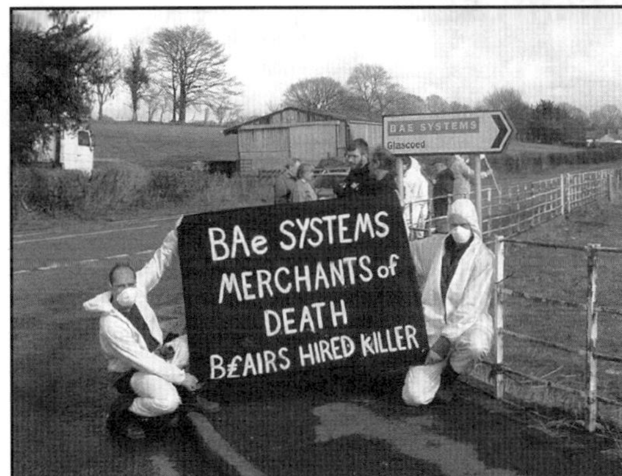

March 1st 2003: **The British Aerospace munitions factory in Glascoed gets a weapons inspection.** Seven climb the fence, with two getting into the building and locking on, while another avoided detection and ran around the complex which makes, amongst other weapons, depleted uranium bombs. When they were evicted, they cut another hole and broke back in, which was cheeky, but then the police got involved and there were arrests. BAe didn't press charges because they didn't want the publicity. This action was organised by Campaign Against Arms Trade www.caat.org.uk

THE "AXIS OF OIL" REGIMES...
VENEZUELA, IRAQ and IRAN
POSE A GRAVE DANGER...

...TO THE
GOD GIVEN RIGHT
OF AMERICA AND
OUR ALLIES TO
DRIVE OUR CARS

RAF Fairford

This airbase in the Cotswolds – which is the biggest bomber base in Europe, and the place where the B52 bombers used to bomb Iraq were based – became a big focus for attempts to physically interfere with the war machine, as well as other more theatrical and symbolic anti-war protests. Here is how SchNEWS covered some of the days of action...

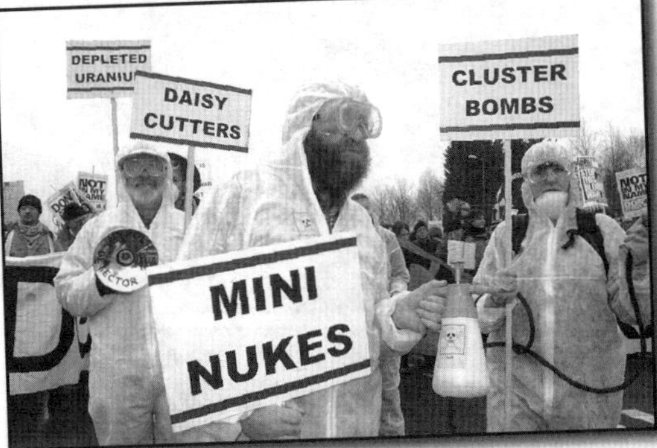

14th December 2002: A cast of 500 people – including the **Gloucestershire Weapons Inspectors** well kitted out with identification equipment – perform a mass citizens' inspection at RAF Fairford Pic: Simon Chapman

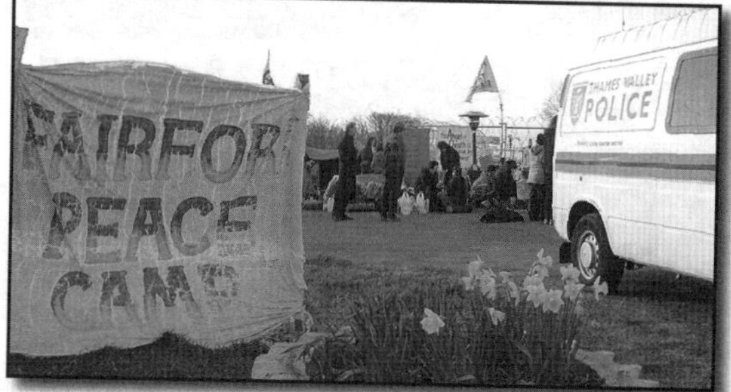

17th February 2003: A peacewatch is set up at Fairford outside Gate 10 to begin monitoring military activity at the base. A permanent camp is established on March the 2nd, the day before the B52 bombers arrive to be based at Fairford for the upcoming war. The camp packed up on the 3rd of May. (Follow the progress in SchNEWS 393, 395, 396)

23rd February 2003: It's a Fairford Cop, Guv! Around 500 people met for a day of direct action at Fairford, a military base in Gloucestershire. After gathering at the main entrance of the base, someone announced that they were weapons inspectors and wanted to inspect the base. An activist told SchNEWS, "We tied ropes to the top of the front gate and started pulling on them and shaking the gate. To everyone's surprise, including the cops, it collapsed on one side and swung open after a few minutes. There was a pause while everyone on the outside watched the horrified expressions on the faces of the police on the other side and then everyone rushed in." While being part of a huge crowd on the streets is an important show of dissent, "direct action allows us to slow down or stop the war machine" as one protestor told SchNEWS, "The best thing was that it was cool to see different types of people working together, protecting each other from being beaten up by police, and fighting back."

It's Sunday morning.

BANG! KNOCK! KNOCK!

Fran! It's 8 o'clock, we're going

Going? (my head hurts...)

Oh yes. We're going to do an independent weapons inspection today.

FAIRFORD is an inoffensive looking town in the Cotswolds which happens to be home to a large air base that sometimes houses American stealth bombers (B2s).

It's one of only 3 forward bases for them outside the USA, so it's likely that in the event of a war with Iraq planes from here will take bombs (possibly nuclear) to the Gulf.

For more info on this see www.cynatech.co.uk/gwi/fairford.htm

Today the area is full of weirdly attired concerned citizens.

We walked through the town, which is tiny, to the base, which is somewhat bigger. Lots of people had brought stuff to decorate the fence with.

We stood around at the gate for a while, then everyone wandered off and the fence magically became more permeable ...

Ooooops

Shall we take the dog for a run dear?

I think so.

Loads of people got in + ran about. For a while it was really anarchic + beautiful.

Have you called for back-up?

Yeah but they're being slow

tee hee

Then we were rounded up + chucked out. Later the police decided to arrest a couple of people in quite a violent way but on the whole it was a really lovely day. More protests are planned at Fairford. See www.gwi.org.uk

FH 10/2/03

26th January 2003: Over 1500 people demonstrate at **RAF Fairford,** fifty of whom manage to get into the base. The day before over 200 had arrived at **RAF St Athans, Wales** for a weapons inspection

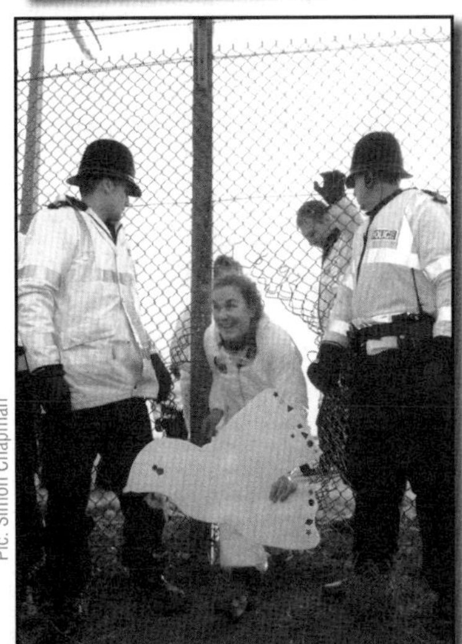

Pic: Simon Chapman

The World's First Ever Sponsored Stop & Search

April 5th 2003: Because everybody around the **Fairford Peace Camp** is getting stopped-and-searched so often by police – sometimes several times a day – they've decided to start getting sponsored for each search, with the money raised going to a selection of charities working in Iraq. Apparently the best way to top up yer earnings is to wear a white boiler suit with padding.

Trainstopping

In the months leading up the war, the US military was busy moving equipment by rail from bases around Europe to ship to Iraq. This called for a bit of... trainstopping

Italy: Trainstopping actions began in Italy on 21st February with hundreds of protesters accosting convoys headed for Camp Darby US military base near Pisa (pic above). The following day direct action against the trains spread to other towns. A train was blocked for hours in Campo di Marte (Padua). There were also successful blockades in Verona, Brescia, Bologna, and Fornovo, all dispersed by police attacks. There were two demos in Pisa, the first in the morning at the military airport, the second in the afternoon, moving from the station to the centre of the town.

On the 23rd the trains were kept stationary due to the 'public disorder situation.'

Antwerp Harbour, Belgium, 16th February: (pic above) 11 peace activists managed to stop a train carrying US military equipment near Antwerp harbour. This train was part of US military transportation towards the Persian Gulf and Turkey, coming from Germany and shipping out of Antwerp. People covered the signal with a cloth and used red lights to signal the driver to halt. With the engine stationary, two people chained themselves to it, while others locked themselves onto the wagons and the military equipment. After 3 hours all 11 were removed and arrested.

Above: Pisa, Italy, February 22nd: 26 convoys of US military equipment were disrupted in Italy.

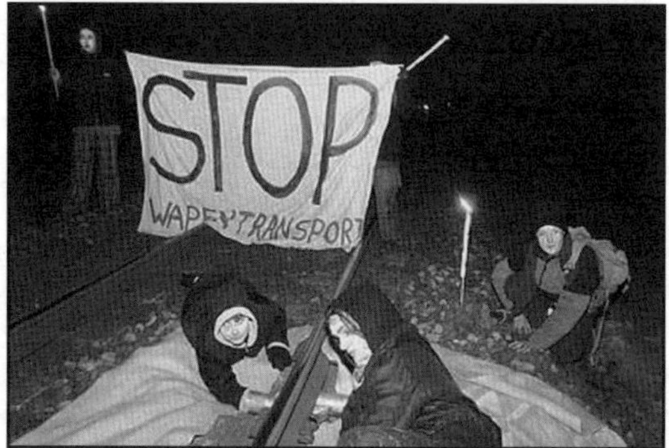

Venlo, Holland April 11th: US military equipment being rail-freighted from German bases to Rotterdam to be shipped to Iraq is halted by people locking onto the track.

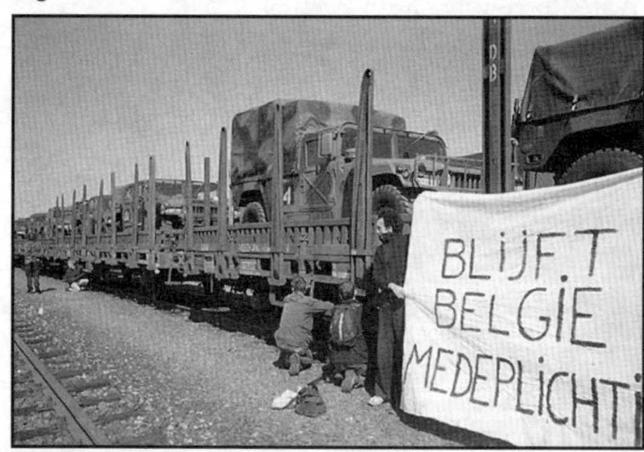

Belgian-German border, 17th April: (pic above) US military equipment being rail-freighted from German bases to Belgian ports gets blockaded for several hours.

Belgium: April 20th, Ostend Airport, being used as a US military transportation node: While fifty disrupt the airport, others climb the fence to get onto the runway.

Bomb stopping – just do it.

(If we did it, you can too...)

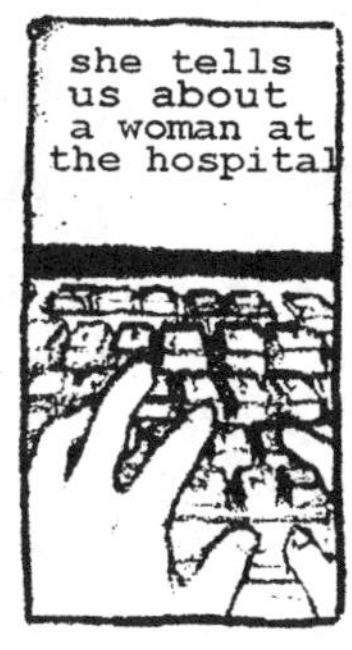

WE WATCH

& WAIT, FOR 6 DAYS

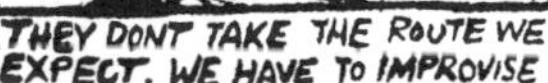

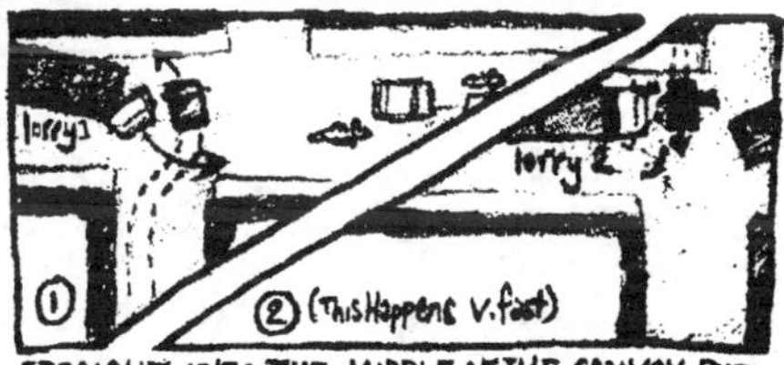

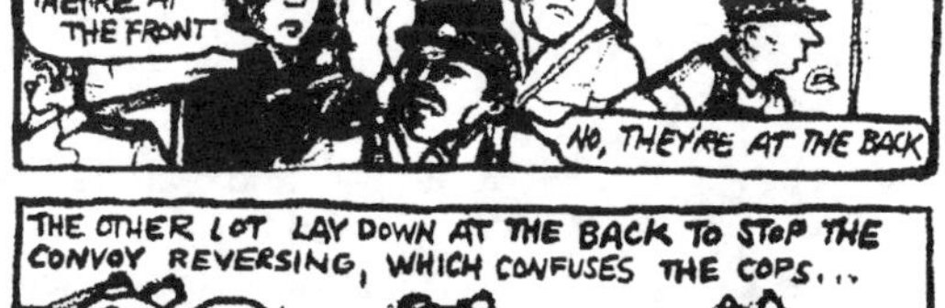

THEY THREATEN TO ARREST US. TAKE OUR DETAILS AND THEN - JUST WALK AWAY

WHICH WAS SURPRISING-

THEY DIDN'T NICK US BECAUSE THEY DON'T WANT PEOPLE TO KNOW IT'S POSSIBLE TO STOP THESE LORRIES. THE CURRENT LEVELS OF BOMBING CAN'T CONTINUE WITHOUT THEM.
WITH MORE OF US WE COULD HAVE STOPPED THE CONVOY.

TO BE CONTINUED...

Cartoon strip: Snook

STOP THE WAR : STOP THE CITY!

MEET 5.30PM : CHURCHILL SQUARE : DAY AFTER WAR IS DECLARED ON IRAQ

BRING POTS AND PANS TO BANG : LETS MAKE SOME NOISE!

PHONE FOR CONFIRMATION
01273 298192
brightonagainstwar@hotmail.com

On the day the invasion begins thousands gather to hear a speech by the statue of Winston Churchill. He obliges the crowd with the line "Success is the ability to go from one failure to another with no loss of enthusiasm." - Winston Churchill

20th March 2003

THIS IS WAR

News that war had started sent a shockwave of protest across the world. In the UK, this felt like the day that people's anger reached its peak. There weren't any licenced demos – people just went out into the streets. We'd all been saying for months that the only real way to confront Tony's war was to bring the whole country to a standstill – this was the closest we came to doing it.

In SchNEWS' hometown it was already kicking off by lunchtime, when hundreds of recently-escaped schoolkids converged at the roundabout in front of the Palace Pier. From there they walked up Grand Parade, the main route into town, and closed the road. They kept it closed all afternoon, despite losing numbers for a bit when some of them ran round the corner to desecrate the American flag hanging outside the American Express building.

Later that afternoon people began gathering outside the shopping centre in the middle of town. When the crowd reached several thousand we moved off, headed by a large samba band. From then the protest stayed mobile into the night, swelling to about 8,000 (if you take the local rag's word for it – we weren't counting.) Outnumbered and unprepared, the police couldn't break up the march, couldn't stop us taking roads, couldn't control the

M32 Motorway occupied, Bristol, 20th March

route, and they couldn't bring in back-up, because all surrounding areas had their own protests to deal with. The march finally stopped at the town hall, which was surrounded, with some people managing to get through police lines and occupy the building. From there several hundred people moved back to the town centre, where the main junction was occupied again, and others moved off through the town, attacking banks and other corporate property.

Similar things were happening all over the country. In Bristol and Glasgow the crowds didn't just shut down the town centres, they also closed motorways. In Lancaster schoolkids shut down the city and occupied the town hall. In Manchester they closed the Hulme bridge, in Rochester they closed the A2. In Cambridge they closed the main road and occupied the Army Recruitment Centre. Edinburgh, Birmingham, Sheffield, Cardiff, Swansea, Leeds, etc., etc., all saw thousands in the streets and drivers turning their engines off for hours. In smaller towns it was a similar picture.

San Francisco, 22nd March 2003

If you want to know about what happened elsewhere in the world that day (in almost obsessive detail), check out *Peace de Resistance*. But a special mention has to go to the residents of San Francisco. The day that war started the whole of San Francisco was shut down for 16 hours. Instead of one mass protest, protesters split into different mobile groups, blocking intersections, occupying buildings, and performing hit-and-run actions on corporate and government targets. One particularly weird group of activists swallowed food dye, went down to the plaza of the Federal Building, took vomit-inducing medicines, and puked red, white and blue. The cops were out-maneuvered and overstretched all day. Many police vehicles were rendered useless by having their windows smashed and tyres slashed. They responded with typical restraint, and arrested about 2,000 people in 24 hours. Don't take our word for it, check out the wicked film about the San Francisco protests, *We Interrupt This Empire…* from www.videoactivism.org

IS WAR MAKING YOU SICK?
FUCK THIS SHIT
IF WAR BEGINS CALL IN SICK!
DON'T GO TO WORK OR SCHOOL
HEAD DOWNTOWN
The morning of the next business day after war begins, mass non-violent direct actions are planned for the downtown area. Meet at Market & Main (Embarcadero BART) at 7:00am, or simply head downtown at any hour. Bring friends, noise, signs, food!

Poster doing the rounds in San Francisco

"Iraqi Oil"

MINORS STRIKE

From Peace de Resistance

March 21st, Westminster Abbey

Perhaps the best thing about the global protests against the War in Iraq was the central role played by schoolchildren. Taking adult activists and headteachers alike by surprise, a pattern was repeated all over the world of kids forming their own groups and sorting out their own actions and protests.

It's hard to say where this wave of schoolkid militancy came from. Some reckon that it's because mobile phones and the internet have given this generation of kids access to new channels of communication that can't be monitored or controlled by adults, allowing them more space to form their own politics and hatch their own plans. Being adults ourselves (well we're trying) SchNEWS doesn't know if that's true or not, but there are two things that are certain: first, whatever the kids were doing, they were definitely doing it for themselves. Even the cops recognised, for the most part, that the schoolkid actions were schoolkid led. Second, in the UK at least, kids have got more than a few things to teach seasoned 'revolutionaries' about 'having it on the streets'. Whilst so-called anti-war unions organised lame rallies outside workplaces, outside working hours, kids sent shockwaves through the education system with a series of illegal student walkouts. In Brighton, on the day the war started, anarchists watched in slack-jawed admiration as GCSE students smashed in the windows of HSBC bank and tore up publicly displayed US flags. Probably not what Tony's cronies had in mind when they added "citizenship" classes to the curriculum last September to combat the "political apathy" of kids today!

There was spontaneous resistance all over the country, without coordination from any one point. One group or another would spring up, and word then passed from school to school, often by email or text messaging.

Kids were already out in force on the February 15th demo in London, making a sizeable presence among the 2 million protestors. Also in February 60 teenagers and students dressed in tiger suits invaded Esso's UK HQ. And this was just the beginning.

On March 5th thousands of children walked out of classrooms nationwide to make their feelings clear. Seven sacks of dung were deposited outside Labour HQ and kids tried to storm Downing Street.

March 19th saw the biggest ever coordinated child demos, with 10,000 kids bolting from classrooms nationwide. Many schools tried to stop them by locking the gates, forcing kids to break out. This was the first truly national protest by children since the 1970s and the media coverage was frenzied, comparing it to the May 68 riots in France which started with schoolkids and university students and almost brought down the government.

While some school heads turned a blind eye, many teachers' unions joined police in condemning this outbreak of freedom. "Treat it as normal truancy and take appropriate action" ordered the draconian secondary heads' association. Several expulsions followed across the country. Kids were given lines: "I will not walk out of school." It didn't stop them.

When the US started bombing on the 20th March, school was out again, with schoolkids playing a major part in the spontaneous protests that brought towns and cities grinding to a halt all over the UK. In Lancaster schoolkids shut down the city for 5 hours and occupied

Hamburg, March 24th – kids visit the US embassy and get hit with water cannons and batons

the town hall; in Brighton the chant of "One two three four Tony Blair is Bush's whore" rang through the streets as kids shredded the stars and stripes hanging outside the American Express building (see SchNEWS 297/8). In Cambridge people as young as 14 were nicked at a sit-down that kept city centre traffic stationary for 6 hours. Glasgow, Bristol, London… the list goes on.

On 24th March police in Bristol decided it was time to find the dangerous and manipulative adult activists behind the continuing under-age unrest, and began questioning onlookers in the city centre where kids had yet again brought traffic to a halt. But the other grown-ups present were as baffled as the cops – the kids were doing it on their own.

Books Not Bombs – Adelaide, March 26th

Anti-war kids in the UK weren't the only ones showing the grown-ups how it's done. Here are some of the global highlights from the playground insurrections that swept the planet:

In Australia 27,000 kids joined a nation wide demonstration called 'Books Not Bombs' on 26th March. Aussie cops proved not to be very child-friendly, with observers saying there was a 'clear attempt to intimidate the kids' with large numbers of mounted police and riot cops. When one kid in Sydney got his first taste of pepper spray his mates fought back and 33 were arrested. Overall 56 kids were nicked on the day, some as young as 11. A day earlier 1,000 angry 12-14 year-olds joined Aboriginals at the entrance of the national parliament in Canberra, and then despite intimidation from the 'Walk Against War Coalition' (!) another 'Books Not Bombs' took place on April the 2nd.

Can someone pass me a chair?
Books Not Bombs, Sydney, March 26th

In Germany it kicked off at a 20,000-strong schoolkid demo in Hamburg on 24th March, when 8,000 kids (according to police) splintered off from the main march and made for the US embassy. The cops (who later claimed that they were pelted with tree branches) then waded in with batons and water cannon, splitting up the group and forcing some onto nearby train tracks and others into a kettle formation. Numerous kids were injured, 36 arrested, and 125 held by police.

In Athens on March 20th a Black Bloc of around 1,000 was joined by unruly schoolkids who helped them 'unrenovate' a recently restored posh hotel, stone the embassies of Italy, Portugal and the UK and set the Ministry of Internal Affairs ablaze with Molotov cocktails. Sadly their plans for the US Embassy were put to a halt by such massive quantities of tear gas that an over-flying pigeon fell out of the sky stone dead!

In Spain there was a series of 'general strikes' by schoolkids and students. The fourth, on March 26th, saw student walkouts in more than 70 towns and cities, with over 1,000,000 kids taking part in protests.

In Bahrain 400 teenagers held a sit-down outside the US embassy, burning US and UK flags.

In Seoul enterprising teenagers eager to occupy the US embassy decided their best bet was to dress up in business suits and pretend they were going in for a meeting – unfortunately the cops thought they were a bit too young and innocent looking to be bona fide fat cats and an unseemly scuffle ensued.

Back in the UK a lot of schools are determined that kids should pay a heavy price for missing the point of the 'political participation' module in Citizenship class. An estimated 30–40 have been suspended or expelled, with one girl from Essex being excluded for 30 days for organising demos even though she was due to sit her GCSEs. She refused to accept her punishment and took the school to high court where the judge ruled in her favour, but not before telling her she was a 'very silly girl'!

Old Steine, Brighton, March 20th. For some it's their third day on strike against the war

SHAKY FOUNDATIONS

***"If GATS gets the green light Europe can kiss goodbye its public health services"* - Susan George, economist.**

After bombing Iraq it's back to bread and butter issues for Neo Labour – flogging off our public services to the lowest bidder.

The new Foundation Hospitals will give private companies a surgical strike on our health service. They will also be able to pull out of nationally agreed pay and conditions for workers. As Allyson Pollock, head of health policy at University College London says "Don't be fooled by the rhetoric: this is about privatisation."

When Prime Sinister Bliar talks about modernisation read privatisation. Such modernisation' has already been the fate of 50 NHS hospitals handed over to companies like Jarvis, Tarmac, Siemens and Rentokil thanks to the Private Finance Initiative (PFI) In a study of the first 15 hospitals put under the PFI operating table a third of hospital beds have so far been amputated.

Foundation Hospitals and PFI's are just what the corporations ordered. These very same corporations are busy pushing for a new round of GATS – the General Agreement on Trade in Services, first signed in 1994 by the World Trade Organisation. GATS aims to remove 'barriers to trade' (which are there to protect us – health and safety rules, environmental laws, planning regulations, etc.) and open up what's left of our public services to private corporations – forever.

Once you've signed away a certain section of your public services to GATS then there is no going back, because the aim of GATS is 'progressive liberalisation' – a way of ensuring that eventually no other model of service delivery other than by the private sector is available. For example despite private companies making a complete pigs ear of our railways, bringing rail maintenance and repair services back under some form of public ownership would breach the UK's existing GATS commitments. The government would then be taken to a World Trade Organisation tribunal made up of unelected trade lawyers who meet in secret and subsequently told to change the offending law or regulation – or face the massive trade sanctions consequences.

Blair Bones

Since the government reckons private companies are obviously the right choice for running our hospitals, here's a little reminder of how corporations have been doing elsewhere. In education, where Local Education Authorities (LEAs) are so under-funded that they cannot afford to put in bids to run their own show, companies like Jarvis are doing a great job. With no previous experience in education, they've recently been awarded a £1.9m contract to provide 'support' for 700 under-performing secondary schools. Surely that's not the same Jarvis that's under investigation for its part in the Potters Bar rail crash? Yep. Or the Jarvis that kept thousands of kids out of school in Liverpool for two weeks and 20 schools in the Huddersfield area closed, because they hadn't completed works on time? The very same. But surely its not the same Jarvis recently joined by two defectors from rival firm WS Atkins. Atkins recently pulled out of their contract to run Southwark LEA after only two years because "We had bitten off more than we could chew" and because there was no profit to be had, which resulted in the company losing 90% of its value in six months, but not before the number of schools in special measures in the borough had risen due to their incompetence? Yes, that Jarvis. Ah, parents can sleep safe at night then.

The school standards minister, David Milibrand, justified Jarvis' appointment by saying that "Ofsted have said there is a real problem in the quality of support going to the lowest-performing schools." Is that the same Ofsted that's farming its school inspections out to companies like Nord Anglia who also run schools? No conflict of interest there then.

Despite an Audit Commission report published in January that found the first PFI schools to be "significantly worse" than other new schools in England and Wales, the government in its wisdom remains convinced that PFI in education is the way forward. Defence and shipping company Vosper Thorneycroft has just won a £100m deal to take over the running of Surrey's LEA, the first award to be made for a successful LEA. Vosper's CEO made no attempt to disguise the motivation behind their bid when he boasted "It is £100m over 7 years. If we are able to catch some of the other LEAs we could double or treble our size over that period of time."

Rotten Boards

They'd better be careful not to fall victim to the level of greed that almost sunk Amey, the company who took on a third share of the London Underground deal, and also went on to grab contracts for the Ministry of Defence, the Edinburgh school system, and Network Rail – including the Croydon Tram service- which almost went belly up when Amey failed for reasons of mis-management and too-fast growth. No contract-breaking penalties for Amey however, instead they were free to sell their contracts on, for £80m to Spanish construction group Ferrovial, the first foreign firm to get their mitts on Britain's public services.

Meanwhile, our old mates WS Atkins are on the loose again, as part of the design team for the new Birmingham Northern Relief Road, the 27-mile motorway that seems set to fail in its objectives before work is completed. The road is being built, despite huge opposition and legal challenges from the local community and environmental groups, by joint venture company CAMBBA (Carillion, McAlpine, Balfour Beatty and Amec) who will also be the operating company after completion. One of the reasons given for building the road was the diversion of heavy polluting trucks off the M6 and out of Birmingham, but the £11 per trip toll that CAMBBA plan to impose on lorry drivers (as opposed to £3 per car) will almost certainly keep those trucks trundling over Spaghetti Junction. And the reasoning behind this can only be guessed at, but Friends of the Earth probably aren't far from the truth: "…a lorry damages the road infrastructure as much as 100 times more than a car. They're going to want to attract cars, which give them revenue, but not lorries, which cause damage."

So, that's health, education, transport – and so to public housing, what's left of it. The government is committing £40m into an estate in Manchester as the first of eight 'social housing' PFI projects. The Grove Village consortium, led by Nationwide Building Society and house builder Gleeson, will revamp the 1,090 home estate, then sell most of it on to private buyers. Jane Robinson from Unison has said that councils have been left with little option but to use PFI through lack of government funding and that the quest for profit by private companies is "not appropriate in public services, where there's a range of other responsibilities to be taken into account." But then we all know that the only responsibility big companies care about is their responsibilities to line the pockets of their shareholders.

She was always off her head

Howzat For A Work Of Art

Forget the faddish fluff of the Turner Prize nominees – this was art event of the year. On the 3rd July 2002 Paul Kelleher took performance art in an exciting new direction when he knocked the head off a statue of Margaret Thatcher; an act which now has taken its place in art history somewhere between Duchamp's urinal and Winston's mohawk.

In February 2003 he was sentenced to three months imprisonment for decapitating the £150,000 statue (see also SchNEWS 394). The judge said, "I don't doubt the sincerity of your beliefs. Many people share them, particularly in relation to what is happening in Third World countries ... and I would be the last person to deny any person the right to freedom of speech and the right to protest against matters which support his beliefs." But he concluded... "The way you acted to knock the head off a valuable statue of a politician who left power over 10 years ago and whose party is no longer the party of government, was very much the wrong way." (That's right – Blair and Neo Labour are the current enemy.)

Defending himself in court, Kelleher insisted he had a lawful excuse for his actions since he believed 'his young son was in "immediate need of protection" from "this stupid world" and the political system represented by Thatcher. The prosecution described the attack as an "ill-conceived publicity stunt" carried out by a man who was "not an avid fan of the former prime minister".

The court heard that on the day of the attack Mr Kelleher arranged a babysitter for his son and purchased a Slazenger V600 cricket bat. Once in the gallery he waited for his "window of opportunity". When the cricket bat "pinged off" the statue, Kelleher picked up a metal crowd barrier and successfully beheaded it. Afterwards he chose not to make a run for it and waited quietly by the statue to be arrested. When police arrived, he told them, "I think it looks better like that."

Thessaloniki Seven

The European Union summit in Thessaloniki in June 2003 was always going get out of control, with thousands of activists from all over Europe travelling to Greece to meet up with fellow protesters and the famously polite Greek police.

The agenda at the EU meeting ranged from expansion to trade liberalisation to immigration and terrorism (which EU governments always treat as the same thing). Since the EU didn't want to invite anyone else to their beachside resort, local anarchists squatted Thessaloniki University and gave visiting protesters a taste of good ole' Greek hospitality.

On the first day of the summit, protestors went to the EU's barricaded beachside a few hundred kilometres out of Thessaloniki. One group decided to try to break into the red zone, but were tear gassed and the demonstration was broken up, leading to running, stone-throwing battles between cops and protesters as locals showered gassed protesters with hose pipes.

On the final day of the summit there were several large demonstrations in the centre of Thessaloniki. The Stalinist Greek Communist Party held a sterile rally, the Greek Social Forum hosted a concert and what started as a boisterous five thousand strong black block march, soon erupted into a ruck with the coppers with molotov cocktails flying one way and tear gas the other.

Dozens of protestors were arrested and many were beaten while in their cells. 27 were charged with 'rioting, defying authority and possession of explosives' regardless of the evidence. Mere participation in the marches was made into a crime punishable by 7-25 years imprisonment. The Greek state was desperate to lock people up, so police systematically went about planting everything from rocks to molotovs in arrestees' bags. Most of those charged were released on bail, but 6 of those nicked—3 Greeks, 2 Spaniards and a Briton—were held for longer awaiting trials. Another two, a Syrian and an American, were threatened with deportation.

One of those was Simon Chapman, an English protestor, whose lawyers had a video from mainstream media showing a policeman placing molotovs in his bag while he lay bleeding on the ground. The judge refused to watch the footage, saying that he'd "seen enough news already." Eventually Simon, and four others went on hunger strike. The five were denied access to mail, toilet privacy and access to their lawyers, and refused water as well as food to win even these basic rights. When word got out that the five only had a week to live, even the mainstream media took an interest.

The Greek Council of Judges ruled for their release after the District Attorney in Athens ordered doctors to force-feed the hunger strikers. That move turned public opinion against the state. The media put pressure on the government, and even members of the government came out to demand their release as well as 28 European Members of Parliament. But it was the solidarity movement in Greece that put pressure on the government, with lots of occupations, demonstrations, actions and publicity while international solidarity campaigns raised awareness and money to help the hunger strikers.

1 Simon Chapman is being beaten by the police. He has a light blue backpack on

2 His original backpack is in the background as a riot cop clearly places a black bag containing molotovs at his feet

Eventually on November 26th all seven were released. Their hunger strike had lasted between 49 and 66 days. Due to their extremely frail health condition they had to stay in hospital for another week or so to recover. They were released without bail but were not allowed to leave Greece before the trial.

The Greek authorities and justice system were made to look totally ridiculous, with clear video and photographic evidence of Simon's innocence being widely circulated. Anyone could see the obvious fit up in the video.

As Indymedia Athens put it, "This is a victory of the struggle for dignity and freedom by the 5 hunger strikers; of the other 2 prisoners; but as well the thousands of people who stood up for them all over the world! It is an outright defeat for the Greek state-repression complex, and for global 'anti-terror' mechanisms. Our passion for freedom was stronger than their prisons".

ARMLESS FUN

"It is like any other trade exhibition. It is like the motor show in Birmingham or exhibitions at Earls Court. This happens to be for the defence industry." - *Paul Beaver, spokesperson for DSEi organisers Spearhead.*

Now – while SchNEWS knows that cars can kill and aren't too good for the environment we reckon that Apache fighter jets, landmines and cluster bombs are just a tad more harmful to civilians. This is the sort of euphemistic blather coming from the suits this week at Europe's biggest arms fair – Defence Systems and Equipment International (DSEi pronounced 'dicey'), the place where state terrorism is labelled 'defence', cluster bombs become 'cargo ammunition' and bombs are creatively called 'air delivered weapons'. This week at the ExCel centre in east London the supposed 'terrorist' regimes were welcomed alongside the 'good guys' alike as 'clients' side by side, queuing up for weaponry. Luckily there were over 2,000 tooled up coppers to hold back the persistent direct action and blockades against the 'fair with the scariest rides in town'.

To get an idea of what gets sold at the arms fair take cluster bombs: they've got a bad name because they contain many bomblets which often don't explode in the initial attack – just like unexploded landmines. Already over 1,000 Iraqi kids have been injured by cluster bomblets since the 'end' of the war on Iraq. Doing a roaring trade in these is Israel Military Industries Ltd who are still licking their lips after flogging loads of cluster bombs to Britain before the war on Iraq. Britain's largest arms company, BAE Systems, bought over 20,000 rounds of Israeli cluster weapons just before the Iraqi war. Then the British army went on to fire over 2,000 of these Israeli cluster bombs during the battle for Basra. DSEi welcomed another sketchy Israeli weapons producer, Rafael, who develop missile systems by testing them on Palestinian civilians. Their most infamous test was the Gill Spike missile test, which they first tested on a civilian home in Beit Jala in 2000.

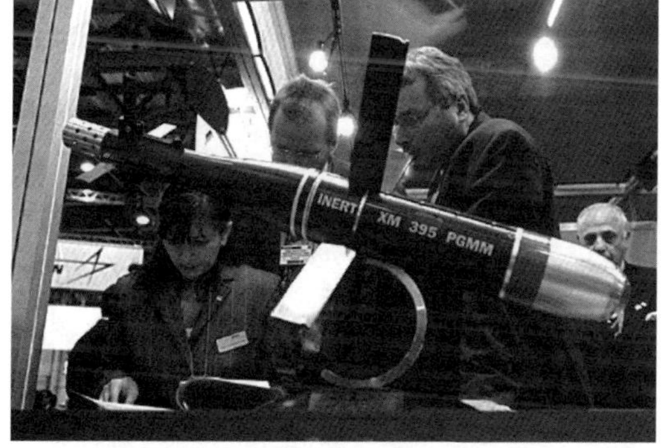

Despite all the deceptive words and oppressive security a few thousand protestors took part in a flood of guerrilla actions and demonstrations over the four day arms fair. The police spokesperson, Greg Pig Trotters, said their operation was "very patient, very sensitive and very low key" – but this came as news to the people of Newham – the borough where the ExCeL exhibition centre is based – who witnessed the biggest ever police operation in the area. As one of the poorest boroughs in London,

IF ORDINARY PEOPLE BEHAVED LIKE- BRITISH AEROSPACE

Newham locals called for the arms fair to be cancelled and would prefer the £1+ million spent on policing DSEi to be channelled into regenerating their neighbourhoods.

Rowed Block

In the run-up to DSEi the death fair's organisers Spearhead had their offices occupied while at the same time people in rubber dinghys blocked DSEi warships. On Saturday morning DSEi attempted to sail 4 warships along the Thames to the ExCel Centre but, alas, 30 water-tight activists were there blocking the lock gates and the swing bridge with good ol' D-locks. There was a four hour window in which the tide allowed entry into the docks so the last 2 ships had to abort their mission. During the week protesters posing as arms dealers joined the hundreds of other dealers and buyers on the trains to the ExCel Centre. Three suited protesters couldn't wait for the fair and started selling their wares on the train: Announcing they had arms for sale they opened their brief cases revealing dismembered Barbie dolls' arms.

Tuesday was declared a 'day of non-violent direct action' against DSEi with a Campaign Against the Arms Trade march attracting about 2,000 protesters. This culminated in the 'Fluffy DSEi' action, with the aim of blockading DSEi, where a crowd of about 1,000 protesters blocked the Connaught Bridge entrance to the fair. For the next few hours it was a game of cat 'n' mouse between agile glittery protesters and stroppy cops as protesters blockaded roundabout after roundabout, occupying a different main road every time the cops threatened arrests.

Wednesday, the 'no rules direct action day', started with an uncontrollable critical mass outside ExCel, and a protest at the London office of Israeli weapons make Rafael by Palestinian Solidarity group ISM. Meanwhile the suits streamed into the centre, many using the Docklands Light Rail (DLR), which was just asking for some direct action to blockade it. Over the course of the day the transport police had their work cut out removing locked-on protesters from the DLR carriages as loadspeakers at the stations apologised for delays saying it was due to – wait for it – 'passenger action'.

While entry to the conference by train was being derailed, another sorted crew pushed a car out onto the road to block the eastern entrance of the centre, which was the beginning of a several hour blockade of the entrance. Meanwhile the road outside the centre was blocked at several points during the day.

Meanwhile six cunning activists had formed their own 'arms company' – the Affinity Group – with their own official website and business cards, and then applied for invitations to the death fair. They waltzed in, suited and accredited, and went on to occupy two tanks, daubing them in 'Stop Death' banners before they were chucked out by security.

Later in the day there was excitement at the Canning Town roundabout when the flyover above was shut down with a banner as a crowd stormed the roundabout until the robocops – tooled up and outnumbering protesters – pushed the line back. Then minutes later like the cavalry coming over the hill, the sound of samba drums and a flash of pink and silver saw the samba block take the roundabout again, though again the sheer number of coppers stopped anything lasting very long. Meanwhile local rudeboys from the nearby estate tucked in, egging on protesters and throwing eggs at coppers. Other locals took part in the actions while many sat on balconies shouting stuff like "Those coppers are denying you your rights, mate!"

While some of the actions were inspirational and we caused serious disruption at times, we didn't shut down DSEi. We needed more people – what ever happened to the one million plus who marched against the war on Iraq in February? With 10,000 people in the Docklands on Wednesday instead of 1,000 we could have kicked the arms dealers out of London for good. We need to take the opportunity to kick the war-profiteering scumbags where it hurts, and the weapon should be mass direct action. At the next DSEi arms fair in two years, it's up to us to make sure that the death fair bites the bullet.

Dicey Manoeuvre

The last time that DSEi, the international arms supermarket, had come to London was in 2001 and the protests then had not worked out too well. The main focus of protests had been only on one day and at one main point, which gave the cops an easy opportunity to herd everyone into a police cordon to escort us to the other side of the conference centre away from the delegates. It felt pretty humiliating. There were a few people who boarded trains and caused some chaos, but generally most people felt disheartened and disappointed about our impact on DSEi (not to mention that we were slightly outdone that day by the World Trade Centre being flattened).

So when it came along again in September 2003 (it happens every 2 years) people started to think more laterally. One of the main objectives was to stop the delegates from getting to the conference which is held in the Excel centre, bang in the middle of the docklands in East London. There were roads and train lines into the conference centre that needed to be blocked. There were already big protests planned for the roads which would bring traffic to a standstill; which left the train lines…

The docklands light railway is the line that goes straight to the centre and was the obvious target. People from around the country planned an on-going blockade of the trains throughout the 3 days of the conference. Different tactics were discussed: blocking doors (useless), setting off alarms (doesn't work), getting on top of trains (very effective), or putting chains through doors to keep them open (also effective). Time slots were arranged, so we vaguely knew when we were supposed to go into action, but even the most well laid plans don't always work! All day we tried to do what we had planned but it was farcical, every time we approached a station we heard the tanoy announce the train was delayed because of passenger action. The train line was closed down most of the day so we hadn't had an opportunity to do our action.

Just as we approached Canning Town station we heard the trains start up again and realised it was now or never. As one train pulled in someone stood in the doors to keep it from moving and two of us jumped up on the roof. Easy! We managed to get up onto the station infrastructure which made it harder for the scab climbers to get us down and forced them to close down the whole station. It was also great timing as many DSEi delegates were leaving and had to use the roads only to be met by a few hundred protestors. We were up there for an hour-ish which doesn't seem long but with lots of people doing similar things over the next 3 days, the train lines were in chaos.

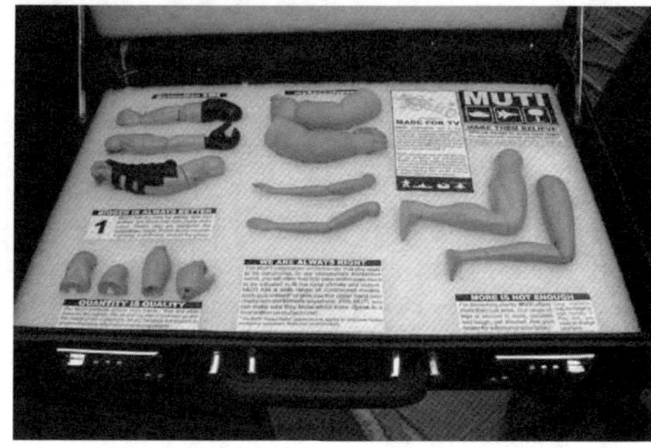

Street hawkers were also selling arms outside the arms fair as well

The conference was not closed down, and the deals were probably done, but a huge amount of disruption that was caused might put cities off holding events like this in the future. So let's organise for the next DSEi with more people…..

As a footnote…

Legal support around and after DSEi was really impressive particularly setting up an email list for people who got arrested and the huge support we found to help us and other people fundraise for our fines. It felt like the Women's Institute but we had pizza nights, jumble sales, and gigs to raise the money for us and other people. It's a choice to pay or not but if you decide to pay, then it shouldn't just be responsibility of those nicked to pay those fines.

"I am crying out my words to you, that have for so long boiled in my body... My warning goes out to all citizens that human beings are in an endangered situation. That uncontrolled multinational corporations and a small number of big WTO Members are leading an undesirable globalization that is inhumane, environmentally degrading, farmer-killing, and undemocratic. It should be stopped immediately."
- 56-year-old Korean farmer Lee Kyung-hae, who took his life in Cancun.

FLUSHED DOWN THE CAN–CUN

Outside thousands were pulling down the fences. Inside the poorer countries from the majority world (the so-called third world) were coming together to demand a better deal. By Sunday afternoon the talks at the fifth ministerial of the World Trade Organisation (WTO) in Cancun, Mexico had collapsed. "You are small fish in a big pond. You eat when the big fish decide" Pascal Lamy, the EU Commisioner for Trade, informed the Africa, Caribbean and the Pacific Group. But this time the small fish weren't biting the bait.

SchINTERVIEWS in CANCUN

One SchNEWS scribe got to Cancun – here are a couple of quick interviews he managed in between pulling down fences and sampling the local tear gas.

SchNEWS: What does the WTO mean to you?

S. Korean farmer: WTO means the colonisation of the Third World. That means the US trying to dominate all Third World Countries. Their strategy is one of colonisation through opening up the market. I've been a farmer for fifteen years. When I started there were 10 million farmers but now there are only 3 million of us as a result of this 'openness'. This spells the death of all South Korean farmers.

Sch: Why only 3 million now?

Farmer: First, our revenues are getting lower and lower. Second, we cannot afford health and education so many farmers are leaving for the city to try and earn enough money to survive. Third, Korean farmers have very little land compared to US farmers, so we cannot compete. In this situation the Korean government is trying to open the market more and more and free up competition. The government is not interested in the lives of small farmers. They are just interested in corporate companies.

Sch: What do you think of bio-technology?

Farmer: The US already dominates the seed industry, if TRIPS* is completed then their power will be strengthened. There is a new kind of rice, 'Reunification Rice' made in the Philippines supported by the US Before this arrived, we farmers didn't use fertilisers. Now we have been led to believe that we have to use them. I think this is very bad for us and for the land. The land is becoming very infertile and very acidic after using these products. The US built a fertiliser factory in Korea and the farmers use their products. Many believe we have no choice even though we can see we are killing our land. In the past we thought the US was a good country which helped us, because they built the fertiliser factory, but we don't think this now. All the profits leave Korea for the US.

Our masked-up geezer also spoke to a Mexican campesino/farmer from the Chiapas region.

Sch: What do you grow?

Campesino: Maize, beans and coffee.

Sch: How does the WTO affect you?

Campesino: The WTO is pushing prices down. The market is now flooded with cheap GM maize so I don't have anywhere to sell my produce. Now I only grow maize for my family and my one pig. Likewise the beans I grow now are just for us. My main production used to be coffee. In 1994 I received

In the WTO's ideal world there would be two kinds of agriculture systems – the rich countries would produce staple foods for the world's 6 billion plus people, and majority world countries would mainly grow cash crops like tomatoes, cut flowers, strawberries and vegetables to export to the west. The money that majority world countries would earn from exporting these crops would eventually be used to buy foodgrains from the west. And guess what? The poorer nations would be unable to feed themselves and would be forever dependent on the west not just for patented seeds, patented medicines and patented technology but also for much of its staple food. Food sovereignty? Forget it!

Previous WTO negotiations were always characterized by the US and the EU isolating poorer countries and forcing through one-sided agreements which benefit western investment and corporations. But this time the G22 (a group of African, Asian and South American countries), in coalition with an African bloc, stood firm, refusing to budge until the question of the west's unfair agricultural subsidies was dealt with. Nearly seventy other nations in addition to the G22 refused to sign the final US and EU-written accord in Cancun. When the WTO decided to address 'Western' issues of investment and competition instead of agriculture it was the final straw and the talks collapsed.

Outside of the WTO fortress the thousands ripping down fences, running the eco-village, holding alternative conferences and spreading the news were also playing their part. According to Peter Muchoki Njorage, Deputy Commisioner for Kenya's Ministry of Finance and Planning, "Sometimes we think we are going mad. They bully us, play with our minds and tell us that we don't understand. But what you, Civil Society, do reminds us that we are right, that we are not going mad. Your actions are very important."

One chuffed fence puller described the scene to SchNEWS "With the Interminable Noise Machine grinding out their Mad Max battle calls in the Caribbean humidity, the slack is taken up on hundreds of yards of rope, an instruction is shouted, and three hundred people go to work. The four metre wide three metre high metal barrier, separating the protesters from the WTO delegates finally gives way and for the second time in four days the barricades are

---

35 Pesos per Kilo and now it is only worth 5 Pesos. Then 95% of Mexico's coffee consumption was home grown but now it is down to 45% due to people buying cheap imported coffee. There is a big problem with the US border. Many campesinos cannot survive here so try to cross the border to find work but are shot and never return. Their deaths are not reported. There is little alternative work here and everything is getting more expensive – like soap and clothes. It is very hard for me to look after my family. Since 2002 the Mexican government have been moving people out of my region to flood the land and build hydroelectric power stations. The electricity is used by US corporate companies here and in the States.

Sch: What do you think of bio-technology and TRIPS*?

Campesino: They are selling GM food and many people are getting ill in our communities. People are conned into using insecticides on the land and this is poisoning them. I have always grown organically and the land is rich and fertile. I see no reason for using fertilisers and insecticides in Chiapas. Before 1994 the coffee I grew was enough to look after my family now we are struggling to survive.

Sch: Who do you think benefits from the WTO?

Campesino: Capitalists from the US, The World Bank and the Banco de Desarollo Interamericana (Development Bank).

* **WTO Vocab Watch: TRIPS** – Trade Related Aspects of Intellectual Property Rights (see SchNEWS 420), an 'agreement' pushed by the US which has seen corporations patenting everything from indigenous peoples' rice seeds to publicly-funded AIDS drugs and then demanding absurd prices from the people it ripped off in the first place.

breached. The team made up of hardened Mexican students, campesinos from Chiapas and Black Block anarchists is organised and led by Korean farmers. Meanwhile hundreds of women methodically bolt crop and hammer their way through other sections of the fence and news filters through that members of Korean Civil Society have succeeded in entering the ministerial conference centre."

On A Knife-Edge

56-year-old Korean farmer Lee Kyung-hae was among the group of about 150 Koreans in the frontline, pulling down the security fences. Climbing to the top of the fence, Lee turned to his compatriots and said: "Don't worry about me, just struggle your hardest." He then stabbed himself in the chest with a knife hoping to focus the world's attention on the hidden misery of what the World Trade Organisation really means to millions.

Lee Kyung-hae had always dreamed of revitalising farming in his hometown and returned from agricultural college in 1974 to put his ideas into practice turning a patch of harsh mountain land into a thriving farm. Seoul Farm became a teaching college and in 1988 he received a UN award for rural leadership. The Lees, now with three daughters, were prospering. Their herd had expanded to 300 cattle and the fame of the charismatic farm leader who had mastered a hostile land was growing. But then Korea was flooded with foreign imports and he was ruined. Koreans are up to their necks in debt and with the US and EU subsidising agribusiness at $1 billion per day, imported rice has been wiping out formerly self-sufficient Korean farmers. In Lee's town the population has almost halved while farmers commit suicide or run off in the middle of the night because they cannot make their interest repayments. One of Lee's sisters said the collapse of his farm prompted him to throw himself with more fury into organising unions, influencing government policy and opposing trade liberalisation.

One Korean farmer told SchNEWS "It is very difficult for Western people to understand what he did. In Korean history if people want to show their strong will, they sometimes give their lives. Now more and more people think the WTO is a very bad thing and needs to be protested against. What he did is like a burning candle. He had to sacrifice himself to make the world shine." Han Gyuha, a town official added, "Lee knew the Korean countryside is slowly dying, that farmers are living lonely, miserable lives. He wanted to tell the world. That is why he sacrificed himself and that is why we call him a hero."

Lee's sacrifice helped focus the world on the plight of the poor suffocating under the belly of a corporate-stuffed WTO. The collapse of the talks is undoubtedly a victory for the new unity of the majority world but it will come under increasing strain in the coming months with the US and the EU resorting to 'divide and rule' tactics – picking off individual countries for bilateral and regional trade deals. It's also true that G22 countries such as India, Brasil and China don't have a common negotiating position. However, united as 22 countries plus the 70 other states that supported them, the majority world countries have the possibility of wringing out concessions from the west, using a combined threat of non-payment of their foreign debts. This victory wouldn't have happened without the grassroots global justice movement – written off after September 11 – as it intelligently mobilised worldwide against two sides of the same dollar coin – capitalist war and capitalist economics. Cancun represented the wonderful diversity of this movement – campesinos and US anarchists opposing the talks of the power-drunk, while proposing their own empowering alternatives – from the Zapatista's radical municipalities to the New Agriculture movement in Bangladesh. And this movement doesn't put all its faith in detached representatives. It will be there in force when America hosts the Free Trade Agreement of the Americas in December.

AND ANYONE WHO SAYS OTHERWISE IS A DANGEROUS, NAÏVE, WOOLY MINDED, BLEEDING HEART TROUBLEMAKER

Constant Harassment

"Being kicked off land you own and live on, having your dwellings destroyed and concrete obstructions placed to stop you getting vehicles back onto your land, or court injunctions to stop you even going on your land. The reason: officially because you haven't got planning permission to live there. Unofficially because you and your way of life are being ethnically cleansed."

The Criminal Justice and Public Order Act 1994 removed the obligation on local authorities to provide sites for travellers and gave the police greater powers to seize and impound vehicles. Ten years on and the evictions and harassment continue, with travellers finding their way of life becoming ever more criminalised.

Current government policy recommends that travellers should house themselves on their own land, yet Gypsy families who attempt to do so are repeatedly denied planning permission. While over 80% of planning applications from settled people are granted consent more than 90% of applications from Gypsies are refused.

Take the twenty-seven Gypsy families who purchased Woodside, a 17-acre touring caravan park with full planning permission in 1997. When they moved on to the park, Mid-Bedfordshire council claimed they did not have permission for permanent occupation and issued enforcement notices. Woodside is unlike any of the 325 council Gypsy sites in this country. It isn't surrounded by barbed wire fences and isn't near a sewage works or other industrial facility. It looks, in fact, more like a modern hamlet than a ghetto, except that the homes are on wheels rather than stone foundations. At the centre of the community is a large green where children play in safety. Yet the council wants the site removed on the grounds that it is having an adverse impact on the environment and has spent nearly a million pounds trying to close Woodside down.

In January, travellers fought an eviction at Bulkington Fields in Warwickshire with seven foot wide trenches and burning barricades. The eviction eventually went ahead in June with bailiffs and 50 coppers trashing the site with JCBs and evicting the six families. The travellers had bought the land nearly three years ago, but as per usual were unable to get the 'planning permission' to officially live there.

The same month 30 people were kicked off the Meadowlands Caravan Park in Waltham, despite the fact that once again some families actually owned the land. Resident Kathy Buckland said that around fifty coppers "smashed and kicked everything up. My two-year-old was hysterical. I was pregnant with my fourth child. I felt like they were trying to sweep us away into a sewer, that they were not treating us like humans".

To help with evictions 'gypsy and squatter eviction specialists' Constant And Co are often brought in. When the bailiffs took the site in Meadowlands, it was agreed after negotiations that the ten caravans still there would be taken by the company to another site. Instead, several caravans were burnt out on the nearby roadside where Constant had left them after towing them a short distance away (see pic above). Constant then claimed that the caravans were torched by the travellers themselves!

To compensate the travellers for the inconvenience of being made homeless, Chelmsford Council set up a "homeless office" in nearby Great Waltham at the parish hall. However, they omitted to tell the travellers the facility was available, and anyway there was a roadblock stopping them getting there! A few travellers were then sent to the Silverwood motel in Essex, but after only two nights, and during mid winter snowfall, they were being forced to provide ID, proof of income, and proof of links to Meadowlands, for the privilege of continuing their stay. There is also a chance that the council will exercise their legal right to repossess the land to pay for the eviction, which cost £100,000. The site is conveniently worth £90,000.

Launching the commission's first strategy on Gypsies and Travellers earlier this year, the Commission for Racial Equality Chairman Trevor Phillips said: "There is no question that Gypsies and Travellers are probably the single most intensely discriminated against group in the country. I've described it as a case of Gypsies and Travellers in the UK being akin to [what] black folk were in the deep south of the US 40 years ago."

Meanwhile Kit Sampson, who has spent decades campaigning for Gypsies, has returned her MBE for a second time. She originally handed it back when the Criminal Justice and Public Order Act became law. She was persuaded to take it back when Neo Labour came to power, but now says "This government is exactly the same as the last one."

Friends, Families, and Travellers: www.gypsy-traveller.org

SPELLBOUND

This is the frontline. It's not just about trees. If people want to continue anti-war protests, it doesn't take much to make the connection between this and the war for oil. This is the Anti-Roads Movement Part II. Cast your mind back to the early nineties — the first Gulf War had just ended, there was a Climate Change Summit. Now things have turned a full circle and a whole new generation are on board." **- Holly, protester at Blackwood Protest Camp.**

This week there are three separate protest camps all on urgent eviction alert: ecological direct action camps at Blackwood near Newport, Sherwood Forest in Nottingham, and Nine Ladies in Derbyshire – all competing for limited amounts of people and resources. Are we back to the protest camp halcyon days of the nineties?

BLACKWOOD MAGIC

Five acres of St Davids Wood in Blackwood, south Wales, is currently under threat of being trashed for the sake of an access road to an industrial park – and would already be gone if it wasn't for some hardy protesters and a ten-year local campaign which involved two High Court battles. This camp needs urgent help to protect the site – but before you go down to the woods, you'd better leaf through the dusty pages of Hogwart's book on tree protest wizardry...

We now know that magic can happen in the woods, but things got truly surreal this week when Harry Potter weaved a spell into the story. This new development has come about because contractors Costain and the Caerphilly Borough Council have used the obscure 'Harry Potter ruling' to secure a High Court civil injunction on the entire camp. In the Harry Potter case, some of the kid wizard books went missing from the publishing company Bloomsbury and were then given to the press before publication. Because the company didn't know the specific names of the persons who had taken the books, they simply described them to the court. The court then decided for the first time that persons described, rather than actually named, could be defendants to an injunction. This means an injunction can be served against anybody – no names are needed – so therefore any person entering or remaining in a specified area (the woodland at Blackwood, in this case) can be immediately removed. Bindmans, the solicitors giving free legal advice to the camp, told SchNEWS "it's the first time the 'Harry Potter ruling' has been used against protesters."

The injunction is a useful legal tool for companies wanting to get rid of pesky protesters. In the hearing for the Blackwood case, the judge only heard evidence from the 'interested party' – the developers – leaving the defendants (the protesters) with no chance to defend themselves. It is possible to later appeal the injunction in court – but it becomes a David and Goliath battle between a cashed up company and a campaign which doesn't get legal aid.

The woodland under threat – owned by Costain and under the spell of Harry Potter – is now 'protected' from protesters, but while the trees are still under threat, the protest camp itself is on adjoining land NOT owned by Costain, making it safe from eviction for the moment.

Currently, the anti-roads campaigners are trying furiously to mix a legal potion to fight the Harry Potter ruling – throwing in such ingredients as the Section 6 status of the camp and the presence of dormice on Costain's woodland site. It's a shame that the dormice can't get an injunction so they can live undisturbed. Work stopped on the site when dormice were found. Legally, dormice are protected and they must be "re-located" (evicted) if the chopping of the trees is to continue – but work has continued, around their habitat. The presence of dormice has meant that a wildlife group is taking Costain to court and maybe even criminal proceedings will occur, but don't hold your breath as courts tend to be more chummy with the likes of Costain than dormice-lovers.

We asked one protester on site, Holly, if the protest camp was mostly made up of Twyford Down or Newbury veterans like herself? She told us that while there is unbelievable local support, there is also a whole new generation of protesters present. This is the generation who took the anti-war protests by storm last year, so watch out cos hopefully there are plenty more where they came from.

People and climbing equipment are needed at the camp now. To contact the camp phone 07952 774525 or 07708 420446 For a map and details visit www.schnews.org.uk/pap/protestcamps.htm

MORE ROADWORKS AHEAD

A Reflection On Blackwood and a decade of protest camps

Back in 1991/2, the first Gulf War had recently ended, with people mobilising around a 'No War for Oil!' banner. The sustainable development conference in Rio had happened, where climate change, voracious habitat loss and environmental degradation were identified, but there had been little policy change. Quite the contrary, in the UK the building of new roads, the inducement of extra traffic, and general green belt development formed a key part of the Conservative governments' policy agenda, as identified in the infamous and outrageous document "Roads to Prosperity".

This was the background context for the flashpoint at Twyford Down in 1992 which catalysed a massive anti-roads movement and set the scene for a decade of direct action where we increasingly got our shit together and got an awareness of 'the bigger picture' – the types of macro-structural, political, social and economic issues which interlinked to cause human rights abuses and eco devastation worldwide. Hence, over the next decade we "rent-a-mobbed" our way around a wide set of targets and got our heads around Neo-liberalism, leading to the cycle of anti-capitalist protests set off at the G8 in Birmingham in 1998.

Fast forward to 2004. Er, we've just had another war in the Gulf, and this time round, many more 'ordinary people' got mobilised, which I think our movements can take some credit for. We've had another sustainability summit, again business as usual for the usual suspects and post-Kyoto, climate change is once again big on the political agenda in terms of hot air spoken. And guess what, New Labour has revived the road-building programme and is fast building houses and shopping malls on greenbelt land for all the nice commuters. Before February this year (2004), I was having something of a bad time, wondering what precisely I'd managed to achieve in over a decade of direct action. But I'd also spotted the spooky similarity in global and domestic events, and had been thinking for some time that more protests against roads were a possibility.

In fact, as I thought about it, the more it seemed like a really important strategy for the direct action movement to get into anti-roads activity again. In a nutshell, we've got our stuff together over a long time and have taught ourselves and others, that issues like oil and war and climate change and capitalism are all interconnected; they feed off each other. Ideologically, we've never been stronger, and our strategies for positive change make sense (especially with Bush's 'war on terror' as the competing ideological position).

The broad alliances and massive demos of our "alternative globalisation movement" have been an extremely strong strategic success, but we have to adapt our strategy or die. That's in fact our greatest strength: our ability to be fluid and biodegrade into new networks and campaigns. I feel that on the streets, in mass demos, we are predominantly out-manoeuvred by the State (though DSEi-style affinity group tactics rock, so I am not saying we can't get past that), and that whilst we demonstrate about global capitalism and try to make it immediate and real to people, generally our demos are tactically symbolic. Which is great, but we need to get back to DOING stuff, and STOPPING CRAP THINGS HAPPENING, to regain the strategic/tactical upper hand, and to highlight how specific issues – like new roads, airports, PFI hospitals etc. – link back to the bigger picture, something that we are much better able to do, a decade on. That's why I don't think this is just wheel reinvention, because we are so much stronger as a movement now.

And suddenly, in late January this year, an email pops up on our Cardiff Anarchist Network list saying that some people want to take direct action at Blackwood, where a bypass is cutting through ancient woodland. Despite the whole rationale just outlined, I ignore the email. January? Direct action? Roads? Good luck to 'em, but forget it – doomed to failure, massive drain of resources, too much to mobilise against, freezing rain, blah blah blah. A day later and another email – two people stopped work all day, they need help urgently. Fuck! Within 24 hours I am poring over maps of the route on my living room floor with them – two "Borises", talking about camps and poly-prop and networks and contractors, while one "Boris" fills me in on the background – the usual story of an unnecessary road promising the ever-elusive 'economic development', the road meant to go through a beautiful stretch of ancient woodland filled with huge trees, and a community that has fought the scheme for 11 years, with the classic stalwarts re-mortgaging their houses to pay for court costs at failed House of Lords appeals, writing protected species letters to Europe (for bats & dormice), the whole thing. But work had already started with old friends Costain the main contractors.

NO U-TURN
D-LOCKS AHEAD

CAN (Cardiff Anarchist Network) activists rally round and over the first week, two or three people at a time manage to stop all work – the two chainsaw guys just give up whenever they come near. By the time I blag off work to get up there on the Friday, dragging kettles, waterbutts and all of that palaver, there is already a rhythm going, resources arriving, plastic bags with sweetly eclectic gifts of food from the locals, and bemused looking Costain workers. I sort the fire out and put the kettle on. Meanwhile all "Borises" on site, freed by the arrival of reinforcements, have thundered off to stop work at the other end of site. In two hours I am re-tying knots in the drizzle and Section 6-ing off areas of land. I haven't had so much fun in years, I had forgotten how effective this could be, what a buzz it is to do this stuff right under their noses, the top brass are obviously shitting themselves…

There is a poncey academic term for our ability to get our shit together like that – we have 'mobile social capital'. We don't have many classic resources, i.e. money, but we know how to network and use the resources we do have. And there were a whole set of resources and circumstances, which meant that over the next few weeks, Blackwood kicked off into a national campaign. Firstly, and probably most importantly, there was massive local support, I have never seen anything like it – people were so supportive, so clued-up. Some of them got into stopping work too. The local teenagers were so into it; these were their woods and they cared about them. The camp would have gone under without them, especially during the first couple of weeks (and a luckily timed half-term) while it was taking time to mobilise activist networks nationally. They bunked off school, stayed the night in freezing tents, learned how to climb trees and tie knots, keep fires going, and on their own initiative stopped work and dealt with hassle from the workers and eventually bailiffs. This is the next generation of activists and the durability of the links they've made with existing networks is crucial. Secondly, we networked like crazy and had enough of a strong local group to chuck resources, including our own time at it. No doubt also that digi videos, cameras and internet access made a massive difference to our ability to network effectively and well.

Extremely crucially, tactics we'd given up on years ago because we'd been out-manoeuvred at them, worked like a dream. We had a repertoire of tactics – section 6's, camping, lock-ons, the simplicity of simply going up and stopping the work – which we knew about, could pass on to others quickly, and which left the opposition reeling. Leave? Naff off mate – this is our land now! YOU leave. High court injunctions? Going damp and mouldy on the floor of a tent somewhere. For whatever reason, we were lucky that generally the cops weren't into nicking us, so we got away with loads. A main reason why protest camps declined in the late 90s was that it increasingly took us more time and resources than seemed worth it to try and hold things together – static camp-sitting and just maintaining the site for years, followed by evictions where their equipment was always better than ours and it was impossible to stop work because of the numbers of security hired. We were burned out, drained. At Blackwood all of our tactics worked cos the contractors and the local council didn't expect them at first. It's a PFI scheme so they didn't have

masses of public money to chuck at it, and because of that it was fun, easy, and lots more people with more energy got involved in maintaining the camp and taking action.

Inevitably, and even as we got more consolidated and better activated, it became harder to stop work as Costain got more manpower to keep us at bay. It hurts to think that with more numbers in those first few weeks we could have stopped all work completely, but as soon as patches of big trees started to go it felt like they would be finishing what they started. Though I have to say that I really did think we could have won this one – I still think this now – if we'd had more numbers, and the energy to organise more public meetings and so on. The stories of the Blackwood campaign and eviction, and of all the posses of people who blatted down and put their energy into the site, are all over the UK and Bristol IMC sites. I could go on and on. The trees are mostly all cut down now which is extremely painful.

I want to finish by talking about follow-up. I noticed a post on Bristol IMC saying, "We should have been better organised. Why wasn't there an eviction phone tree?" To which the answer is of course, good idea, why didn't you do it? When I think what we achieved in a matter of weeks from ground zero, we were stretched to the limit; there was always more to do. But yes, better planning, tactics, resources – all necessary, and I hope that this means people will go into the next protest more prepared, having had Blackwood as their learning curve (and I am thinking about the bypass at Bargoed, the next valley along from here for starters) – in fact I know that's the case. Some dreary inevitability about this next bit – after the eviction people buggered off, leaving tat lunched everywhere, so the communal harnesses, the donated climbing ropes, the pots, pans, tents and bowsaws – essential tat – have mostly disappeared, which is just awful. Some stuff got saved, but not much. Still another learning curve but one that I hate to see repeated. The direct actions that happened at Twyford were actually most effective after the first eviction, when the land was already mostly trashed: it was then that stopping work in 'flying pickets' of digger-divers came into its own, slowing work, forcing the re-hiring of extra security and costing a lot of money. Similarly direct action has continued at Blackwood, though smaller in scale, and the coordination of national days of action at the site now would be an extremely important move for some motivated activists with time on their hands.

A public meeting in Blackwood itself would also be a good idea, some film-showings, talks, discussions on how the money could have been spent in other ways to create local jobs, exhibition boards, that kind of thing. This is an essential follow-up for grassroots community networking. They supported us when we had little time to give accounts of ourselves and then we buggered off. We owe it to them to reconnect. This is the sort of follow through which is essential if we are ever to achieve lasting social change. It'll be a good way to make sure everyone local stays in touch with action networks too. This needs to happen!

But there's a whole generation of younger activists who can tie figure-8 knots, like trees and are anti-capitalists. Got a road scheme going on near you? Sure you have, and it'll be interesting to see how Bilston Glen, Nine Ladies and Sherwood camps fare.

Bilston Glen Protest Camp, near Edinburgh
www.bilstonglen-abs.org.uk

Nine Ladies

Nine ladies anti-quarry camp was set up back in 1999 to stop the destruction of Stanton Moor hillside in Derbyshire's Peak District National Park, which is under threat from the possible re-opening of two dormant quarries.

Nine Ladies Stone Circle is one of several neolithic stone circles which make Stanton Moor recognised as an SSSI (Site of Special Scientific Interest).

Before the Peak District National Park was created, there was quarrying in this area up until fifty years ago, but it has completely re-generated and blended back in with the surrounding area.

The proposed quarry is only 200m from Nine Ladies and 30m from the North Circle, another of five original stone circles, of which four remain. Also nearby are a Bronze Age burial site (45 mounds, mostly excavated), 5 badger setts, bat habitats and a herd of wild Norwegian Fallow Deer.

The protest camp is now very established with a range of implausible treehouses including a three-storey suspended platform (pic below right), a hanging caravan – 'the beast', and other mad constructions masquerading as treehouses. When Jo Makepeace went to the camp this year she described the treehouses as "Lord of the Rings meets Mad Max".

Like most camps Nine Ladies welcomes new people, and always needs useful tat and equipment so make your way down there soon.

The legal case to fight the quarry goes on, but we won't give the latest developments in the saga here because it will probably have all moved on by the time you're reading this. Suffice to say that the legal wrangles are more complicated than some of the treehouse structures.

To find out more about Nine Ladies visit: www.nineladies.uklinux.net

FASLANE PEACE CAMP

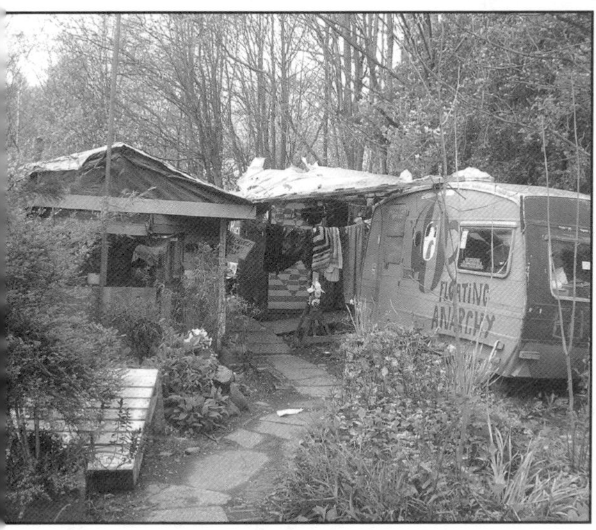

Faslane Peace Camp began life in 1982 when a group of anti-nuclear protesters pitched camp on a small strip of land near Faslane naval base on the Clyde in Scotland, where Britain's four Trident nuclear submarines are based. The original intention of the campers was to stay for just two weeks. Twenty-two years later and the peace camp is still there!

The camp has always been an organising base for direct action protests against the nuclear presence: everything from mass actions and breaking into the base, trying to disable the submarines to chasing nuclear convoys around the country. On a day to day basis the camp keeps a log of submarine movements at the base, as well as other activity in there – just as the base has permanent surveillance on the camp.

Currently the site has eleven caravans, a bus, a tepee, a bender, a tree house and various sheds and self-built structures – anybody is welcome to go and stay for as long or short a time as they can spare.

www.faslanepeacecamp.org.uk

Faslane Focus – would have to be the funniest campaign-based zine in the country, and made in a caravan on the site

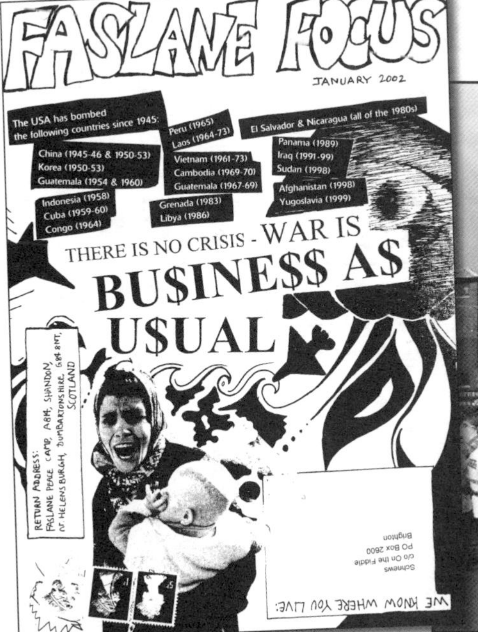

One of the many **Trident Ploughshares** actions at the base. The **'Big Blockade'** at the Faslane naval base on 23rd August 2004 shut down the entrsance for the day with 76 arrests

Part 5...
Behind the Scenes at SchNEWS

That's the real world out of the way, now it's time to look behind the scenes, get a bit of insight into how SchNEWS works, and how it started – and hear from some of the people who have traded in their hairlines, waistlines, youth, chance of a normal life and mental health to make SchNEWS what it is today.

The SchNEWS office - everything here except for the boxes of books at the back is out of a skip bin.

IF ORDINARY PEOPLE BEHAVED LIKE- SONY

WAKE UP! WAKE UP! – IT'S YER TYPICAL SchNEWS WEEK...

Forget about the glamour of writing the SchNEWS. What about all those boring jobs that have to get done every week to keep the presses rolling? Time for some truthful gripes from our regular helpers.

Getting Another Issue Together...

Liz usually comes in on Monday or Tuesday to help go through the vast pile of e-mails that we receive each week.

"Depending on the quality of stuff we get it can either be really interesting or incredibly boring. I pick out and file the pieces that I think would make good articles for the next issue. The only challenge is fighting the will to delete a lot of the mail straight off – we get a lot of people sending in their life stories and rants which aren't really that relevant to anything. We also get a lot of people asking the most random questions, but, you know, being a community-spirited bunch, we try and get back to everyone."

Chris has been involved in SchNEWS for five years and comes in at least every Wednesday "I write articles, but somehow I've managed to end up doing loads of crappy office work, probably cos no-one else bothers to do it. I open the post each week and nearly every week we get a random conspiracy theory – you can spot them a mile off 'cos they always just jump straight into the middle of a story without having an introduction and generally they make absolutely no sense at all!

I also tidy the office a lot. People who work at SchNEWS tend to be really crap at keeping anything in an ordered manner. So it is often down to me to sort out the piles of books, back issues and random bits of paper lying around the office that get thrown away but, inevitably, have some sort of really important phone number scribbled on a coffee stained corner."

John: "Because SchNEWS is an information node, with our 'party & protest' listing being the main thing of its kind in Britain, people treat our number like a citizen's advice bureau, or at least a first point of contact. Which means when you're trying to get something done, and the bloody phone rings all day – apparently it used to be even worse. People ring through bulletins about actions and events of course (as you do), but you also get people on the line who've just got out of a police cell and need a solicitor, or someone's being sectioned against their will and desperately needs advice. Or else it's journalists – 'we're doing a lifestyle piece about anti-capitalist demonstrators' or call centre workers ringing from India, with whom we chat about globalisation."

Pascal, joined the SchNEWS team back in January, after reading about one of the training days run at SchNEWS Towers.

"Having all the writing ability of a pre-school George W Bush, it was probably best that I got asked to do the desktop publishing. Getting the front page, SchNEWS in brief, Positive SchNEWS and the Crap Arrest to fit into two A4 pages is a tight squeeze, but we always seem to find a way.

I come in at about 4pm and get on with proof reading the article, as the strain of producing SchNEWS each week has clearly taken its toll on the writing team's grammar and spellin'! Once all the words are in the right place I'll put them in the slick, glossy format that you have come to expect!

The headlines are written once all the writing is in. This is the hardest part of the day as it involves going through some really cringe worthy efforts until

A Sch-New Way Of Doing Things

Wednesday and Thursday is when that week's issue gets written. A list emerges of the stories we want to cover, coming from range of sources: people phoning or emailing through stuff, our own reports back, and various sources of news bulletins which need follow up research.

SchNEWS is produced in such a way that if you are precious about your work being edited then this is the wrong place for you, on the other hand if you're stuck there's others to help out. It's written collectively, so that anyone who comes in the office gets to have a look, change stuff, correct mistakes, add a comment or joke, think of a headline, so the articles are always evolving and hopefully getting stronger. The first day a new person comes in they're working on a story, and as they get more confident they take bigger ones on. Normally before going to print an article has been emailed to people who are at the event, or those with a bit more knowledge on the subject than us, to make sure there aren't any howlers.

We reckon this collective editorial style is unique and means that those that are new in the office get a say, along with the old gits that have been here since the beginning of time.

we come up with the one that makes us laugh the most (G8 My Hamster anyone?). We always have to check the SchNEWS archives just to make sure that we haven't used the same Hackney-ed line before!"

John: "When there's a draft of the front page knocking around on Thursday afternoon me and Phil use various ways and means to get the creative juices flowing, and come up with a graphic. Either we have a really complicated idea which is fiddly to draw, or it's simple and iconic. Some subjects are tricky, how do you get a joke out of the General Agreement on the Trades on Services?! Other things are hard to joke about – like ID Cards. Thanks to Steve Bell, Dubya is very easy to draw. The biggest buzz is when you find people have pinched our graphics for things like zines, record covers or flyposters."

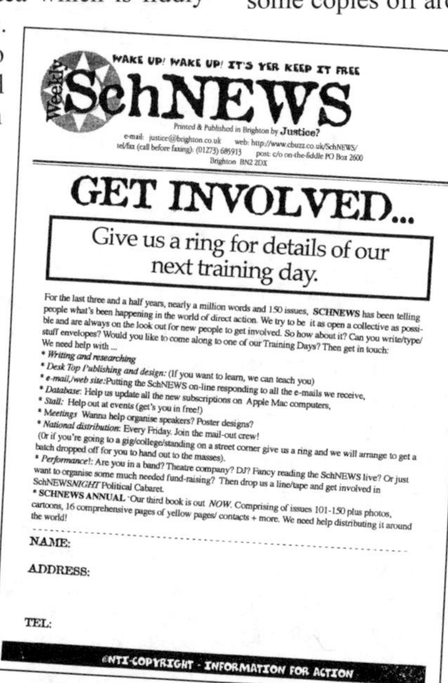

WAKE UP! WAKE UP! IT'S YER KEEP IT FREE

Weekly SchNEWS

Printed & Published in Brighton by Justice?

e-mail: justice@brighton.co.uk web: http://www.cbuzz.co.uk/SchNEWS/
tel/fax (call before faxing): (01273) 685913 post: c/o on-the-fiddle PO Box 2600 Brighton BN2 2DX

GET INVOLVED...

Give us a ring for details of our next training day.

For the last three and a half years, nearly a million words and 150 issues, **SCHNEWS** has been telling people what's been happening in the world of direct action. We try to be it as open a collective as possible and are always on the look out for new people to get involved. So how about it? Can you write/type/stuff envelopes? Would you like to come along to one of our Training Days? Then get in touch:

We need help with ...

* *Writing and researching*
* *Desk Top Publishing and design:* (If you want to learn, we can teach you)
* *e-mail,/web site:* Putting the SchNEWS on-line responding to all the e-mails we receive,
* *Database*: Help us update all the new subscriptions on Apple Mac computers,
* *Stall:* Help out at events (get's you in free!)
* *Meetings* Wanna help organise speakers? Poster designs?
* *National distribution*: Every Friday. Join the mail-out crew! (Or if you're going to a gig/college/standing on a street corner give us a ring and we will arrange to get a batch dropped off for you to hand out to the masses).
* *Performance!*: Are you in a band? Theatre company? DJ? Fancy reading the SchNEWS live? Or just want to organise some much needed fund-raising? Then drop us a line/tape and get involved in SchNEWS*NIGHT* Political Cabaret.
* **SCHNEWS ANNUAL** Our third book is out *NOW*. Comprising of issues 101-150 plus photos, cartoons, 16 comprehensive pages of yellow pages/ contacts + more. We need help distributing it around the world!

NAME:

ADDRESS:

TEL:

ANTI-COPYRIGHT · INFORMATION FOR ACTION

Once the issue has been DTP'd, it's time for the webmasters to do their job, as Iain explains:

"I found out about SchNEWS at the Lizard festival in Cornwall in 1999 where they had a big stall and marquee. I took a SchNEWS, read it and liked it, bought the book read it and liked it, and moved to Brighton six months later, partly because of the SchNEWS connection. I knew they needed someone to do their website so got in touch and have pretty much been doing it every Thursday since.

The issue is in various states of disrepair when I get there early evening – sometimes it's all finished, sometimes it seems like it's hardly been started... After it's been DTP'd I copy it onto the website which takes a couple of hours if you've got a straight run.

Then there's the party and protest guide that gets updated every week, as well as other bits – protest camps, what's happening in your area, the contacts list, the DIY guide etc that get updated regularly. And on top of that there have been extra bits like the Worst Britons poll and the "when the war starts" pages just to keep us on our toes. A recent addition to the site is the SchMOVIES section which contains films we showed on the tour and some we shot on the tour.

I also send SchNEWS out on our two email lists – one is just plain text, the other is PDF which means you can print it out and looks like the paper issue and you can copy it and distribute it yourself which, happily, people do. There are 10,000 people on these lists. There's other work during the week too, with at least a couple of hundred emails a week sent to the webmaster account, subscribing and unsubscribing people etc.

Doing the website isn't very complicated but is really important for distribution, with about 30,000 visits a month."

Friday is the day of printing, stuffing envelopes and updating the database:

Tim "...got involved because as a reader it was the least I could do. My contribution is pretty small – a few hours each week, usually printing and dropping some copies off around Brighton bars, pubs & cafes. The worst experience was printing about a million before the anti war demo and the best is the reaction from people when handing them out or on stalls, sometimes you can't get rid of them quick enough."

Russell comes after his post-round to have some fun stuffing envelopes, while Cath has the job of updating the database.

"SchNEWS is mailed out on a weekly basis, worldwide, to political prisoners, bookshops and subscribers.

After ten years the operation runs smoothly, yeah right, about as smooth as a cat's tongue. In fact this is how it feels to lick 500 stamps in one afternoon! Every week the task of delivering SchNEWS is a battle against multi-national corporations and conglomerates: there's Microsoft and their program glitches and the Post Office which keeps changing its prices.

Our printers don't help much either. SchNEWS has a subscriber's database; it contains all the names and addresses of the people who subscribe to SchNEWS. (We know where you live!). All the relevant address labels are printed out, but because the database and printer are temperamental often the irrelevant ones are as well. If it wasn't for our stubbornness we'd be writing all the labels by hand and probably drawing the stamps as well, but we can never find a pen that works!

Volunteers that make up the mail-out crew come and go and we are always grateful for their help (hint hint). A few though, are surprised it's not all excitement and glamour in the world of independent media. Surprisingly, SchNEWS still gets to you despite all this chaos."

And then there's all the other jobs...

John: "On the subject of sexy jobs – I keep the computers alive. Back in the supposedly good-ol days, they were struggling with one flakey computer and no internet to do SchNEWS. These days – the office looks like a call centre because really unless you're sitting round drinking tea or rolling spliffs, you need to be on a computer – and it needs to be on the internet. So we have six blagged virus-battered

The SchNEWS festival set-up in full flight: info stall, and marquees for schmovies and kids area/chill out Glastonbury 2004

frankensteins made of mongrel bits. I keep an eye out in skip bins – because it's such a shockingly throwaway society, it's all there for the taking. To be producing a newletter, books, websites, SchMovies and all the rest on what we've got is a proper bit of DIY. Same goes for skipped office chairs, of which I've become an expert 'ooh that one's got the mark three armrests'."

Lesley first got involved after coming to a Justice meeting at the Courthouse, and ten years on is still helping out.

"I started helping SchNEWS by giving a hand to paint the newly acquired office at the Metway (which er, hasn't been painted since), then with the stall in the North Laine in Brighton on a Saturday. I also used to help out with the mailout every Friday, and distributed SchNEWS around town for many years until I got sick of the sight of my own face!

Now I help to organize festivals and keep the plants alive in the office. Took over the not-so-sexy job of looking after the accounts, 'cos someone needed to. I'm continually being inspired to keep going by endless support from letters to the office and from meeting so many enthusiastic people at festivals."

One plus point to all these great jobs is free tickets for festivals!

Chris: "SchNEWS manages to blag into festivals – but it's not all an easy ride. We take marquees along for a chill-out space, run our free info-stall and show SchMovies. This year's Glastonbury was a laugh, we turned up in the pouring rain and had to wait 24 hours to put up the first marquee, then when we tried to put up the second marquee it was so windy the pegs kept ripping out of the ground, it took a whole morning to get it up."

John: "Doing info-stalls at festivals is more fun than it looks – it's a great way to chat to half the people on the site. You find out first hand what's going on around the country – and catch up with our mates from crews like Veggies, Squatters Advisory Service, Totnes Genetics, Kebele and others who are always in the same field as us. People drift past all day for a chat, though you do have to put up with the odd well-meaning bore chewing your ear off. We also do stalls at various types of gigs and events. When you're doing a stall at a party by about 3-30am you attract that small percentage who aren't staggering about on ketamine or anything else, and in fact are desperate for a sensible chat!!"

Iain: "Doing the festies is a game of two halfs really. On one hand you've got to negotiate with the organisers, explaining that it takes more than 4 people to put up 2 marquees, deal with power, show films and man a stall all week, then you've got to organise a crew, food, power, transport, the stall stuff etc. When you get there you've got to try to get the marquees up in less time than it takes you to get too drunk to do it. And at the end you've got to take it all down and squeeze it all in the van again, usually with a somewhat dazed and confused feeling. That's the not-so-fun stuff. But while the festival's going you're in the perfect spot to enjoy it with a steady flow of people to chat to, fewer than average worries about having your tent slashed and the warm glow of doing something more productive than just beating your most trashed ever record. Though some people manage to do both."

FULLY BOOKED OUT

For a few months of each year as well as producing the weekly newsletter, we're burning the midnight fair-trade coffee putting together another annual. Here we speak to John whose been involved in the last few...

Who does SchNEWS reach with its annual books?

They have a different function to the weekly newsletter, or the website. We end up distributing them ourselves mostly – selling them on our stalls, posting mail orders, posting to bookshops – and many go out for free to campaign groups, info-centres, and prisoners. And the blag list is endless! We try to get them to new places – like social centres in eastern Europe or the Philippines. Someone once found a SchNEWS book in a temple in India. So they're not instant, like the weekly, but they have a more long-term existence, and they do get around.

What's the job of the annuals?

It's to bring together the year's fifty issues – and to add the things which the weekly issues can't have… like photos, cartoons and more in depth articles. I always say the annuals are like me – they get fatter every year.

How do they come together?

Each one is different, and a learning curve cos of course we're not trained to do these things. But it usually comes from building up a list which we think were important from the past year, working out what sorts of articles would compliment the actual SchNEWS issues, and either commissioning, writing, borrowing or pinching articles which will do the job. Then there's building up piles of photos and cartoons, and bringing all these things into the mix. What you have in mind at the beginning, and what you end up with at the end are two totally different things – you have to be flexible.

The books are an experiment in using all yer right-on decentralised non-linear ways to do things which might otherwise be done very rigidly in the structure of a publishing house. So you're playing 'editor' to people who aren't 'proper' writers, but people actually involved in the issues. Which means you have to cope with sliding deadlines, hippy time and other er variables. On the other hand you're always dealing with people who really do give a shit about the stuff.

Sitting on a computer for months drinking coffee and dealing with things like fonts and images isn't very 'direct action' is it?

To be honest when I spend four or five months solid stuck in here on a book, I think it's about as mad and bloody-minded as spending how ever long down a road protest tunnel or where ever. That might be 'direct action' in the normal sense of the word, but there are a range of frontlines. Some people I know might not agree with this, because of a suspicion amongst 'activists' of alternative media – as though it's a training ground for 'medya' jobs. This is sometimes justified, but there's a big difference between a multi-media yuppie flirting with liberal politics till a real job comes along and a form of action going back to Calvert and the pamphlets makers in the 1600's. In the present day it's yer zine makers, billboard redecorators, independent video makers, subversive websites… genuine on-the-case people trying to bring positive social change, by bypassing the mainstream media.

SchNEWS doesn't come from a zine background, but from people doing direct action who also do a newsletter… doesn't it?

Yes it definitely arose from the need of a political movement to have a media outlet. But at the same time something like SchNEWS takes people with a range of talents, who are prepared to take on a range of tasks in a sustained way – like envelope stuffing. As it turns out hardly anyone who's been involved comes from an alternative media background apart from me - although some people have done zines. Previous to this I was involved in a satirical magazine in Australia – Lies – which we ended up getting into newsagents across the country, but produced it totally independently, and never let it get distorted by commercial pressures. Recently I spoke to a comedian from there who told me that as a teenager in a shitty outer suburb of Perth, him and his friends were into Lies. I thought - if we were reaching kids in places like that - fucking great.

KINKY KINKY

I like to go in the THIRD WAY.

020 7555 44443

TELL ME ALL ABOUT IT

You were at Newbury in a climbing harness? Come on over ECO LOVER

DIAL: 0234 234 234 234

TALK BUSINESS

I'll part privatise your private parts

Call DTI NOW: 020 7215 5000

CHAT

Bore me all night about May 68 and the Situationists and pay 60p a minute to hear me say 'amazing' occasionally.

0888 85434 3332

ZAPATISTA FETISHISTAS

I've been to Chiapas too.

0798 400 86338

DOMINATRIX

If it's not hurting it's not working.

01273 685 913

ASIAN GIRL

gets under $1 a day working for Nike - what are you going to do about it?

phone: 07958 556756

www.nosweat.org.uk

Some of the classified ads in SchNEWS Of The World

The good thing about SchNEWS is that it doesn't compromise content, but yet manages to reach a wide audience - even though it gets called 'populist' by people whose worthy little papers reach tiny numbers. It's no good to just preach to the converted – you need to get out to 'real' people.

Back to the annuals. What were some of the different aspects to the various books?

The first two I was involved with (SchQUALL and Yearbook 2001) were combined books with Squall (www.squall.co.uk). We meshed Squall articles, which covered many of the same things as the SchNEWS articles. This worked well – because Squall also had good photographers – so it all tied together easily.

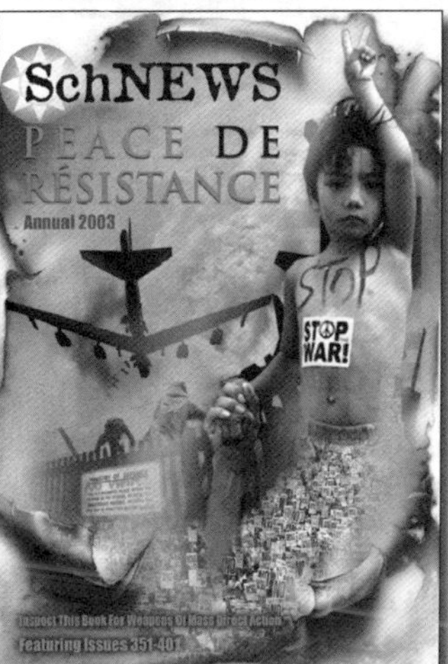

With SchNEWS Of The World a huge wish list of extra articles was drawn up – which all had to be written or sourced. There were 140, and I think we ended up getting 110 of them – which in retrospect was ridiculous. In the end I was just so up to my eyeballs in the project, like a bull terrier not letting go I hung on until all these articles came together. But I was very proud of it and Joe Plant's cover was incredible.

That book was a game of two halves - one was the deadly serious articles about world issues, the other was the tabloid pisstake side of it which the satirical stuff came from. I was buying the odd copy of the Sun for a few months to get the tabloid flavour - but at that time every day the Sun was finding an excuse to print Kylie's bum. It was torture - it just reminds you why we do SchNEWS.

With Peace De Resistance we decided to rein in the scope of the book and concentrate on the anti-war protests which were in full swing at the time. And we upped the font size. We drew up a plan, aiming to have the book for Glastonbury that year, and sure enough we got to share that sweet moment where you've got the new copies in the middle of the festival. Comedians Mark Thomas and Rob Newman kindly came down to Brighton to do a big launch gig for us.

Because each annual is a kind-of one-off, this 10th anniversary year we decided to do a completely different type of thing. Again, a whole new set of things to get our heads around: doing interviews, going through archives, and finding out how the years of caning it have affected peoples' memories.

How many do you usually sell?

The last four have had print runs of 3000. We don't maintain sales records – we're not a small business – but we eventually get through the boxes. We're very lucky to get big donations from anonymous sources, which takes away most of the 'financial viability' burden which normally kills things like this. So thankfully without that worry – the main aim is to get the books out there – which includes everything from using distro people like Active or AK down to much smaller efforts: like when Warren visits shit-hole towns following Slough Town football club around the country he donates SchNEWS books to charity shops – and if some kid takes it home for 50p then you might be reaching someone completely new.

What's a favourite moment from the books?

I love doing the photo stories. 'Carry On Bombing' involved spending a week in the scary world of 'Carry On' fans, who it turns out have regular conventions, often in Brighton because 2 films were shot here. I emailed the website asking to be told about the next Brighton convention because I said "I could come quite easily".

Carry On Bombing: the photostory from 'Peace De Resistance' which tells the story of the invasion of Iraq in see-em-coming-a-mile-off double entendres with a simpering Kenneth Williams as Tony Blair, a guffawing Sid James as Bush, a gawky Charles Hawtrey as Jack Straw, an eye-popping Barbara Windsor as Condaleeza Rice, a groping Benny Hill as Hans Blix, an imbecilic Manuel as ex-Spanish leader Charles Aznar and Donald Rumsfeld playing himself as Dr Evil

Will The Real Jo Makepeace Please Stand Up?

Jo Makepeace is the editor of SchNEWS, but she's actually a very hard person to track down. Because SchNEWS is anonymous, often people don't really have an image of the people behind SchNEWS. There's probably been about fifty people who have been involved in some sort of sustained way around the office over the years, and hundreds more who are involved in distribution around the country/world, and writing or sending things in. Then there's the thousands who float about trying to blag their way into gigs and journalism courses because they once handed out SchNEWS at a gig five years ago.

Anyway out of all those people, here are some often quite personal interviews with just a few of those who have been involved, and give you an idea of the sorts of characters this place attracts...

After the first 50 issues, some of the key people moved on, but thankfully Pete and Tammi got involved and gave some serious commitment to the newsletter...

So when did you come to SchNEWS?

Pete: End of 1995. I was involved from issue 50. I was up in Manchester at the time and we got issues three onwards sent up to us and we thought this was a bit good. We always wondered who were the miscellaneous nutcases putting this together. About a year later I came down and found out, literally. One of them was me!

Tammi: At the beginning of 1996. I moved to Brighton in '96, and had seen SchNEWS in obscure places around town (buses, toilets, that kinda thing) and I thought that it was probably a more productive thing to do than sitting at home smoking dope and talking about putting the world to rights. I arrived with a packet of bourbons and the tradition lives on...

How did you get involved in the direct action movement?

Pete: I was fresh out of university and thought I'd try to do something useful for society. I knew about Twyford Down but at the time I was busy doing my finals at the time. I was a Green Party member but only by bunging 'em eight quid every year.

Tammi: My mum wouldn't let me go on a Greenham Common march when I was 15, so I became vegan, tithed my meagre Saturday job wages to the cause and plotted my escape. My first direct action was leading a school protest in the mid 80's, which resulted in a suspension, lots of street cred and front page in the Leicester Mercury.

So you weren't aware of direct action yet, Pete?

Pete: I got involved with the Green Party in planning for the public enquiry against the Worthing bypass and learning about how public enquiries were hideously unfair, and how in those days there'd only been one that had refused a road. And you think, 'This is horseshit'.

You realised that you weren't going to win by using the usual channels?

Pete: Yes, so the initial thing was how to plan a disruption of the public enquiry. I'd seen the Oxford Direct Action video (the pre-runner to Undercurrents) round somebody's house and that was like – bloody hell, people jammed into canoes stopping logging ships. I'd never seen anything like it before in my life – it was very inspiring.

So you ended up doing a lot of stuff around Manchester at this time?

Pete: I was involved in a lot of campaigns – we did the ethical shoplifting of mahogany, Critical Mass bike rides, something different every week. 1994 was the most incredible, mad year of my entire life. I spent the whole year running around the country getting arrested. Thirteen arrests in the end, six convictions. Got arrested twice in one day once!

The first actual action I did was a lock-on at a Texas Homecare – locking yourself around the neck with a bicycle -lock to a mahogany stand and the manager coming along and cutting, or trying to cut it with a hacksaw. And you're absolutely pooing yourself – it made very little difference to the D-lock but you're like, 'This is going to cut my bloody head off'!

So what other things were you up too?

Pete: Amazing campaigns like the M11, which was my favourite. This series of streets in East London where, no cars went up or down. And it was a genuine community. There was a jazz café which was self-funding through various means, which we won't go into. There were days of action, and by the end of each day you could tell how much fun someone had had by whether or not they were covered head-to-toe in crane grease. I was living on the M11 for three months, but it wasn't like living in London. It was like Lord of the fucking Rings.

Thinking back, the roads budget in '93 was £23 billion and by 95-96 it was down to £4 billion. The M11 was built – but it was the longest eviction post-World War II and cost £4 million, and that was just for three days. And god knows how much Newbury cost. It was millions of pounds. At the end of the day the Worthing Bypass was not built.

Tammi: I was living in Luton at the time, heavily involved with the free party collective Exodus. The fight against the CJA was on top. There was a lot of police stress at some of the parties when you knew that the directives were coming from a higher place than the local police beat. The parties took all the crap away from the estates and directed all that energy into something positive. Crime figures for the wards with the biggest council estates were dramatically down on the night of a 'do'.

Talk about the SchNEWS production schedule then.

Pete: SchNEWS would take a couple of days to put together and there'd already have been a bit of initial work going on already from the week before. A lot of it would be the slog of getting it down to two sides. And then – knocking the headline together – and you'd come up with a good headline and because it's only an A4 newssheet you'd have to shorten it. My favourite headline was 'Police Enter Dead Woman's Bottom', and 'Sheriff Sore After Seven Day Shafting'.

There'd be times when a more pressing story would develop over those two days, and you'd have to sack the front page and start another one. No two weeks would be the same. A bit like giving birth – some babies just pop out, others are 72 hours of grunting, straining and crying!

Tammi: For me the best was the collaborative method of writing and editing. Time would be spent getting the bare bones of the story down onto the computer, then other people would add a quote or a bit of attitude or comment. The final edit was often two or three of us poring over words, trying to make it all fit, sometimes not leaving till 6 in the morning.

Tam, can you talk about some of SchNEWS work at festivals?

Tammi: In the first years, a lot of the times we'd get offered a few free tickets for one festival or another, print up a few extra thousand copies and just walk around giving them out. You'd go and hand 'em out, go and talk to punters – or just shake the donation bucket. Sometimes you'd get people who were really mashed up going 'Oh you're doing really fucking good work' and stick a fiver in – it was a really good way to get a load of positive feedback.

Tammi: I had my first baby in 1997. I kept thinking that as soon as the baby settles, I could just go back to doing one night a week at the office... how naïve I was! I recall sitting in the office with a 5 month baby balanced on my head (I am not making this up!) trying to type in an article I had written the previous night whilst breastfeeding. So I bowed out of action, and did a permaculture course. I still get involved with family-friendly actions, but on the sidelines.

Cosmo gets serious as Flannel liven up an RTS Street Party, Brighton, 1996

Cosmo got involved in the Courthouse and helped out with SchNEWS but is most well known for fronting 'punk rock pop with cheese on top' band Flannel.

What got you into SchNEWS and doing direct action?

Cosmo: I was hanging about in Brighton working and playing in bands. I had a certain amount of political awareness, but I was so cynical that it never translated into actually doing anything. At the time someone said, "Get yourself down the Courthouse, there's a big squat going on, loads of things happening." So I went down there one afternoon and, like lots of people, my life was completely transformed. There was so much positive happening as a reaction to the CJB. As a result it ended up politicising people who had never really thought about stuff in this way before – myself included. By the next year I was working on SchNEWS, then I'd moved off to Wales to help defend a piece of land in Wales that was going to be opencast mined and formed an anarcho-narcho-funk-punk-pop band! Help!!

What did you do with SchNEWS?

Around 1995 I got involved. An incredibly poignant moment happened one day when I turned up at the SchNEWS office and found out that a woman called Jill Phillips had died. She was a single mum who had been run over during a protest by a lorry carrying live calves for export. I found it so tragic and shocking that someone had died in this way, standing up for something I felt strongly about. In a lot of ways it was an intense time filled with so many extreme feelings and life changing moments. This was a big political lesson I learned at the time – sometimes it takes something to affect you and the people around you so that you become aware of the shit that goes down elsewhere in the world.

I was never much good at writing about news issues because my journalism skills were not up to much. Everytime I wrote something it was always edited a lot, but that was cool 'cos I got to learn about how these things work. The main thing I learned from writing SchNEWS was that in order to understand the most important things happening in the world, you have to go out and experience them for yourself.

Your band and your direct action were intertwined...

Flannel worked like an activist cell or affinity group, because we were trying to challenge the way a lot of bands operated. We'd do PAs for Reclaim the Streets, play at protest camps and do publicity stunts that had a real political edge to them. We were trying to bring a bit of humour into things, and were inspired by what was happening at the time on the direct action scene. There was lots of laughter and people weren't up their own backsides too much. While not trying to belittle the seriousness of the issues, there were times when doing actions was like a cross between the Krypton Factor and It's a Knockout!

Here's an example of the sort of direct action punk Flannel got up to... 'And Finally' from issue 192, 19th November 1998:

" Tony Blair's employment revolution took a bizarre turn in the North East last week. Reeling from a post gig knees-up in Darlington, aggro-pop group Flannel decided to take out their comedowns on scabs at Magnet Kitchens, who replaced the 300 skilled workers sacked by management three years ago. "I wouldn't have a Magnet kitchen fitted in my own shithouse," explained bassist Bloke to customers, as they invaded the showroom in drag and serenaded people with Spanish love songs. Jumping on a display bed, Fat Stan and Cosmo cried "We were gonna have a bit of nookie on this but we don't think the workmanship's up to it!" Police eventually bundled them out, but a local boycott has ensured there's only about two customers a fortnight.

The previous day, the band blagged a gig at Sunderland's New Deal Employment Revolution Showcase, where they were hoping to play their anti-work song Hold It Down. On arriving however, they found a few displays and a crowd of 30 people, so they quickly set up a SchNEWS stall and distributed anti-casualisation leaflets from the Simon Jones Memorial campaign. Two middle aged suits from the local enterprise services came by saying "Aye, we fooking agree with yous! Thatcherism totally fucked this part of the country up!" and proceeded to play Black Sabbath songs on the band's equipment. Watch out for the Surreal New Deal for musicians in April. Sex and drugs and on the dole?"

Tell us about that Justice? meeting at the police station?

Cosmo: Justice? was meeting at various places and usually it was cool but the police weren't averse to leaning on landlords or club owners to try and stop things if they felt like throwing their weight around.

One time Justice? was told we couldn't meet in this pub and everyone was like – What the hell do we do now? So some bright spark suggested we go and hold the meeting in the foyer of the police station. About forty or fifty of us traipsed into the foyer of the cop shop and basically had the meeting there. It was surreal. It was quite tense, but deep down everyone was suppressing a laugh. We went through the agenda, everyone said their bit and we fucked off when it was done. If you have nothing to hide, you have nothing to fear, as they say! Fantastic! The desk sergeant looked on with a forced-looking smile fixed to his face. A load of freaks had just made full use of the facilities and there was nothing he could do!

Jon moved to Brighton new year 1997 and started helping out with SchNEWS straight away. Despite moving town and country a couple of times since, he always seems to come back to Brighton, and when he's got time, back to the office.

Jon: At the time I only knew two people in Brighton, but it was either there or go back to Nottingham where I'd been involved in running the Hunt Sabs' national office. As usual, everyone had fallen out with each other in a storm of bitter paranoia and I really wanted to go somewhere new. So Brighton it was. I'd come across SchNEWS in the scene over the years and those two people I knew in Brighton were both involved, so I was up in the office within my first week in town. I was sharing a flat with a communist, so anything to get out of the house!

What period of SchNEWS was this?

Jon: This was about issue 102-103. It was quite a regular crew then and a really good laugh. Pete and I had a similar sense of humour, which we would bend over backwards to accommodate into whatever we were writing. This would wind up politicos across the country no end. There'd always be complaints, generally coming from Manchester Earth First!, complaining in a very 'disgusted of Tunbridge Wells' manner about our perceived political incorrectness. It's not that we were deliberately 'un-PC', more that we regarded it as an irrelevance. I'd been involved in political stuff since I was 15 but was sick to the back teeth of the po-faced miserablism that most people seem to see as de rigueur when dealing with all this fucked-upness. When I first came across SchNEWS, it seemed like a breath of fresh air; it was very symbolic of a whole shift that seemed to come with the anti-CJB campaigns.

How did you get involved with the 'Movement'?

Jon: Like lots of people of my generation I was politicized by punk rock. I grew up in a crappy little dormitory village in Buckinghamshire. A bloke in my class had played me a tape by this band called Flux Of Pink Indians, who were part of the whole anarcho-punk scene. This would have been 1982-3. I went out and started buying loads of records with my pocket money, and they all came with these little booklets full of political ranting. It was all very DIY, all cut-and-pasted and photocopied. The forerunners of stuff like SchNEWS, except at this time everything was deadly serious. There were people churning out these things all over the country, questioning everything in society.

The big things at the time were the anti-nuclear movement and animal rights. I quickly went veggie and started going to gigs. I somehow ended up on a bus full of anarcho-punks organised by High Wycombe CND going to a big anti-nuclear demo at Aldermaston. I kind of by-passed the whole 'peaceful protestor' phase most people go through cos as soon as we were off the bus we were ripping down fences, shouting abuse at cops and being told off by CND officials. I guess I fell in with the wrong crowd.

I soon got into Hunt Sabbing and Animal Rights. Then I ended up in Cardiff where there was a local Class War group (all of us were middle class, naturally) and the Cardiff Solidarity Group, which was a forum for anarchists. This consisted mainly of strange, silent pipe-smoking bearded types who churned out pamphlets urging the bombing of shopping centres. And everything was incredibly academic, dry and deadly serious. Anarchism seemed at the time like a very small pigeonhole occupied entirely by turgid ideologues. It was easy for ordinary people to dismiss.

Then this big change seemed to happen, which turned everything on its head and suddenly the counter-culture became a positive, vibrant, imaginative force again.

What was that?

Jon: Well, as far as I can remember it was the Criminal Justice Bill, and the road protest movement starting at Twyford Down. First thing I knew about it was a little article in Freedom – the world's dullest paper – telling everyone to go to Twyford. Anyway, I just suddenly remember the old guard getting overtaken; suddenly there were loads of things springing up, with all completely new people. I moved to Nottingham, helped run the Hunt Sabs office and was sabbing four days a week. The grand old days of the dole. I was really conscious of a growing gap between the 'new' movement and the last vestiges of the 'old'; the sabs was full of 'up for it' old punks used to violence and the 'eco warriors' seemed to be coming from this 'fluffy' standpoint which seemed to me like naivety verging on stupidity. So I unfairly ignored it all for ages. My loss. Still, I loved the creative and vibrant side of it all, the DIY culture, and so I hung out more and more with them and was called a hippy by my mates.

What was SchNEWS like to work on when you first arrived?

Jon: The thing I remember about SchNEWS was the phone never stopped ringing. It really felt like you were involved in something relevant & vital; people would be phoning in with stories, or asking for contacts, or the straight media would be after information. It was great to be feeling that we were really getting to people, helping people open up their minds and ask questions. I was so used to being involved in the 'old school', where everything was coming from the perspective of guilt-tripping people into getting involved. Now we were getting letters at SchNEWS from 15-year-old kids in some godforsaken place, saying how they were excited by what was going on and really wanting to get involved. They all pointed out how SchNEWS dropping through their door every week was a vital link. That spurs you on.

And vital to that was the fact that SchNEWS was so accessible. Not just in terms of it coming in the mail every week, but in terms of it being written in what I would call a 'friendly' or 'down to earth' way. We

deliberately avoided all the dry academic stuff that was part and parcel of radical political media. We were actually reaching people, and that was what mattered.

Any Particular Favourite Issues?

Jon: I was very proud of the J18 issue (SchNEWS 217). The whole thing was so widely reported by every media outlet in the nation, radical and mainstream, and so many little things happened, that it seemed pointless trying to write a 'standard' report. So instead we opted for taking the piss out of the media hysteria, in the form of an over-the-top burst of indignant outrage worthy of the Daily Mail.

I remember dealing with an irate telephone complaint about 'Down the Cakehole & Up The Duff'. Everything we wrote pissed someone off. Usually from Manchester.

Misty got involved with SchNEWS in 2001. Being American gave every one else in the office the chance to try out all their great anti US jokes, but she paid us all back by being the most pedantic editor since Gibby.

Misty: I got involved when a friend of mine had invited me to Rebel Alliance, a meeting of radical groups that used to happen in Brighton every month or so, and introduced me to one of the SchNEWS crew. A few days later I found myself standing at the door of the office, wondering how so many people, magazines, computers, dogs and bits of paper could fit into such a small space. My greeting was far from friendly – I remember a few grunts from the furiously typing group and the ear-piercing bark of Scruffy the dog. Once everyone figured out that I might be around to stay, they warmed up pretty quickly, treating me to their merciless piss-taking and cutting British wit without restraint. At first no one could seem to get over the fact that I was American, and the jokes about McDonald's, Mickey Mouse, and Phil's endless comments about Vietnam never ended. But once they got to know me, they started to take the piss out of me for far more interesting things – my obsessive interest in correct grammar and the fact that in 2 1/2 years of working together, I probably offered to make tea for everyone a grand total of once.

I will never forget my worst SchNEWS experience. It was late one Thursday night and we had, as usual, just spent the last two days researching, writing, and editing the issue for that week. Suddenly all the computer screens began flashing and freaking out, and by the time we'd sorted them out, we realized that we'd lost the ENTIRE issue. EVERYTHING!! There were only about three or four of us left in the office, and under different circumstances we might have just decided to forget it. But this was the issue that was supposed to be going to the Anarchist Bookfair, or some such, so we decided to brew a hell of a lot of coffee, and re-write the entire fucking thing. None of us got any sleep that night, but SchNEWS came out the next day, same as usual.

And what is my favourite thing about SchNEWS? The way that everyone is given an equal say. Yeah, okay, some people have been around for longer than others, which means that their opinion might get sought out more, but one thing that struck me right from the beginning was how much responsibility and faith new people are given, right from the start. Everyone gets thrown in at the deep end!! Just got here today? Here, why not write this piece on striking workers in Colombia? Don't feel comfortable writing just yet? Here, why not call this traveller and ask her what's up with the possible eviction of her site? That's what I love about SchNEWS – how it's a bunch of people sharing responsibility and writing tips and generally making it up as they go along...

Adrian and Liz are two of the newest recruits, coming to a training day at the beginning of this year – and unlike the majority of people who come to have a look round, drink our tea, eat our biscuits and never return, they've actually stayed to help out.

Ade: I first picked up a copy of the SchNEWS in summer '95. The arrestometer for the CJA caught my attention and it was great to see that people were still fighting. I'd been terrified that the summer of '94 would be my last free party, but the fact that I was in town for a free party and had read SchNEWS helped things look up again.

I like to write about globalisation and Latin America in particular. Corrupt politicians and their corporate interests have taken the piss so badly over there that people have noticed. The policy of the United States in continuing the history of economic pillage in the region is too obvious, when it makes the majority of the population too poor to eat. It's just bound to kick off over there, it always does.

Liz: I moved to Brighton two years before to do a politics degree, and started to educate myself a lot more about things that were going on in the world. I read a lot of morbid books, and it got to the point where I was so angry about what was going on that it was either read Heat magazine, buy some new shoes and forget it all, or do something about it…

Anyway I was reading an issue of SchNEWS and saw that they were looking for more people to help out. The way it works is quite different from anything I'd done before. Choosing what I wanted to do, being expected to use my initiative – a million miles away from a de-humanising minimum wage job. I started off checking e-mails every week and have now started to write occasionally as well. Although non-hierarchical, SchNEWS is incredibly organised, and it's a constant inspiration to be working with people who have gotten off their arses and done so much stuff.

Phil has been licking stamps, thinking of headlines and handing out SchNEWS since the very beginning. So, why did you get involved, Phil?

Phil: I was reading the Brighton Argus and there was a bit about Justice?, the old Courthouse squat and the

Criminal Justice Bill and it looked like fun. It reminded me of stuff from the past so I thought I'd take my two year old son down and meet new people. I was always interested in art and communication and it was in my horoscope that I'd get involved in a newsletter that would be international! I went to a meeting where it was mentioned that the Levellers had given Justice? free office space, and it seemed a scam-free, honourable enterprise that needed long-term commitment.

Ten years later and Phil's still here. How did you first help SchNEWS?

Phil: Giving out copies, helping with the stall, signing cheques and buying sellotape for the mail out.

Ah the mailout...the amount of times we've put a bit in SchNEWS pleading for more people to help with the mail out.

Phil: It isn't as exciting as writing, but ultimately it's just as fucking important! The mail out was first done on index cards and we used sellotape and tatty old envelopes, then we transferred it to a computer and someone trained me up to use it. Every week was a nightmare with something going wrong. It turned me into an alcoholic.

A typical Friday would be me making sure that I had my beer to bring to the office, getting here for 12 and starting to update the database and having an hour on my own to sort things out. I'd go though the letters, decipher people's handwriting, update the database, calculate their subscriptions, and work out if we had enough money. One nice thing about the database is reading all the lovely letters from subscribers and all the letters from prisoners, learning all about prison and what is does to people.

In the middle of the printer chewing up the mail out list, journalists would ring asking some crappy question. They always ask for Jo Makepeace and I wonder why they never think it's odd that Jo keeps changing sex or is always on holiday!

One of the strangest conversations I'd ever had was with a 'journalist' who obviously wasn't. He refused to give his name or the paper he worked for and asked me what we knew about the acts of terror planned for the George Bush visit. I asked him what did he know about the acts of terror planned by Bush? After further interrogation the 'journalist' slammed down his phone in disgust.

For a while Justice? was listed in the DIY column in the Yellow Pages. One time this guy rang wanting to buy some melamine board and I had to explain to him that I was working for an anarchist newsletter. He still demanded to speak to my boss so I told him that he'd gone to play golf with his secretary.

Phil eventually started branching out from stuffing envelopes and started to help with the writing.

Eventually the cheeky school kid came out of me and started punting out headings, wake ups and disclaimers and I turned into a punster monster fuelled by beer and ganja, with Roget's Thesaurus as a first aid kit. I wonder if people realise that headlines are sometimes instantaneous but often require two to three hour debates with thirty to forty permutations. As the years have gone by, SchNEWS' message has remained the same, but we've had time to develop our own style. At the end of the day, we've been saying the same thing every week for ten years, so we've got to come up with some clever ways of saying it differently! I sometimes wonder that Justice? started by saying deeds not words and yet here we are, still scribbling away."

Tony Rebel Green is one of the original Brighton punks – he was an extra in Quadrophenia "I played a rude boy" and well known around town for having bright green hair (it's his natural colour) and handing out SchNEWS for eight years.

I handed 'em out in the Laines and Churchill Square. Sometimes I even used to put 'em through letter boxed in houses around my area.

Did you ever get any hassle?

The police drove me fucking nutty. They used to follow me around when I was handing SchNEWS out, and I was nicked at a Brighton Reclaim The Streets.

How did you get involved?

I've been a punk since 1976 – fucking anarchy – so I wasn't happy with the CJB. I went on a march and found out about the Courthouse and met Warren – but he's got a lot to learn. Brighton was kicking off.

How has Brighton changed?

In the late seventies it was all punks, hippies and mods. Now it's all got a bit snotty. CCTV cameras everywhere, a lot of London yuppies have moved in.

Tony is a closet royalist.

I fucking loved the Queen Mum. When she died they shouldn't have buried her, they should have stuffed her. I was gonna get the Queen Mum tattooed on my bum.

How would you describe anarchy?

I don't want to live under a nanny state. Anarchy's about doing whatever the fuck you like.

I hate New Labour – they are the toilet party – they are the same as the Tories.

there's SO MUCH going on

SchNEWS Tour 2004

22 days on the road, 21 different places, 5 (or so) people, 1 van, nearly 2,000 miles, loads of drugs (echinacea mostly) this was going to be proper rock and roll mayhem! Hang on, 21 places in 22 days, what were we thinking of?!?

Fortunately we didn't have time to think. Get the van packed, pick everyone up, get to Bath, find the pub, set up the stall, set up the equipment, it doesn't work, pull hair out, finally get it all sorted, huge sigh of relief. Almost ready to start, everyone gets together – "What are we going to say?" "We should say why we're on tour." "Why ARE we on tour?" Unanimous: "Dunno". Shit!

It did all come together though. Short films, SchLIVE reading, the history of SchNEWS and how it comes together every week. Followed by a discussion on direct action and other mostly related stuff evolved into being what we were doing on the tour. Glad we got that sorted!

Why then? Well, we wanted to get SchNEWS out to a wider audience, and were inspired by original SchLIVE tour of 1996, so we gave it another go. First thing was to organise a warm up date, somewhere from which we could all skulk back from if it all went horribly wrong. "Southampton?!" everyone said, "Nothing happens in Southampton!" How wrong they were…

We did a shout out in SchNEWS asking if someone was up for sorting out a venue, publicising the event and finding us somewhere to stay. We got a handful of responses and a couple of months later it happened. There were the usual technical hitches but the venue was packed and the night went really well. One highlight was a burly, bomber jacket-wearing bloke saying, without a hint of irony, that he was there to dispel the stereotypes about hunt sabs…

So that's how it all happened. We had a good discussion on the way home and were totally inspired (if a little worse for wear) and agreed that things were pointing to 'do it'. We agreed that the ideal places for the tour would be towns that didn't have a big activist scene so we wouldn't be preaching to the converted. In the end we went to anywhere people asked us to.

Even having done the Southampton date and being aware of the first SchLIVE tour, we had no idea what to expect. We had a video projector and a few short films on a laptop. We had a range of things we wanted to talk about – genetics, the Dissent network and the G8 Summit, and the history and production of SchNEWS. The idea would be to inspire people to do direct action and alternative media, and bring them into already existing networks.

On The Road

Every night was different – the venues, the crowds, the discussions everything. The venues ranged from established set-ups like Kebele in Bristol and the Sumac Centre in Nottingham to a new space in Gloucester called 11A which was bringing together West Indian people and Forest of Dean troublemakers.

Iain: "We hoped that we'd inspire people to take to the streets; we didn't expect it to happen as fast as it did in Oxford though. 12 hours after the show, and following a late night meeting in a squat, a demo was organised for Oxford centre where people read out parts of Jo Wilding's harrowing eye witness report from Fallujah in Iraq from the previous week."

John: "Some of the starkest juxtapositions were only a gig apart – like from the well-heeled arts centre at Leamington Spa to the allotment focused/ multi-ethnic community centre in Bolton. There was just so much going on."

Iain: "Yep, the north south divide was pretty apparent going from Leamington to Bolton. We didn't see any solar-powered crystal turning machines in Bolton for a start. The focus on allotments that came up in Bolton came up throughout the tour, not just because we were missing ours terribly, because people all over the country want to do something about the fact that supermarkets are shit and their food is rubbish."

Paul: "Everywhere was different, reactions were surprising sometimes. But we all knew that everyone was behind us and willing to make it work. I think we left each venue with a sense of a job well done. Well, I hope we did."

John: "As we went, we would keep the new material coming in. We'd have the new issue of SchNEWS when they came out (of course), we'd get on the web and get new stories, and as the tour went on we'd have bits to read from stuff we'd actually seen. We meshed the news reading with the videos, and title screens for stories to make a more cohesive satirical news show. Because we were doing it every fucking night, it was actually functioning as a proper news service – because we were literally going 'and today… this happened…' and getting updates each day. It was never in danger of going stale anyway because each venue and crowd was so totally different."

Caley: "Though we were reciting 'Crap Arrests' in our sleep & singing along to the 'Consumption' video, it still seemed fresh (though we maybe weren't) with the anticipation of each new place, some new material and our increasing dementia! The show was pretty interactive thanks to John encouraging heckling... keeping it lively and sometimes a little scary..."

Paul: "It was a lot like the last tour and then of course it was all so very different. (there's a stupid thing to say) One thing that was so different was the technology. Back in 96 we stuck a ropey tape into a dodgy VHS and prayed it didn't snarl up. On this tour we had the laptop. Press a button, and instant movie. The headlines were eventually created on the lap top. Previously we had just written them up in felt tip. I dunno what I preferred really. Both were good."

Top of the SchPOPS

Iain: "Though not part of the main tour, Southampton was the best night for me. Having been persuaded that no-one would be interested in SchNEWS in Southampton the place was packed and the discussion at the end was really inspiring. It was all topped off by a guy saying that he'd not been involved with direct action for years but was so inspired by the night that he wanted to start things happening. What more could we ask?"

"...When we read out Crap Arrests remember that we're smiling through our teeth with our tongues firmly in our cheeks..."

Caley: "Nine Ladies left me speechless, it was such a beautiful spot and brought it home that you can read all about the injustices done to the environment daily and feel really pissed off about it but it's not until you are in a place that's gonna be ripped apart – for money. In the case of the Nine Ladies quarry site, for stone to build more sacred McDonald's in the US. You really feel the fury and are sick at the tragic ridiculousness of corporate capitalism's destruction."

Paul: I liked Sheffield. The SchLIVE thrives in a good old pub atmosphere with plenty of people to make it happen. There was heckling from the audience that kept ya on ya toes. The discussion at the end was inspiring. The debate on BNP and Simon Jones' brother who gave a measured account of his experiences with direct action were moving and important. I wish also we had more time to spend at Bilston Glen and Nine Ladies. I felt we got there, got a sense of the atmosphere and had to leave. It made you want to go back. I hope the films get this across."

John: "I don't know which our best show was 'cos some were great fun to do even if the audience weren't particularly enthusiastic, and sometimes it was the other way around! I really enjoyed Liverpool, Oxford, Norwich… Newcastle was a blur – it was a lunchtime gig, and we'd driven from Edinburgh that morning, and I was totally catatonic. When the gig finished I demanded our hosts let me borrow a bed immediately and slept for 16 hours straight. Imagine trying to be in a satirical news show when you're slurring and your eyes are rolling."

"...Good morning Bolton... hang on a minute – it's evening and it's Leeds... but don't take it from us... go out and see for yourselves..."

SchMOVIES

Most of the films we showed were, erm, 'acquired' from the Internet. We did a shout out months before the tour asking people to send in what they had, and we used some of them too. Then while we were on the road various people asked us to show their films and let us take copies.

Iain: "The film about the protest against a JNF (Jewish National Fund) event by the Glasgow based Camcorder Guerrillas stood out for me. The event was a fundraiser to make money to buy land which excludes Arabs, a clearly racist policy, and the protest against it was very powerful."

Caley: "A continual highlight throughout the tour was a clip from a Bayer occupation film when a young cop tries to intimidate the guy filming with various threats of arrest but the cameraman had been reading his 'police handbook' while the cop clearly hadn't! He was made to look the idiot he was; we never tired of it and it brought a cheer every time we showed it; reminding us all, fresh faced or seasoned, that you don't have to take their crap if you know yer shit."

The Big Issues

There were a number of issues that kept being brought up by audiences, these were:

Rise Of The Far Right: In practically every place, there was discussion about the rise of the far right. It was a month or so before the local elections, and the BNP were leafleting the estates everywhere, latching onto genuine issues like unemployment, and preying on peoples' weakness for nationalism.

Social Centres: Half way through the tour, the Dissent Network meeting in Manchester had brought up the issue of a national network of social centres as a long-term priority. We were performing or staying in a whole range of new or established centres and comparing them with the Cowley Club in Brighton.

Dissent Network: During the tour it was still very early days, but we were discussing the forthcoming G8 Summit in Scotland in 2005

Community Allotments: from Bolton to Norwich people were encouraging new people to get involved with organic food projects.

Lessons Learnt

John: "You don't want to be coming from yer activist bubble in Brighton and going out like a missionary spreading the good word. Whether it's promoting SchNEWS or libertarian ideas like direct action... cos when we were in Liverpool someone quite rightly said that they associate 'direct action' with middle class white ex-students... when in fact in that city the focus was more on community level activities. The further we got into the tour the more I preferred to listen, rather than spout about what people could do in their city."

Iain: "There were a few reality check moments where I was reminded that the people who say we're just a bunch of whinging students causing trouble are very wrong. There are people battling to hold down jobs and feed their kids but are still fighting the same fight as us."

Caley: "I was pleased to meet genuine folks – resisting in inventive, persistent and real ways... From the school girl in Norwich who was on her own in her beliefs, having no help from her school in trying to combat racism and intimidation, but still tried to organise; to food growing projects with refugees in Bolton having to deal with narrow minded allotment traditionalists; to the guys in Liverpool who'd seen a thing or two and who talked of cheating the system daily and creatively as an important part of resistance... it's all part of the same thing."

Paul: "Like the last tour, networking was the key issue for me. Establishing or re-establishing contacts around the country. Making friends and creating a platform for people to speak and get involved. I really liked the history of SchNEWS and the discussion after the SchLIVE. This was something we didn't do on the last tour. It was fucking excellent to hear the debates unfold, voices found."

Jo Makepeace (SchNEWS' long suffering elusive co-editor): "Nothing! That lot buggered off on the road for 3 weeks leaving me to do all the work. The least I expected was for them to do was return with some biscuit money. What did they return with? Nothing." (i.e. the tour was self-funding – we left with no money and returned with no money. The books etc we sold while we were away covered fuel and other costs almost to the penny. Good planning? Hmmm.)

Top Tour Tips

Iain: "Get a publication with a big circulation (us?) to advertise it. Get the regional organisers to do as much of the work as possible. There's no way we could have found venues and done local publicity for all (any?) of the dates we did. Be flexible – things never go quite to plan."

John: "The only way to learn how to do it is to get out and do it – just like anything else really. Don't waste energy over-preparing it, save your energy and spontaneity for the audiences."

Paul: "Don't let it overwhelm you as an idea. Make sure that the venue is in place at the other end. Make sure you are adaptive because things do change along the way. Remember that you are doing this because you want to and not make everything a chore. Have fun with it because you could be working in some shitty office job for the rest of your life."

Thanks to everyone who organised the shows and put us up

A series of short films were produced from the tour – see below....

SchMOVIES

SchMOVIES is a new medium for SchNEWS. Having filmed the SchNEWS tour this April it became apparent that within the tour footage there were short films that needed to be put together and shown. In this accidental way SchMOVIES were launched – short information pills produced and edited by us here at the office.

SchMOVIES are eclectic, covering road protests, quarry actions, community events, anti-war demos and promoting up and coming events such as the G8 Summit in Scotland in 2005.

We're also interested in any raw footage that you might have and not know what to do with. If ya can get it to us we will put it together and come up with something.

Putting together the retrospective SchNEWS film has exposed the huge mass of archive material that was simply sitting under peoples' beds gathering dust. If you have some great footage which never saw the light of day – get it out, transfer it to DV tape (or let us do it) and send it to us. We are currently building a data base of film that can be accessed for screenings and research. Footage filmed by us will be copyleft/anti-copyright – but you can decide what 'rights' your stuff has – have a chat with us if you're not sure.

From October 2004 onwards we will also be releasing The Justice? Files, featuring archive material that has not been seen for god knows how long. Rare footage of when Justice? invaded Newsnight for instance. In November we hope to unveil the 45 minute SchNEWS at Ten film "Whose in Charge?" covering the early origins to the present day. It will also give you an idea of how the SchNEWS is put together each week. Check out the weekly SchNEWS for more details.

If you don't manage to catch any of our screenings at festies and gigs, feel free to contact us if you want copies for yer own screenings. Or invite us to screen them for you – we like to get out of the office now and again. If you live in the Brighton area and want to get involved by all means do.

SchMOVIES are downloadable free off the web – simply log on to our website, click the SchMOVIES icon and you're in. www.schnews.org.uk/schmovies

Part 6
GRASSROOTS RESISTANCE

As we said at the beginning of the book, it's not all about big, high profile international actions, at the expense of getting involved in your own community.

Regardless of whether hack journalists in the corporate media are pronouncing the 'anti-capitalist movement' dead or not - or that anarchism is only about putting bricks through windows - there is constant grassroots activity going on, even in the least 'happening' places you'd expect.

So what do these troublemakers get up to when they aren't rioting on the streets or planning to overthrow the government? Here are a few examples of people involved in their local communities...

SCRATCHING THE SURFACE
Seaside Town In Naughty Newsheet Shocker

The sleepy seaside town of Worthing has been voted "the most boring place to live" with one magazine saying that "If a town has a personality, Worthing's is that of a majestic middle-aged matron – wearing hot-pants". When SchNEWS recently visited the town, one young activist told us "There's nothing really to do, really crap clubs, not much variety, no alternative scene whatsoever – I don't plan being here forever!"

Yet, despite this, the town has been blessed over the past few years with squatted social centres, a deluge of anarchist postering and graffiti, constant signs of healthy cynicism towards those in authority, a steady stream of new local protest groups, cannabis cafes and demos that don't just begin and end with a bit of banner waving. Could this be anything to do with the town's radical monthly-ish newssheet 'The Porkbolter'? SchNEWS went to investigate.

The Porkbolter gets its name from a real historic term for Worthing people and the newsletter's "aim is to encourage the good folk of this town to take control of their own lives." The Porkbolter is unashamedly anarchist, up for direct action and very sarcastic "We tend to get excited about minor, unfashionable causes like freedom, justice and nature. In the light of this, it should come as no surprise to learn that we have got nothing to do with any political party of any persuasion." The first issue came out seven years ago although "obviously the history of doing things in Worthing didn't start with the Porkbolter". "We distribute 1,500 to 2,000 per issue in the street, in shops, in colleges, the library; anywhere we think would be a good place we leave a bundle out. We have no idea who a lot of the people who read it are, but we do get the impression that they are not necessarily activist types. In fact we know they're not, otherwise there would be a lot more on all the demos! We get a couple of letters from little old ladies that like us slagging off the council and agree with the message – maybe we come across as more respectable than we are!"

SchNEWS was in town during another demo against plans to stick 800 houses on Titnore Woods – the last bit of woodland in the borough. Of course, this wouldn't be just a banner waving event. Instead, after a photocall and some megaphone action, about 50 assorted individuals marched along blocking

---

IF ORDINARY PEOPLE BEHAVED LIKE- L'ORÉAL

traffic, avoiding the town hall and ending up at a disused shopping centre. "The Council say there is no alternative to 800 houses at Titnore woods but there is – Teville Gate is lying empty. There are ways round problems and we try to get people to look at wider issues – like why are the houses at Titnore really being built." "We try to expose the whole thing about democracy, to show people that it doesn't work, even if you do what the authorities say – write your letters, have your petitions, even vote for the party who said they were against the development, who soon as they got in power said they couldn't do anything about it!"

WHAT'S REALLY GOING ON IN WORTHING

The Pork-BolTeR

ISSUE 11 | OCTOBER 1998 | FREE/DONATION

ROTARY CHIEF TRIES TO BAN WORTHING'S GREEN BANK HOLIDAY BASH

RON'S BIG EGO-FESTIVAL

A SURPRISE comedy act was top of the bill at Worthing's Eco-Festival in Homefield Park. But Rotarian clown Ron Noakes didn't turn up to make people smile. He was trying to get the event banned at the last minute!

Not only was this astonishing attack on Friends of the Earth completely ignored by the local mainstream media, but they couldn't even bring themselves to report that this unique and newsworthy Festival had so much as taken place.

This is the disgraceful truth behind events at Homefield Park on Monday August 31, hidden so far from the thousands of Worthing people who will have seen and enjoyed the superb environmental showcase laid on for their benefit by hard-working volunteers.

just beginning to set things up for the bank holiday fun, when in walked Ron Noakes, chairman of Worthing Rotary Fair. Witnesses say he had obviously taken an instant dislike to the alternative goings on shaping up for the festival and projected bad vibes before he even opened his mouth.

This is perhaps not surprising, for we have since found out that he is an ex-copper and the state-enforcers-in-blue are already well known to our readers (and the world as a whole) for their fun-busting frolics.

When he did speak, the verbal diarrhoea lasted for 20 unsavoury minutes, culminating in the immortal rant: "I work for 24 hours a day, you lot just claim the dole!". *Wrong, Ron!* Firstly, many of those involved have full-time jobs, secondly if you really worked 24 hours a day you would undoubtedly be *dead*, which while arguably not a bad thing in itself would have made it impossible for you to be standing there picking fights with common unwashed eco-swine!

Ron, *supposedly representing a charitable organisation*, then made even more of an authoritarian fool of himself. He and his mates told FoE volunteers they couldn't sell their vegetarian food because there was a burger van on the Rotary

ROCKET RON GETS A PORKIN'

"When we first started we caused a few shockwaves – we knew someone who worked for the council, and he said that every time the new Porkbolter came out there was a special meeting to discuss the contents, which is really gratifying that some people getting together with a word processor can put out an A4 sheet and have that effect."

Then there's the story about Rocket Ron of the Rotarians. "A few years back some people who we knew came together under the umbrella of Worthing Friends of the Earth and asked if they could do an eco fair on the corner of the same field as the Rotarians' event. The Council said yes cos it sounded harmless and fluffy, but when the Rotarians turned up there were big anarchy flags between the trees and a sort of protest camp in the middle of Worthing – they just freaked! One rather rotund Rotarian businessman, went round at 7 in the morning to speak to them but ran off after being verbally assaulted by a very sleepy and angry young woman – that's where he got the nickname Rocket Ron. So the next year we decided to do a special issue about Rocket Ron and leaflet the Parade. As we started handing out Porkbolters, the Rotarians on their double decker bus started shouting through a megaphone 'don't take it, don't take their leaflet, it's all lies!' which made people want to read it. We didn't keep up with the procession, but as they disappeared into the distance we could hear them still shouting through the megaphone about us! Moments like that make it all worthwhile."

So a message to others who live in sleepier parts of the country: "Just do it, keep doing it and don't give up, it's a cumulative effect and you've got to be patient. It's not like a revolution has happened in Worthing because of the Porkbolter, but I do feel it's been worthwhile. Stuff like marching in the street because we've done it before and it's been reported in the press means people think 'oh that's normal' – it just normalises stepping up things a wee bit which is quite important rather than asking the council for permission. Stuff we put out in our newsletter and at our meetings hopefully is normalising our views as opposed to the media and government's plans which are to marginalise and criminalise protesters."

For copies of the Porkbolter send an SAE to PO Box 4144, Worthing, West Sussex BN14 7NZ or check out www.eco-action.org/porkbolter

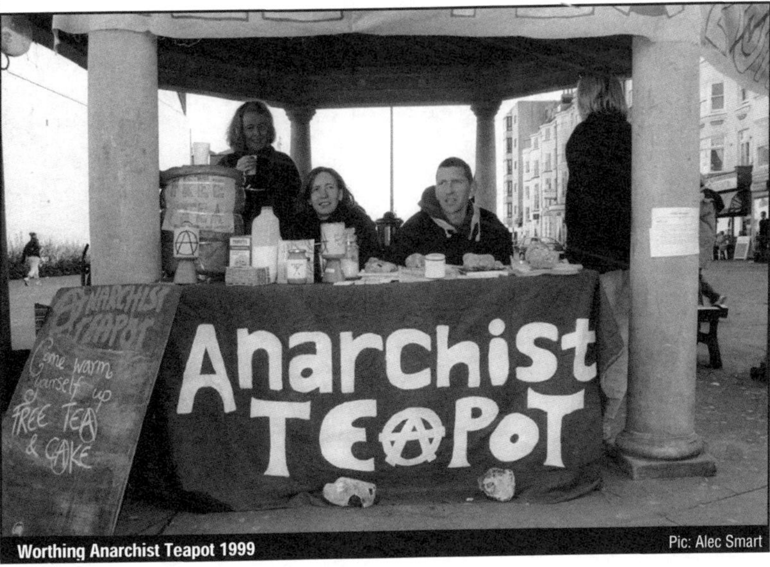

Worthing Anarchist Teapot 1999

Pic: Alec Smart

RESIDENTS TAKE OVER!

Imagine strong and lively communities, and control over our own lives and neighbourhoods...

Can people getting together to moan about dog-shit, broken street lights and fly-tipping ever change the world? How does working with others in our communities who don't share radical views help build an anti-capitalist movement? What are 'radical' views anyway – are they based on people's lifestyles, or on their conditions of life? Whatever happened to 'common sense'? Why are most of the popular, grass roots struggles we read about 10,000 miles away in Chiapas and Argentina, or buried in UK history books? One anarchist who's been involved in residents groups in London for many years reckons working in our local communities can be inspiring, and more importantly, is absolutely essential if we ever want to make lasting change...

The world is in a terrible mess because we're not running our own lives, directly controlling the resources and decision-making for the benefit of all. Currently governments and big-business boss everyone around for their own benefit. So what can people do to get back control? Obviously we can't expect someone to jet in and liberate us, or wait for some cataclysmic 'collapse' of the system in some way off future. By patiently building up grass roots solidarity and mutual aid, we can sow and grow the seeds of the new society within the shell of the old. We have to act for ourselves, in the here and now.

Here – and now? We need to focus on where there is a real need, and a real untapped potential to fight back, where people can empower each other and spread alternative ideas. This means here within our local communities, and now – on a day to day basis in our everyday lives.

I'm involved in Haringey Solidarity Group, an open anarchist/libertarian/socialist collective that grew out of the huge and successful anti-poll tax campaign 13 years ago. We produce leaflets and newsletters, and support a whole range of activities going on in the borough. In the last few years I've put most of my efforts into being involved in street-level activity in my local neighbourhood.

Street Level

The front line of politics is outside your door. And also in workplaces – but that's another matter. If we base our political activity around where people actually are, we can achieve a lot. That doesn't mean we can't get involved in other things, but at the end of the day we have to have a strategy to actually change the world, for people to take over all the decision-making themselves. After all, everyone is an expert about their own lives and their own street.

People have concerns, which may be surprisingly similar to those of other people in their neighbourhoods: they want more control over their lives, to be part of a safe and friendly community, in a decent environment with good local services and facilities, etc. The ruling system only wants obedient consumers and workers, where all the decisions are made from on high in their own selfish and greedy interests. People are not encouraged to feel that they can band together and make changes themselves. There's always someone else claiming to 'represent' people or act for them; politicians, Council officers, the media, professional NGO's that pay people to organise campaigns and publicity… even direct action groups can be seen to be a specialist lifestyle choice that most people can't relate to or take part in. All of which takes the power away from the people who really count: the majority, in particular working class people and other oppressed sections of the population.

The real challenge is: how does this translate to action on a street level that can be taken up

DIY COMMUNITY ACTION

In almost any community a whole range of positive, practical things can be organised and encouraged which bring people together, build up community spirit and improve our local neighbourhoods.

Here are some examples of things you could do that are already going on in local areas around the country:

- encourage lots of informal discussion and communication on the street and in each others' homes
- do local door-to-door leaflets and newsletters
- hold public meetings on topical issues
- organise street parties and other events
- set up skills and resources sharing schemes
- campaign for youth facilities and activities
- demand traffic calming
- set up housing solidarity and action groups
- resist obnoxious development schemes
- defend useful facilities threatened with closure
- promote recycling projects
- develop informal gathering places (in or around local shops, parks etc)
- organise picnics and other activities in local parks
- set up parents' groups in schools and play centres

by millions of people? For me, the answer is to try and build up grassroots action groups and associations that are open and relevant to everybody in the community. It may not always be easy, but unfortunately no-one's yet found any successful short cuts from here to the revolution.

The proof of the pudding

Residents groups have often been seen as linked to the council, or as just complaining bodies with limited concerns, or with only a couple of people running the show. But they can also be solidarity organisations in which people support each other and take up a range of local issues important in improving the conditions and quality of life in the neighbourhood. The potential is definitely there for all kinds of street level residents' action groups, associations and networks.

For about five years I was involved in a residents network where we built up a membership of 250 on an estate of about 1500 homes. We organised regular meetings, usually in each other's homes every three weeks, covering a huge range of issues. They were always minuted and all the members got these minutes so you are building up a network of people that are well informed and encouraged to take part in any way they want to. We succeeded in getting a million pounds for traffic calming, a youth club, and helped get environmental improvements to a local park. We organised an annual 'Home Is Where The Art Is' exhibition of residents' creativity, a local history day and various public meetings. It really brought people together, especially the 20 or so who were most involved.

In 2003 I moved to another part of Tottenham and helped set up a residents association which now has 80 members out of 230 homes. We meet every 3 weeks, and leaflet every house in the area every six weeks encouraging people to come along. There are about 8-10 regulars. We also have an internal email list. We've got the Council to agree to plant more trees in the streets, we monitor street lighting and rubbish dumping, and are about to get traffic calming measures put in. We campaigned to save the local pub from being demolished for yet another block of flats, and mounted a strong campaign to try to save the local sub-Post Office – including holding a 100-strong march round our local streets. Both campaigns failed to win, but were successful in helping to galvanise people into action. The council

- do residents' opinion surveys
- organise local art and creativity exhibitions
- plan community murals
- set up local clubs/interest groups (gardening, music, sports etc)

The possibilities are endless…

Kicking off

The trick is to get organised and active! By encouraging neighbours to get involved, being as friendly as possible with everyone, and avoiding getting bogged down with bureaucracy or politicians of any stripe, it is amazing what people can achieve.

Why not get together with a couple of neighbours you know and start meeting regularly in each other's homes or in a friendly local neighbourhood centre? Give yourselves a name. Discuss what people feel are the important issues, and things you can start to do together – post reports of these discussions to all interested neighbours. Encourage initiative. Gradually build up a list of more and more contacts. Organise public meetings and events, local campaigns and so on. Leaflet door-to-door. Most importantly, stick at it.

In this way we can patiently build up a strong and vibrant grass-roots movement in every neighbourhood.

recently tried to quadruple the rent of a popular café in the local park, but as a result of protests and pressure they've backed down.

In May this year, we and other nearby residents groups helped organise our second annual community festival in the local park – it was bloody fantastic, and attended by about three thousand people. About 20 to 30 of us worked together on quite libertarian lines, organising it collectively with people volunteering to take on different responsibilities. I helped set up a 'speakers forum' tent, and there were stalls, music, crafts, treasure hunts, sports and a carnival-ish procession.

It's not all positive. Anti-social behaviour can also be a big problem in some neighbourhoods. It needs to be addressed because if we can't come up with solutions that we can do ourselves, people are going to say we need more police, we need more CCTV, etc. It's good to support anyone harassed, and to campaign for more youth facilities and so on – but sometimes groups of people that are causing the problem may need to be challenged.

Digging in for the duration

If you're going to start something new it's good to concentrate on positive stuff, things that can build up community strength and empower people. Then you can try and tackle the difficult stuff that takes a long time to make progress on. If you just focus on that at first it can demoralise people and that's when you might become just a moaning group. There can be different ways of doing similar things, some of it is empowering and some of it is frustrating, so patience and persistence are real virtues. After all, it's your neighbourhood – so get stuck in!

Every area is different – differing size neighbourhoods (from a single block of flats to a whole 'ward'), differing geography and populations, and differing issues that are relevant. Build up a list of contacts/members. Try to make every meeting open to everybody, with open agendas, minutes circulated etc. That way your activities are accountable to your community, and its more likely the group will be strongly supported and become a real influence.

Don't moan – organise

The fundamental challenge for any residents' group is to be active and well supported, but to not get sucked into the way the authorities would like it to be. They want you to have low expectations, limit your agenda, leave it to 'professionals and experts', and think that politics is about voting in elections and talking to Councillors. What I like about people involved in residents groups is that if you say to them, 'We should be independent, build up community spirit, support each other and co-operate. We are all equals; we should make all the decisions about our area together, with the decisions based on our community's real needs', then nearly everybody agrees – it's all common sense! In fact, such common-sense ideas are actually a radical basis for alternative politics, for a real counter-power and a new society if acknowledged and built on. Yet if you were to ask the same people what their ideological or political beliefs were, they would cover the whole range of parties, beliefs and religions etc. Somewhere along the line we've allowed our common sense to be suppressed, or hijacked.

Throughout this whole process, the most important thing is local people coming together as equals with a common interest in the local neighbourhood, meeting in each others houses, getting to know each other, spreading a positive atmosphere, because a lot of people are very demoralised and think they can't change anything. But when they come together, they start bringing out their own experiences, their own skills, time and resources, their own views, and they start feeling that there are ways of changing the world and supporting each other based on different principles from profits and power. Working together, face to face, and respecting each other generally works because as neighbours you have common interest with people of all ages, all backgrounds, and all colours in a crazy, unjust and alienating world.

A movement of millions?

In Haringey alone there are 120 residents associations, 20 'friends' groups of local park users, as well as local action groups campaigning for traffic calming measures or against various urban and commercial developments, mobile phone masts etc. This involves a membership of thousands, and annual distribution of tens of thousands of leaflets and newsletters. Across the whole country this amounts to a self-organised and independent movement of millions of people speaking and acting for themselves and their communities. In this way people are able to directly challenge, influence and potentially eventually make all the decisions that affect them and their communities. Anarchists should be fully involved. At the same time as building up people's self-confidence, solidarity and mutual aid, we should be encouraging people to demand not just a few crumbs off the table, or even the whole cake, but the entire bakery.

SITA ON MY FACE

Brighton's refuse workers went to work this Monday to find that SITA – the French multinational with the contract to clean Brighton's rubbish – had imposed increased workloads that the workers knew would be impossible to deliver. One typical run would involve one driver and two others sweeping a major part of the sea front, an entire estate and a bit more for luck. As one refuse worker told SchNEWS, *"What would you do if you went into work and were told you had to clean 18 miles of streets a day?"*

What 11 workers did was refuse to do these impossible rounds – and they were promptly suspended. When the rest of the 160-strong GMB workforce protested against this, SITA's management sacked the lot. It was the last straw – the workforce occupied the depot. They demanded that SITA, who have cost local people an extra £1.8m a year since they took over Brighton's street cleaning, get the sack and that they get back to the job of cleaning streets – instead of increasing some company's stock market value.

SITA brought in bin lorries to a nearby industrial park where they tried to get employment agency workers to scab against the strike. It didn't work.

A key event was the blockade of the rubbish trucks caused by a local lad called "Jamie" who got up at 5am to lock onto one of the trucks for five hours, preventing the rest from moving. As one striker put it, "This fellow is crazy but what he has done is much appreciated".

Faced with a determined strikeforce occupying its depot with enormous local support, SITA's bullying started to crack. Employment agencies started refusing to have anything to do with them. SITA workers in neighbouring areas suddenly developed strange, short-term illnesses when asked to scab. The local council held hours of secret meetings with SITA but couldn't come up with a way to beat the strike.

By Thursday evening, SITA and the council had caved in. All the workers were reinstated, getting full pay for the time they were on strike. SITA were given 11 weeks notice that their contract was being terminated – and that they could forget their new work practices in the meantime.

GMB official Gary Smith told SchNEWS, *"SITA deliberately provoked this dispute by trying to lock members out. Unfortunately for them, the workers decided to lock themselves in. We had enormous public support from the local unemployed centre, direct action people and loads of different communities who are fed up with their services being run for profit. We should take inspiration from this fight, because it shows that when people get together we can stop privatisation in its tracks."*

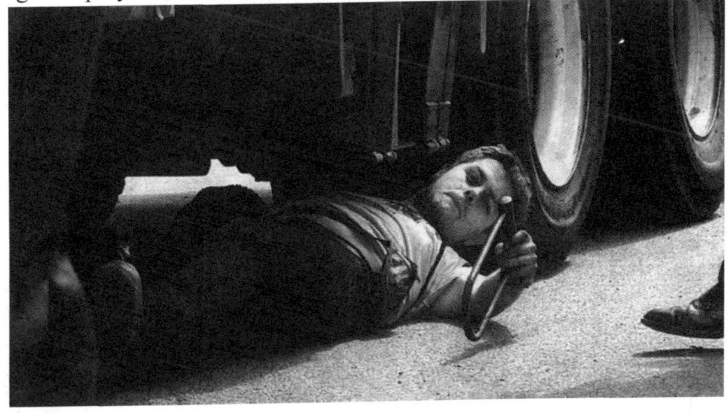

Part 7 ...And Finally...

A Word From Our Panel Of Experts

After ten years of writing SchNEWS, and generating over two million words, you'd think that we'd be able to stand back and offer some blinding bit of insight into how to right all the wrongs of the world. But one thing we've learned is that the ten years we've been going – which might seem like an eternity to some of us – are just a blip in the scheme of things. And the world's problems weren't going to be solved before the novelty of dabbling in radical politics wore off, letting us all go back to 'normal lives'. So nevermind any definitive statements about saving the planet or pompous profundities, here is a discussion with a few of the people who got the SchNEWS ball rolling, catching them in a reflective moment between the second and third pint.

Warren moved to Brighton and helped set up the Courthouse squat, but didn't get involved in SchNEWS "till issue two." Before that he'd been living in Slough, trying to make his local residents group a bit more radical, as well as standing quite a few times for the local Green Party – once somehow getting 16% of the vote! Colin has also been involved in Justice? and SchNEWS for a long time and can claim to be the only communist who ever got involved! Gibby was one of the founders of SchNEWS and is now working with Al-Jazeera in Brazil.

In the early part of this book we covered some of the history about the resistance to the Criminal Justice Act in Britain, and Brighton's active and high profile part of that, Justice? Looking back, big breakthroughs were made in those days, a sea-change in the types of groups emerging and the way people were working. What are your most vivid memories of this?

WARREN: The levels of activity were amazing – during the Courthouse people were out probably seven nights a week – leafleting, doing stalls, collecting money, all in effort to raise awareness about the Criminal Justice Act. The local paper gave it a lot of prominence.

There was a really wide range of people involved – Marxists, anarchists, people who got involved 'cos they thought 'Shit, this is going to stop my free parties.' And there was a couple of key players who brought all these people together and banged their heads together and managed to get stuff going and get loads of people involved. Gibby and Gail have the sort of personalities that draw people in. They knew lots of people and wouldn't condemn you if you hadn't read the whole works of Kropotkin.

There were political discussions going on in that building 24-7. We'd have meetings in the café when people were just eating – big meetings about how to run the place. But the arguments were just unbelievable. I couldn't handle a lot of the meetings. I'd go and do the door or sweep up or help in the kitchen 'cos the meetings were doing my head in but, having said that, they were really important for people to formulate their ideas.

The other great thing was that when the Courthouse got evicted, everyone worked together as a team. In the pub afterwards it was probably the first time the autonomists and the fluffies (or whatever you wanna call them) were actually speaking and working together. OK, they evicted us eventually, but there were people on the roof all day, and loads of us outside. It brought people together. A bit like when I interviewed the Liverpool Dockers and they said that people used to squabble over people who'd been

dead for 150 years – but when push came to shove and there was a battle to be won, they forgot all their political differences and worked together. Fighting evictions engenders solidarity as well – squat and protest camp evictions were a really good bonding thing and if you chat to people who were on those things you find a lot of people have done amazing stuff since then.

COLIN: There's a saying, "Action is the enemy of words". Divisions come out when people have got nothing better to do than sit around and argue and blame other people for what's gone wrong. It was really noticeable in the Courthouse when there were discussions about violence and non-violence, and whether to talk to the media or not – the two big arguments which have sustained hours of boring meeting time for years. But when it came to it, after these enormously vitriolic arguments, ninety-nine percent of people thought, 'Well, we're not gonna just start thumping police for the hell of it, but on the other hand if they attack our mates we're gonna defend them.' In practice things work themselves out – it's a common sense thing.

One of the big stories that gets told about the start of SchNEWS is the story of the Women Against Pit Closures coming to Brighton and telling Justice? to start a newsletter.

COLIN: During the Courthouse, some women from Women against Pit Closures came down to give a talk. I think they'd just dug up Heseltine's garden and were going round doing direct action against pit closures so we thought we'd ask them down and pick their brains. There were a couple of hundred people at the meeting. During the discussion a few people were saying, "When the cops come to chuck us out, I think it's really important we keep the moral high ground and leave peacefully" and the women just laid in. They said emphatically, "No, you don't do that – you stand up for yourselves!" I have this vivid memory of these people looking like they'd just been told off by their mum! Then one of the women said, "And how do you tell everyone what's going on? Have you got a newsletter?" And people were shaking their heads and looking at the floor, and they said "Well you'd better bloody get one together then!" Quite soon after that SchNEWS started. That was certainly part of the reason it came about.

GIBBY: At the time there was a lot of energy – so when someone says 'Let's do a newsletter' you'd have loads of people going 'Wicked, I'd be up for that!' It was just that period of time – I think there are moments in history when things come together and you've just got to be there at the right moment, or better still, help create that moment.

How has the role of SchNEWS changed? For the first year or two SchNEWS was really the newsletter of the anti-Criminal Justice Act movement.

WARREN: A lot of the anti-CJA stuff eventually became the anti-capitalist stuff. People moved away from single issue campaigning, as you do when you start to realise just how the world is run. SchNEWS has tried to reflect and report on these changes, and hopefully have some influence!

Other publications or political groups come and go. What's been the key to SchNEWS lasting? Being flexible and adaptable? Being in the right place at the right time, being a format which is do-able every week, being lucky enough to attract the right people? Or is it that there is such a desperate need for unbiased media that people will embrace it, however flawed?

WARREN: Having enough people to do the thing every week has to be the number one priority. We've also kept it simple so even if there's just a few people in the office we are able to get an issue out. Being in Brighton also helps – people are always moving here, and it has an active political scene with people willing to help out. On the other hand a few people obviously haven't got anything better to do as they've just carried on year after year!

What story for you stands out as being the most important?

GIBBY: A pivotal point for SchNEWS was when a load of us went to the first People's Global Action conference in Geneva in March '98. After about 20 seconds of going to shit boring meetings, we went around interviewing as many people as we could from different countries and put together a little booklet. We met people from all around the world and it was a real eye-opener and really inspirational. This was also when the Internet was coming into its own and so we could now get stories from around the world quickly. Those two things together brought a real pivotal change to SchNEWS.

During that period in the late nineties when the big road protests were starting to wind down, did you hope that something else was going to come up at that point?

WARREN: There are always peaks and troughs, but people who say that there's less stuff going on have usually stopped doing things themselves – there's always something happening. It might be a local community complaining about a hedgerow being cut down. We might not hear about that – stuff that isn't as spectacular as, say, the Newbury bypass campaign, but still, stuff is always going on.

When people look at the past with rose tinted glasses, it's good to remind them of what's going on right now. What about the successful anti GM campaign this year against Bayer which forced the company to close up shop in this country? And then of course there's last year's anti-war movement. I don't usually have a lot of time for marching from A to B, but that was a really powerful demonstration. Having said that, what SchNEWS and others did was try to get more people involved in taking direct action against the war. We were encouraging people to go down to Fairford, to try to shut down the bases there. It's a shame more people weren't involved. The school kids were a big exciting part of the anti-war movement – and who knows what that lot will get up to in the next few years. I haven't got much patience with people getting all nostalgic.

How do you keep SchNEWS connected, avoiding the traps of academics and journalists?

WARREN: SchNEWS is an open collective. We organise training days and are always getting new people involved, which is very important, and hopefully we're always open to new ideas. For instance, after the most recent SchNEWS tour we talked about the things that were happening around the country that we thought were important.

One thing we watch out for, which others get caught up in is... there're a lot of postings on the Indymedia newswire about Palestine or Iraq, while ignoring local everyday issues like education or transport. It's good to talk about Iraq etc., but I think it's more important to talk about things that affect people in their everyday life if we're ever going to have an effect or reach out to new people.

The way SchNEWS is written – sometimes there are not enough of us, and stuff gets in that's not as well written as we'd like it to be. It's anonymous and people are constantly editing each others' articles, thinking how to word things better, or make them funnier, put a better punch line in – it's a collective effort. It's not like 'I've written my article, and if you take it out I'm gonna have the hump.' It's an evolving thing over the two production days and when it's working really well – say for instance with the 'Battle of Seattle' issue when all the people in the office who'd been at Seattle put in their two-penny's worth – I knew because of the way we were working together that something good was written.

Someone I know works for The Sun and he recently told me that SchNEWS is 'very well written', although I don't know whether to take that as a compliment! But the idea of SchNEWS has always been to make it simple, make it accessible, and have a few things to make people laugh like "crap arrest" so people will at least pick it up for that and maybe read a bit more about the politics. At the end of each article we always try to give a phone number or website in case people want to find out more and get involved. Someone recently had a go at me in a pub for SchNEWS being too populist, as if somehow being popular was a bad thing. Too much radical literature is dull and complicated, no one really understands it, and apart from a few politicos, no one reads it – SchNEWS wants to be populist. I want my nan reading it!

A lot of the time we get blinded by boredom – MAI, NAFTA, WTO – what the fuck does it mean to people? It's easy to write about an exciting Reclaim the Streets party or the Battle of Seattle, but to think, 'right I'm gonna write an article on the North American Free Trade Agreement' and try to make it exciting, or relevant to people, or easy to understand, it's actually very difficult. To make it relevant to peoples' lives, and make them go, 'Fucking hell, that's really bad' is hard, which is one of the reasons these subjects are often ignored by the corporate media.

One woman we know, who'd been campaigning against the IMF and World Bank meetings for years, said that they used to have just twenty people in a picket. A few years later, there's fucking ten thousand of us in Prague trying to shut it down. Because we haven't stopped banging on about these boring subjects, we hope we have helped to get people to target organisations like the World Trade Organisation or the IMF.

Where does SchNEWS get its information from and how can we trust it?

WARREN: SchNEWS has always been info for action – get off your arse and go see things for yourself. But obviously this isn't always possible, so we have to rely on people we trust. At the Rio +10 Summit in South Africa, a friend interviewed various people and emailed them to us. An old SchNEWS hack was living in Guatemala, and heading for the WTO protests in Cancun so we asked him to send a report and do some interviews. Another was in Washington at protests against the IMF. We're not saying we always get it right, but we do our best. In fact it's paid journalists with hardly any time who have to become experts on a subject in minutes, who people should be weary of trusting. For example we once had the Financial Times ring up the office for a quote, and I made up a load of rubbish – hey presto, it's in the paper the next day.

GIBBY: I've always hated speed journalism; big - cock - I - was - there - first - today - whatever - it - is journalism. I'm - just - doing - a - job journalism. SchNEWS is honest propaganda. It says 'Don't believe anything we say. Go out and see for yourself!' It's never been allied to anything but itself. It only survives because people want it to. It doesn't have to sell the news. It's just information for action.

COLIN: One of the big strengths of SchNEWS is that it comes out regularly, compared to most volunteer-run, 'activist' based publications. It's also short, which means you can't ramble on which is a real bonus for readers. It's accessible, well written, clear, and funny. We always had this idea that we wanted to communicate with other people like ourselves rather than make people think we were clever because they couldn't understand what we were saying. It also helped that The Levellers gave us a free office. They never would have thought we'd be going ten years later – they only asked us to start paying rent last year after we'd been getting it free for nine years!

GIBBY: We try to remind people of the lessons of the past, so we don't continually repeat the failures. When you initially get involved in something, you

think you're the first person that's ever done this, but it's generally not true, and I hope we bring in these lessons.

SchNEWS is just following on from the radical media from the past couple of hundred years. We're part of that tradition, just as struggle is part of it.

And direct action is always a bit more sexy than the usual run-of-the-mill politics…

WARREN: Sexy?! At least a couple of days a week we're fucking stuck in the office. The writers' job is probably the best thing, but the people doing the printing, or stuffing the envelopes or updating the database or putting it up on the web – they've got very unsexy jobs and probably the best thing is that we've just kept on doing it over and over again so it's reached more people.

The thing is that a lot of politics is very mundane, very day to day. When I was involved in my local residents groups, I was just delivering leaflets through people's doors and being a street rep and chatting to people – they're not very sexy things and the newspapers are never going to write about things like that, but at the end of the day they're really important.

You either let the BNP move into an area, or you get involved in local boring politics to say there's another way. That's when you need to be in your residents groups and things like that, arguing and involved actively in saying 'Hang on, we can't blame the asylum seekers because there are other reasons for our troubles'. That's when the really important politics come through. When I used to hear people say things they'd read in the Daily Mail I'd be, 'Well I don't agree. I don't think that's true' – challenging people but not screaming and shouting at them.

It's a bit of a worry that people rallied around for the CJA ten years ago but at the moment we've got the same type of legislation coming thick and fast, but nothing similar has happened in response...

COLIN: There've been 600 new criminal offences introduced since Labour came to power.

With all these curfews and police cracking down on youths, the government must be trying to force a punk movement to happen – they're provoking a reaction. What could SchNEWS or anyone else do to help channel these youths into something positive – like a punk movement?

WARREN: All we can do is keep pointing out what we think is wrong with the world and how we can try and change it. We've also got to remain open to new ideas and people, and not become the boring old farts in the office. If a new punk type movement happens, great.

How does the Direct Action Movement relate to workers' struggles?

WARREN: I think the direct action/anti capitalist movement has been very good at making links. The Liverpool Dockers were over the moon with our support. After the first anniversary, when we went up there in September 1996, they said we were the only people to offer proper physical support. They were saying 'We've had all the blah, we've had money from all round the world, but you lot have got onto the fucking roofs, joined the picket line, tried to stop scab lorries, got nicked and beaten up by coppers.' Bonds were formed. For me it was one of the most brilliant days ever, even though I got arrested and got a bit of a kicking. But afterwards this felt like a very special moment in time.

I remember sitting in that 'Reclaim The Futures' squat in Liverpool watching the scouse Dockers and southern crusties trying to work together – and the image of 'patchouli oil and water' came to mind.

COLIN: What we noticed when we started getting involved in supporting the Liverpool Dockers and other strikers like the Magnets workers and others was that they had all been shafted by their own unions, so they turned to us. Some people like to believe that there are big battalions of unions out there waiting to go into action and we'll get our way – a lot of the left is based on this myth – whereas in fact unions are mostly against rocking the boat and often oppose workers who fight for a better deal. It's noticeable that the unions in Venezuela have sided with the bosses against Chavez, who is beginning to give food and education and health care to the poor in the shantytowns. You'd be surprised how often people tell us, "I'd love to get involved in this action for basic workers' rights but I can't, I'm in a union."

WARREN: We never went to one of these strikers and said, "Listen to us, we know what's best". Instead it was, "We just support what you're doing, how can we help?" So people did what they were good at, like getting onto roofs and causing chaos. Because I got arrested in Liverpool, I had to go up there quite a lot for my trials. I saw their beer guts getting bigger and bigger, and they were like, 'We don't wanna go back to work. Work's a load of shit'. And I was like, 'That's what we've been saying all along'.

But I can't see a proper continuing link with workers struggles since then though. Take the firemen last year, and you've got the bus drivers

in Sheffield this week – there are workers struggles – but they don't get the support the Dockers did.

WARREN: I think that's because the dockers' strike went on for over two years. But look at the recent Brighton bin strike. Within half a day of the dustmen going on strike the Anarchist Teapot had gone down there, saying, 'We can help you cook food'. They weren't saying 'Buy our papers' they just went down, and we said we'd help on picket lines, and some people D-locked onto scab trucks. I remember one day when there were about thirty of us chasing after scab dust trucks around Brighton. Can you believe this – we're running around after rubbish trucks to try and D-lock ourselves onto them to stop them working, and some of us looked as though we were dressed from the rubbish bins!

COLIN: We had two Liverpool Dockers that came down and talked at a gig in Brighton. The more experienced speakers of the Dockers were going to union branches, but these two were really nervous, saying they'd never done a speech. So anyway, one of them got up and said, "Listen, the reason you should support us is because without us you'd never get any drugs into the country" and it really broke the ice and after that we all got on brilliantly!

WARREN: What about the woman who came down to speak for the Magnet workers? She was a fifty-year-old grandmother, and her husband had been on strike for twelve months. They'd all been sacked, and she just went and talked at a meeting, and she was one of the best public speakers I had ever heard. She spoke at our direct action conference, and at a Mark Thomas gig. She brought people to tears, she was so fucking brilliant, so powerful – and this was just some grandmother who didn't know she was such a good speaker. That's one thing with capitalism and work, it sets peoples' expectations so low, you're shoehorned into shitty little jobs. Then if things kick off they actually find that they've got loads of skills and are capable of getting up in front of loads of people and saying something. It just came from the heart, what she said, and it was so brilliant – she was such a laugh.

How do you deal with the established left wing political parties?

COLIN: We don't have much to do with them. They take anger and resistance and channel it into something ineffective. That's why we published the Monopolise Resistance booklet a few years ago about the SWP's front group Globalise Resistance.

The left often can't think beyond marches. You can see that in the way the history of the anti-war movement in Britain is being reduced to basically one big march. It was much more than that, most of it not organised by any coordinators in London. Take the school students. No-one predicted that, no-one. It was a worldwide phenomenon, school students from Camden to Korea taking unplanned direct action against the war. It was massive, utterly uncontrolled; it just happened, everywhere. Apart from that there was direct action up and down the country – some people did some damage at RAF Fairford before they essentially introduced martial law in the Cotswolds to deal with protesters.

The thing is that in rich countries like Britain and the United States you've got very strong forces that want to oppose some of capitalism's nastiness, but not too much, not so it would upset things. These people are very good at controlling activities. If you're running a campaign and it starts getting popular, before you know it they'll have elected themselves to be the steering committee and everyone else gets told what to do at meetings where they're just the audience. If the direct action movement is anything, it's a rejection of that controlling, pulling-back, moderating approach that destroys so many grassroot initiatives.

The state was terrified of direct action against the war. That's why they took so many steps to criminalise protesters who were, in fact, acting entirely in line with international law. If there'd been another ten thousand people at RAF Fairford where the bombers were leaving from, who knows what would have happened? If the Asian youth in northern cities had taken to the streets, you may well have seen this country's government forced to obey international law. But it didn't happen, for various reasons.

How do you think SchNEWS sits alongside the current array of alternative media such as Indymedia, and campaign-specific websites like Dissent?

WARREN: Hopefully it compliments them, but the main difference is that we're weekly and so we can respond to events quickly. We have work experience kids coming in often – they do a bit of writing, help with the layout, help with the website, and the next day the thing they've written – with a bit of help or whatever – appears in print. It's very immediate, that's the beauty of it.

ADVERTISEMENT

Does your memory let you down?

DO YOU FIND YOURSELF, for example, talking about complex issues like waging a war against the axis of evil, yet forgeting relatively simple things like the name of your grandfather and what it was he used to do for a living?

Our simple technique can help you remember such details as the fact that his name was Prescott Bush, and that his Union Banking Corporation raised $50 million for the Nazis by selling German bonds to Wall Street investors until outlawed by the 1942 "Trading With The Enemy Act." By simple concentration tricks you can even remember who was your grandad's partner in UBC's financing of the Axis Powers. His name was George Walker – hence the W in your own.

No problems remembering pop's name of course, he's the fellah indicted for war crimes in East Timor. Remember when you mistakenly opened the letter from the World Court thinking it was for you and that you were in Really Big Trouble? Remember how terrified you were for a few moments? Okay, well think terrified, terror, terrorist campaign, war on terror, me, same-name-as-me: dad. (But remember: the Butcher of Baghad isn't the one whose sanctions and bombings have killed more children than died in Hiroshima.)

.... And remember the nice Saudi oil millionaire who you had all those meetings with and whose family always kept in touch with your oil millionaire family? Well, he's not a nice man. Confusing, isn't it?

It needn't be. John Negroponte is your Anti-Terrroist Tzar. Remember his terror campaign in Honduras? Think "Tzar of all the Russias". Think Cold War. Think military necessity.

Send off today and we can rush our memory enhancement system to you within days. Then again, think of the Enron case. How much do you want to remember here? Are you sure? Better keep cocaine-blitzing your head until you're not even sure if you put a pretzel in there or not.

How has SchNEWS' role changed?

GIBBY: You have to remember that SchNEWS was born in an era without mobile phones or the internet being the norm. It was a big effort in communication. It was lumping down the printers on a Friday morning. It was a monster mailout. It had strength and a loyal following before everyone became info-swamped. It was, along with Earth First Action Update, the prime source of any news on what was going on and what to do about it. Indymedia, for example, was a good five years away.

Being 'information for action', SchNEWS has always put further links and contacts at the end of each article, so the reader can actually get involved in what they're reading about, as opposed to the mainstream media which is normally 100% about passive consumption.

COLIN: There's a photo of people at Newbury during the anti-bypass protests where there are fifteen people just reading SchNEWS which had just arrived. People know SchNEWS is *theirs*.

How do you deal with the criticism that by doing alternative media, you're more like an onlooker rather than someone actually doing it?

WARREN: I know that the vast majority of us involved in SchNEWS are also involved in direct action and doing stuff in our local community as well, or helping out with the Cowley Club etc. Nobody does SchNEWS in isolation, then goes home. It's written by activists – as much as I hate that word – it's not written by journalists, though we've had wannabe career journalists pass through. One even works for Al-Jazeera now! But on another level, I think things like the monthly Porkbolter (in Worthing) is as important if not more important than SchNEWS. I wish there was a weekly Brighton anti-capitalist newsletter – I wish every town had something like the Porkbolter.

* If you want to set up your own local newsletter check out the SchNEWS DIY Guides on our website www.schnews.org.uk

Bibliography

This isn't by any means comprehensive, but is some of the stuff we reckon compliments this book.

Books

'We Are Everywhere' (Verso 2004) Stories of movements and rebellions from every continent on the front lines of resistance against capitalism and economic globalization **www.weareeverywhere.org**

'Stonehenge – Celebration and Subversion.' (Alternative Albion 2004) Andy Worthington's lively history book about Stonehenge, from the ancient myths through to the Battle of the Beanfield. **www.hoap.co.uk/alternative.htm**

'Do Or Die' issue 10 – the last edition of the annual tome covering ecological direct action around the world. **www.eco-action.org/dod**

'Big Bad World' (New Internationalist 2002) Polyp's book of razor-sharp political cartoons. "Anti-American, unbalanced and unreasonable" - Coca Cola.

'Days of War, Nights of Love:- Crimethink for Beginners' Full of exciting ideas and amazing tales related with passion and humour. **http://crimethinc.com/a/days/**

'DIY Culture: Party & Protest in Nineties Britain.' (Verso 1998) A collection of articles by people involved in some of the key events of the period edited by George McKay

'Battle For The Trees' (Godhaven Ink 1996) Merrick's funny and intimate account of life at the Newbury Bypass protest. **www.godhaven.org.uk**

'Distant Voices' (1992), **'Hidden Agendas'** (1998) and **'The New Rulers of the World'** (Verso 2002) by John Pilger. Hard hitting but immensely readable accounts about who really runs the world. **http://pilger.carlton.com/**

'Killing Hope: US Military and CIA Interventions Since World War II' (Common Courage Press 2003) by William Blum **www.killinghope.org**

'Fierce Dancing' by CJ Stone (Faber and Faber '96) Entertaining account of the counter culture. **www.cjstone.co.uk**

Currently out of print, but worth hunting around for

'Copse' Cartoonist Kate Evan's great book about the big road protest of the mid nineties.

'On Fire' Accounts from on the ground at the G8 summit at Genoa in July 2001.

Online

Indymedia – an international network of regional websites providing alternative independent news uploaded by the readers. Visit **www.indymedia.org** to find the regional Indymedia in your area/country.

A-Infos – www.ainfos.ca – Regular anarchist newsfeed over the internet in various languages.

Squall – Online magazine presenting radical journalism, photography and culture with content. **www.squall.co.uk**

Wildfire – Read about Jo Wilding's firsthand accounts from Iraq, Palestine and more – **www.wildfirejo.org.uk**

Zmag – "an independent political magazine of critical thinking on political, cultural, social, and economic life in the United States". Massive archive of news, analysis, and comment. **www.zmag.org**

Urban 75 – London site packed with several key discussion lists and lots more – **www.urban75.com**

Greg Palast - US investigative journalist digging the dirt on international politics **www.gregpalast.com**

Corporate Watch – Excellent UK research organisation investigating and exposing corporate power. **www.corporatewatch.org.uk**

Statewatch – monitoring the state and civil liberties in the European Union **www.statewatch.org**

Infoshop – **www.infoshop.org** – US anarchist website

Subvertise.org – **www.subvertise.org** – subverts from around the world

Videos (to get 'em try **www.cultureshop.org**)

Guerillavision – On The Barricades – A compilation of three films **- Big Rattle In Seattle –** closing down the WTO summit in Seattle in Nov 99 **/ Capital's III** – riots at World Bank/IMF meeting in Washington DC in April 2000 **/ Crowd Bites Wolf -** World Bank/IMF meeting in Prague gets a hammering in September 2000.

Life In The Fast Lane – the amazing story of the No M11 Campaign, trying to stop a road ploughing through east London

Not This Time – The Story Of The Simon Jones Memorial Campaign (2002 Update). The direct action campaign for justice for Simon Jones - killed on his first day as a casual worker at Shoreham docks. **www.simonjones.org.uk**

Undercurrents – direct action video magazine which has been going for ten years. **'Undercurrents News Network 1'** seeks out and distributes cutting edge documentaries and animations – **www.undercurrents.org/unn/**

Operation Solstice (Battle of the Beanfield). The horrific story of the police attack on travellers on their way to the Stonehenge Free Festival in June 1985. **http://tash.gn.apc.org/op_solstice.htm**

We Interrupt This Empire... The San Francisco Video Activist Network presents the story of their city getting shut down as the invasion of Iraq begins in March 2003. **www.videoactivism.org/empire.html**

McLibel – Two Worlds Collide – the story of the longest libel trial in British history between two individuals and the fast food giant McDonald's. ***See also*** **McSpotlight** – the site for the McLibel campaign which is now an internationally run public relations nightmare for McDonald's. **www.mcspotlight.org**

GNN Guerilla News network – www.guerrillanews.com – Films, news and images

SchMoovies – download our short punchy vids for free at **www.schnews.org.uk/schmovies**

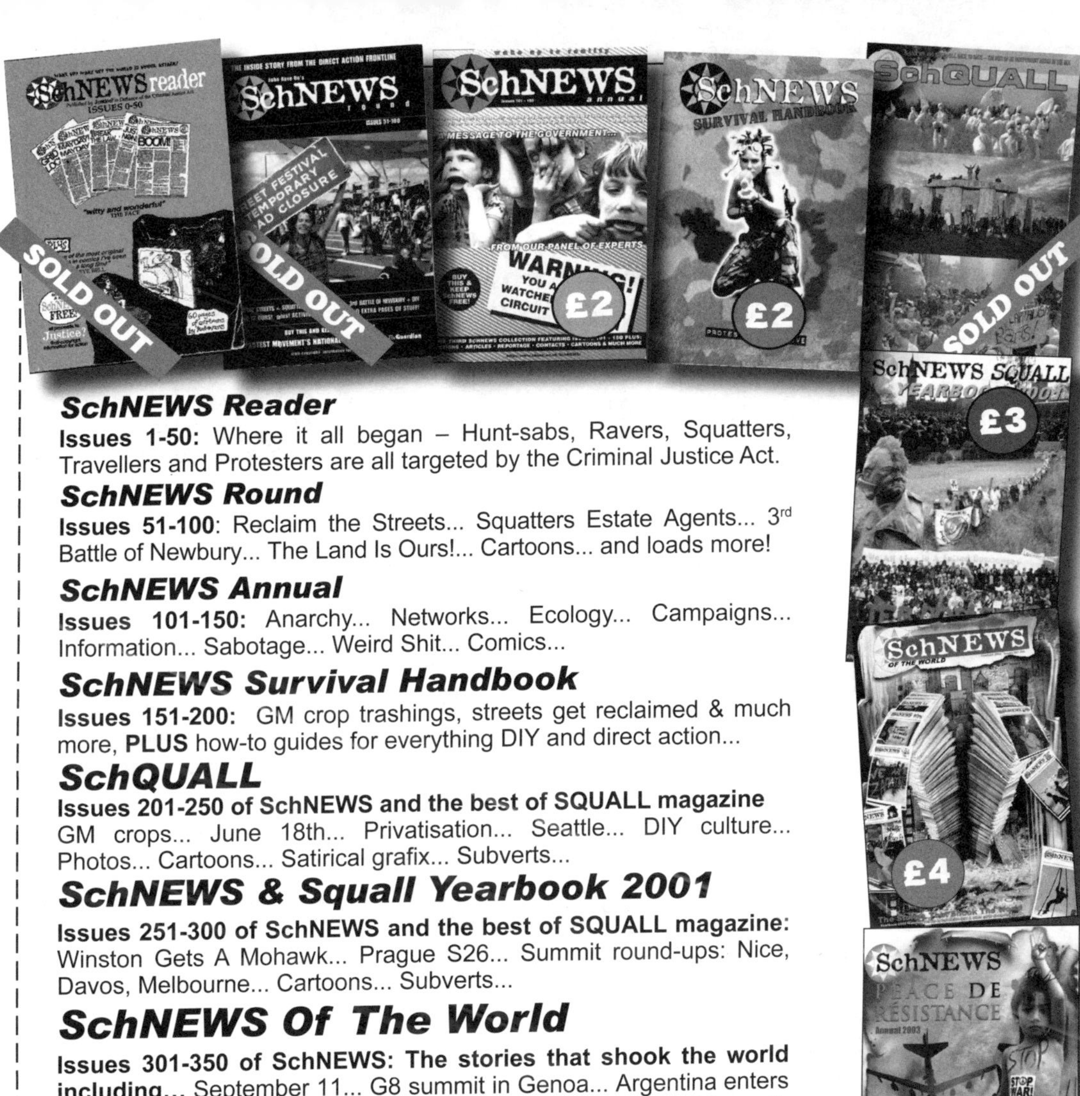

SchNEWS Reader

Issues 1-50: Where it all began – Hunt-sabs, Ravers, Squatters, Travellers and Protesters are all targeted by the Criminal Justice Act.

SchNEWS Round

Issues 51-100: Reclaim the Streets... Squatters Estate Agents... 3rd Battle of Newbury... The Land Is Ours!... Cartoons... and loads more!

SchNEWS Annual

Issues 101-150: Anarchy... Networks... Ecology... Campaigns... Information... Sabotage... Weird Shit... Comics...

SchNEWS Survival Handbook

Issues 151-200: GM crop trashings, streets get reclaimed & much more, **PLUS** how-to guides for everything DIY and direct action...

SchQUALL

Issues 201-250 of SchNEWS and the best of SQUALL magazine
GM crops... June 18th... Privatisation... Seattle... DIY culture... Photos... Cartoons... Satirical grafix... Subverts...

SchNEWS & Squall Yearbook 2001

Issues 251-300 of SchNEWS and the best of SQUALL magazine: Winston Gets A Mohawk... Prague S26... Summit round-ups: Nice, Davos, Melbourne... Cartoons... Subverts...

SchNEWS Of The World

Issues 301-350 of SchNEWS: The stories that shook the world including... September 11... G8 summit in Genoa... Argentina enters meltdown... international activists go to Palestine... the rise of the anti-war movement...

Peace De Resistance with CD-ROM!

Issues 351-400: A global anti-war movement reaches crescendo as Iraq gets invaded... Genetics... Carry On Bombing... Worst Britains...

PRACTICALLY GIVING 'EM AWAY OFFER

SchNEWS Annual, Survival Handbook, Yearbook 2001, SchNEWS of the World and Peace De Resistance for just £15 incl. P&P

Name..

Address..

....

....

....

....

Cheques/postal orders payable to 'Justice?' c/o On the Fiddle, PO Box 2600, Brighton, East Sussex, BN2 0EF.

N.B. If you can't afford to buy the books then order them for your local library and spread the words.

Razz us over the following books to put in the bog:

SchNEWS Annual ISBN: 0 9529748 1 9	Number of copies @ £2 plus £1.70 p&p each................
SchNEWS Survival Guide ISBN: 0 9529748 2 7	Number of copies @ £2 plus £1.70 p&p each................
SchNEWS & Squall Yearbook 2001 ISBN: 0 9529748 4 3	Number of copies @ £3 plus £1.70 p&p each................
SchNEWS of the World ISBN: 0 9529748 6 X	Number of copies @ £4 plus £1.70 p&p each................
Peace De Resistance ISBN: 0 9529748 7 8	Number of copies @ £7 plus £1.70 p&p each................

Or – what the hell I'll have the "practically giving 'em away" offer for £15:
Number of sets @ £15 **incl.** p&p ....
(offer only for UK addresses)

Total................

Photocopy to save cutting up yer book!

Legal Warning

Section 6 Criminal Law Act 1977
As amended by the
Crmininal Justice And Public Order Act 1994

TAKE NOTICE

THAT: ***we live in this house,*** **it is our home, and** ***we intend to stay here.***

THAT: ***at all times there is at least one person in this house.***

THAT: ***any entry into this house without our permission*** **is a CRIMINAL OFFENCE as any of one of us who is in physical possession is opposed to any entry without their permission.**

THAT: ***if you attempt to enter by violence*** **or by threatening violence we WILL PROSECUTE YOU, you may receive a sentence of up to SIX MONTHS IMPRISONMENT and/or a FINE of up to £5,000.**

THAT: ***if you want us to leave*** **you will have to take out a summons for possession in the County Court or in the High Court, or produce to us a written statement or Certificate in terms of Section 12a Criminal Law Act 1977 (as inserted by Criminal Justice And Public Order Act 1994.)**

THAT: **it is an offence under Section 12a (8) Criminal Law Act 1977, (as amended), to knowingly make a false statement to obtain a written statement for the purposes of Section 12a. A person guilty of such an offence may receive a sentence of up to SIX MONTHS imprisonment and/or a fine of up to £5,000.**

The Occupiers

N.B. SIGNING THIS LEGAL WARNING IS OPTIONAL; IT IS EQUALLY VALID WHETHER IT IS SIGNED OR NOT.

Squatting is still legal, necessary and free.

Advisory Service for Squatters:
tel: **020 7359 8814** ***web:*** **www.squat.freeserve.co.uk**

YELLOW PAGES

DON'T JUST LET YOUR FINGERS DO THE TALKING

The SchNEWS Yellow Pages is information for action - a list of hundreds of groups and resources to inform and inspire you to put down this book and get up and do something positive. This contacts list is a selection of the full list of over 800 entries on our website. Hopefully this categorised version is more useful than an A-Z list, but obviously a lot of the categories overlap. Many of the groups listed can put you in touch with more specific or local groups. This list is constantly updated and is never 'complete', if you want to see your group added (or your details change) please get in touch.

The categories are: Anti-War / Anarchism / Animal Rights / Anti-Capitalsim / Anti-Racism / Bookshops / Cafes & Clubs / Children & Parenting / Community Groups / Culture / Disability Rights & Action / Drugs / Economics / Education / Energy / Environment / Food & Farming / Forests & Woodlands / Gardening / Genetics / Health / Housing & Homelessness / Human Rights / Indigenous Peoples / Media / Networking Support / Prisoner Support / Refugees / Sexuality / Transport / Travellers / Women / Workers Rights.

The format of the entries are: **Name** Address. T phone number F fax number email@address www.website *Description*.

ANARCHISM

5th May Group (Turkish and Kurdish Anarchists in Exile) P.O. Box 2474, London, N8. T 020 8374 5027 *We mostly campaign around local issues (eg: JSA, New Deal etc). We also campaign against Compulsory Military Service in Turkey, and propagandise anarchist ideas.*

Active Distribution BM Active, London, WC1N 3XX www.activedistribution.org jon@activedistribution.org *Anarchist (DIY) distribution, mailorder, wholesale, stalls etc of a non-profit, Books, Mags, Music, Badges t-shirts etc. Send SAE for a catalogue.*

A-Infos www.ainfos.ca *Regular anarchist newsfeed over the internet in various languages.*

Alternative Network For Eastern Europe www.alter.most.org.pl/fa/ *A network to coordinate anarchist activities in the region of Eastern Europe, and to make communication between groups of different countries easier, and to encourage the free movement of people and ideas from one community to another.*

Alternative Network for Eastern Europe (Alter-EE) www.alter.most.org.pl/ hydrozag@poczta.onet.pl *Created to help to coordinate anarchist activities in the region of Eastern Europe.*

Anarchist Black Cross Bialystok (ABC-Bialystok) PO Box 43, Bialystok 26, Poland 15-662. T +48 604 142 155 www.czarnyblok.prv.pl soja2@poczta.onet.pl *Support for class struggle prisoners, campaigns against prisons itself, publishing a info bulletin in English about Poland.*

Anarchist Communitarian Network The P.O. Box 2159, Louisa, VA 23093 www.anarchistcommunitarian.net anarchistcommunitariannet@hotmail.com *To facilitate the integration of the anarchist ('libertarian socialist') and the intentional communities ('cooperative living') movements.*

Anarchist FAQ www.anarchistfaq.org *Frequently Asked Questions about anarchism. Its aim is to present what anarchism really stands for and indicate why you should become an anarchist.*

Anarchist Federation (AF) c/o 84b Whitechapel High St, London, E1 7QX. T 07946 214590 www.afed.org.uk anarchistfederation@bigfoot.com *Class struggle anarchists aiming to abolish capitalism and all oppression to create a free and equal society. This is Anarchist Communism.*

Anarchist Federation (Ireland) PO Box 505, Belfast, BT12 6BQ. T 07951 079719 www.afireland.cjb.net ireaf@yahoo.ie *Irish Anarchist Federation.*

Anarchist Information Network (AIN) Box EMAB, 88 Abbey Street, Derby DE22 3SQ. www.ain.20fr.com ain@ziplip.com *AIN is a network of Anarchists from different traditions, Individualist, Social, Green, Syndicalist working together to promote and develop Anarchism.*

Anarchist Studies c/o Dr S. Gemie, Humanities, University of Glamorgan, Pontypridd CF37 1DL www.lwbooks.co.uk sgemie@glam.ac.uk *Anarchist-academic journal; six monthly; cover anarchist theory, politics and culture.*

Anarchist Teapot Mobile Kitchen PO Box 74 Brighton BN1 4ZQ. anarchistteapot@yahoo.co.uk *Catering collective based on volunteer labour to cook vegan, mostly organic food for events we care about. Can cook outside, inside, anywhere for up to 300 people.*

Anarchist Yellow Pages ayp.subvert.info/ *Your Guide to Anarchists and Troublemakers around the Globe.*

Anarchy: A Journal of Desire Armed C.A.L. Press, PO Box 1446, Columbia, MO 65205-1446, USA. www.anarchymag.org jmcquinn@coin.org *Anti-ideological anarchist publishing (magazines & books).*

Aotearoa Anarchist Portal www.anarchism.org.nz yuda@anarchism.org.nz *News and information resources on Anarchist theory, history, culture, organisation for those new to Anarchism and Anarchistsalike.*

Bellow Box 35, 82 ColstonStreet, Bristol, BS1 5BB. Bellow1@bigfoot.com *Radical women's newsletter, instigated by Women Speak Out - FREE, available for photocopying/ distribution - hardcopy or PDF.*

Black Cat Collective Box 22, Green Leaf Bookshop, Colston Street, BS1 5BB T 07905 720575 Black_Cat_Collective@yahoo.co.uk *Anti-reformist loose anarchist collective. Hold monthly open forums, carry-out actions and spread ideas to inspire insurrection.*

Black Flag BM Hurricane, London WC1N 3XX flag.blackened.net/blackflag blackflageds@hushmail.com *Class struggle anarchist quarterly magazine with strong international coverage, recently revamped. Contact us for subs info. Comprehensive list of UK Anarchist groups.*

ChiapasLink PO Box 79, 82 Colston St, Bristol, BS1 5BB. www.chiapasnews.ukgateway.net chiapaslink@yahoo.com *Chiapaslink hopes to provide a link between the Zapatista struggles in Chiapas, Mexico and in the UK.*

Collective for libertarian Ideas kolektiv_za_slobodarska_ideja@hotmail.com *(K.S.I. - Kolektiv Za Slobodarska Ideja) the first anarchist collective in Macedonia*

Czechoslovak Anarchist Federation (CSAF) P.O.Box 223, 111 21 Praha 1, Czech Republic. www.csaf.cz/english intersec@csaf.cz *Anarchist propaganda, street actions, publishing anarchist materials, ABC group.*

Daily Bleed's Anti-Authoritarian Encyclopedia recollectionbooks.com/bleed/gallery/galleryindex.htm

Diggers & Dreamers BCM Edge, London, WC1N 3XX T 07000 780536 F 0870 163 4661 www.diggersanddreamers.org.uk info@diggersanddreamers.org.uk *Diggers & Dreamers - the Guide to Communal Living in Britain? and books on related subjects.*

Dorks Advocating Total Anarchy(DATA) www.antimedia.net/data karen@antimedia.net *Tech support for the revolution.*

Enrager.net www.enrager.net admin@enrager.net *Enrager.net is an online info-hub project to enable better communication and networking within the anti-authoritarian and anti-capitalist movement in Britain, as well as provide an easy and clear introduction for people to revolutionary ideas.*

Federation Collective Rampenplan P.O. Box 780, 6130 At Sittard, The Netherlands T +31 46 452 4803 F +31 46 451 6460 www.antenna.nl/rampenplan ramp@antenna.nl *Federation based on basic democracy and anarchism. Includes a mobile vegetarian/vegan ecological kitchen, anarchist/environment book publisher and a video action newsgroup.*

Freedom anarchist fortnightly 84b Whitechapel High St, London, E1 7QX. T 020 8771 8317 F as phone FreedomCopy@aol.com *Britain's most frequent anarchist paper carries news and views from a growing range of activists. All contributions welcome.*

Grauzone Postfach 705, 6021 Innsbruck, Austria.. T 0699-11617169 www.catbull.com/grauzone infoladen_grauzone@catbull.com *Infoshop, Anarchist and Cultural Collective.*

Green Anarchist Green Anarchist, BCM 1715, London WC1N 3XX. www.greenanarchist.org *UK's original and best (apparently) anarcho-primitivist paper - uncensored forum for direct action news and discussion.*

Green Anarchist (GA) 9 Ash Avenue, Galgate, Lancaster LA2 0NP, UK T 01524 752212 website.lineone.net/~grandlaf/Sotiga.htm grandlaf@lineone.net *Quarterly magazine reporting on environmental issues, anarchism, animal rights, community resistance. With emphasis on positive empowerment and improving our lives.*

Guerillavision Box 91, Green Leaf Bookshop, 82 Colston St, Bristol BS1 5BB guerillavision@angelfire.com *Er... troublemakers with other people's dv cameras...*

Hereford Anarchists c/o PO Box 7, Pontypool, Gwent, NP4 8YB www.herefordanarchists.cjb.net herefordanarchists@hotmail.com *Local group campaigning for an anarchist world through propaganda and action.*

International Smiley Zippy Party smileyzippy@postmaster.co.uk *Web humour and philosophy: Epicureanism, permaculture, autonomous living, alternative economics, quantum psychology and situationist art. Features Pete Loveday's Russell.*

Kate Sharpley Library (KSL) BM Hurricane, London, WC1N 3XX. Or PMB 820, 2425 Channing Way, Berkeley CA 94704, USA. www.katesharpleylibrary.net/ info@katesharpleylibrary.net *Archive of Anarchist and related material, reclaiming Anarchist history to inform current struggles. Write for details of our (many!) publications.*

London Class War P.O. Box 467, london E8 3QX. T 07931 301901 www.classwaruk.org classwaruk@hotmail.com *Exists to promote class consciousness and working class control over our day to day lives. Publish Class War paper.*

Maloka Anarcho Collective BP 536, 21014 Dijon Cedex, France T +33 3 8066 8149 F +33 3 8071 4299 www.chez.com/maloka maloka@chez.com *French anarchist collective from Dijon.*

New York Surveillance Camera Players [SCP-New York] POB 1115, NYC 10009-9998, USA. T 001 212 561 0106 www.notbored.org/the-scp.html notbored@panix.com *Situationist-inspired anti-surveillance camera group.*

News and Views www.newsviews.prv.pl *Information about eastern Europe with links to lots of eastern Europe anarchist groups.*

No God-No Master PO Box 300, East Brunswick, Victoria 3057, Australia. www.punk.gr/nogod-nomaster anthropia@hotmail.com *Anarchist bulletin and publication of small Pamphlets in Greek.*

Norwich Anarchists PO Box 487, Norwich, NR2 3AL. T 07941 657485 *Produce a community based newspaper. Also run advice line on benefits, employment law, squatting and baliffs.*

Now or Never Norwich Anarchists, PO Box 487, Norwich, NR2 3AL. twotins.tripod.com/id4.html *Newspaper of Norwich Anarchists - Fighting molotov and half-brick for the people of Norwich.*

Social Anarchism Atlantic Center For Research and Education, 2743 Maryland Avenue, Baltimore MD 21218, USA, www.nothingness.org/sociala spud@nothingness.org *As both political philosphy and personal lifestyle, social anarchism promotes community self reliance, direct participation in political decision-making, respect for nature. Produce magazine.*

Solidarity Federation (SolFed) PO Box 469, Preston PR1 8XF. T 01772 739724 www.solfed.org.uk solfed@solfed.org.uk *Anarcho-syndicalist federation of groups (contact us for your nearest). Dedicated to an anti-authoritarian future based on mutual aid and individual freedom.*

Surrey Anarchist Group (SAG) PO Box 375, Knaphill, Woking, Surrey. GU21 2XL. saggymail@hushmail.com *Focus on both local and national actions and campaigns.*

Walthamstow Anarchist Group (WAG) PO Box 35832, London E11 3WT. T 07810 288889 www.walthamstowanarchy.org.uk wag@fuckmicrosoft.com *Local group who publish the bi-monthly newsletter The Underdog and run the Middle Finger radio collective among other things.*

Warhead PO Box 43, 15-662 Bialystok, Poland soja2@poczta.onet.pl *Anarchist news service for Poland.*

Wombleswww.wombles.org.ukwombles@hushmail.com *Non-doctrine led, horizontally organised anarchist collective against all institutions which destroys peoples lives and dreams.*

Zabalaza Books Postnet Suite 116, Private Bag X42, Braamfontein, 2017, Johannesburg, South Africa. www.struggle.ws/africa/safrica/zababooks/HomePage.htm zabalaza@union.org.za *Publishers of Anarchist writings/pamphlets on the various issues effecting the building of a free and equal non-statist society under workers self-management.*

ANIMAL RIGHTS

Animal Contacts Directory Veggies, 245 Gladstone Street, Nottingham NG7 6HX: T 0845 458 9595 www.veggies.org.uk acd@veggies.org.uk *The essential guide to thousands of animal welfare rights campaigns across the world available online or as a book from Veggies*

Animal Defender 261 Goldhawk Rd, London, W12 9PE. T 020 8846 9777 F 020 8846 9712 www.animaldefenders.org.uk info@animaldefenders.org.uk *Undercover investigations and campaigning to end the suffering of animals and to protect the planet.*

Animal Liberation Press Office BM4400, London, WC1N 3XX. T 01623 746470 mobile: 07752 107515 F as phone *Media contact for the ALF and other radical animal rights groups. Supplies speakers for groups, rallies, etc.*

Animal Rights Calendar c/o Veggies, 245 Gladstone Street, Nottingham NG7 6HX. T 0845 458 9595 www.veggies.org.uk/calender Arc@veggies.org.uk *Comprehensive, monthly diary of UK animal rights events. Also appears in ARC News*

ARCNEWS P.O.Box 339, Wolverhampton, WV10 7BZ T 0845 458 0146 www.arcnews.co.uk james@arcnews.co.uk *The UK's only independent animal rights magazine aimed at grass-roots campaigning. Available on subscription of ú10 per year or on line.*

Arkangel Arkangel Magazine,BCM 9240.London WC1N 3XX www.arkangelweb.org/ info@arkangelweb.org *Magazine for animal liberation.*

British Anti-Vivisection Association (BAVA) PO Box 73 Chesterfield S41 0YZ. www.bava.pwp.blueyonder.co.uk/ BAVA@blueyonder.co.uk *Organisation trying to expose the uselessness and counterproductiveness of animal experimentation in regards to human health.*

British Union For The Abolition of Vivisection (BUAV) 16a Crane Grove, London, N7 8NN. T 020 7700 4888 F 020 7700 0196 www.buav.org campaigns@buav.org *The BUAV is the leading anti-vivisection organisation specialising in public campaigning, hard-hitting undercover investigations, political lobbying and legal/scientific expertise.*

Coalition of Badger Action Groups PO Box 129, PLYMOUTH, Devon PL1 1RY. T 07817 858166 www.badger-killers.co.uk cbag@webtribe.net *Take non violent direct action against DEFRA's unscientific and cruel badger slaughtering program. We 'monitor' the killing areas and individuals take action to save badgers' (and other animals) lives.*

Compassion in World Farming Charles House,5A Charles Street, Petersfield, Hampshire GU32 3EH T 01730 264208/268863 F 01730 260791 www.ciwf.co.uk info@ciwf.co.uk *Campaigning to end the factory farming of animals and long distance transport through hard-hitting political lobbying, investigations and high profile campaigns.*

Farmed Animal Action PO Box 27, Tonbridge, Kent TN12 5WJ. T 0845 4560284 www.farmedanimalaction.co.uk info@farmedanimalaction.co.uk *Educate the public in the interests of farmed animals, who are often the forgotten victims of animal abuse.*

Gay Veggies & Vegans BM Box 5700, London, WC1N 3XX. *Newsletter and magazine promoting humane diet and living among lesbian, gay and bisexual people.*

Greyhound Rescue UK www.greyhoundrescue.co.uk jill@rigolo.f9.co.uk *Donate free Internet presence to any non-profit making organisation or charity for Greyhound rescue in the UK. List of local contacts.*

Hunt Saboteurs Association (H.S.A) BM HSA, London, WC1N 3XX. T 0845 4500727 /Press office only: 0961 113084 F as phone - call first. www.huntsabs.org.uk info@huntsabs.org.uk *The H.S.A is dedicated to saving the lives of hunted animals directly, using non-violent direct action.*

Judicial Inquiry Campaign PO Box 38552 London SW1W 9YQ www.vivisection.info cat@vivisection.info *Demand the truth about animal experiments, based on the scientific evidence of it's failings.*

London Animal Action (LAA) BM Box 2248, London, WC1N 3XX T 0845 458 4775 F as phone LondonAnimalAction.org.uk info@londonanimalaction.org.uk *Campaign on legal basis for animal rights, support people imprisoned for animal liberation and have monthly newsletter and meetings.*

National Anti-Hunt Campaign (NAHC) 27 Old Gloucester Street, London WC1N 3XX. T 01442 240 246 nahc@nahc.freeserve.co.uk *Peaceful campaigning against all hunting with hounds through petitioning, demonstrations, investigations, lobbying and civil disobedience. Info pack on request.*

Save The Newchurch Guinea Pigs (SNGP) PO Box 74EveshamWorcestershireWR11 3WF T 01902 564 734 www.liberation-now.org info@liberation-now.org *Campaign to close down the Newchurch Guinea Pig farm where thousands of animals are tested on each year.*

Seriously Ill Against Vivisection (SIAV) PO Box 116, High Wycombe, Bucks, HP14 3WX. T 0845 4581720 www.siav.org info@siav.org *Campaigning for a ban on all vivisection. We want non-animal, scientific methods of research to establish cures for disease.*

Shoreham Protester, The c/o 7 Stoneham Rd, Hove, Sussex, BN3 5HJ T 01273 885750 F as phone shorehamprotestr@ntlworld.com *Fortnightly newspaper reporting local and national animal rights news, especially reports from demonstrations. Input welcomed*

SPEAK SPEAK CampaignsPO Box 6712NorthamptonNN2 6XR T 0845 330 7985 www.speakcampaigns.org.uk/ info@speakcampaigns.org.uk *Migrating from Cambridge work for animal rights within the public and political arena through pro-active campaigning.*

Stop Huntingdon Animal Cruelty (SHAC) 6 Boat Lane, Evesham, Worcs WR11 4BP T 0845 4580630 www.shac.net info@shac.net *SHAC campaigns to close down the animal testing lab Huntingdon Life Sciences, and target anyone connected with them.*

Uncaged Campaigns St Matthew's House, 45 Carver St, Sheffield S1 4FT. T 0114 272 2220 F 0114 272 2225 www.uncaged.co.uk info@uncaged.co.uk *Not for profit organisation dedicated to bringing about the abolition of vivisection by democratic means.*

Vegan Prisoners Support Group (VPSG) P.O.Box 194, Enfield, EN1 3HD T 020 8292 8325 F as phone www.vpsg.org info@vpsg.org *VPSG assists vegan animal rights prisoners either held in police custody or within the prison system.*

Viva! 8 York Court, Wilder St, BristolBS2 8QH T 01273 777688 F 01273 776755 www.viva.org.uk info@viva.org.uk *Organisation campaigning to end the factory farming of animals and promote the vegetarian and vegan diets.*

World Animal Net 24 Barleyfields, Didcot, Oxon, OX11 0BJ. T 01235 210775 www.worldanimal.net info@worldanimal.net *The world's largest network of animal protection societies with over 1700 affiliates in more than 90 countries campaigning to improve the status and welfare of animals.*

ANTI-CAPITALISM

Adbusters 1243 West 7th Av, Vancouver, BC, V6H 1B7, Canada. T 604 736 9401 F 604 737 6021 www.adbusters.org info@adbusters.org *A global network of artists, activists, writers, pranksters, educators and entrepreneurs who aim to launch the new social activist movement of the information age.*

Alliance for Workers' Liberty PO Box 823, London SE15 4NA. T 020 72073997 Mob 07748 185553 F 020 72074673 www.workersliberty.org office@workersliberty.org *Agitating, organising, educating, to rebuild the labour movement so it can lead the self-liberation of the working class.*

Anti-Corruption Network P.O.Box 187, Chesterfield, Derbyshire, S40 2DU. T 01246 555713 F as phone. *The title says it all.*

Aufheben P.O.Box 2536, Rottingdean, Brighton, BN2 6LX lists village.virginia.edu/%7Espoons/aut_html *Not an organisation, but a magazine dedicated to the theory and practice of revolutionary class struggle*

Autonomous Centre of Edinburgh (ACE) 17 West Montgomery Place, Edinburgh, EH7 5HA T 0131 557 6242/Pager 07626 128984 www.autonomous.org.uk ace@autonomous.org.uk *Campaign base for social and ecological resistance with a view to bring about the revolutionary overthrow of capitalism.*

Bilderberg www.bilderberg.org *Research into The Power Elite's secretive Bilderberg Conferences*

Catalyst Collective PO Box 29, South-west PDO, Manchester M15 5HW. T 07984-675281 www.solfed.org.uk solfed@solfed.org.uk *Free bulletin of the anarcho-syndicalist Solidarity Federation. Particular focus on anarcho-syndicalist ideas and action at work.*

Communication Workers' Network (CWN) PO Box 29, South-west PDO, Manchester M15 5HW. T 07984 675281 www.solfed.force9.co.uk/cwn.htm solfed@solfed.org.uk *Network of communication/postal workers in Solidarity Federation. Contact CWN for free bulletins.*

Counter Information Agency (CIA) squat.net/cia *Collective of projects based in Amsterdam, each with diverse ways of presenting alternative non-mainstream information as a catalyst for people to take action.*

Dissent! - A Network of Resistance Against the G8 www.dissent.org.uk *Formed to build resistance to the 2005 G8 Summit in the UK, and to help build a lasting anti-capitalist network in Britain.*

Earth First! Action Update (EF! AU) PO Box 487 Norwich, NR2 3AL T 01603 219811 www.eco-action.org/efau efactionupdate@bigfoot.com *A monthly round-up of ecological and other direct action from around Britain. Has list of contacts of all UK Earth First groups.*

Eurodusnie Postbox 2228, 2301 CE Leiden, The Netherlands T + 31 (0)71 5173019 F as tel eurodusnie.nl info@eurodusnie.nl *Dutch anti-authoritarian organisation fighting against economic globalisation. Dutch and international links.*

Haiti Support Group P.O. Box 29623, London, E9 7XU. T 020 7525 0456 www.gn.apc.org/haitisupport haitisupport@gn.apc.org *Solidarity with the Haitian people's struggle for justice, real democracy and equitable development.*

Industrial Workers of the World PO Box 74, Brighton, BN1 4ZQ. T 01202 257556 www.iww.org.uk brightoniww@yahoo.uk *Union for all run by its members. For the abolition of wage-slavery through global solidarity, direct action and industrial democracy.*

Mannequin Republic 2 Combe Farm Cottages, Alldens Lane, Godalming, Surrey GU8 4AP. T 07810 595392 black_star_news@hotmail.com *Socio-democratic, anti-capitalist, anti-IMF. We stage local demos, various other mischief, and publish a monthly newsletter, Black Star News.*

McLibel Support Campaign 5 Caledonian Rd, London, N1 9DX T 020 787131269 F as phone www.mcspotlight.org mclibel@globalnet.co.uk *Encouraging people everywhere to see the sordid reality behind corporate propaganda, and to fight back against McWorld.*

Motkraft www.motkraft.net *The internet infocenter of the Swedish libertarian left. Publish news and information about actions, lectures, etc.*

Movement Against the Monarchy (MA'M) P.O. Box 14672, London, E9 5UQ T 07931 301901 www.geocities.com/capitolhill/lobby/1793/index mam_london@hotmail.com *Local and national direct action against the parasitic, undemocratic Royals; preparing major anti-Golden Jubilee 2002 activity.*

Peoples' Global Action c/o Canadian Union of Postal Workers, 377 Bank Street, Ottawa, Ontario, Canada www.agp.org pga@agp.org *A global instrument for communication and co-ordination for all those fighting against the destruction of humanity and the planet by the global market.*

Radical Activist Network London-based group active in anti-capitalist and anti-war movements which emphasises democracy, pluralism and a non-sectarian approach. www.radicalactivist.net info@radicalactivist.net

Reclaim the Streets (London) P.O.Box 9656, London, N4 4JY T (020) 7281 4621 www.reclaimthestreets.net rts@gn.apc.org *Direct-Action for global and local social-ecological revolution(s) to transcend hierarchical and authoritarian society, (capitalism included), and be home in time for tea...*

Red Star Research BCM Box 3328 London WC1N 3XX. T 07960 865601 www.red-star-research.org.uk info@red-star-research.org.uk *Information about the Labour Party's shift to the right wing of politics. identifies the links and networks of wealth and power and helps you to uncover the connections.*

Revolutionary Communist Group (RCG) BCM Box 5909, London WC1N 3XX. T 020 7837 1688 F 020 7837 1743 www.revolutionarycommunist.com rcgfrfi@easynet.co.uk *RCG supports Cuba, the Palestinian people, the fight against racism and against poverty pay. It is against Labour's imperialist wars. It publishes Fight Racism! Fight Imperialism!*

Rock around the Blockade c/o FRFI, BCM Box 5909, London WC1N 3XX. T 020 7837 1688 www.ratb.org.uk office@ratb.org.uk *Rock around the Blockade was founded in 1995 and is open to anyone who supports Cuba's socialist revolution.*

RTMark www.rtmark.com *RTMark supports the sabotage of corporate products, with no risk to the public investor*

Subvertise! c/o PO Box 68, Headington, Oxford OX3 7YS, UK www.subvertise.org webmaster@subvertise.org *An archive of 100s of subverts, political art, cartoons and articles.*

Transnational Resource and Action Centre PO Box 29344, San Francisco, CA 94129, USA www.corpwatch.org corpwatch@corpwatch.org *Holding corporations accountable.*

World Development Movement (WDM) 25 Beehive Place, London, SW9 7QR T 020 72747630 F 020 72748232 www.wdm.org.uk wdm@wdm.org.uk *Campaigns to tackle the root causes of poverty. Are currently campaigning to rewrite global trade rules to put people before profits.*

World Socialist Web Site www.wsws.org editor@wses.org *Provides analysis of major world*

events, comments on political, cultural, historical and philosophical issues.

Yes Men, The www.theyesmen.org administrative@theyesmen.org *The Yes Men are a genderless, loose-knit association of some three hundred impostors worldwide. Eg. Send spoof WTO delegates to conferences.*

ANTI-RACISM

1990 Trust, The Suite 12, Winchester House, 9 Cranmer Road, SW9 6EJ. T 020 7582 1990 F 0870 127 6657 www.blink.org.uk blink1990@gn.apc.org *A national Black (African, Asian & Caribbean) organisation to increase the capacities of the Black communities to combat racism.*

Antifa UK Box 36, 84b Whitechapel High Street T 07950 836455 www.antifa.org.uk info@antifa.org.uk *A collective of militant anti-fascists committed to opposing the rise of the far-right in Britain and abroad.*

Birmingham Racial Attacks Monitoring Unit (BRAMU) P.O. Box 9289, Birmingham, B15 5AE T 0121 622 4981 www.bramu.fsnet.co.uk harjinder@bramu.fsnet.co.uk *An independent, voluntary organisation, offering free, confidential help, support and advice to anyone suffering racial harassment in Birmingham.*

Black Women's Network St Chad's Court, 213 Hagley Road, Edgbaston, Birmingham B16 9RG. T 0121 695 2239 F 0121 695 2253 bwn@bbcha.nhs.uk *Supporting and providing networking, and other, opportunities for organisations that work for the benefit of Black women living in Birmingham.*

Campaign Against Racism & Fascism (CARF) BM Box 8784, London, WC1N 3XX. T 020 7837 1450 F 0870 052 5899 www.carf.demon.co.uk info@carf.demon.co.uk *CARF magazine exposes racism in multicultural Britain. Details the European offensive against refugees and shows how the domestic fight against racism is shaped by international forces.*

Institute of Race Relations 2-6 Leeke Street, London WC1X 9HS. T 020 7278 0623 F 020 7278 0623 www.irr.org.uk info@irr.org.uk *The IRR carries our research into issues of racism, from the rise of racial violence to the plight of asylum seekers. The IRR publishes Race & Class and the European Race Bulletin.*

Minority Rights Group International 379 Brixton Rd, London, SW9 7DE T 020 7978 9498 F 020 7738 6265 www.minorityrights.org minority.rights@mrgmail.org *Work to secure rights for ethnic, religious and linguistic minorities world wide, and educating people about minority issues in order to counter racism and prejudice.*

National Assembly Against Racism (NAAR) 28 Commercial St, London, E1 6LS T 020 7247 9907 F 020 7247 9907 www.naar.org.uk *Aims to initiate campaigns, set agendas and raise awareness on the whole range of anti-racist issues affecting British society.*

Newham Monitoring Project (NMP) 63 Broadway, Stratford, London, E15 4BQ T 020 8555 8151 F 020 8555 8163 nmp@gn.apc.org *Local grassroots anti-racist organisation, offers independent advice and casework support for victims of racial harassment, police harassment and civil injustice*

Notes From the Borderland Bm Box 4769, London, WC1N 3XX T (Pager) 07669-175886 www.borderland.co.uk larry@borderland.co.uk *We publish cutting edge parapolitical research into the secret state, fascists, etc - material that is too sharp for Guardian/Red Pepper*

Sunderland Fans Against Racism PO Box 601, Sunderland SR2 7XY T 07967 886257 www.sfar.org.uk sunderland_fans_against_racism@hotmail.com *We are a group of Sunderland Fans committed to tackling the problems of racism and fascism amongst supporters of our favourite football team, Sunderland.*

The Monitoring Group (TMG) 14 Featherstone Rd, Southall, Middx, UB2 5AA. T 020 8843 2333 Emergency Helpline 0800 374618 www.monitoring-group.co.uk *A leading agency helping victims of racial harassment, police misconduct, domestic violence and immigration detention.*

ANTI-WAR

Abolition 2000 (A2000 UK) 601 Holloway Rd, London, N19 4DJ T 020 7281 4281 www.gn.apc.org/abolition2000uk A2000UK@gn.apc.org *To achieve for the 21st century a global treaty to abolish nuclear weapons.*

Aid Convoy (was **Brighton Lifeline Humanitarian Aid**) 4 Atlingworth Street, Brighton, UK BN2 1PL T +44 (0)1273-680414 www.aidconvoy.net brighton@aidconvoy.net *Taking aid directly to, and working with people and projects trying to rebuild sustainably. So far, Albania, Macedonia, Kosova, and Ukraine (around Chernobyl).*

Aldermaston Women's Peace Camp c/o 157 Lyndhurst Rd, Worthing, W. Sussex BN11 2DG. T 0845 4588362 / 07904 450307 www.aldermastonwpc.gn.apc.org awpc@gmx.co.uk *Based around a monthly peace-camp at AWE Aldermaston - opposes Britain's nuclear weapons through campaigns and nonviolent direct action.*

Brighton Peace & Environment Centre 39-41 Surrey StreetBRIGHTON BN1 3PBU.K. T 01273 766610 www.bpec.org info@bpec.org *Promoting public awareness of peace, social justice, sustainable development and environmental issues.*

Campaign Against Arms Trade (CAAT) 11 Goodwin St, London, N4 3HQ. T 020 7281 0297 F 020 7281 4369 www.caat.org.uk enquries@caat.demon.co.uk *Broad coalition of groups and individuals committed to an end to the international arms trade, together with progressive demilitarisation within arms-producing countries.*

Campaign for Nuclear Disamament (C.N.D) 162 Holloway Rd, London, N7 8DQ T 020 7700 2393 F 020 7700 2357 www.cnduk.org enquiries@cnduk.org *Campaigns non-violently to rid the world of nuclear weapons and other weapons of mass destruction and to create genuine security for future generations.*

Campaign for the Accountability of American Bases (CAAB) 8 Park Row, Otley, West Yorkshire LS21 1HQ. T 01943-466405 or 01482-702033 F 01482-702033 www.caab.org.uk anniandlindis@caab.org.uk *Working for accountability of American bases through the systems and structures available and taking direct action when these fail.*

Central Committee for Conscientious Objectors 405 14th St. #205, Oakland, CA 94612, USA. T +1 510 465 1617 www.objector.org/ info@objector.org *Supports and promotes individual and collective resistance to war and preparations for war.*

Conscience - The Peace Tax Campaign Archway Resource Centre, 1b Waterloo Rd, London, N19 5NJ T 0870 777 3223 F 020 7281 6508 www.conscienceonline.org.uk info@conscienceonline.org.uk *Campaigns for right of conscientious objectors to war to have the military part of their taxes spent on peacebuilding initiatives.*

Faslane Peace Camp A814, Shandon, Nr Helensburgh, Dumbartonshire, G84 8NT. T 01436 820901 www.faslanepeacecamp.org faslanepeacecamp@hotmail.com *We live across the road from Britain's nuclear arsenal, stop nuclear convoys, generally harrass the MoD.*

Free Flyingdales Network www.freefylingdalesnetwork.co.uk *A small organisation that aim to stop America's 'Son of Star Wars' Plans and, in particular, the use of RAF Fylingdales in North Yorkshire as part of this plan.*

Friends of Al Asqa PO Box 5127, Leicester, LE2 0WU T 07711 823524 F 0166 2537575 *Friends of al Aqsa is a non profit making organisation concerned with upholding the human rights of the Palestinians and the defence of al Aqsa Mosque in Jerusalem.*

Gush Shalom POB 3322 Tel-Aviv 61033 Israel. www.gush-shalom.org info@gush-shalom.org *Aims to influence Israeli public opinion and lead it towards peace and conciliation with the Palestinian people.*

Housmans Peace Resource Project (HPRP) 5 Caledonian Rd, Kings Cross, London, N1 T 020 7278 4474 F 020 7278 0444 worldpeace@gn.apc.org *Produces World Peace Database: 3500 organisations in 170 countries (includes major environmental & human rights groups) - abbreviated annual Directory appears in Housmans Peace Diary.*

Iraq Occupation Focus Iraq Occupation Focusc/o PO Box 304SouthallUB2 5YR www.iraqoccupationfocus.org.uk iraqfocus@riseup.net *Iraq Occupation Focus was formed in the spring of 2004 by a group of activists from across the anti-war movement who were spurred into action by the revelations of human rights abuses coming out of Iraq, the growing evidence of plunder by US corporations and the appaling death toll inflicted by the occupying military forces.*

Israel Imperial News www.israelimperialnews.org tzabar@israelimperialnews.org *A magazine edited by Israeli dissidents, against the illegal Israeli occupation of Palestinian, against Israel's cruel treatment of the Palestinians and against Israel's policy of ethnic cleansing.*

Justice Not Vengeance 29 Gensing Road, St Leonards on Sea, East Sussex TN38 0HE. T 0845 458 9571 www.j-n-v.org info@j-n-v.org *Opposes the US-UK 'war on terrorism', and campaigns for a peaceful resolution of international conflicts, based on justice and equality.*

Nonviolent Action (NVA) 5 Caledonian Rd, Kings Cross, London, N1 9DY T 020 7713 6540 F shared fax please mark for NvA 020 7278 0444 nva@gn.apc.org *Magazine serving campaigners seeking positive social change through nonviolent means with news of activists and activities - and a stimulus to thought and action.*

Non-Violent Resistance Network (NVRN) 162 Holloway Rd, London, N7 8DQ T 020 7607 2302 F 020 7700 2357 c/o cnd@gn.apc.org *To network non-violent direct action activists in the UK and supply with information about NVDA events.*

Nuclear Information Service (NIS) nis@gn.apc.org *Not-for-profit, independent information service, which works to promote public awareness and foster debate on nuclear disarmament and related safety and environmental issues.*

Other Israel, The P.O. Box 2542, Holon 58125, Israel. other_israel.tripod.com AICIPP@igc.org *Bi-monthly peace movement magazine (hardcopy), for free sample send address.*

Peace Brigades International British Section (PBI) 1b Waterlow Rd, London, N19 5NJ T 020 7281 5370 F 020 7272 9243 www.igc.org/pbi pbibritain@gn.apc.org *Send teams of international observers to provide protective accompaniment to local human rights defenders who are at risk as a result of their work for social justice.*

Peace Museum, The Office: Jacob's Well, Manchester Rd., Bradford, BD1 5RW. Visitor Gallery: 10 Piece Hall Yard, Bradford Centre, BD1 1PJ T 01274 780241 www.peacemuseum.org.uk peacemuseum@bradford.gov.uk *Covers peace history, nonviolence, conflict resolution. Four travelling exhibitions. Educational outreach. Open 11-3 Wed and Fri or by appointment.*

Peace News 5 Caledonian Rd, London, N1 9DY T 020 7278 3344 F 020 7278 0444 www.peacenews.info admin@peacenews.info *Radical, international, anti-militarist, quarterly magazine. For nonviolent revolution. Bringing activists and campaigners together worldwide, sharing ideas, theories, and tactics.*

Scientists For Global Responsibility PO Box 473, Folkestone CT20 1GS. T 07771 883696 www.sgr.org.uk/ info@sgr.org.uk *Organisation promoting ethical science and technology, based on the principles of openess, accountability, peace, social justice, and environmental sustainability.*

Scottish Campaign for Nuclear Disarmament (CND) 15 Barrland Street, Glasgow G41 1QH. T 0141 4231222 F 0141 4332821 www.banthebomb.org scnd@banthebomb.org *Largest Peace organisation in Scotland. Campaign against Trident at Faslane, co-ordinates the Coalition for Justice Not War. Supports direct action and political action.*

Solent Coalition Against Nuclear Ships (SCANS) c/o 30 Westwood Rd., Southampton, SO17 1DN T 023 8055 4434 Mob. 07880 557 035 F same as Tel nis@gn.apc.org *Awareness to stop nuclear powered sub. from using Southampton docks*

Trident Ploughshares 42-46 Bethel St, Norwich, Norfolk, NR2 1NR T 0845 4588366 F 0845 4588364 www.tridentploughshares.org tp2000@gn.apc.org *Open, accountable & non-violent disarmament of the British nuclear Trident system.*

Truth Justice Peace Action - Human Shields www.humanshields.org/ human@humanshields.org *Mass direct action, in conflict zones, with the objective of protecting life by getting in the way.*

Voices in the Wilderness UK 16b Cherwell St, Oxford, OX4 1BG T 0845 4582564 www.viwuk.freeserve.co.uk voices@viwuk.freeserve.co.uk *Breaks sanctions by taking medical supplies to Iraq without export licences. Regular newsletter and briefings.*

Women In Black www.womeninblack.net *An international peace network. Women in Black is not an organization, but a means of mobilization and a formula for action.*

WoMenwith Womyn's Peace Camp PO Box 105, Harrogate HG3 2FE. T 01943 466825 cndyorks.gn.apc.org/mhs/index.htm *Camp against the world's largest spy base. Operated by the US government and based in the Yorkshire Moors.*

World Court Project UK 67 Summerheath Rd, Hailsham, Sussex BN27 3DR T 01323 844269 F 01323 844269 www.gn.apc.org/wcp geowcpuk@gn.apc.org *Working to have implemented the Advisory Opinion of the International Court of Justice that nuclear weapons are illegal.*

Youth & Student Campaign for Nuclear Disarmament (Y) 162 Holloway Rd, London, N7 8DQ T 0207 607 3616 F 0171 700 2357 www.youthstudentcnd.org.uk/ info@youthstudentcnd.org.uk *Campaigning to trash Trident through* *actions, demonstrations, awareness raising & letter writing. New volunteers are welcome.*

BENEFITS

Brighton Against Benefit Cuts Brighton & Hove Unemployed Workers' Centre, 4 Crestway Parade, Hollingdean, Brighton, BN1 7BL T 01273 540717 babc99@yahoo.co.uk *Organizing resistance to the New Deal workfare and other attacks on benefits. Support autonomous action by claimants and resistance by JobCentre staff.*

Dartford Unemployed Group c/o 34 Saxon Place, Horton Kirby, Dartford, DA4 9JG. T 01322 861415 *Support and campaigning for all claimants.*

Edinburgh Claimants c/o ACE, 17 West Montgomery Place, Edinburgh, EH7 5HA T 0131 557 6242 www.autonomous.org.uk/ec *We encourage claimants to stick together to overcome benefits hassles, we resist benefit cuts and compulsory workfare schemes e.g New Deal.*

Newham and District Claimants Union Durning Hall, Earlham Grove, London, E7 9AB. *Meetings 7.30 pm alternate Thursdays. Work as a collective to get benefits from DSS, Council or anywhere else.*

Oxford Claimants Union East Oxford Community Centre, Princes St., Oxford, OX4 1MU. T 01865 723750 F 01865 724317 *Benefits advice/ representation, Outreach community work, Community social events and Campaigns.*

BOOKSHOPS

56a Infoshop 56 Crampton St, London, SE17 www.safetycat.org/56a 56a@safetycat.org *Books, tea, zines, info, empties, bikes, library, history, action, people.....sometimes cafes...sometimes otherthings...*

Avalon 73 Fawcett Rd, Southsea, Hants, PO4 0DB T 02392 293673 F 02392 780444 info@avalonheadshop.co.uk *Portsmouth's only head shop. Stock Undercurrents; distribute SchNEWS as well as information on local, national and international campaigns.*

Blackcurrent Bookshop 4 Allen Rd, Abington, Northampton NN1 4NE. T 07833 17328 *Specialises in radical and independent books, comix, cards, badges, tapes and CDs.*

Commonweal Collection c/o JB Priestley Library, University of Bradford, Richmond Rd, Bradford, BD7 1DP T 01274 233404 F 01274 233398 www.brad.ac.uk/library/services/commonweal/ commonweal@bradford.ac.uk *Promoting nonviolent social change, peace and justice, by providing literature, resources and other support to activists, academics and the public.*

Eco-Logic Books 10-12 Picton St, Bristol, BS6 5QA T 0117 9420165 F 0117 9420164 www.eco-logicbooks.com books@eco-logic.demon.co.uk *Publishes and sells mail order books on practical solutions to environmental problems, sustainability, permaculture, organic gardening, etc.*

Freedom Book Company 73 Fawcett Rd, Southsea, Hants, PO4 0DB T 023 92780600 F 023 92780444 www.freedombooks.co.uk info@freedombooks.co.uk *Massive range of informative drugs related books and magazines (cultivation, legality, effects etc), Undercurrents videos, radical magazines and periodicals.*

Freedom Press 84b Whitechapel High St, London, E1 7QX T 020 7247 9249 F 020 7377 9526 www.enrager.net/hosted/freedom/press.php distro@freedompress.org.uk *Anarchist publishers and propagandists since 1886, through our periodicals, books and pamphlets, available from our bookshop or by mail order. Contact us for free sample copy of 'Freedom'.*

Green Books Foxhole, Dartington, Totnes, Devon, TQ9 6EB T 01803 863260 F 01803 863843 www.greenbooks.co.uk paul@greenbooks.co.uk *Publishers of a wide range of books on politics, ecology, economics, eco-philosophy, eco-building, renewable energy and the environment.*

Green Leaf Bookshop 82 Colston St, Bristol, BS1 5BB. T 0117 921 1369 F 0117 9460001 www.greenleafbookshop.co.uk *Radical bookshop. Mail order. Very fast customer order service - from U.S & U.K.*

Housmans Bookshop 5 Caledonian Rd, King's Cross, London, N1 9DX T 020 7837 4473 F 020 7178 0444 shop@housmans.idps.co.uk *London's oldest radical bookshop, home to the weird & the wonderful, publisher of annual Housmans Peace Diary.*

Little Thorn Books 73 Humberstone Gate, Leicester, LE1 1WB. T 0116 251 2002 F as phone *Leicester radical bookshop.*

News From Nowhere Bookshop 96 Bold Street, Liverpool, L1 4HY T 0151 708 7270 www.newsfromnowhere.org.uk *Long established, busy radical community bookshop run by a women's co-operative. Books, magazines, world music CDs and more. Open Mon-Sat 10am-5.45pm.*

R.E.C.Y.C. 54 Upperthorpe Rd, Sheffield, S6 3EB. T 0114 263 4494 *Re-use and second hand, recycling, waste campaigns, newsletter.*

Reading International Solidarity Centre (RISC) 35-39 London St, Reading, Berks, RG1 4PS T 0118 9586692/0118 9569800 F 0118 9594357 www.risc.org.uk admin@risc.org.uk *Development Education Centre with World Shop selling fair trade products, books and teaching materials, Global Caf?, community meeting space.*

Slendermans www.slendermeans.org.uk info@slendermeans.org.uk *Political and punk book and free info stall and website.*

Word Power Bookshop 43 West Nicholson St, Edinburgh, EH8 9DB. T 0131 6629112 F as phone www.word-power.co.uk books@word-power.co.uk *Scotland's radical bookshop and mail order. Organise Edinburgh Radical Book Fair in May each year.*

CHILDREN & PARENTING

Association of Radical Midwives 6 Springfield Road, Kings Health, Birmingham, B14 7DS. T 0121 444 2257 www.radmid.demon.co.uk/ sarahmontagu@postmaster.co.uk *Committed to improving the maternity care provided by the NHS. Primarily a support group for people having difficulty in getting or giving good, sympathetic, personalised midwifery care.*

Baby Milk Action 23 St. Andrew's St, Cambridge, CB2 3AX. T 01223 464420 www.babymilkaction.org info@babymilkaction.org *Aims to save lives and to end the avoidable suffering caused by inappropriate infant feeding.*

Green Parent www.thegreenparent.co.uk editor@thegreenparent.co.uk *Website about natural parenting and environmental issues.*

Hands Up For... 76 Blenheim Gdns, Willesden Grn, London NW2 4NT. T 07708 718231 or 07960 732767 www.messengers.org.uk/ hands_up_for@hotmail.com *A campaign run entirely by young people to encourage political participation,democracy and debate throughout society.*

Informed Parent, The P.O.Box 870, Harrow, Middlesex, HA3 7UW. T 020 8861 1022 F as phone www.informedparent.co.uk *Quarterly newsletter to help parents make a decision regarding vaccination based on knowledge, not fear.*

Real Nappy Project PO Box 3704, London SE26 4RX. www.realnappy.com *Central source of information and advice on all nappy-related issues, for local authorities, health professionals, the media and individuals.*

Woodcraft Folk, The 13 Ritherdon Road, London, SW17 8QE. 13 Ritherdon Rd., London, SW17 8QE. T 020 8672 6031 www.woodcraft.org.uk info@woodcraft.org.uk *We aim to develop self-confidence in young people and aim to bulding a sustainable world basd on equality, peace, social justice and co-operation.*

COMMUNITY GROUPS

Bolton Gathering of Organic Growers (GOG) T 7736685538 bolton-organics.org.uk mail@bolton-organics.org.uk *a community co-operative formed to co-ordinate and better promote the activities of its local groups which consist of community gardens, local neighbourhood food and health co-operatives, home-growing schemes and educational projects. GOG was founded by local community activists, many of whom were involved in the food co-ops.*

Campaign Against Criminalising Communities (CACC) c/o Haldane Society, Conway Hall, Red Lion Square, London WC1 T 020 7586 5892 www.cacc.org.uk knklondon@gn.apc.org *The supposed war on terrorism is in reality a war on dissent and holds inherent dangers for everyone's civil liberties.*

Confederation of Indian Organisations 5 Westminster Bridge Road, London, SE1 7XW T 020 7928 9889 F 020 7620 4025 www.cio.org.uk enquiries@cio.org.uk *Working with south asian voluntary organisations in the UK*

Crystal Palace Campaign 2 Hogarth Court, Fountain Drive, London SE19 1UY www.crystal.dircon.co.uk crystal@crystal.dircon.co.uk *A voluntary group of local people opposed to a plan to build a huge leisure complex on the historic site of the old Crystal Palace in south London.*

Cuba Solidarity Campaign Red Rose Club, 129 Seven Sisters Road, London N7 7QG. T 020-7263-6452 www.cuba-solidarity.org.uk office@cuba-solidarity.org.uk *Provide material aid to Cuba, fundraising and produce a magazine called Cuba Si.*

Haringey Solidarity Group (HSG) PO Box 2474 London N8. T 020 8374 5027 hsg.cupboard.org hsg@globalinternet.co.uk *Local working class group encouraging radical solidarity, co-operation, and mutual aid in our community, workplaces, and lives.*

Kebele Kulture Projekt 14 Robertson Rd, Eastville, Bristol, BS5 6JY T 0117 939 9469 www.kebele.org info@kebele.org *Anarchist collective run drop-in and meeting centre, vegan cafe, bike workshops, anarchist library, housing co-op, exhibitions, campaign catering, political activities and more.*

Lancashire SF PO Box 469, Preston PR1 8XF. T 01772 739724 F as phone mysite.freeserve.com/LancashireSF/index.jhtml lancashiresolfed@hotmail.com *Solidarity Federation group in Lancashire - includes Preston, Burnley, Lancaster etc. (see also Solidarity Federation under anarchism).*

Manchester Environmental Resource Centre initiative (MERCi) Bridge-5 Mill, 22a Beswick Street, Ancoats, Manchester, M4 7HR T 0161 273 1736 F 0161 274 4598 www.bridge-5.org/ merci@bridge-5.org *North West's leading sustainable development innovator and the largest membership based environmental charity in Manchester.*

Manchester SF PO Box 29, SW PDO, Manchester M15 5HW. T 07984 675281 www.manchestersf.org.uk manchestersf@manchestersf.org.uk *Solidarity Federation group in the Manchester area (see also Solidarity Federation under anarchism).*

North & East London Solidarity Federation P.O. Box 1681, London, N8 6LE. T 020 8374 5027 solfed@solfed.org.uk *Solidarity Federation group in North London.*

Red & Black Club PO Box 17773, London SE8 4WX. T 020 7358 1854 solfed@solfed.org.uk *Solidarity Federation group in south London (see also Solidarity Federation under anarchism).*

Sheffield SF PO Box 1095, Sheffield S2 4YR. solfed@solfed.org.uk *Solidarity Federation group in Sheffield/south Yorkshire (see also Solidarity Federation under anarchism).*

South Herts SF PO Box 493, St Albans ALl 5TW. T 01727 862814 solfed@solfed.org.uk *Solidarity Federation group in South Herts (see also Solidarity Federation under anarchism).*

South West Solidarity, Box 43, 82 Colston St, Bristol BS1 5BB. solfed@solfed.org.uk *Solidarity Federation group in the Bristol and Avon area (see also Solidarity Federation under anarchism).*

Sumac Centre 245 Gladstone St., Nottingham, NG7 6HX. T 0845 458 9595 F as tel -phone first www.veggies.org.uk/sumac sumac@veggies.org.uk *Resource centre for local groups campaigning for human and animal rights, the environment, peace, etc.*

Truth & Reconciliation Commission for Stonehenge (TRCS) 96 Church Road, Redfield, Bristol BS5 9LE. T 0117 9542273 www.greenleaf.demon.co.uk george@greenleaf.demon.co.uk *Open forum for resolution of Stonehenge conflict by discussion with all people including officials.*

West Yorks Solidarity Federation PO Box 5, Hebden Bridge, W. Yorks HX7 8YN. solfed@solfed.org.uk *Solidarity Federation group in West Yorkshire, including Bradford and Leeds (see also Solidarity Federation under anarchism).*

CULTURE

Albion Community Arts Trust The Greenhouse, 42-46 Bethel Street, Norwich, NR2 1NR. T 01603 717074/01603 409060 www.albionarts.org info@albionarts.org *To encourage community involvement in the creative arts and to provide platforms where these projects may be viewed.*

Banksy www.banksy.co.uk *Political graffiti artist.*

Banner Theatre Company The Friends Institute, 220 Moseley Rd, Highgate, Birmingham, B12 0DG T 0121 440 0460 www.bannertheatre.co.uk voices@btinternet.com *Promotes political change in support of disenfranchised sections of society, through the use of documentary, multi-media cultural productions rooted in radical experiences.*

Brighton Alliance of Sound Systems (BASS) 43 Park Crescent Road, Brighton, BN2 3HE. bass23.org info@bass23.org *BASS is about positive free party politics. BASS generates funds to pay for communal safety equipment and courses.*

Buddhafield PO Box 27822, London SE24 9YZ. T 020 8671 7144 Mobile 07768 200797 F 020 8671 7144 www.buddhafield.com info@buddhafield.com *Buddhafield runs a festival cafe and the 'Buddhafield Festival', also Buddhaseeds Permaculture and various retreat camps through the year.*

Cartoon Art Trust 7 Brunswick Centre, Bernard St, London, EC1N 8JY T 020 7278 7172 F 020 7278 4234 cartooncentre@freeuk.com *Exhibitions of cartoons, comics & animation; children's classics & adult courses; talks, fairs, auctions, sales & awards.*

Cartoon Kate www.cartoonkate.co.uk kartoonkate@fastmail.fm *Political cartoons by Kate Evans.*

Chumbawamba PO Box TR666, Armley, Leeds, LS12 3XJ. www.chumba.com chumba@chumba.demon.co.uk *A popular combo influenced by Black lace and the Zapatistas.*

Common Ground Gold Hill House, 21 High Street, Shaftesbury, Dorset SP7 8JE. T 01747 850820 F 01747 850821 www.commonground.org.uk kate.ofarrell@commonground.org.uk *Common Ground offers ideas, information and inspiration to help us learn about, enjoy and take more responsibility for our own localities.*

Continental Drifts Hilton Grove Business Centre, London, E17 4QP T 020 8509 3353 F 020 8509 9531 www.continentaldrifts.co.uk chris@continentaldrifts.co.uk *Not for profit organisation representing the finest in UK underground performing arts from outside the mainstream.*

Fanclub www.fanclubbers.org mail@fanclubbers.org *Fusing art and activism to create culture-jams with a focus on surveillance and the excesses of consumer culture.*

Festival Eye BCM 2002, London, WC1N 3XX. T 0870 737 1011 F 0870 7371010 www.festivaleye.com editor@festivaleye.com *Published each May (ú3 + SAE) with the most comprehensive listings of UK festivals side by side with beautiful artwork, photography and reviews.*

Festival Zone, The www.thefestivalzone.com info@thefestivalzone.com *Website listing rock festivals in Europe.*

Green Road Show Ham Mill's Yard, Bowlish, Shepton Mallet, Somerset BA4 5JH. T 01749 343953 Mobile 07831 405661 or 07778 765724 www.greenroadshow.co.uk andy@greenroadshow.demon.co.uk *Environmental education and family entertainment based in, and around, the Worlds only Wind and Solar powered Circus Top.*

Guilfin PO Box 217, Guildford, Surrey GU1 1WS. T 07957 193195 www.guilfin.net moneypenny@mi5.uk.com *The essential alternative guide to what's going on in the South East's underground scene.*

Headspace www.headspace.org.uk mail@headspace.org.uk *Live audio visual entertainment, VJ's, installations at parties, clubs, festivals and galleries.*

Infokiosk Bokal 3 rue Lazare Carnot, 01 000 Bourg, France. T 06 20830843 www.chez.com/lebokal lebokal@chez.com *Independent, self-rule and non-profit association whose aim is to promote and diffuse alternative ideas and underground musics.*

Innerfield Soundsystem T 01273 697579 F 07092 184075 www.innerfield.co.uk mail@innerfield.co.uk *Music, management and equipment for free parties, festivals and other events using unique technology.*

Kingston Green Fair 75a Terrace Road, Walton On Thames, Surrey KT12 2SW. T 01932 229911 www.kingstongreenfair.org info@kingstongreenfair.org *The Green Fair has been in operation since 1987, attracting nearly 15,000 visitors each year making it the UK's most successful one-day green family event!*

Levellers 55 Canning Street, Brighton, BN2 0EF. T 01273 608887 www.levellers.co.uk otf@levellers.co.uk *Band. Produce a magazine, sell merchandise.*

Network 23 www.network23.org *Free party network*

Network 23 - Brighton www.partyvibe.com/brighton23 info@spiralize.co.uk *Free party and autonomous events in Brighton*

Northern Arts Tactical Offensive (NATO) www.nato.uk.net tacticalarts@yahoo.co.uk *A collective resurgence of radical art.*

Panic! Brixton Poetry homepages.which.net/%7Epanic.brixtonpoetry panic.brixtonpoetry@which.net *Panic! is committed to free expression and a radical engagement against oppression.*

Partyvibe collective, The www.partyvibe.com/freeparties.htm *Bringing together partygoers, musicians and artists. This site is dedicated to offering resources to the free party community.*

Raise Your Banners 641 Ecclesall Road, Sheffield, S11 8PT. T 0114 249 5185 www.ryb.org.uk pete@ryb.org.uk *Biennial festival of political song.*

Rhythms of Resistance www.rhythmsofresistance.co.uk info@rhythmsofresistance.co.uk *Radical pink and silver samba band that uses percussion and carnival to mobilise and move people on demos/actions.*

SCRAP Records PO Box 2023, Brighton, BN1 1AA. www.dirtysquatters.com dirtysquatters@hotmail.com *Hardcore underground label bringing music and culture for your hot, drowning planet.*

Sound Conspiracy www.soundconspiracy.freetekno.org soundcode99@hotmail.com *European travelling soundsystem*

Spiral Objective P.O.Box 126, Oaklands Park, South Australia 5046 T +618 8276 5076 www.spiralobjective.com spiralob@adelaide.on.net *DIY fanzine, record label, mailorder, distro and umbrella organistaion for travelling activist theatre group.*

Stonehenge Campaign c/o 99 Torriano Av, London, NW5 2RX. T 07970 378572 www.phreak.co.uk/stonehenge/psb/stonecam.htm stonehenge@stones.com *Meet at Solstice and Equinox sunrises at Stonehenge, want more Free Festivals at Stonehenge, and free access into the Stones for all who come in peace.*

Sunrise Screenprint Workshop The Old Schoolhouse, Kirkton of Menmuir, by Brechin, Angus, Scotland, DD9 7RN www.menmuir.org.uk/sunrise/ sunrise@gn.apc.org *We're vegans who print t-shirts inc. lots of animal rights/anarchist/stonehenge designs and print for groups and campaigns using environmentally safe inks.*

sw@rm www.subdimension.com/community/subversion/swarm swarm@subdimension.com *Mobile radical infospace and information for action! Send an email to swarmlist-subscribe@yahoogroups.com to get regular updates.*

Underground Literary Alliance c/o King Wenclas, POB 42077, Philly, PA 19101, USA. literaryrevolution.com kingwenclas@yahoo.com *The ULA is creating a literary movement. The goal is to overthrow the literary establishment and get access for real writers.*

URBAN 75 www.urban75.com contact@urban75.com *Serves up non-mainstream viewpoint on a wide range of issues including environmental action, rave culture and civil rights. Plus drug information, cartoons, short stories and useless games.*

William Morris Society Kelmscott House, 26 Upper Mall, Hammersmith, London, W6 9TA T 020 8741 3735 F 020 8748 5207 www.morrissociety.org william.morris@care4free.net *To stimulate interest in the life and work of William Morris: Victorian designer, poet and socialist.*

Wolfs Head Press P.O.Box 77, Sunderland, SR1 1EB wolfsheadpress@hotmail.com *Fanzine (Wearwolf), music (Frankenstein Sound Lab), mail art and other stuff with a home made slant.*

Zion Train (Universal Egg) PO Box 3, Whitland, Dyfed, SA34 OYU T 01994 419800 F 01994 419357 wobblyweb.com perch@wobblyweb.com *Dub musicians with a conscience. Check out the Wobbler newsletter on the web.*

DISABILITY RIGHTS & ACTION

British Council of Disabled People (BCODP) Litchurch Plaza, Litchurch Lane, DerbyDE24 8AA. T 01332 295551 Minicom: 01332 295581 F 01332 295580 www.bcodp.org.uk general@bcodp.org.uk *Run entirely by disabled people of all impairments to promote our full equality and participation in UK society. Represent some 126 groups run by disabled people in the UK at national level.*

DIAL UK St Catherine's, Tickhill Road, Doncaster, South Yorkshire, DN4 8QN. T 01302 310123 F 01302 310404 www.dialuk.info/ enquiries@DIALuk.org.uk *A national organisation for a network of 160 local Disability Information and Advice Line services (DIALs) run by and for disabled people.*

DisabilityInformation.Com www.disabilityinformation.com/ *Website dedicated to the Disabled Peoples' Movement in the United Kingdom.*

Disabled Peoples Direct Action Network- DAN DAN NATIONAL OFFICE30 Hayward Rd.Whetstone, London,N20. 0HA andy.gill@fsmail.net *Direct action network for disabled people. Promotes non violent direct action and civil disobedience.*

Federation of Deaf People PO Box 11, Darwen, Lancs BB3 3GH. F 01254 708071 www.fdp.org.uk contact@fdp.org.uk *A voluntary organisation that campaigns for Deaf people's rights, funded by donations and membership.*

Incapacity Action 104 Cornwallis Circle, Whitsable, Kent CT5 1DT. T 01227 276159 F as phone incapacity action@onetel.net.uk *Campaign for rights to benefits, independent living/home care supoprt, other resources and linking with anti-war struggle.*

Mad Pride www.madpride.org.uk madpridelondon@hotmail.com *Committed to ending discrimination against psychiatric patients, promoting survivor equality and celebrating Mad culture*

DRUGS

Cannabis in Avalon (CIA) PO Box 2223, Glastonbury, BA6 9YU. T 01458 833236 www.freecannabis.com freecannabis23@hotmail.com *We aim to manifest the total liberation of cannabis to save the planet, heal the body & free the mind.*

Drug Culture www.drugculture.net *A non profit making website to collect names and emails addresses of people who feel that cannabis should be totally de-criminalised*

Green Party Drugs Group c/o 1a Waterlow Rd, London, N19 5NJ T 020 8671 5936 F phone first www.greenparty.org.uk/drugs greenpartydrugsgroup@gn.apc.org *Promote and sell ecstasy testing kits, part of core group for annual Cannabis March and Festival, info stalls & e testing at clubs, provide speakers, change drug policy.*

Legalise Cannabis Alliance (LCA) PO Box 198, Norwich, NR2 2DH T 01603 442215 www.lca-uk.org lca@lca-uk.org *A political party dedicated to campaigning for the full legalisation and utilisation of cannabis (hemp) - standing candidates in elections.*

Release 388 Old St, London, EC1V 9LT T 020 7729 525524 24 Hour Helpline: 020 7729 9904 Drugs In Schools Helpline: 0808 8000 800 Sex Workers & The Law Advice Line: 020 7729 9904 F 020 7729 2599 www.release.org.uk *24 hour drugs and legal helpline.. Also produces publications, such as the bustcard, and runs training programmes.*

Transform Easton Business Centre, Felix Road, Easton, Bristol, BS5 OHE T 0117 9415810 Mob 07980213943 F 0117 9415809 www.transform-drugs.org.uk info@transform-drugs.org.uk *Transform is the UK's leading campaign for a just and effective drug policy including the legalisation of all drugs.*

ECONOMICS

Aston Reinvestment Trust (ART) Freepost MID 16184, The Rectory, 3 Tower St, Birmingham, B19 3BR T 0121 356 2444 F 0121 359 2333 www.reinvest.co.uk reinvest@gn.apc.org *Provides loans to Birmingham based small businesses and social enterprises that are unable to access finance from the banks.*

ATTAC London Flat 1A, Rose Court, 34 Woodside, London SW19 7AN. attac.org.uk info@attac.org.uk *ATTAC campaigns for economic reforms, in order to reconquer space lost by democracy to the sphere of finance.*

Corporate Europe Observatory Paulus Potterstraat 20, 1071 DA Amsterdam, Holland T +31 20 612 7023 www.corporateeurope.org ceo@corporateeurope.org *Targeting the threats to democracy, equity, social justice and the environment posed by the economic and political power of corporations and their lobby groups.*

Corporate Watch 16b Cherwell St, Oxford, OX4 1BG T 01865 791391 www.corporatewatch.org mail@corporatewatch.org *Research organisation investigating and exposing corporate power. Website for anti-corporate campaigners. Publishes bi-monthly newsletter (sub. ú5/year).*

Ecology Building Society 18 Station Rd, Cross Hills, Keighley, BD20 7EH T 0845 674 5566 F 01535 636166 www.ecology.co.uk info@ecology.co.uk *A mutual building society dedicated to improving the environment by promoting sustainable housing and sustainable communities.*

Ethical Consumer Unit 21, 41 Old Birley St, Manchester, M15 5RF. T 0161 226 2929 F 0161 226 6277 www.ethicalconsumer.org mail@ethicalconsumer.org *The UK's only alternative consumer organisation looking at the social and environmental records of the companies behind the brand names.*

Ethical Junction 1st Floor, Dale House, 35 Dale Street, Manchester, M1 2HF. T 0161 236 3637 www.ethical-junction.org info@ethical-junction.org *Ethical Junction is a one-stop shop for ethical organisations and ethical trading.*

Fairtrade Foundation, The Suite 204, 16 Baldwin's Gardens, London, EC1N 7RJ. T 020 7405 5942 F 020 7405 5943 www.fairtrade.org.uk mail@fairtrade.org.uk *The Fairtrade Foundation exists to ensure a better deal for marginalised and disadvantaged third world producers.*

GetEthical.Com Unit A2, 2nd floor, Linton House, 39-51 Highgate Rd, London NW5 1RS. T 020 7419 7258 www.getethical.com info@getethical.com *The on-line shopping and consumer information site for the Big Issue and Red Pepper magazines.*

Green Guide Publishing Ltd 271 Upper St, London, N1 2UQ. T 020 7354 2709 F 020 7226 1311 greenguide.co.uk sales@greenguide.co.uk *Covers environmental, ethical and fairtrade products and services and provides the latest news, reviews, stories and information.*

LETSlink UK 12 Southcote Road, London N19 5BJ. T 020 76077852 Mob 07966 216891 F 020 76097112 www.letslinkuk.org letslink@synergynet.co.uk *National Development Agency and support network for Local Exchange Trading Schemes and other forms of local currency in the UK.*

New Economics Foundation (NEF) Cinnamon House, 6-8 Cole St, London, SE1 4YH T 020 7089 2800 F 020 7407 6473 www.neweconomics.org info@neweconomics.org *NEF works to put people and the environment at the centre of economic thinking.*

Poor People's Economic Human Rights Campaign Kensington Welfare Rights Union, P.O. Box 50678, Philadelphia, PA 19134, USA. T +1 215 203 1945 F +1 215 203 1950 www.kwru.org kwru@kwru.org *A national effort led by poor and homeless women, men and children of all races to raise the issue of poverty as a human rights violation.*

Public Citizen's Global Trade Watch 1600 20th Street NW, Washington DC, 20009, USA. T +1 202 588 1000 www.tradewatch.org *Educates the American public about the enormous impact of international trade and economic globalization on jobs, the environment, health and democratic accountability.*

Shared Interest Society Limited 25 Collingwood St, Newcastle upon Tyne, NE1 1JE T 0191 2339101 F 0191 2339110 www.shared-interest.com post@shared-interest.com *Co-operative lending society, lending money on fair terms to enable Third World producer groups to pay for labour, materials and equipment.*

UpStart Services 1 Court Ash, Yeovil, Somerset, BA20 1HG. T 0845 4581473 F 01935 431222 users.cooptel.net/upstart upstart@co-op.org *Provide help for people starting or running co-operatives and non-profit businesses, especially those with ecological or social change objectives.*

Women's Development Service No.30 Galtota Mulla, Kandy Road, Yakkala, Sri Lanka T +94 33 27962 jana womented@lanka.ccom.lk *Movement of poor mothers united together to develop themselves and their families, economically, socially and culturally. An alternative banking system for elevation out of poverty.*

EDUCATION

Arts Factory Ltd 11 Highfield Industrial Estate, Ferndale, Rhonda, CF43 4SX T 01443 757954 F 01443 732521 www.artsfactory.co.uk info@artsfactory.co.uk *Environmental design, graphic design, training, woodwork, learning for life classes, community organisation*

Cannabis Campaigner's Guide (CCGUIDE) LCA, PO Box 198, Norwich, Norfolk NR2 2DII T 01603 442214 www.ccguide.org.uk alun@ccguide.org.uk *A cannabis information and news site for campaigners, students, researchers and general public.*

Centre for Human Ecology 12 Roseneath Place, Edinburgh, EH9 1JB T 0131 624 1972 F 0131 228 9630 www.che.ac.uk info@che.ac.uk *The Centre for Human Ecology is an international institute for transformative education and research.*

Education Otherwise PO Box 7420, London N9 9SG www.education-otherwise.org enquiries@education-otherwise.org *UK-based membership organisation which provides support and information for families whose children are being educated outside school.*

Educational Advice for Travellers PO Box 36, Grantham, Lincs NG31 6EW. T 01558 650621 *Providing educational advice and resources to home-educated travellers families.*

Educational Heretics Press 113 Arundel Drive, Bramcote Hills, Nottingham, NG9 3FQ. T 0115 9257261 edheretics.gn.apc.org *Questions the dogmas of schooling in particular, and education in general, and to develop the logistics of the next learning system.*

Emerson College Trust Ltd Forest Row, East Sussex, RH18 5JX T 01342 822238 F 01342 826055 www.emerson.org.uk bmail@emerson.org.uk *An international centre for adult education, especially in the areas of Biodynamic Organic Agriculture and Steiner Waldorf Teacher Training.*

Feminist Library, The 5-5a Westminster Bridge Rd, London, SE1 7XW. T 020 7928 7789 feministlibrary@beeb.net *Largest lending and reference library of contemporary feminist material in the UK, both fiction and non-fiction.*

Free Range Education www.free-range-education.co.uk AskFredService@AOL.COM *Home education site - stacked with resources, links, information, qualified legal help and an e-mail support service called Ask FREd.*

Home Education Reading Opportunities (H.E.R.O Books) 58 Portland Rd, Hove, East Sussex, BN3 5DL T 01273 775560 F 01273 389382 *Home education books via mail order. For a catalogue and list of local newsletters send a large SAE. Free Range Education book on how to home educate ú13.20 inc. postage.*

Human Scale Education Fairseat Farm, Chew Stoke, Bristol BS18 8XF. www.hse.org.uk Info@hse.org.uk *Promotes smaller structures in education and a more holistic approach to learning.*

Institute for Social Ecology 1118 Maple Hill Road, Plainfield, Vermont, 05667, USA. T +1 802 454 8493 www.social-ecology.org *Independent institution of higher education dedicated to the study of social ecology, committed to the social and ecological transformation of society.*

Letterbox Library 71-73 Allen Rd. London, N16 8RY. T 020 7503 4801 F 020 7503 4800 www.letterboxlibrary.com info@letterboxlibrary.com *Workers' co-op providing multicultural and non-sexist books for children - offering essential topics and titles which were sadly neglected by mainstream booksellers.*

Lifecycles PO Box 77, Totnes, Devon, TQ9 5UA T 01803 840098 www.lifecycles.info people@lifecycles.info *A pedal powered cinema and outreach collective dedicated to the pursuit of sustainability and sequins.*

Media Lens www.medialens.org editor@medialens.org *Correcting for the distorted vision of the corporate media.*

Permaculture Association (Britain) BCM Permaculture Association, London, WC1N 3XX T 0845 4581805 F as phone www.permaculture.org.uk office@permaculture.org.uk *Support people and projects to learn about and use permaculture in their homes, gardens, schools, business, farms and communities.*

Photon Press 37 The Meadows, Berwick-Upon-Tweed, Northumberland, TD15 1NY. PHOTON.PRESS@VIRGIN.NET *Publish Light's List of 1500 independent press magazines world-wide printing fiction, poetry, art, reviews etc. ú2.50 inc. postage.*

Scientists for Global Responsibility (SGR) P.O. Box 473, Folkestone, CT20 1GS. T 07771 883696 www.sgr.org.uk info@sgr.org.uk *Promotes the ethical practice and use of science and technology.*

SELFED Collective (SelfED) P.O. Box 1095, Sheffield, S2 4YR www.selfed.org.uk selfed@selfed.org.uk *For self-education ideas and practice, developing real alternatives to state-sponsored education. Courses, self-help materials, workshops, etc?*

Slough Environmental Education Development Service (SEEDS) 1st Floor, 29 Church St, Slough, Berkshire, SL1 1PL T 01753 693819 F as phone theseedstrust@netscapeonline.co.uk *To protect & improve the natural and living environment through education, awareness raising and community based project.*

Student Action India c/o Voluntary Services Unit, UCL Union, 25 Gordon Street, London WC1H 0AY. T 0781 3395957 F 8701353906 www.studentactionindia.org.uk info@www.studentactionindia.org.uk *Self-funded volunteers work in India, assisting NGO's with community development schemes, and using their experience to raise awareness in the UK.*

Wild Things (Ecological Education Collective) c/o 15 The Square, Bestwwod Village, Nottm NG6 8TS. T 0845 458 4727 www.wildthings.org.uk info@wildthings.org.uk *Environmental education for primary & secondary school children through hands on projects.*

ENERGY

BioRegional Development Group (BDG) 24 Helios Road, BedZED, Wallington, Surrey SM6 7BZ. T 020 8404 4880 F 020 8404 4893 www.bioregional.com info@bioregional.com *BioRegional aims to bring local sustainability into the mainstream. We offer solutions to make sustainable living easy, attractive and affordable.*

Campaign for Real Events www.c-realevents.demon.co.uk info@c-realevents.demon.co.uk *Providing renewable energy support for art projects and producing free DIY plans for pedal generators and other renewable energy devices.*

Coltek Systems/K.S.N Graystone, Molsey Rd, Walton on Thames, Surrey KT12 3PP. T 01932 228879 www.colteksystems.freeservers.com colteksys@hotmail.con *Renewable energy pa, lights, video, power.*

Energy Efficiency Advice Centre T 0845 7277200 www.saveenergy.co.uk *An independent, government-funded body - advice on saving money on your electricity/gas bill. Free action pack*

Energy Saving Trust 21 Dartmouth St, London, SW1H 9BP T 020 7222 0101 F 0207 6542444 www.est.org.uk INFO@EST.CO.UK *Set up by the government to stimulate energy efficiency in UK households and create a market for clean fuel vehicles.*

Environmental Rights Action (ERA) International Secretariat:#214, Uselu-Lagos Road, UgbowoP.O. Box 10577, Benin City, Nigeria T +234-52-600 165 www.eraction.org/eraction@infoweb.abs.net *A Nigerian advocacy non-governmental organisation founded on January 11, 1993 to deal with environmental human rights issues in Nigeria.*

Gaia Energy Center Delabole, North Cornwall, PL33 9DA T 01840 213321 F 01840 213428 www.gaiaenergy.co.uk support@gaiaenergy.co.uk *A centre for the promotion of, and education about, renewable and sustainable energy and energy conservation.*

Green Dragon Energy Ceredigion, Wales. T 01974 821564 www.greendragonenergy.co.uk dragonrg@talk21.com *Electricity from Sun, Wind & Water.*

Green Energy www.greenelectricity.co.uk *Aims to help consumers - domestic or industrial - to find sources of green electricity for their homes and businesses.*

Home Power magazine PO Box 520, Ashland, Oregon 97520, USA. www.homepower.com hp@homepower.com *The Hands-On Journal of Home-Made Power.*

La Petroleuse OILWATCH SECRETARIAT û Casilla 17-15-246-C Quito, Ecuador www.oilwatch.org.ec ivonne.yanez@oilwatch.org.ec *Oilwatch is a resistance network that opposes the activities of oil companies in tropical countries.*

Low Carbon Network T 0870 765 9897 www.lowcarbon.co.uk *Not for profit company promoting the construction of buildings that have dramatically reduced carbon dioxide emissions and are easy to build and run.*

Low-Impact Living Initiative Redfield Community, Buckingham Rd., Winslow, Bucks, MK18 3LZ. T 01296 714184 www.lowimpact.org lili@lowimpact.org *Researching and promoting sustainable, low-impact alternatives to various aspects of everyday life.*

No New Oil T 01865 241097 www.nonewoil.org jo@risingtide.org.uk *Oil, war and climate change gathering - Dismantling the Oil Economy.*

Nuclear Information and Resource Service (NIRS) 1424 16th Street NW, #404, Washington DC20036, USA. T +1 202 328 0002 F +1 202 462 2183 www.nirs.org nirsnet@igc.apc.net *Information and networking center for citizens and environmental activists concerned about nuclear power, radioactive waste, radiation and sustainable energy issues.*

Renewable Energy in the Urban Environment (RENUE) 1929 shop Unit 9, Merton Abbey Mills, Watermill Way, London, SW19 2RD. T 020 8542 8500 F 020 8542 7789. www.renue.org.uk Cleanpower@renue.freeserve.co.uk *Tackling Climate Change at a community level by installing renewable energy systems and energy efficient measures, conducting education and arts projects in Wandsworth and Merton.*

UK Solar Energy Society, The c/o School of Engineering, Oxford Brookes University, Headington Campus, Gipsy Lane, Oxford OX3 0BP. T 01865 484367 F 01865 484263 www.brookes.ac.uk/other/uk-ises uk-ises@brookes.ac.uk *A forum for all those interested in the advancement of the utilisation of the sun's energy.*

unit[e] UK Freepost (SCE9229) Chippenham SN15 1UZ. T 0845 6011410 www.unit-e.co.uk enquiries@unit-e.co.uk *Provides renewable electricity services to domestic and corporate customers.*

Wavegen 50 Seafield Road, Longman Industrial Estate, Inverness IV1 1LZ. T 1463 238094 www.wavegen.co.uk enquiries@wavegen.com *Company researching wave power and building wave turbines.*

World Information Service on Energy *See Nuclear Information and Resource Service*

ENVIRONMENT

A SEED Europe Plantage Doklaan 12 A10 18 CM AmsterdamThe Netherlands T +31 20 6682236 F +31 20 4682275 www.aseed.net aseedeur@antenna.nl *Action for Solidarity, Equality, Environment, and Diversity is a global organisation linking youth groups and individuals on all continents.*

Arid Lands Initiative, The Machpelah Works, Burnley Rd, Hebden Bridge, West Yorkshire, HX7 8AU T 01422 843807 *Environmental type work.*

Black Environment Network (BEN) UK Office, 9 Llainwon Uchaf, Llanberis, Wales, LL55 4LL T 01286 870715 F as phone www.ben-network.co.uk ukoffice@ben-network.org.uk *Established to promote equal opportunities, with respect to ethnic communities, in the preservation, protection and development of the environment.*

Bristol Friends of the Earth 10-12 Picton Street, Bristol BS6 5QA. T 0117 942 0129 F 0117 942 0168 www.bristolfoe.org.uk bristolfoe@btinternet.com *Enviromental campaigns in Bristol, seperatley constituted to national FoE.*

British Trust for Conservation Volunteers 36 St Mary's Street, Wallingford, Oxfordshire OX10 0EU T 01491 821600 F 01491 839646 www.btcv.org.uk info@btcv.org.uk *Practical environmental conservation charity.*

BuryGreen burygreen.org.uk richb@bradgate.u-net.com *A service and gateway to the various groups in and around Bury St Edmunds, Suffolk, dedicated to protecting and improving our environment.*

Centre for Alternative Technology (C.A.T.) Machynlleth, Powys, SY20 9AZ. T 01654 705950 F 01654 702782 www.cat.org.uk info@cat.org.uk *Environmental centre covering renewable energy, building, sewage and water and organic growing. Displays, publications, courses, mail-order, consultancy and free information service.*

Climate Action Network UK 31 Pitfield Street, London N1 6HB T 020 7251 9199 www.climatenetwork.org canuk@gn.apc.org

Climate Care 58 Church Way, Oxford OX4 4EF. T 01865 777770 F 01865 777771 www.climatecare.org mail@climatecare.org *A scheme that lets individuals and companies pay to ?offset' the emissions created by their use of products such as petrol and diesel, electricity and gas, and air travel.*

Climate Independent Media Center www.climateconference.org *The Climate Independent Media Center provides up-to-the-minute independent and honest coverage of the climate summit, the backgrounds, the corporate lobby and the actions.*

Council for the Protection of Rural England (CPRE) Warwick House, 25 Buckingham Palace Rd, London, SW1W 0PP T 020 7976 6433 F 020 7976 6373 www.cpre.org.uk info@cpre.org.uk *Promotes the beauty, tranquillity and diversity of rural England by encouraging the sustainable use of land and other natural resources in town and country.*

dirtonline.org Centre for Environmental Protection (CEP),Working Lives Research Institute, London Metropolitan University,Stapleton House, Holloway Road, London N7 8DS T 020 7133 3086 www.dirtonline.org/ writers@dogmanet.org *aims to draw together the ideas and expertise of the manygroups campaigning against pollution from toxic waste by providing aconstantly updated service of help, information and discussion.*

Dragon Environmental Network 23b Pepys Rd, New Cross, London, SE14 5SA www.dragonnetwork.org adrian@gn.apc.org *Promoting eco-magic - ritual and spellwork for the Earth. Free membership of Network list. Publish The Dragon Eco-magic Journal. Occasional events.*

Earth Centre Denaby Main, Doncaster, DN12 4EA T 01709 513933 F 01709 512010 www.earthcentre.org.uk *Exhibition centre aimed at developing understanding of sustainable development*

Earth Day Network 811 First Avenue, Suite 454, Seattle, WA 98104, USA. T +1 206 876 2000 F +1 206 876 2015 www.earthday.net/events/2001.stm worldwide@earthday.net *Earth Day Network is the non-profit coordinating body of worldwide Earth Day activities.*

Earth First! Journal PO Box 3023, Tucson AZ 85702-3023, USA T 520.620.6900 F 413.254.0057 www.earthfi -rstjournal.org collective@earthfirstjournal.org *The Earth First! Journal is the voice of the radical environmental movement containing direct action reports, articles on preservation of wild places, investigative articles, and discussions on monkeywrenching.*

Ecologist, The 18 Chelsea Wharf, 15 Lots Rd, London, SW10 0QJ T 020 7351 3578 F 020 7351 3617 www.theecologist.org sally@theecologist.org *Investigative journalists, leading thinkers and campaigners are constantly rethinking the basic assumptions which underlie mankind's steady march towards self-destruction.*

Envirolink www.envirolink.org support@envirolink.org *Links to Sustainable Business Network, Animal Rights Resource Site where to buy environmental books. Essential & extensive web directory.*

Environmental Law Foundation Suite 309, 16 Baldwins Gardens, London, EC1N 7RJ T 020 7404 1030 F 020 7404 1032 www.elflaw.org info@elflaw.org *ELF is a national charity that secures environmental justice for communities and individuals through a network of legal and technical experts.*

Environmental Rescue International (ERI) P.O.BOX 894, Benin City, Nigeria. : environmentalrescue@yahoo.co.uk *ERI - local and internationally focus environmental, human rights and community development organisation. Organises research, training, conferences and direct actions regularly.*

European Youth For Action (EYFA) Minahassastraat 1, 1090 GC Amsterdam, The Netherlands, T +31 20 665 7743 F +31 20 6928757 www.eyfa.org eyfa@eyfa.org *Eyfa is a international network of grassroots groups and individuals working on environmental and social justice issues.*

Fairyland Trust PO Box 14, Wells-next-the-Sea, Norfolk, NR23 1LA. T 01328 710165 www.fairylandtrust.org info@fairylandtrust.org *Dedicated to protecting ancient countryside, recreating natural habitats and making the land fit for fairies.*

Friends of River Narmada www.narmada.org *A coalition supporting the Narmada Bachao Andolan (Save the Narmada movement) which has been fighting for the democratic rights those whose lands are threatened by the Narmada dam.*

Friends of the Earth 26-28 Underwood St, London, N1 7JQ T 020 7490 1555 F 020 7490 0881 www.foe.co.uk info@foe.co.uk *Friends of the Earth exists to inspire solutions to environmental problems, making life better for people.*

Friends of the Earth Scotland 72 Newhaven Rd, Edinburgh, EH6 5QG T 0131 554 9977 F 0131 554 8656 www.foe-scotland.org.uk *We stand for environmental justice. And we aim to make the right to a decent environment available to everyone in Scotland and around the globe.*

Green Socialist Network c/o 15 Linford Close, Harlow, Essex CM19 4LR. T 01279 435735 F as phone. pete@petebrown.fsnet.com *Campaigning group for green and left ideas - we believe that environmental protection and issues of social justice are inseparable.*

Green Builder www.greenbuilder.co.uk *Promoting the Green Building message in the UK and get more people building in a green way by making information about builders, techniques, materials and systems more widely available.*

Greenpeace Canonbury Villas, London, N1 2PN T 020 7865 8100 Press office 020 7865 8255 F 020 7865 8200 www.greenpeace.org info@uk.greenpeace.org *Independent non-profit global environmental campaigning organisation that uses non-violent, creative confrontation to promote solution s to environmental issues and bring about change.*

Groundwork 85-87 Cornwall St, Birmingham, B3 3BY T 0121 236 8565 F 0121 236 7356 www.groundwork.org.uk *Environmental regeneration charity making sustainable development a reality in many of the UK's most disadvantaged communities.*

Gwynedd and Mon Earth First! (G+M EF!) c/o The Greenhouse, 1 Trevelyan Terrace, Bangor, Gwynedd LL57 1AX. bangor-werdd@yahoogroups.com *We take direct action on a range of social, environmental and human rights issues at a local and national level.*

Hebden Bridge Alternative Technology Centre Hebble End Mill, Hebden Bridge West Yorkshire, HX7 6HJ. T 01422 842121 F 01422 843141 www.alternativetechnology.org .uk info@alternativetechnology.org.uk *The green centre of the North.*

How to Build a Protest Tunnel www.discodavestunnelguide.co.uk *Online manual on how to dig your own tunnel*

International Institute for Environment and Development (IIED) 3 Endsleigh St, London, WC1H 0DD. T 020 7388 2117 F 020 7388 2826 www.iied.org mailbox@iied.org *Non-profit organization promoting sustainable patterns of world development through collaborative research, policy studies, networking and knowledge dissemination.*

Kent Against a Radioactive Environment (KARE) T 01303 257046 / 07767 604409 F 01303 257046 www.kare-uk.org barrie@botley.freeserve.co.uk *Grassroots anti nuclear group involved in NVDA for ten years. Web site hosts most UK anti nuke news letters and briefings.*

Lamberhurst Bypass Protest www.lamberhurstbypass.com l.b@zoom.co.uk *Lamberhurst bypass will be built summer 2002 through an area of outstanding natural beauty, alongside an SSSI and through National Trust land at Scotney Castle.*

Leeds Earth First! c/o Cornerstone Resource Centre, 16 Sholebroke Avenue, Leeds LS7 3HB. T 0113 262 9365 www.leedsef.org.uk leedsef@leedsef.org.uk *All the normal EF! stuff - direct action for the environment & anything else we're into at the time.*

Llanw'n Codi Gwynedd + Mon Rising Tide, c/o The Greenhouse, 1 Trevelyan Terrace, Bangor LL57 1AX. T 07941-735639 llanwncodi@hotmail.com *We are a local welsh direct action and campaign network raising awareness about climate change and trying to stop it happening!*

Low Level Radiation Campaign The Knoll, Montpellier Park, Llndrindod, Powys, LD1 5LW T 01597 824771 www.llrc.org bramhall@llrc.org *Publicising the effects of radioactivity in the environment; lobbying for use of sound science in setting radiation protection standards for such exposures.*

Low-Impact News Low Impact News, Middlewood, Roeburndale, Lancaster, LA2 8QX, UK T 01324 222479 www.lowimpactnews.org.uk michealmiddlewood@yahoo.co.uk *The bi-monthly magazine for and about UK ecovillages.*

Manchester Earth First! Dept.29, 22a, Beswick Street, Manchester M4 7HS. T 0161 2266814 www.eco-action.org/ef mancef@nematode.freeserve.co.uk *Non-hierarchical direct action to defend people & planet, and create the world we want to live in.*

Marine Conservation Society 9 Gloucester Road, Ross-on-Wye, Herefordshire, HR9 5ZZ. T 01989 566017 F 01989 567815 www.mcsuk.org *Charity dedicated to protecting the marine environment and wildlife.*

Mines & Communities Roger Moody, c/o Partizans, 41 Thornhill Square, London, N1. T 20 7700 6189 F 20 7700 6189 www.minesandcommunities.org info@minesandcommunities.org *Seeks to empower mining-affected communities so they can struggle successfully against damaging proposals and projects. Has links to many anti-mining campaigns.*

Narmada Bachao Andolan (NBA) B 13 Shivam Flats, Ellora Park, Baroda, India 390 007. T +91 7290-222464 nba@lwbdq.lwbbs.net *National coalition of environmental and human rights activists, scientists, academics, and project-affected people, working to stop several dam projects in the Narmada Valley.*

National Federation of Badger Groups (NFBG) 15 Cloisters Business Centre, 8 Battersea Park Rd, London, SW8 4BG T 020 7498 3220/mobile: 0976 153389 F 020 7627 4212 www.badgers.org.uk/nfbg enquiries@nfbg.org.uk *Promote conservation & protection of badgers. Represent 85 local voluntary badger groups. Provide information & advice, membership system.*

National Park www.nationalpark.org.uk *Comprehensive internet resource of links to web sites about the UK's National Parks and AONBs (Areas of Outstanding Natural Beauty).*

Natturuvaktin (Nature Wise) Iceland www.natturuvaktin.com *Icelandic environmental group fighting the building of massive destructive dam building in the Icelandic Highlands*

Natur Cymru - A Review of Wildlife in Wales *Tri-annual magazine in English and Welsh giving you the facts, exploring the issues and unveiling the true meaning of biodiversity. Costs ú3.50 for one issue or ú10 for a year, send cheques to: Radnorshire Wildlife Trust, Warwick House, High Street, Llandrindod Wells, Powys, LD1 6AG.*

Nine Ladies Anti-Quarry Campaign Bramble Dene, Stanton Lees, Matlock, Derbyshire DE4 2LQ. www.nineladies.uklinux.net all@nineladies.uklinux.net *Opposing destruction of ancient landscape at the edge of National Park, endangering standing stones.*

Opposition To Destruction of Open Green Spaces (OTDOGS) 6 Everthorpe Rd, London, SE15 4DA T 020 8693 9412 F as phone *Advising people on how to prevent food giants building on open green spaces.*

Peat Alert c/o crc, 16 Sholebroke Avenue, Leeds, LS7 3HB T 0113 262 9365 www.peatalert.org.uk info@peatalert.org.uk *Information for action against peat mining on Thorne and Hatfield Moors, South Yorkshire*

People Against Rio Tinto and Subsidiaries (PARTiZANS) 41a Thornhill Square, London N1 1BE T 0207 700 6189 F same as phone www.minesandcommunities.org/Aboutus/partizans.htm partizabs@gn.apc.org *Partizans has been campaigning since 1978 against the damage wreaked by the world's most powerful mining company.*

Pesticide Action Network UK Eurolink Centre, 49 Effra Rd, London, SW2 1BZ. T 020 7274 8895 F 020 7274 9084 www.pan-uk.org admin@pan-uk.org *The Pesticides Trust is a scientifically based charity concerned with the health, environmental and policy aspects of pesticide manufacture, trade and use.*

Protect Our Woodland! Aims to protect a woodland threatened by a housing development in Worthing. www.protectourwoodland.fsnet.co.uk/ info@protectourwoodland.fsnet.co.uk

Rainbow Keepers PO Box 52, Kasimov, 391330, Russia. T +7 (09131) 41514 www.chat.ru/~rk2000 rk@lavrik.ryazan.ru *Russian radical ecological movement.*

Resurgence Ford House, Hartland, Bideford, Devon, EX39 6EE T 01237 441293 F 01237 441203 www.resurgence.org postmaster@resurge.demon.co.uk *Resurgence magazine encompasses environmental, social, economic and cultural issues. Thought-provoking and informative, bringing articles which nourish all aspects of your life.*

Rising Tide 16b Cherwell Street, Oxford OX1 1BG. T 01865 241097 www.risingtide.org.uk info@risingtide.org.uk *A network of independent groups and individuals dedicated to taking local action and building a national movement against climate change.*

River Ocean Research & Education (RORE) www.rore.org.uk info@rore.org.uk *A charity dedicated to increasing awareness and encouraging care for our water environments - focussed in the fields of environmental education and research.*

Road Alert www.roadalert.org.uk *An online forum for info on direct action against resurrected government road building plans.*

Save Our World www.save-our-world.org.uk *exists to help protect and sustain the natural world through increasing awareness and caring, and inspiring and empowering people to change attitudes, habits and lifestyles - personally, locally, nationally, globally and spiritually.*

Scottish Opencast Action Group c/o 42 Woolfords, by West Calder, West Lothian, EH55 8LH soag.info@virgin.net *A network of people across Scotland opposed to opencast coal mining. Mainly information exchange & help with opposing planning applications.*

Sea Shepherd Conservation Society PO Box 6095, 4000 HB Tiel, Netherlands. T +31 0344 604130 F +31 344 604808 www.seashepherd.nl info@seashepherd.nl *Dedicated to the protection and conservation of marine ecosystems and biodiversity. Take direct action where authorities are unwilling to enforce conservation regulations.*

Sea Turtle Restoration Project (STRP) PO Box 400, Forest Knolls, CA 94933, USA. T (415) 488 0370 F (415) 488 0372 www.seaturtles.org seaturtles@igc.org *STRP works to protect sea turtle populations in ways that meet the needs of the turtles & the local communities who share the beaches & waters with these endangered species.*

Tourism Concern Stapleton House, 277-281 Holloway Rd, London, N7 8HN. T 020 7133 3330 www.tourismconcern.org.uk info@tourismconcern.org.uk *Tourism Concern is an educational charity promoting awareness of the impact of tourism on people and their environment.*

UK Rivers Network (UKRN) T 07092-335227 F 07092-335227 www.ukrivers.net info@ukrivers.net *Community action, information and networking to improve rivers and inland waters across the UK and Ireland.*

Voice of Irish Concern for the Environment 7 Upper Camden St., Dublin 2, Ireland. T +353 1 6618123 F +353 1 6618114 www.voice.buz.org avoice@iol.ie *Ireland's leading independent environmental organisation with members throughout the country. We are committed to promoting positive solutions to environmentally-destructive activities.*

Vrienden van GroenFront! - EarthFirst! NL Support Group PO BOX 85069, 3508 AB Utrecht, Netherlands. T +31 (0)84 8666018 www.groenfront.nl/ *Earth First! Netherlands. Website has reports of actions, including some reports in English.*

Wildfile www.wildfile.co.uk *Independent website that aims to help internet users to reach information on UK wildlife and other environmental themes. We particularly want to help voluntary and individual sites to gain an internet presence.*

Woman and Earth Global Eco-Network (WE) 467 Central Park West, Suite 7F, New York, NY 10025, USA. T +1 212 866 8130 F as phone www.dorsai.org/~womearth womearth@dorsai.org *Publish Almanac and Succes destime, produce conferences, film festivals, exhibitions, videos/TV series, web site, library/archives, chapters world-wide.*

Women's Environmental Network (W.E.N) PO Box 30626, London E1 1TZ, T 020 74819004 F 020 74819144 www.wen.org.uk info@wen.org.uk *A national UK charity and membership organisation educating, informing and empowering women and men who care about the environment.*

York LEAF (Local Environmental Action Forum) c/o Daw Suu Student Centre, Goodricke College, University of York, YO10 5DD. yorkleaf@yahoo.co.uk *A group with diverse viewpoints, united to combat environmental and social issues/awareness on both local and global levels.*

Zeme Predevsim! (Earth First! Prague) PO Box 237, 160 41 Praha 6, Czech Republic. www.ecn.cz/zemepredevsim zemepredevsim@volny.cz *Radical ecology, anti globalisation campaign, RTS activity, anti nazi activity, information, propaganda, network of Czech activists.*

FOOD & FARMING

An Talamh Glas (Bluegreenearth) 9 Kitchener Road, Ipswich, IP1 4DT. T 01473 436948 www.bluegreenearth.com atgblue@yahoo.com *Empowerment, education, information.*

Banana Link 38 Exchange Street, Norwich, NR2 1AX T 01603 765670 F 01603 761645 www.bananalink.org.uk blink@gn.apc.org *Banana Link works towards environmentally, socially and economically sustainable banana production and trade through campaigns, awareness raising and lobbying.*

ETC Group (Action Group on Erosion, Technology and Concentration) 478 River Avenue, Suite 200, Winnipeg, MB R3L 0C8, Canada. T (204) 453-5259, F (204) 284-7871 www.etcgroup.org *Dedicated to the conservation and sustainable advancement of cultural and ecological diversity and human rights.*

Federation of City Farms and Community Gardens The Green House, Hereford St, Bedminster, Bristol, BS3 4NA T 0117 923 1800 www.farmgarden.org.uk admin@farmgarden.org.uk *Bringing together information on city farms and community gardens across the county.*

Foundation for Local Food Initiatives PO Box 1234, Bristol BS99 2PG. T 0845 4589525 F 0117 9260221 www.localfood.org.uk mail@localfood.org.uk *We are an independent not-for-profit co-operative company promoting and supporting the growth of healthy local food economies.*

Hemp Food Industries Association PO Box 204, Barnet, Herts, EN4 8ZQ T 07050 600418 F 07050 600419 www.hemp.co.uk hemp@hemp.co.uk *Hemp food, fibre, fuel, plastic, paper (+more) information for farmers, manufacturer's, retailers, consumers, press + you.*

Henry Doubleday Research Association Ryton Organic Gardens, Coventry CV8 3LG. T 024 7630 3517 F 024 7663 9229 www.hdra.org.uk enquiry@hdra.org.uk *Europe's largest organic membership organisation. Dedicated to researching and promoting organic gardening, food, and farming.*

Movement For Compassionate Living The Vegan Way (MCL) Burrow Farm, Highampton, Beaworhty, Devon EX21 5JQ. T 01409 231264 www.mclveganway.org.uk *Environmental veganism. Changing ones diet is just first step towards compassionate living.*

National Association of Farmers' Markets South Vaults, Green Park Station, Green Park Road, Bath BA1 1JB. T 01225 787914 F 01225 460840 www.farmersmarkets.co.uk campaigns@buav.org *Promoting and supporting farmers' markets across the UK.*

Permanent Publications The Sustainability Centre, East Meon, Hants GU32 1HR T 0845 4584150 F 01730 823322 www.permaculture.co.uk info@permaculture.co.uk *Publishers and distributors of Permaculture Magazine - solutions for sustainable living and hundreds of books and videos on all aspects of sustainable living.*

Plants For a Future Blagdon Cross, Ashwater, Beaworthy, Devon EX21 5DF. T 0845 458 4719 / 01208 872963 F 01208 872963 (ring first) www.pfaf.org webmaster@pfaf.org *Research and provide information on edible, medicinal and useful plants, woodland gardening and vegan-organic horticulture.*

Primal Seeds 22a Beswick Street, Manchester M4 7HR. www.primalseeds.org mail@primalseeds.org *Information on industrial agriculture with a focus on seeds, and its alternatives.*

Seedy Sunday T 01273 381686 www.seedysunday.org seedysundaybrighton@yahoo.co.uk *We have lost 90% of all ourUK vegetable varieties in last 100 years, this regular event shows howpeople can do something to safeguard our vegetable heritage.*

Single Step Co-Op 78A Penny St, Lancaster, LA1 1XN T 01524 847234 *Selling wholefoods and organics in a democratic, non-hierarchical, workers' co-op stylee. Also stock non-mainstream mags and journals.*

Soil Association Bristol House, 40-56 Victoria St, Bristol, BS1 6BY T 0117 929 0661 F 0117 925 2504 www.soilassociation.org info@soilassociation.org *Campaigning and certification organisation for organic food and farming.*

Sustain 94 White Lion Street, London N1 9PF. T 020 78371228 F 020 78371141 www.sustain.org Sustain@sustainweb.org *Sustain advocates food and agriculture policies and practices, that promote equity and enrich society and culture.*

The Hungerhill Allotments www.staan.co.uk *The oldest and largest allotment site in the country. It is home to several projects including Ecoworks and the community orchard.*

The Wholesome Food Association Ball CottageEast Ball HillHartlandDevon EX39 6BU T 01237 441 118 www.wholesomefood.org.uk/ sky@wholesome-food.org.uk

UK Agricultural Biodiversity Coalition www.ukabc.org ukabc@ukabc.org *Brings together public interest groups concerned with issues related to the Equitable Use of Agricultural Biodiversity for Local Food and Livelihood Security and Food Sovereignty.*

Vegan Society, The Donald Watson House, 7 Battle Rd, St. Leonards On Sea, E. Sussex, TN37 7AA T 01424 427393 F 01424 717064 www.vegansociety.com info@vegansociety.com *Educational charity promoting ways of living whicg avoid the use of animal products - for the benefit of people, animals and the environment.*

Vegan Village www.veganvillage.co.uk postie@veganvillage.co.uk *Website lists organisations in the UK which are run by vegans on vegan principles. Link to the best vegan-run websites.*

Vegetarian Society of the UK, The Parkdale, Dunham Rd, Altringham, Cheshire, WA14 4QG T 0161 925 2000 F 0161 926 9182 www.vegsoc.org info@vegsoc.org *Educational Charity dedicated to the promotion of the knowledge of vegetarianism.*

Veggies Catering Campaign 245 Gladstone Street, Nottingham NG7 6HX T 0845 458 9595 mobile: 0787 0861837 www.veggies.org.uk info@veggies.org.uk *Event catering (all-vegan) and support for human, animal rights & environmental campaigns.*

Wholesome Food Association 1 Barton Cottages, Dartington Hall, Totnes, Devon. TQ9 6ED. T 01803 840427 www.wholesomefood.org info@wholesomefood.org.uk *Campaigning for smaller-scale, sustainable, local food production, with low cost labelling scheme.*

World Wide Opportunities On Organic farms (WWOOF) P.O.Box 2675, Lewes, E. Sussex BN7 1RB. T 01273 476286 F as phone www.wwoof.org/ fran@wwoof.org *Opportunities with vast variety of host organic farms & holdings. Accommodation and food provided in exchange for work.*

FORESTS & WOODLANDS

Agroforestry Research Trust 46 Hunters Moon, Dartington, Totnes, Devon, TQ9 6JT T 01803 840776. F 01803 840776 www.agroforestry.co.uk mail@agroforestry.co.uk *Charity, which researches temperate agroforestry and into all aspects of plant cropping. Produce several publications and a quarterly journal, and also sell plants and seeds*

Forest Stewardship Council (FSC) Unit D, Station Building, Llanidgoes, Powys, SY18 6EB T 01686 413916 F 01686 412176 www.fsc-uk.demon.co.uk fsc-uk@fsc-uk.demon.co.uk *Certifying forests managed to standards which protect people and the environment and identifying timber products from them with the FSC logo.*

Rainforest Action Network 221 Pine St., Suite 500, San Francisco, CA 94104 USA www.ran.org rainforest@ran.org *Working to protect tropical rainforests and the human rights of those living in and around those forests*

Reforesting Scotland 62-66 Newhaven Rd, Edinburgh, EH6 5QB. T 0131 554 4321 F 0131 554 0088 reforestingscotland.gn.apc.org info@reforestingscotland.org *Promote awareness of the deforestation of Scotland and to facilitate ecological restoration and community development through reforestation.*

Tree Council 51 Catherine Place, London, SW1E 6DY. T 020 7828 9928 F 020 7828 9060 www.treecouncil.org.uk info@treecouncil.org.uk *Promoting the improvement of the environment through the care and planting of trees.*

Trees For Life The Park, Findhorn Bay, Forres, Moray, IV36 3TZ. T 01309 691292 F 01309 691155 www.treesforlife.org.uk trees@findhorn.org *A Scottish conservation charity dedicated to the regeneration and restoration of the Caledonian Forest in the Highlands of Scotlan.*

Treesponsibility PO Box 38, Hebden Bridge, West Yorkshire, HX7 8YR. T 01422 843222 treesponsibility.gn.apc.org treesponsibility@beeb.net *Empower people to take responsibility for carbon dioxide emissions through tree-planting, as one urgent response to climate change and to bring back lost woodlands and hedgerows and increase biodiversity.*

GARDENING

Allotments Regeneration Initiative Allotments Regeneration Initiative,54 Allison St, Birmingham B5 5TH. T 0121 643 0402 F 0121 643 0609 www.farmgarden.org.uk/ari/ ari@farmgarden.org.uk *ARI aims to get more people -individuals and community groups -growing on urban allotments.*

Association Kokopelli Ripple Farm, Crundale, Canterbury, Kent, CT4 7EB T 01227 731815 www.terredesemences.com contactus@organicseedsonline.com *Organic seed catalogue with many unusual varieties. Also online gardening advice.*

Composting Association Avon House, Tithe Barn Road, Wellingborough, Northamptonshire, NN8 1DH. T 08701 603270 F 08701 603280 www.compost.org.uk *Information about composting and its benefits*

Forest Garden Network A.R.T., 46 Hunters Moon Dartington, Totnes, Devon, TQ9 6JT. www.agroforestry.co.uk mail@agroforestry.co.uk *An informal network of people planning or already cultivating forest garden, aiming to visit each other's gardens and share knowledge of temperate agroforestry.*

Future Foods Luckleigh Cottage, Hockworthy, Wellington, Somerset TA21 0NN. T 01398 361347 F 01398 361541 www.futurefoods.com enquiries@futurefoods.com *Small independent mail order supplier specialising in rare and unusual edible plants. (Seed company only - do not supply produce.)*

Mushroom Cultivator, The *P. Stamets & J.S. Chilton, (Agarikon Press) - Definitive handbook for growing all mushroom species.*

National Society of Allotment and Leisure Gardeners Ltd, The O'Dell House, Hunters Rd, Corby, Northants, NN17 5JE. T 01536 266576 F 01536 264509 www.nsalg.demon.co.uk natsoc@nsalg.demon.co.uk *National representive body for the allotment movement, representing its members at both national and regional levels. Help and advice service on all allotment matters.*

Naturewise 20 The Triangle, Cromartie Rd, London, N19 3RX. T 0845 4584697 naturewise1@hotmail.com *Promotion of: sustainable land use and lifestyles in cities, growing food in cities, education through permaculture courses. Permaculture consultations given.*

Seedswapper www.seedswapper.com *Free non-commercial seed swapping website (USA).*

Spiralseed 35 Rayleigh Avenue, Westcliff On Sea, Essex, S50 7DS T 01702 303259 www.spiralseed.co.uk landandliberty@ukonline.co.uk *Formerly Land and Liberty. Self published earthrights books, posters, teeshirts, forest gardening, permaculture design, consultancy and teaching.*

Vegan Organic Network (VON) 30 Helvellyn road, Wigan, Lancs WN5 9UR. T 01942 214660 www.veganorganic.net nicsuefox@btopenworld.com *Promoting vegan organic principles - a system of cultivation that avoids artificial chemicals and sprays, livestock manures and animal remains from slaughter houses.*

GENETICS

CBG Network PO Box 15 04 18, 40081 Duesseldorf, Germany. T +49 211 333911 www.cbgnetwork.org CBGnetwork@aol.com *Has been monitoring the chemical and pharmaceutical company Bayer since 1978.*

Genetic Engineering Network (GEN) Archway Resource Centre, 1a Waterlow Road, London N19 5NJ. T 020 7272 1586 F as phone (call first) www.geneticsaction.org.uk genetics@gn.apc.org *Providing information for action for the grassroots campaign against genetic engineering. Has list of contacts and field trial sites.*

Genetic Food Alert (GFA) 4 Bertram House, Ticklemore St, Totnes, Devon, TQ9 5EJ T 01803 868523 www.geneticfoodalert.org.uk coordinator@geneticfoodalert.org.uk *GFA campaigns to keep the UK wholefood trade GM-free, ban GM food & crops and meanwhile introduce full labelling and liability.*

GM Free Scotland pro-Natural Food Scotland, 35 Hamilton Drive, Glasgow G12 8DW www.gmfreescotland.net hotlink@gmfreesctoland.net *Campaigning for a GMO free Scotland.*

GM Watch c/o 26 Pottergate, Norwich, NR2 1DX. T 01603 624021 www.gmwatch.org ngin@gmwatch.org *Exposes the role played by corporate-friendly scientists, industry front groups, PR companies, lobbyists, and political groups in promoting GM technolgy.*

Hemel Hempstead G M Action Group (HHGMAG) T 01442 248657 F 01442 248657 www.mhumphrey.btinternet.co.uk hhgmag@btinternet.com *Campaigning for a GM free Dacorum. (After Dacorum, the world!).*

Human Genetics Alert 22/24 Highbury Grove, 112 Aberdeen House, London N5 2EA T 020 7704 6100 F 020 7359 8426 www.hgalert.org info@hgalert.org *We are a watchdog group for Human Genetics, providing information to the public on the developments and policies.*

Scarborough Against Genetic Engineering (SAGE) c/o 7 Palace Hill, Scarborough, North Yorkshire, YO11 1NL T 01723 375533/865773 sage@envoy.dircon.co.uk *A local campaign against the use of genetic engineering in food and farming.*

Stop Bayer GM T 07092 036576 www.stopbayergm.org contact@stopbayergm.org *A national umbrella campaign for all groups and individuals who wish to stop the commercial growing of GM crops.*

Totnes Genetics Group (ToGG) PO Box 77, Totnes, Devon TQ9 5ZJ T 01803 840098 www.togg.org.uk info@togg.org.uk *A local grassroots Genetics group that publish stuff and do a spot of gardening? G*

HEALTH

Communities Against Toxics (CATS) P.O.Box 29, Ellesmere Port, CH66 3TX T 0151 339 5473 F as phone www.communities-against-toxics.org.uk ralph.ryder@communities-against-toxics.org.uk *Campaigns against unsafe methods of waste disposal, industrial processes and polluting industries. Produces Toxcat newsletetr.*

Consumers for Health Choice 9 Old Queen St, London, SW1H 9JA T 020 7222 4182 www.healthchoice.org.uk Enquiries@healthchoice.org.uk *Promotes the right of consumers to access a wide range of natural health products, including vitamin and mineral supplements and herbal remedies.*

Hazards Campaign, The c/o Greater Manchester Hazards Centre, 23 New Mount Street, Manchester M4 4DE. T 0161 953 4037 F 0161 953 4001 www.hazardscampaign.org.uk *A network of resource centres and campaigners on health and safety at work.*

Herb Society Sulgrave Manor, Sulgrave, Banbury OX17 2SD. T 01295 768899 F 01295 768069 www.herbsociety.co.uk email@herbsociety.co.uk *The Herb Society aims to increases the understanding, use and appreciation of herbs and the benefits to health.*

London Hazards Centre 213 Haverstock Hill, London NW3 4QP. T 020 7794 5999 F 020 7794 4702 www.lhc.org.uk mail@lhc.org.uk *Resource centre for Londoners fighting health and safety hazards in their workplace and community.*

Medecins Sans Frontieres 124-132 Clerkenwell Road, London EC1R 5DJ. T 020 7713 5600 F 020 7713 5004 www.uk.msf.org office@london.msf.org *Independent humanitarian medical aid agency providing medical aid wherever needed and raising awareness of the plight of the people.*

National Gulf War Veterans and Families Association 4 Maspin Close, Kingswood, Kingston upon Hull HU8 8LU T 01482 833812 F 01482 833816 flusem666@aol.com *Support network, proactive at looking into what veterans have been exposed to.*

National Pure Water Association Rose Court, 180 Milton Road, Hoyland, Near Barnsley, South Yorkshire, S74 9BW. T 01226 360909 www.npwa.freeserve.co.uk info@npwa.freeserve.co.uk *Campaign for safe drinking water. AGAINST the artificial fluoridation of water supplies. International contacts.*

Natural Death Centre, 6 Blackstock Mews, Blackstock Road, London N4 2BT, UK T 020 8 208 2853; F 020 8 452 6434 www.naturaldeath.org.uk rhino@dial.pipex.com *Aims to support those dying at home and their carers and to help them arrange funerals. It has as a more general aim that of helping improve 'the quality of dying'.*

Organic Herb Trading Company, The Court Farm, Milverton, Somerset TA4 1NF. T 01823 401205 F 01823 401001 www.organicherbtrading.com info@organicherbtrading.com *Sustainably harvested herbs based on socially just and ecologically responsible principles.*

Sambhavna Trust 44 Sant Kanwar Ram Nagar, Berasia Road, Bhopal, 462001, Madhya Pradesh, India. www.bhopal.org sambavna@sancharnet.in *Sole objective is to improve the health condition of the survivors of the Bhopal disaster.*

Surfers Against Sewage Wheal Kitty Workshops, St Agnes, Cornwall. England TR5 0RD www.sas.org.uk *Formed in 1990, one of the fastest growing pressure groups in the country, SAS call for full non-chemical treatment of sewage discharged into our seas.*

Vaccination Awareness Network UK (VAN UK) 347 Baker Street, Alvaston, Derby, DE24 8SJ. T 0870 444 0894 F 08707 418 415 www.van.org.uk enquiries@van.org.uk *Information about vaccinations and their side effects. Support group, meetings, newsletter.*

Vivisection Information Network (VIN) PO Box 223, Camberley, Surrey, GU16 5ZU. www.vivisection-absurd.org.uk vivisectionkills@hotmail.com *VIN provides information by post and email which proves vivisection is failed and enables ordinary people to prove this.*

What Doctors Don't Tell You (WDDTY) Satellite House, London SW19 4EZ. T 0870 444 9886 F 0870 444 9887 www.wddty.co.uk office@wddty.co.uk *Publishers of Newsletter giving information on alternative health treatments and challenging traditional views on health treatments.*

HOUSING & HOMELESSNESS

[Squat!net] www.squat.net squat@squat.net *An international internet magazine with main focus on squatted houses, car sites and other free spaces.*

Advisory Service for Squatters (A.S.S) 2 St. Paul's Rd, London, N1 2QN T 020 73598814 F 020 73595185 www.squat.freeserve.co.uk advice@squat.freeserve.co.uk *We give legal and practical advice and support to squatters and other homeless people.*

Asian Coalition for Housing Rights (ACHR) 73 Soi Sonthiwattana 4, Ladprao 110, Ladprao Rd Bangkok 10310, Thailand. T 662 538 0919 F 662 285 1500 www.achr.net achr@loxinfo.co.th *A regional network of grassroots community organizations, NGO's and professionals actively involved with urban poor development processes in Asian cities.*

Bristol Housing Action Movement Box 56, Greenleaf Bookshop, 82 Colston Street, Bristol BS1 5BB. T 07985 557450 www.public-interest.co.uk/bham *A non-hierarchical collective of squatters and their supporters which houses and promotes autonomy for homeless people, advises travellers and promotes social centres.*

Cambridge Homeless Partnership (CHP) 19 Silver Street, Cambridge CB3 9EP. T 01223 330802 mob 07759194789 hannah@cambridgehomelesspartnership.org.uk *CHP conducts research into local homelessness issues, works to improve communication between agencies, and gives an independent collective voice for homeless people and service providers.*

Confederation of Co-operative Housing (CCH) Unit 19, 41 Old Birley Street, Manchester, M15 5RF. T 0161 232 1588 F 0161 226 7307 www.cch-uk.org Info@cch-uk.org *CCH is the national representative body for co-operative housing, made up of volunteer co-op members from all over the country.*

Cornerstone Housing Co-op 16 Sholebroke Avenue, Leeds, LS7 3HB T 0113 262 9365 www.cornerstonehousing.org.uk cornerstone@gn.apc.org *Communal housing for people engaged in working for social change. We have a resource centre open to local groups and individuals.*

Defend Council Housing P.O Box33519, London, E8 4XW T 0207 9879989 www.defendcouncilhousing.org.uk info@defendcouncilhousing.org.uk *To oppose transfer of council houses to private landlords & to campaign for more and better council housing.*

Ecovillage Network UK (EVNUK) PO Box 1410, Bristol, BS99 3JP T 0117 3730346 www.ecovillages.org/uk/network evnuk@gaia.org *Sustainable settlement project information/advice service. Our focus is on ecovillages as a way out of cash-based living.*

Empty Homes Agency (EHA) 195-197 Victoria St, London, SW1E 5NE T 020 7828 6288 F 020 7828 7006 www.emptyhomes.com info@emptyhomes.com *Highlight the disgrace of empty, wasted and under used homes and property throughout England.*

Haggerston Tenants Association (HTA) Haggerston Community Centre, 179 Haggerston Rd, London, E8 4JA T 020 7254 2312 F as phone info@haggerstoncommunity.org.uk *Help raise tenancy participation. Fights against privatisation. Defend council housing.*

Mina Housing Co-Op Ltd 160 Gloucester Road, Bishopston, Bristol BS7 8NT. T 0117 9246228 mk.housingcoop @btinternet.com

Namibia Housing Action Group/Shack Dwellers Federation of Namibia P.O. Box 21010, Windhoek, Namibia T 09264 61 239398 F 09264 61 239397 nhag@iafrica.com.na *Support the Shack Dwellers to house themselves.*

Radical Routes c/o Cornerstone Resource Centre, 16 Sholebroke Av, Leeds, LS7 3HB. T 0113 262 9365 www.radicalroutes.org.uk cornerstone@ukf.net *Mutual aid network of radical housing & worker co-ops and social centres. Support, advice & loans to member co-ops.*

Talamh Housing Co-Op (THC) Talamh Housing Co-Op, ML11 0NJ T 01555 820400 F 01555 820400 talamhlifecentre.org.uk talamh@lineone.net *Provide access to housing, land, and resources for low income and unemployed community activists and volunteers.*

UK Cohousing Network www.cohousing.co.uk coordinator@cohousing.co.uk *CoHousing Communities are mutually beneficial neighbourhoods where individual households are clustered around a Common house with shared facilities.*

HUMAN RIGHTS

Action for Southern Africa (ACTSA) 28 Penton Street, London N1 9SA T 020 7833 3133 F 020 7837 3001 www.actsa.org actsa@actsa.org *ACTSA campaigns for peace, democracy and development in Southern Africa and is the successor organisation to the Anti-Apartheid Movement.*

Amnesty International 99-119 Rosebery Avenue, London EC1R 4RE T 020 7814 6200 F 020 7833 1510 www.amnesty.org info@amnesty.org.uk *International organisation promoting human rights. In particular, campaigning to free all prisoners of conscience; ensure fair and prompt trials for political prisoners; abolish the death penalty, torture and other cruel treatment of prisoners.*

Anti-Slavery International Thomas Clarkson House, The Stableyard, Broomgrove Yard, London SE27 9LA T 020 7501 8920 www.antislavery.org antislavery@antislavery.org *Anti-Slavery is committed to eliminating slavery: debt bondage, forced labour, forced marriage, the worst forms of child labour, human trafficking and traditional slavery.*

Burma Action Group 1101 Pennsylvania Ave, SE #204 Washington, DC 20003 T (202) 547-5985 F (202) 544-6118 www.freeburmacoalition.org *An Internet-based organisation who aim to raise awareness about the horrific human rights violations in Burma.*

Burma Campaign UK Third Floor, Bickerton House, 25-27 Bickerton Rd, London, N19 5JT T 020 7281 7377 F 020 7272 3559 www.burmacampaign.org.uk info@burmacampaign.org.uk *Campaigns for human rights and democracy in Burma. We campaign to improve government and commercial policy on Burma.*

Campaign for Freedom of Information Suite 102, 16 Baldwins Gardens, London EC1N 7RJ. T 020 7831 7477 F 020 7831 7461 www.cfoi.org.uk admin@cfoi.demon.co.uk *Campaigns against unnecessary secrecy and for a Freedom of Information Act.*

Coke Watch 733 15th Street NW, Suite 920, Washington, DC 20005 T (202) 347-4100 www.cokewatch.org *Campaigning for the rights and safety of all Coca Cola workers.*

Defy-ID www.defy-id.org.uk/ admin@defy-id.org.uk *Defy-ID is an adhoc network of groups and individuals prepared for active resistance to increasing surveillance and the introduction of identity or æentitlementÆ cards in the UK.*

Electronic Frontier Foundation, The 454 Shotwell Street, San Francisco CA 94110. USA. T +1 415/436 9333 F +1 415/436 9993 www.eff.org eff@eff.org *Created to defend our rights to think, speak, and share our ideas, thoughts, and needs using new technologies, such as the Internet and the World Wide Web.*

Free Burma Coalition 1101 Pennsylvania Ave, SE #204 20003, USA. T 202 547 5985 F 202 544 6118 www.freeburmacoalition.org comments@freeburmacoalition.org *Through public education, policy advocacy, consumer boycotts, and divestment campaigns, FBC works to raise awareness about the horrific human rights violations by Burma's illegitimate military dictatorship.*

Free Tibet Campaign 1 Rosomon Place, London, EC1R 0JY T 020 7833 9958 F 020 7833 3838 www.freetibet.org mail@freetibet.org *An independent membership organisation campaigning in support of the rights of the Tibetan people to freedom and independence.*

Ilisu Dam Campaign Box 210, 266 Banbury Rd, Oxford, OX2 7DL T 01865 200550 www.ilisu.org.uk ilisu@gn.apc.org *Works to stop British involvement in the Ilisu Dam and to highlight sustainable development and for peace and security in SE Turkey.*

INQUEST 89-93 Fonthill Road, London N4 3JH T 020 7263 1111 F 020 561 0799 www.inquest.org.uk inquest@inquest.org.uk *Advice, campaigning and information for bereaved people facing Coroner's Inquests, especially those involving deaths in custody (Police, prison, detained patients).*

Kurdish Human Rights Project (KHRP) 162-168 Regent St, Suite 319 Linen Hall, London, W1B 5TG T 020 72872772 F 020 77344927 www.khrp.org khrp@khrp.demon.co.uk *KHRP is committed to the protection of the human rights of all persons within the Kurdish regions.*

Latin America Solidarity Centre (LASC) 5 Merrion Row, Dublin 2, Ireland. T +353 1 6760435 F +353 1 6621784 www.iol.ie/~lasc lasc@iol.ie *LASC is an initiative for cultural promotion, development education and campaigning solidarity, linking Ireland and Latin America.*

Peace in Kurdistan (PIK) and Kurdistan Solidarity Committee (KSC) 44 Alnger Road, London NW3 3AT. T 020 7586 5892 F 020 7483 2531 knklondon@gn.apc.org *Campaigning for international recognition for the right of the Kurdish people to self-determination in collaboration with the Kurdish community in the UK and Europe.*

People & Planet (P) 51 Union St, Oxford, OX4 1JP. T 01865 245678 F 01865 791927 www.peopleandplanet.org people@peopleandplanet.org *UK student action on world poverty, human rights and the environment.*

Privacy International T 07960-523-679 (London Office) www.privacyinternational.org pi@privacy.org *International anti-surveillance organisation. Campaigns on Big Brother issues like data tracking, ID cards, CCTV, encryption, police surveillance, corporate biometrics.*

Project Underground 1916A MLK Jr. Way, Berkeley, CA 94704, USA. T +1 510 705 8981 F +1 510 705 8983 www.moles.org project_underground@moles.org *Supporting the human rights of communities resisting mining and oil exploitation.*

Rwanda UK Goodwill Organisation, The www.rugo.org rugo_info@yahoo.co.uk *Charity devoted to education and training of people of Rwanda and provision and support of community based projects.*

Scottish Human Rights Centre (SHRC) 146 Holland St, Glasgow, G2 4NG T 0141 332 5960 F 0141 332 5309 www.scottishhumanrightscentre.org.uk info@scottishhumanrightscentre.org.uk *SHRC aims to promote human rights in Scotland through advice/information, research, scrutiny of legislation, monitoring international human rights treaties.*

Stand.org.uk stand@stand.org.uk *Disseminate information and motivate people about issues around privacy and censorship, particularly with respect to the Internet.*

TAPOL, The Indonesia Human Rights Campaign 111 Northwood Rd, Thornton Rd, Surrey, CR7 8HW T 020 8771 2904 F 020 8653 0322 www.gn.apc.org/tapol tapol@gn.apc.org *TAPOL - which means political prisoner in Indonesian - is an English language authority on the human rights situation in Indonesia and East Timor.*

Western Sahara Campaign T 0113 245 4786 www.arso.org *The struggle of the Sahrawi people for Self-determination - Western Sahara former spanish colony is the last African colonized country still waiting for independence.*

INDIGENOUS PEOPLES

Amazon Alliance for Indigenous and Traditional Peoples of the Amazon Basin 1367 Connecticut Ave, N.W Suite 400, Washington DC 20036, USA. T 1-202-785-3334 F 1-202-785-3335 www.amazoncoalition.org amazon@amazonalliance.org *The Amazon Alliance works to defend the rights, territories, and environment of indigenous and traditional peoples of the Amazon Basin.*

Black Mesa Indigenous Support PO Box 23501, Flagstaff, Arizona 86002. USA. T (voice mail)+1 9287738086 www.blackmesais.org blackmesais@yahoo.com *Supporting the sovereignty of the indigenous people affected by mining activities on Black Mesa, who face forced relocation, environmental devastation, and cultural extinction.*

Centre For World Indigenous Studies PMB 214, 1001 Cooper Point Rd, SW Suite 140, Olympia WA 98502-1107, USA. T +1 360 754 1990 www.cwis.org *Non-profit research and education organization dedicated to wider understanding and appreciation of the ideas and knowledge of indigenous peoples*

Dark Night Press P.O. Box 3629, Chicago, IL 60690-3629, USA T 207 839 5794 www.darknightpress.org darknight@igc.org *Under-reported news and unheard voices from indigenous struggles worldwide.*

Ejercito Zapatista de Liberacion Nacional (EZLN) www.ezln.org *The EZLN web provides reliable information on the Zapatista uprising and serves as the mouthpiece for the Zapatistas in cyberspace.*

OPM Support Group (Free Papua Movement) c/o 43 Gardner St, Brighton, BN1 1UN www.eco-action.org/opm opmsg@eco-action.org *Direct action network to support Papuan peoples struggle for freedom. Videos talks and publications available to help start new groups.*

Palestine Solidarity Campaign Box BM PSA, London WC1N 3XX. T 020 7700 6192 www.palestinecampaign.org info@palestinecampaign.org *Aim to build an effective mass campaign, organising protests, political lobbying and raising public awareness.*

Solidarity South Pacific c/o SDEF!, Prior House, 6 Tilbury Place, Brighton E. Sussex BN2 2GY UK T +44 (0)1273 695505 www.eco-action.org/ssp/ ssp@eco-action.org *In active solidarity with indigenous and radical ecological struggles in the Pacific.*

Survival International 6 Charterhouse Buildings, London, EC1M 7ET T 020 7687 8700 F 020 7687 8701 www.survival-international.org info@survival-international.org *Survival International is a worldwide organisation supporting tribal peoples. It stands for their right to decide their own future and helps them protect their lives, lands and human rights.*

Taiga Resue Network (TRN) Box 116, Ajtte, S-962 23 Jokkmokk, Sweden, T +46 971 17039 F 46-971-55354 www.taigarescue.org info@taigarescue.org *The TRN is an international network of non-governmental organisations and indigenous peoples working for the protection and sustainable use of the world's boreal forests.*

Tibet Foundation 1 St. James's Market, London SW1Y 4SB. T 020 7930 6001 F 020 7930 6002 www.tibet-foundation.org enquiries@tibet-foundation.org *Non-political organisation working to preserve Tibetan Culture, and assist the Tibetan People across the world.*

JUSTICE & THE LAW

Bindman & Partners Solicitors 275 Gray's Inn Rd, London, WC1X 8QF T 020 7833 4433 F 020 7837 9792 www.bindmans.com info@Bindmans.com *A solicitor's firm specialising in human rights - including criminal law, protest, civil actions against the police.*

Criminal Cases Review Commission (CCRC) Alpha Tower, Suffolk St, Queensway, Birmingham, B1 1TT. T 0121 633 1800 F 0121 633 1804/1823 www.ccrc.gov.uk info@ccrc.gov.uk *An independent body responsible for investigating suspected miscarriages of criminal justice in England, Wales and Northern Ireland.*

Earthrights Solicitors Little Orchard, School Lane, Molehill Green, Takeley, Essex, CM22 6PS T 01279 870391 pager - 07669 127601 F 01279 870391 www.earthrights.org.uk earthrights@gn.apc.org *Together with the EarthRights charity, to provide legal advice and assistance to the environment movement and landrights campaigners.*

Eddie Gilfoyle Campaign c/o Susan Caddick PO Box 1845, Stoke on Trent ST7 4EG. T 0781 501 2372 Paul.Caddick@btinternet.com *Campaigning for the release of Eddie Gilfoyle who was wrongly convivted of murder in 1993.*

Environmental Law Centre (ELC) PO Box 267, Southport PR8 1HY. T 01704 547418 F 01704 549091 www.elc.org.uk info@elc.org.uk *Health, Environmental Law and People in the Human and Fundamental rights area.*

Freedom To Be Yourself, The 13 C, Pioneer House, Adelaide Street, Coventry T 07788 557078 www.geocities.com/thehumanmind thehumanmind@yahoo.co.uk *The right to be unclothed in all public places. Human skin. Body visibility. The human race: Every BODY!*

Friends of Zimbabwe (FOZ) P O Box 50218, Waterfront, Cape Town 8002, South Africa. T 27-83-7090507 F 27-83-87090507 friendsofzimbabwe@hotmail.com *Pressure group promoting democratic principles and culture in Zimbabwe.*

Howard League For Penal Reform The 1 Ardleigh Rd, London, N1 4HS T 020 7249 7373 F 020 7249 7788 www.howardleague.org howard.league@ukonline.co.uk *The Howard League works for humane, effective and efficient reform of the penal system.*

Injustice : T 020 7254 9701/07770 432 439 (evenings-w/ends) www.injusticefilm.co.uk *A film about the struggle for justice by the families of people that have died in police custody.*

Innocent Dept. 54, PO Box 282, Oldham OL1 3FY innocent.org.uk innocent@uk2.net *Mutual support group which offers advice and assistance to the families and friends of prisoners who have been wrongly convicted of serious crimes.*

Irwin Mitchell Solicitors St. Peter's House, Hartshead, Sheffield, S1 2EL T 0114 276 7777/273 9011 F 0114 275 3306 www.imonline.co.uk *Produce Claiming Compensation For Police Misconduct- A Guide To Your Rights, a booklet of civil liberties when dealing with the police.*

Legal Defence & Monitoring Group (LDMG) BM Haven, London, WC1N 3XX T 020 8245 2930 www2.phreak.co.uk/ldmg/index.php ldmgmail@yahoo.co.uk *Legal monitoring at demos & advice for others doing so plus advice on police tactics, prisoners & legal stuff*

Liberty 21 Tabard St., London, SE1 4LA T 020 74033888 F 020 74075354 www.liberty-human-rights.org.uk info@liberty-human-rights.org.uk *Lobbies Parliament on proposed legislation and takes test case litigation to domestic and European Courts*

Lydia Dagostino c/o Kellys Premier House, 11 Marlborough House, Brighton, BN1 1UB T 01273 608311 F 01273 674898 l.dagostino@talk21.com *Solicitor with experience in defending protestors 24 hour helpline 0800 387463.*

Miscarriages of Justice UK (MOJUK) Tardis Studios, 52-56 Turnmill St., London, EC1M 5QR T 0121 554 6947 F 0870 055 4570 www.mojuk.org.uk *Founded by Paddy Hill, one of the Birmingham 6, they fight for people who are wrongly imprisoned.*

Public Law Project (PLP) 266-268 Holloway Road, London, N7 6NE. T 020 7697 2190 F 020 7697 2199 www.publiclawproject.org.uk admin@publiclawproject.org.uk *Undertakes specialist research, training and information, advice and representation in public law to access justice for poor and disadvantaged people.*

Statewatch P.O.Box 1516, London, N16 0EW T 020 88021882 F 020 88801727 www.statewatch.org office@statewatch.org *Statewatch monitors the state and civil liberties in the UK and Europe*

United Families and Friends Campaign (UFFC) c/o inquest, Ground Floor, Alexandra National House, 330 Seven Sisters Rd., London N4 2PJ. kevin@copwatcher.org *Vocal campaigning coalition of families and friends of people who have died in police custody, prison or in psychiatric care.*

Walkers Solicitors 2 Bouverie Road, Stoke Newington, London N16 0AJ. T 020 8800 8855 F 020 8800 9955 info@walkerssolicitors.co.uk *Specialist advice & representation in animal rights, political defence, etc.*

LAND RIGHTS & PLANNING

Boycott Israel www.boycottisrael.co.uk *Info for people who want to boycott produce from Israel and illegal Israeli settlements in the West Bank and Gaza and an educational resource about Israel and Palestine.*

Land Is Ours, The (T.L.I.O) 16B Cherwell St, Oxford, OX4 1BG T 07961 460171 www.tlio.org.uk office@tlio.demon.co.uk *Campaigns peacefully for access to the land, its resources and the decision making processes affecting them, for everyone - irrespective of race, age, or gender.*

Mast Action UK 20 Outwood Road, Radcliffe, Gtr. Manchester M26 1AQ. www.mastaction.org webmaster@mastaction.org *Voluntary organisation dedicated to supporting, advising and actively aiding and representing local campaigns fighting the current mobile phone mast invasion that is sweeping the country.*

Open Spaces Society (OSS) 25A Bell St, Henley-On-Thames, Oxon, RG9 2BA T 01491 573535 F 01491 57305 www.oss.org.uk hq@oss.org.uk *Exists to protect common land and public rights of way.*

Ramblers' Association 2nd floor Camelford House, 87-90 Albert Embankment, London SE1 7TW. T 020 7339 8500 F 020 7339 8501 www.ramblers.org.uk ramblers@london.ramblers.org.uk *Encouraging walking, protecting rights of way, defending the beauty of the countryside and campaigning for freedom to roam over uncultivated open country.*

Royal Town Planning Institute (RTPI) 41 Botolph Lane, London, EC3 8DL T 020 79299494 www.rtpi.org.uk online@rtpi.org.uk *To provide free and independent town planning advice to groups and individuals that cannot afford professional fees*

Spitalfields Market Under Threat (SMUT) T 020 7613 5897 www.smut.org.uk smut@smut.org.uk *Oppose the destruction of three-fifths of the historic old covered market to make way for yet another office development.*

Sprawl Busters 21 Grinnell St, Greenfield, MA 01301, USA. T +1 413 772 6289 www.sprawl-busters.com info@sprawl-busters.com *Help local community coalitions on-site to design and implement successful campaigns against megastores and other undesirable large-scale developments.*

Tinkers Bubble Little Norton, Stoke-Sub-Hamdon, Somerset, TA14. T 01935 881975 *Community small holding. We live in low-impact dwellings and try to earn our livings through sustainable forestry, organic growing, processing, & woodcraft. We invite willing workers - call first.*

Who Owns Scotland T 0131 538 5175 www.whoownsscotland.org.uk andywightman@caledonia.org.uk *Reveals all about landownership in Scotland.*

MEDIA - DISTRIBUTION AND PUBLISHERS

AK Distribution P.O.Box 12766, Edinburgh, EH8 9YE. T 0131 5555165 F 0131 5555215 www.akuk.com ak@akedin.demon.co.uk *Co-operative who distribute & publish a wide range of radical politics: books, mags. audio & t-shirts. Send for free mail-order catalogue.*

Autonomedia P.O. Box 568, Williamsburg Station, Brooklyn, New York 11211-0568, USA T 718-963-2603 www.autonomedia.org info@autonomedia.org *Publishes books related to oppositional culture, and maintains a website devoted to the same, with discussion, links, and surprises!*

Barricada P.O. Box 73, Boston, MA 02133, USA. www.barricada.org barricadacollective@hotmail.com *Publishers of North America's only Revolutionary Anarchist monthly magazine.*

Edge of Time Ltd BCM Edge, London WC1N 3XX T 07000 780536 F 0870 1634661 www.edgeoftime.co.uk sales@edgeoftime.co.uk *Distributes books on communal living and other items associated with cultural change.*

Emjay Reprographics 117 Harwill Crescent, Aspley, Nottingham NG8 5LA. T 0115 978 1305 *Specialises in low-volume print-runs of booklets, periodicals and monographs.*

Enabler Publications 3 Russell House, Lym Close, Lyme Regis, Dorset, DT7 3DE. T 01297 445024 F as phone members.aol.com/adearling/enabler adearling@aol.com *Books about counter culture, Travellers, protest and creative work with young people.*

Godhaven Ink Rooted Media, The Cardigan Centre, 145-149 Cardigan Rd, Leeds, LS6 1LJ T 0113 278 8617 www.godhaven.org.uk merrick@stones.com *Publishers of cheap books and zines about direct action and other countercultural stuff. Promoting a feeling of well-being since 1994.*

La Petroleuse La Petroleuse BP04 86800 St Julien L'Ars (France) www.la-petroleuse.com contact@la-petroleuse.com *An online counterculture bookstore which distribute books, videos and magazines in french or english from independant and underground publishers celebrating counter cultures and social fights.*

National Small Press Centre, The BM Bozo, London, WC1N 3XX *Publishes small press handbook with information on thousands of small presses worldwide.*

Pluto Press 345 Archway Rd, London, N6 5AA. T 020 8348 2724 F 020 8348 9133 www.plutobooks.com pluto@plutobooks.com *One of the UK's leading independent publishers. Committed to publishing the best in critical writing across the social sciences and humanities.*

Rationalist Press Association Bradlaugh House, 47 Theobold's Road, London WC1 8SP. T 020 7430 1371 F 2074301271 www.rationalist.org.uk info@rationalist.org.uk *Produce print and on-line humanist magazines and rationalist books.*

Revolutions Per Minute BCM Box 3328, London WC1N 3XX T 07967 886257 www.red-star-research.org.uk/rpm revopermin@ukonline.co.uk *A radical publishing project, which aims to help liberate the working class. Books on strikes, fox-hunting and anti-racism.*

Rural Media Company, The Sullivan House, 72-80 Widemarsh St, Hereford, HR4 9HG. T 01432 344039 F 01432 270539 www.ruralmedia.co.uk info@ruralmedia.co.uk *We are a National Media Communications Charity, we cover print, web publishing, video production and multimedia production.*

Zed Books, 7 Cynthia St, London, N1 9JF T 020 7837 4014 F 020 7833 3960 www.zedbooks.co.uk/ *Independent workers co-op publishing annually 50+ scholarly, critical books on international issues, politics, the environment, feminism and 'the third world'*

MEDIA - FILM, VIDEO & TV

Beyond TV www.beyondtv.org mick@beyondtv.org *A website hosting alternative news features - in an online database linking features to campaigns, upcoming events and current projects.*

Brighton Arts Resources Technology (Brighton ART) T 01273 697579 F 07092 184075 www.brightonart.org info@brightonart.org *Websites, audio/video production, workshops, and software with friendly rates for charities, arts organisations and voluntary groups.*

Cultureshop.Org PO Box 29683, London E2 6XH. T 07950 699562 www.cultureshop.org *Online distribution to allow progressive film makers to sell there work, may be extended to other forms of media soon.*

Exploding Cinema, The c/o 26 Fairwall House, Peckham Road, London SE5 8QW. T 020 7708 3501/020 7732 8058 www.explodingcinema.org explodingcinema@hotmail.com *Open Access Screenings for Short Films.*

I-Contact Video Network c/o 76 Mina Rd, St. Werburghs, Bristol, BS2 9TX. T 0117 9400636 www.videonetwork.org I-contact@videonetwork.org *A non-profit making initiative set up to provide support for those using video for positive change.*

Reclaim the Streets - The Film T 07092 044579 www.urban75.com/rtsfilm/ reclaim_streets_film@yahoo.com *Video clips, background info and ordering details for this essential documentary, taking a frantic look at RTS actions in the UK and abroad.*

SKA TV Suite 75 Trades Hall Carlton Vic 3053 Australia T 61 3 9663 6976 www.accessnews.skatv.org.au accessnews@skatv.org.au *A grass-roots community organisation using TV and video as tools for social change; training, screenings, broadcast, distribution..*

Turn Off Your TV www.turnoffyourtv.com *Articles on issues such as the role of advertisers, corporate ownership of mass media, and the potential effects of images on children.*

Undercurrents alternative video news 16B Cherwell St, Oxford, OX4 1BG. T 01865 203661/203662 www.undercurrents.org underc@gn.apc.org *Produce and distribute videos and CD-ROM on direct action. Organise BeyondTV video activist festival.*

Undercurrents foundation www.undercurrents.org undercymru@joymail.com *Train activists how to use video for social change.*

White Dot PO Box 2116, Hove BN3 3LR. www.whitedot.org info@whitedot.org *International campaign against television.*

MEDIA - INTERNET NEWS SERVICES

Alternet www.alternet.org *San Fransisco alternative media site with hard-hitting news and investigations not covered in the mainstream press, fiery columns, insights into cultural trends.*

GreenNet 56-64 Leonard Street London EC2A 4JX T 0207 0650 935 F 0207 0650 936 www.greennet.org.uk info@gn.apc.org *GreenNet is an internet service provider that specialises in Internet services for organisations involved in Peace, The environment, Human Rights and Development.*

Guerilla News Network www.guerrillanews.com *An underground news organization whose mission is to expose people to important global issues through guerrilla programming on the web and on television.*

IFI Watch www.ifiwatch.tv eyes@ifiwatch.org, *'Eyes on International financial Institutions' - web portal to independent film and video on the World Bank, IMF etc. Get stuff here for radical/educational screenings.*

Indymedia www.indymedia.org *A collective of independent media organizations and hundreds of journalists offering grassroots, non-corporate coverage - links to Indymedia outlets around the world.*

Monbiot, George www.monbiot.com *Journalist/academic writing on a range of topics including corporate power, globalisation, landrights and planning, transport and more.*

Protest.Net www.protest.net rabble-rouser@protest.net *A site to help progressive activists by providing a central place where the times and locations of protests and meetings can be posted.*

SchNEWS c/o on the fiddle, P.O.Box 2600, Brighton, E. Sussex, BN2 0EF T 01273 685913 www.schnews.org.uk schnews@brighton.co.uk *The UK's weekly direct action newsletter.*

Spunk Library, The www.spunk.org spunk@spunk.org *Collects and distributes literature in electronic format, with an emphasis on anarchism and related issues.*

SQUALL Magazine P.O.Box 8959, London, N19 5HW www.squall.co.uk mail@squall.co.uk *Regularly updated online magazine presenting radical journalism, photography and culture with content.*

Straight Goods www.straightgoods.com *Canada's independent on-line source of news*

Z Magazine 18 Millfield Street, Woods Hole MA 02543, USA. T +1 508 5489063 www.zmag.org sysop@lol.shareworld.com *Z is an independent political magazine of critical thinking on political, cultural, social, and economic life in the United States, Z accepts no paid advertising.*

MEDIA - OVERSEAS

A4 Newsbot c/o L38 Squat Infoshop, Via Giuliotti, 8-00143 Roma, Italy. www.tmcrew.org/laurentinokkupato/a4newsbot a4newsbot@paranoici.org *A SchNEWS inspired quarterly A4 multi-language publication distributed on paper, e-mail, website and PDF about social, eco, anarchists issues.*

Alternative Press Review PO Box 4710, Arlington, VA 22204, USA. T 703-553-2945 F 703-553-0565 www.altpr.org editors@altpr.org *Your Guide Beyond the Mainstream! Each issue is packed with creative ideas, fresh perspectives, insightful analysis and pointed humor.*

An Phoblacht (Republican News) 58 Parnell Square, Dublin 1 T +353 1 873 3611 F www.irlnet.com/aprn aprn@irlnet.com *Ireland's biggest selling political weekly newspaper has been a source of uncensored news on world affairs and the Irish struggle for national self-determination for over 25 years.*

Art of Resistance www.squat.net/cia/aor *The Arts of Resistance web site is a site for Music Poetry Theatre writers and other creative activists celebrating resistance today.*

Community Access Technology www.cat.org.au/main.html *Low tech grass roots net access for real people. Pedestrians, public transport and pushbikes on the information super hypeway.*

Eat The State! P.O Box 85541, Seattle, WA 98145, USA T (206) 215 1156 eatthestate.org ets@scn.org *We want an end to poverty, exploitation, imperialism, militarism, racism, sexism, heterosexism, environmental destruction, television, and large ugly buildings.*

Factsheet 5 PO Box 4660 Arlington, VA 22204, USA. T 703-553-2945 F 703-553-0565 www.factsheet5.org twbounds@pop.mail.rcn.net *Comprehensive quarterly guide to zines/alternative publications. Each issue packed with reviews/contact/ordering info for hundreds of independent publications.*

Green Pepper CIA Office, Overtoom 301, 1054 HW Amsterdam, The Netherlands. T +31 (0)20 665 7743 F +31 (0)20 692 8757 www.greenpeppermagazine.org / contact@greenpeppermagazine.org/ *An environmental and social justice magazine focussing on a different (anti-neoliberal/activist friendly) topic every edition.*

Indymedia Ireland www.indymedia.ie *Grassroots, non-corporate coverage of Irish life politics and protest. Indymedia is a democratic media outlet for the creation of radical, accurate, and passionate tellings of truth.*

KUD Anarhiv Metelkova ulica 6, SI-1000 Ljubljana, Slovenia. T +386 1 434 03 45/+386 1 432 33 78 F +386 1 432 33 78 www.ljudmila.org/anarhiv anarhiv@mail.ljudmila.org *Our main project, Elf's reading room is a resource centre for radical social change. We also publish a magazine and organize events.*

Organic Chaos Network PO Box 234, 2300 AE Leiden, Netherlands, T +31-6-12520674 www.organicchaos.org ocn@antenna.nl *Video action news group, part of Federation Collective Rampenplan*

Tactical Media Crew c/o Radio Onda Rossa, Via dei Volsci, 56, Roma 00185, Italy. www.tmcrew.org tactical@tmcrew.org *A collective of media and political activists from the radical autonomous/anarchist scene of Rome.*

MEDIA - UK LOCAL NEWS

Bangor-Werdd groups.yahoo.com/group/bangor-werdd *North Wales email discussion network of non-violent direct action protesters including peace, environment and animal rights.*

Bristle Box 25, 82 Colston St. Bristol, BS1 5BB www.bristle.org.uk editor@bristle.org.uk *Quarterly magazine for Bristol activism and anarchism treating all relevant subjects from news to campaigns.*

Bristol Indymedia bristol.indymedia.org *Bristol's own Indy Media site with news from Bristol and beyond*

Cardiff Activists Network www.geocities.com/bozavine/can/index.html bozavine@yahoo.co.uk *For everyone interested in direct action based in Cardiff - allowing information about future actions to be advertised and planned.*

Elffinews PO Box 923, Luton, LU2 0YQ. T 01582-512184 Mob: 07903 382228 F 01582 619218 elffinews@aol.com *Activist news letter for Luton and Dunstable. Scurrilous! A community based monthly mewsletter, reporting on local activists' actions.*

Eroding Empire c/o 56a Crampton St. London. SE17 3AE. www.eroding.org.uk eroding@eroding.org.uk *Monthly listings/classifieds for London area, diy, actions, centres, gigs.*

Global Action Scotland www.egroups.com/invite/globalactionscotland *an email discussion group for global justice Visit the website to sign up.*

Interference FM Box 6, Green Leaf, 82 Colston St, Bristol, BS1 5BB. *Bristol's anarchist pirate radio station.*

Pork-Bolter, The P.O.Box 4144, Worthing, West Sussex, BN14 7NZ www.eco-action.org/porkbolter porkbolter@eco-action.org *Radical local newsletter with historically-vindicated pig obsession. Rages against CCTV, Big Business, councils, police etc. etc. Free with SAE.*

Radio 4A T 07980 168115 www.piratetv.net *Monthly pirate radio with a substantial speech output. Open access, non-profit and broadcasting live as well as creating programmes. 106.6FM in Brighton or webcast on www.piratetv.net*

MEDIA - UK NATIONAL

ActivistNetwork.org.uk www.activistnetwork.org.uk info@activistnetwork.org.uk *ActivistNetwork.org.uk is a non profit making organisation that seeks to promote the values of peace, equality and social justice.*

Alan Lodge (Tash) T 0115 9113804 tash.gn.apc.org tash@gn.apc.org *Photographer (One Eye On The Road): travellers, festivals, raves, environmental direct actions and protest. & Police surveillance methods.*

AntiFa.net www.antifa.net *Portal to anti-fascism and anti-racism on the web. Offer secure web hosting to anti-fascists.*

Big Issue, The T 020 75263200 www.bigissue.com editorial@bigissue.com *UK's biggest current affairs weekly, with 1.2 million readers. Campaigning for social justice. Sold by homeless vendors who keep 70p of each issue.*

Black Information Link (BLINK) Suite 12, Winchester House, 9 Cranmer Road, SW9 6EJ, T 020 7582 1990 F 0870 127 6657 www.blink.org.uk blink1990@gn.apc.org *A national Black (African, Asian & Caribbean) organisation to increase the capacities of the Black communities to combat racism.*

Caduceus T 01926 451897 www.caduceus.info *Magazine about healing for people, community and planet.*

Corner House, The Station Rd, Sturminster Newton, Dorset DT10 1YJ. T 01258 473795 F 01258 473748 www.thecornerhouse.org.uk cornerhouse@gn.apc.org *Research, advocacy and solidarity work on social & environmental justice issues. Publish regular briefing papers. Free via email.*

Counter Information c/o ACE, 17 West Montgomery Place, Edinburgh, EH7 5HA T 0131 557 6242 www.counterinfo.org.uk ci@counterinfo.org.uk *Free anarchist newssheet reporting on struggles from around the world.*

Direct Action Collective PO Box 29, SW PDO, Manchester. M15 5HW. T 07984 675281 www.direct-action.org.uk da@direct-action.org.uk *DA - magazine of the anarcho-syndicalist Solidarity Federation. No political parties or dogma. Packed with positive anti-authoritarian ideas, news, comment and actions.*

Do or Die c/o Prior House, 6 Tilbury Place, Brighton, East Sussex, BN2 2GY www.eco-action.org/dod doordtp@yahoo.co.uk *Voices from the Ecological Resistance - an annual magazine crammed with reports and analysis from the worldwide ecological frontlines.*

Guardian Media Guide, The The Guardian, 119 Farringdon Rd, London, EC1R 3ER. *Lists contacts of all media organisations, plus government, publishers, business and action contacts.*

Index on Censorship 6-8 Amwell Street, London EC1R 1UQ United Kingdom T 020 7278 2313 F 020 7278 1878 www.indexonline.org/ rohan@indexoncensorship.org *Publish a magazine, run a website and organise events on free expression and censorship around the world.*

Indymedia UK www.indymedia.org.uk reports@indymedia.org.uk *An evolving network of media professionals, artists, and DIY media activists committed to using technology to promote social and economic justice.*

INK - Independent News Collective 13 Brecknock Road, London N7 0BL T 020 7561 0683 www.ink.uk.com *Umbrella organisation for the alternative press. Deals with marketing and publishing, but not editorial matters.*

Inkthief Rm 304, Maryland House, Manbey Park Road, London E15 1EY. T 020 8223 6011 / 07984 875471 contact@inkthief.org.uk *Designers committed to social and environmental justice who formed a professional design agency for socially progressive organisations.*

Lobster www.lobster-magazine.co.uk *The journal of parapolitics, intelligence, and State Research.*

New Internationalist Tower House, Lathkill St, Market Harborough, LE16 T 01858 438896 F 01858 461739 www.newint.org newint@subscription.co.uk *Monthly informative magazine reporting on issues of world poverty and inequality; focusing attention on the unjust relationship between the powerful and the powerless in both rich and poor countries.*

Positive News 5 Bicton Enterprise Centre, Clun, Shropshire, SY7 8NF T 01588 640022 F 01588 640033 www.positivenews.org.uk office@positivenews.org.uk *A free quarterly newspaper which publishes good news stories from around the world to do with peace, environment, health & education.*

Red Pepper 1b Waterlow Rd, London, N19 5NJ T 020 72817024 F 020 72639345 www.redpepper.org.uk redpepper@redpepper.org.uk *Green - left monthly magazine.*

Somewhere.tv www.somewhere.tv *New open collective website 'by the people, for the people'. Read and write on virtually any subject of interest, including: Art, Environment, Health, Money, Obsessions, Sport, Technology, True Sci-Fi, Work etc...*

YearZero (YZ) P.O. Box 26276, London, W3 7GQ. www.yearzero.org feedback@yearzero.org *The disobedient current affairs quarterly.*

NETWORKING SUPPORT

Active.org.au PO Box 303, Enmore, NSW 2042, Australia www.active.org.au webkids@active.org.au *Provides online interactive open-publishing forums for information and inspiration about social change in cities around Australia.*

Blatant Incitement Project (BLINC) Dept.29, 22a Beswick Street,Manchester M4 7HS. T 0161-226 6814 www.eco-action.org/blinc doinit@nematode.freeserve.co.uk *Empower people to organise themselves without hierarchy, for radical action towards social ecological change, by sharing skills, knowledge, and inspiration.*

Cynefin y Werin Uned 2, gwasg Dwyfor, Stad Ddiwydiannol, Penygroes, Gwynedd LL545 6DB. T 01286 882359 Pager 07669 179015 benica@gn.apc.org *All Wales network for organisations working on international peace, solidarity and social justice.*

Direct Action Scotland groups.yahoo.com/group/directactionscotland *A discussion and information email list focusing on direct action and protest in Scotland.*

Edinburgh CITY (Change IT Yourselves) c/o ACE, 17 West Montgomery Place, Edinburgh EH7 5HA. www.edinburghcity.org.uk info@edinburghcity.org.uk *A new independent forum with no set agenda. Monthly discussion/social evening for people interested in social change.*

EYFA Postbus 94115, 1090 GC Amsterdam, The Netherlands, T +31 20 665 7743 www.eyfa.org eyfa@eyfa.org *European-wide network of individuals and grassroots groups active on social and environmental issues.*

FutureManchester www.futuremanchester.org.uk *Site dedicated to signposting you to others working for positive change in Manchester*

LeftDirect www.leftdirect.co.uk *More than just a comprehensive directory of all left, radical and progressive organisations in the UK.*

Nottingham Association of Subversive Activists (NASA) members.tripod.co.uk/NASA13 nasa13@lycosmail.com *Network of Nottingham-based campaigners, meeting monthly for mutual aid on issues of social justice.*

Seeds for Change Network 96 Church Street, Lancaster, LA1 1TD. T 0845 3307853 www.seedsforchange.org.uk lancaster@seedsforchange.org.uk *Free training + support on campaign planning, tactics, non-hierarchical organising, consensus and facilitation plus advice on low cost computing and free software (linux).*

Sustainable London Trust 7 Chamberlain Street London NW1 8XB. T 020 7722 3710 F 020 7722 3959 www.london21.org admin@london21.org *A user-focussed sustainability network for London, to find mutual support and link work with the actions of others who have similar goals.*

PRISONER SUPPORT

Anarchist Black Cross Network c/o Austin ABC, P.O. Box 19733, Austin, TX 78760-9733, USA. www.anarchistblackcross.org abc-help@anarchistblackcross.org *Network of ABC organisations, has list on website of all ABC groups.*

Anarchist Black Cross, Brighton PO Box 74, Brighton BN1 4ZQ. www.brightonabc.org.uk mail@brightonabc.org.uk *Support group for anarchists, black liberation activists, anti-fascists and others we feel an affinity with who have ended up in prison.*

Anarchist Black Cross, Czech (ABC-CSAF) PH, P.O.Box 41, 565 01 Chocen, Czech republic. www.csaf.cz/english abc@csaf.cz *Helping anarchist prisoners, collecting money for legal defense, publish ABC bulletin.*

Animal Liberation Front UK Supporters Group BM 1160, London WC1N 3XX. T 0870 1385037 F as phone info@alfsg.co.uk *Info about animal rights prisoners and defence funds plus articles/news in bi-monthly newsletter.*

Break the Chains Free, Critter and Rob Legal Defense Committee, P.O. Box 11331, Eugene, Oregon 97440, USA. www.breakthechains.net *Northwest USA anarchist POWs website, a resource for, by and about anarchist political prisoners in the Northwest.*

Campaign Against Prison Slavery PO Box 74, Brighton, East Sussex, BN1 4ZQ. T 07944 522001 www.againstprisonslavery.org againstprisonslavery@mail.com *The Campaign Against Prison Slavery exists to challenge and bring about an end to forced prison labour, and to expose the companies that exploit it.*

Campaign Against Prison Slavery PO Box 74, Brighton BN1 4ZQ. T 07944 522001 www.enrager.net/hosted/caps// againstprisonslavery@mail.com *Exists to challenge and bring about an end to forced prison labour, and to expose the companies that exploit it.*

Campaign to Free Vanunu & for a Nuclear Free Middle East 185 New Kent Rd, London, SE1 4AG T 020 7378 9324 F as phone www.vanunu.freeserve.co.uk campaign@vanunu.freeserve.co.uk *Campaign for the release of Vanunu, the Israeli nuclear whistleblower who, in 1986 was sentenced for 18 years imprisonment for revealing Israel's nuclear stockpiles.*

Earth Liberation Prisoners BM Box 2407, London, WC1N 3XX. www.spiritoffreedom.org.uk earthlibprisoner@mail.com *Supports people who have been arrested and imprisoned for acts of direct action in defence of animals and the earth.*

Haven Distribution 27 Old Gloucester St, London, WC1N 3XX. *Supplies free educational literature to prisoners in UK and Ireland. Donations make this possible.*

International Concerned Family & Friends of Mumia Abu-Jamal www.mumia.org *Information and networking to save this journalist/activist's life.*

Leonard Peltier Defense Committee P. O. Box 583, Lawrence, Kansas KS 66044, USA T +1 785 842 5774 www.freepeltier.org lpdc@freepeltier.org *Framed for killing two FBI agents at the Pine Ridge Reservation, despite the government saying they do not know who is responsible for the deaths of the agents.*

Mumia Must Live! BM Box 4771, London, WC1N 3XX www.callnetuk.com/home/mumia mumia@callnet.uk.com *Mumia Abu-Jamal is a political Prisoner facing death row in the USA. This is a coalition fighting to free Mumia and end the racist death penalty.*

Outside Chance Second Floor, 164-166 King Street, Hammersmith, London W6 0QU. T 020 8563 7700 F 020 8563 7755 www.outsidechance.org outsidechances@aol.com *A self-help organisation, offering advice, practical support and guidance to juvenile and young adult offenders and ex-offenders.*

REFUGEES

Asylum Aid 28 Commercial St, London, E1 6LS T 020 7377 5123 F 020 7247 7789 www.asylumaid.org.uk info@asylumaid.org.uk *rovides free legal advice and representation to refugees seeking safety in the UK from persecution and campaign for fair treatment of refugees in the UK.*

Asylum Support www.asylumsupport.info *Online information focusing on all matters that concern people*

Brighton and Hove Committee to Defend Asylum Seekers c/o 4 Crestway Parade, The Crestway, Brighton BN1 7BL. T 01273 540717 bton_def_asy@hotmail.com *Campaiging group set up to provide a local response to the growing xenophobia of our government and media.*

Campaign to Close Campsfield c/o 111 Magdalen St, Oxford T 01865 558145/557282/378734 www.closecampsfield.org.uk info@closecampsfield.org.uk *Campaign for the closure of Campsfield House Immigration Detention Centre and for the end of detention of refugees nationwide..*

Close Down Harmondsworth Campaign 10 Endsleigh Rd, Southall UB2 5QL. T 07960 309457 F 08701 643017 closedownharmondsworth@hotmail.com *Campaigning against imprisonment of asylum seekers and others in racist detention centre.*

International Federation of Iranian Refugees (IFIR) PO Box 27236, London N11 2ZF. T 07730 107337 F 0870 1394253 www.hambastegi.org ifir@ukonline.co.uk *Committed to organizing the protests of Iranian refugees and asylum seekers in support of political and social campaigns.*

National Coalition of Anti-Deportation Campaigns (NCADC) 110 Hamstead Road, Handsworth, Birmingham B20 2QS. T 0121 554 6947 F 0121 554 7891 www.ncadc.org.uk Ncadc@ncadc.org.uk *Bringing together families and individuals fighting deportation.*

No Border Network www.noborder.org *Tool for all groups and grass root organizations who work on the questions of migrants and asylum seekers.*

Refugee Council 3 Bondway, London SW8 1SJ. T 020 7820 3000 F 020 7582 9929 www.refugeecouncil.org.uk info@refugeecouncil.org.uk *Largest organisation in the UK working with asylum seekers and refugees.*

SEXUALITY

Intercourse: talking sex c/o 17 West Montgomery Place, Edinburgh EH7 5HA. www.intercourse.org.uk info@intercourse.org.uk *Encourages comfortable and positive ways of thinking and talking about sex by organising discussions and events and producing literature.*

OutRage! P.O.Box 17816, London, SW14 8WT T 020 8240 0222 www.outrage.org.uk outreach@OutRage.org.uk *World's longest surviving queer rights direct action group, dedicated to fighting homophobia and achieving equal civil rights.*

Queeruption 56a Infoshop, 56 Crampton Street, London SE17 5AE. T 07949 976016 www.queeruption.com info@queeruption.com *Radical queer network. Organising the queeruption gatherings, parties, actions, alternative pride, cabaret, street intervention, cafe, squat and generally being sexy!*

Sexual Freedom Coalition BM Box Lovely, London, WC1N 3XX www.sfc.org.uk info@sfc.org.uk *Coordinating the groups who campaign for the sexual freedom of consenting adults, providing a back-up force when problems occur.*

Stonewall Lobby Group ltd . 46-48 Grosvenor Gardens, London , SW1W 0EB. T 020 7881 9440 F 020 7881 9444 www.stonewall.org.uk info@stonewall.org.uk *Working towards the advancement of the civil, political, economic, social and cultural rights of lesbians and gay men.*

SOCIAL & COMMUNITY CENTRES

1in12 Club 21-23 Albion St, Bradford, BD1 2LY T 01274 734160 www.1in12.go-legend.net info@1in12.com *Members social club based on the principles of self-management.*

Community Composting Network 67 Alexandra Road, Sheffield, S2 3EE. T 0114 2580483 www.othas.org.uk/ccn Ccn@gn.apc.org *Help and support on all issues around involving your local community in managing its organic resources, through composting.*

Dyfi Eco-Valley Partnership (Ecodyfi) Unit 1, Dyfi Eco Park, Machynlleth, Powys, SY20 8AX. T 01654 705018 F 01654 703000 www.ecodyfi.org.uk ecodyfi@gn.apc.org *Sustainable community regeneration in the Dyfi valley, mid Wales.*

Envolve - Bath Environment Centre Green Park Station, Green Park Road, Bath, BA1 1JB. T 01225 787910 F 01225 460840 www.envolve.co.uk office@envolve.co.uk *Working with schools, community groups, youth groups, businesses and individuals on projects that touch people's lives and benefit the environment.*

Fair Trade Cafe 2 Ashgrove, Bradford, BD7 1BN T 01274 727034 www.fairtradecafe.org.uk *Not-for-profit cafe that exists to raise awareness about fair trade & other related issues. A largely volunteer run community cafe that aims to provide cheap, healthy, ethical and delicious food.*

Groundswell Elmfield House, 5 Stockwell Mews, London SW9 9GX. T 0207737 5500 F 020 7733 1305 www.groundswell.org.uk groundswell@home-all.org.uk *Supporting & promoting self help approaches to takcling homelessness and poverty. Info & advice, publications, grants, exchanges, training and networking events.*

Lancaster Resource Centre 78a Penny St, Lancaster LA1 1XN. www.eco-action.org/lancaster *LaRC is a collectively run resource centre and meeting space in Lancaster. Open every Wednesday 4-7pm.*

Living Streets 31-33 Bondway, London, SW8 1SJ, T 020 7820 1010 F 020 7820 8208 www.livingstreets.org.uk info@livingstreets.org.uk *We help people improve the safety and condition of local streets and public spaces through information and local support.*

London Action Resource Centre 62 Fieldgate St, London E1 1ES. T 020 7377 9088 www.londonarc.org info@londonarc.org *Collectively-run building providing space and resources for people and groups working on self-organised, non-hierarchical projects for radical social change.*

Okasional Caf? Dept. 29, 22a Beswick Street, Manchester, M4 7HS. T 0161 2266814 Okasional-caf?@nematode.freeserve.co.uk *Occasional squat cafes & reclaimed autonomous spaces in Manchester.*

Social Centre Autonomous Network The Midnight Star Social Centre, 55-57 Parramatta Rd., Homebush, NSW, Australia. T 0415-882-901 scan.cat.org.au squatasocialcentre@yahoogroups.com *We are squatting activists and autonomously organised groups who make decisions through the network to occupy and organise around squatted social centres.*

Steward Wood Moretonhampstead, Newton Abbot, Devon TQ13 8SD. T 01647 440233 Mob 07050 674464 www.stewardwood.org affinity@stewardwood.org *Demonstrating positive sustainable alternatives - a vegan community based in a woodland in Dartmoor. Permaculture, renewable energy, organic growing, low impact living. Visitors welcome.*

TRANSPORT

A27 Action Group 56 Firle Village, Lewes, BN8 6LG T 01273 858365 F as phone *We aim to stop with research into the departments facts and figures the building of a new A27 between Lewes and Polegate.*

Cambridge Cycling Campaign PO Box 204 Cambridge CB4 3FN T (01223) 690718 F as tel www.camcycle.org.uk *An organisation of volunteers campaigning for the rights of cyclists and promoting cycling in and around Cambridge.*

Campaign Against Tube Privatisation (CATP) T 07961 440868 www.catp.org publictube@aol.com *Founded in 1999 by London Underground workers so they could campaign together with the travelling public against the Blair government's planned privatisation of the tube.*

Car Busters Magazine and Resource Centre Kratka 26, 100 00 Praha 10, Czech Republic T +420 2 7481 0849 F +420 2 7481 6727 www.carbusters.ecn.cz carbusters@ecn.cz *A quarterly multilingual magazine and resource centre for the international anti-car movement. To facilitate exchange & co-operation, inspire, reach out, and change the world.*

Castlecliff Bicycle Workshop 25 Johnstone Terrace, Edinburgh. T 07887 500667 F 0870 1254360 www.castlecliff.org.uk home@castlecliff.org.uk *Reconditions old bicycles that can be bought or exchanged for volunteer labour etc. Volunteers always needed, no experience necessary as training is given.*

Environmental Transport Association Services Ltd (ETA) 10 Church St, Weybridge KT13 8RS. T 01932 828882 www.eta.co.uk *The ETA is the only British provider of breakdown services that campaigns for environmentally sound transport.*

EVUK www.evuk.co.uk editor@evuk.co.uk *Campaign for REAL, long-distance electric vehicles.*

Green Skies c/o Aviation Environment Federation, Sir John Lyon House, 5 High Timber Street, London EC4V 3NS. T 020 7248 2223 F 020 7329 8160 www.greenskies.org info@greenskies.org *GreenSkies is a worldwide information network of environmental organisations concerned with aviation's environmental effects.*

Nukewatch c/o 30 Westwood Road, Southampton, SO17 1DN. T 023 80554434 F 023 80554434 cndyorks@gn.apc.org *Website: see Scottish CND. A national network that monitors nuclear warhead and materials convoys, informs the public, local authorities and media of their movements and campaigns against them.*

Re-Cycle 60 High St, West Mersea, Essex, CO5 8JE. T 01206 382207 F 01206 382207 www.re-cycle.org info@re-cycle.org *Sends second hand bicycles to Less Developed Countries and teach local people skills to maintain and repair them.*

Road Rage www.roadrage.org.uk *Loads of links to help people quickly navigate to information on these issues and find out about 'green' road transport campaigns*

RoadPeace POBox 2579, London NW10 3PW. T 020 8838 5102/Support line: 020 8964 1021 F 020 8838 5103 www.roadpeace.org info@roadpeace.org *Supporting those bereaved or injured in a road crash. Working for Real Road Safety.*

Slower Speeds Initiative (SSI) PO Box 19, Hereford HR1 1XJ. T 0845 345 8459 www.slower-speeds.org.uk info@slower-speeds.org.uk *Lower speeds make walking and cycling safer, provide alternatives to road-building, support local economies and reduce CO2 emissions.*

South Coast Against Roadbuilding (SCAR) PO Box 4144, Worthing. West Sussex. www.scar-uk.fsnet.co.uk info@scar-uk.fsnet.co.uk *An umbrella group to local groups fighting the threat of a superhighway along the south coast of England.*

Sustrans 35 King Street, Bristol BS1 4DZ T 0117 926 8893 F 0117 929 4173 www.sustrans.org.uk *Sustrans is a civil engineering charity which designs and builds routes for cyclists, walkers, and people with disabilities.*

Transport 2000 Impact Centre, 12-18 Hoxton St, London, N1 6NG T 0207 613 0743 F 0207 613 5280 www.transport2000.org.uk *Campaigns & lobbies for a sustainable transport policy.*

TRAVELLERS

Friends, Families & Travellers (FFT) Community Base, 113 Queens Rd, Brighton BN1 3XG. T 01273 234777/ mobile: 07971 550328 F 01273 234778 www.gypsy-traveller.org fft@communitybase.org *Advice and Information Unit for Gypsies, Travellers, service providers etc, on issues such as evictions, sites, planning, discrimination. Also lobbying and campaigning on Travellers' rights.*

Gypsy Council, The (GCECWCR) 8 Hall Rd, Aveley, Romford, Essex, RM15 4HD T 01708 868986 F as phone www.btinternet.com/~thegypsycouncil enquiries@thegypsycouncil.org *Advocates, liason, contact point resource centre for Gypsies and people supporting/ working with Gypsies.*

New Futures Association The Cottage, Glaneirw, Tan-y-groes, Ceredigion. T 01239 810548 mail@newfutures.fsnet.co.uk *Established a resource centres for nomadic people to encourage training, education and self-help. Supports travellers by providing information and advice and through campaigning.*

Traveller Law Research Unit (TLRU) www.cf.ac.uk/claws/tlru *Research and publication of Traveller-related legal issues.*

Travellers' School Charity Hayne Farm, Morebath, Tiverton, Devon. EX16 9DA T 01398 332347 / 0845 2818571 F 0870 7064782 www.tsct.co.uk info@tsct.co.uk *The Travellers' School Charity's aim is to support traveller families access opportunities, freedom and choice through education.*

TravellerSpace c/o Henjy, Near Hayle, Kernow TR27 6LZ. T 01736 711378/741151 travellerspace@linuxmail.org *Independent project that works with and supports Gypsies and Travellers in Cornwall. We offer on site play and art sessions, basic IT training, a lending library of books for children and adults and support in accessing health, education and welfare services.*

WOMEN

Anarcha-Feminist Health Care Collective T 01273 205651 *Non-hierarchical collective, meeting to gather, share info and experiences of our health and understand it in the political context of patriarchy and capitalism.*

Black Women's Rape Action Project Crossroads Women's Centre, 230A Kentish Town Rd, Lonon NW5 2AB. T 020 7482 2496 F 020 7209 4761 www.bwrap.dircon.co.uk bwrap@dircon.co.uk *A grassroots Black and immigrant women's organisation aiming to win justice for rape survivors and to get rape recognised as persecution and therefore grounds for asylum.*

Crossroads Women'sCentre PO Box 287, London NW6 5QU. T 020 7482 2496 F 020 7209 4761 allwomencount.net crossroadswomenscentre@compuserve.com *Lively, welcoming, anti-sexist anti-racist home of a number of organisations which highlight the needs and concerns of grassroots women especially.*

English Collective of Prostitutes Crossroads Women's Centre, P.O.Box 287, London, NW6 5QU. T 020 7482 2496 F 020 7209 4761 allwomencount.net crossroadswomenscentre@compuserve.com *Campaign for sex workers to be recognized as workers; for civil and economic rights and the abolition of the prostitution laws*

Global Women's Strike Crossroads Women's Centre, 230A Kentish Town Road, London Postcode: NW5 2AB T (020) 7482 2496 F (020) 7209 4761 womenstrike8m.server101.com womenstrike8m@server101.ocm *Women everywhere strike annually on 8 March, to value all women's work and against no pay, low pay and overwork.*

International Wages for Housework Campaign (IWFHC) Crossroads Women's Centre, 230A Kentish Town Road, London, NW5 2AB T 020 7482 2496 F 020 7209 4761 allwomencount.net crossroadswomenscentre@compuserve.com *International multi-racial grassroots women's network campaigning for governments to recognise and pay wages for all women's unwaged work.*

Wages Due Lesbians Crossroads Women's Centre, 230A Kentish Town Road, London, NW5 2AB T 020 7482 2496 F 020 7209 4761 allwomencount.net crossroadswomenscentre@compuserve.com *Multi-racial network campaigning for social, economic, civil and legal rights for lesbian/bisexual women and against all forms of discrimination.*

WinVisible: Women with Visible and Invisible Disabilities Crossroads Women's Centre, 230A Kentish Town Rd, London, NW5 2AB. T 020 7482 2496 womenstrike8m.server101.com rossroadswomenscentre@compuserve.com *Multi-racial self-help network of women with visible and invisible disabilities. Want the caring work we do recognised and paid for.*

Women Against Rape (WAR) PO Box 287, London NW6 5QU. T 020 7482 2496 F 020 7209 4761 www.womenagainstrape.net crossroadswomenscentre@compuserve.com *Grassroots multi-racial women's organisation provides counselling, legal advocacy, and campaigns for justice, protection and compensation for survivors of sexual violence.*

WORKERS' RIGHTS

CASA Club 29 Hope St, Liverpool. T 0151 709 2148 www.gn.apc.org/initfactory dockers@gn.apc.org *Club run on co-operative principles, run by sacked Liverpool dockers. Profits go toward an employment training centre.*

Claimants Action Nottingham (NCAJSA) www.geocities.com/ncajsa/ *NCA believes in fighting the imposition of the Job Seekers Allowance (JSA) benefits regime, and attempts by the DSS to force claimants on to 'workfare' schemes like the Tories' previous Project Work pilots or New Labour's Welfare to Work, part of their bogus New Deal. We changed our name from Nottingham Campaign Against the Job Seekers Allowance (NCAJSA) so as to reflect the wider struggle.*

Education Workers Network PO Box 29, Southwest PDO, Manchester, M15 5HW. T 07984 675 281 www.ewn.org.uk ewn@ewn.org.uk *Network of education workers who favour collective direct action for decent education. Contact EWN for free bulletins.*

Institute of Employment Rights (IER) 177 Abbeville Rd, London, SW4 9RL T 020 7498 6919 F 020 7498 9080 www.ier.org.uk ier@gn.apc.org *A trade union supported think tank acting as a focal point for the spread of new ideas in the field of labour law.*

Iranian Workers News PO Box 23734, London SW5 9GB. www.iranian-workers-news.net editor@iranian-workers-news.net *Solidarity campaign with Iranian workers.*

LabourStart www.labourstart.org ericlee@labourstart.org *Online global labour news service and portal.*

No Sweat PO Box 36707, London, SW9 8YA. T 07904 431959 www.nosweat.org.uk admin@nosweat.org.uk *Campaigning against child and sweated labour at home and abroad through direct action, organisation and making practical solidarity.*

Public Service Workers' Network (PSWN) PO Box 469, Preston PR1 8XF. www.solfed.force9.co.uk/pswn.htm Solfed@solfed.org.uk *Network of public service workers in Solidarity Federation. Contact PSWN for free bulletins (see also Solidarity Federation).*

Simon Jones Memorial Campaign P.O.Box 2600, Brighton, BN2 2 DX T 01273 685913 F as phone www.simonjones.org.uk action@simonjones.org.uk *Campaigns for justice for Simon Jones, killed on his first day as a casual worker on a Shoreham dock, and to expose the dangers of casualisation.*

Tools For Solidarity (TFS) Unit 1B1, Edenberry Industrial Estate, 326 Crumlin Rd, Belfast, BT14 7EE T 028 9074 7473 *Refurbishes unwanted hand tools and sewing machines for skilled tradespeople in Africa. Committed to the equal distribution of power and resources.*

Pic: Andrew Testa